SCIENCE
ACTIVITIES
FOR ELEMENTARY STUDENTS

Eleventh Edition

George C. Lorbeer
California State University
Northridge

Boston   Burr Ridge, IL   Dubuque, IA   Madison, WI   New York   San Francisco   St. Louis
Bangkok   Bogotá   Caracas   Lisbon   London   Madrid
Mexico City   Milan   New Delhi   Seoul   Singapore   Sydney   Taipei   Toronto

McGraw-Hill Higher Education

A Division of The **McGraw-Hill** *Companies*

SCIENCE ACTIVITIES FOR ELEMENTARY STUDENTS, ELEVENTH EDITION

 This book is printed on recycled, acid-free paper containing 10% postconsumer waste.

1 2 3 4 5 6 7 8 9 0 QPD/QPD 0 9 8 7 6 5 4 3 2 1 0

ISBN 0–697–37789–X

Editorial director: *Jane E. Vaicunas*
Sponsoring editor: *Beth Kaufman*
Editorial coordinator: *Teresa Wise*
Marketing manager: *Daniel M. Loch*
Project manager: *Mary E. Powers*
Senior production supervisor: *Sandra Hahn*
Designer: *K. Wayne Harms*
Senior photo research coordinator: *Carrie K. Burger*
Compositor: *Shepherd, Inc.*
Typeface: *10/12 Times Roman*
Printer: *Quebecor Printing Book Group/Dubuque, IA*

Cover designer: *Sean M. Sullivan*
Cover photograph: *Ross Whitaker/Image Bank and PhotoDisc*
Photo research: *Mary Reeg Photo Research*

Page: 1; © PhotoDisc, Inc.; p. 70: © PhotoDisc, Inc.; p. 78: © PhotoDisc, Inc.; p. 145: Dr. Nelson; p. 186: Rebecca St. George; p. 194: George Lorbeer; p. 295: Dr. Nelson; p. 317: © PhotoDisc, Inc.; p. 323: Dr. Nelson; p. 352: Dr. Nelson; p. 358: © PhotoDisc, Inc.; p. 365: Dr. Nelson; p. 374: Dr. Nelson; p. 374: Dr. Nelson; p. 374: Dr. Nelson; p. 374: Dr. Nelson; p. 382: Photo courtesy of NASA; p. 382: Dr. Nelson; p. 398: George Lorbeer.

Some of the laboratory experiments included in this text may be hazardous if materials are handled improperly or if procedures are conducted incorrectly. Safety precautions are necessary when you are working with chemicals, glass test tubes, hot water baths, sharp instruments, and the like, or for any procedures that generally require caution. Your school may have set regulations regarding safety procedures that your instructor will explain to you. Should you have any problems with materials or procedures, please ask your instructor for help.

Library of Congress Cataloging-in-Publication Data

Lorbeer, George C.
    Science activities for elementary students / George C. Lorbeer.—
11th ed.
        p.   cm.
    Rev. ed. of : Science activities for children. 10th ed. 1996.
    Includes index.
    ISBN 0–697–37789–X
    1. Science—Study and teaching (Elementary)—United States
Handbooks, manuals, etc.   2. Teaching—Aids and devices Handbooks,
manuals, etc.   3. Science—Study and teaching—Activity programs—
United States Handbooks, manuals, etc.   I. Lorbeer, George C.
Science activities for children.   II. Title.
LB1585.3.L67   2000
372.3′ 5044—dc21   99–30368
                                                    CIP

To my wife, Dottie, THANKS.

Without her continuous moral support this book would never have been completed.

Contents

Preface   xi

![tree icon] PART I: PHYSICAL WORLD

Ref. No.	Activity	Page

SECTION A: MATTER

Ref. No.	Activity	Page
I-A-1	What Are the Three States of Matter?	2
I-A-2	What Are Atoms? Molecules?	3
I-A-3	What Are Elements? Compounds? Mixtures?	4
I-A-4	Can Matter Be Changed from One State to Another?	5
I-A-5	Can a Gas Change to a Liquid? A Liquid to a Gas? A Gas to a Solid? What Is Condensation? Dew?	6
I-A-6	Do All Solids Melt at the Same Temperature?	7
I-A-7	Do All Liquids Boil at the Same Temperature?	8
I-A-8	How Do Materials Combine?	9
I-A-9	What Is a Chemical Change?	10
I-A-10	What Is a Physical Change?	11
I-A-11	What Is a Solution?	12
I-A-12	What Matter Is Acidic? What Matter Is Alkaline?	13
I-A-13	How Does Living Matter Differ from Nonliving Matter?	14
I-A-14	How Can We Make Invisible Ink?	15
I-A-15	What Is Diffusion?	16
I-A-16	What Are the Tiniest Pieces of Matter?	18

SECTION B: AIR

Ref. No.	Activity	Page
I-B-1	What Is Air? What Are Its Characteristics?	19
I-B-2	How Does a Chimney Work?	20
I-B-3	Does Air Take Up Space?	21
I-B-4	Does Air Have Weight?	22
I-B-5	How Does Air Help Us?	23
I-B-6	Does Warm Air Rise or Fall? Expand or Contract?	24
I-B-7	How Do Hot Air Balloons Ascend and Descend?	26
I-B-8	What Is Suction?	27
I-B-9	How Can People Work Under Water?	28
I-B-10	Can Air Pressure Hold Water in an Inverted Glass?	29
I-B-11	Can Air Pressure Lift Heavy Objects?	30
I-B-12	Can Air Pressure Crush a Can?	31
I-B-13	How Does Air Pressure Hold Water in a Can?	32
I-B-14	How Does Air Pressure in a Bicycle Tire Hold Up the Bicycle?	33
I-B-15	Can a Shelled, Hard-Boiled Egg Be Put into a Small-Mouthed Bottle Without Breaking the Egg?	34
I-B-16	How Does a Siphon Work?	35
I-B-17	What Is Sideways Air Pressure?	36
I-B-18	How Much Oxygen Is in the Air?	37
I-B-19	In Which Direction Does Moving Air Exert the Most Pressure?	38

SECTION C: WATER

Ref. No.	Activity	Page
I-C-1	What Are the Main Sources of Water?	39
I-C-2	When Water Freezes Does It Expand or Contract?	40
I-C-3	At What Temperature Does Water Freeze? Boil?	41
I-C-4	What Is Bouyancy?	42
I-C-5	What Objects Float? What Objects Sink?	43
I-C-6	Why Do Heavy Ships Float?	44
I-C-7	Why Does Solid Water (Ice) Float?	45
I-C-8	Why Can We Swim Easier in Salt Water?	47
I-C-9	What Color Marble Sinks Faster?	48
I-C-10	What Causes Evaporation?	49
I-C-11	How Does Wind Help Drying?	51
I-C-12	How Can We Measure the Volume of Irregularly Shaped Objects?	52
I-C-13	What Makes a Submarine Go Up and Down?	53
I-C-14	The Sailor's Dilemma	54
I-C-15	What Is the "Water Cycle"?	55

SECTION D: MAGNETISM

Ref. No.	Activity	Page
1-D-1	What Are Magnets? How Do They Work?	56
1-D-2	Do Like Poles on Magnets Attract or Repel Each Other?	57
1-D-3	What Kinds of Substances Do Magnets Attract?	58
I-D-4	Is the Earth a Magnet?	59
I-D-5	How Can We Make a Compass?	61
I-D-6	Can a Paper Clip Defy Gravity?	62
I-D-7	What Is a Magnetic Field of Force?	63
I-D-8	Through What Kinds of Substances Do Magnetic Lines of Force Pass?	64

SECTION E: STATIC ELECTRICITY

Ref. No.	Activity	Page
I-E-1	What Is Static Electricity?	65
I-E-2	What Causes Static Electricity?	66
I-E-3	Do Like Charges Repel or Attract Each Other?	67
I-E-4	Can Static Electricity Be Produced by Friction?	68
I-E-5	Does Static Electricity Affect Water Flow?	69

![atom logo] # PART II: ENERGY

Ref. No.	Activity	Page

SECTION A: SOURCES

Ref. No.	Activity	Page
II-A-1	What Are Nonrenewable Sources of Energy?	71
II-A-2	What Are Renewable Sources of Energy?	72
II-A-3	Can Energy Be Changed from One Form to Another?	73
II-A-4	What Is Kinetic Energy? Potential Energy?	74
II-A-5	How Can We Use Solar Energy?	75
II-A-6	What Are Fossil Fuels?	76
II-A-7	Is Nuclear Energy Safe or Harmful?	77
II-A-8	Is Wind a Good Source of Energy?	78

SECTION B: FIRE AND HEAT

Ref. No.	Activity	Page
II-B-1	What Is Heat? What Is Temperature?	79
II-B-2	What Is the "Fire Triangle"?	80
II-B-3	How Does Heat Move?	81
II-B-4	What Is the Difference Between a Celsius (Centigrade) and a Fahrenheit Temperature Scale?	82
II-B-5	What Happens to Solids When They Are Heated? Cooled?	84
II-B-6	What Happens to Liquids When They Are Heated? Cooled?	85
II-B-7	What Happens to Gases When They Are Heated? Cooled?	86
II-B-8	What Causes a Candle to Burn?	87
II-B-9	What Is Smoke?	88
II-B-10	Does Color Affect Heat Absorption?	89
II-B-11	Do Some Substances Conduct Heat Faster Than Others?	90
II-B-12	Is Carbon Dioxide Heavier Than Air? Will Carbon Dioxide Gas Support Combustion (Burning)?	91

SECTION C: LIGHT AND COLOR

Ref. No.	Activity	Page
II-C-1	Does Light Travel Only in a Straight Line?	92
II-C-2	What Causes a Shadow?	93
II-C-3	What Colors of Light Are in Sunlight?	94
II-C-4	What Makes Colored Light?	95
II-C-5	How Can We Make Different Colors? Are Some Colors "Warmer" Than Others?	96
II-C-6	What Is the Difference Between Source Light and Reflected Light?	97
II-C-7	How Does Light Cause Reflections?	98
II-C-8	What Is the Difference Between a Concave and a Convex Lens?	99
II-C-9	How Can We Make a Periscope? Can Light Be Bent?	101

Ref. No.	Activity	Page
II-C-10	How Can We Make a Single-Colored Picture Disappear?	102
II-C-11	How Can We Make a Simple Magnifying Glass?	103

SECTION D: SOUND

Ref. No.	Activity	Page
II-D-1	What Are Some of the Sounds We Hear Each Day on the Way to School?	104
II-D-2	What Causes Sound? How Are Sounds Made?	105
II-D-3	Does Sound Travel Through Solids? Liquids? Gases?	106
II-D-4	How Do We Communicate By Using Sound?	107
II-D-5	What Causes Sounds to Vary in Pitch?	108
II-D-6	What Makes Sounds When We Speak?	109
II-D-7	How Does a Stethoscope Work?	110
II-D-8	How Can We Make Pop Bottle Music?	111
II-D-9	How Do Vibrating Wires Make Different Sounds?	112
II-D-10	How Can We Make a Simple Telephone?	113

SECTION E: SIMPLE MACHINES

Ref. No.	Activity	Page
II-E-1	How Do Simple Machines Help Us?	114
II-E-2	How Do Levers Make Work Easier?	115
II-E-3	How Do Inclined Planes Help Us Do Work?	116
II-E-4	How Do Pulleys Help Us in Lifting Weights?	117
II-E-5	How Does the Wheel and Axle Help Us Do Work?	119
II-E-6	How Do Gears Help Us?	120

SECTION F: MOVEMENT AND RESISTANCE

Ref. No.	Activity	Page
II-F-1	What Makes Objects Move?	121
II-F-2	What Prevents, Slows, or Stops Movements?	122
II-F-3	What Is Inertia? Momentum?	123
II-F-4	How Do Inertia and Momentum Affect Us?	124
II-F-5	What Is Sliding Friction? Rolling Friction?	125
II-F-6	How Does Friction Help Us? Hurt Us?	126
II-F-7	How Does Friction Vary With Pressure?	127
II-F-8	Are There Forces Without Movement of Objects?	128
II-F-9	Does Steam Exert a Tremendous Force?	129
II-F-10	What Are Newton's Laws of Motion?	130
II-F-11	How Can We Make Steam-Propelled Toys?	131

SECTION G: CURRENT ELECTRICITY

Ref. No.	Activity	Page
II-G-1	What Is Electricity?	132
II-G-2	How Many Electrical Appliances Do We Have in Our Homes?	133
II-G-3	How Do We Use Electricity to Communicate?	134
II-G-4	How Can We Make a Simple Electric Circuit?	135
II-G-5	What Is a Series Circuit?	136

Ref. No.	Activity	Page
II-G-6	What Is a Parallel Circuit?	137
II-G-7	How Does a Fuse Work?	138
II-G-8	What Materials Conduct Electricity?	139
II-G-9	How Do Batteries Work?	140
II-G-10	Can We Make Some Simple Batteries?	141
II-G-11	How Can We Make a Model Telegraph?	142
II-G-12	How Can We Make an Electromagnet?	143
II-G-13	How Does an Electric Doorbell Work?	144

PART III: PLANTS

SECTION A: PARTS AND CLASSIFICATION

Ref. No.	Activity	Page
III-A-1	How Do We Classify Living Things?	146
III-A-2	How Are Plants Classified?	148
III-A-3	What Kinds of Plants Are Found in Our Neighborhood?	149
III-A-4	What Are the Main Parts of Plants?	150
III-A-5	What Parts of Plants Do We Eat?	151
III-A-6	What Are Grasses?	152
III-A-7	Do All Plants Change Color in the Fall?	153

SECTION B: SEEDS AND REPRODUCTION

Ref. No.	Activity	Page
III-B-1	How Many Different Kinds of Flowers Are Found in Our Community?	154
III-B-2	Where Do Seeds Come From?	155
III-B-3	How Do Plants Reproduce?	156
III-B-4	How Do Bees Help Plant Reproduction?	157
III-B-5	How Do Seeds Travel?	158
III-B-6	What Conditions Lead to Mold Growth?	159

SECTION C: SOILS AND GERMINATION

Ref. No.	Activity	Page
III-C-1	How Do We Plant Seeds?	160
III-C-2	Do Different Soils Affect Germination?	161
III-C-3	How Does Water Affect Germination?	162
III-C-4	How Does Air Affect Germination?	163
III-C-5	How Does Light Affect Germination?	164
III-C-6	How Do Seeds Start to Grow?	165
III-C-7	Are Some Soils Better than Others for Holding Water?	166

SECTION D: GROWTH

Ref. No.	Activity	Page
III-D-1	What Do Plants Need to Grow?	167
III-D-2	Do Plants Need Sunshine?	168
III-D-3	Can Plants Live Without Water?	169
III-D-4	How Does Water Move in Plants?	170
III-D-5	Do Plants Need Air to Grow?	171
III-D-6	What Kinds of Classroom Plants Should We Raise?	172

SECTION E: ROOTS, STEMS, AND LEAVES

Ref. No.	Activity	Page
III-E-1	What Are the Different Types of Roots?	173
III-E-2	Do Roots Seek Water?	174
III-E-3	How Quickly Does Water Move in Stems?	175
III-E-4	How Do Stems of Plants Differ?	176
III-E-5	Do Leaves Give Off Water?	177
III-E-6	How Do Leaves Vary in Size, Shape, and Edges?	178

SECTION F: FUN WITH PLANTS

Ref. No.	Activity	Page
III-F-1	How Can We Make a Decorative Sweet Potato Plant?	179
III-F-2	How Can We Start a Pineapple Plant?	180
III-F-3	What Can We Make With Gourds?	181
III-F-4	How Do We Make a Simple Plant Terrarium?	182
III-F-5	How Can Leaves Be Preserved?	183
III-F-6	How Can We Make a "Spray Print"?	184
III-F-7	How Can We Make Mounts for Plants?	185

PART IV: ANIMALS

SECTION A: CLASSIFICATION

Ref. No.	Activity	Page
IV-A-1	What Is the Difference Between Living and Nonliving Things?	187
IV-A-2	How Many Different Species of Animals Are There?	188
IV-A-3	What Animals Can We Find on Our School Campus?	189
IV-A-4	How Do Animals Move?	190
IV-A-5	How Do Animals Communicate?	191
IV-A-6	How Do Animals Protect Themselves?	192

SECTION B: PETS

Ref. No.	Activity	Page
IV-B-1	What Kinds of Pets Does Our Class Have in Their Homes?	193
IV-B-2	What Kind of Pet Should I Have?	194
IV-B-3	How Do We Care for Dogs and Cats?	195
IV-B-4	How Do We Care for Hamsters, Guinea Pigs, Gerbils, and/or Mice?	196

SECTION C: INSECTS AND SPIDERS

Ref. No.	Activity	Page
IV-C-1	How Do Spiders Differ from Insects?	197
IV-C-2	How Do Ants Live?	198
IV-C-3	How Do Bees Live?	199
IV-C-4	How Do Moths Differ from Butterflies?	200
IV-C-5	How Can We Collect Moths, Butterflies, Other Insects, and Spiders?	201

Ref. No.	Activity	Page

SECTION D: REPTILES

IV-D-1	What Are Reptiles?	202
IV-D-2	What Are Some Characteristics of Snakes?	203
IV-D-3	How Do We Make a Terrarium for Reptiles?	204
IV-D-4	What Do We Know About Dinosaurs?	205

SECTION E: WATER ANIMALS (FISH AND AMPHIBIANS)

IV-E-1	How Can We Identify the Different Species of Fish?	206
IV-E-2	How Should We Collect Seashells?	207
IV-E-3	What Are the Differences Between Frogs and Toads?	208
IV-E-4	How Do We Care for a Fresh-Water Aquarium?	209

SECTION F: BIRDS

IV-F-1	How Do Birds Differ from Other Animals?	211
IV-F-2	How Do We Classify Common Birds?	212
IV-F-3	What Can We Learn from Birds' Beaks and Feet?	213
IV-F-4	Why Do Birds Migrate?	214

SECTION G: MAMMALS

IV-G-1	How Do Mammals Differ from Other Animals?	215
IV-G-2	What Are Some Common Jungle, Farm, and Sea Mammals?	216
IV-G-3	Are Human Beings Mammals?	217
IV-G-4	How Do Mammals Protect Themselves?	218

SECTION H: WORMS AND SNAILS

IV-H-1	How Can We Make an Earthworm Home?	219
IV-H-2	What Are the Main Characteristics of Snails?	220

SECTION I: STORAGE AND CARE

IV-I-1	How Do We Make a Simple Vivarium?	221
IV-I-2	How Do We Build a Small, Simple Cage?	222
IV-I-3	How Do We Make a Wire Cage for Small Animals?	223
IV-I-4	How Do We Make a Cage for Medium-Sized Animals?	224
IV-I-5	What Should We Feed Captured Animals?	225

SECTION J: RESOURCES

IV-J-1	How Do Animals Help People?	227
IV-J-2	Why Do We Hunt and Fish for Certain Animals?	228
IV-J-3	Should Animals Be Protected?	229

PART V: HEALTH

Ref. No.	Activity	Page

SECTION A: BODY STRUCTURE AND FUNCTION

V-A-1	What Are the Different Systems in Our Body?	231
V-A-2	What Different Kinds of Bones and Joints Do We Have?	232
V-A-3	How Does Our Heart Work?	233
V-A-4	How Can We Find Our Pulse?	234
V-A-5	How Much Air Do Our Lungs Hold?	235
V-A-6	How Does Our Skin Help Us?	236
V-A-7	Are All Fingerprints Different?	237
V-A-8	What Are Cells, Tissues, and Organs?	238

SECTION B: SENSES

V-B-1	How Many Senses Do We Have? How Do We Receive Information About Our Environment?	239
V-B-2	Why Do the Pupils of Our Eyes Change Size?	240
V-B-3	How Do We See Color?	241
V-B-4	How Do Our Eyes Blend Separate Colors?	242
V-B-5	Are There Blind Spots in Our Eyes?	243
V-B-6	Do Our Eyes Ever Deceive Us?	244
V-B-7	How Do We See Motion?	245
V-B-8	How Well Do We Hear?	246
V-B-9	What Can We Learn About Our Sense of Touch?	247
V-B-10	How Do We Use Our Sense of Smell?	248

SECTION C: NUTRITION

V-C-1	What Kinds of Foods Do Our Bodies Need?	249
V-C-2	What Is the "Food Pyramid?"	250
V-C-3	What Foods Contain Carbohydrates (Starches and Sugars)?	251
V-C-4	How Do We Test Foods for Fats?	252
V-C-5	How Do We Make Butter?	253
V-C-6	How Is Food Preserved?	254
V-C-7	Are "Fast Foods" Good for Us?	255
V-C-8	If I'm Overweight or Underweight, What Should I Eat?	256
V-C-9	What Should We Look For on Food Labels?	257

SECTION D: PERSONAL HEALTH

V-D-1	How Can We Stay Healthy?	258
V-D-2	How Can We Protect Our Eyes?	259
V-D-3	How Can We Protect Our Hearing?	260
V-D-4	What Kind of Clothing Should We Wear?	261
V-D-5	How Do We Properly Care for Our Teeth?	262
V-D-6	Is Smoking Bad for Our Health?	263

Ref. No.	Activity	Page
V-D-7	How Can We Protect Our Skin?	265
V-D-8	How Can I Improve My Posture?	266
V-D-9	Why Should We Wash Our Hands Frequently?	267
V-D-10	Is Liquor Bad for Our Health?	268

SECTION E: PUBLIC HEALTH

V-E-1	What Makes People Ill?	269
V-E-2	How Can We Prevent Disease?	270
V-E-3	How Can We Fight Disease?	271
V-E-4	How Does the Government Protect Our Health and Safety?	272

SECTION F: FIRST AID

V-F-1	What Can You Do for a Cold?	273
V-F-2	What Should We Do for Cuts and Wounds?	274
V-F-3	What Should You Do if You Get Something in Your Eye?	275
V-F-4	What Should You Do in Case of a Nosebleed?	276
V-F-5	How Can We Help a Person with Injuries to the Arms or Legs?	277
V-F-6	What Should We Do in Case of Burns? Scalds?	278
V-F-7	What Should We Do for a Bite or a Sting?	279
V-F-8	How Can Breathing Be Restored in Drowning or Shock?	280

SECTION G: SAFETY

V-G-1	What School Safety Drills Should We Know?	281
V-G-2	How Can We Prevent Accidents?	282
V-G-3	What Traffic Signals Should We Know?	283
V-G-4	What Safety Precautions Should We Take When Riding Bicycles, Skateboards, or In-Line Skates?	284
V-G-5	Should We Be Friendly with Strangers?	285
V-G-6	What Should We Do if We Get Lost in the Woods?	286

PART VI: ECOLOGY

SECTION A: ECOSYSTEMS

VI-A-1	What Is the Balance of Nature?	288
VI-A-2	What Is the "Triangle of Life"?	289
VI-A-3	What Is "Biological Diversity"?	290
VI-A-4	What Are the Largest Ecosystems in the World?	291
VI-A-5	How Do We Make a Simple Ecosystem?	292
VI-A-6	Do We Belong to an Ecosystem?	293
VI-A-7	How Do People Destroy Habitats?	294
VI-A-8	What Controls Animal Populations?	295
VI-A-9	Are Any Animals Threatened with Extinction?	296
VI-A-10	Is There a World Population Explosion?	297

SECTION B: CONSERVATION

VI-B-1	How Does Running Water Affect Our Soil?	298
VI-B-2	How Does Moving Air Affect Our Soil?	299
VI-B-3	How Can We Conserve Our Wildlife?	300
VI-B-4	How Can We Conserve Energy (and Money) in Our Homes?	301
VI-B-5	How Can We Conserve Our Oceans?	302
VI-B-6	How Can We Conserve Our Forests, Especially the Rain Forests?	303
VI-B-7	How Can We Protect Our Wetlands?	304
VI-B-8	How Can We Conserve Our Natural Resources?	305
VI-B-9	How Can We Conserve Our Fresh Water?	306
VI-B-10	What Is Recycling? Salvaging?	307

SECTION C: POLLUTION

VI-C-1	What Are the Main Pollution Problems?	308
VI-C-2	What Are Nonrenewable Resources? Renewable Resources?	309
VI-C-3	How Do Automobiles Pollute the Air?	310
VI-C-4	How Are Our Homes Adding to the Pollution Problems?	311
VI-C-5	What Is Global Warming (the "Greenhouse Effect")?	312
VI-C-6	Are Our Lakes and Rivers Becoming Polluted?	313
VI-C-7	How Safe Is Our Drinking Water?	314
VI-C-8	What Is Happening to Our Topsoil?	315
VI-C-9	How Does Pollution Affect Food Chains and Food Webs?	316
VI-C-10	What Should We Do with Our Wastes?	317
VI-C-11	Are There Hazards in Using Nuclear Energy?	318
VI-C-12	What Is the Ozone Problem?	319
VI-C-13	Is Noise Pollution a Problem?	320

SECTION D: POLLUTION SOLUTIONS

VI-D-1	How Can We Help Solve the Pollution Problems?	321
VI-D-2	What Is the Best Way to Get Rid of Our Nontoxic Wastes?	323
VI-D-3	How Can We Save Diminishing Species?	324
VI-D-4	How Can We Protect Our Oceans and Beaches?	325
VI-D-5	Are Detergents Harmful to Our Environment?	326
VI-D-6	What Better Ecological Means of Land Transportation Do We Have other Than Automobiles?	327
VI-D-7	What Is "Sustainability"?	328

PART VII: EARTH AND SPACE

Ref. No.	Activity	Page

SECTION A: UNIVERSE

Ref. No.	Activity	Page
VII-A-1	How Big Is the Universe?	330
VII-A-2	What Kinds of Heavenly Bodies Are There?	332
VII-A-3	Why Do Stars Move?	333
VII-A-4	How Can We Find the North Star?	334
VII-A-5	What Are Constellations?	335
VII-A-6	What Are Galaxies?	336

SECTION B: SOLAR SYSTEM

VII-B-1	What Are Planets?	337
VII-B-2	How Is the Earth Different from Other Planets?	338
VII-B-3	Is the Earth Round?	340
VII-B-4	Does the Sun Revolve Around the Earth?	341
VII-B-5	What Makes Day and Night?	342
VII-B-6	How Does the Sun Help Us?	343
VII-B-7	How Does the Length of Day and Night Change from Season to Season?	344
VII-B-8	Why Is the Sky Blue?	345
VII-B-9	How Does the Moon Travel?	346
VII-B-10	Why Does the Moon Appear to Change Shape?	347
VII-B-11	What Causes an Eclipse?	349
VII-B-12	What Causes Tides?	350

SECTION C: EARTH'S CRUST

VII-C-1	What Are the Natural Surfaces Found on the Earth's Crust?	351
VII-C-2	What Kinds of Rocks Are There?	352
VII-C-3	What Are Some Characteristics of Oceans?	354
VII-C-4	Where Do We Get Our Natural Gas?	355
VII-C-5	What Causes Earthquakes?	356
VII-C-6	What Causes a Volcano to Erupt?	357
VII-C-7	What Are Geysers?	358
VII-C-8	What Is the "Water Table"?	359

SECTION D: GRAVITY

VII-D-1	Do Heavy Objects Fall Faster than Light Ones?	360
VII-D-2	Does Gravity Always Work in the Same Direction?	361
VII-D-3	How Does Gravity Affect the Time of Falling Sticks of Different Lengths?	362
VII-D-4	How Does Gravity Affect Swinging Objects?	363
VII-D-5	How Fast Is Gravity?	364
VII-D-6	Can You Balance a Pencil on the Tip of Your Finger?	365
VII-D-7	Is It Easy to Become a Gymnast?	366
VII-D-8	Why Does This Can Defy Gravity?	367
VII-D-9	Do People Have a Center of Gravity?	368

Ref. No.	Activity	Page

SECTION E: WEATHER

VII-E-1	What Makes the Wind Blow?	369
VII-E-2	How Can We Make a Wind Vane?	370
VII-E-3	Is There Water in the Air? What Causes Dew?	371
VII-E-4	Where Does Rain Come From?	372
VII-E-5	How Can We Measure Rainfall?	373
VII-E-6	How Are Clouds Formed? What Kinds of Clouds Are There?	374
VII-E-7	What Causes a Rainbow?	375
VII-E-8	What Is Lightning?	376
VII-E-9	What Is Thunder?	377
VII-E-10	Why Are Summers Warmer than Winters?	378
VII-E-11	How Is Fog Formed?	379
VII-E-12	How Do We Read a Weather Map?	380
VII-E-13	What Are "Warm Fronts" and "Cold Fronts"?	381

PART VIII: AVIATION, SATELLITES, AND SPACE TRAVEL

SECTION A: AVIATION

VIII-A-1	What Are the Different Kinds of Aircraft?	383
VIII-A-2	What Are the Main Parts of an Airplane?	384
VIII-A-3	How Does an Airplane Get "Lift" from Its Wings?	385
VIII-A-4	How Does a Pilot Control an Airplane?	386
VIII-A-5	How Does an Airplane Propeller Work?	387
VIII-A-6	How Does a Parachute Work?	388

SECTION B: SATELLITES

VIII-B-1	Why Does Water Stay in a Fast-Swinging Bucket?	389
VIII-B-2	What Direction Will a Circular Moving Ball Go if All External Forces Are Removed?	390
VIII-B-3	How Does a Rocket Work?	391
VIII-B-4	How Is a Spaceship Launched?	392
VIII-B-5	What Is a Space Station?	393
VIII-B-6	What Keeps a Satellite in Orbit?	394
VIII-B-7	What Good are Artificial Satellites?	395

SECTION C: SPACE TRAVEL

VIII-C-1	How Is Our Planet (Earth) Like a Spaceship? How Is It Different?	396
VIII-C-2	What Are Some of the Problems of Space Travel?	397
VIII-C-3	What Is a Space Shuttle?	398
VIII-C-4	How Do Astronauts Maneuver Spacecraft?	399

Preface

The repair of the Hubble Telescope in space, discoveries in the structures of the genes, the finding of the last quark, the predictions of population growth, the findings of new galaxies in our expanding known universe, the cloning of animals, the critical loss of wildlife, and the launching of the first section of the space station are only a few of the scientific events that have been incorporated in this eleventh edition of *Science Activities for Elementary Students.*

Not since Sputnik has there been so much emphasis on science. We are living in a scientific and technological world, and the trend portends that it will be essential for all people to understand these areas in order to maintain even the basic necessities of life. The main problem stems from the fact that we are NOT providing our students with fundamental scientific background and problem-solving skills. This book can help reverse this trend.

The major emphasis of this edition is still a hands-on, minds-on approach. Dewey's statement: "We learn by doing," is the focal point of this book. Students learn best by direct, first-hand experiences. While a teacher's scientific explanation of natural phenomena may be interesting, it often lacks substance and meaning to the students. This book has been designed to provide teachers, student teachers, and students with many complete activities so that even the neophyte in science can perform them successfully. The materials needed are mostly common, inexpensive items found in the home, local market, or the classroom. Activities can be used as student experiments, group activities, and/or teacher demonstrations. This book can provide many ideas to enrich school science programs for curriculum workers, science supervisors, and other school administrators. Parents, too, who want to help their children enrich their knowledge of science will find these activities interesting and motivating.

What Is Science?

1. Science is the study of the biological environment from the tiniest living organisms to the largest life-being, and the physical environment from the smallest speck of matter to the immense universe.
2. Science is a method of solving problems. It requires using all the materials and procedures necessary and available. It is not a predetermined, sequential, step-by-step process. If this were so, all of the world's problems would have been solved long ago. It includes hypothesizing, investigating, collecting, and interpreting data. It is a continuous refinement of a problem studied by testing, narrowing the hypotheses in numbers and scope, retesting, etc., until conclusions based on objective evidence are reached. Since "The Scientific Method" is so important and can be used in a multitude of Activities found throughout this book, the following are some of the steps that could also be included in using "The Scientific Method."
   a. Sensing problems of a scientific nature
   b. Inquiring into strategies for problem solving
   c. Seeking assistance from others who are considered experts
   d. Clarifying problems and sub-problems
   e. Speculating on possible hypotheses
   f. Using books, periodicals, etc. as sources for information
   g. Selecting promising alternative(s) for testing
   h. Experimenting and observing in order to gather data
   i. Using new tools and techniques
   j. Gathering facts under controlled conditions
   k. Looking for irregularities, deviations, or exceptions
   l. Checking "cause and effect" relationships
   m. Measuring and recording findings
   n. Interpreting and organizing data
   o. Verifying findings with reliable sources
   p. Reporting findings accurately
   q. Predicting on the bases of gathered information
   r. Testing results with new applications
   s. Developing "models"
3. Science is an art in that it provides many internal satisfactions. A student who constructs a simple telegraph or organizes a collection of butterflies feels the same internal satisfaction as a student who composes a basic melody or paints a simple picture. Science activities can produce intrinsic satisfactions that are as enjoyable and productive as any other art form. Do not discount this phase of science education.
4. Science is an attitude based on facts. The ability to understand and interpret natural phenomena alleviates misconceptions and unreasoning fears. The student who understands the cause of thunder and has learned this in a meaningful way by popping a paper bag, is less likely to be frightened during a storm. When a student learns that animals are not apt to sting or bite except in self-defense, he/she is less apt to fear animals.
5. Science is a pragmatic philosophy. We all need a sound philosophy of life. Science can play an important role in this development by yielding

information about life itself, the difference between living and nonliving things, the elements that make a healthy organism, and the dangers to living individuals from external sources or self-imposed deleterious substances and behaviors.

Objectives of Science Education

In planning any science program, the first step for the teacher is to determine what objectives are to be achieved by each student. While the teacher may want to develop a personal list of goals, the following objectives are highly recommended:

1. *Developing personal strengths.* This includes not only the basics of reading, writing, and arithmetic skills, but also communication skills, social activities, critical attitudes about work, problem-solving skills, and satisfying psychological needs such as recognition, affection, security, belonging, etc.

2. *Becoming aware of the natural environment and social realities.* Students are naturally curious about their environment, and they are anxious to learn about it—IF we don't stifle their individual initiative. Students are continually asking: "Why?" "How?" "When?" "What?" The wise teacher can direct students down the discovery path to develop personal skills and acquire basic scientific knowledge. We, as educators, should use this natural curiosity as a prime motivating device in science and all the other disciplines as well.

3. *Having fun in games, contests, hobbies, and recreation.* Science is fun! Students enjoy creating projects and performing experiments. Much scientific knowledge can be acquired through games and contests. Many students have hobbies that involve science, e.g., collecting rocks, raising pets, and building model airplanes, crafts, etc. Recreational activities such as swimming, backpacking, surfing, skating, etc. all have scientific implications which could be used by the classroom teacher.

4. *Enjoying artistic experience.* There are satisfying science implications in all art forms. Colors in painting, sounds in music, and movements in dance interrelate with science.

5. *Living healthfully and safely.* Science educators can help students by teaching them about food, rest, exercise, accident prevention, first aid, causes of disease, etc. Indoctrination about drugs and smoking can spell the difference between success and failure, life and death, even to very young students.

6. *Learning that science is involved in all vocations.* Science is involved in all walks of life from performing menial tasks to working with nuclear energy.

7. *Acquiring the basic facts about the biological and physical environments.* By building on basic facts, students will begin to develop fundamental concepts which expand with each related new fact; concepts are developed from facts—not vice versa. One of the major problems in teaching science is the selection of appropriate facts which will develop desired concepts.

8. *Developing a scientific attitude.* Students begin to learn cause and effect relationships, increase their natural curiosity, suspend judgment, develop the desire to search for valid answers, approach problems with an open mind, and accept "The Scientific Method" as a basic approach to solve *factual* problems. A scientific attitude can eliminate superstition, remove unfounded fears, and prevent individuals from jumping to erroneous conclusions.

9. *Using "The Scientific Method."* This cannot, and is not intended to solve all the problems people face, however, learning the basic procedures in "The Scientific Method" can help individuals solve many of them. It will enable students to become aware of problems, hypothesize about them, devise possible solutions, conduct tests, make accurate observations, collect data, avoid misleading clues, and find the correct answers, if not on the first attempt, then on subsequent studies of the problem(s). "The Scientific Method" can help find facts; it can never solve problems on the level of *values.* Science can never determine what is good or bad, right or wrong, better or worse—these are value judgments whose answers must be left to philosophers. Problems stimulate thinking, and never before in our history has critical thinking been so sorely needed.

10. *Building a sound personal, pragmatic philosophy of life.* This is the summation of all previous objectives. It leads to wisdom and social concerns based on facts, concepts, a scientific attitude, and the knowledge and use of "The Scientific Method."

Ideals of Science Education (Professional Recommendations)

Many excellent recommendations regarding science education have been noted in the professional field. The author has incorporated many of these in this book. Some of the important ones are:

1. *Bloom's Taxonomy of Educational Objectives* beginning with the most specific pieces of information and leading toward abstract relations.

2. *National Research Council, Teaching Standards* particularly in orchestrating student involvement in each Activity.

3. *National Science Education Standards* with emphasis on student participation.
4. *California Academic Standards Commission, Science Standards* in its recommendations for scope and sequence of science content.
5. *American Association for the Advancement of Science (AAAS):* Benchmarks for Science Literacy.
6. *National Science Teachers Association*—their recommendations for science teaching.

A composite of the above guidelines (or "Standards") and mine would include:

1. Incorporating student experiences
2. Challenging students to predict the outcome of each Activity
3. Focusing on the student rather than on the subject content
4. Planning for the diversity of students
5. Designing lessons to permit student designs of investigations
6. Focusing on the scientific methods for solving problems
7. Stimulating student discussions on each step of the procedure
8. Promoting skepticism
9. Considering the teacher to be a resource person, not just a dispenser of information
10. Rewarding curiosity
11. Using as many resources as practical: multisensory aids, reference materials, and knowledgeable personnel in and out of school
12. Encouraging extended investigations
13. Ensuring a safe working environment
14. Developing small group activities
15. Making each Activity open-ended and not giving students the answers prematurely in planning, investigating, or reaching conclusions
16. Evaluating all phases of the learning process, not just factual accumulation

The Design of the Book

The physical makeup of the book has been created to make it especially easy for teachers to use. It is divided into eight major Parts. Each Part contains many carefully pretested Activities. (See Table of Contents.) Each Activity has nine major divisions. Each Activity is significant because it is related to other Activities and to life itself. It is rare that a single Activity can be very meaningful to the student if it is taught in isolation.

1. Problem
   Each Problem is stated in the form of a typical question which could be raised by an inquiring student. This enables the teacher to select the appropriate Activity and helps in lesson planning.

2. Materials Needed
   In Materials Needed, the supplies and equipment needed to perform the Activity are listed. Most materials are simple, inexpensive, and easy to obtain.

3. Procedure
   This is a step-by-step process that can be used to develop each Activity. The focus is on the student. It combines the utilization of:
   a. The process approach
   b. Open-mindedness
   c. "Hands-on, minds-on focus
      The students are encouraged to establish their own procedures and try them out even if failure results. The only failure in science is the student who won't try again. Failure is not terminal; it is a step in the solution of almost every problem. It is not an insurmountable fence. If students' procedures continuously lead to failure, the Procedures in the text can be utilized. Students should be continuously lauded for their attempts whether successful or not.

4. Results
   The Results are the observed conclusions of the Procedure. Other results of different procedures may be obtained, and they may yield the correct answer(s) to the particular problem or question.

5. Basic Facts and Supplementary Information
   The teacher and/or student is provided with additional background information that will help to complete the understanding of the particular problem involved. It includes scientific principles, handy hints, and safety precautions.

6. Thought Questions for Classroom Discussions
   These are included so that teachers may add thought-provoking questions, especially if they prefer the *inquiry* techniques to challenge students to think about possible solutions to other practical problems. This encourages students and teachers to do more critical thinking. Critical thinking is at the heart of all scientific testing, and consequently, it is a vital part of each Activity.

7. Related Ideas for Further Inquiry
   This has been added to enrich each Problem. Activities can be correlated to show the interrelationships of science activities, consequently, the students will gain a better comprehension of each area and not view each Activity as an isolated one. Teachers who prefer "teaching units" will find this most helpful.

8. Vocabulary Building—Spelling Words
   We need to help students improve their language skills in every possible way, and science instruction can be one of the vehicles for the student to develop in this area, therefore, Vocabulary Building—Spelling Words has been

included to integrate science and language arts, particularly, spelling.

9. Thought for Today

These statements are essentially philosophical and/or humorous in nature. They have been added to provide enjoyment as well as thought for the teacher and the students. These "Thoughts" have been used in classrooms for years, and have proven to be an excellent initiatory activity. Statements can be modified, depending on the level and understanding of the students.

One of the major problems facing new science teachers is the element of time. It would be ideal if students could raise problems, plan the investigations, conduct the tests, collaborate with other students and resource specialists, do the necessary research, collect the data, interpret the findings, and be completely satisfied with the entire process, as defined in most professional "standards." However, there is not enough classroom time available, and consequently, teachers must balance the "ideals" of "standards" with the "realities" of time, resources, and "desired" objectives.

There are three main parts of every successful lesson:

1. Objectives—what you hope to accomplish
2. Activities—how you are going to accomplish the objectives
3. Evaluation—determines how well the objectives were accomplished

This book focuses on the Activities which are at the heart of every science lesson.

In summary, science helps us to understand our environment. It enables us to solve problems with an open mind, helps us to appreciate the natural order and beauty of the universe, helps us to live in a more intelligent manner, teaches us respect for all creatures and our natural, physical environment, and encourages us to conserve our resources now and for future generations.

For the student, science should be a "rediscovery of the known by the uninformed." Students are not like sponges—they do not automatically absorb knowledge. They are individuals who learn best by firsthand, hands-on experiences. All of the Activities in this book were developed to raise and answer scientific questions that might arise in daily living.

The science teacher should be a director of learning, an agent of interaction, a motivator, a guide, a resource person, and rarely if ever, a storyteller. The teacher must recognize that students differ in experiences, learning rates, interests, abilities, backgrounds, etc., and must take each of these factors into consideration.

This book is not designed to cover all the science activities for any one grade. Instead, it offers typical, effective, proven activities from the various areas of science to give a teacher sufficient ideas to initiate a meaningful program of science education with a feeling of confidence. A teacher at any level of instruction can modify any Activity, making it either easier or more complex, depending on the age and maturity of the students. It must be remembered that these Activities are for young students who have a high level of curiosity and like to have fun while learning.

Reviewers

I am grateful to the following reviewers for their helpful comments and suggestions:

Lance Bedwell—Coastal Carolina University
Marilyn Lisowski—Eastern Illinois University
Albert Nous—The University of Pittsburgh

George C. Lorbeer

PART I

PHYSICAL WORLD

SECTION A	Matter	2
SECTION B	Air	19
SECTION C	Water	39
SECTION D	Magnetism	56
SECTION E	Static Electricity	65

SECTION A: MATTER

Activity

A. Problem: *What Are the Three States of Matter?*

B. Materials Needed:
1. Chalkboard
2. Chalk
3. Collection of materials: solids, liquids, and gases. (See drawing.)

C. Procedure:
1. Make a chart showing the three states of matter as illustrated.
2. Briefly describe the three states of matter: solids, liquids, and gases.
3. Have the students classify each of the materials by its state.
4. Add other items to each classification heading until you are sure the students have learned the differences between the states of matter.

D. Result:

The students learn the different states of matter as they develop the chart.

E. Basic Facts and Supplemental Information:

Each state of matter has its own unique characteristics and can be readily distinguished. Solids have definite shapes; liquids assume the exact shape of the containers they occupy; and gases expand to fill the space of the container. In warming, states of matter usually change from solids to liquids and liquids to gases. In cooling, the reverse takes place. Dry ice (carbon dioxide) at room temperature changes directly from a solid to a gas. This is called "sublimation."

F. Thought Questions for Class Discussions:
1. What are some other differences among solids, liquids, and gases?
2. Is ice a liquid or a solid?
3. Can we change the states of matter, that is, can we change a solid to a liquid or a liquid to a gas?
4. How can you change water from a liquid to a solid?
5. How can you change water from a liquid to a gas?
6. Why is air needed in a bicycle tire?
7. Can air hold water?

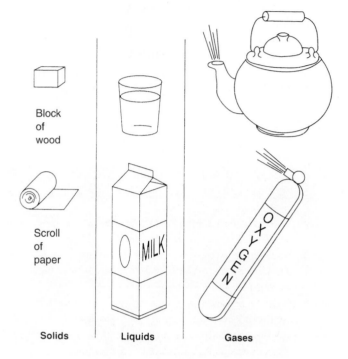

Block of wood

Scroll of paper

MILK

OXYGEN

Solids   **Liquids**   **Gases**

G. Related Ideas for Further Inquiry:
1. Blow air into a paper or plastic bag. Seal the top. Study the air's properties,—i.e., size, weight, warmth.
2. Put a straw into a glass of water, blow into it, and describe what happens.
3. Study the characteristics of carbon dioxide. Why is it used in soft drinks?
4. List the ways compressed air works for us.
5. Study: Activity VIII-A-3, "How does an airplane get lift from its wings?"
6. Study: Activity I-B-18, "How much oxygen is in the air?"
7. Drop a balloon filled with water and a firm sponge. Discuss the differences in shapes as they hit the floor.

H. Vocabulary Builders—Spelling Words:
1) **solids**   2) **liquids**   3) **gases**   4) **steam**
5) **oxygen**   6) **containers**   7) **expand**   8) **contract**

I. Thought for Today:

"The American Dream is not over: America is an adventure."

A. Problem: *What Are Atoms? Molecules?*

B. Materials Needed:

1. Styrofoam balls
2. Water paints
3. Thin wire
4. Iron
5. Zinc
6. Reference material(s) showing the electrons, protons, and neutrons of atoms.
7. Copper
8. Water
9. Salt
10. Baking soda

C. Procedure:

1. Briefly explain the three different states of matter: solids, liquids, and gases.
2. Define and describe atoms and molecules.
3. Show sketches or models of atoms such as iron, copper, zinc, etc.
4. Show sketches or models of molecules such as water, salt, baking soda, oxygen gas (O_2), nitrogen gas (N_2).
5. Have students blow against their hands and describe what they feel. Tell them that they are feeling molecules in motion.
6. Have each student build a mobile of a different atom using the reference materials as a guide.
   a. Use styrofoam balls for protons, neutrons, and electrons using a different color for each. (Electrons could be painted red; protons, blue; and neutrons, orange.)
   b. Arrange the protons and neutrons in a small inner circle as shown in the drawing. Any means of attachment is all right: drilling or punching holes in styrofoam balls, taping, etc. This circle represents the nucleus where the protons and neutrons are bunched together.
   c. Attach "electrons" to a much larger wire circle so that they are evenly spaced so that their number is equal to the number of protons.
   d. Attach the "nucleus ring" to the "electron ring."
   e. Affix this mobile to the ceiling or to a high point in the room.

D. Results:

1. When students blow air against their hands they are making air molecules move.
2. Students will learn about atoms through actual construction and display of mobiles.

E. Basic Facts and Supplemental Information:

1. Atoms are the basic components of molecules.
2. Molecules are combinations of atoms.
3. There are now 112 known elements: 92 occur naturally; the rest have been synthesized in the laboratory.

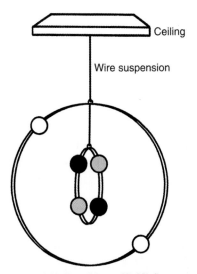

A Helium "Atom Mobile"
Electrons in outer orbit
Protons (light-colored) and
Neutrons (dark-colored) in
inner portion (nucleus)

4. Atoms or molecules are so small that we cannot see them.
5. A million atoms are about the size of the period at the end of this sentence.
6. Molecules are in constant motion regardless of whether they are in a solid, liquid, or gaseous state.
7. The smallest particle of matter that can be divided and still retain the properties of matter is called a molecule.

F. Thought Questions for Class Discussions:

1. If molecules didn't move, could laundry be dried outside?
2. Is all matter composed of molecules?
3. If all molecules are in motion, why don't all solids dissipate and disappear?

G. Related Ideas for Further Inquiry:

1. Study Activity I-A-1 "What are the three states of matter?"
2. Study Activity I-A-4 "Can matter be changed from one state to another?"
3. Study Activity I-A-16, "What are the tiniest pieces of matter?"

H. Vocabulary Builders—Spelling Words:

1) **atoms**   2) **molecules**   3) **elements**   4) **electrons**
5) **protons**   6) **neutrons**   7) **orbits**   8) **evaporation**

I. Thought for Today:

"Do not put off until tomorrow what you can do today."

Activity

I A 3

A. Problem: *What Are Elements? Compounds? Mixtures?*

B. Materials Needed:

1. Glass jar
2. Bits of paper
3. Paper clips
4. Spoon
5. Water
6. Marbles
7. Tacks
8. Sand
9. Salt
10. Sugar
11. Iron filings
12. Copper pennies
13. Magnifying glass
14. Reference materials including the Periodic Table

C. Procedure:

1. Define terms:
   a. **Element**—basic unit of matter of atom consisting of electrons, protons, and neutrons.
   b. **Compound**—basic unit of molecule with atoms in fixed chemical proportions.
   c. **Mixture**—a combination of two or more ingredients, not in a fixed proportion, with each part retaining its identity.
2. Identify each of the substances listed in "Materials Needed" as to whether it is an element, compound, or mixture.
3. Look at the sand with a magnifying glass. Do all the particles look the same?
4. Look at the sugar with a magnifying glass. Do all particles look the same?
5. Put the paper clips, bits of paper, marbles, and tacks into a half-filled glass of water.
6. Stir vigorously. Did they change appearance?

D. Results:

1. The sand particles were varied in appearance.
2. The sugar particles were identical in appearance.
3. All of the materials in the glass retained their individual identities.

E. Basic Facts and Supplemental Information:

1. Common elements found in the home are products that consist of copper, zinc, lead, iron, etc.
2. Common compounds found in the home are salt, baking soda, ammonia, water, etc.
3. Common mixtures found in the home are liquid soap, detergents, paints, soup, salad dressing, milk, etc.

F. Thought Questions for Class Discussions:

1. Is a mixture the result of a physical change or a chemical change?

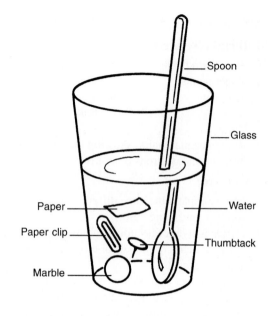

2. How does a mixture differ from a solution?
3. How many mixtures can you name?
4. Is air a mixture or a compound?

G. Related Ideas for Further Inquiry:

1. Have students make a chart of the first 10 elements in the Periodic Table showing differences in atomic number, weight, number of protons, number of electrons, number of neutrons, and the number of electrons in the outer ring.
2. Discuss what elements, compounds, and mixtures are found in sea water.
3. Make a list of 10 compounds found in the home.
4. Make a list of 10 mixtures found in the home.
5. Make a list of 5 elements found in the home.
6. Study Activity I-A-2, "What are atoms? molecules?"
7. Study Activity I-A-9, "What is a chemical change?"
8. Study Activity I-A-10, "What is a physical change?"
9. Study Activity I-A-11, "What is a solution?"

H. Vocabulary Builders—Spelling Words:

1) **elements** 2) **compounds** 3) **mixtures**
4) **iron** 5) **copper** 6) **sand** 7) **sugar**
8) **marbles**

I. Thought for Today:

"Education is not training but rather the process that equips you to entertain yourself, a friend, and an idea."

A. Problem: *Can Matter Be Changed from One State to Another?*

B. Materials Needed:
1. Heat source
2. Sauce pan
3. Small pieces of ice
4. Thermometer, upper range over 212° F. or 100° C.

C. Procedure:
1. Put the pieces of ice in the sauce pan.
2. Record the temperature reading of the ice in the sauce pan.
3. Heat the sauce pan slowly.
4. Check the temperature at regular intervals until all the ice is melted.
5. Record the temperature when all the ice has changed to water.
6. Continue to apply heat.
7. Check the temperature at regular intervals until most of the water has been changed to steam. (Do this carefully. Steam can burn your hands.)
8. Record this temperature.

D. Results:
1. The temperature of the initial pan of ice will be close to 32° F. or 0° C.
2. The ice will change to water as heat is applied. Little or no temperature change will occur until all the ice has melted.
3. The water will change to steam as more heat is applied.
4. The temperature of water changing to steam will be close to 212° F. or 100° C.
5. It is almost impossible to get accurate temperatures in regular classroom testing.

E. Basic Facts and Supplemental Information:

Heat causes molecules of substances to move faster and farther apart. Sufficient heat can change a solid to a liquid and then to a gas. Various substances have different melting points and different boiling points. The melting point is the point at which a solid changes to a liquid. The boiling point is the temperature at which a liquid changes to a gas. Some substances change directly from a solid to a gas. This is called "sublimation." These are physical changes. See Activities I-A-9 and I-A-10 for physical and chemical changes.

Changes in the states of matter can be very helpful. Fire extinguishers are designed so that burning gases are changed back to liquids or solids that do not burn.

Ice

Water

Steam

Ice is a solid. Ice skaters cannot skate on a solid surface. They are able to "ice skate" because the ice under the blades or runners changes to a liquid.

F. Thought Questions for Class Discussions:
1. Can all matter exist in three states (solids, liquids, and gases)?
2. Is heat, or the reduction of heat, a cause of the change of state of matter?
3. Can you name any other matter, except water, that exists as a solid, liquid, and a gas?

G. Related Ideas for Further Inquiry:
1. Mothballs can be placed in the room and observed daily. They change from a solid to a gas at room temperature.
2. Changes in matter can be reversed. Steam can be condensed on a cold object and then frozen with ice and table salt. Take temperatures as this is done.
3. Make a list of items that you know exist in two or more states: solid and liquid, liquid and gas, or solid and gas.
4. Study how dew, frost, and snow are formed.
5. Study Activity I-A-1, "What are the three states of matter?"
6. Study Activity I-A-10, "What is a physical change?"

H. Vocabulary Builders—Spelling Words:
1) **sublimation** 2) **physical** 3) **chemical**
4) **change** 5) **molecules** 6) **melting**
7) **boiling** 8) **steam** 9) **temperature** 10) **ice**

I. Thought for Today:
"The family fireside is the best of schools."

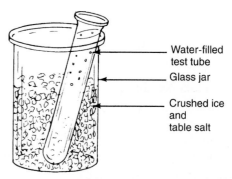

Water-filled test tube
Glass jar
Crushed ice and table salt

Procedure One

A. Problem: *Can a Gas Change to a Liquid? A Liquid to a Gas? A Gas to a Solid? What Is Condensation? Dew?*

B. Materials Needed:

1. Water
2. Crushed ice
3. Table salt
4. Paper towels
5. Glass jar
6. Test tube
7. Heat source
8. Sauce pan
9. Pane of glass
10. Gloves (for handling hot materials and pane of glass)

C. Procedure One:

1. Fill a glass jar with crushed ice.
2. Mix a generous amount of salt with the ice.
3. Place a water-filled test tube upright in the ice.
4. Wrap paper toweling or other insulation around the glass jar.

Procedure Two:

1. Partly fill a sauce pan with water.
2. Apply heat till the water boils.
3. Wearing gloves, carefully hold the pane of glass over the boiling water.
4. Collect the water that runs off into a cup.
5. When the water has cooled, taste it. Does it taste "pure"? It is chemically pure.

D. Results:

1. After several minutes the water in the test tube will become frozen. (Procedure One)
2. Drops of water will condense and collect on the cold glass and run off into the cup. (Procedure Two)

E. Basic Facts and Supplemental Information:

1. Ice around the test tube will cool the water. Salt in the ice lowers the water temperature below the freezing point of water. When the water temperature is cooled to its freezing point (0° C. or 32° F.) the water will freeze (turn into ice). The wrapper helps prevent outside heat from warming the ice-salt mixture. *Note:* Put distilled water in the test tube for best results. The "snow" from a freezer is a good source of mineral-free water. A cool pane of glass, or a cool lid, held several inches above boiling water will cool the vapor rising above the boiling water enough to condense the vapor, i.e., change its state from gas to liquid by lowering the temperature of the gas.
2. When small liquid droplets come together to form larger drops, they are said to have condensed. When water vapor in the air is cooled and

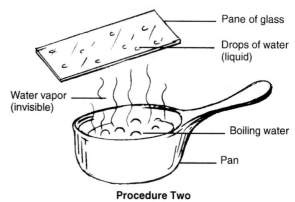

Pane of glass
Drops of water (liquid)
Water vapor (invisible)
Boiling water
Pan

Procedure Two

condensed on cold surfaces such as plants, cars, cement, etc., it is called "dew."

F. Thought Questions for Class Discussions:

1. Is this principle used in making homemade ice cream?
2. Why is the insulation wrapped around the jar?
3. What makes an object hot or cold?
4. What is meant by "dew point"?
5. Does pressure affect condensation?
6. Could we convert salt water to fresh water using this technique? One method is shown in Procedure Two.

G. Related Ideas for Further Inquiry:

1. Wet a piece of cloth and hang it out to dry.
2. Make some ice in a refrigerator freezer at school or have students make some at home.
3. Boil some water. Add several tablespoons of salt. What happens immediately? (Stops boiling)
4. Study Activity I-A-16, "What are the tiniest pieces of matter?"
5. Study Activity I-A-10, "What is a physical change?"

H. Vocabulary Builders—Spelling Words:

1) **liquid**   2) **solid**   3) **condensation**   4) **dew**
5) **crushed**   6) **sauce**   7) **vapor**   8) **boiling**

I. Thought for Today:

"All that humankind has done, thought, gained, or been, can be found in the pages of books."

A. Problem: *Do All Solids Melt at the Same Temperature?*

B. Materials Needed:

1. Water glasses
2. Double boiler or small frying pan
3. Source of heat
4. Ice cubes
5. Thermometer (cooking)
6. Butter
7. Wax
8. Sugar
9. Other substances to be tested
10. Gloves (for handling hot materials)

C. Procedure:

1. Put the ice into a glass and record temperatures as ice melts.
2. Pour the water out.
3. Have students wear gloves as a safety precaution as some substances may splatter when heating.
4. Put the butter in the double boiler or frying pan.
5. Heat it until the butter melts.
6. Have a student note the temperature at which the butter melts.
7. Continue this process with other substances to be tested.
8. Make a graph or table showing the melting point of each of the substances used in the experiments.

D. Result:

Each substance melts at a different temperature.

E. Basic Facts and Supplemental Information:

1. Various materials require different amounts of heat before melting begins.
2. Care must be used in taking the temperatures of these melting points. Several attempts should be made on each trial to ensure accuracy.
3. The melting point is a characteristic which is used to help identify each substance.
4. Melting is a process used in industry to separate and purify materials.

F. Thought Questions for Class Discussion:

1. Does iron have a melting point?
2. Can dry ice be melted?
3. Do you know any solid substance which cannot be melted?

Ice melting

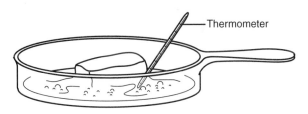

Butter melting

G. Related Ideas for Further Inquiry:

1. Discuss the temperature at which snow melts.
2. Discuss the temperature at which chocolate melts.
3. Study "fractional distillation" in refining fossil fuels.
4. Different solids melt at different temperatures and different liquids vaporize at different temperatures. Scientists use these differences of physical characteristics to separate the various components of mixtures. This is called "fractional distillation."

H. Vocabulary Builders—Spelling Words:

1) **splatter** 2) **physical** 3) **change**
4) **boiling point** 5) **melting point**
6) **thermometer** 7) **temperature** 8) **identify**

I. Thought for Today:

"An ounce of prevention is worth a pound of cure."

A. Problem: *Do All Liquids Boil at the Same Temperature?*

B. Materials Needed:
   1. Large glass jars or beakers
   2. Hot plate (Do not use open flame)
   3. Water
   4. Test tube or small glass container
   5. Rubbing alcohol
   6. Thermometer
   7. Gloves

C. Procedure:
   1. Use gloves as a safety precaution.
   2. Boil some water.
   3. Record the temperature of the water when it boils.
   4. Pour water to the depth of several inches in glass jar or beaker.
   5. Put some alcohol into a small container or test tube and then place the container or tube in the beaker.
   6. Place these two containers over heat. (Be sure the alcohol vapor is not exposed to open flame.)
   7. Record the temperature at which the alcohol boils.

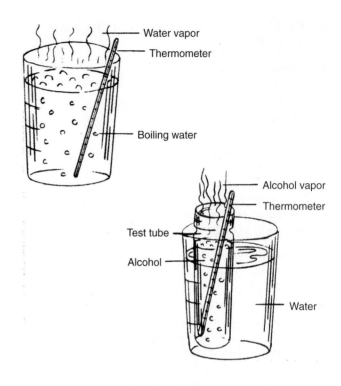

D. Result:

The two liquids boil at different temperatures.

E. Basic Facts and Supplemental Information:
   1. At standard pressure, water boils at 100° C. (212° F.). Rubbing alcohol's boiling point varies because it is a mixture. It usually boils around 78° C.(173° F.).
   2. Each substance has its own boiling point.
   3. Each substance has its own melting point.
   4. Scientists use these points to help identify different substances.
   5. Evaporation is different from boiling. Evaporation is the movement of a liquid into air. Boiling is the changing of the state of matter from a liquid to a gas.
   6. Since each substance has its own melting point and boiling point, we can use these properties to separate a mixture of different substances by heating and/or cooling the mixture. This process is called "fractional distillation."

F. Thought Questions for Class Discussions:
   1. Can all substances be changed into gases?
   2. What would happen in this experiment if the water and alcohol were mixed together in one container and then heated?
   3. Is gasoline made by "fractional distillation"?

G. Related Ideas for Further Inquiry:
   1. Determine the boiling points of other liquids.
   2. Test to find out if milk boils at the same temperature as water.
   3. Investigate evaporation by filling two jars half-full of water and covering one. Place both in the sun for a few days. Check results.
   4. Study the principle of a "vacuum bottle" (thermos bottle).
   5. Study Activity I-A-1, "What are the three states of matter?"
   6. Study Activity I-A-6, "Do all solids melt at the same temperature?"

H. Vocabulary Builders—Spelling Words:
   1) **distillation**   2) **fractional**   3) **boiling point**
   4) **mixture**   5) **alcohol**   6) **jars**   7) **test tube**

I. Thought for Today:

"The written word can be erased; not the spoken one."

Activity

A. Problem: *How Do Materials Combine?*

B. Materials Needed:

1. Sulfur powder
2. Iron filings
3. Two test tubes
4. Magnet
5. Saucer
6. Ring stand
7. Paper towels
8. Hammer
9. Hot plate or Bunsen burner
10. Goggles

C. Procedure:

1. Mix sulfur and iron filings in a test tube.
2. Shake the two elements together.
3. Pour them into a saucer.
4. Using a magnet, separate the iron filings from the sulfur.
5. Put twice as much sulfur as iron filings into a second test tube.
6. Heat this one over a hot plate or Bunsen burner. (Only the teacher or older student under the supervision of the teacher should do this part.)
7. Let cool.
8. Wrap the test tube in paper towels.
9. With hammer, break it as gently as possible.
10. Using the magnet, try to separate the iron filings from the sulfur.

D. Results:

1. When the iron and sulfur were mixed in the first test tube, the magnet attracted all the iron filings.
2. When the iron and sulfur were mixed in the second test tube and heated, a change in color occurred. The magnet was unable to separate the iron filings from the sulfur. They had chemically combined to form iron sulfide.

E. Basic Facts and Supplemental Information:

1. A mixture is the placing together of two or more materials with each material retaining its individual properties. A compound is the union of two or more elements by chemical change, each element no longer retaining its original characteristics.

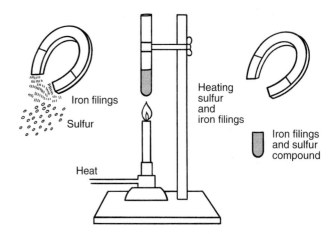

Iron filings

Sulfur

Heating sulfur and iron filings

Iron filings and sulfur compound

Heat

2. A solution is a special kind of mixture. It usually consists of solid materials dissolving in a liquid. Salt water is a good example of this type of mixture. A liquid can be combined with another liquid to form a solution, which is a "physical change." Putting milk into a cup of coffee would be a good example of a physical change. Two liquids could be combined as a result of a chemical change. Mixing an acid with a base would yield this kind of "combination."

F. Thought Questions for Class Discussions:

1. How do we know a chemical change has taken place?
2. What is the difference between a chemical and a physical change?
3. Why won't the magnet attract the iron sulfide compound?

G. Related Ideas for Further Inquiry:

1. Study home food recipes for mixtures.
2. Study mineral ores for compounds.
3. Study Activity I-A-9, "What is a chemical change?"
4. Study Activity I-A-10, "What is a physical change?"

H. Vocabulary Builders—Spelling Words:

1) **materials**   2) **combine**   3) **elements**
4) **compounds**   5) **mixtures**   6) **ores**
7) **magnet**   8) **sulfur**   9) **filings**

I. Thought for Today:

"Those who do not learn from the mistakes of the past are condemned to repeat them."

Activity

A. Problem: *What Is a Chemical Change?*

B. Materials Needed:

1. Heat source (Bunsen burner, Sterno, or alcohol lamp)
2. Tablespoon
3. Cube of sugar
4. Tongs or clothespin
5. Goggles

When sugar is heated it changes chemically and becomes a new substance.

C. Procedure:

1. Hold tablespoon with tongs or clothespin (safety precaution).
2. Place the sugar in the spoon.
3. Hold it over the flame.
4. Notice the changes that take place in the sugar.

D. Result:

The sugar first turns to dark brown and then to black.

E. Basic Facts and Supplemental Information:

The heat causes a chemical change in the sugar. The sugar molecules are broken down and lose hydrogen and oxygen, which are contained in the original sugar molecule. The black substance which is left on the spoon is mainly carbon. Chemical changes may or may not involve heat.

When metals rust or tarnish, a chemical change is taking place. When apples turn brown after being peeled, a chemical change is taking place. When candles burn, chemical changes occur. There are many chemical changes taking place all the time. Our bodies are really chemical factories with their digestive, respiratory, nervous, and muscular systems all involving complex chemical reactions which take place because of the food we eat, the air we breathe, and the water we drink.

F. Thought Questions for Class Discussions:

1. Will heat cause chemical changes to take place in other substances such as salt or sand?
2. How does the change in the sugar compare with melting a substance, such as melting a piece of ice?
3. How many chemical changes can you name?
4. Does a chemical change take place when gasoline burns in an automobile engine?
5. Does a chemical change take place when bread is toasted?

G. Related Ideas for Further Inquiry:

1. Name some chemical changes in which heat is involved.
2. The teacher can separate mercury from mercuric oxide by heating.
3. Examine some iron rust and discuss whether this is a chemical change. (Iron rust can be made quickly by placing steel wool in a solution of water, bleach, and vinegar.)
4. Demonstrate how yeast is used in cooking and describe the chemical change that takes place. Yeast, a fungi, feeds on sugars, and produces alcohol (ethanol) and carbon dioxide. The alcohol is driven off, the carbon dioxide causes the dough to rise, and the yeast is finally killed by the prolonged heating.
5. Study Activity I-A-8, "How do materials combine?"
6. Study Activity I-A-10, "What is a physical change?"

H. Vocabulary Builders—Spelling Words:

1) **molecules** 2) **decomposition** 3) **dehydration**
4) **tablespoon** 5) **clothespin** 6) **chemical**
7) **sugar** 8) **heat** 9) **substance**

I. Thought for Today:

"The difference between genius and stupidity is that genius has limits."

A. Problem: *What Is a Physical Change?*

B. Materials Needed:
1. Water glass
2. Paper napkins
3. Teaspoon
4. Measuring cup
5. Sugar
6. Clean sand
7. Iron filings
8. Magnet
9. Water

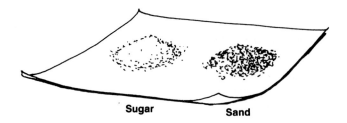

Sugar   Sand

C. Procedure:
1. Mix two teaspoons of sugar with two teaspoons of sand on a paper napkin.
2. Fill the measuring cup half-full with water.
3. Put the mixture of sugar and sand into the water, and stir for a few seconds.
4. Let the mixture settle until the solution is clear.
5. Pour the liquid part of the solution into the glass.
6. Taste a drop of solution from the glass.
7. Mix the iron filings and the sand.
8. Use a magnet and remove the iron filings.
9. Discuss other examples of physical change such as:
   a. pumping up bicycle tires
   b. turning on a light bulb
   c. mowing the lawn
   d. sharpening a pencil
   e. writing answers on an examination paper
   f. drawing pictures on the chalkboard

D. Results:
1. With the sand and the sugar mixture, the sand was not dissolved in the solution, and when the stirring was stopped it settled to the bottom.
2. The sugar dissolves in the solution. It remains as sugar so the water tastes sweet.
3. The iron filings are extracted by the magnet.

E. Basic Facts and Supplemental Information:
1. The sugar can be recovered to its solid state by placing the solution in a pan over low heat and evaporating the water slowly. (See Activity I-A-11, "What is a solution?") Crystals of sugar will form in the bottom of the pan.
2. Physical changes do not change the basic physical material(s), but may change its shape, condition, etc.
3. A mixture is a combination of materials which changes none of the characteristics of the substances of which it is made.

Sugar solution

F. Thought Questions for Class Discussions:
1. How can we separate a mixture of iron filings and sand?
2. How can we separate a mixture of golf balls and tennis balls?
3. Is air a mixture?

G. Related Ideas for Further Inquiry:
1. Put dissolved materials aside and let the water or solvent evaporate naturally.
2. Discuss more examples of physical change found in the classroom:
   a. heating or cooling the room
   b. writing with pens
   c. tossing paper into the wastebasket
3. Study Activity I-A-8, "How do materials combine?"
4. Study Activity I-A-9, "What is a chemical change?"
5. Study Activity I-A-11, "What is a solution?"

H. Vocabulary Builders—Spelling Words:
1) **solvents** 2) **solute** 3) **evaporate** 4) **iron**
5) **filings** 6) **sugar** 7) **sand** 8) **magnets**

I. Thought for Today:
"Technological progress has given society a more efficient way of going backwards."

Activity

A. Problem: *What Is a Solution?*

B. Materials Needed:
1. Water glass
2. Water, warm
3. Teaspoon
4. Sugar
5. Measuring cup

C. Procedure:
1. Fill the water glass with warm water using the measuring cup to fill the glass to the brim, but not overflowing.
2. Fill the teaspoon with sugar.
3. Slowly and carefully add the sugar to the water.
4. Wait until it dissolves completely.
5. Add a second teaspoon of sugar slowly and carefully.
6. Sometimes a third teaspoon of sugar can be added depending on the size of the glass and the temperature of the water.
7. Ask the class, "Where did the sugar go? Why doesn't the water overflow?"

D. Results:
1. The first teaspoon of sugar will dissolve quickly.
2. The second teaspoon of sugar will dissolve but will take a little more time.
3. Usually, the third teaspoon of sugar will cause the water to overflow.

E. Basic Facts and Supplemental Information:
1. A solution is a liquid containing a dissolved substance. The substance can be a solid, liquid, or a gas.
2. In solids, molecules are packed tightly together.
3. In liquids, molecules are wider apart, thus leaving "holes" or "openings."
4. In gases, molecules become disconnected, and they will dissipate anywhere they can.
5. In this activity, the solid sugar molecules find the "holes" or "openings" and do not take up any more volume.
6. When these are full, the water can no longer hold any more sugar, so the volume increases and the water overflows.
7. The warmer the water, the larger the "holes" or "openings" and the more sugar can be added.
8. Whenever a solid substance is homogeneously mixed with a liquid and does not precipitate out, it

Sugar dissolving in water

is known as "dissolving" the substance in the liquid. The resulting liquid is a combination of the original liquid, plus the solid, which has been dissolved in it. This is known as a solution. Liquids can hold only so much dissolved material for each temperature.
9. There are many solutions we come in contact with daily in our homes, in our schools, and in our neighborhoods. In our homes, liquid detergents, hair sprays, soft drinks, liquid medicines, bleaches, chocolate milk, and some salad dressings are good examples of solutions.

F. Thought Questions for Class Discussions:
1. What would happen in a "saturated solution" if the liquid solvent were cooled?
2. Can air hold water? Can water hold air?
3. Is a solution a mixture?

G. Related Ideas for Further Inquiry:
1. Study solutions found in the home.
2. Study why some solutions are thicker or thinner (viscosity).
3. Study Activity I-A-2, "What are atoms? molecules?"
4. Study Activity I-A-4, "Can matter be changed from one state to another?"
5. Study Activity I-A-10, "What is a physical change?"

H. Vocabulary Builders—Spelling Words:
1) **solution** 2) **solvent** 3) **solute** 4) **dissolve**
5) **molecules** 6) **movement** 7) **teaspoon**
8) **sugar**

I. Thought for Today:
"Chemistry is no field for people with shaky hands."

A. Problem: *What Matter Is Acidic? What Matter Is Alkaline?*

B. Materials Needed:
1. Three water glasses
2. Red litmus paper
3. Blue litmus paper
4. Vinegar
5. Ammonia or baking soda
6. Salt
7. Water

C. Procedure:
1. Prepare a salt water solution by placing one-half teaspoon of salt in a glass of water.
2. Dip a piece of red and a piece of blue litmus paper into this solution.
3. In a second glass of water place a small amount (one-quarter of a teaspoon) of vinegar.
4. Dip a piece of blue litmus paper into this solution.
5. In a third glass of water place about a quarter of a teaspoon of baking soda or ammonia.
6. Dip a piece of red litmus paper into this solution.
7. Dip a piece of red litmus in the vinegar.
8. Dip a piece of blue litmus in the baking soda or ammonia solution.

D. Results:
1. In the salt water solution the red and blue litmus papers did not change color.
2. In the vinegar solution the blue litmus paper turned red.
3. In the ammonia or baking soda solution the red litmus paper turned blue.
4. See "Basic Facts and Supplemental Information" for other test results.

E. Basic Facts and Supplemental Information:
1. Ions are atoms or molecules that have gained or lost electrons from their original outer shell.
2. Solutions usually have hydrogen or hydroxide ions. If they have hydrogen ions they are acidic. If they have hydroxide ions they are alkaline (basic).
3. Litmus paper turns blue in the presence of alkaline solutions and red in the presence of acids. We can say then that acids turn blue litmus red and bases turn red litmus blue.
4. We can conclude in these procedures that vinegar is acidic and that ammonia (or baking soda) is basic.

Salt water

Red and blue litmus paper remain the same.

Vinegar

Blue litmus paper turns red.

Ammonia

Red litmus paper turns blue.

5. Other liquids can be tested to determine if they are acidic or basic.
6. Water (H_2O) has the form H-OH. In solutions it becomes H^+ ("H-Plus"), a hydrogen ion and OH^- ("OH Minus"), a hydroxide ion.
7. Some tap water may be naturally acidic or naturally basic. If so, bottled or distilled water will have to be used.

F. Thought Questions for Class Discussions:
1. Why do we need to know whether a substance is acid or alkaline?
2. If acid is spilled, how can we prevent it from causing damage?
3. What color would litmus paper test with lemon juice? Why?

G. Related Ideas for Further Inquiry:
1. Test other liquids to determine if they are acidic or alkaline.
2. Research other chemical tests for determining acidity or alkalinity of liquids.
3. If you put blue litmus paper in lemon juice, it turns red, showing that lemon juice is acidic.
4. If you put red litmus paper in a test solution and it turns blue, this proves the solution is alkaline (basic).
5. Study Activity I-A-2, "What are atoms? molecules?"
6. Study Activity I-A-11, "What is a solution?"

H. Vocabulary Builders—Spelling Words:
1) **acidic** 2) **alkaline** 3) **alkalinity** 4) **basic**
5) **litmus paper** 6) **vinegar** 7) **ammonia**
8) **baking soda** 9) **lemon juice**

I. Thought for Today:
"If people learn from their mistakes, many are getting a fantastic education."

A. Problem: *How Does Living Matter Differ from Nonliving Matter?*

B. Materials Needed:
1. Books
2. Pencils
3. Rocks
4. Small plants
5. Classroom animals
6. Pictures of students' pets
7. Plastic items (comb, ruler, etc.)
8. Miscellaneous items

C. Procedure:
1. Have class make a list of:
   a. nonliving things
   b. plants
   c. animals
2. List the characteristics of each group.
3. Compare and contrast their differences.

D. Results:
1. The pupils will recognize the differences between living and nonliving things and between plants and animals.
2. They will understand that most known living things are classified as either plants or animals.
3. Students will learn that many scientists today classify all living things in five main kingdoms: a. Monera, b. Protista, c. Fungi, d. Plants, e. Animals.

E. Basic Facts and Supplemental Information:
1. Living things are alike in some respects and different in others.
2. Nonliving things have very few characteristics of living things.
3. Animals move about; plants do not.
4. Animals have senses for locating food and the means of locomotion to obtain it.
5. Most plants make their own food.
6. Living matter will have the following characteristics: (a) reproduce, (b) feed, (c) react to stimuli (irritability), (d) grow, (e) develop, (f) acquire energy, (g) have cells (or are one), (h) respire (breathe), (i) have complex structure (protoplasm), (j) die (may omit this for younger students).
7. All living matter can be divided into three main classes:
   a. Producers (plants, fungi, algae)
   b. Consumers (most animals, including people)
   c. Reducers-decomposers (bacteria, fungi, etc.)

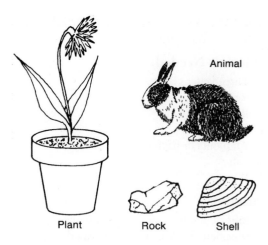

Animal

Plant   Rock   Shell

8. If it weren't for reducers-decomposers we would be living in one big garbage pile.

F. Thought Questions for Class Discussions:
1. How do some nonliving things move?
2. What is the biggest living thing you know about? the smallest?
3. What is the largest nonliving thing? the smallest?
4. Do nonliving things ever affect other nonliving things?

G. Related Ideas for Further Inquiry:
1. Look at some nonliving things with a microscope or magnifying glass.
2. Do some research on the biggest and smallest living things and nonliving things.
3. Younger students can collect pictures of plants and animals.
4. Students can study the "growth patterns" of plants and animals.
5. Study Activity III-A-1, "How do we classify living things?"
6. Study Activity IV-A-2, "How many different species of animals are there?"

H. Vocabulary Builders—Spelling Words:
1) **nonliving** 2) **locomotion** 3) **stimuli**
4) **respiration** 5) **protoplasm** 6) **irritability**

I. Thought for Today:
"One of the secrets of a long and fruitful life is to forgive everybody everything every night before you go to bed."—Ann Landers

A. Problem: *How Can We Make Invisible Ink?*

B. Materials Needed:
1. Lemon
2. Toothpicks
3. Shallow dish
4. White paper
5. Heat source (light bulb)

Secret writing

C. Procedure:
1. Squeeze the juice from half a lemon into the shallow dish.
2. Use the juice to write. (A toothpick makes a good pen for invisible ink.)
3. Set aside the paper with the writing on it to dry.
4. Heat the paper by holding it over a light bulb.
5. Move the paper around so that all the invisible writing gets warm.

D. Results:
1. As the lemon juice dries it becomes invisible.
2. As the paper heats, the writing becomes visible.

E. Basic Facts and Supplemental Information:
1. The heat causes a chemical change in the lemon juice which makes it turn brown. The writing, therefore, becomes visible. This system can be used to send "secret messages." This is a simple chemical experiment. The heat "burns" the chemicals so that they become visible.
2. The browning of the dried juice when heated is due to the caramelizing of the sugars in the liquid.
3. Many other liquids can be used:
   a. grapefruit juice
   b. lime juice
   c. onion juice
   d. milk

F. Thought Questions for Class Discussions:
1. Will sugar in water have the same result as the lemon juice?
2. Will white vinegar yield the same result?
3. What other substances change color when heated?

4. Will plain water work?
5. What are some other safe sources of heat that could be used in this activity?

G. Related Ideas for Further Inquiry:
1. Students can write "secret" messages to one another using this procedure.
2. Study Activity I-A-4 "Can matter be changed from one state to another?"
3. Study Activity I-A-9, "What is a chemical change?"
4. Study Activity I-A-11, "What is a solution?"
5. Other types of communication can be explored:
   a. telegraph
   b. signal flags
   c. flares
   d. traffic signs
   e. signal lights
   f. sign language, etc.

H. Vocabulary Builders—Spelling Words:
1) **invisible** 2) **secret** 3) **ink** 4) **lemon**
5) **magic** 6) **toothpick** 7) **fire** 8) **oxygen**
9) **combustible** 10) **shallow** 11) **dish**

I. Thought for Today:
"A person who doesn't read books has no advantage over the person who can't read."

A. Problem: *What Is Diffusion?*

B. Materials Needed, Procedure One:
1. Water glass
2. Medicine dropper
3. Ink or food coloring
4. Water

Materials Needed, Procedure Two:
1. Water glass or beaker
2. Coffee crystals
3. Water

Materials Needed, Procedure Three:
1. Two water glasses or clear plastic containers with tops
2. Mothballs

Materials Needed, Procedure Four:
(See following page for Activity)
1. Bulletin board
2. 100 cutout disks
   a. red color preferred
   b. about one and a half inches in diameter
3. 100 straight pins

C. Procedure One:
1. Fill one of the glasses two-thirds full of water.
2. Put some ink or food coloring in the medicine dropper and place several drops on the surface of the water.
3. Set glass aside and observe after several hours.

Procedure Two:
1. Place some coffee crystals in a water glass or beaker.
2. Slowly pour water over the crystals and let stand. Observe results immediately and again after several hours.

Procedure Three:
1. Place one mothball in each of two containers, capping one of them.
2. Let stand for several days or weeks and note any changes.

Procedure Four:
1. Pin 100 disks on the bulletin board in ten rows of ten disks to a row closely packed together (see sketch). Do not discuss this with anyone.
2. On day two, spread the disks apart, leaving about an inch between each of the disks. Again avoid any conversations regarding them.

Ink or food coloring diffusing

Procedure One

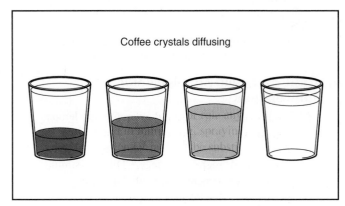

Coffee crystals diffusing

Procedure Two

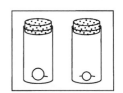

The mothball in the capped jar becomes smaller.

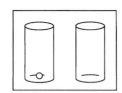

The mothball in the uncapped jar disappears.

Procedure Three

3. On day three, move the disks so that there are three or more inches between the disks.
4. On the fourth day, pin the disks all over the bulletin board in random fashion. Now discuss what has been happening. Diffusion!!!
5. Ask the class if they know what "diffusion" is.

6. Challenge the class to teach others about diffusion. (Added incentives often help.)
7. Pin one of the disks on the clothing of each student; have students wear the disk for one school day. When anyone asks them what it is, tell the students they will have to explain "diffusion" to that person. To verify that this is being done, the "nonclass" person who asked what the disk was for would be requested to initial the back of the disk. When a student has five initials on his/her disk, it can be taken off. The author knows of one teacher who was promoted primarily on the basis of this activity. Everyone in that teacher's school knew the meaning of "diffusion."

D. Results:

1. When drops of ink or food coloring are placed on the surface of the water, the molecules in a liquid state (ink or food coloring) move through the water.
2. When some coffee crystals are placed in a glass of water, the molecules in a solid state (coffee) move through water.
3. In the activity with mothballs, the mothball in the uncovered jar will eventually disappear. The mothball in the covered jar will become smaller. Mothballs change to a gas and dissipate in time.
4. In Procedure Four, everyone learns the meaning of "diffusion."

E. Basic Facts and Supplemental Information:

1. Molecules are so small that we cannot see them.
2. Molecules are in constant motion regardless of whether they are in a solid, liquid, or gaseous state.
3. In Procedures One, Two, and Three we can think of the ink or food coloring, coffee crystals, or mothballs as clumps of molecules.

F. Thought Questions for Class Discussions:

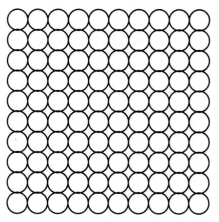

Diffusion disks

Procedure Four

1. Why do clothes dry faster outside?
2. Where does all the water go when it rains?
3. Would perfume be valuable if it didn't diffuse?

G. Related Ideas for Further Inquiry:

1. Study Activity I-A-1, "What are the three states of matter?"
2. Study Activity I-A-2, "What are atoms? molecules?"
3. Study Activity I-A-10, "What is a physical change?"
4. Study: Activity I-A-11, "What is a solution?"

H. Vocabulary Builders—Spelling Words:

1) **diffusion** 2) **mothballs** 3) **coffee** 4) **crystals**
5) **disks** 6) **dissolving** 7) **evaporation**
8) **molecules**

I. Thought for Today:

"Do not put off until tomorrow what you can do today."

A. Problem: *What Are the Tiniest Pieces of Matter?*

B. Materials Needed:
1. Paper
2. Pencils (black and colored)
3. Drawing compasses
4. Reference materials on atomic structure

C. Procedure:
1. Describe and define atoms and their subatomic particles.
2. Have students read about atomic structure.
3. Have students draw the four sketches after they have read the characteristics of each.
4. Using whatever color code you wish, color the various parts of each drawing.
5. Mount the better drawings on the bulletin board.

D. Results:
1. Students will learn about the tiniest pieces of matter by studying and drawing the present information we have on atomic structure.
2. Students will learn that matter is composed of large pieces which can be broken down into smaller and smaller pieces.

E. Basic Facts and Supplemental Information:
1. Scientists have determined that atoms are the smallest particles of matter that still retain the characteristics of the larger piece of matter.
2. Atoms are composed of protons and neutrons in a nucleus and electrons orbiting around the nucleus.
3. Neutrons and protons collectively are called "nucleons."
4. All nucleons consist of quarks and leptons.
5. A proton consists of a(n):
   a. electron (charged lepton)
   b. electron neutrino (neutral lepton)
   c. up quarks (two of them)
   d. down quark (one of them)
6. A neutron consists of a(n):
   a. electron (charged lepton)
   b. electron neutrino (neutral neutrino)
   c. down quarks (two of them)
   d. up quark (one of them)
7. Gluons bind the quarks together.
8. Over 100 types of atomic particles have been identified.
9. Scientists have been able to identify different particles by pictures taken in "atom smashers."

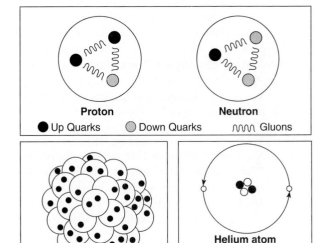

Proton
● Up Quarks ◐ Down Quarks 〰 Gluons

Neutron

Nucleus of a large atom

Helium atom
● - Protons
○ - Neutrons
○ - Electrons in orbit

10. Most of these particles exist only for a fraction of a second.
11. We still don't know all the subatomic particles and how they are related to each other.
12. In German, "quark" means "cottage cheese."

F. Thought Questions for Class Discussions:
1. Do you think that leptons and quarks can be subdivided? New evidence suggests this.
2. Do our bodies contain leptons and quarks?
3. Is there anything that doesn't contain leptons and quarks?
4. How do scientists find out about subatomic particles, particles that are too small to be seen with the naked eye?

G. Related Ideas for Further Inquiry:
1. Study the different "families" of matter.
2. Students can make models of atoms by using clay, styrofoam, or paper mobiles.
3. Study Activity I-A-1 "What are the three states of matter?"
4. Study Activity I-A-3, "What are elements? compounds? mixtures?"
5. Study Activity I-A-15, "What is diffusion?"

H. Vocabulary Builders—Spelling Words:
1) **atoms** 2) **electrons** 3) **protons** 4) **neutrons**
5) **leptons** 6) **quarks** 7) **neutrinos** 8) **gluons**

I. Thought for Today:
"The impossible is often the untried."

A. Problem: *What Is Air? What Are Its Characteristics?*

B. Materials Needed:
1. Water glass
2. Straw (plastic)
3. Matches
4. Paper windmill
5. Water, colored

C. Procedure:
1. Fill the glass with water.
2. Place the straw in the glass of water.
3. Blow through the straw.
4. Ask students what causes the bubbles.
5. Place your index finger over the top of the straw.
6. Lift the straw above the glass.
7. Ask class what holds the water in the straw.
8. Lift your finger off the top of the straw.
9. Ask students why the water now falls.
10. Have students blow against their hands.
11. Ask class what they felt on their hands.
12. Light a match carefully.
13. Ask class why it burns.
14. Blow out the match.
15. Blow against the paper windmill.

D. Results:
1. Bubbles will be seen in the glass of water.
2. The water will remain in the plastic straw until finger is removed from the top—then the water will run out.
3. Students will feel pressure against their hands when they blow on them.
4. The match burns until the gas from the wood is removed by blowing.
5. The paper windmill will rotate.

E. Basic Facts and Supplemental Information:
1. We are living in an ocean of air.
2. Air is all around us.
3. Air is found in the ground.
4. Air is found in water.
5. All living things need air.
6. Moving air is called wind.
7. We cannot see air but we can feel it.
8. Air is composed primarily of gases:
   a. 78% is nitrogen
   b. 21% is oxygen
   c. traces of other gases: argon, neon, carbon dioxide, ozone, carbon monoxide, etc. make up the other 1%.

9. Air also contains tiny particles of solid matter held in suspension:
   a. salt
   b. dust
   c. soot
   d. ash, etc.
10. Air has weight.
11. Air takes up space.
12. The air surrounding the Earth is about 500 miles high. This is called our atmosphere.
13. The atmosphere also holds water vapor which has been obtained through evaporation.

F. Thought Questions for Class Discussions:
1. Do animals need air?
2. Do people need air?
3. Do plants need air?
4. Do fires need air for combustion?
5. Besides breathing, how else do people use air?

G. Related Ideas for Further Inquiry:
1. Study Activity I-B-5, "How does air help us?"
2. Study Activity I-B-12, "Can air pressure crush a can?"
3. Study Section VIII-A, "Aviation."

H. Vocabulary Builders—Spelling Words:
1) **atmosphere**   2) **compression**   3) **nitrogen**
4) **carbon dioxide**   5) **oxygen**

I. Thought for Today:
"Air travel is wonderful; it allows you to pass motorists at a safe distance."

Activity

A. Problem: *How Does a Chimney Work?*

B. Materials Needed:
1. Metal funnel
2. Saucer
3. Small pencils (three or four)
4. Candle
5. Piece of cotton or woolen cloth
6. Matches
7. Tongs

C. Procedure:
1. Secure a small candle in an upright position on the saucer. (The candle must be short enough so that the funnel will fit over it.)
2. Light the candle.
3. Place the funnel over the candle in such a way that the edge of the funnel sits directly on the saucer. Note what happens to the flame.
4. Carefully remove the funnel.
5. Place the small pencils on the saucer so they will support the funnel as shown in the drawing. The funnel must be clear of the candle.
6. Light the candle again.
7. Carefully place the funnel over the candle and on the small pencils.
8. Using tongs to be safe, carefully light the cotton or woolen cloth.
9. As soon as it begins to burn, blow it out.
10. Place the smoldering piece of cloth just under the lower edge of the funnel and note how the smoke travels.

D. Results:
1. When the funnel is placed over the candle without any air space underneath, the candle is quickly extinguished because its oxygen supply is cut off.
2. When the base of the funnel is resting on the pencils and is placed over the candle, air travels underneath the funnel and smoke comes out of the opening at the top end of the funnel.

E. Basic Facts and Supplemental Information:
1. When no air is allowed to flow underneath the funnel, the candle is extinguished because the oxygen required to support combustion is not available. As soon as air is allowed to enter under the funnel, the path of air can be traced and this

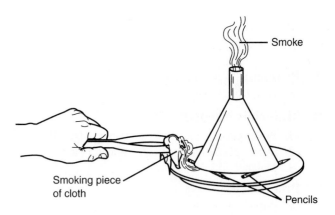

Smoke

Smoking piece of cloth

Pencils

indicates that air travels below the funnel and out the top. As long as air reaches the candle it will continue to burn. The candle uses the oxygen in the funnel, and if a fresh supply of air is not available the candle will go out.
2. Chimneys work on this principle. Air containing oxygen is drawn to the fire by the rising warm air. This reduces the air pressure at the fire which produces a circulation of air. Some heat is radiated into the room, but most of the heat goes up the chimney. Chimneys have "drafts" which minimize heat loss and control the speed of circulation.

F. Thought Questions for Class Discussions:
1. With vertically opening windows, why do people open them both at the top and at the bottom?
2. Does hot air rise or fall? Why?
3. What is smoke?

G. Related Ideas for Further Inquiry:
1. Shake a little talcum powder in the air and see what happens. Now using a heat source that has been on for a few minutes, shake some fine talcum powder over it. What does it do? Rise or fall? Why?
2. Discuss why heavy hot air balloons rise.

H. Vocabulary Builders—Spelling Words:
1) **extinguish**   2) **combustion**   3) **candle**
4) **funnel**   5) **saucer**   6) **circulation**
7) **smoke**   8) **drafts**   9) **chimney**

I. Thought for Today:
"A laugh at your own expense costs you nothing."—Mary H. Waldrip

Activity

A. Problem: *Does Air Take Up Space?*

B. Materials Needed:
1. Small aquarium or large, clear bowl
2. Bottle (small, thin-necked)
3. Water
4. Two large water glasses

C. Procedure One:
1. Fill the aquarium with water.
2. Invert the small bottle and move it down to the bottom of the aquarium.
3. Slowly move the bottle to an upright position.
4. Observe results.

Procedure Two:
1. Continue to use the aquarium.
2. Turn one water glass upside down and push it to the bottom of the aquarium. You will have to hold it down. It will stay full of air.
3. While holding the first glass down, slowly fill the second glass with water. When it is filled, move it face down to the bottom of the aquarium.
4. Move the second glass close to the first glass, keeping both of them face down.
5. Tilt the first glass so that the air from this glass rises into the second glass.
6. Observe results.

D. Results:
1. In Procedure One, air bubbles will rise to the surface and water will fill the bottle.
2. In Procedure Two, the air from the first glass will replace the water in the second glass.

E. Basic Facts and Supplemental Information:
1. Air takes up space.
2. We can't see, smell, or feel air unless it is in motion.
3. Air has weight.
4. Air is composed of many gases.
5. Nitrogen constitutes about 79% of air; oxygen 20%.
6. Air pressure is 14.7 pounds per square inch at sea level.
7. This pressure forced the water out of the second glass in Procedure Two.

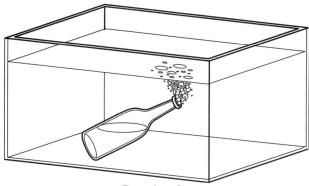

Procedure One

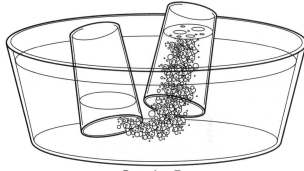

Procedure Two

F. Thought Questions for Class Discussions:
1. Can we weigh air?
2. How do we use air pressure?
3. Can two objects occupy the same space at the same time?

G. Related Ideas for Further Inquiry:
1. Study Activity I-B-11, "Can air pressure lift heavy objects?"
2. Study Activity I-B-12, "Can air pressure crush a can?"
3. Study Activity I-B-l0, "Can air pressure hold water in an inverted glass?"

H. Vocabulary Builders—Spelling Words:
1) **air** 2) **space** 3) **water** 4) **pressure**
5) **bottle** 6) **aquarium** 7) **tilt** 8) **glasses**

I. Thought for Today:
"Castles in the air cost a vast deal to keep up."

Activity

A. Problem: *Does Air Have Weight?*

B. Materials Needed:

1. Two balloons (same size)
2. Thin table or bench
3. Long dowel (longer than the width of table or bench)
4. Short dowel, 10″–12″
5. Tape
6. Two cans (same size)
7. String
8. Needle or pin
9. Pencil

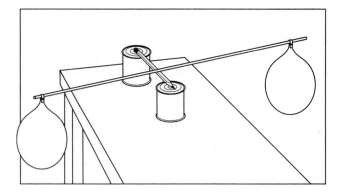

C. Procedure:

1. Place the two cans about eight inches apart toward one end of the table or bench.
2. Tape the short dowel to the tops of the cans so it can't move.
3. Mark the middle of the long dowel with a heavy pencil mark.
4. Blow up both balloons fully and secure them with string so that they are air-tight.
5. With other pieces of string tie the necks of the balloons, making a loop so that the loops can be slipped on the edges of the long dowel. (See drawing.)
6. Slip each balloon on one edge of the long dowel, balancing it by the center pencil mark.
7. You may have to adjust one balloon or the other to get them to balance.
8. While holding the two dowels lightly, either you or one of your students should puncture one balloon so that the air will rush out.

D. Results:

1. The air will rush out of the punctured balloon.
2. The second balloon will drop down.

E. Basic Facts and Supplemental Information:

1. This proves that air has weight.
2. There is no loss of weight from either balloon after the air is released from one.
3. Air molecules are affected by gravity.
4. Air exerts pressure in all directions.
5. Wind is moving air.

6. When air is moving in one direction, it exerts less pressure perpendicularly. This is called "Bernoulli's Principle."
7. Air is a composition of many gases, some water vapor, and many kinds of small solid particles.
8. If you don't want to puncture the balloon, you can untie the string of one, let the air out, and then replace it on the dowel.

F. Thought Questions for Class Discussions:

1. Do inflated tires weigh more than deflated ones?
2. Do compressed air tanks weigh more when filled than empty?
3. Is air pressure related to air weight?

G. Related Ideas for Further Inquiry:

1. Study Activity I-B-1, "What is air? What are its characteristics?"
2. Study Activity I-B-3, "Does air take up space?"
3. Study Activity I-B-10, "Can air pressure hold water in an inverted glass?"
4. Study Activity I-B-16, "How does a siphon work?"
5. Study Activity I-B-19, "In which direction does moving air exert the most pressure?"

H. Vocabulary Builders—Spelling Words:

1) **weight** 2) **pressure** 3) **dowel** 4) **balance**
5) **balloon** 6) **Bernoulli's Principle**
7) **puncture** 8) **dowel** 9) **loop**

I. Thought for Today:

"A student will study more if you pull a few cords: computer, television, telephone, etc."

Activity

A. Problem: *How Does Air Help Us?*

B. Materials Needed:
1. Tire pump
2. Model airplane
3. Inflated ball
4. Elongated balloon
5. Diving mask
6. Bicycle tire
7. Atomizer
8. Model automobile
9. Model submarine
10. Picture of deep sea diver
11. Other objects, models, or pictures of ways in which air helps us.

C. Procedure:
1. Place all the objects on a "science table" or "learning center."
2. Ask class what all these objects have in common.
3. Discuss how air is used in the home:
   a. cooking
   b. vacuuming
   c. hair dryers
   d. clothes dryers
   e. paint sprays
   f. air hoses
   g. siphoning
   h. air conditioners
   i. furnaces
   j. aerosol sprays
4. Discuss how parents use air in their work.
5. Discuss how air is used in recreation.

D. Results:
1. Students will learn that people use air in many ways.
2. Pupils will gain a better respect for this natural commodity.

E. Basic Facts and Supplemental Information:
1. Air is a combination of many gases, primarily nitrogen and oxygen.
2. We are polluting our air with automobile exhausts, industrial wastes, and trash burning.
3. The primary sources of oxygen in our air are from phytoplankton and trees.
4. If we pollute our oceans, destroy the phytoplankton and cut down our trees, what will happen to our oxygen supply?
5. The primary component of weather is air.

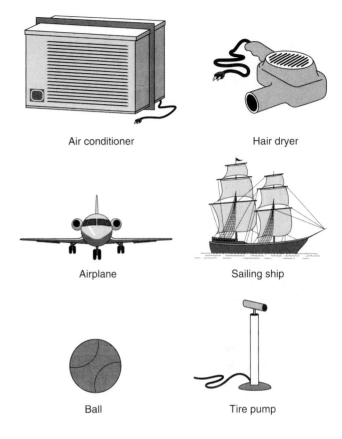

Air conditioner

Hair dryer

Airplane

Sailing ship

Ball

Tire pump

F. Thought Questions for Class Discussions:
1. Could we talk to each other if there were no air?
2. Could we live without air?
3. What can we do to keep our air pure?
4. How does warming and cooling of our air affect our weather?
5. Is smog dirty air?

G. Related Ideas for Further Inquiry:
1. Study all Activities in this Section I-B, "Air."
2. Study Section VII-C, "Earth's Crust."
3. Study Section VII-E, "Weather."

H. Vocabulary Builders—Spelling Words:
1) **inflation** 2) **compression** 3) **pressure**
4) **siphon** 5) **weather vane** 6) **airplane**

I. Thought for Today:
"The wife of an airplane pilot is the only person who likes to see her husband down and out."

Activity

A. Problem: *Does Warm Air Rise or Fall?*
Expand or Contract?

B. Materials Needed, Procedure One:
1. Thread or string
2. Yardstick or meterstick
3. Pencil
4. Several books
5. Table
6. Two paper bags of equal size and weight
7. Candle
8. Matches
9. Coat hanger (wire)
10. Wooden block
11. Scissors

Materials Needed, Procedure Two (next page):
1. Thin paper, 4″ × 4″
2. Scissors
3. Candle
4. Matches
5. Thread
6. Pencil or pen
7. Supporting device

C. Procedure One:
1. Make a loop out of a 12″ piece of thread or string and use it to support the yardstick or meterstick at the halfway mark.
2. Tie the other end of the thread in a loop and attach over a pencil, supported under several books set near the end of the table.
3. Make two pin-sized holes in the bottom of each of the bags; run a piece of thread through the holes and make the thread into a loose loop.
4. Hang both bags on the yardstick or meterstick as shown in the diagram. If the bags are exactly the same weight, they should make the yardstick or meterstick balance when they are placed one inch from each end. You may have to adjust one bag slightly until you get them balanced.
5. Hold a lighted candle a foot or more below the mouth of one open bag until the air inside is warmed. *Be careful with flame!*
6. Remove the candle and extinguish the flame.
7. When the bags are balanced again, place the lighted candle a foot or more below the mouth of the other bag. Again, be careful with flame!
8. Remove the candle and extinguish the flame.

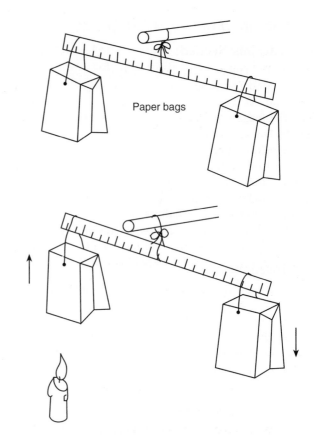

Paper bags

Procedure One

Procedure Two:
1. Cut a circular piece of paper about four inches in diameter.
2. Starting from the outside of the circle, cut a continuous strip about an inch wide.
3. Cut and bend the wire coat hanger so that you have one long, straight piece.
4. Staple or nail this to the baseboard, bending the end at right angles for support.
5. Place one end of the spiral on top of the wire without puncturing the strip.
6. Light a candle beneath the strip.

D. Results, Procedure One:
1. The bag with the warm air will rise.
2. When the candle is removed and the warm air is dissipated (in a few seconds) the bags will again be balanced.

3. When the air in the second bag was warmed, it rose higher than the other.
4. When air is warmed, the molecules move farther apart; consequently warm air expands and rises.

Results, Procedure Two:

1. The "paper snake" will slowly start to turn.
2. It will continue to rotate as long as the candle remains lighted.

E. Basic Facts and Supplemental Information:

The bag with the warm air rises; therefore, it must be lighter than the air in the other bag. Heat causes air to expand. As air expands it becomes lighter because there are fewer molecules per unit of volume. Cold causes air to contract. As air contracts it becomes heavier. Air has weight. Air has pressure because it has weight and movement. Most draft furnaces in houses operate on this heat principle. As the air is heated it becomes lighter and rises. Cold air comes in from the sides or below, and thus a circulation of air takes place. This is very different from the principle of radiant heating by which the house is heated by radiation instead of air circulation.

There are three ways that heat travels:

1. convection
2. conduction
3. radiation

In both these activities it is "convection" that causes the bag to rise and the "paper snake" to rotate.

F. Thought Questions for Class Discussions:

1. What problems do people have who fly hot air balloons?
2. What happens to tires on a car or bicycle when the tires heat up or cool down?
3. Can you think of any other ways that warm or hot air works for us?

G. Related Ideas for Further Inquiry:

1. Check the air temperature in different places around the school.
2. Check air movement in your classroom. (Hold a thin strip of paper or light piece of thread in test area.)
3. Study Activity VII-E-1, "What makes the wind blow?"
4. Study Activity I-B-7, "How do hot air balloons ascend and descend?"

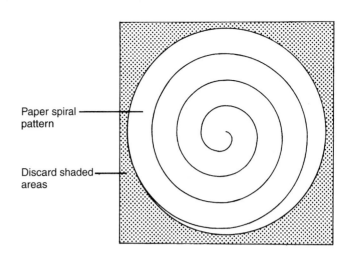

Paper spiral pattern

Discard shaded areas

Procedure Two

H. Vocabulary Builders—Spelling Words:

1) **ascend** 2) **descend** 3) **convection**
4) **candle** 5) **matches** 6) **spiral** 7) **conduction**
8) **radiation**

I. Thought for Today:

"A teacher affects eternity: no one can tell where his influence stops."—Henry Adams

Activity

A. Problem: *How Do Hot Air Balloons Ascend and Descend?*

B. Materials Needed:

1. Tissue paper
2. Scissors
3. Hair dryer
4. Cellophane tape
5. Pen or marking device
6. Long ruler, yardstick, or meterstick
7. Long piece of heavy thread

C. Procedure:

1. If a large piece of tissue is available, lay out the pattern as shown in the drawing, using the measuring stick and pen or marking device.
2. Cut the pattern out carefully.
3. Make slight folds in the tissue paper pattern along the four arms as shown by the dots in the drawing.
4. Fold the arms in an upright position to form a rectangular box.
5. Carefully tape each upright arm to an adjacent arm to prevent any possible air loss.
6. Turn the "balloon" over and tape one end of the long thread to the top of the "balloon."
7. Affix the other end of the thread to the ceiling or other supporting device.
8. Holding the "balloon" steady, turn on the hair dryer under the "balloon."
9. When the air is "hot," release the balloon.

D. Results:

1. The balloon will rise.
2. As the air cools, it will descend.

E. Basic Facts and Supplemental Information:

1. Hot air rises because it is less dense than cold air.
2. Recreation and commercial balloons are heated by large air heating systems.
3. In March of 1999, Bertrand Piccard, a Swiss psychiatrist and Brian Jones, a British balloon instructor/pilot circumnavigated the globe from Chateau d'Oex in Switzerland to Mauritania in North Africa in 20 days in the Breitling Orbiter 3, a 180 foot-high hot air balloon finally landing in Egypt.

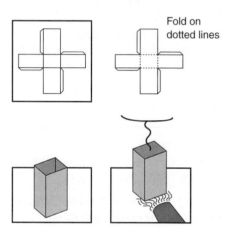

Fold on dotted lines

F. Thought Questions for Class Discussions:

1. How do home furnaces work?
2. Do home air conditioners use this same principle?
3. How are weather and hot and cold air related?

G. Related Ideas for Further Inquiry:

1. Study Activity I-B-6, "Does warm air rise or fall? expand or contract?"
2. Study Activity I-B-2, "How does a chimney work?"
3. Study Activity VII-E-1, "What makes the wind blow?"

H. Vocabulary Builders—Spelling Words:

1) **balloon**   2) **rise**   3) **ascend**
4) **descend**   5) **thread**   6) **scissors**
7) **pattern**   8) **furnace**   9) **sail**

I. Thought for Today:

The right angle to approach a difficult problem is the "try-angle."

Activity

A. Problem: *What Is Suction?*

B. Materials Needed:
1. Two plungers
2. Small amount of water
3. Chair
4. Piece of porous material such as wire screen

C. Procedure:
1. Wet the bottom rubber ring of each plunger and push these ends together.
2. Have two members of class try to separate plungers, pulling straight out. (It is a good idea to have another student stand behind each in case plungers come apart quickly and forcibly.)
3. Observe results.
4. Have one student press a plunger against the seat of a chair.
5. Try to lift chair with the plunger.
6. Observe results.
7. Try to lift porous material.
8. Observe results.

D. Results:
1. When a partial vacuum is created on the inside of the two plungers by pushing them together, the pressure on the outside will be great enough so that two students of ordinary strength cannot pull them apart.
2. The chair can be lifted with the plunger.
3. The plunger will not be able to lift porous materials.

E. Basic Facts and Supplemental Information:
1. The expulsion of air from the inside of the plunger reduces the pressure within and a greater relative pressure is exerted without. These activities prove that suction is really a differential in air pressure.
2. Suction, the difference of pressure of gases or liquids, is used in many ways in the home, in businesses, industries, etc. Water pumps, gasoline pumps, and air lifts are but a few examples of how suction helps us in our everyday lives. The following are a few ways that "suction" (differences of gaseous or liquid pressures) helps us in our homes:

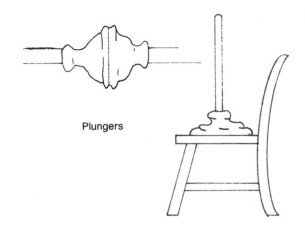

Plungers

a. vacuum cleaners	f. air conditioners
b. atomizers	g. refrigerator pumps
c. water faucets	h. water closets (toilets)
d. gas stoves	i. paint sprayers
e. fans	

F. Thought Questions for Class Discussions:
1. What is a vacuum?
2. Can you think of any other ways in which rubber suction cups are used?
3. How do we use vacuums to help us?
4. Is there any other way we can get the plungers apart?

G. Related Ideas for Further Inquiry:
1. Explain how a plunger works.
2. Study Activity I-B-10, "Can air pressure hold water in an inverted glass?"
3. Study Activity I-B-12, "Can air pressure crush a can?"
4. Study Activity I-B-16, "How does a siphon work?"

H. Vocabulary Builders—Spelling Words:
1) **suction**   2) **partial**   3) **vacuum**   4) **plunger**
5) **porous**   6) **pressure**   7) **chair**   8) **screen**
9) **lift**

I. Thought for Today:
"Children need love, especially when they don't deserve it."

Activity

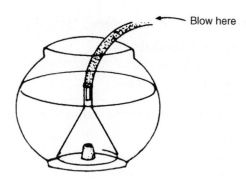

Blow here

A. Problem: *How Can People Work Under Water?*

B. Materials Needed:
1. Large glass container
2. Water
3. Cork
4. Glass or plastic funnel
5. Plastic tubing

C. Procedure:
1. Attach plastic tubing to the small end of funnel.
2. Fill the container about two-thirds full of water.
3. Place the cork on water's surface.
4. Place funnel over the cork.
5. Push funnel to the bottom of the container and hold it there.
6. Blow air into end of plastic tubing.
7. Pinch tubing or hold thumb over the end.

D. Results:
1. When funnel is first inserted it will fill up with water and cork will float to the top of the funnel.
2. When air is blown into the funnel, water will be forced out.
3. Air bubbles will rise to the surface.
4. The cork will descend to the bottom of the container as the water is expelled from funnel.

E. Basic Facts and Supplemental Information:
1. Air pressure may displace water in an enclosed underwater area. This area will remain dry as long as the pressure is maintained. Under actual working conditions, pressure must be increased and decreased very slowly, a process requiring several hours. People can work in a compressed air chamber only a short time.
2. Deep sea divers who descend into very deep waters must do so very slowly so that the pressure inside the body can adjust to the outside pressures. After they have worked in deep waters and have had a high compression air supply, they must ascend very slowly or they will get the "bends" which is a "decompression sickness" caused by the release of air bubbles from the blood. These bubbles are primarily nitrogen which do not combine with the blood or other body tissues.

F. Thought Questions for Class Discussions:
1. What will happen to people in an underwater chamber if the air hose leaks or breaks?
2. If the air hose is sealed tightly, will the people suffocate or drown? Why?
3. How do divers get their fresh air? What are the dangers in obtaining this air?
4. What causes an object to sink or float?
5. Why does gaseous air hold the liquid water out?

G. Related Ideas for Further Inquiry:
1. Push a water glass down over a cork floating in a glass container. The air in the glass will keep most of the water out and the cork will drop to the new water level.
2. Study Activity I-B-13, "How does air pressure hold water in a can?"
3. Study Activity I-B-10, "Can air pressure hold water in an inverted glass?"
4. Study Activity I-B-12, "Can air pressure crush a can?"

H. Vocabulary Builders—Spelling Words:
1) **suffocate** 2) **compression** 3) **displace**
4) **bottom** 5) **funnel** 6) **cork** 7) **tubing**
8) **chamber**

I. Thought for Today:
"Failing is not the worst possible outcome; not trying is."

A. Problem: *Can Air Pressure Hold Water in an Inverted Glass?*

B. Materials Needed:

1. Water glass
2. Water
3. Cardboard (or heavy paper)
4. Basin or sink

C. Procedure:

1. Fill the glass tumbler completely with water.
2. Place a piece of cardboard or heavy paper on top of the glass and hold it in place with your hand.
3. Over a basin or sink, being careful not to let any bubble of air enter between the cardboard and the glass, invert the glass while holding the cardboard in place.
4. Remove your hand carefully from below the paper or cardboard, being careful not to jar either the glass or the cardboard.

D. Result:

The cardboard and the water will remain in place.

E. Basic Facts and Supplemental Information:

1. The water is held in the glass because the pressure of the air outside the glass against the cardboard was greater than the pressure of the water against the cardboard. It is important to seal the cardboard tightly against the glass. If any air gets in between the cardboard and the edge of the glass, this will not work.
2. The glass has only the weight of the water in it. Atmospheric pressure is excluded from the inside of the glass. Outside atmospheric pressure (14.7 lbs. per square inch at sea level) has only the weight of a glass of water to work against and therefore *pushes* the cardboard firmly against the glass.
3. Air pressure is tremendous. The reason our bodies don't collapse from the great pressure is because the pressure inside our bodies is equal to the outside pressure.
4. Deep sea divers must descend and ascend slowly to enable their bodies to adjust to changes in air pressure, otherwise they get the "bends" (bubbles in the blood and cells).

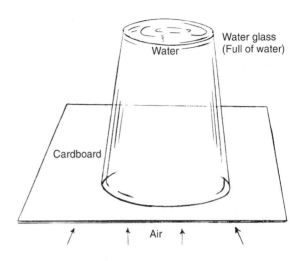

F. Thought Questions for Class Discussions:

1. How much does air weigh?
2. What would happen if the water glass were only half-full?
3. What would happen if the water glass were turned sideways slowly and carefully after the cardboard adhered to the glass?

G. Related Ideas for Further Inquiry:

1. Study the pressures working on a submarine.
2. What protection would be necessary for people constructing a tunnel or tube under water?
3. Study Activity I-B-11, "Can air pressure lift heavy objects?"
4. Study Activity I-B-12, "Can air pressure crush a can?"
5. Study Activity I-B-15, "Can a shelled, hard-boiled egg be put into a small-mouthed bottle without breaking the egg?"

H. Vocabulary Builders—Spelling Words:

1) **pressure** 2) **drinking** 3) **air** 4) **atmospheric**
5) **exerted** 6) **cardboard** 7) **sink** 8) **glass**

I. Thought for Today:

"If April showers bring May flowers, what do May flowers bring? Pilgrims."

A. Problem: *Can Air Pressure Lift Heavy Objects?*

B. Materials Needed, Procedure One:

1. Brick or other similar object
2. Small rubber balloon
3. Piece of plastic tubing
4. String

Materials Needed, Procedure Two:

1. Tire pump
2. Hot water bottle
3. Board, approximately 12″ × 18″

C. Procedure One:

1. Place the plastic tubing in the neck of the balloon.
2. Put the brick on top of the deflated balloon.
3. Secure the neck with string.
4. Inflate the balloon by blowing into the tubing.

Procedure Two:

1. Attach an air pump to the rubber tubing of a hot water bottle.
2. Place a board on the top of the empty hot water bottle.
3. Have a student stand on the board.
4. Pump air into the hot water bottle.

D. Results:

1. The balloon will expand by air pressure, and as it inflates it will lift the brick.
2. The air forced into the hot water bottle exerts enough pressure to lift the board and the student several inches.

E. Basic Facts and Supplemental Information:

The rubber balloon has elastic sides and, therefore, when air is blown into it, it will expand. Because the walls of the balloon expand, the air pressure inside is almost the same as that outside of the balloon. The only difference lies in the extra pressure needed to expand the elastic of the balloon. Air pressure is used to inflate tires on automobiles, bicycles, airplanes, etc.

F. Thought Questions for Class Discussions:

1. What happens if too much air is put into the balloon?
2. If the weight is extra heavy, will the student have to blow harder to raise the object? Why?
3. In what other ways are heavy objects raised?
4. Where is air used to lift heavy objects?
5. Why is it smoother to ride on a tire filled with air than a solid one?

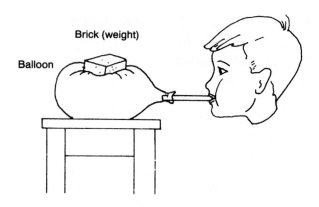

Procedure One

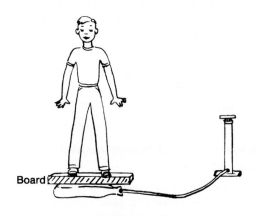

Procedure Two

6. How are cars lifted in service stations when they are to be lubricated or repaired?
7. Does the tire pump get hot or cold? Why?

G. Related Ideas for Further Inquiry:

1. Check an electric fan. Does it exert air pressure?
2. Check the exhaust side of a vacuum cleaner. Does it exert air pressure?
3. Study Activity I-B-12, "Can air pressure crush a can?"
4. Study Activity I-B-14, "How does air pressure in a bicycle tire hold up the bicycle?"

H. Vocabulary Builders—Spelling Words:

1) **elastic**   2) **pump**   3) **balloon**   4) **tire**
5) **board**   6) **pressure**   7) **tubing**   8) **expands**

I. Thought for Today:

"The mediocre teacher tells.
The good teacher explains.
The superior teacher demonstrates.
The great teacher inspires."

A. Problem: *Can Air Pressure Crush a Can?*

B. Materials Needed:
1. One-gallon tin can
2. Stopper to fit can
3. Pair of pot holders
4. Hot plate, gas burner, or canned heat
5. Water

C. Procedure:
1. Put about a quarter-inch of water in the can.
2. Heat the can over heat source until the water reaches the boiling point and steam comes out of the opening.
3. Using pot holders, carefully remove the can from the heat and close the opening with the stopper; make sure this is an airtight fit. *This is very important.*
4. Watch carefully as can cools after removing from heat source.

D. Result:
The can will slowly crinkle and collapse.

E. Basic Facts and Supplemental Information:
1. The air pressure inside and outside were equal at the start, when the water was added, and when the water was steaming.
2. The steam forces most of the air out of the can.
3. After the can was sealed, the steam condensed, causing a partial vacuum; the volume of air and steam was reduced, causing the inside pressure to decrease. (One c.c. of water will make about 1500 c.c. of steam; c.c. stands for cubic centimeter.)
4. The condensation reduces the pressure inside, and the outside pressure, being greater, crushes the can.
5. If any outside air enters the can, a balance of forces will take place, causing the can to remain intact.

F. Thought Questions for Class Discussions:
1. How is a partial vacuum created on the inside of a can?
2. Why is it necessary to boil the water before sealing the can?
3. Why must the can be airtight?
4. If air has a pressure of 14.7 pounds per square inch, how much pressure was exerted on this can? (Hint: How many surfaces does a can have?)

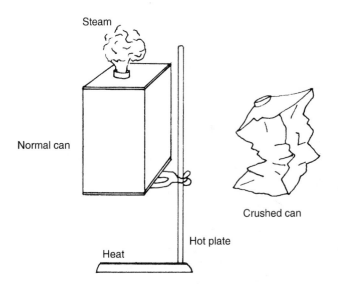

G. Related Ideas for Further Inquiry:
1. Pour several ounces of water in a can with a push-down top or use a loosely fitted cork. Place over heat source. Take precautions, for the cork will be blown out of can.
2. Study Activity I-B-11, "Can air pressure lift heavy objects?"
3. Study Activity I-B-17, "What is sideways air pressure?"

H. Vocabulary Builders—Spelling Words:
1) **partial** 2) **vacuum** 3) **condensation**
4) **steam** 5) **precautions** 6) **boiling point**
7) **heat**

I. Thought for Today:
"It is harder to conceal ignorance than to acquire knowledge."

Activity

A. Problem: *How Does Air Pressure Hold Water in a Can?*

B. Materials Needed, Procedure One:

1. Small metal can or plastic bottle with removable top or cork
2. Water
3. Awl
4. Sink, tray, or bucket to catch water

Materials Needed, Procedure Two:

1. Empty soft drink can
2. Awl
3. Adhesive, cellophane, or duct tape
4. Sink, tray, or bucket to catch water

C. Procedure One:

1. Punch a small hole near bottom of the plastic bottle or metal can.
2. Put finger over hole and fill bottle or can with water.
3. With top off, remove finger from hole and watch water flow from it in a steady stream.
4. Refill bottle or can with finger over the hole.
5. Fasten top to it securely. (Finger must be over hole while refilling.)
6. Remove finger from hole and observe results.

Procedure Two:

1. In soft drink can punch three small holes vertically, one near the bottom, one near the middle, and one near the top.
2. Tape holes individually and securely.
3. Fill the can with water.
4. Place can near sink, tray, or bucket.
5. Remove bottom tape and observe results.
6. When empty, replace bottom tape, fill the can, and quickly remove bottom and middle tapes. Observe results.
7. When empty, replace both tapes, fill the can, and quickly remove all the tapes. Observe results.

D. Results, Procedure One:

1. On first attempt with top off bottle or can, water flows from the hole in a steady stream.
2. On second attempt, and with top on the bottle or can, water does not flow from the hole.

Results, Procedure Two:

1. When can is full of water and all holes taped, nothing happens.
2. When the bottom tape is removed, water streams out the bottom hole.

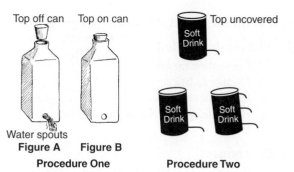

Top off can   Top on can   Top uncovered

Water spouts
Figure A   **Figure B**
Procedure One   **Procedure Two**

3. When the middle and bottom tapes are removed, water streams out both holes with the lower stream being stronger: it shoots out further.
4. When all the tapes are removed water streams out of all holes with the bottom one being stronger, the middle one next, and the top one the weakest.

E. Basic Facts and Supplemental Information:

1. In Procedure One, the bottle or can has no top on it; the weight of the water and air pressure will force the water out of the small hole in a steady stream. When the top is on, the air pressure cannot exert a downward force on the water in the can or bottle. Air pressure acting against the water in the hole does not permit any water to escape.
2. In Procedure Two, the air pressure is the same in all trials, but the weight of the water adds to the force of the stream so that the bottom stream has a total greater force acting on it, and so the stream is longer and stronger.

F. Thought Questions for Class Discussions:

1. Does altitude have any effect on this experiment?
2. Why do we punch two holes on the top of any can holding a liquid?
3. Can water ever run uphill?
4. What would happen if the bottle or can were covered during the experiment?

G. Related Ideas for Further Inquiry:

1. Punch holes in a horizontal line and test.
2. Punch horizontal holes close together and squeeze the streams. The streams will flow together and appear as a knot.

H. Vocabulary Builders—Spelling Words:

1) **atmospheric**   2) **pressure**   3) **stream**
4) **punched**   5) **finger**   6) **soft drink**   7) **cork**

I. Thought for Today:

"Without experience one gains no wisdom."

Activity

A. Problem: *How Does Air Pressure in a Bicycle Tire Hold Up the Bicycle?*

B. Materials Needed:

1. Bicycle tire on bicycle
2. Hand tire pump

C. Procedure:

1. Deflate one bicycle tire.
2. Feel the tire.
3. Attach hose of hand pump to air valve of deflated tire.
4. Inflate the tire using hand pump.
5. Stop when inflated tire has normal appearance.
6. Have students feel the bicycle tire and the tire pump.

D. Results:

1. Students can see and feel that air pressure in the tire does hold up the bicycle.
2. The pump gets hot due to the compression of the air by the pump.

E. Basic Facts and Supplemental Information:

1. Automobile tires work in the same way as bicycle tires.
2. Air pressure can hold up heavy objects. Some types of lifts use this principle. If time permits, you may wish to have students study how an air pump works.

F. Thought Questions for Class Discussions:

1. Why does a bicycle tire get flat only on the bottom?
2. What might cause a tire to go flat?
3. Is the air pressure in the tire greater than the air pressure outside the tire?
4. How is air pressure measured?

G. Related Ideas for Further Inquiry:

1. Try the same test with an automobile tire tube, if one is available.
2. Try the same test with an air mattress.
3. Try the same test with a beach ball.
4. Study Activity I-B-11, "Can air pressure lift heavy objects?"
5. Study Activity I-B-12, "Can air pressure crush a can?"

H. Vocabulary Builders—Spelling Words:

1) **bicycle**   2) **tire**   3) **inflate**   4) **deflate**
5) **attach**   6) **automobile**   7) **compression**

Bicycle

Tire pump

I. Thought for Today:

"A mistake is evidence that someone has tried to do something."

A. Problem: *Can a Shelled, Hard-Boiled Egg Be Put into a Small-Mouthed Bottle Without Breaking the Egg?*

B. Materials Needed:
1. Small-mouthed bottle (slightly smaller than the egg)
2. Medium-sized wad of paper
3. Matches
4. Hard-boiled egg with shell removed

C. Procedure:
1. Show the pupils that the egg will not fit into the bottle without being crushed.
2. Light the wad of paper and carefully insert it into the bottle.
3. Place the egg on the mouth of the bottle immediately.
4. Have students observe the results.

D. Result:
The egg will bob up and down, then slowly descend into the neck of the bottle, and finally pop into the bottle with a loud plunk.

E. Basic Facts and Supplemental Information:
1. The bobbing up and down of the egg is due to the fact that as the heated air expands, the air bubbles out from beneath the egg. When the paper stops burning, the air within the bottle cools and the inside pressure is reduced. However, the normal air pressure on the top and sides of the egg remains unchanged. The egg, therefore, is forced into the bottle.
2. A good challenging question is how to get the egg back out without breaking the egg. This can be accomplished by inverting the bottle and blowing hard into its mouth; the increased air pressure on the inside will force the egg out. (Don't forget to duck or move head quickly to the side.)
3. The teacher can start this activity with an "unshelled," hard-boiled egg first and then compare results. The unshelled egg will not move because the air pressure is not strong enough to compact the egg and there is always a little air seepage. With the shelled egg, the fit becomes very tight and the outside pressure is allowed to act on it.
4. Air pressure equals 14.7 pounds per square inch (at sea level).

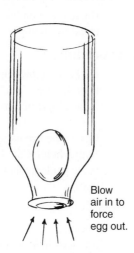

Blow air in to force egg out.

5. Air pressure acts in all directions—down, up, sideways, every way.

F. Thought Questions for Class Discussions:
1. What would happen to the egg if you tried to push it into the bottle with your hands?
2. Is the egg "sucked" into the bottle or is it pushed in by the outside air pressure?
3. Why aren't soft items crushed by the great air pressure that surrounds them?

G. Related Ideas for Further Inquiry:
1. Place a small candle in a shelled, hard-boiled egg. Light the candle and place an inverted bottle over the egg and the lighted candle.
2. Study Activity I-B-12, "Can air pressure crush a can?"
3. Study Activity I-B-10, "Can air pressure hold water in an inverted glass?"
4. Study Activity I-B-14, "How does air pressure in a bicycle tire hold up the bicycle?"
5. Study Activity I-B-16, "How does a siphon work?"

H. Vocabulary Builders—Spelling Words:
1) **expand** 2) **descend** 3) **bottle**
4) **hard-boiled** 5) **breaking** 6) **wad** 7) **shelled**
8) **force**

I. Thought for Today:
"Education is what survives when what was learned has been forgotten."—B. F. Skinner

Activity

A. Problem: *How Does a Siphon Work?*

B. Materials Needed:
1. Three feet of plastic tubing
2. Two glass jars
3. Water

C. Procedure:
1. Fill one jar with water.
2. Put about one inch of water in the other jar.
3. Place the full jar at a higher level than the other one. (See drawing.)
4. Fill the plastic tubing with water. (Must be completely filled.)
5. Cover each end of the tubing with your thumbs.
6. Insert one end of the tubing into the higher level jar, and the other end into the lower level jar. Be sure the tubing in the lower level jar is below the level of the water level in the upper jar.
7. Take thumb away from tubing in the lower level jar; then take thumb away from tubing in the higher level jar.

D. Result:
The water will flow from the jar filled with water into the jar containing an inch of water until the water is at the same level, even though the quantity in the jars will not be the same.

E. Basic Facts and Supplemental Information:
1. In the "Before" drawing, the water will flow downward due to the force of gravity and the atmospheric pressure, P. As the water flows down, this will create a partial vacuum in the tube. The atmospheric pressure P exerted on the surface of the water L will force water up the tube and along the tube in direction D. This will cause a continuous flow of water as long as the level of M is lower than the level of L.
2. It is often stated that water cannot run uphill. Well, this activity disproves this concept. What does the water do in this siphoning activity from the start of the siphoning from the water level in the top of the first jar to the top of the tubing? It runs uphill. Actually it is "pushed" uphill by atmospheric air pressure.

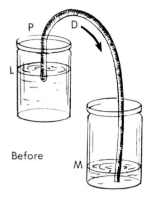

Before

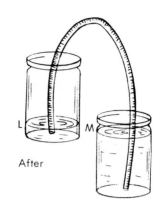

After

3. Siphons are a main part of many water supply systems for municipalities and outlying areas. Large pumps are used to initiate the siphoning action and to keep the water flowing.

F. Thought Questions for Class Discussions:
1. What will happen if the jars are alternately raised and lowered?
2. Will this siphon work if one of the jars becomes empty?
3. Why won't the siphon work if some air gets in the tubing?
4. How do water pumps use this principle?
5. Are there other ways to start a siphon?

G. Related Ideas for Further Inquiry:
1. Practice siphoning your classroom aquarium when it needs cleaning.
2. Discuss the dangers of siphoning gasoline from an automobile.
3. Study Activity I-B-1, "What is air? What are its characteristics?"
4. Study Activity I-B-8, "What is suction?"
5. Study Activity I-B-10, "Can air pressure hold water in an inverted glass?"

H. Vocabulary Builders—Spelling Words:
1) **siphon**   2) **vacuum**   3) **pressure**   4) **plastic**
5) **tubing**   6) **thumb**   7) **gravity**   8) **atmosphere**

I. Thought for Today:
"School is a place where children live."

Activity

A. Problem: *What Is Sideways Air Pressure?*

B. Materials Needed:
1. Wooden spool
2. Thin cardboard
3. Common pin or thumbtack

C. Procedure:
1. Cut a piece of cardboard approximately two inches square.
2. Push the pin or tack through the center of the cardboard.
3. Place this over one end of the spool with the pin inside the hole in the spool. (This keeps the card from sliding sideways.)
4. Blow a steady stream of air into the opposite end of the spool as card is held as shown in drawing.
5. Release the cardboard but continue to blow.

D. Results:
1. The cardboard seems to cling to the spool.
2. The harder you blow, the tighter the cardboard clings to the spool.
3. When the blowing stops, the cardboard falls.

E. Basic Facts and Supplemental Information:

The blown air moves out the sides between the spool and cardboard, and not downward. The more air going out the side, the less pressure is exerted downward. The normal air pressure from below pushes upward, keeping the cardboard near the spool. When the blowing is stopped, the weight of the cardboard causes it to drop because the air pressure above and below is then equal and gravity takes over.

Bernoulli's Principle has become one of the basic laws of science. In essence, it states that the faster a stream of gas moves in one direction, the less the pressure of the gas in a perpendicular or "sideways" direction. This activity is a prime example of Bernoulli's Principle.

F. Thought Questions for Class Discussions:
1. Is this experiment related to two passing trains?
2. If two automobiles pass too close to each other, what might happen?
3. Would children on passing bicycles be affected by this phenomenon?

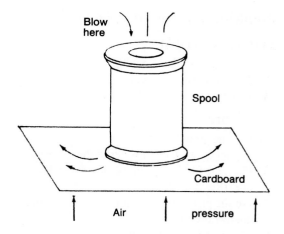

G. Related Ideas for Further Inquiry:
1. Look up "Bernoulli's Principle" and describe it in simple terms.
2. Place a ping-pong ball in a funnel with the stem below and the mouth pointing straight upward. Try to blow the ping-pong ball out of the funnel.
3. Place a ping-pong ball in an inverted funnel with the stem on top, and while holding the ball in the cup, blow steadily on the stem and release the ball.
4. Another exciting activity is to place a fully inflated balloon in an air stream created at the exhaust end of a vacuum cleaner with the air stream pointing straight up.
5. Study Activity I-B-11, "Can air pressure lift heavy objects?"
6. Study Activity I-B-8 "What is suction?"
7. Study Activity I-B-10, "Can air pressure hold water in an inverted glass?"
8. Study Activity I-B-19 "In which direction does moving air exert the most pressure?"

H. Vocabulary Builders—Spelling Words:
1) sideways   2) pressure   3) spool
4) wooden   5) thumbtack   6) cardboard
7) upward   8) Bernoulli's Principle

I. Thought for Today:

"Give a man a fish and he eats for a day; teach him to fish and he eats for a lifetime."

A. Problem: *How Much Oxygen Is in the Air?*

B. Materials Needed:
1. Widemouth jar (quart size)
2. Pyrex dish or metal pan
3. Matches
4. Candle
5. Water to fill dish halfway
6. Food coloring

C. Procedure:
1. Light candle.
2. Set candle on melted drippings in the center of dish or pan.
3. Fill pan half-full of water.
4. Add food coloring to water for better effect.
5. Place widemouth jar over lighted candle.
6. Observe results.

D. Results:
1. The candle will cease burning.
2. Water will rise in the jar.

E. Basic Facts and Supplemental Information:

The candle flame has removed most of the oxygen from the air in the jar. The pressure of the air left inside the jar has been reduced below that of the air outside. Carbon dioxide, CO_2, is also formed. Air heated by the candle escapes under the lip of the jar. Water rises in the jar about one-fifth of the way so we could conclude that oxygen makes up 20% of the air. While this is true in our atmosphere, there are several other factors that must be taken into account for these results to be definitive in this activity such as heat, incomplete combustion, composition of the candle, etc. Much of the remaining air is nitrogen, which makes up about 79% of the normal air constituency. Other gases found in the air in small quantities are carbon dioxide, neon, krypton, argon, xenon, and ozone.

F. Thought Questions for Class Discussions:
1. Why does the candle go out?
2. Why does the water rise in the jar?
3. Is there any change in water level if the jar partially filled with water is allowed to remain for a while? Why? Check level(s) with rubber band(s) around the jar.
4. What are the "products of combustion"? Do they have any effect in this activity?

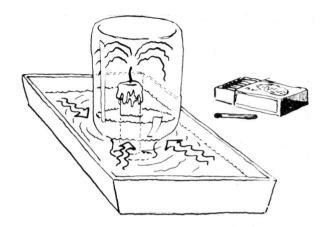

G. Related Ideas for Further Inquiry:
1. Study and give examples of the "Fire Triangle"— the three requirements needed for combustion to take place.

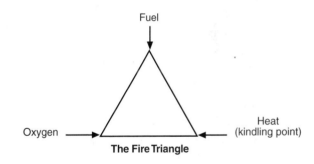

The Fire Triangle

2. Using the "Fire Triangle," cite some examples of how combustion could be controlled or eliminated in practical situations such as forest fires, home fires, picnic fires, etc.
3. Discuss how welders use oxygen.
4. Discuss how oxygen is a vital factor in space exploration.
5. Study Activity I-B-12, "Can air pressure crush a can?"
6. Study Activity I-B-15, "Can a shelled, hard-boiled egg be put into a small-mouthed bottle without breaking the egg?"
7. Study Activity I-B-2, "How does a chimney work?"

H. Vocabulary Builders—Spelling Words:
1) **oxygen** 2) **nitrogen** 3) **carbon** 4) **escapes**
5) **combustion** 6) **rises** 7) **estimate** 8) **Pyrex**

I. Thought for Today:
"Education makes people easy to lead but difficult to drive; easy to govern but impossible to enslave."

Activity

A. Problem: *In Which Direction Does Moving Air Exert the Most Pressure?*

B. Materials Needed, Procedure One:

1. 5″ × 7″ card
2. Soda straw
3. Table or desk top

Materials Needed, Procedure Two:

1. Two ping-pong balls
2. Cellophane tape
3. Thread
4. Book
5. Table or desk top

C. Procedure One:

1. Fold the card so that one-half inch at each end of the card is perpendicular to the card itself.
2. Place the card on the desk or table so that the folded card makes a little platform.
3. Using the soda straw, blow vigorously through the straw and under the card.

Procedure Two:

1. Tape a piece of thread to each ping-pong ball. (See drawing.)
2. Let them hang down from desk or table by placing the threads underneath the book so that the ping-pong balls will be separated by about one inch.
3. Have a student, using the soda straw, blow vigorously between the two ping-pong balls to try to blow them apart.

D. Results, Procedure One:

The harder one blows, the faster the air moves under the card and the more the card bends down toward the current of air.

Results, Procedure Two:

The harder one blows between the ping-pong balls, the closer they will move together.

E. Basic Facts and Supplemental Information:

1. In Procedure One, a rapidly moving current of air reduces the sideways pressure under the card, thus the normal pressure above is greater and pushes the card downward.
2. In Procedure Two, the normal pressure between the ping-pong balls is reduced, consequently the outside pressure is greater, causing the balls to

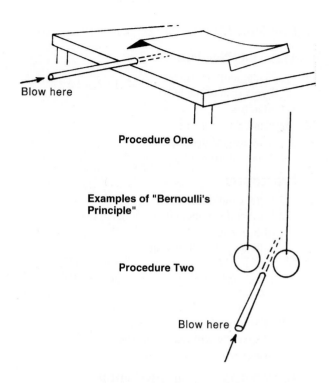

Blow here

Procedure One

Examples of "Bernoulli's Principle"

Procedure Two

Blow here

come closer together. This is called "Bernoulli's Principle." It is the same principle that operates in Activity I-B-17.

F. Thought Questions for Class Discussions:

1. What would happen to a person who stands too close to a moving train?
2. What would happen if a person got too close to the jet stream of an airplane?
3. What happens when two automobiles, moving in opposite directions, pass close together?

G. Related Ideas for Further Inquiry:

1. Hold a sheet of paper in front of your lips, let it droop, then blow briskly over the top.
2. How does this principle affect airplanes?
3. Study other Activities in this section, especially I-B-8, I-B-10, and I-B-16.

H. Vocabulary Builders—Spelling Words:

1) **Bernoulli** 2) **principle** 3) **direction**
4) **exert** 5) **pressure** 6) **ping-pong**
7) **thread** 8) **vertical** 9) **moving**

I. Thought for Today:

"It is useless to try to reason a person out of a thing that a person was never reasoned into."

Activity

A. Problem: *What Are the Main Sources of Water?*

B. Materials Needed:

Pictures, resource books about:

1. Oceans
2. Streams and rivers
3. Clouds
4. Rain
5. Lakes and ponds
6. Underground water (springs, wells, etc.)
7. Aquifers
8. Wetlands
9. Bays and estuaries

C. Procedure:

1. Have students discuss places where they have seen water.
2. Discuss where the water comes from.
3. Discuss where we get water for our homes.
4. Discuss all the uses of water:
   a. drinking
   b. laundry
   c. bathing
   d. food processing
   e. industrial uses
   f. recreation
   g. gardening, etc.
5. Describe the different states of water (ice, water, steam).
6. Discuss who or what needs water (people, plants, animals).
7. Have students study plants and animals that live in water.
8. Discuss water for recreation, transportation, etc.
9. Describe some of the problems of water supplies and shortages:
   a. floods
   b. droughts
   c. contaminations
   d. increasing demand due to enlarging populations

D. Result:

Students will learn that water covers 70% of the Earth's surface; it comes from many sources, and supplies many needs.

E. Basic Facts and Supplemental Information:

1. Water makes up a good portion of all plants and animals.
2. About 65% of the human body is water.
3. Water is essential for life.
4. Not all water is safe to drink.

A hydroelectric dam holding large lake behind.

5. Water dissolves many substances.
6. Fresh water is distributed unevenly throughout the world.
7. Pure water supplies are being depleted by increasing demands and contamination.
8. Millions of deaths occur annually throughout the world because of water shortages, food shortages, and distribution inadequacies.
9. Only about 3% of our water is safe to drink.

F. Thought Questions for Class Discussions:

1. Are you concerned about our fresh-water supplies?
2. Are you concerned about the gradual deterioration of our fresh-water supplies?
3. Do you think we will be able to use the salt water oceans for fresh-water supplies? What is this process called? (desalinization)

G. Related Ideas for Further Inquiry:

1. Study Part VI, "Ecology."
2. Have students collect information about how we are contaminating our fresh-water supplies by:
   a. agricultural wastes
   b. pesticides
   c. chemical processing
   d. industrial runoff

H. Vocabulary Builders—Spelling Words:

1) **fresh-water** 2) **supplies** 3) **aquifers**
4) **contamination** 5) **drought** 6) **floods**
7) **bathing** 8) **serious** 9) **radiator**

I. Thought for Today:

"It isn't falling into water that drowns a person; it is staying under water."

Activity

A. Problem: *When Water Freezes Does It Expand or Contract?*

B. Materials Needed, Procedure One:

(Can be done at school or home)

1. Two jars
2. Water
3. Refrigerator
4. Heating device

Materials Needed, Procedure Two:

(Good homework assignment)

1. Two small cans
2. Labels or marking pens
3. Refrigerator

C. Procedure One:

1. Fill one jar with hot water, the other with cold.
2. Label one jar "HOT" and the other "COLD."
3. Cover both bottles.
4. Place aside and observe the following day.

Procedure Two:

1. Fill the two cans exactly to the top.
2. Place one can in the freezing compartment of a refrigerator.
3. Place the second can in the cold (regular) compartment.
4. Let the cans stand until the next day (or until the one placed in the freezing compartment is frozen).

D. Results:

1. In Procedure One, the jar marked "HOT" will show a lower water level than the one marked "COLD."
2. In Procedure Two, the water placed in the cold (regular) compartment of the refrigerator will have contracted so it is not quite to the top of the can. The water which was frozen will be pushed out so that it extends above the top of the can.

E. Basic Facts and Supplemental Information:

Water expands slightly when heated and contracts slightly when it is cooled. In cooling, the molecules move closer together. When the temperature gets down to 4° C. or 39° F., it begins to expand rather than contract further. From this point to the freezing point it can cause damage to containers such as water pipes, radiators, batteries, etc.

F. Thought Questions for Class Discussions:

1. Why does ice float if water normally contracts and gets heavier (per volume) as it cools?

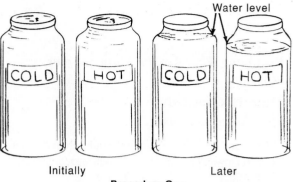

Water level

COLD HOT COLD HOT

Initially   Later

Procedure One

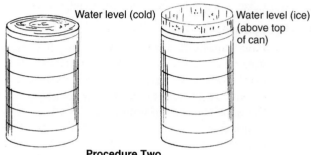

Water level (cold)   Water level (ice) (above top of can)

Procedure Two

2. What happens when water in an automobile radiator freezes?
3. What does antifreeze do when added to water in a radiator?
4. Why do icebergs float?
5. What causes some water pipes to break in cold weather?

G. Related Ideas for Further Inquiry:

1. Have students check level of any liquids in the refrigerator and then again when they have warmed up to room temperature.
2. Repeat Procedure Two using old capped jars enclosed in heavy duty freezer bags.
3. Discuss how ice cream is made at home and why salt is added to the ice.

H. Vocabulary Builders—Spelling Words:

1) **liquid**   2) **bottle**   3) **freezing**   4) **temperature**
5) **contract**   6) **expand**   7) **refrigerator**
8) **molecules**   9) **Celsius**   10) **Fahrenheit**

I. Thought for Today:

"The art of teaching is the art of assisting discovery."—Mark Van Doren

Activity

A. Problem: *At What Temperature Does Water Freeze? Boil?*

B. Materials Needed, Procedure One:

1. Paper towel
2. Beaker or glass jar
3. Crushed ice
4. Salt
5. Test tube
6. Water
7. Thermometer

Materials Needed, Procedure Two:

1. Heat source
2. Small pan
3. Water
4. Thermometer
5. Gloves

C. Procedure One:

1. Fill the beaker or glass jar with crushed ice.
2. Put some water in the test tube.
3. Put a thermometer in the test tube in such a manner that it can be read. Observe temperature.
4. Place the test tube in the ice in the beaker.
5. Stir a generous amount of salt into the crushed ice. Note the temperature of the water in the test tube.
6. Immerse the test tube in the mixture of crushed ice and salt. Let it stand for several minutes, then note the temperature.

Procedure Two:

1. Fill the pan one-half full of water.
2. Heat the pan until the water boils.
3. Using gloves, carefully place the thermometer in the boiling water.
4. Record the temperature.
5. Compare the thermometer readings of Procedure One and Procedure Two.

D. Result:

1. As long as the water in the test tube is immersed in the beaker or jar with crushed ice, the temperature will not go below 32° F. or 0° C. and cause the water to freeze. As the water in the test tube is placed in the mixture of salt and ice, the temperature of the water is lowered below the freezing point and the water in the test tube will freeze. The temperature at the time the water freezes is 32° F. or 0° C.
2. The water in Procedure Two will boil at 212° F. (100° C.).
3. The difference in temperature of frozen water (ice) and boiling water is 180° F. (100° C.)

E. Basic Facts and Supplemental Information:

1. Salt lowers the freezing point of water. This causes the water in the test tube to freeze. When

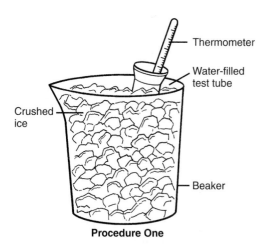

Thermometer

Water-filled test tube

Crushed ice

Beaker

Procedure One

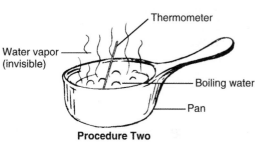

Thermometer

Water vapor (invisible)

Boiling water

Pan

Procedure Two

water freezes, it expands. This phenomenon causes a lot of problems for water pipes in cold climates because the pipes often are cracked by the expanding water.
2. Boiling water will scald a person. Consequently gloves must be worn for Procedure Two.

F. Thought Questions for Class Discussions:

1. Will a large amount of salt added to ice create a lower temperature than a small percentage of salt added to the ice?
2. In making homemade ice cream, why are the ingredients packed in salt?
3. Do you think salt lowers or raises the boiling point of water?

G. Related Ideas for Further Inquiry:

1. Study Activity I-C-2 "When water freezes does it expand or contract?"
2. Study Activity II-B-4 "What is the difference between a Celsius (Centigrade) and Fahrenheit temperature scale?"
3. Study Activity II-B-6, "What happens to liquids when they are heated? Cooled?"

H. Vocabulary Builders—Spelling Words:

1) **crushed** 2) **beaker** 3) **test tube**
4) **freezing** 5) **mixture** 6) **thermometer**

I. Thought for Today:

"Education is a chest of tools."—Herbert Kaufman

Activity

I C 4

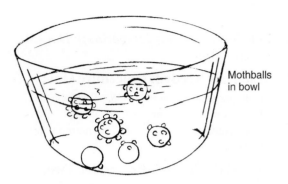

Mothballs in bowl

A. Problem: *What Is Buoyancy?*

B. Materials Needed:

1. Citric acid or vinegar (clear)
2. Baking soda
3. Mothballs
4. Food coloring
5. Two large clear bowls
6. Toy ship

C. Procedure:

1. In a large bowl make a solution using one teaspoon of citric acid or vinegar and one teaspoon of baking soda for every quart of water.
2. Add food coloring.
3. Place 5 or 6 mothballs in this solution.
4. Observe the results.
5. Place the toy ship in the second bowl, which contains water only.

D. Results:

1. When the mothballs are placed in the solution, they sink to the bottom. After a few moments, one by one, they slowly rise to the top. As they come to the surface, they roll over again and sink. A moment or two on the bottom and they rise again.
2. The ship will float on the water.

E. Basic Facts and Supplemental Information:

The mothballs are heavier than the solution. When they are dropped in the bowl they sink to the bottom. A chemical reaction takes place with citric acid and soda which causes carbon dioxide to form. The bubbles of carbon dioxide collect on the mothballs, and these bubbles lift the mothballs to the surface of the water. As the balls reach the surface, the bubbles of gas disappear into the air and the mothballs drop again to the bottom. A light ship or a heavy ship will not sink because it is lighter than the volume of water it has displaced. A ship's weight includes the metal, wood, contained air, passengers, crew, etc.

F. Thought Questions for Class Discussions:

1. Does this principle of buoyancy have anything to do with submarine submersion?

2. As the bubbles of gas form, why don't the bubbles of gas rise to the surface instead of collecting on the mothball?
3. Is carbon dioxide heavier or lighter than air?

G. Related Ideas for Further Inquiry:

1. Cover the first bowl tautly with plastic wrap. Does this affect the test in any way?
2. In a tall jar or graduated cylinder add some water, then some corn oil, then some rubbing alcohol, then baby oil, and observe what happens. (Each layer should float on the earlier addition.)
3. Another example of this can be adding raisins to a glass full of clear, carbonated soda. The raisins will rise and fall.
4. A fascinating activity on buoyancy is to use a tall graduated cylinder or thin bottle. Place a little mercury in it. Float a steel ball on it. Add carbon tetrachloride (CCl_4) to this. Float a mothball on it. Add water. Float a wooden ball on it. Add alcohol. Float a cork on it. You will have four levels of liquids with objects floating on each level.
5. Study also Activities I-C-1, I-C-5, and I-C-6.

H. Vocabulary Builders—Spelling Words:

1) **citric acid**   2) **baking soda**   3) **mothball**
4) **submarine**   5) **chemical reaction**   6) **bubbles**

I. Thought for Today:

"As spring approaches, the boys begin to feel more gallant, and the gals more buoyant."

Activity

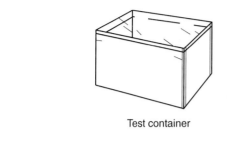

A. Problem: *What Objects Float?*
What Objects Sink?

B. Materials Needed:

1. Aquarium or large clear bowl
2. Twigs
3. Leaves
4. Cork
5. Small piece of paper
6. Wooden and plastic buttons
7. Piece of glass
8. Aluminum cup
9. Metal jar lid
10. Water
11. Medicine bottle with eyedropper
12. Other small objects to test

Test container

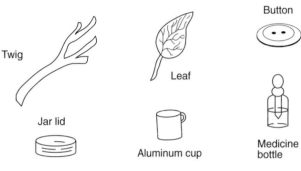

Twig

Leaf

Button

Jar lid

Aluminum cup

Medicine bottle

C. Procedure:

1. Place articles in aquarium or large bowl of water, one at a time.
2. Observe which of them floats.
3. Place aluminum cup right-side up in the water, then upside down.
4. Do the same thing with the screw-type jar lid.
5. Place empty medicine bottle with eyedropper in aquarium or large bowl.
6. Remove from water.
7. Add a little water to medicine bottle and close with eyedropper.
8. Place in the aquarium or large bowl.
9. Repeat steps 6, 7, and 8 until the bottle with eyedropper sinks.
10. Other small objects may be tested for flotation.

D. Results:

1. The twigs and the cork will float.
2. Leaves and paper will float until they become waterlogged.
3. Wooden buttons float; most plastic buttons sink.
4. The aluminum cup and the bottle cover will float when their open ends are up, but when inverted they will fill with water and sink.
5. The closed medicine bottle floats with some water, but when more water is added, it will become too heavy and sink.

E. Basic Facts and Supplemental Information:

Objects float in water if they are lighter than an equal volume of water. Some objects sink after they become waterlogged because the light air is replaced by heavier water.

F. Thought Questions for Class Discussions:

1. Why do leaves and paper float for a brief time and then sink?
2. How does a submarine submerge? rise? stay half-submerged?
3. Why do heavy objects sink?

G. Related Ideas for Further Inquiry:

1. Test other objects for flotation such as a sponge, bar of soap, piece of cloth, paper clip, etc.
2. Ask pupils if they can float in a swimming pool.
3. Study Activity I-C-4, "What is buoyancy?"
4. Study Activity I-C-6, "Why do heavy ships float?"

H. Vocabulary Builders—Spelling Words:

1) **buoyancy**   2) **flotation**   3) **medicine**
4) **twig**   5) **eyedropper**   6) **leaves**   7) **plastic**

I. Thought for Today:

"The only ones who don't change their opinions are the dead and the foolish."

A. Problem: *Why Do Heavy Ships Float?*

B. Materials Needed:
1. Large bowl or aquarium
2. Water
3. Clay
4. Toy boat

C. Procedure:
1. Fill the bowl or aquarium with water.
2. Place the toy boat in the bowl or aquarium.
3. Ask the class why it floats.
4. Shape the clay into a boat.
5. Float it on the water.
6. Ask the class why it floats.
7. Roll the clay boat into a ball and place it in the water.
8. Ask the class why it sinks.
9. Tell the class the clay weighs the same whether it is in the shape of a boat or ball.
10. Tell the class the water didn't change.
11. Again pose the question of the buoyancy of a piece of clay.

D. Results:
1. The toy boat floats.
2. The clay boat floats.
3. The clay ball sank.

E. Basic Facts and Supplemental Information:
1. Archimedes' Principle is the answer.
2. Archimedes' Principle states that the buoyancy of any object depends on the weight of the object and the weight of the volume of water it displaces.
3. Let's assume that clay is twice as heavy as an equal volume of water. If the clay weighs 100 grams, an equal volume of water would weigh 50 grams. If the ball of clay would be placed in the water, it would sink.
4. If, however, the clay boat is placed in the water and it displaces 101 grams of water, it will float.

F. Thought Questions for Class Discussions:
1. Why don't heavy ships sink?
2. Why do some logs float but sink after they become waterlogged?
3. How can submarines float on the surface of the water?
4. Why do icebergs float?
5. What must people do to float? Aren't they heavier than water?

G. Related Ideas for Further Inquiry:
1. Study Activity I-C-4, "What is buoyancy?"
2. Study Activity I-C-7, "Why does solid water (ice) float?"
3. Study Activity I-C-13, "What makes a submarine go up and down?"

H. Vocabulary Builders—Spelling Words:
1) **Archimedes** 2) **floating** 3) **sinking**
4) **waterlogged** 5) **weight** 6) **volume**

I. Thought for Today:
"Think big but relish small pleasures."

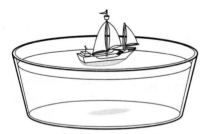
Toy boat floats.

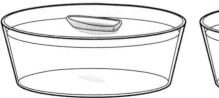
Clay boat floats.

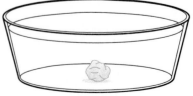
Clay ball sinks.

Activity

A. *Problem: Why Does Solid Water (Ice) Float?*

B. Materials Needed:

1. Three water glasses
2. Ice cubes
3. Water
4. Pictures of icebergs
5. Toy ship
6. Sponge, ice cube size
7. Rubber eraser (ice cube size)
8. Reference materials on water, icebergs.

C. Procedure:

1. Fill all three glasses about 2/3 full of water.
2. Place the sponge in one water glass.
3. Place the rubber eraser in the second glass.
4. Place several ice cubes in the third glass.
5. Discuss why the sponge floats.
6. Discuss why the eraser sinks.
7. Discuss why the ice cubes float.
8. Discuss densities of liquids and solids.
9. Discuss some of the reading materials on icebergs:
   a. causes
   b. drifting
   c. dangers
   d. global warming problems
   e. visibility above the water line
   f. percentage of mass below the water line

D. Results:

1. The sponge floats.
2. The eraser sinks.
3. The ice cubes float.
4. The students will learn about the nature of and problems with icebergs.
5. When the ice cubes melt, the water will not overflow. The level of water stays about the same.

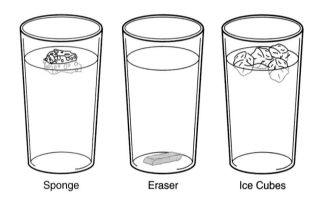

Sponge   Eraser   Ice Cubes

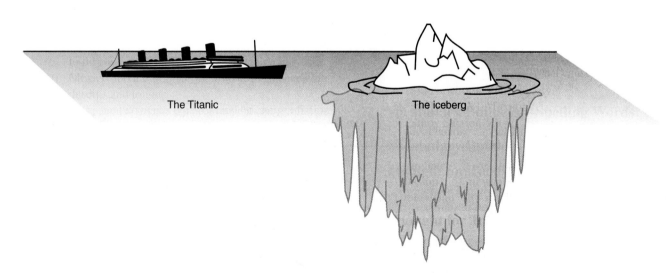

The Titanic   The iceberg

E. Basic Facts and Supplemental Information:

1. When water freezes it expands.
2. Ice takes up more space than it did as water, consequently it is less dense than water and so it floats.
3. Ice is about 9/10 as dense as water.
4. Icebergs are about 9/10 as dense as water; therefore approximately 9/10 of an iceberg is below water level.
5. The Titanic struck an iceberg on April 14, 1912, causing the loss of an estimated 1,515 lives.

F. Thought Questions for Class Discussions:

1. Should submarines stay away from icebergs?
2. How is global warming affecting icebergs?
3. Why do some water pipes break in freezing weather?

G. Related Ideas for Further Inquiry:

1. Study Activity I-C-2, "When water freezes does it expand or contract?"
2. Study Activity I-C-3, "At what temperature does water freeze? boil?"
3. Study Activity I-C-4, "What is buoyancy?"
4. Study Activity I-C-5, "What objects float? What objects sink?"

H. Vocabulary Builders—Spelling Words:

1) **icebergs**   2) **freezing**   3) **expands**
4) **contracts**   5) **surface**   6) **submarine**
7) **dangerous**   8) **melting**   9) **lighter**

I. Thought for Today:

"You can't enjoy being idle unless there is plenty of work to do."

A. Problem: *Why Can We Swim Easier in Salt Water?*

B. Materials Needed, Procedure One:

1. Two water glasses
2. Water
3. Two hard-boiled eggs (unshelled)
4. One tablespoon of salt

Materials Needed, Procedure Two:

1. Two water glasses
2. Water
3. Two pencils
4. One tablespoon of salt
5. Two thumbtacks

C. Procedure One:

1. Fill each glass two-thirds full of water.
2. Add one tablespoon of salt to one of the glasses.
3. Place one egg in the fresh water.
4. Place the other egg in the salt water.

Procedure Two:

1. Fill each glass two-thirds full of water.
2. Add one tablespoon of salt to one of the glasses.
3. Stick thumbtacks in rubber erasers on the pencils.
4. Place one pencil in the fresh water.
5. Place the other pencil in the salt water.

D. Results:

1. In Procedure One, the egg placed in the fresh water will sink, but the egg in the salt water will be partially buoyed up.
2. In Procedure Two, the pencil in salt water will float higher than the one in fresh water.

E. Basic Facts and Supplemental Information:

1. Each glass of water is a simple hydrometer— a device for measuring the density of a liquid. The denser the water, the greater the buoyancy. Buoyancy is determined by the density of the liquid involved. Battery hydrometers use this principle. The denser the liquid, the stronger the battery.
2. If you have ever swum in the ocean, you have found out that it is easier to keep afloat in salt water than it is in fresh water. The reason for this is that salt water is denser than fresh water. The heavier the liquid, the greater the buoyancy. A solid iron bar will float in liquid mercury.

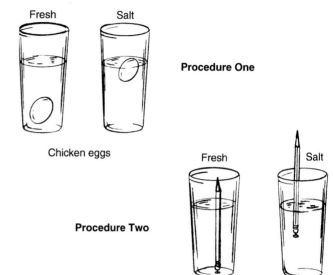

Fresh   Salt

Procedure One

Chicken eggs

Procedure Two

Fresh   Salt

Pencils with thumbtack

F. Thought Questions for Class Discussions:

1. Is salt water denser (heavier) than fresh water?
2. Is salt water denser (heavier) than an egg?
3. Why is salt water heavier than fresh water?
4. Why is water mixed with alcohol lighter than fresh water?

G. Related Ideas for Further Inquiry:

1. Have class relate experiences in swimming in salt water and fresh water.
2. Compare densities of different liquids: oil, molasses, alcohol, mercury, etc.
3. Make a simple hydrometer using a plastic straw, sealing it at one end, and adding sand to it until it acts like the pencil (or egg) described in the activity.
4. Study Activity I-C-5 "What objects float? What objects sink?"
5. Study Activity I-C-4 "What is buoyancy?"
6. Study Activity I-C-13 "What makes a submarine go up and down?"
7. Study Activity I-C-14 "The sailor's dilemma."

H. Vocabulary Builders—Spelling Words:

1) **buoyancy**   2) **density**   3) **hard-boiled**
4) **afloat**   5) **tablespoon**   6) **hydrometer**
7) **thumbtack**   8) **partially**   9) **swimming**

I. Thought for Today:

"A school is a building with four walls with tomorrow inside."—Len Waters

A. Problem: *What Color Marble Sinks Faster?*

B. Materials Needed:

1. Five tall water glasses (clear)
2. Five marbles, all different colors
3. Rubbing alcohol
4. Water
5. Salad oil
6. Mineral oil
7. Light color corn syrup
8. Paper towels
9. Spoon (to retrieve marbles)

C. Procedure:

1. Tell class, "We want to have a contest to see which color marble sinks faster."
2. Select five students as contestants.
3. Select three other students as judges.
4. Fill the water glasses to within a half inch of the top with the liquids cited in "Materials," e.g., one with water, one with alcohol, etc.
5. Place the glasses far enough apart so that students won't bump into each other.
6. Hand each contestant one of the marbles.
7. Tell them that each of them is to place his/her marble just above the surface of the liquid. Then when you say "GO," each is to release the marble to see which marble is heaviest and sinks fastest.
8. When everything is set, say, "GO."
9. You may have to have several contests to determine the winner and the rankings.
10. Wipe off the marbles with the paper towels after each contest.
11. You can also change contestants. Tell the class that different people have different reaction times, i.e., time between a stimulus and the reaction to it.

D. Results:

1. The marbles will sink at different rates.
2. The thicker the liquid, the slower the descent of the marble.

E. Basic Facts and Supplemental Information:

1. The speed of descent of each marble will depend on the viscosity (density, thickness) of the fluid, not the color of the marble.
2. Many scientific investigations are like this one. The real factor is hidden; the obvious one is called a "red herring" which has nothing to do with the item under study.
3. Viscosity is the resistance to flow.

Colored marbles in different liquids

4. Viscosity plays a major role anytime liquids are involved in lubricating, spraying, etc.
5. Long, slender jars can be substituted for water glasses.
6. If tall graduates are available, they make excellent test equipment. (Graduates are glass or plastic measuring devices for determining quantities of liquids.)

F. Thought Questions for Class Discussions:

1. What other liquids could be tested in this experiment?
2. What determines whether an object sinks or floats?
3. Do heavier things sink faster?

G. Related Ideas for Further Inquiry:

1. Study all Activities in Section I-A, "Matter" and in this Section I-C, "Water."
2. Study Section VII-C, "Earth's Crust."

H. Vocabulary Builders—Spelling Words:

1) **viscosity** 2) **density** 3) **thickness**
4) **marbles** 5) **liquid** 6) **reaction**

I. Thought for Today:

"If you are going around in circles, you are cutting too many corners."

Activity

I **C** 10

A. Problem: *What Causes Evaporation?*

B. Materials Needed, Procedure One:
1. Rubbing alcohol
2. Water

Materials Needed, Procedure Two:
1. Two teaspoons
2. Candle
3. Matches
4. Water
5. Spring-type clothespin or tongs
6. Small supporting device (eraser, block of wood, book)

Materials Needed, Procedure Three:
1. Two teaspoons
2. Water
3. Small supporting device (eraser, block of wood, book)
4. Plastic or vinyl cover for desk or table

C. Procedure One:
1. Place some rubbing alcohol on the back of one hand.
2. Place some water on the back of the other hand.
3. Notice the difference in feeling.

Procedure Two:
1. Place one teaspoon full of water on book as shown in drawing.
2. Using clothespin or tongs, hold a second teaspoon of water over a candle.

Procedure Three:
1. Spread one teaspoon of water over as wide an area as possible on a tabletop.
2. Place a book or other supporting device on the tabletop.
3. Using the supporting device, place a second teaspoon, full of water, on the tabletop.
4. Observe the rate of evaporation of each.

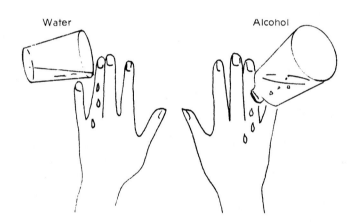

Procedure One

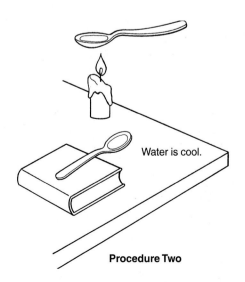

Procedure Two

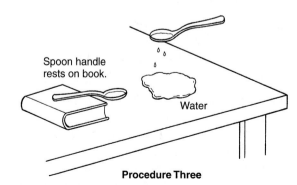

Procedure Three

Physical World **49**

D. Results:

1. The hand with rubbing alcohol will feel cool compared to the hand with water, and the alcohol will evaporate faster than the water.
2. The water over the flame will evaporate more quickly than the water which remains unheated.
3. The water on the table will evaporate and disappear quickly. The water in the spoon will remain for a much longer period of time.

E. Basic Facts and Supplemental Information:

1. Evaporation is the result of molecules which are in constant motion.
2. When liquid molecules move into the air, we call this process "evaporation."
3. Because molecules vary in size and energy, they evaporate at different rates.
4. The more energy a molecule has, the faster it moves and consequently the faster the rate of evaporation.
5. The faster liquids evaporate, the greater the cooling effect.
6. In emergencies an alcohol rub can lower a person's body temperature.

F. Thought Questions for Class Discussions:

1. Will alcohol boil at a lower temperature than water?
2. Why does the heated water evaporate faster?
3. Where does the water go that evaporates?
4. Where does the water come from when it rains?

G. Related Ideas for Further Inquiry:

1. Study Activity I-C-1, "What are the main sources of water?"
2. Study Activity I-C-3, "At what temperature does water freeze? boil?"
3. Study Activity I-C-4, "What is buoyancy?"
4. Study Activity I-C-11, "How does wind help drying?"

H. Vocabulary Builders—Spelling Words:

1) **evaporation** 2) **temperature**
3) **testing** 4) **surface** 5) **area**
6) **amount** 7) **heat** 8) **teaspoon**

I. Thought for Today:

"If all the world is a stage, a lot of people need lessons on how to act."

Activity

A. Problem: *How Does Wind Help Drying?*

B. Materials Needed:
1. Fan
2. Water
3. Pot or pan

C. Procedure:
1. Wet both hands with water.
2. Place one hand in front of a fan.
3. Let the other wet hand remain still and away from the breeze.
4. Feel the difference on your hands.

Fan

Water

Wind dries hands.

D. Result:
The wet hand placed in the path of the moving air will feel cool and will dry more rapidly. The other hand will remain wet for a much longer period of time.

E. Basic Facts and Supplemental Information:
Moving air produces faster evaporation than still air because of the increase in movement of the water molecules. This is why clothes will dry faster on a windy day than on a calm day.

F. Thought Questions for Class Discussions:
1. Why does the hand in front of the fan dry more quickly?
2. Why does the same hand feel much colder than the other hand?
3. When swimming at the beach, why do we feel colder on a windy day than on a non-windy day, even if the temperature is the same?

G. Related Ideas for Further Inquiry:
1. Have students discuss with their parents how they dry clothes outside.
2. A good activity is to test the difference in drying time among different fabrics: cotton, polyester, rayon, silk, etc.
3. Study Activity I-C-10, "What causes evaporation?"
4. Study Activity I-C-1, "What are the main sources of water?"
5. Study Activity I-C-2, "When water freezes does it expand or contract?"

Wind dries clothes.

H. Vocabulary Builders—Spelling Words:
1) **moist** 2) **moisture** 3) **temperature**
4) **wind** 5) **drying** 6) **speed** 7) **time** 8) **help**

I. Thought for Today:

"We all admire the wisdom of people who come to us for advice."

Activity

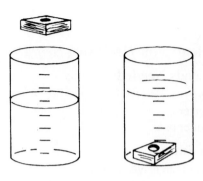

A. Problem: *How Can We Measure the Volume of Irregularly Shaped Objects?*

B. Materials Needed:

1. Measuring cup or graduate (scaled cylinder used in science)
2. Irregularly shaped object (rock, nut, seashell, etc.)
3. Water

C. Procedure:

1. Fill the container with water to about two-thirds full (less if a large object is used).
2. Record the reading (volume).
3. Place the object gently in the container.
4. Record the reading (volume).
5. Subtract the first reading from the last.
6. The difference is the volume of the object.

D. Results:

1. Water will rise in the container.
2. The difference in water level tells you the volume of the irregularly shaped object.

E. Basic Facts and Supplemental Information:

1. Objects which sink displace water equal to their volume.
2. The increase in water volume equals the volume of the irregular object.
3. Archimedes discovered this principle when he was taking a bath and the water overflowed.
4. The volume of regularly shaped objects are as follows:
   a. The volume of a box or cube is:

   Volume = length × width × height

   b. The volume of a cylinder is: the area of a circle times its height.

   V = (Pi) × R² × height (Pi = 3.1416) or (3 1/7)

   c. The volume of a sphere is: (4/3) × Pi × R³
   d. For advanced students, the formula for the volume of a cone is:

   V = 1/3 × Pi × R² × H

F. Thought Questions for Class Discussions:

1. Does the weight of an object in this activity make any difference?
2. How can you measure the volume of an irregularly shaped object that floats?
3. Can you accurately measure tablespoons of butter in a cooking recipe by this procedure?

Water level rises.

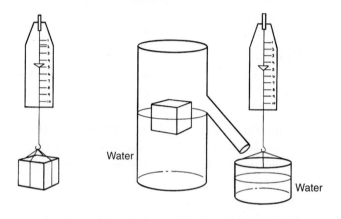

Weight in air   **Weight of object equals weight of displaced water.**

4. How do ship designers decide on whether a ship will sink or float?

G. Related Ideas for Further Inquiry:

1. Measure the volume of many irregularly shaped objects.
2. Use both our system and the metric system for reporting answers.
3. Test using several other types of liquids.
4. Compute the volume of regularly shaped objects such as a box, book, can, ball, etc.
5. Weigh a floatable object. Place it in a full container of water. Measure the overflow. (Archimedes' Principle: the weight of the overflow will equal the weight of the object.)
6. Study Activity I-C-14, "The sailor's dilemma."

H. Vocabulary Builders—Spelling Words:

1) **irregular**   2) **shape**   3) **Archimedes' Principle**
4) **volume**   5) **measure**   6) **metric system**

I. Thought for Today:

"Not only is there an art in knowing a thing, but also a certain art in teaching it."—Cicero

Activity

A. Problem: *What Makes a Submarine Go Up and Down?*

B. Materials Needed:
1. Tall glass or one-quart canning jar
2. Eyedropper
3. Water
4. Rubber balloon
5. Rubber band

C. Procedure:
1. Fill the glass or jar to about 1/2″ from the top.
2. Place the eyedropper in the water with enough water in it so that it barely floats. (You'll have to make several trials to adjust it properly.)
3. Observe the air pocket inside.
4. Cut the balloon and make a rubber cap for the jar. Secure with a rubber band.
5. Push cap down and keep it depressed.
6. If "diver" (eyedropper) sinks, release pressure on top of glass or jar.

D. Result:
The eyedropper goes into its dive when the rubber top is depressed. When the rubber top is released, the eyedropper will rise near the surface of the water.

E. Basic Facts and Supplemental Information:
1. The increase in air pressure forces more water into the eyedropper making it heavier, consequently it sinks to the bottom. When the cap is elevated, the air pressure is decreased in the jar. The air in the eyedropper then forces the water out and the eyedropper becomes lighter and consequently rises.
2. The flotation device is called a "cartesian diver." It can be made with a piece of glass tubing and a cork that fits on the top of the tubing. It is necessary to adjust the size of the cork so that the diver just barely floats. This can be accomplished by using a large cork and gradually filing off small pieces until the diver just floats. To make this device more visible to the students, make circles on the diver with red fingernail polish.
3. A third type of "diver" can be fashioned by using the top of a ball point pen and a piece of clay for "ballast."

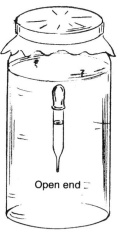

Open end

Cartesian diver

F. Thought Questions for Class Discussions:
1. Why is it important to adjust the eyedropper so that it just barely floats at the beginning of the experiment?
2. Can you do this experiment without having a little air in the eyedropper?
3. How do submarines use this principle?
4. What happens to the water level in the eyedropper?

G. Related Ideas for Further Inquiry:
1. Discuss what makes any object sink or float.
2. Study deep sea diving and how divers descend and ascend.
3. Interview scuba divers.
4. Study Activity I-C-5, "What objects float? What objects sink?"
5. Study Activity I-C-4, "What is buoyancy?"
6. Study Activity I-C-14, "The sailor's dilemma."

H. Vocabulary Builders—Spelling Words:
1) **submarine**   2) **eyedropper**   3) **rubber**
4) **ascend**   5) **descend**   6) **cartesian diver**
7) **surface**

I. Thought for Today:
"Every adult needs a child to teach; it's the best kind of adult education."

Activity

A. Problem: *The Sailor's Dilemma*

B. Materials Needed:

1. Toy sailboat
2. Modeling clay
3. Large bowl or aquarium
4. Water
5. Tall, wide jar
6. Tall, narrow can that will fit inside jar
7. Weights (paper clips, nails, or metal tacks)
8. Marking pen or pencil

C. Procedure:

1. Show the sailboat to the class.
2. Place the sailboat in the large bowl or aquarium.
3. Fashion a small boat of clay simulating the sailboat.
4. Partially fill it with weights.
5. Place this in the large bowl or aquarium.
6. Now pose this "challenging dilemma" to the class: "If this were a real boat on a real lake, and instead of nails and paper clips there were a real anchor in the boat, would the water level of the lake rise, fall, or remain the same if its anchor were taken out of the boat and dropped into the lake?"
7. After the class has made "guesses" (hypotheses), the guesses can be tested by using the tall jar as the lake, the can as the sailboat, and the weights as the anchor.
8. Float the can with weights inside in the tall jar, marking the water level.
9. Dump the weights in the bottom of the jar and with the can still floating mark the new water line.
10. Compare levels.

D. Result:

The water level in the jar will—DROP!

E. Basic Facts and Supplemental Information:

1. When the anchor is in the boat, the weight of the anchor will displace water equal to the weight of the anchor. If the anchor weighs 100 grams, the weight of the volume of water displaced would be 100 grams.
2. Water weighs 1 gram per cubic centimeter.
3. 100 grams of water would occupy 100 cubic centimeters.
4. When the "anchor" is dropped overboard, the anchor still weighs 100 grams but it displaces the volume of water occupied by the anchor. If the "anchor" weighs twice as much as the water, the water displaced would be only 50 grams or 50 cubic centimeters.

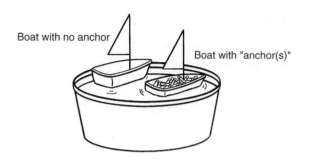

Boat with no anchor

Boat with "anchor(s)"

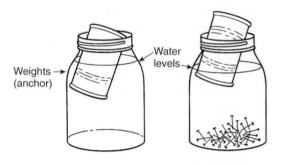

Weights (anchor)

Water levels

5. This being so, the water level would be less when the anchor is in the water. Originally the water level would be the level of the lake plus 100 cubic centimeters. With the anchor overboard the water level would be the level of the lake plus 50 cubic centimeters.

F. Thought Questions for Class Discussions:

1. How can heavy ships float?
2. Do shippers need to be concerned about the weight in their cargoes?
3. Could a boat sink if only water were added to its weight? Why?

G. Related Ideas for Further Inquiry:

1. Study Activity I-C-5, "What objects float? What objects sink?"
2. Study Activity I-C-4, "What is buoyancy?"
3. Study Activity I-C-6, "Why do heavy ships float?"
4. Study Activity I-C-13, "What makes a submarine go up and down?"

H. Vocabulary Builders—Spelling Words:

1) **sailor** 2) **dilemma** 3) **displace** 4) **weights**
5) **volume** 6) **mass** 7) **gram** 8) **centimeter**

I. Thought for Today:

"It is easier to build a child than to repair a man or woman."

Hydrological Cycle

A. Problem: *What Is the "Water Cycle?"*

B. Materials Needed:

Large sketch as shown in drawing

C. Procedure:

1. Discuss water:
   a. covers two-thirds of the Earth
   b. vital to life
   c. two-thirds of the human body is water
2. Discuss:
   a. water cycle
   b. oxygen cycle
   c. carbon cycle
3. Discuss the details of the water cycle:
   a. evaporation from surface water
   b. collects on particles in the air
   c. condenses in air by cooling
   d. falls on land and water surfaces
   e. on land, picked up by plants and animals
   f. on water, evaporates to start another cycle
   g. some plant food (with water) eaten by animals and is involved in the carbon cycle

D. Result:

Students learn about and should be able to sketch a Water Cycle.

E. Basic Facts and Supplemental Information:

1. Heat speeds water evaporation.
2. Humidity is water in the air.
3. Relative humidity is the amount of water in the air compared to the amount it could hold for that temperature. It is recorded in percents.
4. Wind speeds evaporation.
5. Dew and frost are forms of water that have condensed from the air.
6. Hail is frozen raindrops.
7. Snow is frozen water crystals that fall to the Earth in soft, white flakes and spreads upon the ground as a white layer.
8. Water is becoming one of the most critical problems facing the world.
9. Only 3% of all water is fresh.
10. As our population increases, the demands for fresh water will increase.
11. More and more areas of the world are suffering from water shortages because of changes in the weather, El Niño, global warming, etc., water contamination from industrial and agricultural runoffs, and depletion of our water wells from increasing use.

F. Thought Questions for Class Discussions:

1. What forms of water leave the air as frozen particles?
2. What is the difference between precipitation and condensation?
3. What factors affect the water cycle?

G. Related Topics and Activities:

1. Study Section VII-E, "Weather."
2. Study Activity VI-A-10, "Is there a world population explosion?"
3. Study other Activities in this Section.

H. Vocabulary Builders—Spelling Words:

1) **water** 2) **cycle** 3) **precipitation**
4) **condensation** 5) **oceans** 6) **transpiration**

I. Thought for Today:

"The secret of education is respecting the child."— *Emerson*

SECTION D: MAGNETISM
Activity
I D 1

A. Problem: *What Are Magnets? How Do They Work?*

B. Materials Needed:
1. Bar magnet
2. Horseshoe magnets
3. Other magnets if available
4. Iron or steel materials
5. Lodestone (if available)
6. Alnico
7. Compass

C. Procedure:
1. Describe and briefly show the kinds of magnets:
   a. Permanent magnets
      1) lodestone
      2) steel
      3) alnico
   b. Temporary magnets (electromagnets)
   c. Earth as a magnet (use compass to prove)
2. Show how magnets are made:
   a. stroking iron or steel with another magnet
   b. electric current passing through an insulated wire coiled around an iron bar
3. Discuss actions of magnets:
   a. kinds of materials magnetism will pass through
   b. north and south poles
   c. laws of attraction of poles
   d. usefulness of magnets

D. Result:
Students will get a quick overview of magnets. For more specifics do the Activities that follow in this Section.

E. Basic Facts and Supplemental Information:
1. Magnets have many uses.
2. Magnetism and electricity are interrelated.
3. Magnets pull toward each other which we call "attraction" or push away from each other which we call "repulsion." The action verbs are "attracting" and "repelling."
4. Since magnets and electricity are interrelated, everything that uses electricity has some relationship with magnets, be they home appliances, business machines, automobiles, etc.

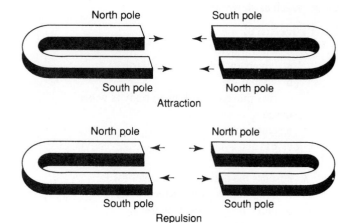

Laws of attraction and repulsion

F. Thought Questions for Class Discussions:
1. Do all electric motors have magnets?
2. What is the difference between a temporary magnet and a permanent magnet?
3. Can a magnet lift heavy things?
4. Does a compass prove that our Earth is a magnet?

G. Related Ideas for Further Inquiry:
1. Study Activity I-D-2, "Do like poles on magnets attract or repel each other?"
2. Study Activity I-D-4, "Is the Earth a magnet?"
3. Study Activity I-D-7, "What is a magnetic field of force?"
4. Study Section II-G, "Current Electricity."
5. Study Section VII-C, "Earth's Crust."

H. Vocabulary Builders—Spelling Words:
1) **magnets** 2) **magnetism** 3) **attraction**
4) **attracting** 5) **repulsion** 6) **repelling**
7) **temporary** 8) **permanent** 9) **lodestone**

I. Thought for Today:
"The full development of each individual is not only a moral right but a legal duty of society."

Activity

A. Problem: *Do Like Poles on Magnets Attract or Repel Each Other?*

B. Materials Needed:
1. Two bar magnets
2. String, one foot in length
3. Means of suspension
4. Compass
5. Marking pens or pencils

C. Procedure:
1. Lay one of the bar magnets on the table.
2. Place the compass about one inch from the end of this magnet.
3. If the "north pointer" on the compass points to this end, mark this end with an "S" for south, and the other end with an "N" for north.
4. If the "north pointer" on the compass points away from this end, mark this end with an "N" for north and the other end with an "S" for south.
5. Repeat this test with the second bar magnet, marking the ends appropriately.
6. Suspend one magnet horizontally so that it can swing freely.
7. Approach the suspended magnet with the second magnet slowly, end to end.
8. When the suspended magnet moves, note the letters on the magnets and their relative positions.
9. Remove the second magnet and when the first (suspended) magnet stops swinging, repeat the procedure using the other end of the second magnet.
10. Note the relative positions of the two magnets and their markings.

D. Results:
1. "Like" poles will repel each other (two "norths" or two "souths").
2. "Unlike" (opposites) will attract each other (one "north" and one "south").
3. The north pole of the compass will be attracted to the south pole on the magnet. The north pointer on the compass is really a north-seeking compass. The north pole of a magnet is really a north-seeking edge. Consequently, the north pointer of a compass will be repelled by the north edge of the magnet.

E. Basic Facts and Supplemental Information:
1. This proves one of the laws of magnetism: unlike magnetic poles attract; like magnetic poles repel.
2. Many games and home devices use magnetism.

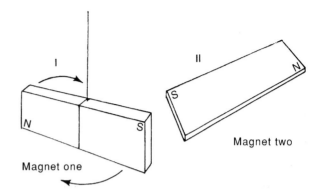

Magnet one

Magnet two

F. Thought Questions for Class Discussions:
1. How can you test an unmarked magnet to find which is the north pole and which is the south pole?
2. Is a freely swinging bar magnet like a compass?
3. Why do compasses always point toward the north if no interference?

G. Related Ideas for Further Inquiry:
1. Test a bar magnet with a horseshoe magnet in checking poles.
2. Rub a rubber rod briskly and place between two closely suspended pith or styrofoam balls.
3. Check to see if the rod has become magnetized.
4. An enjoyable activity can be devised by obtaining two small plastic cars and taping a bar magnet on the roof of each car and then attempting to bring the cars together. Depending on the position of the poles, the cars will either attract or repel each other rather forcibly.
5. Study Activity I-D-3, "What kinds of substances do magnets attract?"
6. Study Activity I-D-7, "What is a magnetic field of force?"
7. Study Activity I-D-5, "How can we make a compass?"
8. Study Section I-E, "Static Electricity."

H. Vocabulary Builders—Spelling Words:
1) **magnets** 2) **horseshoe magnet** 3) **attraction**
4) **repulsion** 5) **repel** 6) **north-seeking**
7) **south-seeking** 8) **pith** 9) **styrofoam**

I. Thought for Today:
"The clash of ideas is the sound of freedom."

Activity

A. Problem: *What Kinds of Substances Do Magnets Attract?*

B. Materials Needed:
1. Table
2. Magnet
3. Nails
4. Pins
5. Pencils
6. Copper
7. Aluminum
8. Dime
9. Other small objects

C. Procedure:
1. Place the objects on the table.
2. Touch the magnet against each object.
3. Observe the results.

D. Result:
Objects made of iron and steel will be attracted by the magnet; others will not.

E. Basic Facts and Supplemental Information:
1. Magnets attract iron and steel objects, but do not attract wood, copper, silver, or other objects which do not contain iron.
2. We still don't know what causes magnetic attraction and repulsion.
3. Lodestone, or magnetite, is an iron oxide material that has magnetic properties. The most common form is Fe_3O_4. There are other natural minerals which contain iron oxides that also have magnetic properties. These have been known since 500 B.C.
4. Iron is the most abundant element that can be magnetized. Nickel and cobalt can also be magnetized.
5. Substances made of these elements can be magnetized by rubbing them in one direction with one pole of a magnet.
6. Magnetism is caused by electrons whirling around the atoms and lining up in small parts called "domains." If a magnet is cut in two, these domains line up to form a new magnet with each part.

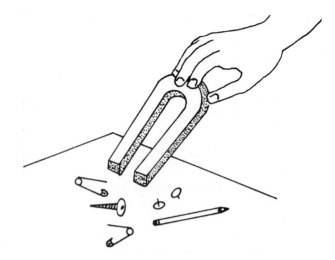

F. Thought Questions for Class Discussions:
1. How can we test a metal to see if it contains iron?
2. How could a magnet be used to find a lost needle?
3. Why are magnets often used to separate iron or steel from wood or other nonmagnetic materials?
4. Does it make any difference what shape the magnet has?

G. Related Ideas for Further Inquiry:
1. Test other objects made of rubber, brass, paper, etc.
2. Test to determine if both ends of a horseshoe magnet have the same or different poles.
3. Make an electromagnet. See Activity II-G-12, "How can we make an electromagnet?"
4. Study Activity I-D-7, "What is a magnetic field of force?"
5. Study Activity I-D-8, "Through what kinds of substances do magnetic lines of force pass?"
6. Study Activity I-D-6, "Can a paper clip defy gravity?"

H. Vocabulary Builders—Spelling Words:
1) **attraction**   2) **magnets**   3) **magnetism**
4) **repulsion**   5) **aluminum**   6) **copper**

I. Thought for Today:
"I have never let schooling interfere with my education."—Mark Twain

A. Problem: *Is the Earth a Magnet?*

B. Materials Needed:
1. Map of magnetic poles
2. Ball of yarn
3. Bar magnet
4. Long knitting needle

C. Procedure:
1. Work the bar magnet through the ball of yarn so that equal ends are protruding.
2. With the bar magnet slanting slightly to one side, insert the knitting needle through the center of the ball of yarn. This is a model of the Earth and its magnetic poles.
3. Discuss true north direction. (We can determine by the North Star.)
4. Discuss magnetic north direction. (We can determine by a compass.)
5. Discuss variation. (This is the difference in degrees between true north and magnetic north.)
6. Show the class the "model" of the Earth.
7. Explain that the knitting needle represents the axis of the Earth on which the Earth rotates.
8. Point to the bar magnet and tell the class that the Earth acts very much like the bar magnet having a north pole, a south pole, and a magnetic field.
9. Study the map on the following page.

D. Results:
1. Students will find that the magnetic North Pole lies about 15° south of the true North Pole and the magnetic South Pole lies about 24° north of the true South Pole.
2. Students will learn that the variation differs greatly and there is no regular pattern.
3. Pupils will find that while most variations are small, some are very large—over 100° of longitude.

E. Basic Facts and Supplemental Information:
1. Even the magnetic poles are not fixed.
2. The magnetic poles are believed to be caused by the mineral deposits within the Earth.
3. The magnetic poles even change during the Earth's revolution.
4. Variations are measured in degrees east or west of the true direction.
5. The North Pole of a magnet is named because it points to magnetic north.

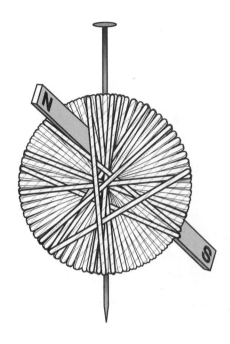

6. The Earth's North Magnetic Pole is in the Canadian Arctic, about 1,600 km. (1,000 mi.) from the true, or geographic North Pole.
7. The Earth's South Magnetic Pole is in Adelie Land about 2,400 km. (1,500 mi.) from the geographic South Pole in Central Antarctica.
8. The Earth's magnetism is produced by molten metal deep within the Earth's core. As the Earth spins, electric currents produce the Earth's magnetic force.

F. Thought Questions for Class Discussions:
1. Do you think early sailors had trouble navigating?
2. What are gyrocompasses?
3. Would magnetic compasses be effective on the moon?
4. Are we living on a huge magnet?

G. Related Ideas for Further Inquiry:
1. Study Section I-A, "Matter."
2. Study Section VII-C, "Earth's Crust."
3. Study Activity I-D-1, "What are magnets? How do they work?"
4. Study Activity I-D-5, "How can we make a compass?"
5. Study Activity I-D-7, "What is a magnetic field of force?"

H. Vocabulary Builders—Spelling Words:

1) **North Pole** 2) **South Pole** 3) **magnetic**
4) **variation** 5) **deviation** 6) **Arctic** 7) **Antarctic**

I. Thought for Today:

"Imagination was given to us to compensate for what we are not, and a sense of humor to console us for what we are."

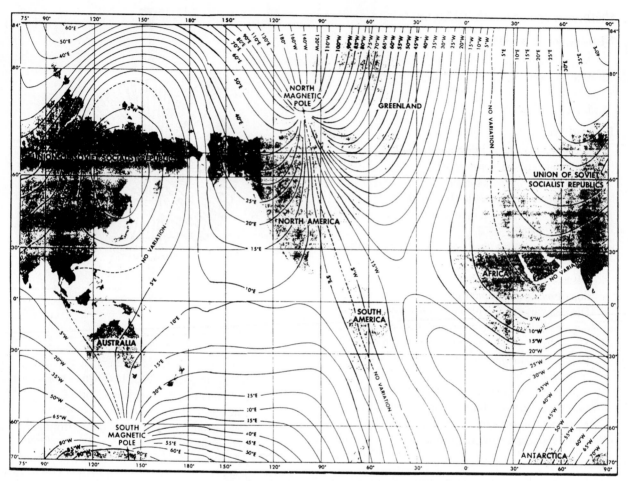

The Earth's magnetic poles do not correspond to the regular north and south poles. The difference is called "variation."

A. Problem: *How Can We Make a Compass?*

B. Materials Needed:

1. Magnet
2. Needle
3. Cork
4. Water
5. Sheet of paper
6. Magnetic compass
7. Knife
8. Shallow dish

C. Procedure:

1. Rub a needle in one direction over a magnet until the needle becomes magnetized. Test it with a compass.
2. Trim a slice of the cork and float it in the dish of water.
3. Place the needle across the cork.
4. Mark the corners of the paper "N" for North, "E" for East, "S" for South, and "W" for West.
5. Add water to dish.
6. Set the dish on the paper and allow the needle to come to rest.
7. Lift the saucer without disturbing the needle and move the paper around until the N (North) and the point of the needle are in line.
8. Move the cork and the needle so that they point to various directions; release the cork and let the needle swing freely.

D. Results:

1. The needle and cork will swing to a north-south line. (This can be tested by the magnetic compass.)
2. The floating magnetized needle will become a simple compass.

E. Basic Facts and Supplemental Information:

1. A needle can be magnetized by rubbing it on a magnet in one direction only.
2. It acts as a compass in that it continues pointing north as the dish is moved.
3. Styrofoam may be substituted for cork.

F. Thought Questions for Class Discussions:

1. Why must the needle be placed on a cork on the water?
2. Will a magnet held close to a compass keep the compass from pointing north and south?
3. Why does the magnetized needle point north and south instead of east and west?

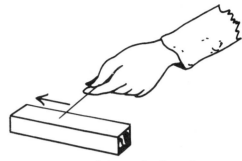

Rub needle in one direction only.

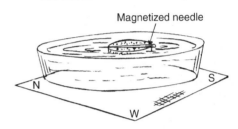

Magnetized needle

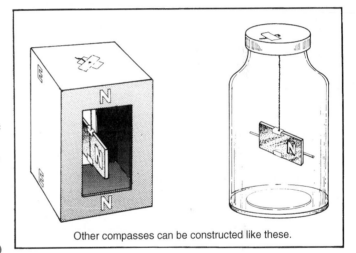

Other compasses can be constructed like these.

G. Related Ideas for Further Inquiry:

1. Magnetize a needle. Cut it in two very carefully with cutting pliers. Check each piece for magnetic poles.
2. Make a map of the schoolyard using a compass.
3. Many types of simple compasses can be constructed.
4. Study all Activities in this Section.

H. Vocabulary Builders—Spelling Words:

1) **bowl** 2) **needle** 3) **compass** 4) **measuring tape** 5) **protractor** 6) **measure** 7) **knife** 8) **saucer**

I. Thought for Today:

"If two people agree on everything, you may be sure that one of them is doing all the thinking."

Activity

A. Problem: *Can a Paper Clip Defy Gravity?*

B. Materials Needed:
1. Paper clips
2. Permanent magnet (preferably a bar magnet)
3. Piece of thread
4. Ring stand and a clamp
5. Small box

C. Procedure:
1. Support the magnet in the ring stand and clamp as shown in the diagram at right.
2. Secure a paper clip to a piece of thread and secure the thread to the base of the ring stand. The thread should be just long enough so that the paper clip cannot quite touch the tip of the magnet.
3. Cover the magnet with a small box so that the class can't see the top of the apparatus.
4. Drop several paper clips away from apparatus and have class note that they fall.
5. Raise paper clip with thread close to box and have class note that it does not fall.
6. Ask class why? Is this magic?
7. If class guesses correctly, then remove box.

D. Result:
If the magnet is reasonably strong, the paper clip will be held in the position shown.

E. Basic Facts and Supplemental Information:
A magnet can attract a magnetic substance without touching it. Magnetic lines of force surround any magnet. There are many kinds and shapes of magnets. These include:

1. bar magnets
2. cylinder magnets
3. horseshoe magnets
4. disk magnets

There are also countless varieties of electromagnets.

F. Thought Questions for Class Discussions:
1. Does the strength of the magnet make any difference in this experiment?
2. Does the paper clip have to be magnetized?
3. Will it make any difference whether the north or south pole of the magnet is used?

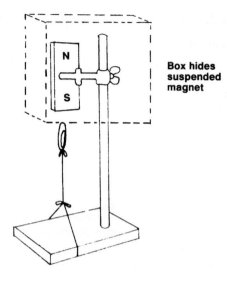

Box hides suspended magnet

4. Can this experiment be used to help determine how strong a magnet really is?
5. How far can the magnet be moved from the paper clip before the paper clip will fall?
6. Where are magnets used in the home?

G. Related Ideas for Further Inquiry:
1. A good follow-up Activity is I-D-8, "Through what kinds of substances do magnetic lines of force pass?"
2. Study Activity I-D-3, "What kinds of substances do magnets attract?"
3. Study Activity I-D-5, "How can we make a compass?"
4. Study Activity I-D-7, "What is a magnetic field of force?"
5. Study Activity II-G-8, "What materials conduct electricity?"

H. Vocabulary Builders—Spelling Words:
1) **magnet**   2) **paper clip**   3) **thread**
4) **suspension**   5) **magic**   6) **permanent**   7) **defy**
8) **clamp**   9) **touch**   10) **apparatus**   11) **raise**

I. Thought for Today:
"One of the things a person notices when he visits a 'backward' country is that the children still obey their parents."

Activity

A. Problem: *What Is a Magnetic Field of Force?*

B. Materials Needed:
1. Bar magnet
2. Sheet of paper or thin cardboard
3. Iron filings
4. Compass
5. Table
6. Pencil

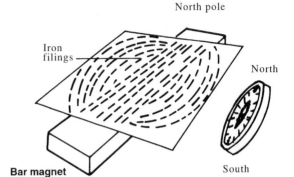

Compass to check direction

C. Procedure:
1. Place the compass near the edge of the table.
2. Place the bar magnet so that the north pole of the magnet is pointing north as indicated on the compass. The north pole of the magnet is the "north-seeking" pole.
3. Confirm poles by checking with compass.
4. Cover the magnet with the paper or cardboard.
5. Sprinkle iron filings evenly on the paper or cardboard.
6. Shake or tap the paper or cardboard lightly.
7. With pencil, draw lines alongside iron filings.
8. Remove iron filings and study pencil lines.

D. Results:
1. The iron filings will arrange themselves along the magnetic lines of force.
2. The lines will look like those in the drawing.
3. The filings point toward the poles.
4. When equal attractions from the poles occur, the lines will appear as shown in the middle of the drawing. Note that the filings seem to stand on end at the poles of the magnet.

E. Basic Facts and Supplemental Information:
1. A magnet has a field of force. This will be shown by the iron filings being drawn together in lines, extending along the magnet. A little farther away from the magnet the iron filings will look just as they did when they were sprinkled on the cardboard. The force of the magnet did not move them. The force becomes weaker the farther we get from the magnet, finally becoming so weak it will not move the filings at all.
2. When a bar magnet is bent into a "U" shape it is called a "horseshoe magnet." This type of magnet will have greater attraction power because the two poles are closer together. By using iron filings it can be shown that the lines of force are closer together.

F. Thought Questions for Class Discussions:
1. Does the strength of the magnet have any effect on the magnetic field?
2. How does the magnetic field of the bar magnet differ from that of the horseshoe magnet?
3. Where in your home can you find practical uses for magnets?

G. Related Ideas for Further Inquiry:
1. Repeat test with a horseshoe magnet.
2. Pencil or ink lines can be drawn near iron filings for a permanent record.
3. Study Activity I-D-3, "What kinds of substances do magnets attract?"
4. Study Activity I-D-2, "Do like poles on magnets attract or repel each other?"
5. Study Activity I-D-8, "Through what kinds of substances do magnetic lines of force pass?"
6. Study Activity I-D-5, "How can we make a compass?"

H. Vocabulary Builders—Spelling Words:
1) **iron filings**   2) **magnetic field**   3) **compass**
4) **horseshoe**   5) **bar**   6) **sprinkle**   7) **direction**

I. Thought for Today:
"A smile is an inexpensive way to improve your looks."

Activity

ı D 8

A. Problem: *Through What Kinds of Substances Do Magnetic Lines of Force Pass?*

B. Materials Needed, Procedure One:

1. U-shaped magnet, small
2. Paper clip
3. Cup hook
4. Thread or string
5. Thin pieces of wood, glass, leather, iron, rubber, paper, cloth, copper, steel, aluminum, etc.

Materials Needed, Procedure Two:

1. Large wide-mouth jar
2. Iron filings
3. U-shaped magnet, large
4. Water

C. Procedure One:

1. Make a wooden support as shown in Fig. 1.
2. Attach cup hook to the top.
3. Attach thread or string to the base.
4. Attach a paper clip to thread or string so it reaches about halfway to the top of the wooden support.
5. Hang horseshoe (U-magnet) from the top so that there is a strong attraction to the paper clip but still enough room to insert test materials.
6. Insert test materials between the magnet and the paper clip.

Procedure Two:

1. Place filings in jar and cover with water to a depth of several inches. (The depth will depend on the strength of the magnet.) See Fig. 2.
2. Hold magnet just above the water.

D. Results:

1. Procedure One:
   a. The magnet will attract through paper, cloth, glass, thin plywood, rubber, and nonferrous materials.
   b. The magnet will not attract materials through iron, steel, nickel, or cobalt.
2. Procedure Two:
   The iron filings will be attracted through the water to the magnet.

E. Basic Facts and Supplemental Information:

1. Several other metals besides iron are capable of becoming magnetized. Among them are cobalt and nickel.
2. Most metals are not magnetic.
3. Sometimes magnetic boards are used in a classroom. If a teacher wants to make a combination magnet and flannel board, steel screening can be placed under the flannel. Because magnetic lines of force

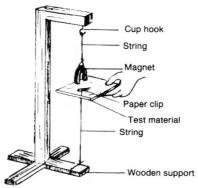

Fig. 1

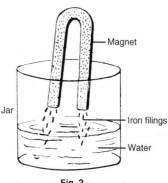

Fig. 2

travel through the flannel, magnets can still be used on the flannel board. To stimulate curiosity, you may want to combine this Activity with I-D-6.

F. Thought Questions for Class Discussions:

1. Why will a magnet attract an iron object through a piece of paper?
2. Can you think of any places in your home where there are magnets?
3. Do motors have magnets?
4. Does a doorbell use electromagnetism?

G. Related Ideas for Further Inquiry:

1. Many commercial products use magnets. Have students do some research in this area.
2. Discuss how iron and steel objects could be located under water.
3. Study Activity I-D-3, "What kinds of substances do magnets attract?"
4. Study Activity II-G-13, "How does an electric doorbell work?"

H. Vocabulary Builders—Spelling Words:

1) **attract**   2) **lines of force**   3) **support**
4) **iron filings**   5) **paper clip**   6) **magnetic**

I. Thought for Today:

"The primary purpose of a liberal education is to make one's mind a pleasant place in which to spend one's leisure."

64   *Magnetism*

SECTION E: STATIC ELECTRICITY
Activity

A. Problem: *What Is Static Electricity?*

B. Materials Needed:
1. Two thin books
2. Piece of heavy glass
3. Small torn bits of tissue paper
4. Piece of silk cloth

C. Procedure:
1. Place books parallel on table leaving a space between them.
2. Place torn bits of paper on table between the books.
3. Place glass on books over the paper bits.
4. Rub glass briskly with silk cloth.

D. Result:
The pieces of paper dance or attach themselves to the glass when the cloth is rubbed on the glass.

E. Basic Facts and Supplemental Information:
1. Electricity can be produced by rubbing silk on glass. Rubbing the glass with silk causes the electrons to be rubbed off the glass and the glass becomes positively charged. This attracts the negative charges of the neutral paper and hence, unlike charges attract.
2. Some static on radio and snow on television is caused by static electricity. Lightning is a huge spark of static electricity being generated in the clouds. The relationship of weather to the success of the experiments can be discussed: dry weather gives the best results.
3. Water in the air tends to neutralize the effects of static electricity.

F. Thought Questions for Class Discussions:
1. Will it make any difference if the cloth used in this experiment is a different kind of material?
2. Does the direction the glass is rubbed make any difference, i.e., up and down, side to side, or in a circular motion?
3. What are the differences between static electricity and regular (current) electricity?

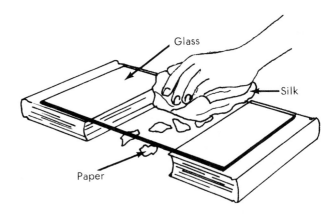

Glass

Silk

Paper

G. Related Ideas for Further Inquiry:
1. Students can divide into groups and experiment by combing their hair briskly and then picking up tissue paper with the combs they used.
2. Students may try rubbing materials other than silk on the glass (see Procedure 4 in this Activity).
3. Have students rub a piece of tissue paper against a blackboard with a piece of silk cloth.
4. Sprinkle a little salt and some finely ground pepper in a dish. Rub a plastic comb or pen with felt or wool very briskly. Place comb or pen near the salt and pepper. The finely ground pepper will "jump up" to the object used.
5. Suspend two balloons from a common point with light thread. Rub each facing side of the balloons with wool or silk. (They will repel each other, i.e., move apart.)
6. Many other experiments which illustrate static electricity can be tried.
7. Study Activity I-E-2, "What causes static electricity?"
8. Study Activity I-E-4, "Can static electricity be produced by friction?"

H. Vocabulary Builders—Spelling Words:
1) **static** 2) **electricity** 3) **positive** 4) **negative**
5) **neutral** 6) **spark** 7) **briskly** 8) **parallel**
9) **circular** 10) **glass** 11) **attraction**

I. Thought for Today:
"A generation ago most people who finished a day's work needed rest; now they need exercise."

A. Problem: *What Causes Static Electricity?*

B. Materials Needed:
1. Two rubber or plastic combs
2. Two glass rods
3. Thread
4. Supporting device
5. Piece of wool cloth

C. Procedure One:
1. Attach the two combs to the supporting device so that they are close together but not touching.
2. Rub the two combs briskly with the wool cloth.
3. Observe the results.

Procedure Two:
1. Attach the two glass rods to the supporting device so that they are close together but not touching.
2. Rub the two glass rods briskly with the wool cloth.
3. Observe the results.

Procedure Three:
1. Attach one comb and one glass rod to the supporting device so that they are close together but not touching.
2. Rub these two items briskly with the wool cloth.
3. Observe the results.

D. Results:
1. In Procedure One, the two combs will move apart (repel each other).
2. In Procedure Two, the two rods will move apart (repel each other).
3. In Procedure Three, the comb and the glass rod will move closer together (attract each other).

E. Basic Facts and Supplemental Information:
1. All material is made up of atoms.
2. All atoms have electrons (negative charges) on their outermost parts.
3. When the wool cloth rubs against these electrons it moves the electrons from one object to another.
4. One object becomes negatively charged (has excess electrons) and the other object becomes positively charged (has lost electrons).

F. Thought Questions for Class Discussions:
1. What is the difference between static electricity and current electricity?
2. Can other types of material be charged with "static electricity"?

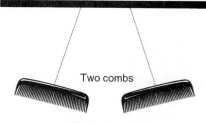

Two combs

Like charges repel

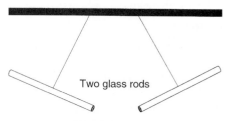

Two glass rods

Like charges repel

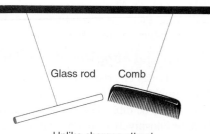

Glass rod   Comb

Unlike charges attract

3. Does a simple telegraph key use static or current electricity?

G. Related Ideas for Further Inquiry:
1. Test how long the comb and the glass rod hold their charges.
2. Study other Activities in this Section.
3. Study Activity I-A-2 "What are atoms? molecules?"
4. Study Section II-G, "Current Electricity."

H. Vocabulary Builders—Spelling Words:
1) **static**   2) **electricity**   3) **attraction**
4) **repulsion**   5) **comb**   6) **briskly**

I. Thought for Today:
"The thing to try when all else fails is again."

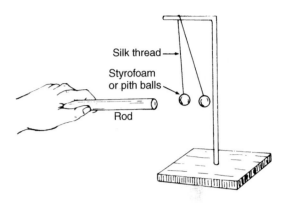

Silk thread →

Styrofoam or pith balls →

Rod

A. Problem: *Do Like Charges Repel or Attract Each Other?*

B. Materials Needed:

1. Pith balls (Can be obtained at school supply stores or made from dry cornstalks.) (May substitute styrofoam balls.)
2. Thread
3. Cellophane tape, glue, or clay
4. L-shaped glass or plastic tubing (support)
5. Glass rod
6. Wooden base
7. Small piece of wool fabric

C. Procedure:

1. Secure the support to the base with tape or glue or small mound of clay.
2. Fasten a pith ball to each end of a piece of thread about 12″ long with cellophane tape or glue.
3. Hang them from a support made of wood or glass as shown in the accompanying illustration.
4. Rub the rod briskly with a piece of wool. This will cause the rod to become negatively charged.
5. Bring the rod near the pith or styrofoam balls.

D. Results

The pith balls will be first attracted to the rod, and then after a little while they will be repelled. Sometimes it is necessary to allow the balls to roll along the rod and to rub the rod several times. Soon both the balls secure the same charge as the rod, and they are repelled by the rod and by each other.

E. Basic Facts and Supplemental Information:

1. Substances with like charges repel each other. Substances with unlike charges attract each other. The charge of any substance is determined by the electrons (negative) on the surface of the materials. If the electrons are rubbed off, the substance loses negative charges and becomes positively charged. If the surface picks up electrons it becomes negatively charged.
2. Benjamin Franklin, American statesman and scientist, was the first to suggest the idea of positive and negative charges. He is noted for demonstrating that lightning is a form of static electricity by flying a kite in an electric storm.

F. Thought Questions for Class Discussion:

1. What is the difference between negative and positive charges of static electricity?
2. How are negative and positive charges of static electricity involved in lightning storms?
3. How can one tell what is positively charged and what is negatively charged?

G. Related Ideas for Further Inquiry:

1. Blow up several balloons. Rub them briskly against your clothing. Try adhering them to a wall.
2. Have students discuss times they have walked across rugs and touched a metallic object and received a little shock.
3. Study Activity I-E-1, "What is static electricity?"
4. Study Activity I-E-2, "What causes static electricity?"
5. Study Activity I-E-5, "Does static electricity affect water flow?"

H. Vocabulary Builders—Spelling Words:

1) **repel** 2) **attract** 3) **pith balls** 4) **support**
5) **styrofoam** 6) **thread** 7) **tubing** 8) **wooden**

I. Thought for Today:

"The greatest resource any country can have is its children."—Danny Kaye

Activity

A. Problem: *Can Static Electricity Be Produced by Friction?*

B. Materials Needed:
1. Two rubber balloons
2. Piece of thread
3. Piece of wool or silk cloth
4. Pieces of newspaper, thin manila paper, or tissue paper.

C. Procedure One:
1. Inflate balloons and tie them together with thread. (See drawing.)
2. Space them so that they can swing and touch each other freely.
3. Rub balloons with wool or silk cloth.
4. Have student raise a hand directly over balloons.

Procedure Two:
1. Select a flat spot on wall or chalkboard.
2. Place paper on this area.
3. Rub paper briskly with silk or wool cloth, being sure that paper is flat on wall or chalkboard.
4. Observe what happens.

D. Results:
1. In the first experiment, the balloons follow the student's hand after the balloons are rubbed with wool.
2. In the second experiment, the paper will cling to the wall for a short period of time.

E. Basic Facts and Supplemental Information:
1. The paper has a charge, but the wall is neutral. It should be remembered that before carrying out this experiment the paper should be thoroughly dry for best results. It can be concluded from the experiments that electricity can be produced by friction. This static electricity is the result of producing electric charges by rubbing materials briskly, which moves the outer electrons of atoms.
2. By rubbing any object briskly, usually the outer electrons are removed and picked up by another object. One object becomes positive and the other becomes negative. Either will attract a neutral object, because the latter will move most of its electrons to one side and will become positive on one side and negative on the other.

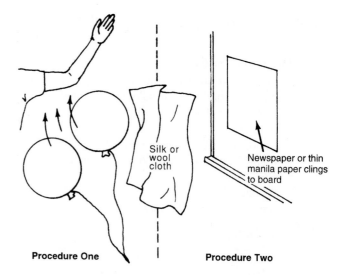

Procedure One

Silk or wool cloth

Newspaper or thin manila paper clings to board

Procedure Two

F. Thought Questions for Class Discussions:
1. How can you determine which materials rubbed together will cause static electricity?
2. What makes your hair crackle when you comb it briskly?
3. When one walks on carpeting and then touches a metal object, a "crackle" is heard and a tiny spark is seen. What causes this?

G. Related Ideas for Further Inquiry:
1. Test any material by rubbing it briskly and checking to see if it can pick up paper bits.
2. Study about lightning and find the causes of its existence.
3. Make two pith balls out of cornstalks and test them by stringing them together and then charging them with a comb after it has been used briskly in combing hair.
4. Study Activity I-E-1, "What is static electricity?"
5. Study Activity I-E-2, "What causes static electricity?"
6. Study Activity I-E-3, "Do like charges repel or attract each other?"

H. Vocabulary Builders—Spelling Words:
1) **electron** 2) **charges** 3) **positive** 4) **negative**
5) **attraction** 6) **repel** 7) **candle** 8) **wool**

I. Thought for Today:
"If you can tell the difference between good advice and bad advice, you don't need advice."

Activity

A. Problem: *Does Static Electricity Affect Water Flow?*

B. Materials Needed:

1. Plastic comb
2. Bits of paper
3. Stream of water

C. Procedure One:

1. Adjust the faucet stream so that it flows steadily in a small stream.
2. Vigorously comb your hair.
3. Hold the comb near the stream of water.
4. Observe the flow of water.
5. Slowly move comb horizontally toward and then away from the stream of water.
6. Observe any changes in the flow of water.

Procedure Two:

1. Lay the bits of paper on a table or desk top, scattering them slightly.
2. Comb hair briskly and immediately hold comb near bits of paper.
3. Observe results.
4. Move comb slowly around the bits of paper.
5. Again observe any changes.

D. Results:

1. When the comb is used briskly in combing one's hair, the comb becomes negatively charged.
2. In Procedure One, the stream of water will bend toward the comb as long as the comb is nearby.
3. In Procedure Two, when the comb is placed near the bits of paper, the bits of paper will "jump up" to the comb and adhere to it briefly.

E. Basic Facts and Supplemental Information:

1. Static electricity is caused by rubbing the electrons of atoms of one material and causing them to move toward other materials that have fewer electrons closer to them.
2. Running water has a neutral charge. When the negatively charged comb is placed near the water, the electrons on the atoms of the water move to the opposite side, leaving the side nearest the comb positively charged. The attraction between the negatively charged comb and the positively charged side of the atoms of the water cause the water to "bend" toward the comb.

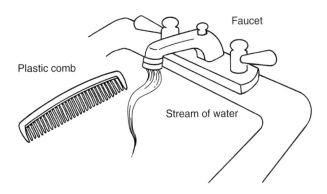

Faucet

Plastic comb

Stream of water

Procedure One

Plastic comb

Bits of tissue paper

Procedure Two

F. Thought Questions for Class Discussions:

1. How do lightning rods work?
2. Where does the electricity come from that is in the clouds?
3. Can you make a balloon cling to a wall by rubbing it briskly against your clothing and then placing it on the wall?

G. Related Ideas for Further Inquiry:

1. Suspend one comb with a thin thread. Have a student comb his/her hair briskly with a second comb and bring it immediately near the first comb.
2. Study Section II-G, "Current Electricity."
3. Study all other Activities in this Section.

H. Vocabulary Builders—Spelling Words:

1) **static**   2) **comb**   3) **faucet**   4) **vigorously**
5) **briskly**   6) **stream**   7) **negatively**   8) **positively**

I. Thought for Today:

"The bigger a person's head gets, the easier it is to fill his/her shoes."—Anne Bancroft

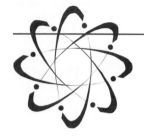

PART II
ENERGY

SECTION A   SOURCES   71

SECTION B   FIRE AND HEAT   79

SECTION C   LIGHT AND COLOR   92

SECTION D   SOUND   104

SECTION E   SIMPLE MACHINES   114

SECTION F   MOVEMENT AND RESISTANCE   121

SECTION G   CURRENT ELECTRICITY   132

$$E = mc^2$$

SECTION A: SOURCES

Activity

II **A** 1

A. Problem: *What Are Nonrenewable Sources of Energy?*

B. Materials Needed:
1. Pictures of:
   a. Coal
   b. Oil wells
   c. Natural gas derricks
   d. Nuclear power plants
2. Reference materials about the above.

C. Procedure:
1. Discuss some of our present sources of energy.
2. List the nonrenewable sources of energy:
   a. fossil fuels
   b. coal (actually a fossil fuel)
   c. natural gas
   d. nuclear power plants
3. Compare the renewable and nonrenewable sources of energy. (See Activity II-A-2.)
4. Discuss the problems of using up our nonrenewable sources of energy.
5. Discuss the problems of nuclear energy:
   a. production
   b. disposal of nuclear wastes
   c. limited life of nuclear power plants
   d. leaks, spills, etc.
   e. radioactivity
   f. thermal pollution
6. Discuss the increasing energy needs of people everywhere.
7. Cite uses of energy inside and outside the home: appliances, power tools, lawn mowers, snow blowers, automobiles, etc.
8. Have students make a list of energy uses in their homes.

D. Results:
Students will learn that:
1. Most of our current energy use is from nonrenewable sources.
2. We are going to deplete our fossil fuels in the very near future.
3. Our only present large supply of energy from a nonrenewable source is coal.
4. There are many ways in which energy is used in and around the home.

E. Basic Facts and Supplemental Information:
1. Most of our electric power plants are run using oil, coal, natural gas, and atomic energy—all nonrenewable sources of energy.

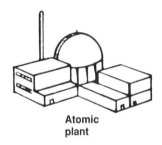

Atomic plant

2. In the United States the demand for energy is increasing about 7% per year.
3. Burning fossil fuels causes air pollution.
4. The Earth's population is expected to double in the next 35 to 50 years; consequently the demand for energy will increase and fuel costs will rise because of limited supplies.
5. Many "poor" countries that lack energy sources are resorting to the burning of biomass—trees, shrubs, plants, etc. They are stripping the land of vital soil-holding power, consequently erosion and flooding are increasing, thus compounding the situation.
6. Disposal of radioactive wastes is a very serious problem because they remain radioactive for thousands of years.

F. Thought Questions for Class Discussions:
1. Should energy be rationed?
2. What are some practical, renewable sources of energy?
3. What can we do if we run out of fossil fuels (gasoline and oil) for our automobiles?
4. Should we practice conservation of energy by cutting down on the amount of time spent watching TV, playing electronic games, using computers, listening to radios, stereos, CDs, etc.?

G. Related Ideas for Further Inquiry:
1. Study Activity II-A-2, "What are renewable sources of energy?"
2. Study Activity II-A-4, "What is kinetic energy? potential energy?"
3. Study Activity II-A-5, "How can we use solar energy?"
4. Study Section VII-C, "Earth's Crust."

H. Vocabulary Builders—Spelling Words:
1) **renewable**   2) **nonrenewable**   3) **natural**
4) **nuclear**   5) **derrick**   6) **radioactivity**
7) **fossil fuels**   8) **energy**   9) **atomic**

I. Thought for Today:
"One thing most children save for a rainy day is energy."

Activity

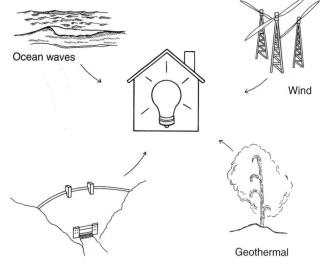

Ocean waves

Wind

Geothermal

Hydroelectric

A. Problem: *What Are Renewable Sources of Energy?*

B. Materials Needed:
1. Pictures of:
   a. Solar panels
   b. Windmills
   c. Geothermal spouts
   d. Hydroelectric dams
   e. Biomass (trees, shrubs, etc.)
   f. Ocean waves
2. Reference materials about the above.

C. Procedure:
1. Discuss some of our present sources of energy.
2. List the renewable sources of energy:
   a. sun
   b. wind
   c. dams
   d. oceans
   e. biomass
3. Review Activity II-A-1, "What are nonrenewable sources of energy?"
4. Compare renewable and nonrenewable sources of energy.
5. Discuss the consequence of using up all of our nonrenewable energy sources.
6. Have students make a list of energy uses in their home appliances, e.g., TV, VCRs, CDs, computers, etc.

D. Results:
1. Students will learn the difference between renewable and nonrenewable resources.
2. Students will realize that we are running out of our nonrenewable resources, especially our fossil fuels.
3. Students will learn that there are many uses of electrical energy in our homes.

E. Basic Facts and Supplemental Information:
1. The sun is our basic source of energy.
2. Geothermal energy could be an important energy source.
3. Geothermal energy is produced by molten rock that lies deep within the Earth.
4. Eighteen countries are already using geothermal energy.
5. Molten rock, called magma, lies 15 to 25 miles beneath the Earth's surface. In some places, it pushes even closer to the surface of the Earth in the forms of hot springs and geysers.
6. Ethiopia has enough geothermal sources to supply all of Africa with electricity.
7. Hydroelectric power is a limited potential. If we built all the dams possible and they ran to maximum capacity every day, they would supply only 30% of our energy needs.
8. Ocean waves and tides have been used to produce energy, but they both produce very limited quantities of electricity.
9. Biomass is the last major renewable source of energy. Anything organic can be burned, and the heat derived therefrom can produce energy. The big problem is that many "poor" countries are using more "biomass" energy than they are replenishing.

F. Thought Questions for Class Discussions:
1. What is the difference between renewable and nonrenewable sources of energy?
2. Should we ration our renewable sources of energy?
3. Do we need local, state, national, or international control of our energy resources?

G. Related Ideas for Further Inquiry:
1. Study Activity II-A-1, "What are nonrenewable sources of energy?"
2. Study Activity II-A-3, "Can energy be changed from one form to another?"
3. Study Activity II-A-5, "How can we use solar energy?"
4. Study Section VII-C, "Earth's Crust."

H. Vocabulary Builders—Spelling Words:
1) **solar** 2) **wind** 3) **hydroelectric** 4) **biomass**
5) **oceans** 6) **renewable** 7) **nonrenewable**

I. Thought for Today:
"The person who sees both sides of an issue is very likely to be on the fence or up a tree."

A. Problem: *Can Energy Be Changed from One Form to Another?*

B. Materials Needed:
1. Light bulb
2. Toy paddle wheel or picture of a dam
3. Flashlight
4. Toy generator
5. Guitar or other stringed instrument

C. Procedure:
1. Define energy (ability to do work).
2. Discuss the different forms of energy:
   a. mechanical   e. sound
   b. chemical   f. electrical
   c. heat   g. nuclear
   d. light
3. Turn on the electric light.
4. Trace the energy from its source.
5. Feel the heat given off.
6. Turn on the flashlight.
7. Trace the changes of forms of energy.
8. Strum a guitar or other stringed instrument.
9. Trace the changes of forms of energy.
10. Show how a paddle wheel or a dam could be used to turn generators.

D. Result:
Students will learn that energy can be changed from one form to another.

E. Basic Facts and Supplemental Information:
1. There are many other possibilities that can show changes of forms of energy.
2. The basic source of most of the energy on our planet comes from the sun.
3. A toy generator can be made by placing tin vanes on a movable cork which rotates on a dowel when steam is directed at the vanes through a steam-producing source.

F. Thought Questions for Class Discussions:
1. Does the energy from electric lights originate from the sun?
2. Where do our bodies get their energy?
3. What is the original source of energy that powers our automobiles?

G. Related Ideas for Further Inquiry:
See other Sections that discuss each of the specific forms of energy cited in "Procedure."

H. Vocabulary Builders—Spelling Words:
1) **mechanical**   2) **chemical**   3) **electrical**
4) **nuclear**   5) **generator**   6) **electricity**

I. Thought for Today:
"Drowning problems in an ocean of information is not the same as solving them."

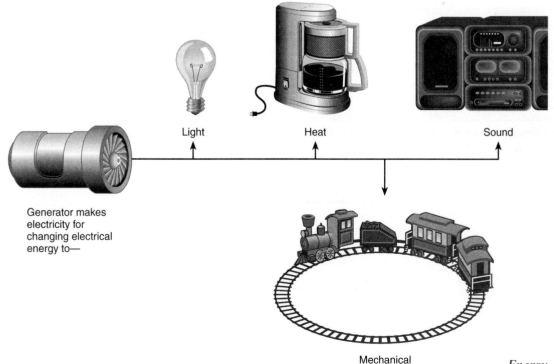

Light   Heat   Sound

Generator makes electricity for changing electrical energy to—

Mechanical

Energy **73**

Activity

A. Problem: *What Is Kinetic Energy? Potential Energy?*

B. Materials Needed:
1. Toy car
2. Toy train
3. Heavy object (old book)
4. Small object (pencil)
5. Bicycle

C. Procedure:
1. Drop the small object on the floor.
2. Drop the heavy object on the floor.
3. Move the toy car.
4. Move the toy train.
5. Define "kinetic energy" and "potential energy." (See "Section E. Basic Facts and Supplementary Information.")
6. Have a few students stand in front of class.
7. Have these students slowly walk around the room or up and down an aisle.
8. If convenient, have a student ride a bicycle near the classroom.
9. Have him/her explain the type or types of energy, potential or kinetic, involved in moving from a motionless starting point to a riding position, and returning to a complete stop.
10. Ask the students what causes objects to move.

D. Results:
1. The dropped objects will fall to the floor.
2. The shoved objects will move as directed.
3. The bicycle rider will move forward.

E. Basic Facts and Supplemental Information:
1. Any object moves because it has **kinetic energy.** If there were no kinetic energy (stored up, potentially usable energy) there would be no movement. When an object moves it has kinetic energy. When an object has the ability to move, but is not moving, it has **potential energy.**

A moving train has kinetic energy.

2. Gases move about because they have stored up energy.
3. People move about because they have stored up energy.

F. Thought Questions for Class Discussions:
1. Does the Earth have kinetic energy?
2. Do the dropped objects have kinetic energy when they have fallen halfway?
3. Does an automobile at rest have any kinetic energy?
4. When does a person have kinetic energy?
5. When does a person have potential energy?

G. Related Ideas for Further Inquiry:
1. Study Section II-E, "Simple Machines."
2. Study Section II-F, "Movement and Resistance."
3. Study Activity II-A-1, "What are nonrenewable sources of energy?"
4. Study Activity II-A-2, "What are renewable sources of energy?"
5. Study Activity II-A-6, "What are fossil fuels?"

H. Vocabulary Builders—Spelling Words:
1) **kinetic** 2) **potential** 3) **energy**
4) **dropped** 5) **falling** 6) **movement**

I. Thought for Today:
"The best way to double your money is to fold it and put it in your pocket."

Activity

A. Problem: *How Can We Use Solar Energy?*

B. Materials Needed:
1. Two cans (medium-sized)
2. Aluminum foil
3. Black drawing paper
4. Two thermometers
5. Cellophane or masking tape
6. Water
7. Ice pick

C. Procedure:
1. Fill both cans with water.
2. Wrap one can with aluminum foil (sides and top).
3. Secure with cellophane tape.
4. Wrap the other can with black paper (sides and top).
5. Secure with cellophane or masking tape.
6. Using the ice pick, punch a hole in each top (aluminum foil and black paper).
7. Insert a thermometer in the hole on top of each can.
8. Leave thermometers in cans for a few minutes.
9. Record temperature readings in both cans.
10. Place both cans in the sun.
11. Let the cans stay in the sun as long as possible.
12. Observe new readings.
13. Compare changes in readings.
14. Remove both thermometers.

D. Results:
1. In the first part of the procedure (see 9 above), the temperature readings will be the same in both cans.
2. In the second part of the procedure (see 12 above), the temperature in both cans will be increased, and the can wrapped in black paper will show the greater rise.

E. Basic Facts and Supplemental Information:
1. The basic source of our energy comes from the sun. It costs us nothing to produce, only to harness.
2. The sun's energy will last for ten billion years (the anticipated life of the sun).
3. The sun gives off many kinds of radiation.
4. Basically, it is the infrared rays that produce heat.
5. Solar energy is now being used to warm homes, the water in homes, and swimming pools, etc.
6. Solar energy is nonpolluting.

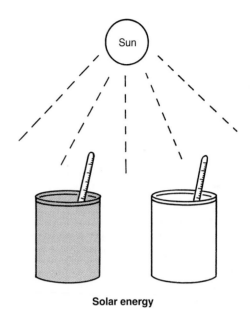

Solar energy

7. We could stretch solar cells across barren desert lands to produce needed energy.
8. Solar photovoltaic cells can generate electric current when exposed to the sun. Virtually every spacecraft and satellite since 1958 uses this kind of energy.

F. Thought Questions for Class Discussions:
1. How can solar energy be stored for use when the sun does not shine?
2. In what areas of the U.S. would solar energy devices be most efficient?
3. Can we use solar energy to generate steam?

G. Related Ideas for Further Inquiry:
1. Study Activity II-A-1, "What are nonrenewable sources of energy?"
2. Study Activity II-A-2, "What are renewable sources of energy?"
3. Study Activity II-A-3, "Can energy be changed from one form to another?"
4. Study Section II-B, "Fire and Heat."
5. Study Section VII-B, "Solar System."

H. Vocabulary Builders—Spelling Words:
1) **solar** 2) **radiation** 3) **panel** 4) **readings**
5) **air conditioners** 6) **radiant** 7) **heat**
8) **deserts** 9) **energy** 10) **infrared**

I. Thought for Today:
"In 40 minutes the sun delivers to the Earth's surface as much energy as humans use in a year."

Activity

A. Problem: *What Are Fossil Fuels?*

B. Materials Needed:
1. Piece of coal
2. Kerosene or lighter fluid
3. Can of oil
4. Picture of shale, tar, sand (optional)
5. Candle or heat source

C. Procedure:
1. Display the materials and show how each is related to energy, and specifically, fossil fuels.
2. Describe burning. All fires (burning) require: a) fuel, b) high temperature, and c) oxygen. These are called the "Fire Triangle." Remove one of these and there is no fire (burning).
3. Discuss our need for energy.
4. Burn a candle and tell class that the wax comes from fossil fuels.
5. Carefully warm some water over a heat source and describe how the energy came from fossil fuels.
6. Discuss how fossil fuels originated from the decomposition of organic materials (plants and animals).

D. Results:
1. Students will learn there are many kinds of fossil fuels.
2. Burning, warming, heating, all require energy, and most of it comes from fossil fuels.

E. Basic Facts and Supplemental Information:
1. Fossil fuels consist primarily of oil and gas. Oils are refined by a process called "fractional distillation" in which oil is heated and the lighter, more volatile substances are removed first, followed by each consecutive product.
2. Gasoline is refined during this process, and several additives are added to make it more efficient for internal combustion engines.
3. Coal, a fossil fuel, is found abundantly in the United States, which has two-thirds of the free world's supply.
4. The United States has about 3.3 trillion (3,300,000,000,000) tons of coal, but about 70 billion (70,000,000,000) tons lie so close to the Earth's surface that it must be "strip-mined."

Hard coal
(Anthracite)

F. Thought Questions for Class Discussions:
1. Think of a hard manual task. Could you devise a means of using energy to do this?
2. What will happen to our world when the Earth's fossil fuels run out?
3. Is gasoline inexpensive now? Will it always be inexpensive as supplies dwindle and demands increase?

G. Related Ideas for Further Inquiry:
1. Study Section II-B, "Fire and Heat."
2. Study Section VI-B, "Conservation."
3. Study Part III, "Plants," and Part IV, "Animals."
4. Study Activity II-A-1, "What are nonrenewable sources of energy?"
5. Study Activity II-A-3, "Can energy be changed from one form to another?"

H. Vocabulary Builders—Spelling Words:
1) **volatile**   2) **fossil fuels**   3) **fractional distillation**   4) **gasoline**   5) **kerosene**

I. Thought for Today:
"It's an odd thing but, internationally speaking, oil seems to cause a lot of friction."

A. Problem: *Is Nuclear Energy Safe or Harmful?*

B. Materials Needed: (about nuclear energy)
 1. Newspaper articles
 2. Radio and television reports
 3. Magazine write-ups

C. Procedure:
 1. Make a collection of articles discussing nuclear energy.
 2. Discuss these articles.
 3. If possible, bring in a film or an outside speaker to discuss nuclear energy for peaceful purposes.

D. Results:
 1. Students will find that there are many accounts of nuclear energy in the public media.
 2. Students will learn that there are many differences of opinion regarding nuclear energy.
 3. Some accounts will state that nuclear energy is beneficial and safe; others that it is harmful.

E. Basic Facts and Supplemental Information:
 1. We need energy. Nuclear energy is one source of energy.
 2. There are inherent problems in producing nuclear energy.
 3. The material used in producing nuclear energy can be used for nuclear weapons.
 4. With India's recent nuclear testing, all of the major countries now have or could easily make atomic bombs.
 5. There have been several major accidents at nuclear plants involving radiation and subsequent deaths.
 6. The disposal of radioactive wastes is a real problem, because these remain radioactive for thousands of years. The United States is planning to dispose of these wastes in a salt mine in New Mexico about 2,000 feet below the surface of the desert.
 7. There are two major types of nuclear energy: fission and fusion. Fission is the splitting of atoms to release energy, which we have achieved. Fusion is the joining of two atoms to produce energy, which we have not yet achieved for practical purposes.
 8. There are about 400 nuclear power plants operating around the world. They don't last forever and have to be retired. The problem is what to do with them.

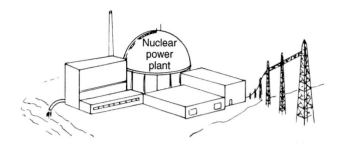

 9. A study by psychiatrists William Beardslee and John Mack has shown that American children become aware of nuclear war before age 12. Half of them say that it affects their future plans. They said that a significant number were "deeply disturbed," "profoundly pessimistic," and "just plain scared."
 10. Nuclear energy is America's third leading source of electricity.
 11. As of this writing, there are approximately 25,000 nuclear warheads stockpiled in the world's arsenal.

F. Thought Questions for Class Discussions:
 1. How should we dispose of old nuclear power plants? (They are radioactive.)
 2. What should we do with the radioactive wastes that are being continually produced?
 3. Would you like to live close to a nuclear power plant?

G. Related Ideas for Further Inquiry:
 1. Study Activity II-A-1, "What are nonrenewable sources of energy?"
 2. Study Activity II-A-2, "What are renewable sources of energy?"
 3. Study Activity II-A-3, "Can energy be changed from one form to another?"
 4. Study Section V-G, "Safety."
 5. Study Part VI, "Ecology."
 6. Study Section VII-C, "Earth's Crust."

H. Vocabulary Builders—Spelling Words:
 1) **nuclear** 2) **reactors** 3) **fusion**
 4) **fission** 5) **newspaper** 6) **radio**
 7) **television** 8) **retired** 9) **disposal**

I. Thought for Today:
 "It's a confusing world—we are running out of electricity and we don't even know what it is."

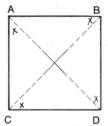 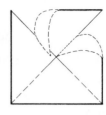 

A. Problem: *Is Wind a Good Source of Energy?*

B. Materials Needed:

1. Wooden dowel or stick about six inches long
2. Straight pin
3. Construction paper

C. Procedure:

1. Cut a piece of construction paper making a 6" square.
2. Draw diagonal lines from A to D and from B to C. (See drawing.)
3. Cut to within 1/2 inch of center point from four corners along these diagonal lines.
4. Fold points X to center and put the pin through the center where lines cross.
5. Attach this pinwheel to the end of the wooden dowel or stick by forcing the point of the pin into the dowel or stick.
6. Blow into the center of the pinwheel or hold pinwheel in any current of air.

D. Result:

Students will learn how to make small paper windmills.

E. Basic Facts and Supplemental Information:

1. Wind (moving air) causes pinwheel to whirl.
2. When the same principle is used on a large scale, the wind can be used to do beneficial work.
3. In some areas where winds are prevalent, many windmills have been constructed for providing energy to nearby communities.
4. Wind power is inexhaustible, clean, efficient, free, and does not pollute the atmosphere.
5. Wind power generators are more efficient than present day solar, nuclear, or fossil fuel generators.
6. The major drawbacks of wind power are the capriciousness of the winds and the limited areas where the winds are continually strong enough to supply more than a fraction of our total needs.
7. Windmills have been used in the past to grind wheat into flour, pump water, and do other jobs.
8. The modern windmill converts wind power into electricity.

F. Thought Questions for Class Discussions:

1. How does wind make this paper windmill operate? What makes it turn?
2. Is this kind of windmill able to do work?
3. What kinds of work are ordinarily done by regular windmills?
4. Where do sailboats get their energy to move?

G. Related Ideas for Further Inquiry:

1. Study Activity II-A-1, "What are nonrenewable sources of energy?"
2. Study Activity II-A-2, "What are renewable sources of energy?"
3. Study Activity II-A-5, "How can we use solar energy?"
4. Study Activity VII-E-1, "What makes the wind blow?"
5. Study Section VII-E-2, "How can we make a wind vane?"
6. Study Part VI, "Ecology."

H. Vocabulary Builders—Spelling Words:

1) **windmill** 2) **construction** 3) **diagonal**
4) **center** 5) **pinwheel** 6) **generator**
7) **capricious** 8) **weather** 9) **vane**

I. Thought for Today:

"The most called upon prerequisite of a friend is an accessible ear."

SECTION B: FIRE AND HEAT

Activity

II B 1

A. Problem: *What Is Heat?*
What Is Temperature?

B. Materials Needed:

1. Candle
2. Matches
3. Flashlight
4. Electric light
5. Toaster
6. Aquarium heater
7. Bunsen burner
8. Alcohol lamp
9. Sterno

C. Procedure:

1. Have all students rub their hands together briskly.
2. Demonstrate how each of the materials cited above can produce heat.
3. Explain that heat is measured by temperature.
4. Describe the two main temperature scales, Fahrenheit and Celsius (Centigrade).
   See Activity II-B-4, "What is the difference between a Celsius (Centigrade) and a Fahrenheit temperature scale?"
5. Have students record the classroom temperature every morning and afternoon at the same time. See chart as an example.

D. Results:

1. The students' hands will become warm.
2. All the materials will become warm and their temperatures will rise.
3. Students will develop a temperature table.
4. Pupils will begin to understand daily fluctuations in temperature.

E. Basic Facts and Supplemental Information:

1. Basically, heat is the speed of molecules in motion. Anything that will increase the speed of molecules will increase its heat. Anything that will decrease the speed of the molecules will decrease its heat. Molecular speed changes can be initiated by many means: chemical, mechanical, light, electrical, radiation, heat, pressure, friction, etc. Temperature measures the amount of heat. Cold is the absence of heat.
2. Every object has some energy because of molecular movement. The faster the molecules move, the more energy it has. Heat and energy are manifestations of molecular movement.

OUR CLASSROOM TEMPERATURE RECORDINGS:		
Month: _____	Week: _____	
Day:	Morning:	Afternoon:
Monday	57°F. = 14°C.	68°F. = 20°C.
Tuesday	54°F. = 12°C.	77°F. = 25°C.
Wednesday	68°F. = 20°C.	98°F. = 37°C.
Thursday	77°F. = 25°C.	86°F. = 30°C.
Friday	86°F. = 30°C.	104°F. = 40°C.

3. There is one theoretical point where there is no molecular movement and that is called "absolute zero." This is –459.67° F. or –273.15° C.

F. Thought Questions for Class Discussions:

1. Does air in a bicycle tire heat up as the bicycle speeds up?
2. Do batteries warm up in toys that contain them?
3. Why doesn't a toaster get hot when not in use?
4. What ways can you speed up the molecules of any substance?
5. Do water molecules move faster in steam than in ice?

G. Related Ideas for Further Inquiry:

1. Study Activity II-B-2, "What is the 'Fire Triangle'?"
2. Study Activity II-B-3, "How does heat move?"
3. Study Activity II-B-5, "What happens to solids when they are heated?"
4. Study Activity II-B-6, "What happens to liquids when they are heated? cooled?"
5. Study Activity II-B-7, "What happens to gases when they are heated? cooled?"
6. Study Section VII-E, "Weather."

H. Vocabulary Builders—Spelling Words:

1) **motion** 2) **heat** 3) **increase** 4) **decrease**
5) **molecules**

I. Thought for Today:

"The direction in which education starts a person will determine his/her future life."

Activity

A. Problem: *What Is the "Fire Triangle?"*

B. Materials Needed:

1. Baking pan
2. Noncombustible protective pad
3. Sheet of newspaper
4. Matches
5. Large glass jar or metal pail

C. Procedure:

1. Discuss local, accidental fires.
2. Have students relate any fires that they are aware of that were serious in nature.
3. Place protective pad on desk or table.
4. Place baking pan in the center of the protective pad.
5. Tear several small strips of paper from the newspaper.
6. Crumple them into a small ball.
7. Carefully ignite the paper ball.
8. Let it burn for several seconds.
9. Before it burns itself out, carefully cover the fire with glass jar or metal pail.
10. After the fire is extinguished, ask the class why the fire went out.
11. Discuss with class how firefighters put out fires.
12. Have class list and discuss the three main elements that are needed for a fire:
    a. combustible material
    b. heat
    c. oxygen
    These make up the Fire Triangle. (See drawing.)

D. Results:

1. When ignited, the newspaper will burn.
2. When the oxygen supply is diminished, the fire will go out.
3. Students will learn the three elements that compose the Fire Triangle.

E. Basic Facts and Supplemental Information:

1. The removal of any one of the three elements of the Fire Triangle will cause the fire to be extinguished.
2. Firefighters use water to reduce the "heat" of the fire below its "kindling point."
3. In some cases, firefighters also use foam to cut off the fire's oxygen supply.
4. Another method of fighting small fires is to use a fire extinguisher. This is effective because it reduces the oxygen supply.

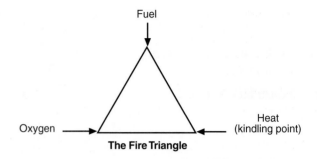

The Fire Triangle

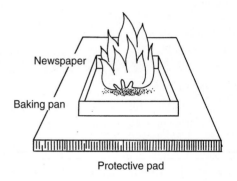

F. Thought Questions for Class Discussions:

1. Do all substances burn?
2. What are some causes of fires in homes?
3. What are some of the causes of forest fires?
4. What are some safety precautions that we can take to prevent fires in our homes, at school, and in our community?

G. Related Ideas for Further Inquiry:

1. Study Activity II-B-1, "What is heat? What is temperature?"
2. Study Activity II-B-3, "How does heat move?"
3. Study Activity II-B-11, "Do some substances conduct heat faster than others?"

H. Vocabulary Builders—Spelling Words:

1) **triangle**   2) **combustion**   3) **oxygen**
4) **temperature**   5) **extinguish**   6) **kindling**

I. Thought for Today:

"The difficulties of life are intended to make us better, not bitter."

Activity

A. Problem: *How Does Heat Move?*

B. Materials Needed:
1. Tea kettle
2. Heat source
3. Water

C. Procedure:
1. Define the three types of heat movement.
   a. Conduction: Transfer of heat (energy) from one object to another by direct contact.
   b. Convection: Transfer of heat (energy) from one object to another through an intermediate medium such as air or water.
   c. Radiation: Transfer of heat (energy) from one object to another by infrared energy such as the sun heating the Earth.
2. Put some water in the tea kettle.
3. Heat slowly.
4. Discuss where heat is and how it moves.

D. Results:
1. Heat moves by *conduction* from heat source to the tea kettle.
2. Warm water moves upward and cold water moves downward by *convection*. Heat moves through the air by *convection*.
3. Heat is passed from the side of the stove to the air by *radiation*.

E. Basic Facts and Supplemental Information:
1. Conduction, convection, and radiation are the three basic ways that heat is transferred from one place to another.
2. Conduction and convection transfer heat by molecular contact.
3. Heat radiation is a form of electromagnetic radiation. It travels through space at the speed of light which is 186,000 miles per second. Everything emits radiant heat.
4. The higher the temperature of a body, the greater the amount of radiant heat given off.
5. Heat is never lost. It is always transferred from one source to another.
6. Heat is kinetic energy. It is molecules in motion. The slower the molecules move, the less heat the substance has; the faster the molecules move, the more heat it has.

Three ways that heat energy is transferred

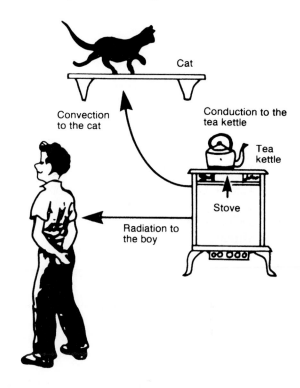

7. People spend a lot of time trying to control heat movement with clothing, air conditioning, furnaces, sunbathing, cooking, freezing, manufacturing, taking baths, drinking water, coffee, or soup, etc.

F. Thought Questions for Class Discussions:
1. What do you do to keep cool in summer? warm in winter?
2. Why don't you like to swim in very cold water?
3. Why don't you like to bathe in very hot water?

G. Related Ideas for Further Inquiry:
1. Have students make a list of ways that heat was transferred in their homes during a 24-hour period.
2. Study Section I-B, "Air."
3. Study Section I-C, "Water."
4. Study other Activities in this Section.

H. Vocabulary Builders—Spelling Words:
1) **radiation**   2) **conduction**   3) **convection**
4) **kinetic**   5) **molecules**   6) **infrared**

I. Thought for Today:
"The human mind is like a parachute—useless until opened."

Activity

A. Problem: *What Is the Difference Between a Celsius (Centigrade) and a Fahrenheit Temperature Scale?*

B. Materials Needed:

1. Fahrenheit thermometer
2. Celsius (Centigrade) thermometer (or one thermometer with both Fahrenheit and Celsius [Centigrade] readings)
3. Water
4. Ice cubes
5. Hot plate or heating device
6. Water glass
7. Pan
8. Stirring rod or spoon

C. Procedure:

1. Put ice in glass of water and stir well.
2. Put thermometers in ice water and take readings.
3. Record findings.
4. Put water in pan and heat gently for about two minutes.
5. Place thermometers in water and record findings.
6. Remove the thermometers from pan and heat the water for several minutes.
7. Place the thermometers in the pan of water and record the temperatures.
8. Remove the thermometers and heat the water again for several minutes.
9. Record the temperatures.
10. Remove the thermometers and heat the water again until it is boiling.
11. Record the temperatures.
12. Remove the thermometers and heat the boiling water for several more minutes.
13. Place the thermometers in the boiling water.
14. Record the findings.
15. Note any difference in water temperature when water starts to boil and after several minutes of continued boiling.
16. Have one student volunteer to take his/her body temperature orally.
17. Record temperature reading.

D. Results:

1. Students will learn that temperatures can be measured on different scales.
2. Pupils might be able to determine the difference between the two readings. (One degree Celsius [Centigrade] = 1.8 degrees Fahrenheit.)
3. Students will learn that ice melts (or water freezes) at 0° C. or 32° F.

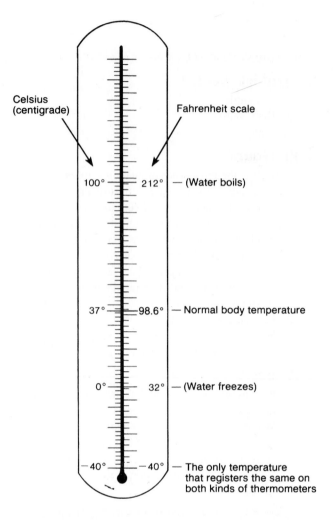

Celsius (centigrade)

Fahrenheit scale

100° — 212° — (Water boils)

37° — 98.6° — Normal body temperature

0° — 32° — (Water freezes)

−40° — −40° — The only temperature that registers the same on both kinds of thermometers

4. Students will learn that water boils at 100° C. or 212° F.
5. Students will learn that boiling water does not change temperature no matter how long the water boils.

E. Basic Facts and Supplemental Information:

1. Scientists sometimes use an Absolute or Kelvin scale. Its degrees are the same size as Celsius but it begins at a point in which there is no movement of the molecules. This point is zero on the Absolute or Kelvin scale, −273.17 on the Celsius or Centigrade scale, and −459.65 on the Fahrenheit scale.
2. Older students may want to convert one scale to another. These are the formulas:
   To convert Fahrenheit to Celsius:

   $C = (F-32) \times 5/9$

   And to convert Celsius to Fahrenheit:

   $F = (9/5 \ C) + 32$

3. Always handle mercury thermometers carefully. They break easily and mercury is a poison.

F. Thought Questions for Class Discussions:

1. What makes the red-colored mercury move in a thermometer?
2. Do all liquids boil at the same temperature?
3. What is normal room temperature in Fahrenheit? Celsius? Absolute?

G. Related Ideas for Further Inquiry:

1. A mock-up of a thermometer can be made by using a tall piece of tagboard and a red ribbon that can be moved up and down. With Fahrenheit readings on one side and Celsius (Centigrade) on the other side, students can quickly compare readings. Slits can be made at the top and bottom of the scales, and a ribbon can be made that is half-white and half-red to fit in slits forming a circle of ribbon that can be easily moved to any temperature reading.
2. Check room temperatures and discuss comfort ranges.
3. Discuss geographical areas students have visited that were "very hot" or "very cold."
4. A simple thermometer can be made by using a jar with a one-holed stopper and a piece of glass tubing. (Colored water can be used for higher visibility.) Wet stopper and then very carefully insert the glass tubing with a twisting motion.
5. Study Activity II-B-1, "What is heat? What is temperature?"
6. Study Activity II-B-2, "What is the 'Fire Triangle'?"
7. Study Activity II-B-3, "How does heat move?"
8. Study Activity II-B-11, "Do some substances conduct heat faster than others?"

H. Vocabulary Builders—Spelling Words:

1) **Fahrenheit** 2) **Celsius** 3) **Centigrade**
4) **Absolute** 5) **Kelvin** 6) **thermometer**
7) **freezing** 8) **boiling** 9) **temperature**

I. Thought for Today:

"We must learn to live together as sisters and brothers or we will perish together as fools."

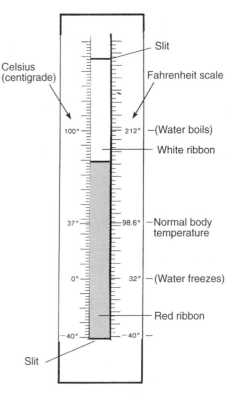

Thermometer mock-up

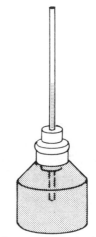

Bottle thermometer and colored water

A. Problem: *What Happens to Solids When They Are Heated? Cooled?*

B. Materials Needed:

1. Piece of uninsulated steel or copper wire
2. Light weight
3. Ruler
4. Two ring stands or other supports
5. Candle
6. Desk or tabletop

C. Procedure:

1. Stretch the wire between two points and secure as taut as possible.
2. Tie a weight in the center of the wire.
3. Measure the distance from the wire to the table.
4. Very carefully use a candle to heat the wire.
5. Move the candle back and forth along the wire so that the wire becomes heated throughout its entire length.
6. Measure the distance from the wire to the table again.
7. Let wire cool, or cool it with ice or cold water.
8. Measure the distance from the wire to the desk or tabletop.

D. Results:

1. When the wire is heated, the weight will move closer to the table. This proves that the wire expands when heated.
2. When the wire is cooled, the weight will move farther away from the desk or tabletop. This proves that the wire contracts when cooled.

E. Basic Facts and Supplemental Information:

1. Metals expand when heated, but contract when cooled. In this case the wire becomes longer when heated and shorter when cooled.
2. This quality is vital in processing all metal products.
3. This procedure is used to remove tight nuts from bolts by heating the nuts. The nuts expand and become looser; both expand, but the nuts expand more.

F. Thought Questions for Class Discussions:

1. Do all solids expand when heated and contract when cooled?
2. Do telephone lines sag more on hot days?
3. If you had to string metal wire, would it be better to string it on a hot or a cold day?

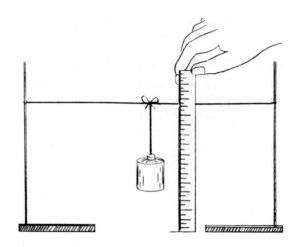

4. How do railroad tracks allow for expansion and contraction?
5. Can this procedure be used to remove metal tops from glass jars? (Metals expand faster than glass.)

G. Related Ideas for Further Inquiry:

1. Study Activity II-B-3, "How does heat move?"
2. Study Activity II-B-4, "What is the difference between a Celsius (Centigrade) and a Fahrenheit temperature scale?"
3. Study Activity II-B-11, "Do some substances conduct heat faster than others?"

H. Vocabulary Builders—Spelling Words:

1) **heating**   2) **cooling**   3) **length**   4) **weight**
5) **candle**   6) **ruler**   7) **desk**   8) **tabletop**

I. Thought for Today:

*EVERYBODY, SOMEBODY, ANYBODY,
AND NOBODY*
*This is a story about four people named Everybody,
Somebody, Anybody, and Nobody.*
*There was an important job to be done and Everybody
was sure that Somebody would do it.*
Anybody could have done it, but Nobody did it.
*Somebody got angry about that, because it was
Everybody's job. Everybody thought Anybody could do
it, but Nobody realized that Everybody wouldn't do it.*
*It ended up that Everybody blamed Somebody when
Nobody did what Anybody could have done!*
—Source unknown.

A. Problem: *What Happens to Liquids When They Are Heated? Cooled?*

B. Materials Needed:
1. Small-necked bottle
2. One-hole stopper (rubber or cork)
3. Water, cold
4. Glass or plastic tubing, 15 cm. (6") long
5. Red food coloring
6. Fingernail polish
7. Thermometer

C. Procedure:
1. Fill the bottle to the top with cold water.
2. Add red food coloring to the water until the water becomes clearly visible.
3. Wet the stopper so that the tubing can be inserted easily by slowly twisting.
4. Insert the tubing into the rubber or cork stopper.
5. Put the stopper with the tubing into the bottle and press down hard enough so that the water will rise halfway up the tubing.
6. Show the class the regular thermometer. Discuss the uses of a thermometer.
7. Have class members discuss their experiences with a thermometer.
8. With the fingernail polish, carefully draw a circle around the water line on the tubing.
9. Place the apparatus in the sun (or use a heating device to warm).
10. Observe the results.
11. Mark the new level of water in the tubing.
12. Cool the apparatus. This can be accomplished by bringing it inside or placing it in ice water, depending on the time available.

D. Results:
1. When the apparatus is heated, the water will rise in the tubing.
2. When the apparatus is cooled, the water level in the tubing will drop.

E. Basic Facts and Supplemental Information:
1. Liquids expand when heated because heat forces the molecules further apart, thus causing the expansion.
2. As heat is removed (or lost) the molecules in liquid move closer together, thus causing the contraction.

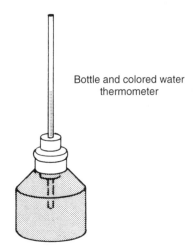

Bottle and colored water thermometer

3. Heat (energy) is never really lost. It is transferred from one object to another.
4. Cold is really the absence of heat. A cold object has less heat (energy) than a hot one.

F. Thought Questions for Class Discussions:
1. Do all liquids boil at the same temperature? freeze at the same temperature?
2. Can liquids change into solids? into gases?
3. Why is alcohol used rather than water to bring a person's temperature down?

G. Related Ideas for Further Inquiry:
1. Study "fractional distillation."
2. Study Activity I-A-2, "What are atoms? molecules?"
3. Study Activity I-A-1, "What are the three states of matter?"
4. Study Activity I-A-7, "Do all liquids boil at the same temperature?"
5. Study Activity II-B-5, "What happens to solids when they are heated? cooled?"
6. Study Activity II-B-7, "What happens to gases when they are heated? cooled?"

H. Vocabulary Builders—Spelling Words:
1) **heated** 2) **cooled** 3) **expands**
4) **contracts** 5) **molecules** 6) **thermometer**

I. Thought for Today:
"One of the most labor saving inventions of today is tomorrow."

Activity

A. Problem: *What Happens to Gases When They Are Heated? Cooled?*

B. Materials Needed:

1. Plastic bottle with small mouth
2. Balloon
3. Bowl
4. Water
5. Ice cubes
6. Heating device
7. Gloves or pot holders

C. Procedure:

1. Blow the balloon up to stretch the rubber.
2. Let the air out.
3. Place the balloon over the top of the bottle.
4. Fill the bowl about two-thirds full of water.
5. Heat the water until it begins to boil.
6. Remove the heating device.
7. Add the bottle with the balloon to the boiling water.
8. Observe results.
9. After several minutes, using gloves or pot holders, CAREFULLY remove the bottle and empty the boiling water.
10. Place bottle in bowl.
11. Add ice to the bowl.
12. Observe results.

D. Results:

1. The balloon on the bottle in the boiling water will inflate.
2. The balloon on the bottle in the bowl of ice will deflate.

E. Basic Facts and Supplemental Information:

1. Gases expand when heated.
2. Gases contract when cooled.
3. In expanding, the air in the balloon needs more space so it inflates the balloon.
4. In contracting, the air in the balloon needs less space so the balloon becomes smaller.
5. Sometimes in cooling, the balloon may be forced into the bottle.

F. Thought Questions for Class Discussions:

1. Will the balloon expand more if a larger glass flask is used?
2. What happens to the size of weather balloons when they rise into colder air?
3. Do automobile tires expand and contract?

Room temperature

In boiling water

In ice water

4. Do bicycle tires expand and contract?
5. Does air in our atmosphere expand and contract?

G. Related Ideas for Further Inquiry:

1. Put a stretched balloon over the neck of an empty plastic bottle. Place this apparatus in a refrigerator overnight. The next day, let the bottle stand in a warm room. Observe results.
2. Study Section I-B, "Air."
3. Study Activity II-B-5, "What happens to solids when they are heated? cooled?"
4. Study Activity II-B-6, "What happens to liquids when they are heated? cooled?"
5. Study Activity II-B-11, "Do some substances conduct heat faster than others?"
6. Study Activity VII-E-1, "What makes the wind blow?"
7. Study Activity VII-E-13, "What are 'warm fronts'? 'cold fronts'?"

H. Vocabulary Builders—Spelling Words:

1) **expand** 2) **contract** 3) **balloon** 4) **bottle**
5) **temperature** 6) **inflate** 7) **deflate** 8) **plastic**

I. Thought for Today:

"Science teachers teach 'what is.' Philosophy teachers teach 'what should be.' "

Activity

A. Problem: *What Causes a Candle to Burn?*

B. Materials Needed:
1. Candle
2. Match
3. Several pieces of paper or 4" × 5" index cards
4. Tongs or clothespin
5. Saucer or tray
6. Small bucket with a little water

C. Procedure One:
1. Light candle carefully.
2. Place candle on saucer or tray, affixing it with hot wax from candle.
3. Let the candle burn for a minute or two, then snuff it out.
4. Immediately after snuffing out candle, CAREFULLY hold a lighted match about an inch or less over the extinguished flame.

Procedure Two:
1. Light candle carefully.
2. Place candle on saucer or tray affixing it with hot wax from candle.
3. Holding the paper with tongs or clothespin, thrust it quickly about 1/4 inch above the flame with as little side movement as possible. *Caution:* Have a safe place close by to dispose of paper in case it bursts into flame. A small bucket with a little water in it is excellent.
4. Quickly remove paper as soon as it begins to scorch.
5. Try several textures of paper.

D. Results:
1. In Procedure One, the candle will again become lighted.
2. In Procedure Two, a distinct charred ring will form with an unscorched center.

E. Basic Facts and Supplemental Information:
1. There is still a supply of inflammable gas present immediately after you blow out a candle.
2. The heated candle gas is burnable regardless of whether or not the candle happens to be lighted. This is proved when the candle again becomes ignited. Actually it is the gaseous material that burns, not the solid candle. The flame (heat) changes the solid candle to a gas and it is this gas that burns.
3. In Procedure Two, the flame (burning gases) is hollow and rather cool just above the wick. The sides of the flame's merging point can be determined by placing the paper at varying heights. The gas from the burning candle forms a cone shape,

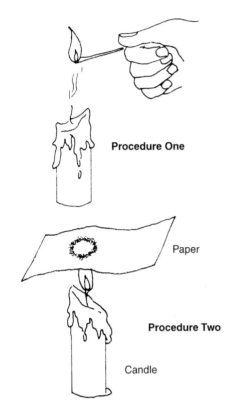

Procedure One

Paper

Procedure Two

Candle

consequently the charred area will vary depending upon the height of the paper above the candle.

F. Thought Questions for Class Discussions:
1. Do any or all liquids burn?
2. Do any or all solids burn?
3. Do any or all gases burn?
4. When gasoline burns, is it the liquid that burns or a gas which is given off by the liquid?
5. In Procedure Two, why is a charred *ring* formed instead of a charred *spot?*
6. Why does the size of the charred ring vary with the height at which the paper is held?
7. Where is the hottest part of the flame?
8. What causes the charred area?

G. Related Ideas for Further Inquiry:
1. Study Section I-B, "Air."
2. Study Section II-A, "Energy: Sources."
3. Study Activity II-B-2, "What is the 'Fire Triangle'?"
4. Study Activity II-B-9, "What is smoke?"
5. Study Activity II-B-1, "What is heat? What is temperature?"

H. Vocabulary Builders—Spelling Words:
1) **flame** 2) **thrust** 3) **caution** 4) **wick**
5) **dispose** 6) **cone** 7) **candle** 8) **charred**

I. Thought for Today:
"It is better to light one candle than to curse the darkness."

Activity

A. Problem: *What Is Smoke?*

B. Materials Needed, Procedure One:

1. Candle
2. Matches
3. Tablespoon
4. Clothespin

Materials Needed, Procedure Two:

1. Matches
2. Newspaper
3. Baking pan
4. Noninflammable pad
5. Paper toweling

C. Procedure One:

1. Light the candle.
2. Affix it to the baking pan or other noninflammable surface.
3. Observe the candle as it burns; particularly, watch the flame.
4. Place the clothespin on the handle of the tablespoon.
5. Hold the tablespoon over the candle's flame for a few seconds.
6. Withdraw the tablespoon and observe the bottom of it.
7. Wipe it clean with paper toweling.

Procedure Two:

1. Place the baking pan in the middle of the protective pad.
2. Crumple a small piece of newspaper and place it in the baking pan.
3. Light the newspaper and let it burn out.
4. Observe the final results.

D. Results:

1. Black material, carbon, collects on the spoon.
2. The newspaper leaves charred black ashes.

E. Basic Facts and Supplemental Information:

1. The main part of the flame is yellow because of chemicals in the candle wax. Most of the chemicals are burned away except for the black carbon remaining on the spoon or left in the pan.
2. The black material which collects on the object is carbon which was removed from the flame before it had a chance to burn.
3. Smoke is actually small solid particles of unburned carbon.
4. The charred newspaper is essentially unburned carbon plus some mineral ashes.

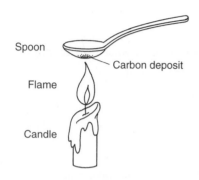

Procedure One

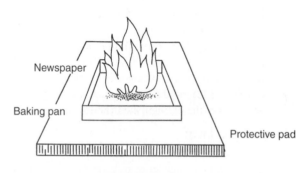

Procedure Two

5. All burning requires:
   a. combustible material (fuel)
   b. supply of oxygen
   c. high enough temperature (kindling point)
6. See Activity II-B-2, "What is the 'Fire Triangle'?"

F. Thought Questions for Class Discussions:

1. Why doesn't all of the carbon burn?
2. How does the carbon get from the candle up to the spoon?
3. Where does the carbon come from in the charred newspaper?
4. What is necessary for complete combustion?

G. Related Ideas for Further Inquiry:

1. Study Activity I-A-1, "What are the three states of matter?"
2. Study Activity II-B-8, "What causes a candle to burn?"
3. Study other Activities in this Section.

H. Vocabulary Builders—Spelling Words:

1) **combustion** 2) **smoke** 3) **carbon**
4) **candle** 5) **newspaper** 6) **flame** 7) **ashes**
8) **particles**

I. Thought for Today:

"There are two ways of spreading light: be the candle or the mirror that reflects it."

Activity

A. Problem: *Does Color Affect Heat Absorption?*

B. Materials Needed:
1. Tin can
2. Black paint
3. Paint brush
4. Candle
5. Matches
6. Wax
7. Two thumbtacks

C. Procedure:
1. Clean the can if necessary.
2. Paint one-half of the can black inside and outside.
3. Drop some candle wax in the bottom of can and secure candle to the wax while it is still warm.
4. Set the can in view of students.
5. Secure the tacks on either side of the can with an equal amount of wax.
6. Tell students that this is going to be a test to tell how effective black is in its ability to absorb or reflect heat.
7. Light the candle.
8. Observe the results.

D. Result:

The tack on the black side will drop off first.

E. Basic Facts and Supplemental Information:
1. Have the students carefully test the sides of the can for warmth. Students will see and feel that the black side absorbed more heat and consequently the tack on the dark side dropped off first.
2. Heat absorption and heat reflection are major considerations in home construction.
3. If the candle does not produce enough heat fast enough, an electric light bulb can be utilized.
4. Heat is a form of energy.
5. Energy cannot be created or destroyed but can move from one object to another.
6. In this Activity, heat moves from the candle to the can to the wax to the tacks.

F. Thought Questions for Class Discussions:
1. Why do people wear dark-colored clothing in winter?
2. Why do people wear light-colored clothing in summer?
3. If you live in a cold climate, what color would be best for your home?

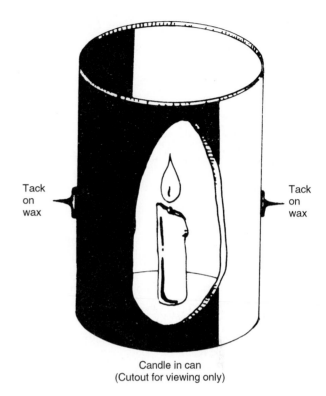

Tack on wax

Tack on wax

Candle in can
(Cutout for viewing only)

4. If you live in a very hot climate, what color car would absorb the least heat?

G. Related Ideas for Further Inquiry:
1. Test other colors for their heat absorption qualities.
2. Study solar panels.
3. Study Activity II-B-1, "What is heat? What is temperature?"
4. Study Activity II-B-2, "What is the 'Fire Triangle'?"
5. Study Activity II-B-5, "What happens to solids when they are heated? cooled?"
6. Study Activity II-B-11, "Do some substances conduct heat faster than others?"

H. Vocabulary Builders—Spelling Words:

1) **black**   2) **silver**   3) **absorption**   4) **energy**
5) **reflection**   6) **tacks**   7) **wax**   8) **conduction**

I. Thought for Today:

"The world seldom notices who teachers are, but civilization depends on what they do."

A. Problem: *Do Some Substances Conduct Heat Faster Than Others?*

B. Materials Needed:
1. Ceramic cup
2. Aluminum cup
3. Thermometer (high level or cooking)
4. Wood bowl
5. Boiling water
6. Heat source

C. Procedure:
1. CAREFULLY pour boiling water into each of the three containers.
2. CAREFULLY feel the outside of the containers.
3. Place the thermometer in one of the containers.
4. Record the temperature and dry the thermometer carefully. Repeat this step with each of the other two containers.
5. Allow the containers to stand for 15 minutes.
6. Record temperatures every 5 minutes.
7. Compare the readings.
8. Determine facts on the rates of conduction of these materials.
9. Carefully empty all containers, dry them, and put an equal amount of crushed ice in each.
10. After the ice has started to melt, insert the thermometer in each container, and record the temperatures every five minutes.
11. Compare the readings.

D. Results:
1. With the boiling water:
   a. All containers will have an equal starting temperature but will feel different as time elapses.
   b. The aluminum cup will lose its temperature the fastest, the ceramic cup next, and the wooden bowl the slowest.
2. With the crushed ice:
   a. All containers will have an equal starting temperature after the ice has melted but will feel different as time elapses.
   b. The aluminum cup will gain heat the fastest, the ceramic cup next, and the wooden bowl the slowest.

E. Basic Facts and Supplemental Information:
1. Aluminum is a better conductor of heat than either ceramic or wood, consequently it will gain (or lose) heat the fastest.

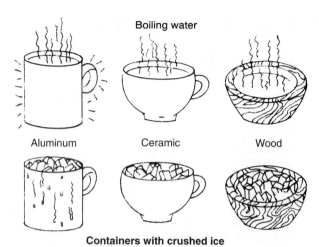

Boiling water

Aluminum   Ceramic   Wood

Containers with crushed ice

2. Ceramic is a better conductor of heat than wood.
3. Wood is the poorest conductor of heat of these three materials, consequently it will gain (or lose) heat the slowest.
4. Coldness is the lack of heat.

F. Thought Questions for Class Discussions:
1. If you want coffee to stay hot, would you put it in an aluminum cup?
2. Why does hot coffee, when served in a metal cup, seem hot at first, but much cooler after a few minutes?
3. Will a cold drink stay cold longer in a metal can or a wooden bowl?
4. How does a thermos bottle keep hot liquids hot and cold liquids cold?

G. Related Ideas for Further Inquiry:
1. Test other materials for conduction such as plastic and steel.
2. Study Activity II-B-4, "What is the difference between a Celsius (Centigrade) and a Fahrenheit temperature scale?"
3. Study Activity II-B-5, "What happens to solids when they are heated? cooled?"
4. Study Activity II-B-3, "How does heat move?"
5. Study Activity II-B-10, "Does color affect heat absorption?"

H. Vocabulary Builders—Spelling Words:
1) **aluminum** 2) **ceramic** 3) **wood** 4) **heat**
5) **plastic** 6) **steel** 7) **conduct** 8) **container**

I. Thought for Today:
"Experience should be a guiding post not a hitching post."

Activity

A. Problems: *Is Carbon Dioxide Heavier Than Air? Will Carbon Dioxide Gas Support Combustion (Burning)?*

B. Materials Needed:

1. Large glass jar
2. Baking soda and vinegar or dry ice (solid form of carbon dioxide)
3. Three candles
4. Wood or cardboard trough (See drawing.)
5. Water glass

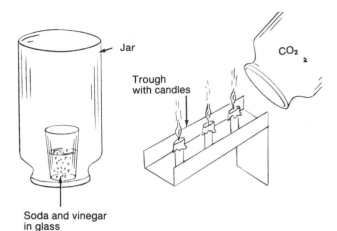

C. Procedure:

1. Attach candles in trough as shown in sketch. (Bottom of candles can be trimmed so that they will stand upright easily.)
2. Use prop to tilt one end.
3. CAREFULLY light candles.
4. If you are using baking soda and vinegar, place several teaspoons of baking soda in glass.
5. Add a half cup of vinegar. (Carbon dioxide is formed when soda and vinegar are mixed.)
6. Place jar over the glass or place a piece of dry ice in the jar and cap it.
7. Wait several minutes so that the jar will fill with carbon dioxide.
8. Remove the lid and gently "pour" the carbon dioxide gas out of the jar and just over the top candle as shown in sketch.

D. Result:

As the carbon dioxide floats down the trough, the candles go out one by one.

E. Basic Facts and Supplemental Information:

1. Carbon dioxide is heavier than air and thus can be "poured" from the jar. Carbon dioxide is effective as a fire extinguisher because it is heavier than air and settles around the flame, shutting off the oxygen supply. This is what happens when the carbon dioxide is poured down the trough.
2. This activity demonstrates two principles:
   a. Carbon dioxide is heavier than air.
   b. Carbon dioxide does not support combustion.

F. Thought Question for Class Discussions:

1. Why is carbon dioxide applied above the flame instead of below the flame?

2. If you knew an excess of carbon dioxide was in the air, would it be better to breathe near the ceiling or near the floor of the room? Why?
3. Do you know any other way of making carbon dioxide?
4. Do our bodies give off carbon dioxide?
5. What would happen if oxygen was used in this Activity instead of carbon dioxide?

G. Related Ideas for Further Inquiry:

1. Study Activity II-B-1, "What is heat? What is temperature?"
2. Study Activity II-B-2, "What is the 'Fire Triangle'?"
3. Study Activity II-B-3, "How does heat move?"
4. Study Activity II-B-8, "What causes a candle to burn?"
5. Study Activity II-B-9, "What is smoke?"
6. Study Activity I-B-2, "How does a chimney work?"

H. Vocabulary Builders—Spelling Words:

1) **support** 2) **carbon dioxide** 3) **combustion**
4) **vinegar** 5) **baking soda** 6) **trough** 7) **jar**
8) **extinguished** 9) **candles** 10) **pour**

I. Thought for Today:

"The key to wisdom is a knowledge of our own ignorance."

SECTION C: LIGHT AND COLOR

Activity

A. Problem: *Does Light Travel Only in a Straight Line?*

B. Materials Needed, Procedure One:

1. Cardboard strips
2. Small flashlight
3. Scissors

Materials Needed, Procedure Two:

1. Piece of garden hose
2. Flashlight

C. Procedure One:

1. Cut small, equal-size holes about 1″ in diameter in the center of four strips of cardboard. (See drawings.)
2. Arrange the cardboard strips so that holes are in a straight line.
3. Turn on flashlight.
4. Look through holes toward flashlight.
5. Move one strip of cardboard out of line and look toward flashlight.

Procedure Two:

1. Look through unbent hose toward flashlight.
2. Keep one end of hose straight, and bend the other end.
3. Hold light against straight end.
4. Look through bent end of hose.

D. Results:

1. When cardboard strips are in a straight line, the light from the flashlight can be seen.
2. When one cardboard strip is moved out of line, the light will not be seen. If the cardboard strip is moved only slightly, only part of the light will be seen.
3. With the garden hose, the light is visible only as long as the hose is perfectly straight. When the hose is bent, the light from the flashlight cannot be seen. If the hose is only slightly bent, only part of the light will be seen.

E. Basic Facts and Supplemental Information:

1. This experiment proves that light rays travel only in straight lines. For advanced students you might want to discuss light waves.
2. The speed of light is the fastest known speed in the universe. It travels at 186,000 miles per second (300,000 kilometers per second).
3. The speed of light is constant. It travels at the same speed no matter where it is in the universe.

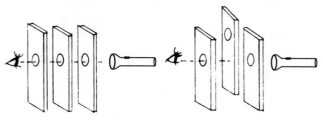

Eye sees light   Eye cannot see light

Procedure One

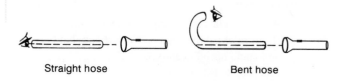

Straight hose   Bent hose

Eye sees light   Eye cannot see light

Procedure Two

4. In Einstein's equation comparing mass and energy ($E=MC^2$), the "C" in this formula is the speed of light. This is why we can get so much energy out of a little mass.

F. Thought Questions for Class Discussions:

1. Where does light come from?
2. Do mirrors make light rays curve or bend?
3. What is the difference between source light, reflected light, and refracted light?
4. Why can't we see around a corner?

G. Related Ideas for Further Inquiry:

1. Conduct some experiments with a magnifying glass.
2. Study Activity II-C-2, "What causes a shadow?"
3. Study Activity II-C-8, "What is the difference between a concave and a convex lens?"
4. Study Activity II-C-9, "How can we make a periscope? Can light be bent?"
5. Study Activity II-C-6, "What is the difference between source light and reflected light?"

H. Vocabulary Builders—Spelling Words:

1) **travel**   2) **intact**   3) **flashlight**   4) **bent**
5) **straight**   6) **hose**   7) **rubber**   8) **cardboard**

I. Thought for Today:

"Most after dinner speakers give off more heat than light."

A. Problem: *What Causes a Shadow?*

B. Materials Needed:

1. White sheet or light-colored background
2. Rope or heavy string, tacks, and safety pins (or device to support sheet)
3. Extension cord with socket, light bulb, and reflector, or a filmstrip projector.
4. If no filmstrip projector or reflector is available, a reflector can be made by cutting a piece of cardboard in an 18″ circle and making a small 1 1/2″ hole in the middle. Secure with cellophane tape and place behind bulb.
5. Flashlight (if no projector available)
6. Yardstick or meterstick
7. Cardboard circle the same size as flashlight or projector lens

C. Procedure:

1. Secure rope across the room and pin sheet to rope, or tack sheet over a doorway.
2. Hold light or place it on the floor about seven or eight feet in front of the sheet.
3. Have a student stand in back of the light.
4. Have another student stand between the sheet and the light.
5. Have this second student move closer to the sheet.
6. Have him/her move farther away from the sheet.
7. Tape small cardboard circle to end of stick.
8. Darken room.
9. Turn on flashlight or projector and aim it toward wall or sheet.
10. Have a student stand in front of the flashlight or projector, holding the circle over the lens.
11. Have student move slowly away from lens and toward the sheet or wall.

D. Results:

1. The student will not cast a shadow when he/she stands in back of light.
2. The student will cast a shadow when he/she stands between the light and the sheet.
3. The circle shadow will become smaller as the student approaches the sheet.

E. Basic Facts and Supplemental Information:

Light rays do not pass through the student, therefore, a shadow is cast on the screen when he/she stands in front of the light. This also demonstrates that light travels in straight lines. Some teachers like to make shadows with their hands forming various animals, objects, etc. Students love to do

Sketch One

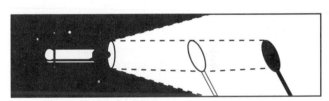

Does shadow get smaller, larger, or stay the same size as object moves closer to the screen?

Sketch Two

this as well. An opaque object will not permit light to pass through; consequently a shadow is formed.

F. Thought Questions for Class Discussions:

1. How can you increase or decrease the height of a shadow?
2. Will moving the light closer to a person cause the shadow to be larger or smaller? Why?
3. How does a sundial work?

G. Related Ideas for Further Inquiry:

1. Change the position of the light or projector and observe size of shadow.
2. Have students write a play using shadow characters.
3. Draw portraits of students by outlining shadows from projector projections. (Makes an excellent present for parents.)

H. Vocabulary Builders—Spelling Words:

1) **shadow**　2) **projector**　3) **flashlight**　4) **sheet**

I. Thought for Today:

"A winner never quits; a quitter never wins."

Activity

A. Problem: *What Colors of Light Are in Sunlight?*

B. Materials Needed:
1. Prism
2. Window
3. Strong sunlight
4. Any movable flat surface

C. Procedure:
1. Select window with strong sunlight passing through.
2. Allow sunlight to pass through prism so that a rainbow is formed on the flat surface.

D. Result:

Sunlight will split into the following sequence of colors: red, orange, yellow, green, blue, indigo, and violet. An easy way to remember this sequence of colors is by the mythical character ROY G BIV.

E. Basic Facts and Supplemental Information:
1. From an experiment such as this one, it can be shown that white light, such as sunlight, is composed not of a single color but of many colors. Whenever light passes at an angle from one substance into another of different density, it is bent; that is, its direction is changed. The different colors are bent differently, the violet being bent most and the red least. Hence, when the light comes out of the prism, the different colors are traveling in somewhat different directions, and they do not strike the flat surface in the same place. This is how the rainbow is produced. The droplets of falling water have the same effect as the prism. All the colors in combination are called a "spectrum."
2. Sunlight, or light from a light bulb, flashlight, or projector appears colorless, but it is actually composed of seven basic colors. When blended under normal circumstances it is called "white light." These individual colors can be separated by a prism, water, glass, or any transparent substance with differences in thickness. Two other kinds of light, ultraviolet and infrared, are also present but can't be seen with the naked eye.

F. Thought Questions for Class Discussions:
1. How can we see various colors?
2. Are there other kinds of light rays which we don't see?
3. If we put two prisms together in opposite directions, what color(s) of light would appear?

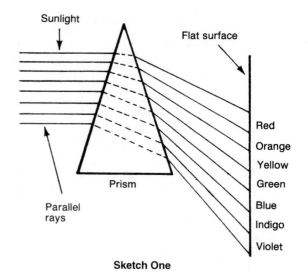

Sketch One

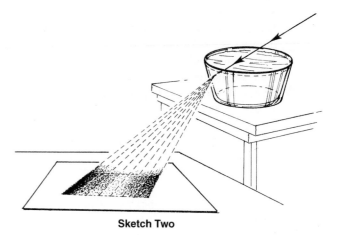

Sketch Two

G. Related Ideas for Further Inquiry:
1. On a sunny day, fill a glass bowl with water and set it on the edge of a counter so the sunlight can strike the water. Place a white sheet of paper so that the refracted light will strike it. Results: sunlight will be broken into its component colors. (See sketch two.)
2. Have class discuss rainbows they have seen.
3. Study other Activities in this Section, especially II-C-1, II-C-2, and II-C-4.

H. Vocabulary Builders—Spelling Words:
1) **prism** 2) **refraction** 3) **rainbow** 4) **angles**
5) **spectrum** 6) **ultraviolet** 7) **infrared**

I. Thought for Today:
"Some speakers who don't know what to do with their hands should clamp them over their mouths."

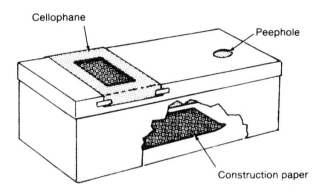

A. Problem: *What Makes Colored Light?*

B. Materials Needed:

1. Shoe box
2. Construction paper squares of five inches of various colors
3. Scissors or knife
4. Cellophane tape
5. Cellophane rectangles 3″ × 5″ of various colors

C. Procedure:

1. Cut a rectangular opening about 2″ × 4″ in the top of the shoe box, about 2″ from one end. (See sketch.)
2. Outline the opening with a cellophane tape border.
3. Cut a two-inch diameter opening at other end of box top (peephole).
4. Place a square of colored construction paper in the center of shoe box.
5. Tape a piece of cellophane (same color as the construction paper in the box) to the rectangular opening in the top of shoe box.
6. Place the shoe box top on the shoe box.
7. In a well-lighted room, look through the peephole at the construction paper square.
8. Repeat the experiment using a different color for the construction paper square and the cellophane.
9. Repeat experiment using different combinations of construction paper and cellophane.

D. Results:

1. If the same color construction paper and cellophane are used, the student will see that particular color.
2. If complimentary colors are used for the construction paper and the cellophane, the student will see only a dark color (almost black). If colors were perfectly complimentary, student would see black, the absence of all colors.
3. If adjacent colors of construction paper are used with a primary color as the cellophane test, only the primary color will be seen.
4. Other unusual and unexpected outcomes will be observed by changing colors of construction paper and cellophane.

E. Basic Facts and Supplemental Information:

1. The primary colors of light are slightly different from paints. They are red, blue, and green.
2. If the colors appear too dark, point the box toward a window.

3. White light, from the sun or light bulbs, is composed of all colors and can be separated into its component colors by passing it through a prism. See Activity II-C-3.
4. The color(s) of any object is (are) actually the complimentary color(s) we see. An object that reflects red light actually has absorbed colors that make it green.
5. A white object looks white because it reflects all colors in white light. A black object appears black because it absorbs all of the colors of white light and reflects none of them.

F. Thought Questions for Class Discussions:

1. Why do we see the clouds as white?
2. What is the real color of a red dress?
3. If we say an object is blue, is it really blue?

G. Related Ideas for Further Inquiry:

1. Another excellent activity is to place six different colored squares on the wall, then using a flashlight covered with one color cellophane, shine it on the squares with the lights on and then off. Repeat with other squares, other colors of cellophane, and with lights on and off.
2. Study Activity II-C-10, "How can we make a single-colored picture disappear?"
3. Study other Activities in this Section.

H. Vocabulary Builders—Spelling Words:

1) **complimentary** 2) **construction** 3) **rectangle**
4) **diameter** 5) **cellophane** 6) **shoe box**

I. Thought for Today:

"Science is a creation of the human mind."

Activity

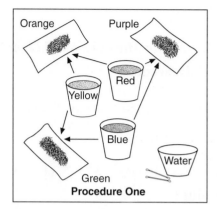

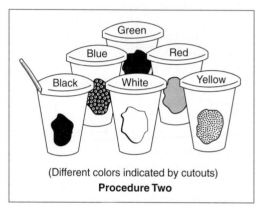

A. Problem: *How Can We Make Different Colors? Are Some Colors "Warmer" Than Others?*

B. Materials Needed:
1. Cotton swabs
2. Water
3. Paper cups with lids
4. Paper towels
5. Six cups of tempera paint (black, white, red, yellow, blue, and green)
6. Scrap paper
7. Color wheel
8. Paint brushes
9. Thermometer

C. Procedure One:
1. Place cups of primary paint colors (red, yellow, and blue) on the table.
2. Divide the class into four to six groups.
3. Instruct the students to be careful of their clothing—young students should wear aprons.
4. Explain that with the primary colors, all other colors can be created.
5. Have all students mix different primary colors to see what the secondary color will be.
6. Have students mix secondary colors (green, orange, and purple) in varying amounts.
7. Show the students the color wheel. They might make one for themselves as they progress.

Procedure Two:
1. Paint each cup a different color.
2. Paint a lid to match each cup.
3. Put 3/4 cup of cold water in each cup.
4. Take temperature of each cup with thermometer. All cups should have same temperature.
5. Set the cups in strong sunlight.
6. Record the temperature of the water in each cup at half-hour intervals.

D. Results:
1. The students will see that by mixing two of the primary colors, a third color (secondary color) is obtained. Yellow and blue will make green. Yellow and red will make orange. Red and blue will make purple. Two secondary colors when mixed will produce a third color.
2. The water in the black cup will get warmest in the shortest amount of time.

E. Basic Facts and Supplemental Information:
1. The primary colors of paint are different from the primary colors of light.
2. The so-called "hot" color red is not nearly as warm as black. White is the coolest color of all.

F. Thought Questions for Class Discussions:
1. What will happen if primary colors are mixed together in unequal amounts?
2. How can colors be darkened? lightened?
3. What color clothing should one wear on hot days? cold days? Why?
4. If two objects are exposed to the sun, which one would become warmer; a light colored one or a dark colored one?
5. Can a person get sunburned on a cloudy day?

G. Related Ideas for Further Inquiry:
1. Combine color mixing with art work.
2. Mix different food colorings.
3. Make colored disks that can be attached to a hand drill using various combinations of colors. Disks can be rotated quickly and colors will seem to blend.
4. Study all Activities in this Section.

H. Vocabulary Builders—Spelling Words:
1) **primary** 2) **secondary** 3) **tertiary** 4) **paint**
5) **different** 6) **darkened** 7) **lightened** 8) **mix**

I. Thought for Today:
"Love most the unlovable."

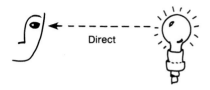

Sketch One

A. Problem: *What Is the Difference Between Source Light and Reflected Light?*

B. Materials Needed:

1. Light bulb
2. Mirror
3. Reflector for the light bulb

C. Procedure:

1. Tell the students that you are going to show them two different types of light.
2. Demonstrate source light by lighting the light bulb and having the students look directly (very briefly) at the light.
3. Next, using the reflector to hide the light bulb from the students' view, turn the bulb so that the light is reflected by the mirror.
4. Have the students look at the mirror.
5. Discuss the differences involved in direct light and reflected light.

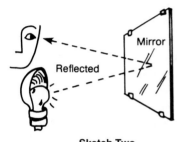

Sketch Two

D. Results:

1. The light will come from the bulb directly.
2. The light from the mirror will be reflected light from the bulb.

E. Basic Facts and Supplemental Information:

1. We receive light by two means: direct and reflected. This Activity will help students understand direct light and indirect light. Many things are visible because they give off their own light, e.g., the sun, electric light, candles, flashlights, etc. (These are all luminous.)
2. Most substances are visible because they reflect light from one of the luminous sources. We can see things in the light because of reflections from luminous objects, but we can't see the same objects in the dark.

F. Thought Questions for Class Discussions:

1. Why is reflected light from the mirror practically the same strength as direct light?
2. Is the sun direct (source) light?
3. Is the moon direct light or reflected light?

G. Related Ideas for Further Inquiry:

1. Have students set up Sketch Two as accurately as possible.
2. Have them discuss source (direct) (luminous) and reflected (indirect) light.
3. Study Activity II-C-1, "Does light travel only in a straight line?"

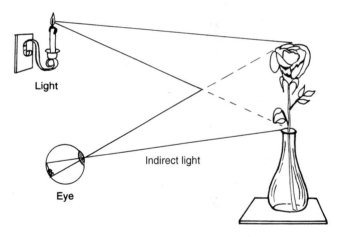

Sketch Three

4. Study Activity II-C-9, "How can we make a periscope? Can light be bent?"
5. Study Activity II-C-3, "What colors of light are in sunlight?"

H. Vocabulary Builders—Spelling Words:

1) **source** 2) **reflected** 3) **emit** 4) **direct**
5) **indirect** 6) **luminous** 7) **bulb** 8) **mirror**

I. Thought for Today:

"Bad officials are elected by people who don't vote."

A. Problem: *How Does Light Cause Reflections?*

B. Materials Needed:

1. Three small dolls or other toys
2. Two or three square mirrors, 4″ square or larger
3. Large mirror
4. Tabletop or desk

C. Procedure:

1. Conduct the following tests followed by class discussions after each:
   a. Place one doll in front of one of the small mirrors.
   b. Place several dolls in front of one small mirror.
   c. Place two mirrors at right angles to each other and place a doll equidistant between them.
   d. Place two mirrors side by side with a doll between them.
2. Move the positions of the mirrors and vary the number of dolls.
3. Vary the positions of the dolls and note the images seen.

D. Results:

1. When a student stands in front of the large mirror, the mirror reverses the image so that the right side appears to be the left and the left side appears to be the right.
2. This is true whether it be a person or a doll.
3. When the mirrors are placed at right angles, the doll will appear as that shown in the drawing.
4. When the two mirrors are placed close together and parallel, and a doll is placed between them, you should be able to see endless reflections.

E. Basic Facts and Supplemental Information:

1. When rays of light strike any surface, they bounce off them. This phenomenon is called "reflection."
2. Surfaces which are highly polished and flat produce the best reflections.
3. Mirrors are usually highly polished glass with metallic or amalgam backing.
4. Mirrors can be curved in many ways to distort objects. You might have seen one of these at a circus side show.

F. Thought Questions for Class Discussions:

1. How many mirrors should a car have for maximum visibility?
2. Should bicycles have mirrors?
3. Why do bathroom mirrors sometimes "steam up"?

G. Related Ideas for Further Inquiry:

1. Study Activity II-C-1, "Does light travel only in a straight line?"
2. Study Activity II-C-8, "What is the difference between a concave and a convex lens?"
3. Study Activity II-C-6, "What is the difference between source light and reflected light?"

H. Vocabulary Builders—Spelling Words:

1) **reflection** 2) **light** 3) **image** 4) **doll**
5) **reverse** 6) **mirror** 7) **square** 8) **source**

I. Thought for Today:

"The person who doesn't read good books has no advantage over the person who can't read them."

A. Problem: *What Is the Difference Between a Concave and a Convex Lens?*

B. Materials Needed:

1. Highly polished spoons
2. Magnifying glass(es)
3. Different lens types (if available)
4. Objects to view with magnifying glass

C. Procedure:

1. If spoon does not have a high sheen, polish it.
2. Pass out spoons to class members. (May have to share if insufficient numbers.)
3. Have pupils look at their image on the inside part of the bowl of the spoon starting at arm's length and slowly moving it closer to their eyes. (Closing one eye and moving toward the other eye gives better results.)
4. Have students note changes in images.
5. Have students repeat, only this time have them rotate spoons so they are looking at the backs (bottom of bowl).
6. Have students note changes in images.
7. Look at several objects with the magnifying glass, moving it closer to and then away from objects, and noting changes in images.
8. The depth and time spent on studying lenses will depend on the level of the students. Younger students can draw spoons and draw the lines where light enters the spoon and the angle(s) it leaves. Middle students can study simple concave and convex lenses. Older students can study complex lenses.
9. Light is reflected off an object at the same angle it enters.

D. Results:

1. In the first part, the image will appear upside down and grow larger, then fill the whole surface; it may reappear enlarged and right side up.
2. On the reverse side, the image will start out small and right side up and get larger as it is moved closer to the eye. It will also have an oval appearance.
3. With magnifying glasses, the images will only appear larger and right side up.

E. Basic Facts and Supplemental Information:

1. Convex lenses bend the light inward.
2. Concave lenses bend the light outward.
3. Magnifying glasses use double convex lenses.

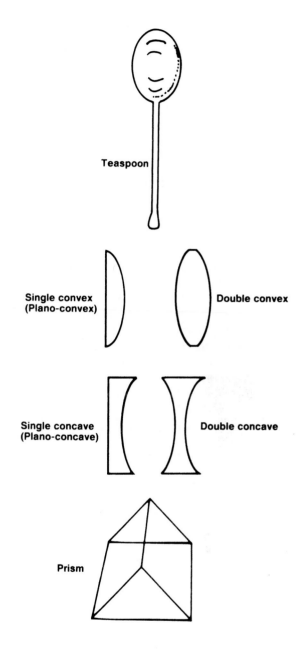

Teaspoon

Single convex (Plano-convex)

Double convex

Single concave (Plano-concave)

Double concave

Prism

4. Slide projectors and film projectors use double convex lenses.
5. Telescopes also use double convex lenses for greater magnification.
6. Double convex lenses appear thicker in the middle and thinner on the edges.
7. Double concave lenses are used in the eyeglasses of nearsighted people.
8. Double concave lenses appear thinner in the middle and thicker on the ends.

9. An "image" is what we see indirectly as our "image" in the mirror.
10. A prism is also a type of lens.
11. A lens that is flat on one side and curved on the other is called "plano-concave" or "plano-convex."

F. Thought Questions for Class Discussions:

1. What kinds of lenses are used in binoculars?
2. Some automobile headlights have complicated lenses. What major types of lenses do they have?
3. Where else might lenses be used?
4. Many side view mirrors on automobiles have the statement: "Objects in the mirror are closer than they appear." Why is this? What kind of "lens" is being used?

G. Related Ideas for Further Inquiry:

1. Examine eyeglasses.
2. Examine projector lenses.
3. Examine flashlight lenses.
4. The magnifying power of a convex lens can be measured by looking at some thin-lined paper and comparing the number of lines outside to the number of lines viewed inside. If, for example, there are five spaces outside to one space inside, the magnifying power is five times. This magnification occurs in all directions.
5. Study Activity II-C-1, "Does light travel only in a straight line?"
6. Study Activity II-C-6, "What is the difference between source light and reflected light?"
7. Study Activity II-C-7, "How does light cause reflections?"
8. Study Activity II-C-9, "How can we make a periscope? Can light be bent?"

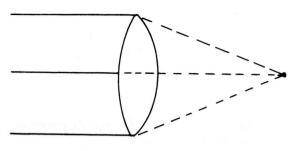

Convex lens makes rays converge

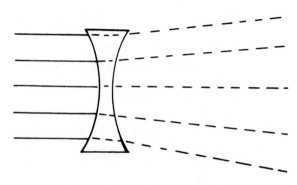

Concave lens makes rays diverge

H. Vocabulary Builders—Spelling Words:

1) **concave** 2) **convex** 3) **plano-concave**
4) **plano-convex** 5) **image** 6) **double concave**
7) **double convex** 8) **prism** 9) **converge**

I. Thought for Today:

"Hardening of the attitudes starts a long time before hardening of the arteries."

Activity

A. Problem: *How Can We Make a Periscope? Can Light Be Bent?*

B. Materials Needed, Procedure One:
1. Cardboard
2. Scissors or single-edge razor blade
3. Two small pocket mirrors
4. Cellophane tape

Materials Needed, Procedure Two:
1. Cardboard box
2. Scissors or single-edge razor blade
3. Small candle or flashlight
4. Matches if using candle
5. Book
6. Four small pocket mirrors

C. Procedure One:
1. Fold the Cardboard and cut diagonal slots in it as shown in the sketches.
2. Place the mirrors in the slot as shown and fasten them securely with cellophane tape. These should be at 45° angles.
3. Cut a square hole for the viewing section.

Procedure Two:
1. Cut cardboard box as shown in sketch.
2. Attach mirrors with cellophane tape with reflecting surfaces facing the inside of the box at 45° angles.
3. Put the top on the box.
4. Shine flashlight in front of one opening.

D. Results:
1. In Procedure One, a periscope will be made as shown in top drawings.
2. In Procedure Two, students will be able to "see through" a solid object.

E. Basic Facts and Supplemental Information:
1. Light travels in straight lines if unhindered.
2. Light rays can be reflected by mirrors.
3. Silver plastic material from greeting cards may be substituted for mirrors.

F. Thought Questions for Class Discussions:
1. How tall can we make a periscope?
2. Does light travel *from* our eyes or *to* our eyes? How can this be proved?
3. Where can periscopes be used?

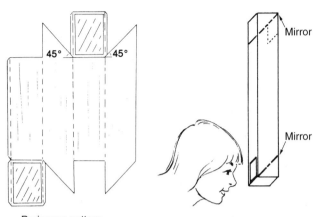

Periscope pattern
how to make a periscope

Completed periscope

Procedure One

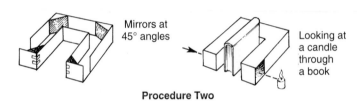

Mirrors at 45° angles

Looking at a candle through a book

Procedure Two

G. Related Ideas for Further Inquiry:
1. If you hold the periscope sideways, you can see around a corner.
2. Study where mirrors are used today.
3. Study Activity V-B-2, "Why do the pupils of our eyes change size?"
4. Study Activity V-B-4, "How do our eyes blend separate colors?"
5. Study Activity V-B-7, "How do we see motion?"
6. Study Activity V-B-5, "Are there blind spots in our eyes?"
7. Study Activity V-B-6, "Do our eyes ever deceive us?"

H. Vocabulary Builders—Spelling Words:
1) **periscope** 2) **mirror** 3) **apparent** 4) **angle**
5) **pattern** 6) **diagonal** 7) **viewing** 8) **locking**

I. Thought for Today:
"It is better to keep your mouth shut and appear to be stupid than open it and remove all doubts."

Activity

II C 10

A. Problem: *How Can We Make a Single-Colored Picture Disappear?*

B. Materials Needed:
1. Various colors of cellophane
2. Simple pictures in color as close to cellophane colors as possible, such as dog, cat, house
3. Bulletin board
4. Thumbtacks
5. Large white sheet of tagboard (or white paper)
6. Red and blue pencils or crayons

C. Procedure:

(Mount all pictures on tagboard.)

1. Draw a picture in red.
2. Look at it through red cellophane.
3. Repeat with other pictures and other cellophane colors using same color for both picture and cellophane.
4. Draw a blue picture.
5. Look at it through a red piece of cellophane.
6. Draw a red bird in a blue cage.
7. Look at it through a piece of blue cellophane.
8. Look at it through a piece of red cellophane.
9. Look at it with a piece of red cellophane covering one eye and a piece of blue cellophane covering the other eye.

D. Results:
1. When a picture is viewed through the same color of cellophane, the picture will "disappear."
2. Using different colors of pictures and cellophane, the pictures will show up as black.
3. Viewing the red bird and the blue cage:
   a. with blue cellophane the cage will disappear
   b. with red cellophane, the bird will disappear
   c. with different colored cellophane over each eye, both bird and cage will be seen

E. Basic Facts and Supplemental Information:
1. The white tagboard reflects all colors.
2. A red picture reflects only the red portion of white light.
3. When the red portion is filtered out with the red cellophane, no color strikes the eye, hence the red picture seems to have disappeared.
4. The same is true for all colors.

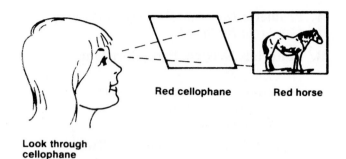

Look through cellophane

Red cellophane   Red horse

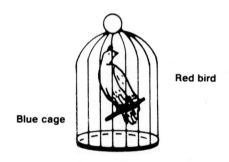

Red bird

Blue cage

F. Thought Questions for Class Discussions:
1. What color would you see in a dark room viewing a multicolored picture if the only light was from a flashlight covered with red cellophane?
2. How would you make a green picture disappear?
3. How would you make a black picture disappear?

G. Related Ideas for Further Inquiry:
1. Try various combinations of pictures and cellophane.
2. Study Activity II-C-1, "Does light travel only in a straight line?"
3. Study Activity II-C-2, "What causes a shadow?"
4. Study Activity II-C-4, "What makes colored light?"
5. Study Activity II-C-5, "How can we make different colors? Are some colors 'warmer' than others?"

H. Vocabulary Builders—Spelling Words:
1) **reflection**   2) **cellophane**   3) **disappear**
4) **filter**   5) **bulletin board**   6) **various**

I. Thought for Today:
"Most people spend more time going around problems than trying to solve them."

102   *Light and Color*

Activity

A. Problem: *How Can We Make a Simple Magnifying Glass?*

B. Materials Needed, Procedure One:
1. One piece of flat glass which has been carefully cleaned (A)
2. Eyedropper (B)
3. Piece of cloth
4. Other objects to examine

Materials Needed, Procedure Two:
1. Nail (large), or dowel (small)
2. Copper wire 6″ approx.
3. Water
4. Objects to examine

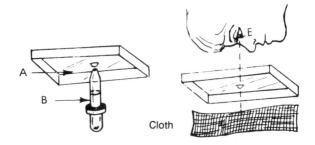

Procedure One

C. Procedure One:
1. Carefully hold the glass in a horizontal position.
2. With the eyedropper just below the glass, squeeze a small drop of water on the glass. (Do not attempt to place the drop of water on the upper side and then turn the glass over; the water will run off the edge.)
3. The surface of this hanging water drop is like the surface of a glass lens. Use it to examine the piece of cloth.
4. Hold your head close to the glass so that one eye is very close to the glass and just above the water drop (E).
5. Hold the cloth just below the glass and very close to the water drop, but do not let them touch.
6. Slowly move the cloth downward until the image is as clear as possible.

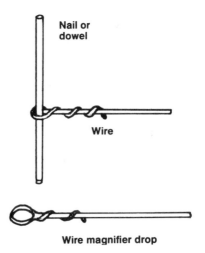

Procedure Two

Procedure Two:
1. Make several turns of wire around the nail or dowel.
2. Remove the wire from nail or dowel.
3. Dip the wire loop into water or use eyedropper to put water in center of loop.

D. Results:
1. The drop of water will magnify the cloth.
2. A simple magnifying glass has been created.

E. Basic Facts and Supplemental Information:
1. These are simple and effective devices.
2. Each student in the class can make one or both magnifying glasses.

F. Thought Questions for Class Discussions:
1. Why does the drop of water act like a magnifying glass?
2. Does the water bend the light rays?
3. How does a magnifying glass magnify?

G. Related Ideas for Further Inquiry:
1. If a regular microscope is available, use it to examine many objects. Care should be taken with regular microscopes because they are expensive—especially the lenses.
2. Study Activity II-C-1, "Does light travel only in a straight line?"
3. Study Activity II-C-8, "What is the difference between a concave and a convex lens?"
4. Study Activity II-C-6, "What is the difference between source light and reflected light?"

H. Vocabulary Builders—Spelling Words:
1) **magnifying** 2) **surface** 3) **eyedropper**
4) **horizontal** 5) **lenses** 6) **dowel**

I. Thought for Today:
"We can do anything we want to do if we stick to it long enough."

SECTION D: SOUND

Activity

A. Problem: *What Are Some of the Sounds We Hear Each Day on the Way to School?*

B. Materials Needed:
1. Bell
2. Pencil sharpener
3. Clock
4. Pictures of objects that make sounds

C. Procedure:
1. Assign students the task of bringing in a picture of an object that makes sound.
2. Collect some pictures of your own.
3. Cite some sound-making objects found in the classroom such as:
   a. clock
   b. pencil sharpener
   c. bell
   d. aquarium aerator
   e. heating unit
   f. air conditioner
   g. students
4. Cite the importance of sound for people.
   a. communication:
      1) voices
      2) television
      3) movies
      4) radio
   b. safety
   c. transportation
   d. health
5. This would be a good time to teach about how loud sounds contribute to hearing loss, especially "boom boxes."
6. Discuss how life would change if we had no sense of hearing.

D. Results:
1. Students will realize that life would be totally different without sound.
2. Students will appreciate their own sense of hearing.

Automobile

E. Basic Facts and Supplemental Information:
1. About 10% of all students have some hearing loss.
2. About 3% of all students need a hearing aid in order to hear well in school.
3. Many students with a hearing loss assume their hearing is normal.

F. Thought Questions for Class Discussions:
1. What would life be like without sound?
2. How do deaf people communicate?
3. How can we protect our sense of hearing?

G. Related Ideas for Further Inquiry:
1. Look up "Krakatoa" (the loudest sound ever recorded on Earth).
2. Study the principles of Sign Language.
3. Have each student learn a few "words" (signs) in Sign Language.
4. Study Activity II-D-4, "How do we communicate by using sound?"
5. Study Activity II-D-6, "What makes sounds when we speak?"
6. Study Activity V-B-8, "How well do we hear?"

H. Vocabulary Builders—Spelling Words:
1) **sound**   2) **communication**   3) **hearing**
4) **deafness**   5) **safety**   6) **dependent**

I. Thought for Today:
"Those who can't laugh at themselves leave the job to others."

Activity

A. Problem: *What Causes Sound? How Are Sounds Made?*

B. Materials Needed:
1. Blade of grass
2. Piece of paper
3. Toy guitar, or other stringed musical instrument
4. Any noisemaker (dried gourd, tonette, rattle, whistle, blocks of wood)
5. Tissue paper over comb
6. Rubber band

C. Procedure:
1. Have students hold a blade of grass or piece of paper between their thumbs, and blow.
2. Have pupils place tissue paper over a comb, hold it to their lips, and hum.
3. Stretch a rubber band around some object, and listen to it as it is plucked.
4. Stop the vibrations and listen again.
5. Pluck a stringed instrument, listen to it; stop its vibrations and listen again.
6. Make sounds with noisemaker(s).
7. Ask the class if they know what all these sounds have in common.

D. Results:
1. These test materials will produce vibrations which cause sound.
2. When vibrations cease, sounds will stop.

E. Basic Facts and Supplemental Information:
1. Sounds travel in air at about 1,600 feet per second.
2. Sound travels faster in liquids and solids.
3. One aspect of sound is *frequency* or *pitch*. It is the number of vibrations (cycles) per second. The more vibrations or cycles, the higher the pitch.
4. Another characteristic of sound is *intensity* or *amplitude*. The greater this is, the louder the sound.
5. The average person has a very limited hearing range and scope.
6. The normal hearing range is between 20 and 20,000 vibrations per second.

F. Thought Questions for Class Discussions:
1. What other vibrating objects will cause sound?
2. Are noises caused by vibrations?
3. Are there any vibrations we can't hear?
4. What is an echo?

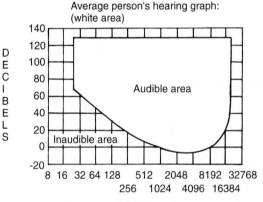

Average person's hearing graph: (white area)

Audible area

Inaudible area

Frequency (pitch) in cycles per second

G. Related Ideas for Further Inquiry:
1. Study the sounds of music.
2. Listen to the sounds of birds, insects, and other animals.
3. Place a finger on your throat and hum.
4. Study Activity II-D-1, "What are some of the sounds we hear each day on the way to school?"
5. Study Activity II-D-3, "Does sound travel through solids? liquids? gases?"
6. Study Activity II-D-5, "What causes sounds to vary in pitch?"
7. Study Activity II-D-6, "What makes sounds when we speak?"

H. Vocabulary Builders—Spelling Words:
1) **frequency**   2) **pitch**   3) **intensity**   4) **sound**
5) **vibrations**   6) **cycles**   7) **amplitude**   8) **listen**

I. Thought for Today:
"Learning is the original and greatest of all 'do it yourself' projects."

Activity

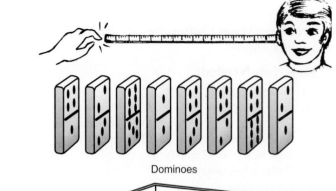

Dominoes

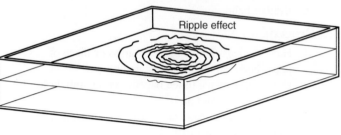

Ripple effect

A. Problem: *Does Sound Travel Through Solids? Liquids? Gases?*

B. Materials Needed:

1. Three or four yardsticks or metersticks
2. Set of dominoes
3. Pan
4. Small rock

C. Procedure:

1. Students in the class should pair off so that two of them working together can be involved in this experiment.
2. Have one pupil hold the yardstick or meterstick close to, but not touching, his/her ear.

Caution: Both students must handle the yardstick carefully to avoid injury.

3. Have the second student scratch the other end of the stick.
4. Have this student move closer and closer to the first student scratching the stick at various points along the way.
5. Set up the dominoes in a straight line so that when one falls it will strike an adjacent one so that it, too, will fall.
6. Topple the first one and start a "chain reaction."
7. Fill the pan with water and drop a small rock in the center.
8. Ask the class how these three activities are related to sound.
9. Discuss how sound needs a medium to travel be it solid, liquid, or gas. Discuss how sounds need molecules to travel and that the closer the molecules are, the stronger the sound.

D. Results:

1. When the yardstick or meterstick is held close to the ear the sound will be quite audible.
2. When the stick is held away from the ear the sound diminishes in direct proportion to the distance from the ear.
3. The dominoes will fall.
4. The rock will cause ripples in the pan of water, similar to sound waves.

E. Basic Facts and Supplemental Information:

1. Actually the sound travels through wood molecules much more easily than it does through air because there are more molecules per given volume.
2. A person with normal hearing can hear sounds between 20 and 20,000 vibrations (cycles) per second.

3. In order to have sound, some medium must carry the sound. This could be a *solid* as in this activity, a *liquid* such as water, or a *gas* such as air.

F. Thought Questions for Class Discussions:

1. Why did some Indians put their ears to the ground when hunting or tracking?
2. When a guitar is played, what substances do the sounds pass through?
3. How do you think fish communicate?
4. Can sound ever become harmful?
5. How can we test our hearing?

G. Related Ideas for Further Inquiry:

1. Make a "hose telephone." Attach a clean funnel to each end of a hose six to ten feet in length and have two students carry on a conversation using each funnel as a mouthpiece and an earpiece.
2. Make a "sound amplifier." Roll a large sheet of paper into a cone-like megaphone. Place the small end on the ear (never in the ear) and put the large end toward a clock, radio, or talking student. Many years ago people with hearing loss used devices like this.
3. Study Activity II-D-2, "What causes sound? How are sounds made?"
4. Study Activity II-D-4, "How do we communicate by using sound?"

H. Vocabulary Builders—Spelling Words:

1) **conduction** 2) **vibrations** 3) **molecules**
4) **liquids** 5) **solids** 6) **cone** 7) **hose** 8) **ear**

I. Thought for Today:

"Nothing lowers the level of conversation more than raising the voice."

A. Problem: *How Do We Communicate by Using Sound?*

B. Materials Needed:

Pictures or drawings of:
1. People in conversation
2. Whistles
3. Bells
4. Horns
5. Telephones
6. Radios
7. Television sets
8. Transcriptions
9. Cassette tapes
10. CDs
11. Computers
12. Musical instruments
13. Megaphones
14. Railroad signals, etc.

C. Procedure:

1. Discuss each item listed above and describe its importance in carrying out phases of living.
2. Discuss other means of communication we use:
   a. gestures
   b. newspapers
   c. magazines
   d. books, pamphlets
   e. mail
   f. signal flags
   g. railroad crossing lights
   h. flares
   i. notes and memos

D. Results:

1. Sound plays a vital part in our lives.
2. Communication may or may not include sound.

E. Basic Facts and Supplemental Information:

1. If we could not communicate with others, we would have to learn everything by ourselves.
2. Sounds can make us happy, sad, irritated, etc.
3. Sounds vary in intensity, pitch, and harmonics.
4. Sounds travel through the air at about 1,100 feet per second.
5. Sounds need a medium to travel: solids, liquids, or gases.

F. Thought Questions for Class Discussions:

1. How do deaf and hard-of-hearing people communicate?

My turn?

2. Do satellites help us communicate?
3. How do ships at sea communicate?
4. What does the term "audiovisual" mean?

G. Related Ideas for Further Inquiry:

1. There are many activities that can be included with sounds from storytelling to news broadcasts.
2. Study Activity II-D-1, "What are some of the sounds we hear each day on the way to school?"
3. Study Activity II-D-2, "What causes sound? How are sounds made?"
4. Study Activity II-D-3, "Does sound travel through solids? liquids? gases?"
5. Study Activity II-D-6, "What makes sounds when we speak?"
6. Study Activity II-D-10, "How can we make a simple telephone?"

H. Vocabulary Builders—Spelling Words:

1) **radio** 2) **television** 3) **records**
4) **transcriptions** 5) **audiovisual**

I. Thought for Today:

"Television is not replacing radio half as fast as it is homework."

A. Problem: *What Causes Sounds to Vary in Pitch?*

B. Materials Needed:
1. Wooden box or shoe box open at top
2. Rubber bands of varied lengths and thicknesses
3. String
4. Wire

C. Procedure:
1. With open end of box up, place one rubber band around the box and pluck.
2. Tighten band by pulling it out to the side, keeping taut on top. Pluck again.
3. Place bands of same length but different widths on box and pluck each one.
4. Place bands of same width but different lengths around box and pluck each one.
5. Place string, wire, and a band around box and pluck each one.

D. Results:
1. The string will not vibrate, consequently, no sound.
2. The wire will vibrate and sound can be heard. Pitch will vary on tautness.
3. Short bands will have a higher pitch than long bands of equal tautness.
4. Tight bands will have a higher pitch than loose bands.
5. Thin bands will have a higher pitch than thick bands.

E. Basic Facts and Supplemental Information:
By observing closely, students will learn that high pitch results from many vibrations and low pitch results from fewer vibrations in the same time interval.

F. Thought Questions for Class Discussions:
1. Why won't a heavy band vibrate as rapidly as a light band?
2. Why will stretching a rubber band or making a wire more taut cause it to vibrate faster?
3. What does this have to do with tuning a violin, guitar, or piano?

G. Related Ideas for Further Inquiry:
1. Study Activity II-D-2, "What causes sound? How are sounds made?"
2. Study Activity II-D-3, "Does sound travel through solids? liquids? gases?"
3. Study Activity II-D-4, "How do we communicate by using sound?"
4. Study Activity II-D-8, "How can we make pop bottle music?"
5. Study Activity II-D-6, "What makes sounds when we speak?"

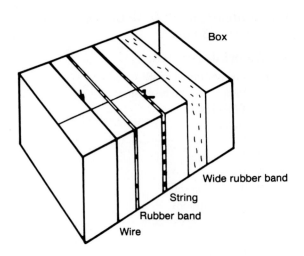

Box
Wide rubber band
String
Rubber band
Wire

PITCH SCALE (VIBRATIONS PER SECOND)	
FREQUENCY	EXAMPLES (SOUND, MUSIC, HEARING)
0 – 15	Below human capabilities
16 – 20	Lower limit of human capabilities

FREQUENCY	EXAMPLES	
21 – 200	Deep bass tones	
256	Middle C = "DO"	
278	C-Sharp, D-Flat	
294	D = "RE"	
312	D-Sharp, E-Flat	
330	E = "ME"	
349	F = "FA"	Musical
370	F-Sharp, G-Flat	Scale
392	G = "SO"	
416	G-Sharp, A-Flat	
440	A = "LA"	
466	A-Sharp, B-Flat	
494	B = "TI"	
512	C = "DO"	

FREQUENCY	EXAMPLES
500 – 3,000	Normal conversation
About 4,000	Highest musical tone
About 8,000	Highest pitch, shrill tone
About 20,000	Upper limit of human hearing
About 30,000	Upper limit of dogs and cats
About 100,000	Upper limit for bats

H. Vocabulary Builders—Spelling Words:
1) **decibel** 2) **threshold** 3) **pain** 4) **whisper** 5) **eardrum** 6) **pitch** 7) **vibrations** 8) **hearing**

I. Thought for Today:
"Intelligence is like a river—the deeper it is the less noise it makes."

A. Problem: *What Makes Sounds When We Speak?*

B. Materials Needed:

1. Pictures of people talking or singing
2. Reference materials showing the anatomical structures of the throat

C. Procedure:

1. Have each member of the class gently grasp his/her throat with the thumb on one side and the rest of the fingers on the other side.
2. Have each student hum softly and feel his/her throat.
3. Have each talk quietly, still holding his/her throat.
4. Have each sing a few lines from a popular song, still holding his/her throat.

D. Results:

Students will feel the vibrations in their throats when they hum, talk, and sing.

E. Basic Facts and Supplemental Information:

1. Sounds are caused by vibrations.
2. Human sounds are caused by the vibrations of the vocal cords.
3. The vocal cords vibrate when air from the lungs rushes against them.
4. Human voices vary in pitch because of the length, thickness, and tautness of the vocal cords.
5. Girls (and women) usually have higher voices than boys (and men) because their vocal cords are shorter and more tightly stretched.
6. Vocal cords are flaps of muscle.
7. In normal breathing, the vocal cords are open.
8. When speaking, the vocal cords are adducted (drawn together).
9. In high-pitched sounds, the space between the vocal cords becomes a narrow slit.
10. Other parts of our anatomy involved in speech are our lips and tongue.
11. Professional singers spend many hours vocalizing to develop their voices by training their vocal cords and respiratory systems.

F. Thought Questions for Class Discussions:

1. Do other animals have vocal cords?
2. How do we hear sounds over a telephone?
3. Why do people's voices change as they grow into adolescence and young adulthood?

G. Related Ideas for Further Inquiry:

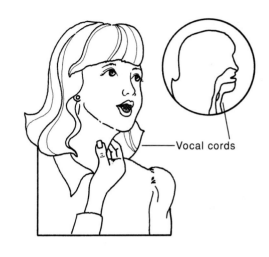

Vocal cords

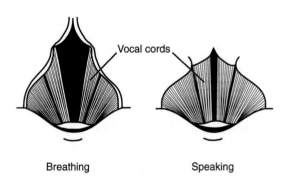

Vocal cords

Breathing   Speaking

1. Study Activity II-D-2, "What causes sound? How are sounds made?"
2. Study Activity II-D-1, "What are some of the sounds we hear each day on the way to school?"
3. Study Activity II-D-4, "How do we communicate by using sound?"
4. Study Activity II-D-9, "How do vibrating wires make different sounds?"
5. Study Activity II-D-5, "What causes sounds to vary in pitch?"

H. Vocabulary Builders—Spelling Words:

1) **vocal cords** 2) **vibrating** 3) **sound** 4) **hum**
5) **voice** 6) **throat** 7) **speaking** 8) **talking**

I. Thought for Today:

"Psychology has proved that if you keep your voice soft, you will not become angry."

Activity

A. Problem: *How Does a Stethoscope Work?*

B. Materials Needed:

1. Three pieces of rubber or plastic tubing, each 8″ long
2. Three medium-sized funnels
3. "Y" joint (glass or plastic tubing)
4. String, rubber bands, or tape
5. Sound makers (harmonica, whistle, tuning fork, etc.)

C. Procedure:

1. Take one piece of rubber or plastic tubing and attach it to one of the funnels on one end.
2. Follow the same procedure for the other two tubing ear pieces (funnels). (See Fig. 1)
3. Now join the three pieces of tubing with the funnels together, using the "Y" joint; fasten all connections with string, rubber bands, or tape.
4. Have students listen to sound makers with this homemade stethoscope. The ear pieces can be held by other students or by an extra large rubber band fitted over the head and under the chin.
5. Listen to a student's heartbeat.
6. Have a student jog in place for two minutes and listen to his/her heartbeat again.
7. Make the apparatus as shown in Fig. 2.
8. Clap your hands in a part of the room that is closer to one funnel than the other.
9. Have students guess where the sound originated.

D. Results:

1. The funnels and tubes will intensify the vibrations of the heart by channeling sound waves through the tubes directly to the ears and eliminating outside noises. Students will get a better concept of how sound can be channeled and intensified.
2. The students will learn that the heart beats more frequently (and louder) after exercise.
3. In reversing funnels, sounds appear to be coming from the opposite direction of the source of the sound.
4. Our brains interpret the sounds our ears hear.

E. Basic Facts and Supplemental Information:

1. Through experiments with the stethoscope, students will learn about sound.
2. They will learn more about their heart rates before and after exercise.
3. Perhaps this will lessen the fears of some students when their doctors use stethoscopes during an examination.

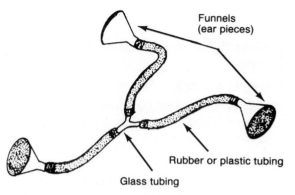

Funnels
(ear pieces)

Rubber or plastic tubing

Glass tubing

Fig. 1

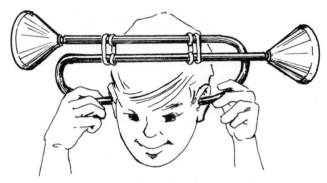

Fig. 2

F. Thought Questions for Class Discussions:

1. How does this instrument (Fig. 1) compare with a doctor's stethoscope?
2. How do you think stethoscopes help doctors?
3. Do all sounds coming through this stethoscope have the same volume? pitch? quality?

G. Related Ideas for Further Inquiry:

1. Study Activity II-D-2, "What causes sound? How are sounds made?"
2. Study Activity II-D-5, "What causes sounds to vary in pitch?"
3. Study Activity II-D-10, "How can we make a simple telephone?"
4. Study Activity II-D-8, "How can we make pop bottle music?"
5. Study Activity II-D-6, "What makes sounds when we speak?"

H. Vocabulary Builders—Spelling Words:

1) **stethoscope**   2) **tubing**   3) **funnel**   4) **plastic**
5) **rubber**   6) **tape**   7) **doctor**   8) **ears**   9) **hearing**

I. Thought for Today:

"Nature gave us two ears and one mouth so that we would listen twice as much as we talk."

Activity

A. Problem: *How Can We Make Pop Bottle Music?*

B. Materials Needed:

1. Eight pop bottles of the same size, shape, and thickness
2. Water
3. Dowel or rod
4. Food coloring
5. Pitcher

C. Procedure:

1. Fill pitcher with water.
2. Color water with food coloring to make water visible.
3. Fill one bottle with water.
4. Lower the depth of the water in the second bottle until the next note of the scale is obtained. Test by blowing over the neck of the bottle or by striking with dowel or rod.
5. Continue lowering the level of water in each successive bottle about an inch each time.
6. This will give the eight tones of the scale which can be tested by blowing on the bottles or striking them with a dowel or rod.
7. Add or remove water until each bottle has correct pitch.
8. Give one bottle to each of eight students.
9. Have each student blow or strike his/her own bottle.
10. Play some simple tunes.
11. Create your own songs using this musical instrument.

D. Results:

1. By having students blow in the bottles or strike them, different notes can be sounded.
2. When the "notes" are arranged, simple tunes can be created and played.

E. Basic Facts and Supplemental Information:

1. The pitch and tone produced from blowing in the pop bottles are due to the size of the resonating chamber within the bottle. The tone and pitch can also be affected by the shape of the chamber and by the material from which the bottle is made.
2. This instrument is a simple xylophone.
3. A simple zampana can be made by taping different length tubes together that have been sealed with modeling clay on one end.

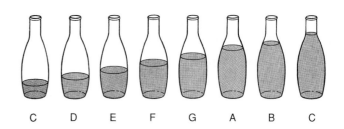

C   D   E   F   G   A   B   C

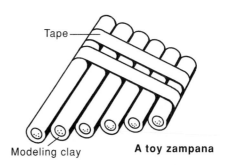

Tape

Modeling clay   **A toy zampana**

F. Thought Questions for Class Discussions:

1. Why does enlarging the air chamber change the pitch?
2. Would a large jug produce a lower or higher pitch than a pop bottle? Why?
3. Does a pipe organ have similar resonating chambers?

G. Related Ideas for Further Inquiry:

1. Study Activity II-D-2, "What causes sound? How are sounds made?"
2. Study Activity II-D-3, "Does sound travel through solids? liquids? gases?"
3. Study Activity II-D-4, "How do we communicate by using sound?"
4. Study Activity II-D-5, "What causes sounds to vary in pitch?"
5. Study Activity II-D-7, "How does a stethoscope work?"
6. Study Activity V-B-8, "How well do we hear?"

H. Vocabulary Builders—Spelling Words:

1) **resonating** 2) **hearing** 3) **depth** 4) **tone**
5) **scale** 6) **xylophone** 7) **notes** 8) **music**

I. Thought for Today:

"Peace comes not from the absence of conflict in life but upon the ability to cope with it."

A. Problem: *How Do Vibrating Wires Make Different Sounds?*

B. Materials Needed:
1. Four wires of the same length.
   a. Two steel wires, same thickness (A and B)
   b. One steel wire, thinner than above two (C)
   c. One copper wire, same thickness as single steel wire (D)
2. Frame as illustrated
3. One light weight and three heavier weights to keep wires taut

C. Procedure:
1. Arrange the four wires on a frame like the one in the sketch. A and B are made of steel of the same length and thickness. A has the light weight on it, B has a heavier weight. When the wire is stretched, we say it has tension. C is also made of steel wire but is not as thick as A or B. D is made of copper wire which is lighter than steel wire.
2. Pluck the various wires and note the differences in pitch.
3. Pluck any one wire and remember the pitch.
4. Press the same wire firmly to the table with your finger and pluck it again.
5. Repeat with the other wires. Listen carefully.

D. Result:
Different pitches will be produced.

E. Basic Facts and Supplemental Information:
1. We know now that four different characteristics regulate the pitch of vibrating strings:
   a. *The tension*—The higher the tension, the higher the pitch (same thickness, length, and materials).
   b. *The thickness*—The thicker the wire, the lower the pitch (same material, same length and tension).
   c. *The material*—The lighter the wire, the higher the pitch (same length, tension, and thickness).
   d. *The length*—The shorter the wire, the higher the pitch (same material, thickness, and tension).
2. The proper tuning of any stringed musical instrument is dependent upon these characteristics.

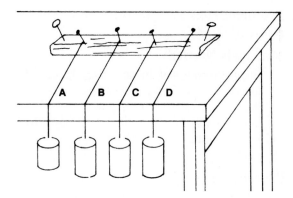

F. Thought Questions for Class Discussions:
1. Does this experiment have anything to do with tuning a piano? Pianos have wires that are struck.
2. If we double the weight, do we double the volume? pitch? (See drawing.)
3. Do we hear the strings vibrating or the air molecules moving?

G. Related Ideas for Further Inquiry:
1. Study how sounds vary with different musical instruments such as:
   a. violin
   b. guitar
   c. banjo
   d. harp, etc.
2. Study Activity II-D-2, "What causes sound? How are sounds made?"
3. Study Activity II-D-3, "Does sound travel through solids? liquids? gases?"
4. Study Activity II-D-4, "How do we communicate by using sound?"
5. Study Activity II-D-7, "How does a stethoscope work?"
6. Study Activity II-D-10, "How can we make a simple telephone?"

H. Vocabulary Builders—Spelling Words:
1) **vibrating** 2) **tension** 3) **material** 4) **length**
5) **width** 6) **thickness** 7) **wires** 8) **size**

I. Thought for Today:
"The only reason some people listen to reason is to give them time for a rebuttal."

A. Problem: *How Can We Make a Simple Telephone?*

B. Materials Needed:

1. Two empty cans
2. String (or waxed dental floss)
3. Wax (not necessary, but helpful)
4. Two buttons
5. Ice pick or can opener

C. Procedure:

1. Punch a small hole in the center of each can at the bottom.
2. Cut string desired length and run wax up and down the string.
3. Put waxed string through the holes in the cans.
4. Tie a button on each end of the string to hold the string firmly in the cans.
5. Keep the strings taut.
6. Have one student talk into one can and another student listen at the other can.

D. Result:

When a student talks into the can, the vibrations from the vocal cords cause the air to vibrate and this makes the bottom of the can vibrate. These vibrations are carried along the waxed string. When they reach the other can, the bottom of the can vibrates, causing the adjacent air to vibrate. When the vibrations reach a person's eardrum at the other end of the string, they reproduce the sound of the voice.

E. Basic Facts and Supplemental Information:

1. Sound must have a medium to vibrate. In this activity we can trace the vibrations through the different media from the vocal cords to the air to the can to the string to the other can to the eardrum.
2. Other equipment can be substituted and the results will be the same. Plastic or paper cups can be used instead of tin cans. Thin wire or very heavy thread can be used in place of the string. Large knots can be tied in lieu of buttons.

F. Thought Questions for Class Discussions:

1. Why does it help to wax the string in order to make this "tin can telephone?"
2. Would fine wire, stretched between the cans, work better than the string?
3. Would this telephone work around corners? Why?
4. What causes sounds to increase when we raise our voices or turn up the volume on the radio, stereo, CD, or television?

G. Related Ideas for Further Inquiry:

1. Have students place their thumb and fingers on their throats. Have them talk, sing, or hum and they will feel vibrations.
2. Discuss how vibrations cause sounds in musical instruments, stereos, radios, television, and telephones.
3. Study Activity II-D-1, "What are some of the sounds we hear each day on the way to school?"
4. Study Activity II-D-2, "What causes sound? How are sounds made?"
5. Study Activity II-D-4, "How do we communicate by using sound?"
6. Study Activity II-D-7, "How does a stethoscope work?"
7. Study Activity II-D-9, "How do vibrating wires make different sounds?"

H. Vocabulary Builders—Spelling Words:

1) **string** 2) **waxed** 3) **listen** 4) **taut** 5) **center** 6) **vocal cords** 7) **vibrations** 8) **speak**

I. Thought for Today:

"In quarreling, the truth is always lost."

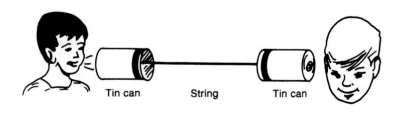

Tin can   String   Tin can

SECTION E: SIMPLE MACHINES
Activity

A. Problem: *How Do Simple Machines Help Us?*

B. Materials Needed:

Pictures or models of:

1. Wheel and axle
2. Levers
3. Inclined planes
4. Pulleys
5. Gears
6. Screws
7. Wedges

C. Procedure:

1. Briefly show how each of these "simple machines" is a device to help people do work more quickly or more easily.
2. Describe and define "work."
3. Discuss how it is easier for "work" to be done over a longer period of time or over a greater distance using simple machines.
4. Have the students cite examples of each simple machine that they have seen.

D. Results:

1. Students will gain a general idea of work, force, time, and distance.
2. Students will develop a new respect for levers, pulleys, gears, and other simple machines.

E. Basic Facts and Supplemental Information:

1. Most simple machines make our work easier.
2. Complicated machinery, like an automobile, uses various combinations of simple machines.
3. To do work you must use effort or "force." Most scientists use "foot-pounds" for a measure of work. If we lift a 50 pound weight 2 feet, we say that we did 100 foot-pounds of work.

4. "Mechanical advantage" is another term used in doing work. If we move a weight 6 feet and it rises 2 feet we say the mechanical advantage is 3.
5. *Science News* reported that some of the oldest tools manufactured by our ancestors, dated 2 million to 2.5 million years ago, were discovered in a rain forest in Zaire.

F. Thought Questions for Class Discussions:

1. Do you know of any machine that uses more than one simple machine?
2. Is a bicycle a simple machine?
3. Is our body made up of simple machines?

G. Related Ideas for Further Inquiry:

1. Make a survey of simple machines found in and around the home.
2. Study the simple machines we use to extract materials from the earth.
3. Study Activity II-E-2, "How do levers make work easier?"
4. Study Activity II-E-3, "How do inclined planes help us do work?"
5. Study Activity II-E-5, "How does the wheel and axle help us do work?"
6. Study Activity II-E-4, "How do pulleys help us in lifting weights?"

H. Vocabulary Builders—Spelling Words:

1) **pulley** 2) **lever** 3) **inclined plane** 4) **work**
5) **wheel and axle** 6) **gear** 7) **wedge** 8) **force**

I. Thought for Today:

"If you are going to let your mind wander, you might just as well go with it."

Wheelbarrow

Hand eggbeater

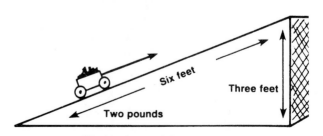

What is the mechanical advantage of this setup?

Activity

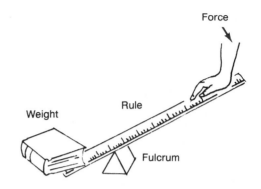

A. Problem: *How Do Levers Make Work Easier?*

B. Materials Needed:

1. Heavy book
2. Yardstick or meterstick
3. Hammer
4. Nutcracker
5. Chart showing 1st, 2nd, and 3rd class levers
6. Several walnuts, unshelled
7. Scissors
8. Tweezers

C. Procedure:

1. Explain that every lever has three important elements: the fulcrum, the force, and the weight or resistance.
2. Allow students to try to crack a walnut by hand.
3. Have students discuss pulling a nail out of a piece of wood by using his/her fingers.
4. Discuss lifting heavy objects without the use of levers or other simple machines.
5. Have students discuss performing these tasks with the use of simple machines.
6. Have students identify the class of lever from the drawings shown.

D. Result:

Students will learn about levers and be able to identify the class of each lever.

E. Basic Facts and Supplemental Information:

1. The force required can be determined by multiplying the weight and the distance to the fulcrum and dividing by the distance the force is applied from the fulcrum. The lever is a form of a simple machine. Several tools use compound levers. (Nutcrackers and scissors are good examples.)

2. The simplest formula is:

   $F \times D_1 = W \times D_2$

   F = Force

   D_1 = Distance of force to fulcrum

   W = Weight (Resistance)

   D_2 = Distance of weight to fulcrum

   or $F = \dfrac{W \times D_2}{D_1}$

3. The force and weight could be in pounds and the distance in feet, or in the metric system, force and weight are in kilograms and distance in meters.

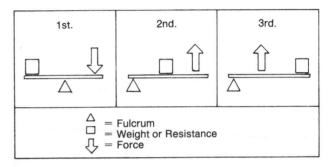

= Fulcrum
= Weight or Resistance
= Force

Classes of levers

F. Thought Questions for Class Discussions:

1. How can a seesaw or teeter-totter be adjusted to accommodate children of different weights?
2. What class of levers are teeter-totters, wheelbarrows, and hammers?
3. What levers can you name that you have in your home?

G. Related Ideas for Further Inquiry:

1. Classify the following objects as to their class of lever:
   a. automobile jack   e. tongs
   b. bottle opener   f. knife
   c. shovel   g. tweezers
   d. pliers   h. can opener
2. Study the human body for different classes of levers. (We have all three types of levers in our arms and legs.)
3. Study all Activities in this Section.

H. Vocabulary Builders—Spelling Words:

1) **force**   2) **weight**   3) **heavy**   4) **fulcrum**
5) **resistance**   6) **distance**   7) **teeter-totter**
8) **scissors**   9) **levers**   10) **balance**

I. Thought for Today:

"Some teenagers are so delinquent that they could go to reform school on a scholarship."

Activity

A. Problem: *How Do Inclined Planes Help Us Do Work?*

B. Materials Needed:

1. Boards of different lengths (See sketches for examples.)
2. Toy wagon—(Roller skates may be used.)
3. Spring scale
4. Cord
5. Books or weights

C. Procedure:

1. Put books or weights in the toy wagon and secure with cord.
2. Weigh the wagon and books. The weight represents the amount of force required to lift wagon and books. (See Figure 1.)
3. Make an inclined plane with the shortest board lengths approximately as shown in drawing.
4. Pull wagon up incline as shown in Figure 2 checking spring scale for reading (force).
5. Record this reading.
6. Use another (longer) inclined plane (Figure 3).
7. Pull loaded wagon up inclined plane checking scale for reading.
8. Check and record data (force).
9. Use a third inclined plane using longest board (Figure 4).
10. Pull loaded wagon up inclined plane checking force required.
11. Record this.
12. Compare results.

D. Result:

Using the same height, 12 inches, the student will find that the sharper the incline, the greater the amount of force will be required to pull the wagon. Or, stating it in another way, as the distance is increased, less force is required to pull the wagon up the same height.

E. Basic Facts and Supplemental Information:

1. While the inclined plane makes it possible to move heavier objects, they must be moved over a longer distance. The total amount of force required to move the object up 12″ therefore, is equal under all circumstances if friction is disregarded. The advantage with the inclined plane is that the force required is less than the weight. In other words the force required at any point to move the weight is less than the weight itself.

Fig. 1

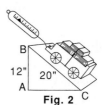

B
12″ 20″
A
Fig. 2 C

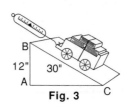

B
12″ 30″
A
Fig. 3 C

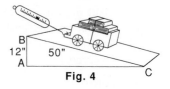

B
12″ 50″
A
Fig. 4 C

2. The mechanical advantage can be computed by simply dividing the length of the inclined plane by the height.

F. Thought Questions for Class Discussions:

1. What would happen if we used a sliding object instead of a wagon?
2. What are some ways in which we can lessen friction in working on an inclined plane?
3. Is it easier to walk straight up a steep hill or circle around it as you go upward?
4. Is the wedge an inclined plane?

G. Related Ideas for Further Inquiry:

1. Repeat the experiment but use a roller skate or skateboard.
2. Study Activity II-E-1, "How do simple machines help us?"
3. Study Activity II-E-6, "How do gears help us?"
4. Study Activity II-F-1, "What makes objects move?"
5. Study Activity II-F-3, "What is inertia? momentum?"
6. Study Activity II-F-5, "What is sliding friction? rolling friction?"

H. Vocabulary Builders—Spelling Words:

1) **inclined plane**   2) **force**   3) **resistance**
4) **scale**   5) **mechanical advantage**   6) **friction**

I. Thought for Today:

"A bargain is something that costs less than the last time you didn't need it either."

Activity

A. Problem: *How Do Pulleys Help Us in Lifting Weights?*

B. Materials Needed:
1. Two single-wheel pulleys (Spools could be used.)
2. Two double-wheel pulleys (Spools could be used.)
3. Small bucket or weight
4. Light rope (or cord)
5. Spring scale
6. Supporting device

C. Procedure:
1. Attach one end of rope to bucket or weight.
2. Attach spring scale to other end of rope.
3. Lift the bucket by the scale and record the weight.
4. Construct apparatus as shown in Figure 1.
5. Lift the weight off the floor or desk and record the reading on the spring scale.
6. Construct the apparatus as shown in Figure 2.
7. Lift the weight off the floor or desk and record the reading on the spring scale.
8. Construct the apparatus as shown in Figure 3.
9. Lift the weight off the floor or desk and record the reading on the spring scale.
10. Construct the apparatus as shown in Figure 4.
11. Lift the weight off the floor or desk and record the reading on the spring scale.

D. Results:
1. In the first reading, the actual weight is determined.
2. The weight recorded in Figure 1 will be the same as its actual weight if friction is disregarded. This merely changes the direction of pull.
3. The reading on the scale in Figure 2 will be half of the original weight if friction is disregarded.
4. The reading on the scale in Figure 3 will also be halved when friction is disregarded.

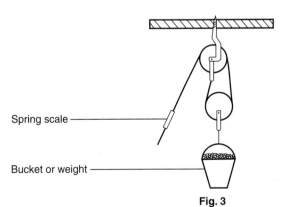

Fig. 1

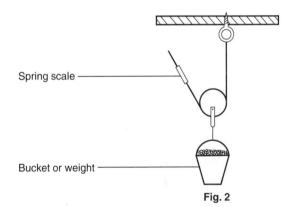

Fig. 2

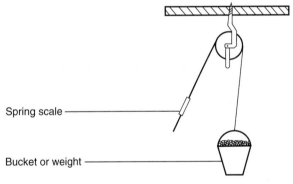

Fig. 3

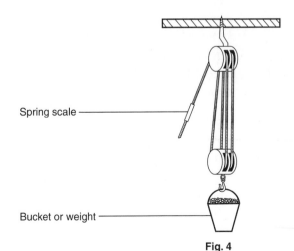

Fig. 4

5. The reading on the scale in Figure 4 will be one-fourth of the original weight if friction is disregarded.

6. The mechanical advantage of a pulley system can be determined by the number of ropes that support the weight. In Figure 1 there is one supporting rope; consequently there is no mechanical advantage. In Figure 2 there are two ropes supporting the weight; consequently the mechanical advantage is two, which means the pull or force to lift the weight is one-half the weight. In Figure 3 there are also two supporting ropes; the mechanical advantage is the same as in Figure 2 but the direction of force has changed. In Figure 4 there are four supporting ropes; consequently, the mechanical advantage is four and the pull or force required to lift the weight is one-fourth. The force or pull is always the inverse of the number of supporting ropes (the mechanical advantage) when friction is neglected. The effects of friction will require some additional force or pull.

E. Basic Facts and Supplemental Information:

1. Fixed pulleys and movable pulleys help us in many ways.

2. The more pulley wheels there are, the easier it is to lift weights.

3. This principle is used for some hoists in garages to lift heavy automobiles.

4. Pulleys are used for lifting and moving freight on docks and on shipboard.

5. Pulleys are used in cranes and derricks to lift heavy loads such as steel sheets or coils.

6. The principles of pulley use are the same whether they are small ones operated by string or rope or large ones which use chains and powerful motors.

F. Thought Questions for Class Discussions:

1. What would be the mechanical advantage of a pulley system that had three supporting ropes?

2. Neglecting friction, how many supporting ropes would be needed in a pulley system to lift a 500-pound weight with a 100-pound pull?

3. How could you test the amount of friction in any pulley system?

G. Related Ideas for Further Inquiry:

1. Have two adults each hold a broomstick horizontally. Have a student wrap a rope around the broomsticks four or five times, leaving one end loose and tying the other end to one broomstick. When the adults try to pull apart, the student should pull on the loose end and will be

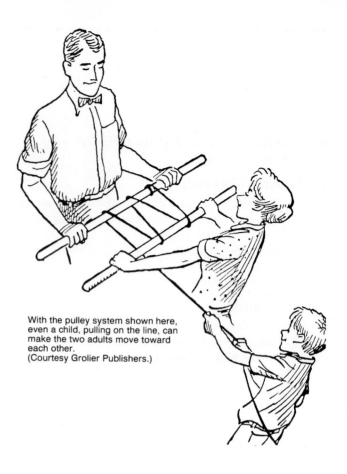

With the pulley system shown here, even a child, pulling on the line, can make the two adults move toward each other.
(Courtesy Grolier Publishers.)

able to force the adults together. If the adults are very strong or the student a little weak, add more loops around the broomsticks.

2. Study Activity II-E-5 "How does the wheel and axle help us do work?"

3. Study Activity II-E-2, "How do levers make work easier?"

4. Study Activity II-E-3, "How do inclined planes help us do work?"

5. Study Activity II-E-6, "How do gears help us?"

6. Study Activity II-F-1, "What makes objects move?"

7. Study Activity II-F-6, "How does friction help us? hurt us?"

H. Vocabulary Builders—Spelling Words:

1) **pulley**   2) **scale**   3) **mechanical**   4) **movable**
5) **advantage**   6) **weight**   7) **toward**   8) **away**
9) **rope**   10) **wheels**   11) **force**   12) **reading**

I. Thought for Today:

"What we know is very little; what we don't know is immense."

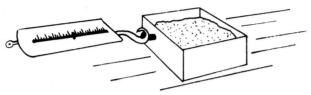

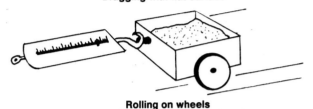

Dragging with flat surface

Rolling on wheels

A. Problem: *How Does the Wheel and Axle Help Us Do Work?*

B. Materials Needed:

1. Two boxes of the same size, one with wheels and axle and one without
2. Some heavy materials such as sand, books, etc.
3. Spring scale

C. Procedure:

1. Place the sand or heavy material in the box without wheels.
2. Attach the scale to one end of the box.
3. Holding the other end of the scale, drag the box a distance of about one yard.
4. Make a note of the number of ounces or pounds indicated by the pointer on the spring scale while the dragging was in progress.
5. Transfer the load to the box with wheels.
6. Move the second box the same distance and speed as the first one.
7. Record the reading on the scale as the box is moving.

D. Result:

The differences in readings will show differences in forces used in pulling two boxes. The amount of energy saved can be computed by comparing the forces. Each force is determined by the formula:

Force = Weight × Distance.

Forces are usually reported in "foot-pounds" or "gram-centimeters."

E. Basic Facts and Supplemental Information:

1. Wheels and axles help objects move easily.
2. More energy was needed to drag the box without wheels than the box with wheels because the entire surface of the base of the box without wheels had to overcome friction, whereas the wheels of the other box reduced the contact area and consequently had less friction to overcome. The wheel and the axle is very important in reducing friction. In fact, it is considered to be among our most important inventions. The applications in automobiles, railroad cars, planes, buses, bicycles, etc., are evident everywhere.
3. Scientists use the term "mechanical advantage" to determine the effectiveness of the "wheel and axle."
4. The mechanical advantage of a wheel and axle is the diameter of the wheel divided by the diameter of the axle. (Corresponding radii or circumferences may be used.)

F. Thought Questions for Class Discussions:

1. Is a ball bearing device an example of using a wheel and axle?
2. Why is grease and/or oil important to use in the wheel and axle?
3. Cite some examples where the wheel and axle is used in your home.
4. Does the handle on a water well use a wheel and axle?

G. Related Ideas for Further Inquiry:

1. Find out how many wheels and axles there are on a bicycle.
2. Can you find any wheels and axles in your classroom?
3. Make a spoolmobile by notching an empty spool of thread and inserting a rubber band through the center securing it with a small stick on one end and a long projecting stick on the other end.
4. Discuss the wheel and axles used on roller skates, skateboards, roller blades, and bicycles.
5. Study Activity II-E-1, "How do simple machines help us?"
6. Study Activity II-F-1, "What makes objects move?"
7. Study Activity II-F-6, "How does friction help us? hurt us?"

H. Vocabulary Builders—Spelling Words:

1) **wheel and axle**   2) **friction**   3) **ounces**
4) **scale**   5) **overcome**   6) **drag**   7) **distance**

I. Thought for Today:

"Human history becomes more and more a race between education and catastrophe."—H. G. Wells

Activity

A. Problem: *How Do Gears Help Us?*

B. Materials Needed:
1. Eggbeater
2. Old clocks and/or watches
3. Pictures of different kinds and sizes of gears

C. Procedure:
1. Show the different kinds of gears:
   a. Pair of same-sized gears when meshed would change directions.
   b. Two gears of different sizes when meshed would change direction and speed.
   c. Gears that can change direction by 90° are called beveled gears.
2. If available, old large clocks have many gears inside that can show how gears mesh or interlock. (Be sure the clock is "run down" as some gears will turn rapidly when the spring is wound up and then released suddenly.)
3. Draw on the chalkboard sketches of three meshing flat gears and have students discuss direction of turning of each.
4. Draw on the chalkboard sketches of different-sized gears with any set number of teeth and have students discuss direction and speed of each, establishing one as the "power gear."

D. Results:
1. Students will learn there are many uses for gears.
2. Students will learn that gears can change speed and/or direction of prior movement.

E. Basic Facts and Supplemental Information:
1. A gear is a toothed wheel.
2. Gears can change direction, speed, and/or power.
3. Most bicycles have multi-gear systems for changing speed so that hill climbing is easier.
4. Gears are frequently used with other simple machines such as pulleys, levers, inclined planes, etc. These are called "compound machines."

F. Thought Questions for Class Discussions:
1. How would a gear perform if a prior gear were smaller?
2. How would a gear perform if a prior gear were larger?
3. If you had five meshed gears in a line, all of the same size, would all odd ones move in the same direction? Same speed?
4. Could you create a "gear system" that could change speed but not direction?

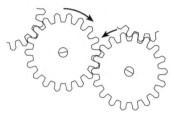

Change of direction

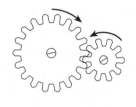

Change of speed and direction

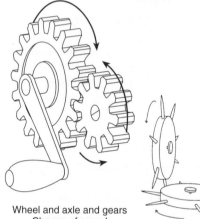

Wheel and axle and gears
Change of speed and direction

Change of direction

G. Related Ideas for Further Inquiry:
1. Sometimes flanged bottle caps can be used to simulate gears by meshing them side by side.
2. A good activity to show how gears can change direction by 90° is to cut two rings out of a potato and insert six to ten toothpicks in each, and arrange them as shown in bottom right drawing.
3. Study Activity II-E-1, "How do simple machines help us?"
4. Study Activity II-E-5, "How do the wheel and axle help us do work?"
5. Study Activity II-F-1, "What makes objects move?"
6. Study Activity II-F-10, "What are Newton's Laws of Motion?"

H. Vocabulary Builders—Spelling Words:
1) **gear** 2) **ratio** 3) **speed** 4) **direction**
5) **meshed** 6) **turning** 7) **power** 8) **driving**

I. Thought for Today:
"Perseverance is not a long race; it is many short races one after another."—Walter Elliott

SECTION F: MOVEMENT AND RESISTANCE

Activity

A. Problem: *What Makes Objects Move?*

B. Materials Needed:

Pictures, models, examples of:

1. Wind
2. Water
3. Machines
4. Electricity (batteries)
5. Heat (sun)
6. Light (sun or lamp)
7. Gravity (in action)
8. Magnets
9. Chalkboard
10. Chalk

C. Procedure:

1. Have the class make a list of ten different objects that move.
2. Put this list on the chalkboard.
3. Go over this list and ask them what makes each of these move.
4. Discuss energy as a force that makes objects move. (A force is a push or a pull.)
5. Show the class the pictures or models that you have collected.
6. Discuss the source of energy that made these objects move.
7. Discuss the forms of energy that parents use in their work.
8. List appliances in homes and discuss how their movements help us.

D. Results:

1. Many things move.
2. There is a reason that things move.
3. The reason is that a force must be applied to an object, otherwise no movement occurs.
4. Students will learn a little about Newton's Laws of Motion.

E. Basic Facts and Supplemental Information:

1. All movements require a force.
2. The movement depends on the mass of the object and the acceleration it has whether this is zero or anything faster.

3. Just as force or energy is needed to start an object in motion, so is force or energy required to stop an object once it is in motion.
4. Newton's Laws of Motion pertain to all matter anywhere in the universe.
5. Planets, satellites, spaceships—all move according to Newton's Laws of Motion.

F. Thought Questions for Class Discussions:

1. What slows down moving objects?
2. What makes a doorbell ring?
3. What makes an automobile run?
4. What role does gravity play in the movement of objects?

G. Related Ideas for Further Inquiry:

1. Study Part II, "Energy."
2. Study Section II-E, "Simple Machines."
3. Study Activity II-F-3, "What is inertia? momentum?"
4. Study Activity II-F-8, "Are there forces without movement of objects?"
5. Study Activity II-F-10, "What are Newton's Laws of Motion?"

H. Vocabulary Builders—Spelling Words:

1) **push**   2) **pull**   3) **force**   4) **resistance**
5) **gravity**   6) **Newton**   7) **energy**   8) **movement**

I. Thought for Today:

"If I had a child who wanted to be a teacher, I would wish him/her Godspeed as if he/she were going to war. For, indeed, the war against prejudice, greed, and ignorance is eternal, and those who dedicate themselves to it give their lives."

Activity

A. Problem: *What Prevents, Slows, or Stops Movements?*

B. Materials Needed:

1. Toy airplane
2. Bicycle (toy or real)
3. Heavy object

C. Procedure:

1. Discuss and demonstrate the forces that affect bicycle riding.
   a. energy
   b. resistance
   c. friction
2. Discuss and demonstrate the forces that affect trying to lift a heavy object.
   a. muscle power
   b. weight of object
   c. gravity
3. Discuss and demonstrate the forces that affect a plane in flight.
   a. gravity
   b. thrust of propeller
   c. lift of wings
   d. drag: air resistance, friction

Weight (gravity)

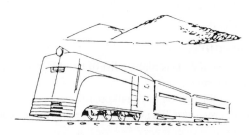

Air resistance and gravity

D. Result:

There are many forces that are continually acting on all objects; some to keep them moving, some to slow them down, some to keep them at rest.

E. Basic Facts and Supplemental Information:

1. Friction slows down moving objects.
2. Gravity affects things trying to rise.
3. Other forces can act on objects to slow them down or speed them up (wind, friction, etc.).

F. Thought Questions for Class Discussions:

1. Why do we need brakes on automobiles and bicycles?
2. What are some ways that we overcome resistance?
3. What items play a role in resistance?

G. Related Ideas for Further Inquiry:

1. Discuss the feasibility of a "perpetual motion machine."
2. Discuss why we use oil in machines.
3. Discuss the advantage of using ball bearings.
4. Study Section II-E, "Simple Machines."
5. Study Activity II-F-3, "What is inertia? momentum?"

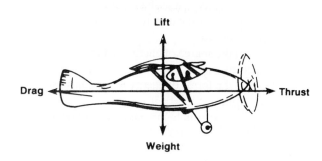

6. Study Activity II-F-4, "How do inertia and momentum affect us?"
7. Study Activity II-F-8, "Are there forces without movement of objects?"

H. Vocabulary Builders—Spelling Words:

1) **resistance**   2) **drag**   3) **thrust**   4) **brakes**
5) **lift**   6) **gravity**   7) **weight**   8) **forces**

I. Thought for Today:

"If you don't stand for something, you will fall for anything."

Activity

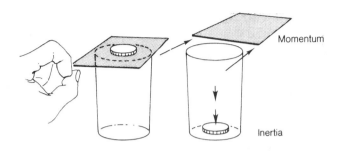

Momentum

Inertia

A. Problem: *What Is Inertia? Momentum?*

B. Materials Needed:
1. Water glass
2. Card, approximately 4″ × 4″
3. Coin

C. Procedure:
1. Explain inertia. (A body in motion tends to stay in motion or a body at rest tends to stay at rest unless acted on by some outside force.)
2. Explain momentum. (The force with which a body moves.)
3. Place card on glass.
4. Place coin in the middle of card.
5. Give the card a quick flip as shown in drawing.

D. Results:
1. The card will be knocked off the glass.
2. The coin will fall into the glass.

E. Basic Facts and Supplemental Information:
1. The force on the card produced enough momentum to knock the card off the glass.
2. The inertia of the coin (the tendency to stay at rest) kept the coin from moving sideways and when it lost its support, gravity caused it to fall into the glass.
3. Momentum is equal to the mass times the velocity.
4. The greater the mass or the greater the speed, the greater will be the momentum of a moving object. The greater the momentum, the greater will be the force required to stop the object.

F. Thought Questions for Class Discussions:
1. When a person first gets on a bicycle does he/she have any inertia? momentum?
2. When he/she is underway riding the bicycle does he/she have any inertia? momentum?
3. When brakes are applied to an automobile in motion, why doesn't it stop instantly?
4. Do spaceships have inertia? momentum?
5. Does our planet have inertia? momentum?

G. Related Ideas for Further Inquiry:
1. Fill the glass half-full of water. Place the card on top of the glass. Cut the cardboard cylinder of a toilet paper core in half and place one-half of it in an upright position on top of the card. Place a hard-boiled egg on top of the cylinder. Strike the card with a quick blow—and duck.
2. Have student ride a bicycle. Discuss the inertia and momentum involved.
3. Discuss sports activities in which inertia and momentum play a part such as:
   a. baseball—sliding into home plate
   b. basketball—ball in motion
   c. football—tackling a ball-carrier
   d. archery—an arrow in a bow
4. Study Activity II-F-1, "What makes objects move?"
5. Study Activity II-F-4, "How do inertia and momentum affect us?"
6. Study Activity II-F-2, "What prevents, slows, or stops movements?"
7. Study Activity II-F-8, "Are there forces without movement of objects?"
8. Study Activity II-F-10, "What are Newton's Laws of Motion?"

H. Vocabulary Builders—Spelling Words:
1) **inertia** 2) **momentum** 3) **body** 4) **rest**
5) **force** 6) **coin** 7) **card** 8) **flip** 9) **glass**

I. Thought for Today:
"The teacher opens the door—you enter by yourself."

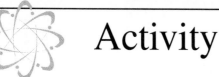

A. Problem: *How 'Do Inertia and Momentum Affect Us'?*

B. Materials Needed:

Pictures of students involved in many recreational activities such as:

1. Baseball
2. Basketball
3. Tennis
4. Volleyball
5. Swimming
6. Skating
7. Running
8. Dancing
9. Gymnastics
10. Badminton, etc.

C. Procedure:

1. Have students make a list of all the recreational activities in which they are, or have been, involved.
2. Cite how inertia and momentum are involved in each activity.
3. As an example—baseball
   a. *inertia:*
      1) sitting on the bench
      2) the batter waiting for the pitch
      3) the first baseman waiting for the batter to hit
      4) a runner waiting for the pitcher to pitch or the batter to hit
   b. *momentum:*
      1) pitcher pitching
      2) runner running
      3) outfielder making a catch
      4) catcher trying to throw a base runner out
      5) umpire signaling a strike
4. Show pictures showing the various activities that can be discussed in a similar fashion.

D. Results:

1. Students will learn that both inertia and momentum are involved in all activities.
2. Students will realize that inertia and momentum are not just scientific terms but a part of all movements.

E. Basic Facts and Supplemental Information:

1. Every movement we make involves inertia and momentum.
2. If a person is motionless, he/she has inertia but no momentum. His/her body tends to stay at rest.

3. Life is full of problems involving inertia and momentum:
   a. braking of automobiles and bicycles—even skateboards
   b. starting to move objects such as elevators or space shuttles
   c. drilling for oil
   d. baking a cake

F. Thought Questions for Class Discussions:

1. How are inertia and momentum affected by friction?
2. What role does gravity play with people's movements?
3. Is heat or light involved with inertia and/or momentum?

G. Related Topics and Activities:

1. Study Activity II-F-1, "What makes objects move?"
2. Study Activity II-F-2, "What prevents, slows, or stops movements?"
3. Study Activity II-F-5, "What is sliding friction? rolling friction?"
4. Study also Section VII-D, "Gravity."

H. Vocabulary Builders—Spelling Words:

1) **inertia**   2) **momentum**)   3) **force**   4) **energy**
5) **initial**   6) **running**   7) **stopping**
Also "recreational items" listed in "Materials Needed"

I. Thought for Today:

"Counting time is not so important as making time count."

Activity

A. Problem: *What Is Sliding Friction? Rolling Friction?*

B. Materials Needed:
1. Sandpaper
2. Matches
3. Two books for support
4. Toy car
5. Flat board
6. Soap or wax
7. Small wood block (same size as toy car)
8. Two wooden blocks (3″ × 4″)

C. Procedure:
1. Hold hands in front of you, palms facing each other—rub hands together.
2. Carefully strike a match.
3. Rub a piece of sandpaper on a block of wood.
4. Rub two blocks of wood together.
5. Rub surfaces of blocks with soap or wax, and repeat above operation.
6. Position a flat board so that one end is higher than the other. (See top drawing.)
7. Place a wooden block about the same size and weight as the car on the top of the flat, inclined board.
8. Place a toy car on the higher end and release the car. (See bottom drawing.)

D. Results:
1. Your hands will become warm.
2. The match will ignite.
3. The blocks will require more force without the use of soap or wax.
4. The block will not slide on the flat board.
5. The car will roll freely.

E. Basic Facts and Supplemental Information:
1. Friction produces heat and causes wear.
2. Lubrication reduces friction, saves wear.
3. Rolling friction is less than sliding friction because there is less surface area contact.
4. Ball bearings and roller bearings are examples of using rolling objects to reduce friction.
5. Rolling friction is present with ball bearings, roller bearings, or rotating wheels.

F. Thought Questions for Class Discussions:
1. What are some other experiments you can devise to compare rolling friction to sliding friction?
2. Why does lubrication reduce friction?

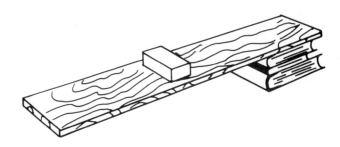

Sliding friction

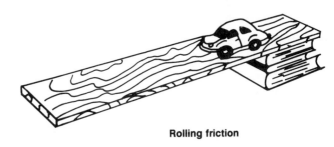

Rolling friction

3. Can water be used as a lubricant?
4. How is friction lessened in engines?
5. Do ships have to overcome friction?

G. Related Ideas for Further Inquiry:
1. Study a roller skate, skateboard, or roller blade and note how it meets with less friction because of the wheels.
2. Repeat experiment with single block of wood, but use a lubricating oil on its base.
3. Increase the angle of the board. Discuss how this affects friction on the blocks of wood and car.
4. Can you find ways that friction helps us?
5. Study Activity II-F-1, "What makes objects move?"
6. Study Activity II-F-2, "What prevents, slows, or stops movements?"
7. Study Activity II-F-3, "What is inertia? momentum?"
8. Study Activity II-F-4, "How do inertia and momentum affect us?"

H. Vocabulary Builders—Spelling Words:
1) **friction**   2) **block**   3) **lubrication**   4) **rolling**
5) **wooden**   6) **board**   7) **incline**   8) **wax**

I. Thought for Today:
"Science solves everything. When they found out they couldn't open windows on railroad cars, they air-conditioned the whole train."

Activity

A. Problem: *How Does Friction Help Us?*
Hurt Us?

B. Materials Needed:
1. Two flat boards for use as testing ramps
2. Items to test:
   a. two small boxes of paper clips
   b. two flat rocks (same size and shape)
   c. two wooden blocks (same size and shape)
   d. two rubber erasers (same size and shape)
   e. two ice cubes
3. Lubricating oil (any kind)

C. Procedure:
1. Apply lubricating oil to the surface of one of the boards.
2. Leave the second board as is.
3. Tell the class you are going to test the two flat boards to see which one will hold the test item longer when the flat boards are raised to an equal height.
4. Place the two ramps parallel and close to each other.
5. Place one box of paper clips near the end of each board.
6. Slowly raise the two boards evenly until one box slides down and off the ramp.
7. Repeat the test with the two flat rocks.
8. Repeat the test with the wooden blocks.
9. Repeat the test with the two erasers.
10. Repeat the test with the two ice cubes.
11. If time permits, other tests can be run with different objects on the same board.

D. Results:
1. Different objects have different surfaces, consequently they vary in the amount of friction involved.
2. The smoother the object the greater the friction because there is more surface contact.
3. In all cases the object on the lubricated board will slide off first.

E. Basic Facts and Supplemental Information:
1. Friction plays an important part in the contact of any two objects.
2. Friction is of great concern in the operation of all machines.

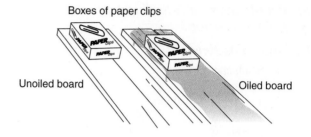

Boxes of paper clips

Unoiled board   Oiled board

3. The rougher the surface, the greater the friction because all surfaces have bumps and hollows and the surfaces of these must be considered in determining the amount of friction involved.
4. Making surfaces smooth and applying lubrication smooths surfaces and reduces friction.
5. Friction is good when it provides traction in walking shoes, automobile and bicycle tires, swimming, turning dials on any piece of equipment, even sitting in chairs.
6. Friction is bad when it wears out clothing, bicycle tires, and moving machine parts.

F. Thought Questions for Class Discussions:
1. Could we live in a frictionless world?
2. What are the advantages of tires on a bicycle?
3. How do highway workers provide or increase friction on icy streets?
4. What role does friction play in sandpapering and in using velcro?

G. Related Ideas for Further Inquiry:
1. Rub your hands lightly together, then increase the pressure. Friction causes the hands to heat.
2. We add oil to automobiles, bicycle wheels, and on all machinery to reduce friction.

H. Vocabulary Builders—Spelling Words:
1) **friction** 2) **oil** 3) **lubrication** 4) **smooth**
5) **hollow** 6) **bumps** 7) **machinery** 8) **surface**

I. Thought for Today:
"One machine can do the work of fifty ordinary people. No machine can do the work of one thinking person."

Activity

A. Problem: *How Does Friction Vary with Pressure?*

B. Materials Needed:

Yardstick or meterstick

C. Procedure:

1. Have one student spread his/her hands about 20″ apart and then have another student place the yardstick or meterstick on top of the first student's index fingers so that the stick is as balanced as possible (See drawing.)
2. Estimate at what point which end of the stick will fall off the student's fingers if he/she moves both hands together slowly at exactly the same rate of speed for each hand.
3. After the estimate is made, have the student move his/her hands together very slowly.
4. Remove the stick from the student's fingers.
5. Discuss what happened.
6. Have another student place his/her fingers several inches apart in a horizontal position and have another student place the yardstick or meterstick on these two fingers.
7. Again guess what will happen if the student slowly moves his/her fingers apart.
8. After the guesses have been made, have the student holding the stick slowly move his/her fingers apart.

D. Results:

1. When the fingers are moved toward the center, the stick will be continually balanced and the fingers will meet in the center without the stick falling in either direction.
2. When the fingers are moved outward, the fingers will both reach the ends of the stick without the stick falling in either direction.

E. Basic Facts and Supplemental Information:

The heavier the weight, the greater the friction. The side that is longer (and heavier) will remain stationary until the other side becomes heavier. Then this (the other side) will move until the first side becomes heavier. This will continue until the index fingers meet in the exact center of the yardstick or meterstick or on its edges when the fingers are moved outward.

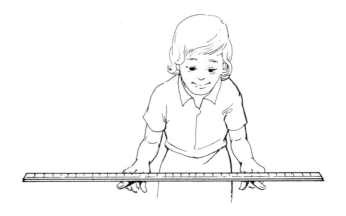

F. Thought Questions for Class Discussions:

1. Why does the stick slide faster over one hand than the other?
2. Can you make the hands not meet in the center of the stick by putting a little oil on one side of the stick or putting a little oil on one side of one finger that comes in contact with the stick?
3. What do you think will happen if you start with three fingers on one side and one finger on the other side?
4. What do you think will happen if you place a little weight in the middle of the stick before you start?

G. Related Ideas for Further Inquiry:

1. Study Activity II-F-1, "What makes objects move?"
2. Study Activity II-F-5, "What is sliding friction? rolling friction?"
3. Study Activity II-F-6, "How does friction help us? hurt us?"
4. Study Activity II-F-8, "Are there forces without movement of objects?"
5. Study Activity II-F-10, "What are Newton's Laws of Motion?"

H. Vocabulary Builders—Spelling Words:

1) **meterstick** 2) **friction** 3) **pressure**
4) **fingers** 5) **stationary** 6) **apart** 7) **together**
8) **balanced** 9) **sliding** 10) **yardstick**

I. Thought for Today:

"The recognition of ignorance is the first spark of enlightenment."

A. Problem: *Are There Forces Without Movement of Objects?*

B. Materials Needed:
1. Book
2. Desk

C. Procedure One:
1. With arms at chest level, have each student hook his/her index fingers. (See drawing.)
2. Have each one try to pull his/her arms apart while still keeping their fingers hooked.

Procedure Two:
1. Have each student hook an index finger with another student.
2. Have them try to keep their fingers hooked while gradually applying force toward themselves but keeping hooked fingers from moving.

Procedure Three:
1. Have a student sit on a desk for a moment.
2. Have the student get off the desk.
3. Place a book on the desk.
4. Remove the book.
5. Ask class what is similar in these actions.
6. Explain force (pushing or pulling on an object).
7. Explain that if forces are equal, there is no movement.

D. Results:
1. In Procedure One, no movement resulted even though forces were applied.
2. In Procedure Two, no movement resulted even though forces were applied.
3. In Procedure Three, there was no apparent movement of the person sitting on the desk or the book lying on the desk even though there were forces acting in both cases.

E. Basic Facts and Supplemental Information:

In Procedure Three, when a person sits on the desk, he/she is exerting a downward force. The desk reacts by pushing upward with an equal force. The same is true of the book. The book pushes down and the desk pushes up with an equal force. It is difficult to believe that the desk can exert differences of force, but that is exactly what happens or there would be movement somewhere.

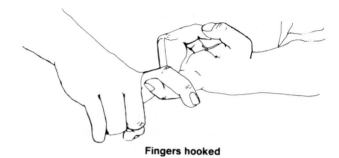

Fingers hooked

F. Thought Questions for Class Discussions:
1. Are there forces acting on a parked car?
2. Why do automobiles and bicycles have brakes?
3. Does it take more force to move a car from a dead stop or to stop it when it is in motion?

G. Related Ideas for Further Inquiry:
1. Have one student place his/her hands on the wall and push. Explain forces.
2. Have one student stand about two feet from the wall, facing it, and have him/her place his/her hands on the wall with outstretched arms. Have three other students line up with each facing the back of the one in front. Have each place arms outstretched on the shoulders of the one in front. Challenge the three to see if they can collapse the arms of the student with the hands on the wall. Discuss with students why they were unsuccessful.
3. Study Activity II-F-1, "What makes objects move?"
4. Study Activity II-F-2, "What prevents, slows, or stops movements?"
5. Study Activity II-F-8, "Are there forces without movement of objects?"
6. Study Activity II-F-10, "What are Newton's Laws of Motion?"

H. Vocabulary Builders—Spelling Words:
1) **stationary** 2) **stationery** 3) **force**
4) **desk** 5) **reaction** 6) **equal** 7) **opposite**

I. Thought for Today:

"Science arises from the discovery of identity amidst diversity."

Activity

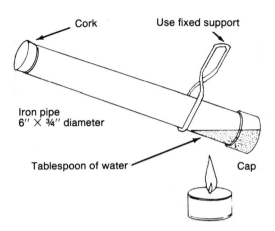

Cork Use fixed support

Iron pipe
6″ × ¾″ diameter

Tablespoon of water Cap

A. Problem: *Does Steam Exert a Tremendous Force?*

B. Materials Needed:
1. Piece of metal pipe six inches long, 1/4″ wide, and threaded on at least one end
2. Cap to fit the threaded end
3. Cork to fit in the other end
4. Bunsen burner or canned heat
5. Tablespoon of water
6. Ring stand and clamps

C. Procedure:
(USE EXTREME CAUTION.)

1. Tighten the cap securely on one end of the pipe.
2. Place a tablespoon of water in the pipe. (See drawing.)
3. Place a cork stopper firmly but not too tightly in the opening of the other end.
4. *Be sure to point the pipe away from people, windows, or other fragile objects. Never hold pipe in hand.*
5. Secure the pipe at an angle to the stand with a clamp.
6. Heat the pipe at the capped end containing the water.
7. Aim corked end of the pipe toward a padded box, safe wall, or outside.

D. Result:
When the pipe has been heated, it will change the water to steam. The steam pressure creates a terrific pressure which forces the stopper out of the "cannon," usually with a loud noise and moderately high velocity.

E. Basic Facts and Supplemental Information:
1. Steam exerts tremendous force.
2. One cannot be too cautious when working with steam.
3. One cubic centimeter of water will convert to 1,500 cubic centimeters of steam. This explains why there is such force behind steam.
4. Old railroad engines were driven by steam because water and wood or coal were cheap and plentiful.
5. Automobiles were tested for steam-driven engines, but that proved to be impractical.
6. We are still trying to develop automobile engines that operate with some source(s) of power that is/are efficient and use a renewable source of energy without being destructive to our environment.

F. Thought Questions for Class Discussions:
1. What can cause the cap on an automobile radiator to blow off?
2. How do they keep a hot water heater from exploding?
3. How is steam harnessed for our benefit?

G. Related Ideas for Further Inquiry:
1. Boil water in a tea kettle without stopping up the spout.
2. Boil water in a pot with a lid on it.
3. An excellent activity to show the force of steam is to make some popcorn. Popcorn is made when the water in corn kernels is heated to steam. It is the steam that explodes the kernels. When water changes to steam it expands greatly and the steam literally bursts the kernels.
4. Study Activity II-F-1, "What makes objects move?"
5. Study Activity II-F-3, "What is inertia? momentum?"
6. Study Activity II-F-4, "How do inertia and momentum affect us?"
7. Study Activity II-F-8, "Are there forces without movement of objects?"
8. Study Activity II-F-11, "How can we make some steam-propelled toys?"

H. Vocabulary Builders—Spelling Words:
1) **threaded** 2) **safety** 3) **precautions** 4) **force**
5) **steam** 6) **cannon** 7) **cork** 8) **careful**

I. Thought for Today:
"The foundation of every nation is the education of its youth."

Activity

A. Problem: *What Are Newton's Laws of Motion?*

B. Materials Needed:
1. Book
2. Marbles
3. Desk

C. Procedure:
1. Discuss how things move.
2. Describe how helpful it would be if we could predict movements.
3. Lay the book on the table.
4. Ask if there are any "forces" acting on it.
5. Push a marble along a table top or the floor.
6. Ask if there are any "forces" acting on it when it is in motion.
7. Push down on the desk.
8. Ask if there are any "forces" acting if there is no movement.
9. Discuss "Newton's Three Laws of Motion." Simplify the laws appropriately for the level of your students. (See Section E below.)

D. Result:
Students will learn that the three Activities portrayed are examples of Newton's Laws of Motion. His Laws are numbered.

E. Basic Facts and Supplemental Information:
1. Sir Isaac Newton (1642–1727) was a physicist who formulated these laws to explain movements of celestial bodies in space as well as movements on Earth.
2. The three laws are:
   a. *First Law of Motion:* A body continues in a state of rest, or in motion at a constant speed in a straight line, except when this state is changed by forces acting upon it.
   b. *Second Law of Motion:* Force is equal to mass multiplied by acceleration. In other words, a given force on a given mass will produce a given acceleration. On twice the mass, it will produce half the acceleration. If the force on a given mass is doubled, the acceleration will double too.
   c. *Third Law of Motion:* To every action, there is an equal and opposite reaction.

F. Thought Questions for Class Discussions:
1. Are there forces acting on everything all the time?
2. Do you know any exceptions to these Laws of Motion?
3. If an arrow is shot in the air, does it conform to the laws of motion?

G. Related Ideas for Further Inquiry:
1. Have a student on skates or a skateboard push against the side of a desk and note results.
2. Drop some nonbreakable objects. Have students explain movement.
3. Have a student ride a bicycle and discuss performance in terms of the Laws of Motion.
4. Study all Activities in this Section.

H. Vocabulary Builders—Spelling Words:
1) **motion** 2) **constant** 3) **speed**
4) **force** 5) **mass** 6) **acceleration**
7) **action** 8) **reaction** 9) **Laws of Motion**
10) **Newton** 11) **inertia** 12) **momentum**

I. Thought for Today:
"One small schoolboy to another: 'It might be unconstitutional but I always pray before a test.' "

Book (at rest)

Marble (in motion)

Action and reaction

Activity

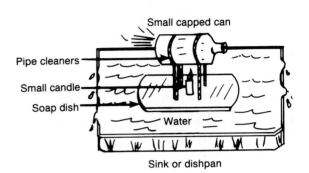

Small capped can
Pipe cleaners
Small candle
Soap dish
Water
Sink or dishpan

Steamboat (Toy One)

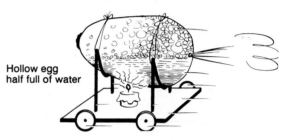

Hollow egg
half full of water

Eggmobile (Toy Two)

A. Problem: *How Can We Make Steam-Propelled Toys?*

B. Materials Needed: (Toy one, see top drawing.)

1. Small can with screw-type lid
2. Soap dish
3. Small candle
4. Pipe cleaners or wires
5. Water
6. Large dishpan or sink
7. Awl
8. Matches

Materials Needed: (Toy two, see bottom drawing.)

1. Hollow eggshell
2. Coat hanger or heavy wire
3. Piece of thin plyboard or heavy cardboard
4. Candle
5. Matches
6. Toy wheels
7. Awl
8. Water
9. Tape (to seal hole in egg)

C. Procedure One:

1. With an awl, punch a small hole near the top edge of the bottom of the can.
2. Place some water in the can. Place lid on can.
3. Mount the can so that it will rest horizontally by twisting the pipe cleaner stems or wires around the can in such a way that they will support the can in the soap dish. (See drawing.)
4. Place this (steam boiler) carefully over a candle in the soap dish boat.
5. Place the soap dish on the water in the dishpan or sink.
6. Light the candle.

Procedure Two:

1. Construct toy as shown in drawing using an awl to make one small hole on each end of the egg, puncturing the yolk and then blowing or using a light stream of water to empty its contents. One hole is then sealed with any strong binding tape.
2. Fill the eggshell half-full of water.
3. Place the candle under the supported eggshell.
4. Place the apparatus in an open space.
5. Light the candle.

D. Results:

1. As the candle heats the water in the can it will change the water to steam. The steam squirts out the hole in the can which causes the whole float to move in the opposite direction.
2. The toy eggmobile will scoot around.

E. Basic Facts and Supplemental Information:

The reason the "steamboat" moves forward is because the steam shooting out from the can creates a propulsion force which causes the steamboat to move in the opposite direction. This is the same principle that permits a rocket to lift off from a launching pad. The fuel in the rocket pushes down on the pad with force which propels the rocket up into space.

F. Thought Questions for Class Discussions:

1. What are the different ways people use to transport themselves?
2. In our culture what are the different kinds of propellant systems used in transportation?
3. Do people use the same systems for propelling themselves on land, on water, and in the air?

G. Related Ideas for Further Inquiry:

1. Study Newton's Third Law of Motion: "For every action there is an equal and opposite reaction."
2. Study where steam is used in our society.
3. Study Activity II-F-1, "What makes objects move?"
4. Study Activity II-F-9, "Does steam exert a tremendous force?"
5. Study Activity II-F-10, "What are Newton's Laws of Motion?"

H. Vocabulary Builders—Spelling Words:

1) **steam** 2) **force** 3) **action** 4) **reaction**
5) **propulsion** 6) **water** 7) **needle** 8) **eggmobile**

I. Thought for Today:

"We judge ourselves by what we are capable of doing, while others judge us by what we have already done."—Longfellow

Activity

A. Problem: *What Is Electricity?*

B. Materials Needed:

1. Electric light bulb
2. Electric fan
3. Toaster
4. Flashlight
5. Electric toy car
6. Short length of garden hose
7. Small marbles to fit inside

C. Procedure:

1. Turn flashlight and classroom lights on and off.
2. Turn electric fan on and off.
3. Turn electric toaster on and off.
4. Turn electric car on and off.
5. Ask class what makes the light come on, the fan to run, the toaster to heat, the flashlight to shine, and the car to run.
6. Pick up the short length of hose.
7. Fill hose with marbles.
8. Shove marble in one end of the hose to force one marble out the other end.
9. Discuss the structure of the atom. Study Activity I-A-2, "What are atoms? molecules?"
10. Compare the movement of the electrons (flow of electricity) to the flow of marbles in the hose.

D. Results:

1. Electricity will flow through all appliances and toy car.
2. Each marble will move in the hose.

E. Basic Facts and Supplemental Information:

1. Scientists are not positive what electricity is.
2. They assume that it is the flow of electrons from individual atoms along a common carrier (wire as a medium) in one direction just as the marbles moved in the hose.
3. Only the electrons move, not the whole atom.
4. When electricity is flowing, the electrons "jump" from one atom to another. As soon as electrons leave one atom other electrons from other atoms take their place. This is necessary to have a "complete circuit." If the circuit is "broken" no electricity will flow. This can be be compared to marbles flowing around a round hose or hula hoop.
5. The energy of the flowing electrons is electricity.
6. Batteries use chemicals to give electrons their push to make them move.

Light bulb

Toaster

Television

Iron

F. Thought Questions for Class Discussions:

1. What is the difference between alternating current and direct current?
2. What causes a short circuit?
3. What is the difference between a parallel circuit and a series circuit?

G. Related Ideas for Further Inquiry:

1. There are many ways to demonstrate electricity with electric appliances. Motion picture projectors, filmstrip projectors, electronic games, and transcription players are usually available in every school.
2. Study Section I-E, "Static Electricity."
3. Study Activity II-G-2, "How many electrical appliances do we have in our homes?"
4. Study Activity II-G-5, "What is a series circuit?"
5. Study Activity II-G-6, "What is a parallel circuit?"
6. Study Activity II-G-9, "How do batteries work?"

H. Vocabulary Builders—Spelling Words:

1) **current**   2) **electricity**   3) **electrons**   4) **circuit**
5) **hose**   6) **series**   7) **parallel**   8) **flow**

I. Thought for Today:

"Joint bank accounts have proved that most spouses are quick on the draw."

Activity

A. Problem: *How Many Electrical Appliances Do We Have in Our Homes?*

B. Materials Needed:
1. Pictures of the types of electrical appliances found in the home
2. A few small electrical appliances
3. Bulletin board
4. Chalkboard and chalk
5. Display area

C. Procedure:
1. Collect pictures of appliances.
2. Post them on the bulletin board.
3. Display the samples of electrical appliances on your science table, science corner, or any convenient location.
4. On the chalkboard make a list of the electrical appliances that students have in their homes.
5. Discuss the conveniences of each.
6. Discuss what life would be like if we had no electricity.

D. Results:
1. A collection of pictures of electrical appliances found in the home will probably include:
   a. In the home:
   1) electric lights
   2) lamps
   3) washing machine
   4) refrigerator
   5) dryer
   6) can opener
   7) toaster
   8) mixer
   9) waffle iron
   10) electric stove
   11) radio
   12) television
   13) transcription player
   14) computer
   15) typewriter
   16) air conditioner
   17) furnace
   18) clocks
   19) dishwasher
   20) blenders, etc.
   b. In the garage and/or shop:
   1) electric lights
   2) garage door opener
   3) sander

   4) saw
   5) drill
   6) router
   7) paint sprayer
   8) insect sprayer, etc.
2. Students will have a deeper appreciation of electricity.

E. Basic Facts and Supplemental Information:
1. We are very fortunate to have electricity for all our home conveniences.
2. Without electricity we would be living as people did in the "horse and buggy" period.
3. Don't forget, battery-driven appliances are also run by electricity. Many of the students' games and toys are run by batteries.

F. Thought Questions for Class Discussions:
1. Without electricity what would we use for transportation?
2. Without electricity what would we do for communication?
3. Could we live without radios, televisions, CDs, and computers?

G. Related Ideas for Further Inquiry:
1. Study Activity II-G-1, "What is electricity?"
2. Study Activity II-G-3, "How do we use electricity to communicate?"
3. Study Activity II-G-5, "What is a series circuit?"
4. Study other Activities in this Section.

H. Vocabulary Builders—Spelling Words:
Use appliance names listed in "Results."

I. Thought for Today:
"Television hasn't replaced radio half as fast as it has homework."

Activity

A. Problem: *How Do We Use Electricity to Communicate?*

B. Materials Needed:
1. Models or pictures of:
   a. television
   b. radio
   c. transcription player
   d. CD
   e. movie projector
   f. filmstrip projector
   g. opaque projector
   h. newspaper
   i. magazine
   j. overhead projectors
   k. home or office speaker systems
   l. telephone
   m. satellites
   n. computers
   o. traffic signals
   p. cell phones, etc.
2. Models or pictures of nonelectrical means of communication such as:
   a. letters
   b. megaphones
   c. Sign Language
   d. musical instruments
   e. signs
   f. bells
   g. horns
   h. smoke signals
   i. flags
   j. voices, etc.
3. Bulletin board
4. Chalkboard and chalk
5. Display area

C. Procedure:
1. Collect models or pictures of electrical means of communication.
2. Collect models or pictures of non-electrical means of communication.
3. Make displays of these on the bulletin board or other convenient sites.
4. Make a list of other items that fall into this classification.
5. Discuss the uses of each of the items in both areas as it pertains to communication.
6. Discuss what life would be like if we had to rely only on the nonelectrical means of communication.

D. Results:
1. Knowledge of all means of communication will be acquired.
2. Students will better appreciate modern means of communication.

E. Basic Facts and Supplemental Information:
1. We are very fortunate to have electrical means of communication.
2. Without electricity we would have to rely on methods listed in "Materials 2" for communication.

F. Thought Questions for Class Discussions:
1. What problems do deaf and hard-of-hearing people have in communication?
2. Can we trust all communication to be honest? truthful? accurate?
3. Should the government regulate all means of communication?

G. Related Ideas for Further Inquiry:
1. Study Activity II-G-1, "What is electricity?"
2. Study Activity II-G-2, "How many electrical appliances do we have in our homes?"
3. Study Activity II-G-8, "What materials conduct electricity?"
4. Study Activity II-G-11, "How can we make a model telegraph?"
5. Study Activity II-G-I3, "How does an electric doorbell work?"

H. Vocabulary Builders—Spelling Words:
Use the names of the means of communication that are appropriate for your class.

I. Thought for Today:
"Three varied forms of communication are telegraph, telephone, and tell a person."

A. Problem: *How Can We Make a Simple Electric Circuit?*

B. Materials Needed:
1. Flashlight battery
2. Electrical wire, 2′ of #16 or #20
3. 1 ½ volt bulb
4. Stripping pliers

C. Procedure:
1. Strip about two inches of the insulation from the ends of the wire.
2. Lay one stripped end on the bottom of the flashlight battery.
3. Wrap the other end snugly around the flashlight bulb.
4. When ready to test, place the wrapped bulb on the center battery terminal.
5. Test the circuit by noting if the bulb lights when placed on the center terminal of the battery.
6. When the bulb lights remove it from the center terminal.
7. Since there is little voltage, there is no danger in handling the wire, battery, or bulb at any time.

D. Results:
1. The wiring circuit will be completed.
2. The bulb will light.

E. Basic Facts and Supplemental Information:
1. A circuit must be complete in order for electricity to flow. In this case the complete circuit follows:
   a. from the bottom of the battery to
   b. the top of the battery to
   c. the base of the bulb to
   d. the filament in the bulb to
   e. the outside wire to
   f. the base of the battery.
   It doesn't make any more difference where you start in the circuitry than where you start when you draw a circle.
2. Electricity is a flow of electrons.
3. Any "break" in the circuit will stop the flow of electrons.
4. Without a circuit there is no flow of electrons.
5. Without a circuit there is no discharge of the battery.

F. Thought Questions for Class Discussions:
1. What could be the problem if the wiring circuit is complete and the bulb doesn't light?

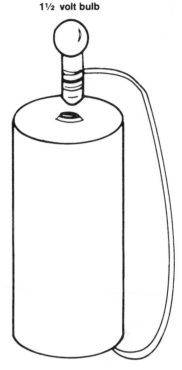

1½ volt bulb

Insulation removed from ends of wire for good contact

Flashlight battery

2. What toys or appliances in your home use dry cell batteries?
3. How strong are the batteries used in regular flashlights? How many are used?

G. Related Ideas for Further Inquiry:
1. Insert a fuse in the circuit.
2. See Section I-E, "Static Electricity."
3. Study Activity II-G-1, "What is electricity?"
4. Study Activity II-G-8, "What materials conduct electricity?"
5. Study Activity II-G-10, "Can we make some simple batteries?"

H. Vocabulary Builders—Spelling Words:
1) **battery** 2) **bulb** 3) **insulation** 4) **electricity**
5) **circuit** 6) **filament** 7) **flashlight** 8) **terminal**

I. Thought for Today:
"Juvenile delinquency is the result of parents trying to train their children without starting at the bottom."

Activity

A. Problem: *What Is a Series Circuit?*

B. Materials Needed:
1. Two dry cell batteries
2. Light switch or a single knife switch
3. Four 3″ lengths of wire (#22 or #24)
4. Two 9″ lengths of wire (#22 or #24)
5. Flashlight bulbs
6. Small bulb bases

C. Procedure:
1. Attach wires as shown in drawing.
   a. Center terminal (positive) on one battery to outside (negative terminal on second battery)
   b. Center terminal (positive) on second battery to first light base
   c. First light base to second light base
   d. Second light base to third light base
   e. Third light base to fourth light base
   f. Fourth light base to knife switch
   g. Knife switch to outside terminal of other battery
2. With light bulbs attached, close knife switch.
3. Observe lights.
4. Open knife switch.
5. Remove one light from base.
6. Close knife switch.
7. Observe remaining lights.

D. Results:
1. If all lights are connected and knife switch is closed, the lights will be on.
2. If one light is removed and knife switch closed, the remaining lights will be out. (Removing the light breaks the circuit and no electricity will flow)

E. Basic Facts and Supplemental Information:
1. In a series circuit, only one wire connects with each light, so if any one light is taken out the circuit is broken and all of the lights will go out.
2. Electricity is a flow of electrons. The atoms don't move, only the electrons do. They act like a bee jumping from flower to flower.
3. Batteries are labeled in volts. Volts are the "pressure" the battery puts out just like the "pressure" in a water hose.

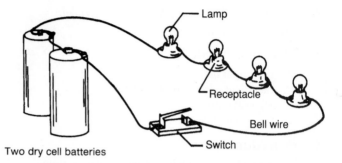

Two dry cell batteries

Lamp

Receptacle

Bell wire

Switch

F. Thought Questions for Class Discussions:
1. If you have one bad bulb, how can you check to determine which one it is?
2. How can you check to determine if one battery is dead?
3. Why do some sets of lights continue to burn even when one bulb is burned out?
4. What is the difference between a series circuit and a parallel circuit?
5. Are your homes wired in series or parallel circuits?
6. What are conductors? insulators?
7. Does your home have fuses or circuit breakers?

G. Related Ideas for Further Inquiry:
1. Double the number of batteries to see how it affects the brilliance of the lights.
2. Check a string of Christmas tree lights. Is the circuit wired in series or parallel?
3. Study Activity II-G-1, "What is electricity?"
4. Study Activity II-G-4, "How can we make a simple electric circuit?"
5. Study Activity II-G-6, "What is a parallel circuit?"
6. Study Activity II-G-7, "How does a fuse work?"
7. Study Activity II-G-9, "How do batteries work?"
8. Study Activity II-G-10, "Can we make some simple batteries?"

H. Vocabulary Builders—Spelling Words:
1) **series** 2) **circuit** 3) **batteries** 4) **knife switch**
5) **parallel** 6) **position** 7) **negative** 8) **terminal**

I. Thought for Today:
"Dancing is wonderful for girls; it's the first way they learn to guess what a boy is going to do before he does it."

Activity

A. Problem: *What Is a Parallel Circuit?*

B. Materials Needed:
1. Two dry cell batteries
2. Knife switch
3. Wire, #22 or #24, six feet long
4. Stripping pliers
5. Four small light bases (sockets)
6. Four small flashlight bulbs

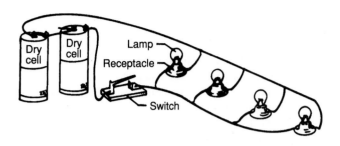

C. Procedure:
(Strip wires at each connection where wires are joined.)

1. Attach wires as shown in drawing.
2. Insert the bulbs in the light bases.
3. Close the knife switch.
4. Observe results.
5. Loosen one bulb at a time, keeping the others tight in their sockets.
6. Record observations.
7. Loosen various combinations of two bulbs, keeping the remaining bulbs tight in the sockets.
8. Record observations.
9. Open knife switch.
10. Hypothesize results.

D. Results:
1. All the bulbs will light when the batteries are connected and the switch is closed.
2. If one or two bulbs are loosened or removed, these light(s) will go out but the remaining one(s) will continue to burn.

E. Basic Facts and Supplemental Information:
Any bulb(s) in a parallel circuit will continue to burn as long as the circuit is complete. When a single bulb is taken out, the electricity will bypass the one bulb and the electricity will continue to operate the other bulbs, because it is able to complete the circuit which is necessary for electricity to flow.

F. Thought Questions for Class Discussions:
1. What makes a complete circuit?
2. What is the difference between wiring bulbs in *parallel* and wiring them in *series*?

3. In the above diagram which bulb(s) will go on and which one(s) will go out if the knife switch is moved to a position on one of the parallel light lines?

G. Related Ideas for Further Inquiry:
1. Change the number of batteries to see if any differences would occur in the brightness of the bulbs.
2. Vary the number of bulbs, connecting them in a similar fashion to determine any changes that occur in the brightness of the bulbs.
3. Connect two lights in parallel and two in series. Observe. Remove one light anywhere and observe results. Repeat with other bulbs.
4. Connect two batteries in series. Connect the other two terminals to a small ball of wool. Observe results. (It will glow!)
5. Study Activity II-G-1, "What is electricity?"
6. Study Activity II-G-4, "How can we make a simple electric circuit?"
7. Study Activity II-G-5, "What is a series circuit?"
8. Study Activity II-G-7, "How does a fuse work?"
9. Study Activity II-G-10, "Can we make some simple batteries?"

H. Vocabulary Builders—Spelling Words:
1) **parallel** 2) **circuit** 3) **removed** 4) **stripping**
5) **pliers** 6) **receptacle** 7) **dry cell** 8) **filament**

I. Thought for Today:
"An expert is one who is just beginning to understand his/her subject."

A. Problem: *How Does a Fuse Work?*

B. Materials Needed:

1. Two dry cells (No. 6 preferably)
2. Four feet of insulated wire
3. Six thin strips of aluminum foil (Cut like fuse in drawing)
4. One piece of wood, 4″ × 4″
5. Knife switch
6. Rubber cement or nail
7. Cork
8. Staples or tape
9. Stripping pliers

C. Procedure:

1. Connect the two dry cells in a series as shown in drawing.
2. Cement or nail cork to block of wood.
3. Staple or tape wires to cork after stripping ends of wire.
4. Connect one wire from cork to dry cell.
5. Connect a second wire from cork to knife switch.
6. Connect last wire from knife switch to terminal on battery.
7. Open knife switch.
8. Put small test strip of foil between the upright stripped ends of the wires on the cork. This will serve as a "fuse."
9. Close knife switch.

D. Result:

When the knife switch is closed, the circuit will be completed and electricity will flow through the fuse. The fuse will not be strong enough to carry the electricity and will overheat, melt, and "blow out" (break).

E. Basic Facts and Supplemental Information:

Care should be taken when touching the wires connected to the dry cell. Sometimes these wires will get hot if the current is left on too long. Fuses and/or circuit breakers are always installed in electric wiring in homes or industry. The fuse or circuit breaker is made so that it will stop the flow of current when the current becomes too strong for the safe operation of lights or appliances. Most homes have circuit breakers rather than fuses. Some appliances still use fuses.

F. Thought Questions for Class Discussions:

1. Why is it necessary to protect wiring systems with fuses or circuit breakers?
2. Should all electric circuits have fuses or circuit breakers?

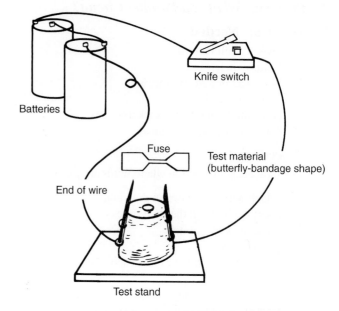

Batteries

Knife switch

Fuse

Test material
(butterfly-bandage shape)

End of wire

Test stand

3. Are fuses used in automobiles?

G. Related Ideas for Further Inquiry:

1. Test other materials to see if they would make good fuses.
2. Find out how a circuit breaker works.
3. Demonstrate a short circuit by bypassing the knife switch.
4. Study Activity II-G-1, "What is electricity?"
5. Study Activity II-G-5, "What is a series circuit?"
6. Study Activity II-G-4, "How can we make a simple electric circuit?"
7. Study Activity II-G-8, "What materials conduct electricity?"
8. Study Activity II-G-9, "How do batteries work?"
9. Study Activity II-G-10, "Can we make some simple batteries?"

H. Vocabulary Builders—Spelling Words:

1) **fuse**   2) **circuit breaker**   3) **insulated**
4) **test**   5) **terminal**   6) **short circuit**
7) **knife switch**   8) **batteries**   9) **cork**

I. Thought for Today:

"Always behave like a duck—keep calm on the surface but paddle like heck underneath."

Activity

A. Problem: *What Materials Conduct Electricity?*

B. Materials Needed:

1. Two 1 1/2 volt batteries
2. Several feet of #20 wire
3. Several pieces of cloth, wood, plastic, rubber, glass, paper, and some nails and pins
4. Flashlight bulb and socket
5. Knife switch
6. Short piece of wire to check test terminals
7. Block of wood
8. Thumbtacks

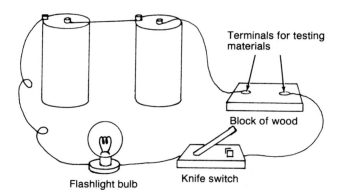

Terminals for testing materials

Block of wood

Flashlight bulb

Knife switch

C. Procedure:

1. Make the following wire connections:
   a. Center (positive) terminal of one battery to outward (negative) terminal of second battery.
   b. Positive cell of second battery to one terminal on block of wood (under tack).
   c. Second terminal on block of wood to open knife switch.
   d. Knife switch to one terminal on socket.
   e. Second terminal on lamp to negative terminal on first battery.
2. Place a piece of wire across the test terminals.
3. Close the knife switch to see if bulb glows and all connections are tight.
4. Open knife switch.
5. Remove test wire.
6. Place a piece of cloth across test terminals.
7. Close knife switch.
8. Record whether bulb glows.
9. Open knife switch.
10. Remove cloth and replace with another test material.
11. Close knife switch.
12. Record whether bulb glows.
13. Repeat procedure for each test material.

D. Results:

1. The bulb will be lighted when a nail or pin is used.
2. The lamp will not glow when paper, wood, glass, plastic, cloth, or rubber are used.

E. Basic Facts and Supplemental Information:

1. Metal (nails and pins) will conduct electric current, whereas nonmetals such as glass, plastic, rubber, wood, paper, and cloth do not conduct electrical current. If you wish, test different kinds

of wires on test terminals; the wires can be left free to touch test materials since there is very little flow of electricity and usually the current cannot even be felt.
2. Materials that allow electricity to flow through them are called conductors. Those that do not are called nonconductors or insulators.
3. More batteries can be added to increase the electrical current.

F. Thought Questions for Class Discussions:

1. Why is it necessary to know which materials are conductors of electricity?
2. How can you determine whether some conductors are more efficient than others?
3. Are human bodies conductors of electricity?

G. Related Ideas for Further Inquiry:

1. With test wires in a glass of distilled water, close knife switch to test.
2. Repeat with tap water, and then with salt water.
3. Test other materials.
4. If you have an "electric identifier" in your classroom, this makes an excellent current tester.
5. Study Activity II-G-1, "What is electricity?"
6. Study Activity II-G-7, "How does a fuse work?"
7. Study Activity II-G-11, "How can we make a model telegraph?"
8. Study Activity II-G-5, "What is a series circuit?"

H. Vocabulary Builders—Spelling Words:

1) **conductor**   2) **insulator**   3) **terminal**
4) **socket**   5) **bulb**   6) **glass**   7) **metals**   8) **rubber**

I. Thought for Today:

"Good teachers cost more. Poor teachers cost most."

Activity

A. Problem: *How Do Batteries Work?*

B. Materials Needed:
1. Salt water (or 1/4 cup of dilute sulphuric acid)
2. Copper strip
3. Zinc strip
4. Electric wires (#22 or #24)
5. Small jar
6. 1 1/2 volt bulb
7. 1 1/2 volt socket
8. Baseboard
9. Screwdriver
10. Two small screws
11. Ice pick or hammer and nail

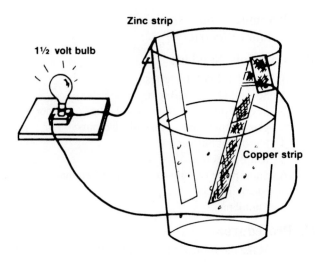

Salt water or weak acid

C. Procedure:
1. Fasten the light bulb socket to the baseboard with screws.
2. Punch a hole in one end of each strip with ice pick or hammer and nail.
3. Fasten an electric wire to the copper strip.
4. Fasten another electric wire to the zinc strip.
5. Pour some salt water or dilute acid solution into the jar.
6. Place the copper and zinc strips into the solution, one on each side.
7. Fasten the other ends of the wires to the socket (or voltmeter).
8. Check all connections to be sure they are tight.
9. Screw the light bulb into the light socket.

D. Result:
The bulb will light or a small electric current will be detected on the voltmeter.

E. Basic Facts and Supplemental Information:
1. This apparatus is called a "voltaic wet cell."
2. Liquids contain ions which are positively or negatively charged. These are called electrolytes.
3. In this case, the zinc strip will dissolve in the battery solution and form zinc ions which are positively charged, and part of the solution becomes negatively charged. The zinc strip becomes negatively charged and the copper strip becomes positively charged.
4. Electrons flow from the zinc to the copper, setting up an electric current.

F. Thought Questions for Class Discussions:
1. Would pure water work as a battery solution?
2. What would happen if both strips of metal were of the same kind?
3. How do dry cells differ from wet cells?

G. Related Topics and Activities:
1. Cut apart an old dry cell and identify its main parts.
2. Study Section I-E, "Static Electricity."
3. Study Activity II-G-1, "What is electricity?"
4. Study Activity II-G-4, "How can we make a simple electric circuit?"
5. Study Activity II-G-5, "What is a series circuit?"
6. Study Activity II-G-8, "What materials conduct electricity?"
7. Study Activity II-G-9, "How do batteries work?"

H. Vocabulary Builders—Spelling Words:
1) **voltaic** 2) **copper** 3) **zinc** 4) **electrons**
5) **bulb** 6) **socket** 7) **electrolytes**

I. Thought for Today:
"Science has produced so many substitutes for what we need that it is hard to remember what we needed in the first place."

Activity

A. Problem: *Can We Make Some Simple Batteries?*

B. Materials Needed:

1. Lemon
2. Potato
3. Zinc strips (2)
4. Copper strips (2)
5. Electric wires (#22 or #24)
6. Voltmeter (current detector)
7. Ice pick or hammer and nail.

C. Procedure: (for Lemon and Potato)

1. Punch a hole in each of the copper and zinc strips.
2. Insert one zinc and one copper strip in the lemon or potato about one-half inch apart.
3. Cut wire in strips with sufficient length to reach the voltmeter.
4. Attach wires to each strip.
5. Connect the wires from the lemon or potato to a voltmeter or current detector.

D. Result:

The voltmeter or current detector will indicate the flow of a small amount of electric current.

E. Basic Facts and Supplemental Information:

These instruments act like the *"voltaic wet cell"* in the previous Activity, II-G-9.

F. Thought Questions for Class Discussions:

1. What do lemons or potatoes have that make this battery function?
2. Would other fruits or vegetables work just as well in this experiment?
3. Can you tell in which direction the electricity flows?

G. Related Ideas for Further Inquiry:

1. With a salt-water-soaked blotter, a penny, and a dime, you can replace the metal strips and an "Eleven Cent Battery" can be made.
2. See Section I-E, "Static Electricity."
3. Study Activity II-G-1, "What is electricity?"
4. Study Activity II-G-4, "How can we make a simple electric circuit?"
5. Study Activity II-G-5, "What is a series circuit?"
6. Study Activity II-G-8, "What materials conduct electricity?"

H. Vocabulary Builders—Spelling Words:

1) **zinc**   2) **copper**   3) **lemon**   4) **potato**
5) **blotter**   6) **current**   7) **voltmeter**
8) **current detector**

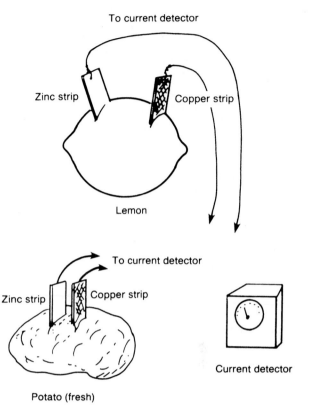

Lemon

Potato (fresh)

Current detector

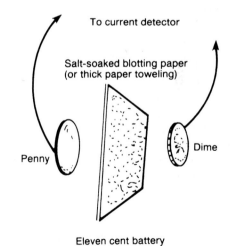

Eleven cent battery

I. Thought for Today:

"The child that strikes the first blow is the one who runs out of ideas first."

A. Problem: *How Can We Make a Model Telegraph*?

B. Materials Needed:
1. Small flat board
2. Small block of wood
3. Thin "T" strip of tin carefully cut from a large "tin" can or piece obtained from a construction supply company.
4. Nails, steel
5. Two thumbtacks or screws
6. Short strip of copper or brass
7. Some light insulated copper wire (#16, #18, or #20)
8. Two dry cell batteries
9. Hammer
10. Tin snips

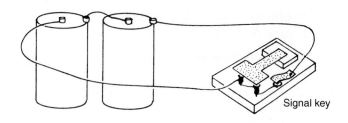

Signal key

C. Procedure:
1. Make the signal key by using a thin metal strip and securing it with a screw. (See drawing.)
2. Place a tack underneath it for the key contact.
3. Nail "T" on block.
4. Drive two nails into the flat board so their heads are just below the tin "T" strip.
5. Nail small wood block on the flat board.
6. Wrap one wire from the dry cell around the two nails and connect to the movable part of the key.
7. Connect the second wire to the stationary part of the key which is the thumbtack or screw.
8. Connect wire from key to batteries as shown in drawing.
9. Press key down and release.

D. Result:
When the key is depressed the current will flow through the strip of metal. It will flow through the wire wrapped around two nails. An electromagnet will be made by the nails and the "T" strip of tin (tin plated iron) being subject to magnetism will click against the nails. As soon as the key is released the electric circuit is broken, the electromagnet is destroyed, and the "T" springs back up.

E. Basic Facts and Supplemental Information:
Several sets of model telegraphs can be hooked together to enable pupils to send and receive coded messages. This device was used as a powerful communication device but is now obsolete. It makes a good toy and demonstrates one application of an electromagnet. To set up two sets, remember that the second key must be depressed to complete the circuit. In the Morse Code, "Dots" (quick depressions) and "Dashes" (long depressions) are used. The Morse Code alphabet and numbers are shown above.

MORSE INTERNATIONAL TELEGRAPH CODE

A	.—	N	—.
B	—...	O	———
C	—.—.	P	.——.
D	—..	Q	——.—
E	.	R	.—.
F	..—.	S	...
G	——.	T	—
H	....	U	..—
I	..	V	...—
J	.———	W	.——
K	—.—	X	—..—
L	.—..	Y	—.——
M	——	Z	——..

Numbers:

1	.————	7	——...
2	..———	8	———..
3	...——	9	————.
4	....—	0	—————
5	.....	Period	.—.—.—
6	—....	Comma	——..——

F. Thought Questions for Class Discussions:
1. What causes the nails to become magnetized?
2. Why does the metal "T" have to be spaced quite close to the nail heads?
3. Will more wraps of wire around the nails enable the set to work better?

G. Related Ideas for Further Inquiry:
1. Make a list of the ways people can communicate on a person-to-person basis. Include electronic and nonelectronic devices such as flags, bells, gestures, etc.
2. Study Activity II-G-3, "How do we use electricity to communicate?"
3. Study Activity II-G-8, "What materials conduct electricity?"

H. Vocabulary Builders—Spelling Words:
1) **telegraph** 2) **model** 3) **Morse Code** 4) **key**
5) **dots** 6) **dashes** 7) **contact** 8) **movable**

I. Thought for Today:
"Success comes in cans, not cannots."

Activity

A. Problem: *How Can We Make an Electromagnet?*

B. Materials Needed:

1. Two dry cell batteries
2. Iron or steel bolt about 2″ long
3. 4′ of insulated copper wire (#24)
4. Assortment of nails, nuts, bolts, pins, tacks, etc.
5. Pocket knife or cutting pliers for stripping wire
6. Knife switch

C. Procedure:

1. Show that the 2″ bolt is not magnetized by attempting to pick up some of the nuts, pins, etc. with this bolt.
2. Strip the ends of the wires that will connect the batteries and knife switch.
3. Connect the two batteries and knife switch as shown in drawing. Remove the insulation from both ends of the wire and connect the center terminal of one battery to the outside terminal of the other battery.
4. Wind the remaining wire around the 2″ bolt, leaving about one foot of free wire at both ends of wire.
5. Strip the insulation from both ends of the wire.
6. Connect one end to the outside terminal of one battery and the other end of the wire to the knife switch.
7. Hold the wired bolt close to the assorted nails, nuts, pins, etc.
8. Close the knife switch.

D. Result:

When the knife switch is closed, the wire-wound bolt will attract the iron and steel objects as does a permanent magnet.

E. Basic Facts and Supplemental Information:

Electricity can be used to create a temporary magnet. This magnet can be strengthened by increasing the number of turns on the bolt or by adding additional dry cells. A knife switch can be made with a metal strip and a screw mounted as shown in drawing.

F. Thought Questions for Class Discussions:

1. Why does increasing the number of wraps around the bolt strengthen the magnet?
2. Can you think of any ways that electromagnets could be used?

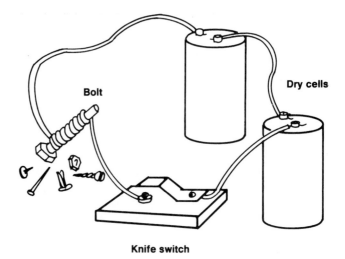

Bolt

Dry cells

Knife switch

3. Would a thicker wire produce more or less magnetic strength?
4. How do junkyards use electromagnets?
5. What is the advantage of using an electromagnet?

G. Related Ideas for Further Inquiry:

1. Demonstrate the difference between an electromagnet and a permanent one.
2. Devise an electromagnet game where objects are moved by an electromagnet such as a football player, a train, checkers, etc.
3. Study Activity II-G-1, "What is electricity?"
4. Study Activity II-G-8, "What materials conduct electricity?"
5. Study Activity II-G-9, "How do batteries work?"
6. Study Activity II-G-11, "How can we make a model telegraph?"
7. Study Activity II-G-13, "How does an electric doorbell work?"

H. Vocabulary Builders—Spelling Words:

1) **electromagnet** 2) **temporary** 3) **permanent**
4) **magnetized** 5) **insulated** 6) **terminal** 7) **bolt**
8) **cells** 9) **stripping** 10) **knife switch**

I. Thought for Today:

"None of us is as smart as all of us."

Activity

A. Problem: *How Does an Electric Doorbell Work?*

B. Materials Needed:
1. Electric doorbell (or drawing)
2. Push button
3. Two dry cells
4. Electric wires (#16 to #22)

C. Procedure:
1. Remove the cover of the doorbell so that working parts can be observed.
2. Connect the two dry cells in series to the doorbell and the push button after stripping ends of all wires. (See drawing.) (Note that the center terminal of one dry cell is connected to the outside terminal of the second.) The push button can be placed anywhere in the circuit. A knife switch can be used instead of a push button.
3. Depress the push button and hold for several seconds.

D. Result:
When the current is connected and is flowing through the wires of the electromagnets (a) they will become magnetized and will attract the iron bar (armature) (d). The armature is pulled toward the electromagnet and the clapper (c) hits the bell. As the armature is pulled away from the contact point (b) which is fastened to it, it is pulled away from the fixed contact point (b). The circuit is broken. Since there is no current flowing through the electromagnets, they no longer attract the armature and it returns to its original position. When the armature returns, the contact points again touch, the circuit is completed, and current flows again through the electromagnets. This attracts the armature to the electromagnets again and the whole cycle of operations is repeated. This continues rapidly as long as the button is pushed and the batteries are strong.

E. Basic Facts and Supplemental Information:
This electric doorbell is one of the most common examples of what happens in creating and destroying magnetic lines of force with electricity. When the current flows, there is a magnet. Without the current, the magnetic lines of force disappear. Alternately applying the current and removing it thus makes the hammer vibrate. This principle is applied to many other household and commercial objects.

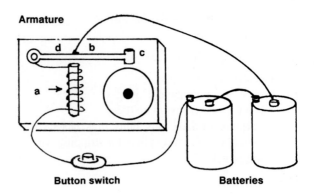

Armature

Button switch   **Batteries**

F. Thought Questions for Class Discussions:
1. How many things do you know that use electromagnets in their operation?
2. How can you increase the rapidity with which the vibration takes place?
3. How does a doorbell differ from a door chime in operation?

G. Related Ideas for Further Inquiry:
1. Repeat Activity but vary the number of batteries.
2. Repeat Activity but vary the number of winds on the armature.
3. Study Activity II-G-1, "What is electricity?"
4. Study Activity II-G-2, "How many electrical appliances do we have in our homes?"
5. Study Activity II-G-3, "How do we use electricity to communicate?"
6. Study Activity II-G-4, "How can we make a simple electric circuit?"
7. Study Activity II-G-12, "How can we make an electromagnet?"

H. Vocabulary Builders—Spelling Words:
1) **doorbell** 2) **push button** 3) **terminal**
4) **clapper** 5) **switch** 6) **contact**
7) **electromagnet** 8) **operation** 9) **circuit**
10) **electric** 11) **batteries** 12) **armature**

I. Thought for Today:
"Horse sense is found in stable situations."

PART III

PLANTS

Section A   Parts and Classification   146

Section B   Seeds and Reproduction   154

Section C   Soils and Germination   160

Section D   Growth   167

Section E   Roots, Stems, and Leaves   173

Section F   Fun with Plants   179

SECTION A: PARTS AND CLASSIFICATION

Activity

A. Problem: *How Do We Classify Living Things?*

B. Materials Needed:

1. Classroom plants
2. Classroom animals
3. Pictures or models of other plants and animals, including microscopic ones
4. Multisensory materials
5. Reference books

C. Procedure:

1. Discuss the different kinds of plants and animals that students know.
2. Discuss where they live.
3. Discuss what they need to survive.
4. List some of the characteristics of living things: (*Refers to animals only)
   a. grow
   b. reproduce
   c. respire
   d. eliminate wastes
   e. locomotion*
   f. communication*
   g. digestion
   h. chemical factories
   i. defense mechanisms
   j. specific life cycles
   k. feed (food and water)
   l. energy transfers
   m. care for young*
   n. sensations
5. Discuss the reasons and general principles of classification.
6. Show any multisensory materials that are available on plants and animals that would be appropriate for this Activity.
7. Have the students research and/or discuss some of the major characteristics of each of the five major kingdoms:
   a. *Monera*
      1) one-celled
      2) no movement capabilities
      3) consumers and producers
      4) procaryotic (lack nuclear membrane) (cell parts appear clumped)
      5) feed by absorption
      6) reproduce by fission (splitting)

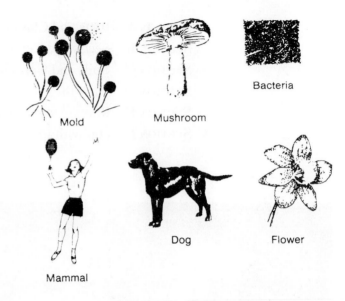

Mold   Mushroom   Bacteria

Mammal   Dog   Flower

   7) Organisms include bacteria and blue-green algae.
   b. *Protista*
      1) one-celled
      2) eucaryotic (have nuclei) (discrete cell parts)
      3) limited movement
      4) Organisms include amoebas, euglena, and diatoms.
   c. *Fungi*
      1) no movement capabilities
      2) have nuclei
      3) made of cells, tubular
      4) Organisms include molds, mushrooms, yeasts, and mildews.
   d. *Plants (Plantae)*
      1) multi-celled, walled cells
      2) no movement capabilities
      3) specialized parts (roots, stems, leaves)
      4) photosynthesis
      5) producers of food
      6) Members include trees, flowers, and legumes.
   e. *Animals (Animalia)*
      1) movement capabilities
      2) consumers of food
      3) various sizes
      4) Organisms include fish, amphibians, reptiles, birds, mammals, etc.
      5) Human beings are mammals.

8. Have the class develop their own organization scheme for any group of objects. See Section G, "Related Ideas for Further Inquiry," for some suggestions.

9. Make a list of terms that the students should become familiar with in their research of living things such as:
   a. predator
   b. prey
   c. consumer
   d. producer
   e. habitat
   f. ecosystem
   g. environment

D. Results:

1. Students will learn about the different forms of living things.
2. Students will learn the general principles of classification.
3. Students will become aware of the different characteristics of living things.
4. Students will learn that there are small, even microscopic organisms other than the former two classifications of the Plant and Animal Kingdoms.
5. Students will learn the difference between living things and nonliving things.

E. Basic Facts and Supplemental Information:

1. This classification system was developed by R. H. Whittaker of Cornell University and has generally been accepted by most life scientists.
2. Young students can develop their own classification system, which could be based on size, color, shape, function, etc.

3. There are about three million species of organisms that are now classified.
4. Some scientists predict that there may be 10 to 15 million species on Earth classified and unclassified. Every year new organisms are discovered and other organisms become extinct.

F. Thought Questions for Class Discussions:

1. What is the largest animal you know about?
2. What is the smallest animal you know about?
3. What is the prettiest plant you know about?
4. Are most of the foods we eat formerly living things?
5. Should we be concerned about plant and animal extinction?
6. What are some factors that cause changes in the life style of organisms?

G. Related Ideas for Further Inquiry:

1. Study seeds and eggs.
2. Examine buds, flowers, and bulbs.
3. Have each student take off one shoe, put it in a pile in the middle of the room. Have them develop a classification for these, i.e., size, color, shape, etc.
4. Have students classify other items such as bottles, rocks, automobiles, etc.

H. Vocabulary Builders—Spelling Words:

1) **classify**   2) **nucleus**   3) **consumers**
4) **producers**   5) **photosynthesis**   6) **organisms**
(also the *names* of the five kingdoms and the *characteristics* of living things in Procedure.)

I. Thought for Today:

"A problem is a chance for you to do your best."

Activity

Flowers

Trees

Grasses

A. Problem: *How Are Plants Classified?*

B. Materials Needed:

1. Pictures of bacteria, fungi, and algae
2. Pictures of different kinds of animals (the more contrasting the better)
3. Pictures, specimens, and full plants

C. Procedure:

1. Describe the five main "living kingdoms" (See Activity III-A-1.)
   a. *Monera* (bacteria, blue-green algae)
   b. *Protista* (amoebas, euglena, and diatoms)
   c. *Fungi* (molds, mushrooms, yeasts, and mildews)
   d. *Plant* (mosses, ferns, and flowering plants)
   e. *Animal* (sponges, sea anemones, jellyfish, coral, flatworms, segmented worms, mollusks, arthropods, spiny skinned animals, fish, amphibians, reptiles, birds, and mammals)
2. Review the Activity III-A-1, "How do we classify living things?"
3. If practical, take a walk around the school campus to study different plants and their plant parts.
4. The school gardener can be a big aid to plant identification.
5. Describe how scientists classify living things in the following sub-classifications:
   kingdom (division)
     phylum
       class
         order
           family
             genus
6. The depth of classification should be determined depending on the age of the students. Older students may want to study a book on plant taxonomy (technical plant classification). Younger students can use common, general subdivisions such as:
   a. *Non-flowering plants:*
      1) liverworts
      2) mosses
      3) ferns
   b. *Flowering plants:*
      1) trees
      2) shrubs
      3) flowers
      4) grasses
7. Have students identify (classify) as many different kinds of plants as their maturity dictates.

D. Result:

Students will become aware of the complex nature of classification.

E. Basic Facts and Supplemental Information:

1. There are about 350,000 different plants now classified.
2. Without plants, animals could not exist.
3. The age, maturity, and interest of your students should be considered in how deeply this Activity should be explored. The protista kingdom is a relatively new concept and even taxonomists are not clear as to what organisms belong in this category.

F. Thought Questions for Class Discussions:

1. Can animals be classified?
2. Can dogs be classified?
3. Can people be classified?
4. Can weeds be classified?

G. Related Ideas for Further Inquiry:

1. Young children can make their own large classifications of trees, shrubs, flowers, vegetables, grasses, etc.
2. Study mushrooms. There is no practical way to tell if they are poisonous or not.
3. Study all Activities in this Section.

H. Vocabulary Builders—Spelling Words:

1) **bacteria** 2) **fungi** 3) **algae** 4) **classification**
(also the terms in 6a and 6b of this Activity)

I. Thought for Today:

"The art of teaching is the art of assisting discovery."

Grass

A. Problem: *What Kinds of Plants Are Found in Our Neighborhood?*

B. Materials Needed:
1. Specimens of local plants
2. Pictures of those not obtainable
3. Reference materials on plants

C. Procedure:
1. Take a walk around the school campus or neighborhood and list the different kinds of plants seen. (Students can study reference materials to identify plants.)
2. Show specimens or pictures of plants.

D. Results:
1. Students will be introduced to the wide world of plants.
2. Students will learn that plants are numerous and vary in size, color, age, flowering parts, leaves, stems, etc.
3. Plant specimens may be collected if permitted.

Foxglove

E. Basic Facts and Supplemental Information:
1. Plants are a vital part of our lives.
2. Animals could not live without plants.
3. Plants make all the air we breathe.
4. All the food we eat are plants or animals that eat plants.
5. Plants live all over the world.
6. Plants take energy from the sun to make their own food.
7. This food is sugar. Different plants make different kinds of sugars.
8. We humans, and all animals breathe out carbon dioxide.
9. Plants breathe in carbon dioxide and give off oxygen.
10. This process is part of photosynthesis.

Pine cones

F. Thought Questions for Class Discussions:
1. What type of plants are the tallest? shortest?
2. What animals eat plants?
3. What products do we get from plants besides food?
4. What would happen if all plants were destroyed?

Dahlia

G. Related Ideas for Further Inquiry:
1. Have students describe some unusual plants they have seen.
2. Visit a nursery.
3. Discuss how plants and animals differ.
4. Study all Activities in this Section.

H. Vocabulary Builders—Spelling Words:
1) **trees** 2) **shrubs** 3) **flowers** 4) **photosynthesis**
5) **grass** 6) **school campus** 7) **garden**
8) **search**

I. Thought for Today:
"A chrysanthemum by any other name would be easier to spell."

A. Problem: *What Are the Main Parts of Plants?*

B. Materials Needed:
1. Potted plants
2. Pictures of plants
3. Specimens of plant parts
   a. Flowers
   b. Seeds
   c. Fruits
   d. Leaves
   e. Stems
   f. Roots

C. Procedure:
1. Discuss the various plant parts.
2. Have students identify the plant parts in the plants, pictures, and specimens.
3. Have each student draw a picture of a specific plant labeling its main parts.

D. Result:
Students will learn the various plant parts and their main functions. These are:

1. Roots—absorb water and minerals; anchor plants.
2. Stems—paths for water and minerals to travel up and down; hold leaves.
3. Leaves—produce food from sunlight.
4. Flowers—attract pollinators to form seeds.
5. Seeds—reproduce plant.
6. Fruit—houses seeds.

E. Basic Facts and Supplemental Information:
1. The roots, leaves, stems, flowers, fruit, and seeds are parts of a plant. Each of these parts may look different on the different kinds of plants, but each kind of plant has these same parts.
2. All plants need food. Leaves make the food for the plant. Leaves need air, sunshine, and water to do this work. All green plants are alike because they need sunshine, water, and air to make their food and to grow.
3. Plants play a vital part in all life cycles, beginning with the smallest phytoplankton, which are microscopic plants that live in the oceans.
4. Plants supply us with oxygen which is needed by all organisms.
5. Plants come in all sizes and shapes, and they are found in almost all parts of the world.

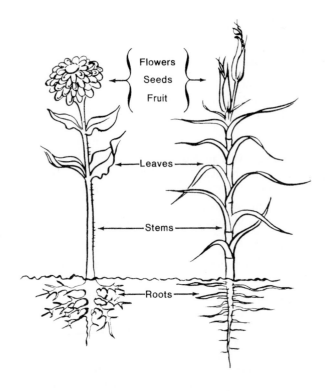

F. Thought Questions for Class Discussions:
1. How do plants get their food?
2. Is a tree a plant?
3. What foods do we eat from each part of the plant?
4. Do plants attract animals?

G. Related Ideas for Further Inquiry:
1. Study grasses.
2. Watch plants grow from season to season.
3. Study how we use plants.
4. Dissect weeds and study their plant parts.
5. Study Activity III-A-1, "How do we classify living things?"
6. Study Activity III-A-2, "How are plants classified?"
7. Study Activity III-A-3, "What kinds of plants are found in our neighborhood?"

H. Vocabulary Builders—Spelling Words:
1) **roots**   2) **stems**   3) **leaves**   4) **flowers**
5) **seeds**   6) **fruit**   7) **specimens**   8) **plants**

I. Thought for Today:
"When the going gets tough, the tough get going."

Activity

A. Problem: *What Parts of Plants Do We Eat?*

B. Materials Needed:

Pictures of food representing plant parts:

1. Roots: carrots, radishes, beets, turnips, etc.
2. Stems: asparagus, celery, etc.
3. Seeds: corn, oats, wheat, rice, etc.
4. Leaves: lettuce, spinach, cabbage, etc.

C. Procedure:

1. Discuss with students the plant parts we eat.
2. Divide the class into four groups: one group to research information in books about those plants which provide us food in the form of seeds, the second group on roots, the third group on stems, and the fourth group on leaves.
3. After the information is gathered, each group should present its findings to the rest of the class.
4. Make a survey of supermarkets to find out how edible plants are processed to sell: cut-up, cooked, canned, cleaned, chopped, frozen, radiated, etc.
5. Have the students make a survey of their homes to find out how plant parts are prepared to make them more palatable.

D. Result:

1. Students learn that people eat only certain parts of specific plants.
2. Students will learn that supermarkets display plant foods to look attractive and palatable.
3. Students learn that there are many ways plant foods can be prepared to eat.

E. Basic Facts and Supplemental Information:

1. People do not eat the whole plant. Some parts may taste good and be nutritionally wholesome, but custom has led us to believe that not all parts of plants are edible.
2. It is essential that we eat fruits and vegetables every day to keep our bodies healthy.
3. Plants are the source of many vitamins and minerals.
4. Plants are a vital part of every food chain and food web.
5. The energy we get originates from plants that collect the sun's energy and through photosynthesis converts this energy to "plant energy."
6. One of the big problems that will face the people of the world is food—plant food. As our population increases and the land now growing food is used to build new homes, highways,

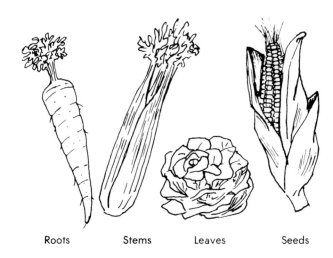

Roots   Stems   Leaves   Seeds

businesses, etc., we are going to have less food for each person.

7. Agriculturists will be of some help by producing more crops per acre, but there is a limit to the amount of food that can be raised per acre even with better fertilizers for old crops and for the development of new crops.

F. Thought Questions for Class Discussions:

1. What plants do we eat that have more than one edible part?
2. Why should we eat vegetables?
3. Does cooking increase or decrease the food value of plant foods?

G. Related Ideas for Further Inquiry:

1. Study Activity V-C-1, "What kinds of foods do our bodies need?"
2. Study Activity V-C-2, "What is the food pyramid?"
3. Study Activity V-C-6, "How is food preserved?"
4. Study Activity III-A-3, "What kinds of plants are found in our neighborhood?"
5. Study Activity III-A-6, "What are grasses?"
6. Study Activity III-A-2, "How are plants classified?"

H. Vocabulary Builders—Spelling Words:

1) **roots**   2) **stems**   3) **seeds**   4) **prepare**
5) **leaves**   6) **edible**   7) **buds**   8) **nutritious**

I. Thought for Today:

"Happiness is not a station you arrive at, but a manner of traveling."

Activity

A. Problem: *What Are Grasses?*

B. Materials Needed:
  1. Seeds, samples, or pictures of living grasses important to people:
     a. wheat
     b. barley
     c. oats
     d. corn
     e. rye
  2. Labels from cereal boxes, bread wrappers, etc. that list specific "grasses" in the ingredients.

C. Procedure:
  1. Have students collect labels cited in the "Materials Needed" section.
  2. Discuss grasses that people eat as food.
  3. Discuss the other ingredients listed that have been added to the grasses in the food.
  4. Discuss other uses of grasses:
     a. medicine
     b. paper
     c. clothing
     d. recreation
  5. Define grasses. Technically they are characterized by jointed stems. Sheathing leaves, flower spikelets, and fruit consisting of seedlike grain, or caryopsis. More simply put, grasses have narrow leaves, hollow jointed stems, and spikes or clusters of membranous flowers.

D. Results:
  1. Students will learn about grasses.
  2. They will learn that cereals are primarily grasses combined with a lot of other ingredients.
  3. They will realize that grasses are a vital part of our food intake.
  4. Students will learn that grasses give us energy, carbohydrates, vitamins, and minerals.
  5. Most important, students will learn how to look for and interpret ingredients listed on food labels.

E. Basic Facts and Supplemental Information:
  1. Grass is the start of many food chains.
  2. When soils are poor for trees, grasses grow.
  3. Grasses sprout from the roots of the plants, and consequently nibbling animals do not destroy the grasses.
  4. Grasses rejuvenate quickly after fires.
  5. Most people don't realize that the cereals we eat come from grass plants.

Corn

Wheat

Barley   **Oats**   **Rye**

F. Thought Questions for Class Discussions:
  1. What vitamins and minerals are found in most grasses?
  2. Are weeds just grasses that people don't like?
  3. What kinds of grasses make the best lawns in your locality?

G. Related Ideas for Further Inquiry:
  1. Compare grasses to other foods.
  2. Study grasses in relation to crop rotation.
  3. Study fungi and algae.
  4. Study all Activities in this Section.

H. Vocabulary Builders—Spelling Words:
  1) **grass** 2) **weed** 3) **barley** 4) **oats**
  5) **wheat** 6) **corn** 7) **rye** 8) **labels**

I. Thought for Today:
  "You cannot stop people from thinking, but you can start them."

152   *Parts and Classification*

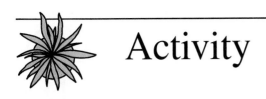

A. Problem: *Do All Plants Change Color in the Fall?*

B. Materials Needed:

1. Leaves
2. Dried corn
3. Small pumpkins (or pictures of)
4. Hay
5. Other plants or plant parts collected by the students that are evidence of the fall season

C. Procedure:

1. During the fall season ask questions such as: "What did you see on the way to school this morning that reminded you of the fall season?"
2. Discuss with class such questions as:
   a. "What happens to leaves in the fall?"
   b. "Why is the season called 'fall'?"
3. Observe the color of leaves and when they fall.
4. Discuss what happens to birds and other animals during the fall season.
5. Discuss how various plants and animals prepare for winter.
6. Observe which plants change color(s) in the fall.
7. Observe if there are any plants that do not change color(s) in the fall.

D. Results:

1. Students will be aware that some plants change color(s) in fall.
2. Students will learn that some plants change drastically while others do not change at all. Deciduous trees are the most obvious plants that change in the fall. Evergreen trees keep their foliage all year long.

E. Basic Facts and Supplemental Information:

1. Seasons are a result of the changing positions of the Earth in relation to the sun.
2. The length of daylight varies with these positions.
3. When daylight periods are shorter, some plants cannot manufacture as much food to sustain themselves as they do in longer daylight hours.
4. Leaves turn color in the fall because "carotenoids" (pigments in cells that are involved in photosynthesis) are present all the time in some plants and are hidden by the green color in chlorophyll. In the fall, chlorophyll production ceases and the colors of the carotenoids manifest themselves in the gorgeous colors of fall: red, yellow, orange, purple, brown, etc.

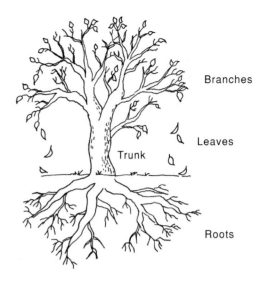

F. Thought Questions for Class Discussions:

1. What causes the change in seasons?
2. Is it the same season everywhere on the Earth at the same time?
3. Does the moon have seasons?
4. What happens to the fallen leaves?
5. What changes in plants do you see in the spring?

G. Related Ideas for Further Inquiry:

1. Ask the students what people do to prepare for each season.
2. Other seasons and their characteristics can be studied.
3. Study Activity VII-B-7, "How does the length of day and night change from season to season?"
4. Study Activity III-A-3, "What kinds of plants are found in our neighborhood?"
5. Study Activity III-A-4, "What are the main parts of plants?"
6. Study Activity III-A-6, "What are grasses?"

H. Vocabulary Builders—Spelling Words:

1) **deciduous** 2) **evergreens** 3) **fall** 4) **spring**
5) **seasons** 6) **leaves** 7) **branches** 8) **colors**

I. Thought for Today:

"The worst area of unemployment is between the ears."

SECTION B: SEEDS AND REPRODUCTION

Activity

A. Problem: *How Many Different Kinds of Flowers Are Found in Our Community?*

B. Materials Needed:
1. Typical specimens or pictures of:
   - a. Roses
   - b. Daisies
   - c. Zinnias
   - d. Irises
   - e. Daffodils
   - f. Hyacinths
   - g. Gladiolas
   - h. Other local flowers
2. Reference materials on flowers (may obtain from nurseries, garden shops, or florists)

C. Procedure:
1. Show the different kinds of flowers listed above.
2. List the way flowers differ:
   - a. color
   - b. size
   - c. shape
   - d. fragrance, etc.

D. Result:
Students will learn the many different kinds of local flowers.

E. Basic Facts and Supplemental Information:
1. Flowers are found almost everywhere.
2. They are found in lakes, deserts, mountains, valleys, etc.
3. They are found in all kinds of climates.
4. Their primary function is to attract insects to aid in pollination.
5. Plants grow, develop, and reproduce.
6. Plant growth is a change in size.
7. Plant development is adding new parts.
8. Plant reproduction is creating new plants.

F. Thought Questions for Class Discussions:
1. Do all plants have flowers?
2. What is your state flower?
3. Do all flowers have the same major parts?
4. Do we eat any flowers?

G. Related Ideas for Further Inquiry:
1. Study monocots (monocotyledons).
2. Study dicots (dicotyledons).
3. Study Activity III-B-2, "Where do seeds come from?"
4. Study Activity III-B-3, "How do plants reproduce?"
5. Study Activity III-B-4, "How do bees help plant reproduction?"
6. Study Activity III-B-5, "How do seeds travel?"

Petunia

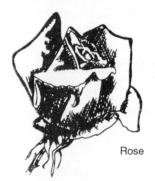

Rose

Tulip

H. Vocabulary Builders—Spelling Words:
1) **monocots** 2) **dicots** 3) **specimens** 4) **flowers**
5) **seeds** 6) **growth** 7) **pollination**
(also the names of local flowers)

I. Thought for Today:
"Some people believe that criticism is more blessed to give than to receive."

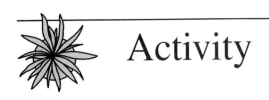

Activity

A. Problem: *Where Do Seeds Come From?*

B. Materials Needed:

1. Tomato
2. Grapefruit
3. Apple
4. Strawberry
5. Avocado
6. Grapes
7. Watermelon
8. Cantaloupe
9. Other seed-bearing fruits and vegetables
10. Seed packets from local nurseries

C. Procedure:

1. Discuss parts of plants.
2. Discuss the function of seeds.
3. Have students report on their experiences with planting seeds.
4. Show class the seeds in the "Materials Needed" list. You may want to dissect the seeds and examine them under a magnifying glass.
5. Discuss the development of seeds from flowers.

D. Result:

Students will learn that there are many kinds of seeds and that seeds are a developing part of the plant itself.

E. Basic Facts and Supplemental Information:

1. A seed is the reproductive structure in plants that consists of a miniature plant, or embryo, usually accompanied by a supply of food and a protective coat.
2. Some of the fresh seeds might be planted to test their germination.
3. The best seeds can be obtained from local nurseries.
4. Seeds should be kept moist during germination.
5. Some plants do not have seeds.

F. Thought Questions for Class Discussions:

1. Do any plants have seeds that develop on the outside of the plant?
2. Do small seeds grow into small plants and big seeds into big plants?
3. What prevents some seeds from germinating?

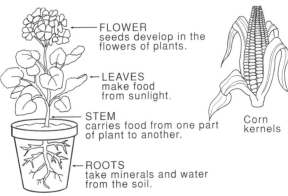

FLOWER
seeds develop in the flowers of plants.

LEAVES
make food from sunlight.

STEM
carries food from one part of plant to another.

ROOTS
take minerals and water from the soil.

Corn kernels

Peas

Strawberry seeds

G. Related Ideas for Further Inquiry:

1. Make a collection of seeds. (Many can be obtained at local nurseries.)
2. Plant some seeds and watch them develop.
3. Classify nut seeds.
4. Study Activity III-B-1, "How many different kinds of flowers are found in our community?"
5. Study Activity III-B-3, "How do plants reproduce?"
6. Study: Activity III-B-4, "How do bees help plant reproduction?"
7. Study Activity III-B-5, "How do seeds travel?"

H. Vocabulary Builders—Spelling Words:

1) **seeds** 2) **pods** 3) **grain** 4) **flower** 5) **nursery**
(Also include items in Materials list.)

I. Thought for Today:

"It costs more to entertain children now than it used to cost to educate their parents."

Activity

A. Problem: *How Do Plants Reproduce?*

B. Materials Needed:

1. Large drawing of a flower of a plant (See drawing.)
2. Large drawing of a stamen of a flower
3. Reference book(s) on plant reproduction
4. Multisensory aids on plant reproduction if available
5. Specimens of flowers (students can collect)

C. Procedure:

1. Present an overview of plants in general.
2. Show any appropriate multisensory aids.
3. Review Activity III-A-3, "What kinds of plants are found in our neighborhood?"
4. Discuss the main parts of the stamen, the male reproductive organ. It is located inside the petals. It consists of the:
   a. "stalk" or "filament"
   b. "anther" which is an enlarged tip at the top of the filament
5. Discuss the main parts of the pistil, the female reproductive organ. It is located in the very center of the flower. It consists of the:
   a. "ovary" which is at the base of the pistil
   b. "style" which is a tender stalk arising from the ovary
   c. "stigma" which is the enlarged portion at the top of the style
6. Show the specimens collected and point out the main parts of the flower's reproductive system.
7. Discuss typical reproductive processes of flowers.

D. Results:

1. Students can collect specimens.
2. Students will learn the main parts of the flower's reproductive system.
3. Students will learn the process of flower reproduction.

E. Basic Facts and Supplemental Information:

1. Pollen grains are produced by the anthers.
2. These grains will form the sperm which are the male reproductive cells.
3. To create seeds, pollen must get from the anther on the stigma to the tip (stigma) of the pistil.

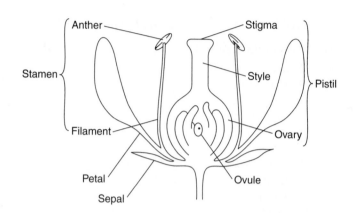

4. This is called "pollination."
5. Pollination may occur on one flower which is called "self-pollination," or between two flowers which is called "cross-pollination."
6. Pollination is the first step in seed development.
7. The sperm which is formed from the pollen grain travels to the ovary, fertilizing the egg, and a seed is formed.

F. Thought Questions for Class Discussions:

1. How are insects important to flowers?
2. How are insects detrimental to flowers?
3. Are flowers important to animals?

G. Related Ideas for Further Inquiry:

1. Study Activity III-A-1, "How do we classify living things?"
2. Study Activity III-B-2, "Where do seeds come from?"
3. Study Activity III-B-4, "How do bees help plant reproduction?"

H. Vocabulary Builders—Spelling Words:

1) **pollen** 2) **grain** 3) **sperm** 4) **ovary**
5) **reproduction** 6) **fertilization** 7) **style**

I. Thought for Today:

"He that climbs a ladder must begin at the first rung."

Activity

A. Problem: *How Do Bees Help Plant Reproduction?*

B. Materials Needed:
1. Pansies, roses, irises, etc.
2. Flower chart with parts labeled

C. Procedure:
1. Divide class into small groups.
2. Pass out flowers to the students.
3. Have them identify the different parts of the flowers such as: petal, stamen, pistil, and sepal.
4. Examine the pistil. (The anther is on the end of the filament.)
5. Ask students to gently touch the pollen with their fingers and observe what actually happens.
6. Ask students if they know what happens when a bee settles on a flower to extract nectar.

D. Results:
1. Students will learn the names of plant parts.
2. It has been shown that pollen will stick to the fingers, thus it will stick to the bees' legs and wings also. Actually it is the hairs on the bees' legs which pick up the pollen.
3. Students will learn that bees and other insects are very important for plant reproduction.

E. Basic Facts and Supplemental Information:
1. Bees are vital to plant reproduction.
2. When pollen from one flower is carried to the stamen of another flower, cross-pollination takes place.
3. Pollination occurs only in seed-bearing plants.
4. Seeds are carried by many insects, birds, and larger animals.
5. Pollination is the transfer of the male's reproductive units to the female's reproductive structures.
6. Pollen is usually yellow or orange.
7. The following terms should be identified and learned:
   Anther—tip of the filament where the pollen is developed
   Filament—thin stalk that holds the anther
   Pistil—Female reproductive organ
   Stamen—Male reproductive organ
   Pollen—Fine grain which develops the sperm on anther

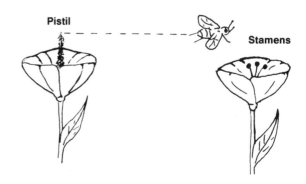

F. Thought Questions for Class Discussions:
1. What other insects carry pollen from flower to flower?
2. Can people carry pollen intentionally?
3. How could we show that cross-pollination is part of plant reproduction?
4. What other animals transfer pollen?
5. Is pollen transferred by means other than by animals?

G. Related Ideas for Further Inquiry:
1. Visit nurseries and floral shops to study flowers.
2. Flowers can be dissected.
3. Flowers can be pressed after studying.
4. Study Activity III-B-1, "How many different kinds of flowers are found in our community?"
5. Study Activity III-B-2, "Where do seeds come from?"
6. Study Activity III-B-3, "How do plants reproduce?"
7. Study Activity IV-C-3, "How do bees live?"

H. Vocabulary Builders—Spelling Words:
1) **bees**   2) **reproduction**   3) **pistil**   4) **stamen**
5) **anther**   6) **pollen**   7) **pollinization**   8) **seeds**

I. Thought for Today:
"Use what talents you possess; the woods would be very silent if no birds sang except those who sang best."

Activity

A. Problem: *How Do Seeds Travel?*

B. Materials Needed:
1. Different types of wild seeds
2. Printed materials about seeds
3. Chart materials

C. Procedure:
1. Have students visit a garden to observe the growth of new seeds.
2. Ask students to gather information concerning seed travel.
3. Have them bring different types of seeds to class.
4. Have students observe which seeds are most likely to travel in the air, or on water, or on animals, or people.
5. Have them make charts of their findings.

D. Result:

Students will learn that seeds travel in many ways.

E. Basic Facts and Supplemental Information:
1. The usual seed cycle consists of:
   a. Seed develops into a plant.
   b. Plant develops a reproductive system.
   c. Plant becomes pollinized.
   d. Plant produces a fruit.
   e. Fruit develops seeds.
   f. Seeds are dispersed.
2. On land, seeds are carried by people and animals. Parachute-type seeds, as well as seeds that come from bursting pods, travel by air. Some float on the surface of the water, while others roll on the ground or are stored in the ground by animals. Some seeds called burrs are carried on the clothing of people or on the fur of animals. Wild seeds can be carried by air, water, and by chance contact with people and animals. This activity is particularly effective in the fall season.

F. Thought Questions for Class Discussions:
1. How does seed travel help maintain a plant species?
2. Can you name some seeds that people eat?
3. Can you name some seeds that animals eat?

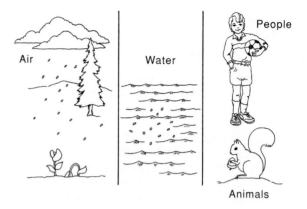

G. Related Ideas for Further Inquiry:
1. Classify seeds in any way the students want (doesn't have to be scientific). They might start with any characteristic such as color, shape, size, texture, weight, etc. and then use the other items as subdivisions (groups).
2. There are many unusual facts about seeds which students can collect. For example, you might ask. "Which fruit has its seeds on the outside?" (Answer: strawberry) or "Which fruit has a very large seed?" (Answer: avocado).
3. An interesting class project is to make a collection of seeds. These can include such seeds as apple, tomato, acorn, wheat grain, strawberry, etc. Be sure the seeds are labeled.
4. Study Activity III-B-1, "How many different kinds of flowers are found in our community?"
5. Study Activity III-B-2, "Where do seeds come from?"
6. Study Activity III-B-3, "How do plants reproduce?"
7. Study Activity III-B-4, "How do bees help plant reproduction?"

H. Vocabulary Builders—Spelling Words:
1) **burrs** 2) **parachute** 3) **bursting**
4) **travel** 5) **pods** 6) **barbs** 7) **air** 8) **water**

I. Thought for Today:

"Teachers' successes are measured by the lack of students' failures."

Activity

A. Problem: *What Conditions Lead to Mold Growth?*

B. Materials Needed:

1. Bread
2. Water
3. Cellophane, or some other airtight covering
4. Magnifying glass
5. Picture, drawing, or sample of mold on bread

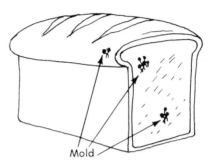

Mold

C. Procedure:

1. Ask the class if they have ever seen any mold. Tell them what it looks like.
2. Discuss their experiences with the mold.
3. Mutually plan to test the various factors in mold development:
   a. Take two moist samples of bread. Seal one in cellophane; expose the other to air.
   b. Expose two more samples of bread, one in strong light, one in the dark.
   c. Expose two more samples of bread; keep one very dry, the other moderately moist.
   d. Expose two more samples of bread, one in a warm, dark place, the other in a cold, dark place, such as a refrigerator.
   e. Examine the bread samples each day with a magnifying glass and record any changes in appearance.

D. Results:

1. Students will share their experiences with molds they have seen.
2. Pupils will help plan the means of determining mold growth.
3. Molds grow best in warm, dark, moist environments.
4. Molds will develop on some of the samples.

E. Basic Facts and Supplemental Information:

1. Molds are part of the classification of fungi.
2. Black mold is probably the best known example of fungi.
3. Sometimes these tests designed in "Procedure" above are slowed because of preservatives now added to bread and other foodstuffs.

F. Thought Questions for Class Discussions:

1. Where and how should bread be stored to keep it free from molds?
2. What other foods do you think might develop molds if left exposed?
3. What methods do people use to preserve their foods?
4. Are all plants green?
5. How do mold seeds get on the food? (Answer: "Airborne.")

G. Related Ideas for Further Inquiry:

1. Discuss other food products on which molds grow.
2. Discuss ways of preserving food.
3. Have students examine molds under a magnifying glass and then draw pictures of the molds.
4. Study Activity III-A-1, "How do we classify living things?"
5. Study Activity III-A-2, "How are plants classified?"
6. Study Activity III-A-5, "What parts of plants do we eat?"
7. Study Activity III-B-3, "How do plants reproduce?"
8. Study Activity III-B-4, "How do bees help plant reproduction?"

H. Vocabulary Builders—Spelling Words:

1) **molds** 2) **moist** 3) **samples** 4) **fungi**
5) **magnifying** 6) **dark** 7) **warm** 8) **conditions**

I. Thought for Today:

"A person who asks a question is a fool for five minutes. A person who does not, is a fool forever."

SECTION C: SOILS AND GERMINATION
Activity

A. Problem: *How Do We Plant Seeds?*

B. Materials Needed:
1. Dried seeds: radishes, lima beans, beets, onions, carrots, etc. (Number and type will depend upon local community. Seeds can best be obtained from a local nursery.)
2. Water
3. Paper cups, small jars, flowerpots, and/or outside garden plot
4. Knives
5. Magnifying glass

C. Procedure:
1. Carefully open a few seeds of each variety with knives to examine and study.
2. Soak other seeds overnight before planting.
3. Plant seeds according to instructions on packets and nursery's recommendations.
4. Plant a group of similar seeds every two weeks from spring until near midsummer.
5. Most vegetable seeds should be planted about one-half inch deep, and if outside, in rows 12 to 15 inches apart. Several seeds should be planted in each spot to assure sprouting.

D. Result:

Students will become junior gardeners as they learn how to plant seeds.

E. Basic Facts and Supplemental Information:
1. Planting seeds involves geography, climate, and soil.
2. This is a good socializing activity because students can work in groups and intra-group communication is excellent.
3. This completed activity is a long-range activity, and most seeds will sprout in about a month's time.

F. Thought Questions for Class Discussions:
1. What factors should be considered in planting seeds: soil, temperature, time, water, etc.?
2. Do vegetables and fruits have the same planting season?
3. Why do farmers cultivate their soil before planting?

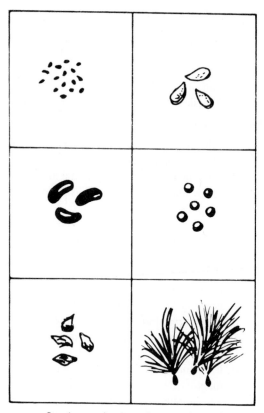

Seeds vary in size, shape, color and mode of transportation.

G. Related Ideas for Further Inquiry:
1. Study pests that attack plants.
2. Study diseases of plants.
3. Have students separate bird seed into types.
4. Study Activity III-C-2, "Do different soils affect germination?"
5. Study Activity III-C-3, "How does water affect germination?"
6. Study Activity III-C-5, "How does light affect germination?"

H. Vocabulary Builders—Spelling Words:
1) **planting**   2) **harvesting**   3) **climate**   4) **soil**
5) **disease**   6) **pests**   7) **nursery**   8) **sprout**

I. Thought for Today:
"Everything is funny as long as it is happening to somebody else."

Activity

A. Problem: *Do Different Soils Affect Germination?*

B. Materials Needed:
1. Eight lima bean seeds from seed packets
2. Four flowerpots or similar containers
3. Four different types of soil: sand, clay, loam, humus

C. Procedure:
1. Fill each container with one type of soil and label it.
2. Plant two seeds in each container. (Seeds sprout more rapidly if soaked overnight.)
3. Keep soils moist.
4. Place pots near window.
5. Keep a chart record of plant growth as soon as the plants appear above the ground.

D. Results:
Different types of soil vary so greatly in texture and fertility that a wide variety of results can be expected. However the usual results are as follows:

1. Plants in the sand stopped growing after the food in the bean was consumed because the sand did not furnish the food necessary for continued growth.
2. Clay soils usually produce very weak, short-lived plants.
3. Humus and loam soils are both very beneficial for plant growth.

E. Basic Facts and Supplemental Information:
1. Rich garden soil can be used for loamy soil. Humus is newly decomposed materials. Leaves, twigs, and old parings can be used.
2. Students can experiment with other types of soil such as gravel, rocks, or even mixtures of various soils cited.
3. Additional beans can be planted and the beans dissected at various stages and in different types of soil. Using these methods, the best type of soil for each plant can be determined.
4. Soil is being treated with more chemicals than ever as herbicides are replacing weeding.
5. Farmers are also using many types of chemicals to enrich soils and stimulate plant growth.

Plant	Soil	Growth per week			
Lima beans		1st	2nd	3rd	4th
	Sand				
	Clay				
	Loam				
	Humus				

6. Farmers also use pesticides to prevent pests from eating plants. This practice is being reduced, and many farmers are now using biological controls for retardation of plant pests.
7. See definition of soils in Activity III-C-7.

F. Thought Questions for Class Discussions:
1. How would knowing the best kind of soil for each plant help farmers?
2. What would happen if a specific plant used up most of a mineral needed for its growth?
3. Is a mixture of soils better than any one type? How can you find out?

G. Related Ideas for Further Inquiry:
1. Many tests can be conducted on soils and germination. In any test be sure to have only one variable.
2. Study Activity III-C-1, "How do we plant seeds?"
3. Study Activity III-C-3, "How does water affect germination?"
4. Study Activity III-C-6, "How do seeds start to grow?"

H. Vocabulary Builders—Spelling Words:
1) **germination** 2) **rate** 3) **soil** 4) **humus**
5) **loam** 6) **different** 7) **clay** 8) **chemicals**

I. Thought for Today:
"In 1851 the modern bathtub was invented; the telephone, not until 1876. Just think, for 25 years you could take a bath without the phone ringing."

A. Problem: *How Does Water Affect Germination?*

B. Materials Needed, Procedure One:

1. Two small flowerpots
2. Soil, humus
3. Lima bean seeds
4. Water

Materials Needed, Procedure Two:

1. Two water glasses
2. Radish seeds
3. Paper towels
4. Water

C. Procedure One:

1. Plant some bean seeds in small flowerpots, some in wet soil, and some in dry soil.
2. Label one pot "Dry" and the other "Wet."
3. Keep temperature, light, and ventilation normal and equal for both pots.
4. Keep "Wet" pot moist, but do not water "Dry" pot.

Procedure Two:

1. Place two small pieces of a folded paper towel in the bottom of each of two glasses.
2. Sprinkle some radish seeds on each pad and cover with another paper towel.
3. Label one glass "Dry" and the other "Wet."
4. Keep the towel in the "Wet" glass moist and the towel in the other glass dry.
5. Keep temperature, light, and ventilation normal and equal for both pots.

D. Result:

In both procedures, only the seeds that were well-watered germinated and grew.

E. Basic Facts and Supplemental Information:

1. Water is necessary for seed germination. Sponge or cotton may be substituted for paper towels. Mustard seed or mixed birdseed may be substituted for radish seeds.
2. One of the big problems in the near future will be the availability of fresh water because we will need more food crops and more food crops will demand more water.
3. Unfortunately, our current supplies of fresh water are being increasingly contaminated.

Dry   Wet

Procedure One

Dry   Wet

Procedure Two

F. Thought Questions for Class Discussions:

1. Do all seeds require the same amount of water for germination?
2. How do farmers control the amount of water they use after planting their seeds?
3. Is ocean water (salt water) good for germination?

G. Related Ideas for Further Inquiry:

1. Test seeds using one group with soil and the other with no soil and an equal amount of water in each.
2. Study Activity III-C-1, "How do we plant seeds?'
3. Study Activity III-C-2, "Do different soils affect germination?"
4. Study Activity III-C-4, "How does air affect germination?"
5. Study Activity III-C-5, "How does light affect germination?"
6. Study Activity III-C-6, "How do seeds start to grow?"
7. Study Section VII-C, "Earth's Crust."

H. Vocabulary Builders—Spelling Words:

1) **germination** 2) **flowerpot** 3) **temperature**
4) **moist** 5) **ventilation** 6) **radish** 7) **seeds**
8) **towels** 9) **water** 10) **humus** 11) **bean**

I. Thought for Today:

"It's nice to be important, but it's more important to be nice."

Activity

III **C** 4

A. Problem: *How Does Air Affect Germination?*

B. Materials Needed, Procedure One:

1. Two jars, one with cover
2. Humus soil
3. Lima bean seeds
4. Water

Materials Needed, Procedure Two:

1. Two jars, plastic or styrofoam cups
2. Cotton
3. Radish seeds
4. Water

C. Procedure One:

1. Plant lima bean seeds in jars with humus.
2. Water both soils fairly well. When air bubbles cease to rise, the air has been expelled from the soil.
3. Cap the first jar. This cuts off the air supply to the plant.
4. Keep the second planting moist by watering as needed.

Procedure Two:

1. Fill the other two jars or cups with water.
2. Place a cotton pad on top of one jar. Sprinkle some radish seeds on the cotton. (This will keep the seeds moist.)
3. Drop seeds into the water of the second container thus eliminating the air.
4. Keep the temperature and light the same for both jars.

D. Results:

1. In Procedure One, the seeds might germinate, but the new plant will quickly die from lack of oxygen.
2. In both procedures, when air is eliminated the seeds will not germinate.

E. Basic Facts and Supplemental Information:

1. Air is essential for germination and growth.
2. It is the oxygen in the air that is required for photosynthesis, the process whereby plants manufacture their own food for their growth and development.

F. Thought Questions for Class Discussions:

1. What other ways might air be eliminated from the jars?
2. Is air ever a problem to the farmer?
3. Would the same results occur with different types of seeds?

G. Related Ideas for Further Inquiry:

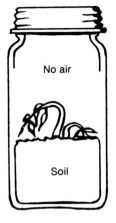

Procedure One

Procedure Two

1. Study the problems of farmers in your area or nearby communities.
2. Study what happens to crops in areas where there is a lot of pollution.
3. Study Activity III-C-3, "How does water affect germination?"
4. Study Activity III-C-5, "How does light affect germination?"
5. Study Activity III-C-7, "Are some soils better than others for holding water?"
6. Study Section III-D, "Growth."
7. Study Section VII-C, "Earth's Crust."

H. Vocabulary Builders—Spelling Words:

1) **germination** 2) **lima bean** 3) **oxygen**
4) **radish** 5) **plastic** 6) **jars** 7) **bowls** 8) **seeds**

I. Thought for Today:

"None is so tall as one who stoops to help a child."

Plants **163**

Activity

Procedure One   Procedure Two

A. Problem: *How Does Light Affect Germination?*

B. Materials Needed, Procedure One:
1. Bean seeds
2. Small flowerpots, cut-out milk cartons, or styrofoam cups
3. Good soil or planter mix
4. Water

Materials Needed, Procedure Two:
1. Grass seeds
2. Two sponges
3. Two bowls
4. Water

C. Procedure One:
1. Plant bean seeds in plant containers.
2. Label one pot "Dark" and the other "Light."
3. Place the appropriately labeled one in the dark, and the other in the light.
4. Keep both pots well-watered and ventilated in normal temperature.

Procedure Two:
1. Wet two sponges and place one in each bowl.
2. Add water to one-half inch depth.
3. Sprinkle each with grass seeds.
4. Place one in the dark and one in the light (not direct sunlight).
5. Keep both bowls well-watered and ventilated in normal temperatures.

D. Results:
1. In Procedure One, seeds germinated both in the light and in the dark.
2. In Procedure Two, seeds germinated both in the light and in the dark.

E. Basic Facts and Supplemental Information:
1. Light is not necessary for germination. In some cases it may even be detrimental.
2. After germination, when growth starts, most plants require light for normal growth and development.

F. Thought Questions for Class Discussions:
1. Why are some flowers planted on the south side of homes? On the north side?
2. Where do grass seeds get their food to germinate?
3. Do you think all seeds need water to germinate?

4. How could you prevent germination of weed seeds in your garden?
5. Where does our natural light come from?

G. Related Ideas for Further Inquiry:
1. Test different soils for the effects of light.
2. Test soils for the effects of different colored lights by shielding them with various colors of cellophane. ("Green light" is disastrous to plants; other colors will vary.)
3. Study Section III-B, "Seeds and Reproduction."
4. Study Activity III-C-1, "How do we plant seeds?"
5. Study Activity III-C-7, "Are some soils better than others for holding water?"
6. Study Activity III-C-4, "How does air affect germination?"
7. Study Activity III-C-6, "How do seeds start to grow?"
8. Study Section VII-C, "Earth's Crust."

H. Vocabulary Builders—Spelling Words:
1) **light**   2) **germination**   3) **flower**   4) **grass**
5) **sponges**   6) **flowerpots**   7) **bowls**   8) **seeds**

I. Thought for Today:
"If you have a job to do you might just as well do it right the first time."

A. Problem: *How Do Seeds Start to Grow?*

B. Materials Needed:
1. Water glass or clear plastic tumbler
2. Sponge that will fit into container (See drawing.)
3. Lima bean seeds
4. Water

C. Procedure:
1. Soak the lima beans in water overnight for easier germination.
2. Place the sponge on the inside of the container curving it to fit the glass or tumbler.
3. Place the lima beans between the container and the sponge.
4. Water slightly until the sponge becomes moist and there is a little water on the bottom to ensure an adequate water supply.
5. Place in a lighted area.
6. Keep a small amount of water on the bottom of glass or tumbler.
7. Observe daily.

D. Results:
1. After several days the seeds will begin to sprout.
2. Water will evaporate, so water must be added as needed to keep the seeds moist.

E. Basic Facts and Supplemental Information:
1. Seeds do need water for germination.
2. Seeds do not need light for germination.
3. The initial food for plant growth is contained in the seed itself.
4. When the food in the seed is used up, the young plant must get additional food from external soils or it will die.
5. Young plants within the seed are called "embryos."

F. Thought Questions for Class Discussions:
1. Do all seeds need water to germinate?
2. Could other seeds be tested in a similar fashion?
3. How could you test the percentage of germination of a particular batch of seeds?
4. Where do farmers get their seeds?

G. Related Ideas for Further Inquiry:
1. Test to determine if size of seeds has anything to do with time of germination.
2. Test with other kinds of seeds like radishes, squash, apples, etc.

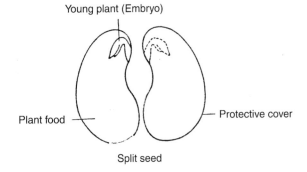

Split seed

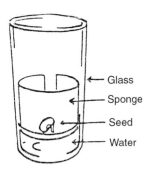

Plant a seed between glass and sponge.

Watch it grow.

3. Study Section III-A, "Parts and Classification."
4. Study Section III-B, "Seeds and Reproduction."
5. Study Activity III-C-1, "How do we plant seeds?"
6. Study Activity III-C-3, "How does water affect germination?"
7. Study Activity III-C-5, "How does light affect germination?"
8. Study Activity III-C-7, "Are some soils better than others for holding water?"

H. Vocabulary Builders—Spelling Words:
1) germination 2) embryo 3) reproduction
4) growth 5) sunlight 6) protective

I. Thought for Today:
"The rooster that crows the loudest is the first to lose its head."

Activity

A. Problem: *Are Some Soils Better Than Others for Holding Water?*

B. Materials Needed:

1. Five clay flowerpots, same size
2. Five glass jars big enough for flowerpots to be set in (See drawing.)
3. Soils:
   a. Clay
   b. Silt
   c. Sand
   d. Loam
   e. Humus
4. Measuring cup
5. Water
6. Watch with second hand

C. Procedure:

1. Place each type of soil in a different flowerpot.
2. Place flowerpots in the glass jars.
3. Pour equal amounts of water into each flowerpot.
4. Observe the amount of water that runs off from each pot, the amount of dirt carried through with the water, and the length of time for the water to seep through.

D. Results:

1. With clay, little soil is washed off; it has little holding power.
2. With silt, a lot of soil is washed off; it has little holding power. Water runs off this type of soil.
3. With sand, a lot of sand is lost; it has little holding power.
4. With loam, a lot of loam is lost; it has little holding power.
5. With humus, little soil is washed off; it is the best soil for holding water.

E. Basic Facts and Supplemental Information:

1. Soil with vegetation will hold water longer and tends to prevent erosion. Leaf matter and remains from trees hold water and become the best watershed materials.
2. The five test soils are:
   a. Sand—fine particles of disintegrated rock or seashells.
   b. Humus—remains of dried plants and animals.
   c. Loam—composition of gravel, sand, and clay.

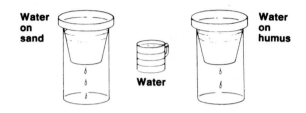

d. Silt—very fine soil and sand deposited by running streams and rivers.
e. Clay—stiff, sticky kind of earth that can be molded.

3. The first eight inches of most farms' soils is called "topsoil." It takes about 500 years to make one inch of topsoil. Modern farming practice is causing the loss of some topsoil.

F. Thought Questions for Class Discussions:

1. What is a watershed?
2. How important is watershed to us?
3. Can farmers with steep slopes on their farms change their soil type?

G. Related Ideas for Further Inquiry:

1. Study soil erosion and methods of prevention.
2. Study how farmers enrich or improve their soils.
3. Study Section VII-C, "Earth's Crust."
4. Study Activity III-C-1, "How do we plant seeds?"
5. Study Activity III-C-2, "Do different soils affect germination?"
6. Study Activity III-C-3, "How does water affect germination?"
7. Study Activity III-C-4, "How does air affect germination?
8. Study Activity III-C-6, "How do seeds start to grow?"

H. Vocabulary Builders—Spelling Words:

1) **humus**   2) **loam**   3) **clay**   4) **silt**
5) **sand**   6) **water**   7) **rate**   8) **topsoil**

I. Thought for Today:

"A weed is a plant whose virtues are yet to be discovered."

Activity

A. Problem: *What Do Plants Need to Grow?*

B. Materials Needed:
1. Lima bean seeds (from seed packets)
2. Five quart-size milk cartons
3. Good soil
4. Water
5. Paper towels
6. Spatula

C. Procedure:
1. Wash cartons. Cut four cartons to the height of 4″ and the other carton to 1″.
2. Put soil in the 4″ cartons.
3. Plant several beans in carton one, labeling with planting date. A spatula will help if available.
4. Repeat with cartons two, three, and four, planting seeds in different cartons each week.
5. Place in light sunny spot and keep soil damp.
6. One week after the last planting, put several seeds in the 1″ carton.
7. Add a small amount of water to sprout the seeds.
8. When plants have reached desired level of growth, uproot them carefully. Wash soil from roots (gently).
9. Place one plant from each stage of growth on a paper towel for each group of students to examine, compare, and discuss.

D. Result:
Plants will be at different stages of growth.

E. Basic Facts and Supplemental Information:
1. Each seed has the potential for developing into a full-grown plant if it is planted in good soil, watered, and kept in the sun. Some plants do not have seeds and reproduce by "vegetative propagation" where some part of the plant develops into a new plant. This may be a root, stem, or leaf. Gardeners and nursery workers use some of these possibilities in budding and grafting.
2. Corn grows fast. It takes 8 weeks to grow from a seed to a full plant with over 1,400 square inches of leaves. It establishes a root system which, if stretched out in one long line, would measure 7 miles. There is a saying that "you can hear the corn grow." Well, some corn plants grow as much as 4 inches in one day.

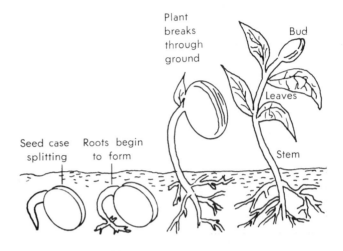

F. Thought Questions for Class Discussions:
1. How fast do the bean plants grow?
2. Do they grow faster during their first week, second week, third week, or fourth week?
3. Do all plants grow at the same speed?

G. Related Ideas for Further Inquiry:
1. Have students describe the growth of plants they have seen.
2. Discuss some ways to get rid of unwanted plants.
3. Have students compare the germination and growth of lima bean seeds from nursery packets and grocery store packets.
4. Have students compare the germination and growth of corn from nursery packets and grocery store "popping corn."
5. Study Activity III-D-2, "Do plants need sunshine?"
6. Study Activity III-E-3, "How quickly does water move in stems?"
7. Study Activity III-D-6, "What kinds of classroom plants should we raise?"

H. Vocabulary Builders—Spelling Words:
1) **growth** 2) **cartons** 3) **beans** 4) **label**
5) **sprout** 6) **days** 7) **weeks** 8) **months**

I. Thought for Today:
"Visits always give pleasure-if not coming, then the going."

Activity

A. Problem: *Do Plants Need Sunshine?*

B. Materials Needed:
1. Growing plant with large leaves
2. Vaseline or grease
3. Black construction paper
4. Paper clips

C. Procedure One:
1. Place green plant in well-lighted place where it can be seen without being handled by students.
2. Carefully cover *both* sides of several leaves with Vaseline or grease.
3. Observe these leaves each day and compare them with uncoated leaves. Notice color and freshness.

Procedure Two:
1. Cut out a pattern on one side of a folded piece of black construction paper. (See "Mask" in drawing, Procedure Two.)
2. Clip the pattern on the leaf and leave it attached for several days.
3. After several days remove the construction paper and observe the results.

D. Results:
1. Procedure One:
   The coated leaves will die and drop off.
2. Procedure Two:
   The masked portions will turn a pale green or brown while the unmasked portions will retain their normal color.

E. Basic Facts and Supplemental Information:
The Vaseline or grease seals the tiny pores in the surface of the leaf and keeps the air out of the leaf. The leaf needs to respire to keep alive, to manufacture food by photosynthesis, thus supplying the total plant the nourishment it needs to survive. Without sunshine, the leaves will die. Leaves are required for plant survival.

F. Thought Questions for Class Discussions:
1. What would happen if only the topside were coated? only the bottom side?
2. Would a leaf continue to die if the coating were removed after one day?
3. What would happen if only half the leaf were covered (half of the topside or half of the bottom side)?
4. What happens to the plant leaf after the mask is removed? Observe for several days.

Procedure One

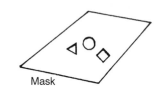

Mask

Mask on leaf

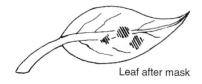

Leaf after mask

Procedure Two

G. Related Ideas for Further Inquiry:
1. Look at leaves of plants to see what damage has been done by insects.
2. Study Activity III-D-1, "What do plants need to grow?"
3. Study Activity III-D-3, "Can plants live without water?"
4. Study Activity III-D-4, "How does water move in plants?"
5. Study Activity III-D-5, "Do plants need air to grow?"

H. Vocabulary Builders—Spelling Words:
1) **sunshine** 2) **leaf** 3) **leaves** 4) **color** 5) **grease**
6) **respire** 7) **photosynthesis** 8) **mask** 9) **pattern**

I. Thought for Today:
"All the flowers of tomorrow are in the seeds of today."

A. Problem: *Can Plants Live Without Water?*

B. Materials Needed:
1. Bean seeds
2. Two small flowerpots
3. Water
4. Soil, humus

C. Procedure:
1. Plant some bean seeds in each of the small pots.
2. Place both plants in the sunshine.
3. Label one flowerpot "water" and the other pot "no water."
4. Water plant "A" lightly each day.
5. Do not water plant "B."

D. Results:
1. Plant "A" will grow large and healthy.
2. Plant "B" will soon die.

E. Basic Facts and Supplemental Information:
1. All plants need water to grow.
2. All plants need sunshine to grow.
3. Plants make their own food by a process called "photosynthesis."
4. Photosynthesis is the plant's ability to combine the carbon dioxide from the air and water from the ground in the presence of sunlight to make plant food.
5. If there were no plant food, there would be no animal food for most animals.
6. If there were no plant food or animal food, there would be no human food.

F. Thought Questions for Class Discussions:
1. Would the same results be possible with different kinds of seeds?
2. Is it possible to give a plant too much water?
3. How can a farmer tell if crops are receiving enough water? not enough water? too much water?

G. Related Ideas for Further Inquiry:
1. Start four lima bean seed plants. Vary the amount of water on each.
2. Add different liquids to different plants such as vinegar, clorox, salt water, etc., to see if it makes any difference in plant growth.
3. Study Activity III-D-1, "What do plants need to grow?"

Before

A is watered.

B is not watered.

After

A is healthy.

B is dying.

4. Study Activity III-D-2, "Do plants need sunshine?"
5. Study Activity III-D-4, "How does water move in plants?"
6. Study Activity III-E-3, "How quickly does water move in stems?"

H. Vocabulary Builders—Spelling Words:
1) **water**   2) **healthy**   3) **plants**   4) **liquids**
5) **vinegar**   6) **flowerpots**   7) **humus**
8) **watered**

I. Thought for Today:
"The easiest way to teach children the value of money is to borrow it from them."

Activity

A. Problem: *How Does Water Move in Plants?*

B. Materials Needed, Procedure One:
1. Carrots, celery, or flowers
2. Calla lilies or white carnations
3. Food coloring
4. Tall, clear plastic or water glass
5. Eyedropper
6. Water

Materials Needed, Procedure Two:
1. Three tall, clear plastic or water glasses
2. Calla lily or white carnation
3. Water
4. Three different colors of food coloring

Carrot   Celery   Flower (Carnation)

C. Procedure One:
1. Fill glass 2/3 full of water.
2. Color water with food coloring.
3. Let carrot, celery, or flower stand in solution for one hour.
4. Remove and make crosscuts to show colored streaks.
5. Put some calla lilies or white carnations in colored liquid for several hours and note results.

Procedure Two:
1. Split the stem of a calla lily or white carnation in three parts. (See drawing.)
2. Fill the liquid containers about 2/3 full of water.
3. Add different food coloring to each container.
4. Place one part of the cut stem in each of the containers.

Red   Green   Blue

D. Results:
1. In Procedure One, the colored fluid travels upward coloring the stem and flower.
2. In Procedure Two, the colored fluids from all containers travel up the stem and produce a blend of all three colors in the flower.

E. Basic Facts and Supplemental Information:
Plants have well-defined passageways through which liquids travel. By using a colored solution we can trace these channels through the plant. These tubes are formed by xylem cells in the plants.

F. Thought Questions for Class Discussions:
1. Do tall trees get their water through xylem cells?
2. What functions do you think the stems and stalks have other than transporting water?
3. What happens to plants during dry seasons? in summer time?

G. Related Ideas for Further Inquiry:
1. Study Activity III-D-1, "What do plants need to grow?"
2. Study Activity III-D-2, "Do plants need sunshine?"
3. Study Activity III-D-3, "Can plants live without water?"
4. Study Activity III-E-3, "How quickly does water move in stems?"
5. Study Activity III-D-6, "What kinds of classroom plants should we raise?"

H. Vocabulary Builders—Spelling Words:
1) **xylem**   2) **calla lilies**   3) **colored**   4) **knife**
5) **eyedropper**   6) **carnations**   7) **stalk**   8) **stem**

I. Thought for Today:
"Facility of speech is not always accompanied by fertility of thought."

Activity

A. Problem: *Do Plants Need Air to Grow?*

B. Materials Needed:
1. Plastic cups (2)
2. Pre-sprouted lima beans
3. Soil, humus
4. Clear plastic bag
5. Rubber band
6. Saucers (2)
7. Knife or scissors

C. Procedure:
1. Cut small holes in bottoms of cups and place on saucers.
2. Put humus soil in cups.
3. Plant beans in cups.
4. Cover one cup with a plastic bag securing with a rubber band.
5. Observe cups for many weeks.

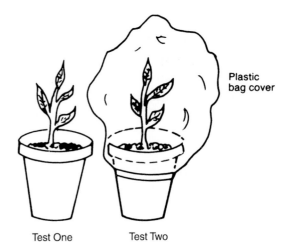

Plastic bag cover

Test One   Test Two

D. Result:

The plant which does not obtain fresh air will not grow and soon dies.

E. Basic Facts and Supplemental Information:
1. Plants need oxygen from the air to grow.
2. Plants need carbon dioxide from the air to grow.
3. During the day, plants give off oxygen and take in carbon dioxide.
4. During the night, the reverse is true; plants give off carbon dioxide and take in oxygen.
5. The two main sources of oxygen in the air are from phytoplankton that live in the water and from trees that are rooted in the land.

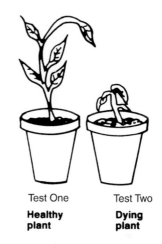

Test One   Test Two

Healthy plant   **Dying plant**

F. Thought Questions for Class Discussions:
1. Could a plant ever get too much air?
2. Do plants breathe?
3. Is the air we breathe in (inhale) the same as the air we breathe out (exhale)?
4. Is the air plants breathe in the same as the air that people breathe in?

G. Related Ideas for Further Inquiry:
1. Could you devise a test in which plants have contact only with oxygen?
2. Could you devise a test in which plants have contact only with carbon dioxide?

3. Study Activity III-D-1, "What do plants need to grow?"
4. Study Activity III-D-6, "What kinds of classroom plants should we raise?"

H. Vocabulary Builders—Spelling Words:
1) **breathe**   2) **inhale**   3) **exhale**   4) **plastic**
5) **humus**   6) **oxygen**   7) **carbon dioxide**

I. Thought for Today:

"It's hard to know exactly when one generation ends and the next one begins, but it is somewhere around nine o'clock at night."

A. Problem: *What Kinds of Classroom Plants Should We Raise?*

B. Materials Needed:
1. Books about plants
2. Gardening pamphlets from local nurseries
3. Chalkboard
4. Chalk

C. Procedure:
1. Discuss with class the value of classroom plants.
2. Have students report on the kinds of plants they have in their homes.
3. Have students report on why these particular plants were selected for their homes.
4. Have them determine the kind of care that is required for house plants.
5. Have several students interview the school gardener for suggestions for classroom plants.
6. If a nursery or florist is nearby, have several students visit there to learn about the best possible classroom plants.
7. List on the chalkboard the criteria for selecting classroom plants.
8. Discuss the different choices available.
9. Students can then select their own classroom plants.

D. Results:
1. The best result is student realization that plants are living things and as such demand care.
2. The range of plants is so great, that lively discussions always result.
3. Students will learn that plants have different:
   a. colors
   b. sizes
   c. shapes
   d. growing seasons
   e. soil requirements
   f. care
   g. leaf shapes and colors
   h. flower shapes and colors
   i. propagation times
4. Students will learn that different containers can be used: pots, jars, terraria, bowls, boxes, etc.

E. Basic Facts and Supplemental Information:
1. Local flower shops can supply needed information.
2. Light is a very important factor in plant growth.
3. Too many of our life science activities are nonliving experiences. This life science activity is living.

F. Thought Questions for Class Discussions:
1. How will the plants be cared for during vacation and holiday seasons?
2. How do plants differ from animals?
3. What is the purpose of "greenhouses"?
4. Ask the school gardener to take the class around the campus to identify different plants.

G. Related Ideas for Further Inquiry:
1. Study the differences between "annuals" and "perennials."
2. Study the pests that might harm the school plants.
3. Discuss the value of various chemical sprays.

H. Vocabulary Builders—Spelling Words:
1) **annuals** 2) **perennials** 3) **gardener**
4) **nursery** 5) **florist** 6) **flowers** 7) **terrarium**

I. Thought for Today:
"You cannot build character and courage by taking away a person's initiative and independence."

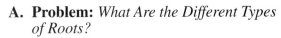
A. Problem: *What Are the Different Types of Roots?*

B. Materials Needed:

Pictures or specimens of:

1. Fibrous root (wheat)
2. Secondary roots (those branchlike roots growing from the main root) (beets, carrots)
3. Taproot (peanuts)
4. Seeds of flowering vegetables (lima beans)

C. Procedure:

1. Discuss plant parts.
2. Study Activity III-A-4, "What are the main parts of plants?"
3. Discuss the role of roots:
   a. Hold plants in ground
   b. Obtain food for growth
   c. Reproduction (in some cases)
4. Discuss the different kinds of roots.

D. Result:

Students will learn that plants have many types of roots and they serve many purposes.

E. Basic Facts and Supplemental Information:

1. Roots are the parts of plants that grow underground.
2. When a seed starts to grow, the first change in the seed splitting is the emergence of a root.
3. If this major root sends out other roots, they are called secondary roots.
4. If many hair-like roots are formed, this is called a fibrous root. The root hairs take up water and minerals from the soil.
5. Some roots store food for plants.

F. Thought Questions for Class Discussions:

1. What roots do we eat?
2. What other uses do people have for plant roots?
3. Can you tell the kind of root by the plant above them?
4. What are "runners" in plant roots? (roots which spread out from main root to start a new plant)

G. Related Ideas for Further Inquiry:

1. Radish seeds can be easily germinated by placing them on moistened blotting paper in semi-darkened place.

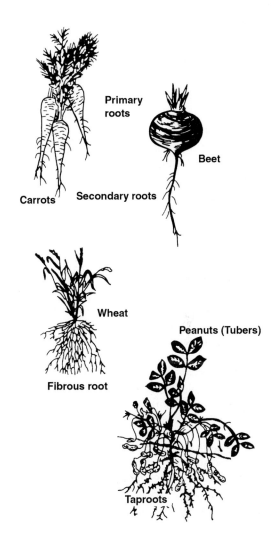

2. Compare the types of roots of plants with climates.
3. Study all Activities in this Section.

H. Vocabulary Builders—Spelling Words:

1) **primary**   2) **secondary**   3) **taproot**
4) **hair root**   5) **vegetable**   6) **fibrous**

I. Thought for Today:

"When asked to start a garden, the first thing people dig up is an excuse."

Activity

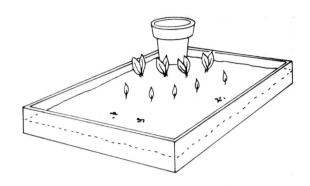

A. Problem: *Do Roots Seek Water?*

B. Materials Needed:
1. Medium-sized plant box
2. Two-inch flowerpot
3. Soil, humus
4. Lima bean seeds (40–50) (They grow fast.)
5. Water

C. Procedure:
1. Place the flowerpot close to one corner of the box.
2. Fill the box with humus soil.
3. Have students plant a number of seeds close to the flowerpot working them down with their fingers.
4. Plant about 10 seeds at each measured distance from the flowerpot. Distances that work well are 3", 6", 9", 12", etc.
5. Fill the flower pot one-half full of water. Do not put any water directly on the soil. The only source of water must come from the flowerpot.
6. Keep the soil close to the flowerpot slightly moist by adding water to the flowerpot as necessary.
7. Check the plants about every three days from each measured distance from the flowerpot beginning around the tenth day, noting particularly the direction of the growth of the roots and root hairs in relation to the flowerpot.
8. Keep a record of these observations.

D. Results:
1. The seeds nearest the water will germinate first, the next row out germinate next, and so on outwards. The seeds farthest out may not germinate because of lack of water.
2. After ten days to two weeks, the roots can be detected growing toward the source of water.
3. After a month the plants closest to the flower pot should have many roots surrounding them.

E. Basic Facts and Supplemental Information:
1. Water dissolves minerals in the soil.
2. Roots grow toward water.

3. Roots pick up water and dissolved materials.
4. Roots store some of the plant's food supply.

F. Thought Questions for Class Discussions:
1. Why do roots surround and sometimes infiltrate clay sewer pipes?
2. Do all seeds under the same conditions germinate at the same time?
3. Why do some seeds produce longer roots?

G. Related Ideas for Further Inquiry:
1. Study Section I-C, "Water."
2. Study Section VII-C, "Earth's Crust."
3. Make a list of the roots we eat. Classify the roots by root type cited in the previous Activity.
4. Study Activity III-E-4, "How do stems of plants differ?"
5. Study Activity III-B-2, "Where do seeds come from?"
6. Study Activity III-C-3, "How does water affect germination?"

H. Vocabulary Builders—Spelling Words:
1) **root** 2) **water** 3) **lima beans** 4) **flower**
5) **pot** 6) **growth** 7) **observe** 8) **seeds**

I. Thought for Today:
"Get acquainted with your neighbors; you might like them."

A. Problem: *How Quickly Does Water Move in Stems?*

B. Materials:
1. Plate, ceramic or plastic
2. Six wooden matches (or toothpicks)
3. Water

C. Procedure:
1. Break five matches half through at the middle.
2. Arrange the five matches symmetrically on the dry plate around a circle about 3/4″ in diameter as shown in drawing.
3. Dip a sixth match into water and use it to wet each of the five matches where they are bent, with a drop or two of water.
4. Leave the matches on the plate for a short time.

D. Result:

The matches partially straighten and thus form the shape of a five-pointed star.

E. Basic Facts and Supplemental Information:

Water enters the dry wood cells in the bent parts of the matches and swells the cells. This swelling and movement, in turn, tends to straighten the matches and makes the ends move apart to form a five-pointed star. Capillarity is the movement of a liquid when in contact with dry cells in plants. In the matches it moves quite quickly.

F. Thought Questions for Class Discussions:
1. Can you think of other examples of water movement in plants?
2. Is this the same reaction that causes water pipes to burst in freezing temperatures?
3. What are the relationships among the terms *capillarity, osmosis,* and *surface tension?*

G. Related Ideas for Further Inquiry:
1. An excellent activity demonstrating osmosis is to take a peeled potato and place it in a glass of very salty water. It will shrink in size. Placing the same-size peeled potato in a similar glass of fresh water and letting it stand for a day will cause the potato to swell. This action of water moving in and out of the potato is called osmosis.
2. Another phenomenon regarding water is "surface tension." Surface tension acts like a "skin" over water. It should be studied. This is caused by water particles attracting each other. Water particles attract each other in all directions. On the surface of the water there are no particles to pull in

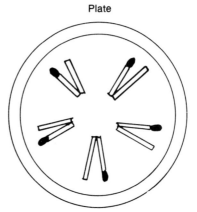
Plate

Wet the broken ends of these matches

Matches form a five-pointed star

the opposite direction. This tension creates the "skin" which is strong enough to support the weight of tiny insects like the water strider. It can also support a flat razor blade if placed on the water carefully, keeping the top side dry.
3. Study Activity III-D-3, "Can plants live without water?"
4. Study Activity III-D-4, "How does water move in plants?"
5. Study Activity III-E-2, "Do roots seek water?"
6. Study Activity III-E-5 "Do leaves give off water?"

H. Vocabulary Builders—Spelling Words:
1) **capillarity** 2) **symmetrical** 3) **star** 4) **liquid**
5) **straighten** 6) **osmosis** 7) **surface** 8) **tension**

I. Thought for Today:

"Keep your words soft and sweet because you'll never know when you will have to eat them."

A. Problem: *How Do Stems of Plants Differ?*

B. Materials:

Pictures or specimens of:

1. Tree stem (horizontal cut)
2. Celery stalk
3. Weed stem
4. Flower stem

C. Procedure:

1. Show the different kinds of stems.
   a. *Woody*
      1) hard
      2) tall
      3) evergreens
      4) have bark
   b. *Herbaceous*
      1) soft
      2) green
      3) clumps
2. Discuss the two major types of stems.
3. Discuss the functions of stems:
   a. support
   b. if green, make food
   c. transportation system for food and water
   d. storage for food and water
4. Study stem growth in plants around the school campus and classroom.
5. Study the different kinds of seeds.
6. If time permits, make soil boxes to plant seeds and study developing stems.

D. Results:

1. Plants will grow.
2. Most stem growth occurs near the tip.

E. Basic Facts and Supplemental Information:

Stems grow in rings from inside to outside. Large plants show green colors of rings in spring, and brown during summer. Older students can study more in detail about the xylem (pronounced *zi-lem*) and phloem (pronounced *flome*). Stems conduct food from the leaves to the roots.

F. Thought Questions for Class Discussions:

1. Which foods do we eat that are basically the stems of plants?
2. What are some uses of plant bark?
3. From what part of the plants do natural ropes come?
4. From what part of plants do we get our lumber?

G. Related Ideas for Further Inquiry:

1. Examine different types of lumber.
2. Cut a piece of celery horizontally and observe the vascular tubes. (small vertical cylinders)
3. Study all Activities in this Section.

H. Vocabulary Builders—Spelling Words:

1) **woody** 2) **herbaceous** 3) **bark**
4) **xylem** 5) **phloem** 6) **stem**

I. Thought for Today:

"All parents believe in heredity until their children start bringing home report cards."

Asparagus   **Celery**

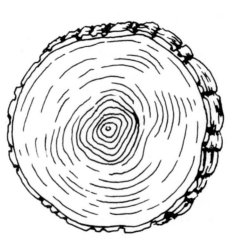

Tree rings (Annual)

Corn stalk

Activity

A. Problem: *Do Leaves Give Off Water?*

B. Materials Needed:
1. Large leaf with stem
2. Four water glasses
3. Cardboard
4. Water

C. Procedure:
1. Put water into a water glass (about 1/3 full).
2. Cut a hole in a piece of cardboard big enough for the stem of the leaf to slip through.
3. Place cardboard across the top of glass and arrange the leaf so that the stem is in the water and the blade is above the cardboard.
4. Set a second glass over the blade of the leaf.
5. Set up a similar piece of apparatus but do not put a leaf in this one.
6. Observe the inside of both upper glasses.

D. Results:
1. The glass on top of the leaf will soon contain droplets of water.
2. No droplets of water form in the glass which contains no leaf.

E. Basic Facts and Supplemental Information:
1. The process of leaves giving off water is called "transpiration."
2. The water which is transpired from the leaf condenses on the upper glass. This indicates that plants give off moisture. A small plant can be substituted for the large leaf. The surface of the leaf determines its rate of transpiration.

F. Thought Questions for Class Discussions:
1. What kind of leaves give off the most water?
2. Does size or color have any effect on the amount of water transpired?
3. Does climate have any effect on transpiration?
4. Do all plants transpire at the same rate?

G. Related Ideas for Further Inquiry:
1. Study Activity III-E-1, "What are the different types of roots?"
2. Study Activity III-E-6, "How do leaves vary in size, shape, and edges?"
3. Study Activity III-A-3, "What kinds of plants are found in our neighborhood?"

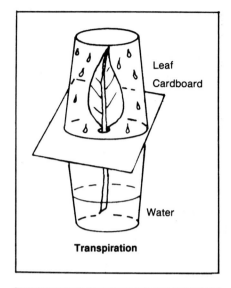

Transpiration

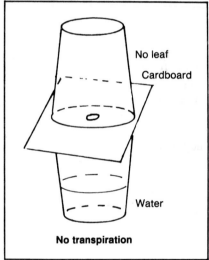

No transpiration

4. Study Activity III-A-4, "What are the main parts of plants?"
5. Study Activity III-A-5, "What parts of plants do we eat?"
6. Study Activity III-A-6, "What are grasses?"

H. Vocabulary Builders—Spelling Words:
1) **transpire**   2) **cardboard**   3) **apparatus**
4) **similar**   5) **droplets**   6) **glass**   7) **condenses**

I. Thought for Today:
"Live your life fully—this life is not a dress rehearsal."

A. Problem: *How Do Leaves Vary in Size, Shape, and Edges?*

B. Materials Needed:
1. Leaves with parallel veins
2. Leaves with branching veins
3. Large leaves
4. Small leaves
5. Narrow leaves
6. Miscellaneous, unusual leaves
7. Bulletin board
8. Reference materials on plants

C. Procedure:
1. Have students bring in as many different kinds of leaves as they can find. You might want to assign a given number of leaves, such as 5 or 10 per student.
2. Have students describe the species of plants from which they collected their leaves.
3. Mount selected leaves on the bulletin board with the names of the students who collected them.
4. Have students study plants and in particular the functions of leaves.
5. Have a class discussion on plants and in particular the functions of leaves.

D. Results:
1. Students will learn that leaves vary in:
   a. size
   b. shape
   c. venation
   d. edges
   e. color
   f. occurrence (singular or multiple)
2. Students will learn that plant leaves are necessary for the production of plant food.
3. Students will enjoy collecting leaves.

E. Basic Facts and Supplemental Information:
1. There are over 850 different species of trees in the United States.
2. Only one-eighth of a tree is or can be used as useful timber.
3. The national flower of the United States is the rose which was adopted on October 7, 1986.

F. Thought Questions for Class Discussions:
1. What is the main function of leaves?
2. What leaves do we eat?
3. How do house plants live without direct sunlight on their leaves?

G. Related Ideas for Further Inquiry:
1. Students may take a walk around campus and collect leaves which are plentiful and will not hurt the plant if removed.
2. This Activity can be combined with an art lesson. Leaves can be drawn, framed, or added to other art work.
3. Study Activity III-A-3, "What kinds of plants are found in our neighborhood?"
4. Study Activity III-A-4, "What are the main parts of plants?"
5. Study Activity III-A-5, "What parts of plants do we eat?"
6. Study Activity III-F-5, "How can leaves be preserved?"
7. Study Activity III-F-6, "How can we make a 'spray print'?"

H. Vocabulary Builders—Spelling Words:
1) **leaf** 2) **leaves** 3) **photosynthesis**
4) **carotenoids** 5) **serrated** 6) **veins**
7) **chlorophyll** 8) **alternate**

I. Thought for Today:
"Oaks are true conservatives; they hold old leaves till summer gives a green exchange."

A variety of leaves

A. Problem: *How Can We Make a Decorative Sweet Potato Plant?*

B. Materials Needed:
1. Quart jar
2. Straight pins, toothpicks, or thin nails
3. Sweet potato
4. Water
5. Supporting device for hanging (if desired)

C. Procedure:
1. Wash sweet potato carefully as some are treated with pesticides.
2. Note eyes or buds which indicate top of potato.
3. Place potato in jar about two-thirds of the way down.
4. Support with pins, toothpicks, or thin nails.
5. Put enough water in the jar so that the potato is half submerged.
6. Place on shelf near window.
7. Keep potato well-watered.

D. Result:

An attractive classroom plant will develop.

E. Basic Facts and Supplemental Information:
1. The sweet potato must be kept watered.
2. The sweet potato should have good sunlight for maximum growth.

F. Thought Questions for Class Discussions:
1. Do you think an avocado seed can be made to sprout in the same way?
2. What other plants might be started in this way?
3. What is hydroponics?

G. Related Ideas for Further Inquiry:
1. Charts can be kept on the number of leaves and roots of the sweet potato.
2. The roots can be studied both macroscopically and microscopically.
3. Plant leaves can be studied for size, shape, growth rates, etc.
4. Study Activity III-F-2, "How can we start a pineapple plant?"
5. Study Activity III-F-3, "What can we make with gourds?"
6. Study Activity III-F-5, "How can leaves be preserved?"

Early growth

Full growth

H. Vocabulary Builders—Spelling Words:
1) **decorative** 2) **sweet potato** 3) **supporting**
4) **device** 5) **preserve** 6) **watered** 7) **observe**
8) **eyes** 9) **toothpicks** 10) **window** 11) **buds**

I. Thought for Today:

"If necessity is the mother of invention, discontent is the father of progress."

Activity

A. Problem: *How Can We Start a Pineapple Plant?*

B. Materials Needed:
1. Ripe pineapple
2. Knife
3. Shallow pan or dish
4. Water

C. Procedure:
1. Cut off the top of a pineapple, leaving about 2" of the fruit attached.
2. Place this piece in the shallow pan or dish.
3. Add water about halfway up the fruit.
4. Check water every few days and add water as needed.

D. Result:
The cut piece of pineapple will start to grow new leaves.

E. Basic Facts and Supplemental Information:
1. After the top of the pineapple has been cut off, the rest of the pineapple should be shared with the students.
2. Pineapples are very rich in vitamin C.
3. Pineapples provide good fiber for helping food digestion.

F. Thought Questions for Class Discussions:
1. How can you tell when a pineapple is ripe?
2. Where do pineapples grow?
3. Why are there holes in canned pineapple slices?

G. Related Ideas for Further Inquiry:
1. If time permits, the top piece of pineapple could be planted in potting soil and placed in a flowerpot or the school garden.
2. Study Section V-C, "Nutrition."
3. Study Activity III-F-1, "How can we make a decorative sweet potato plant?"
4. Study Activity III-F-3, "What can we make with gourds?"
5. Study all other Activities in this Section.

H. Vocabulary Builders—Spelling Words:
1) **pineapple** 2) **saucer** 3) **potting**
4) **soil** 5) **knife** 6) **ripe** 7) **shallow**

Pineapple

Pineapple top
in dish or pan

I. Thought for Today:
"Character cannot be purchased, bargained for, inherited, rented, or imported from afar. It must be home-grown."

Activity

A. Problem: *What Can We Make with Gourds?*
(Gourds are the hard-shelled fruit of certain vines. They are related to cucumbers, squash, pumpkins, and muskmelons. The hard shells of gourds can be used for many things.)

B. Materials Needed:
1. Dry gourd rinds
2. String
3. Yarn
4. Supporting device
5. Dowels or branch for bird feeder
6. Heavy balloon, or heavy plastic sheet
7. String or heavy rubber band

C. Procedure:
1. Cut holes in top half of gourd and suspend for making a bird feeder. (See drawing.)
2. Cut gourds in half and suspend for hanging planters.
3. Stretch the balloon or heavy plastic over the top of a cut half of a gourd to make a drum.
4. Secure with string or heavy rubber band.
5. For table planters, may make legs for support.

D. Results:
Creative projects can be made.

E. Basic Facts and Supplemental Information:
1. Gourds can be obtained in many grocery stores.
2. Gourds can be kept for many years.
3. Even though "gourd" is the name of the whole fruit, many people refer to the rinds as gourds.

F. Thought Questions for Class Discussions:
1. What other items can you create with gourds?
2. Would gourds make good liquid containers?
3. Could other musical instruments be made from gourds?

G. Related Ideas for Further Inquiry:
1. Plan some plants that might be placed in the gourds.
2. Gourds can be painted for artistic activities.
3. Plan other uses for gourd containers.
4. Study all Activities in this Section.

H. Vocabulary Builders—Spelling Words:
1) **gourd** 2) **planters** 3) **hinged** 4) **support**
5) **suspend** 6) **yarn** 7) **string** 8) **hanging**

I. Thought for Today:
"An open mind collects more riches than an open purse."

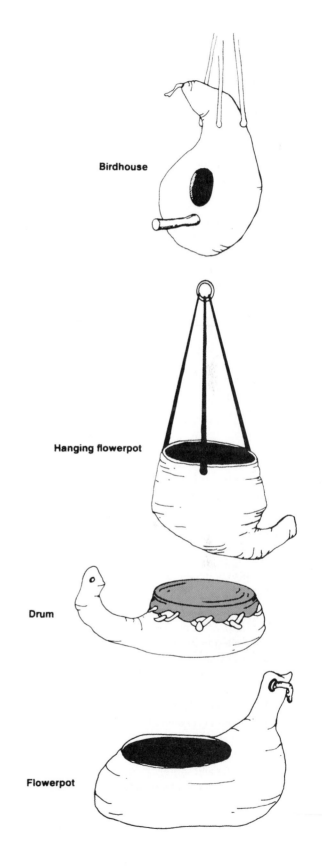

Birdhouse

Hanging flowerpot

Drum

Flowerpot

Activity

A. Problem: *How Do We Make a Simple Plant Terrarium?*

B. Materials Needed:

1. Large clear glass container and lid
2. Different small plants
3. Sufficient soil to fill one-third of container
4. Small trowel or tongue depressor
5. Decorative rocks or driftwood
6. Water can

C. Procedure:

1. Plan with class the interior setting of the terrarium (a wooded area, a desert scene, a farm, or other scene) and the planting arrangement.
2. Put 3″ of soil in the container.
3. Demonstrate proper method of removing plants from pots. (Gently tap sides and bottom with trowel until soil is loosened enough to lift plant from pot.)
4. Plant the plants in container.
5. Arrange rocks and other decorative material.
6. Lightly sprinkle garden.
7. Place lid to one side on terrarium allowing air to get to plants.

D. Result:

Class will have created an artistic terrarium.

E. Basic Facts and Supplemental Information:

1. A small dish garden or terrarium needs little or no water, as it uses the evaporation which condenses as moisture on the underside of the lid. If the terrarium appears dry, add a slight amount of water.
2. The terrarium should be given sufficient sunlight, and the air should be allowed to reach the plants. The terrarium should last for weeks and can be kept indefinitely by replacing the dead plants with live ones. Students will not only learn how to make a terrarium, but will also enjoy watching the plants develop.
3. Three terms are often confused: *vivarium, terrarium,* and *aquarium.*
4. An aquarium is essentially a container with water.
5. A terrarium is essentially a container with dirt, sand, or soil(s).
6. A vivarium is essentially a container that contains both water and soil(s).
7. The plural of each term ends in "ia"—aquaria, vivaria, and terraria.

F. Thought Questions for Class Discussions:

1. What are the differences between a terrarium, a vivarium, and an aquarium?
2. Why are some plants more suited to a terrarium than other plants?
3. What would happen if the terrarium lid were kept on?

G. Related Ideas for Further Inquiry:

1. Collect weeds around the school and plant them in the terrarium.
2. Plant grasses.
3. Plant radish seeds.
4. Study Activity III-C-1, "How do we plant seeds?"
5. Study Activity III-C-2, "Do different soils affect germination?"
6. Study Activity III-C-5, "How does light affect germination?"
7. Study Activity III-D-1, "What do plants need to grow?"
8. Study Activity III-D-6, "What kinds of classroom plants should we raise?"
9. Study all Activities in this Section.

H. Vocabulary Builders—Spelling Words:

1) **terrarium** 2) **vivarium** 3) **aquarium**
4) **trowel** 5) **decorative** 6) **plants** 7) **scene**
8) **bow** 9) **lid** 10) **develop** 11) **garden**

I. Thought for Today:

"It is by logic that we prove, but by intuition that we discover."

Activity

A. Problem: *How Can Leaves Be Preserved?*

B. Materials Needed, Procedure One:

1. Leaves
2. Three or four books
3. Newspapers

Materials Needed, Procedure Two:

1. Leaves
2. Clear plastic container (large enough to hold leaves)
3. Top for container or thin sheet plastic and rubber band
4. Water
5. Glycerin

Materials Needed, Procedure Three:

1. Leaves
2. Clear plastic folder
3. Cellophane tape

C. Procedure One:

1. Place the leaves between sheets of newspaper.
2. Place the books on top of the newspapers containing the leaves.
3. Let stand for several weeks.

Procedure Two:

1. Remove the ends of the long stems of leaves.
2. Fill the container with a solution of 2/3 of hot water and 1/3 glycerin.
3. Place the leaves in the solution.
4. The leaves and the solution should be left to stand for three or four weeks.

Procedure Three:

1. Select the leaves that you want to preserve.
2. Place the leaves in the plastic folder.
3. Trim to size desired.
4. Seal the folder with the cellophane tape.

D. Results:

1. The leaves will be preserved.
2. Some leaves will become brown and brittle with the passing of time.
3. The leaves will make beautiful displays.

Leaf in plastic

Leaves in glycerin solution

E. Basic Facts and Supplemental Information:

1. Most leaves will turn brown in time regardless of the means of preservation due to the withering away of chlorophyll, the active chemical in leaves.
2. Leaves turn sunlight into plant food.
3. Animals that eat plants are really getting energy from the sun which is stored in plants.
4. Leaves provide us with energy.
5. Leaves also supply us with some of the oxygen we need to breathe.

F. Thought Questions for Class Discussions:

1. Could we live without leaves?
2. How many different leaves can you identify?
3. What is the largest leaf you know?

G. Related Ideas for Further Inquiry:

1. Leaves can be used in many artistic projects.
2. Leaves can be copied by free-hand drawing, tracing, pressing, painting, copying, or by other techniques.
3. Study Section III-E, "Roots, stems, and leaves."
4. Study all other Activities in this Section.
5. Students have a lot of fun collecting leaves around the school campus or at home; they love to collect things.

H. Vocabulary Builders—Spelling Words:

1) **leaf** 2) **leaves** 3) **press** 4) **plastic**
5) **glycerin** 6) **newspaper** 7) **container**

I. Thought for Today:

"Happiness in life is not having what you want but wanting what you have."

A. Problem: *How Can We Make a "Spray Print"?*

B. Materials Needed:

1. White or colored construction paper, size 9″ × 12″
2. Spray paint of contrasting color
3. Large leaf with a distinctive outside edge
4. Pins (enough to fasten leaf points)
5. Newspapers

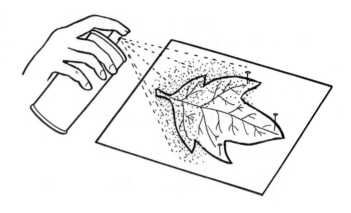

C. Procedure:

1. Place several thicknesses of newspaper on a working surface.
2. Place construction paper on newspaper.
3. Place the leaf on top of the construction paper.
4. Pin the leaf points to keep leaf from moving.
5. Test spray paint on old newspaper to be sure that the proper effect will be achieved when spraying on the leaf.
6. Stand a little in front of the leaf; begin spraying gently and carefully over the leaf.
7. Cover as much of the surface of the leaf as you wish, making sure that the edges are well-defined.
8. Several practice attempts usually need to be made to keep the leaf and background material free from blobs.
9. After the paint has dried, remove the leaf from the paper. The print should be labeled as follows:
   a. type of leaf (oak, elm, etc.)
   b. name of collector
   c. date of collection
10. Prints can be framed.
11. The best specimens can be mounted on the classroom bulletin board.

D. Results:

1. Beautiful colored silhouettes of the leaves will have been created.
2. A lot of enjoyment will have been realized as a result of combining this science and art activity.

E. Basic Facts and Supplemental Information:

1. Leaves can be collected on the campus, in local areas on field trips, and in and around the home.
2. Leaves are very important to us. They collect the energy from the sun which is then available to us. They also supply us with much-needed oxygen.
3. Many other materials have been used to make spray or splatter prints: toothbrushes, old knives, wire screens, shaving brushes, flat sticks, etc.

F. Thought Questions for Class Discussions:

1. What would be some good colors to use as background for green leaves?
2. What other objects might use this technique for outlining them?
3. What other methods could be used for making silhouettes?

G. Related Ideas for Further Inquiry:

1. Make hearts for Valentine's Day, pumpkins for Halloween, turkeys for Thanksgiving, etc. by "spray printing."
2. Study Activity III-A-3, "What kinds of plants are found in our neighborhood?"
3. Study Activity III-A-4, "What are the main parts of plants?"
4. Study Activity III-A-7, "Do all plants change color in the fall?"
5. Study Activity III-D-2, "Do plants need sunshine?"
6. Study all Activities in this Section.

H. Vocabulary Builders—Spelling Words:

1) **spray** 2) **print** 3) **colored** 4) **edges**
5) **construction** 6) **harmony** 7) **knife**
8) **newspaper** 9) **contrasting** 10) **leaves**

I. Thought for Today:

"The only thing most people do better than anyone else is read their own handwriting."

Activity

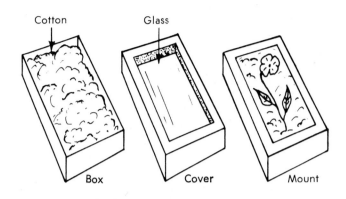

Cotton   Glass

Box   Cover   Mount

A. Problem: *How Can We Make Mounts for Plants?*

B. Materials Needed:
1. Shallow cardboard box of any desired dimensions
2. Piece of glass, clear plastic, or heavy cellophane to fit under cover of cardboard box (If glass is used, an adult should cut it to fit the box cover.)
3. Cotton
4. Razor blade or knife
5. Adhesive tape, masking tape, or glue
6. Dry plant or artificial flower or plant

C. Procedure:
1. Draw 1/2-inch margin along all sides of cover.
2. Cut out along these lines with razor blade or knife. (Be very careful.)
3. Fit glass, plastic, or cellophane cover, taping or gluing it to the bottom side of box cover.
4. Place enough cotton in box to nearly fill it.
5. Arrange the specimen, and label (See E-4 below.)
6. Replace cover.
7. Paint box if desired.

D. Result:
An attractive Riker-type box for storing a plant is made.

E. Basic Facts and Supplemental Information:
1. An inexpensive Riker-type box for mounting leaves, pressed flowers, branches or stems, butterflies, or other insects, shells, etc., for display is easily made.
2. Attractive and durable display boxes can be made from inexpensive or discarded materials.
3. Only a minimum of time and work is needed to make the boxes.
4. Label should contain:
   a. scientific name of specimen
   b. common name of specimen
   c. where found
   d. date
   e. collector's name
5. A "specimen" is a part of an object or an item that is typical of a group.
6. This type of box can also be used for small animals or animal specimens.
7. A similar box with a heavier base and omitting the cotton can be used for mounting insects.
8. Students love to collect things, and teachers should take advantage of this.
9. This is one activity where "intrinsic motivation" is self-evident.

F. Thought Questions for Class Discussions:
1. What kinds of plant specimens could be placed in these mounts?
2. What animal specimens could be placed in this type of mount?
3. What would cause spoilage of specimens in this Riker mount? What could be done to help eliminate this source or sources of trouble? (Answer: mothballs or mothflakes)
4. Could a similar type of box be used for storing other items?

G. Related Ideas for Further Inquiry:
1. Collect and mount butterflies.
2. Collect and mount other insects.
3. Study Activity IV-C-5, "How can we collect moths, butterflies, other insects, and spiders?"
4. Study Activity III-B-4, "How do bees help plant reproduction?"
5. Study Activity III-F-5, "How can leaves be preserved?"
6. Study all other Activities in this Section.

H. Vocabulary Builders—Spelling Words:
1) **Riker box** 2) **plastic** 3) **specimen**
4) **butterflies** 5) **cellophane** 6) **label**
7) **collection** 8) **insect**

I. Thought for Today:
"Snowflakes are one of nature's most fragile things, but just look at what they can do when they stick together."

PART IV
ANIMALS

SECTION **A** Classification   187

SECTION **B** Pets   193

SECTION **C** Insects and Spiders   197

SECTION **D** Reptiles   202

SECTION **E** Water Animals (Fish and Amphibians)   206

SECTION **F** Birds   211

SECTION **G** Mammals   215

SECTION **H** Worms and Snails   219

SECTION **I**   Storage and Care   221

SECTION **J** Resources   227

A. Problem: *What Is the Difference Between Living and Nonliving Things?*

B. Materials Needed:
1. Books
2. Pencils
3. Rocks
4. Small plants
5. Classroom animals
6. Pictures of students' pets
7. Plastic items (comb, ruler, etc.)
8. Miscellaneous items

C. Procedure:
1. Have class make a list of: (a) nonliving things, (b) plants, and (c) animals.
2. List the characteristics of each group.
3. Compare and contrast their differences.

D. Results:
1. The pupils will recognize the differences between living and nonliving things and between plants and animals.
2. They will understand that most known living things are classified as either plants or animals.
3. Students will learn that many scientists today classify all living things in five main kingdoms: (1) Monera, (2) Protista, (3) Fungi, (4) Plants, and (5) Animals

E. Basic Facts and Supplemental Information:
1. Living things are alike in some respects and different in others.
2. Nonliving things have very few characteristics of living things.
3. Animals move about; plants do not.
4. Animals have senses for locating food and the means of locomotion to obtain it.
5. Most plants make their own food.
6. Living things will have the following characteristics: (a) reproduce, (b) feed, (c) react to stimuli (irritability), (d) grow, (e) develop, (f) acquire energy, (g) have cells (or are one), (h) respire (breathe), (i) have complex structure (protoplasm), (j) die (may omit for younger students).
7. All living matter can be divided into three main classes:
   a. Producers (plants, fungi, algae)
   b. Consumers (most animals, including people)
   c. Reducers (bacteria, protozoa)

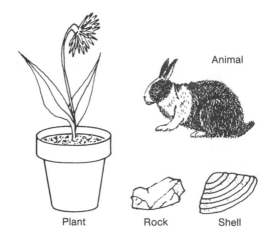

Animal

Plant   Rock   Shell

F. Thought Questions for Class Discussions:
1. How do some nonliving things move?
2. What is the biggest living thing you know about? the smallest?
3. What is the largest nonliving thing? the smallest?
4. Do nonliving things ever affect other nonliving things?

G. Related Ideas for Further Inquiry:
1. Look at some nonliving things with a microscope or magnifying glass.
2. Do some research on the biggest and smallest living things and nonliving things.
3. Younger students can collect pictures of plants.
4. Study Activity IV-A-2, "How many different species of animals are there?"
5. Study Activity III-A-1, "How do we classify living things?"
6. Study Activity VI-A-1, "What is the balance of nature?"

H. Vocabulary Builders—Spelling Words:
1) **nonliving**   2) **locomotion**   3) **stimuli**
4) **respiration**   5) **protoplasm**   6) **irritability**

I. Thought for Today:
"One of the secrets of a long and fruitful life is to forgive everybody everything every night before you go to bed."—Ann Landers

A. Problem: *How Many Different Species of Animals Are There?*

B. Materials Needed:
1. Pictures of different animals
2. Reference materials about animals
3. Newspaper accounts of animals
4. Bulletin board

C. Procedure:
1. Have students collect pictures of different animals and mount these pictures on the bulletin board.
2. Have students watch the media for information about different animals.
3. Discuss how animals differ:
   a. size
   b. weight
   c. mobility
   d. habitat
   e. feeding habits
   f. care of young
   g. relationship to people
   h. color

D. Results:
1. Students will learn that there are millions of different species of animals.
2. Students will learn that there are amazing differences among animals.
3. Students will realize that there are many interrelationships among animals including Homo sapiens (people).

E. Basic Facts and Supplemental Information:
1. Most taxonomists classify animals in the following "classes" and "phyla." Phyla are indicated by an (*). A few examples are:
   a. Porifera* (sponges)
   b. Coelenterata* (jellyfish, coral)
   c. Brachipods* (lingulas)
   d. Cephalopods* (squid, octopus)
   e. Gastropods (snail, sea slug)
   f. Bivalves (clam, scallop)
   g. Annelids (earthworm, leech)
   h. Insects (bee, butterfly, beetle)
   i. Arachnids (spider, scorpion)
   j. Crustaceans (lobster, crab)
   k. Echinoderms* (starfish)
   l. Fish (trout, shark, lamprey)
   m. Amphibians (frog, salamander)
   n. Birds (turkey, eagle, ostrich)
   o. Reptiles (snake, lizard)
   p. Mammals (horse, dog, humans)

2. Taxonomists estimate that there are between 2 and 30 million different kinds of species in all five kingdoms.
3. More than one million species of animals are known to exist today.
4. Arthropods are the most numerous, constituting about 85% of all animals.
5. Insects are the most numerous in this group.
6. Beetles are the most numerous insect.
7. Mammals constitute only about 5% of all animals.

F. Thought Questions for Class Discussions:
1. What relationships do humans have with animals (food, transportation, companionship, etc.)?
2. How have humans caused the extinction of some species?
3. What are "preys?" "predators?"

G. Related Ideas for Further Inquiry:
1. Study Activity VI-A-3, "What is 'biological diversity'?"
2. Study Activity VI-A-9, "Are any animals threatened with extinction?"
3. Study Activity IV-A-3, "What animals can we find on our school campus?"

H. Vocabulary Builders—Spelling Words:
1) **humans** 2) **mammals** 3) **insects** 4) **beetles**
5) **prey** 6) **predator** 7) **extinction** 8) **habitat**

I. Thought for Today:
"It's a crime to catch fish in some lakes and a miracle in others."

Activity

A. Problem: *What Animals Can We Find on Our School Campus?*

B. Materials Needed:

1. Insect nets
2. Collecting jars
3. Riker mounts
4. Notebooks
5. Writing instruments
6. Field guides (books for identification)
7. Magnifying glasses
8. Shoe boxes
9. Metal spoons
10. Tweezers
11. Small cages

C. Procedure:

1. Decide on the amount of time you want to spend on this Activity. (A week is usually enough.)
2. Decide on whether you want to collect the animals or just identify them.
3. Divide the class into four or six groups.
4. Make a contest out of this to see which group can identify the most animals found around the school (or whatever limits you choose).
5. Include specific rules and regulations for safety.
6. Have each group keep a notebook which should include for each animal:
   a. common name
   b. date found
   c. where located
   d. type of animal
      1) very small animal
      2) insect, land
      3) insect, flying
      4) rodent
      5) water animal, etc.

D. Results:

1. Students will learn from this fun Activity for they love to collect things and they enjoy playing games. This "contest" is really a game to them.
2. Students will learn that there are many animals around the school.
3. Students will realize that the vast number of animals are insects.

Fly   Bee

Beetle   Grasshopper

E. Basic Facts and Supplemental Information:

1. Safety of the students is vital:
   a. crossing streets looking for animals
   b. biting or stinging insects
   c. poisonous plants, etc.
2. In watching for animals, it is usually best to pick a spot and sit quietly for a period of time.
3. Listening for animal sounds will help locate and define animals.

F. Thought Questions for Class Discussions:

1. Where does each animal live?
2. What is its primary food source?
3. Is this animal a "prey" or a "predator"? It could be both.

G. Related Ideas for Further Inquiry:

1. Study how animals can be housed.
2. Parents can become involved if you include home areas in your boundaries.
3. Similar activities can be conducted for plants.
4. Study Activity IV-A-1, "What is the difference between living and nonliving things?"
5. Study Activity IV-A-2, "How many different species of animals are there?"
6. Study Activity IV-A-4, "How do animals move?"

H. Vocabulary Builders—Spelling Words:

1) **insects** 2) **spiders** 3) **rodents** 4) **collecting**
5) **searching** 6) **identify** 7) **guides** 8) **ants**

I. Thought for Today:

"It's nice for children to have pets until the pets start having 'children.' "

A. Problem: *How Do Animals Move?*

B. Materials Needed:
1. Pictures of animals that are:
   a. walking
   b. swimming
   c. climbing
   d. swinging
   e. crawling
   f. hopping
   g. slithering
   h. flying
   i. gliding
   j. diving
   k. running
   l. trotting
   m. creeping
   n. stalking
   o. fluttering
   p. rolling
   q. holding
   r. grasping
   s. jumping, etc.
2. Reference materials
3. Multisensory aids:
   a. films
   b. slides
   c. filmstrips, etc.

C. Procedure:
1. Have a general discussion about how animals move i.e., as cited in "Materials Needed 1." above.
2. Discuss the reasons that animals move:
   a. search for food
   b. look for water
   c. means of protection
   d. recreation and exercise
   e. seeking mates
   f. communication, etc.
3. Use whatever multisensory aids are appropriate and available.
4. Have students make a list of five to ten common animals and have them cite how each of these move: Cats, dogs, and horses all use four legs to move; birds, moths, and butterflies have wings to move, etc.
5. Discuss different ways that people move, e.g., run, walk, swim, etc.

D. Results:
1. Students will learn that all animals make many movements.
2. Each movement is usually for a specific purpose.

E. Basic Facts and Supplemental Information:
1. Animals must move for survival.
2. Human beings must move for survival.

3. People not only move their physical bodies themselves, but they also employ electrical and mechanical means to transport them from place to place.

F. Thought Questions for Class Discussions:
1. Do plants move?
2. How many ways can people move?
3. Select your favorite sport. How many movements are involved in it?

G. Related Ideas for Further Inquiry:
1. Study Activity IV-A-1, "What is the difference between living and nonliving things?"
2. Study Activity IV-A-2, "How many different species of animals are there?"
3. Study, Activity IV-A-3, "What animals can we find on our school campus?"
4. Study Activity IV-A-6, "How do animals protect themselves?"
5. Study Activity VI-A-1, "What is the balance of nature?"
6. Study Activity VI-A-3, "What is 'biological diversity'?"

H. Vocabulary Builders—Spelling Words:
1) **walking**   2) **flying**   3) **swimming**   4) **creeping** (also other movements cited in Materials 1.)

I. Thought for Today:
"Jumping to conclusions doesn't make for happy landings."

A. Problem: *How Do Animals Communicate?*

B. Materials Needed:

Pictures of many animals

C. Procedure:

1. Discuss animal characteristics.
2. Discuss the need of animals to communicate with other members of their species.
3. Discuss how many animals are "social" animals.
4. Discuss the various means animals use to communicate such as:
   a. touching
   b. making sounds
   c. lighting (night lights)
   d. pheromones (chemical substances)
      1) lay trails to food
      2) alarms
      3) mating attractants
   e. movements
5. All students have seen dogs associating with one another. Discuss how dogs "communicate": (a) fear, (b) anger, (c) friendliness, (d) need for attention, (e) possessiveness, etc.
6. Pair several students and assign one of them to communicate to the other without using spoken language. This could be inviting one to go to a movie, having a hamburger, playing tennis after school, etc.

D. Result:

Students learn that animals communicate in many ways.

E. Basic Facts and Supplemental Information:

1. Animals need to protect themselves and to protect other members of their species.
2. Since animals prey on other animals, warnings are a vital part of their continued existence.
3. Some animals communicate by running away.

4. Some communication is highly technical such as bees communicating with other bees "telling" them the direction and distance where food has been located.
5. Cats, dogs, and other household pets communicate with people in many ways.

F. Thought Questions for Class Discussions:

1. In what ways do people communicate that are similar to animals?
2. In what ways do people communicate that are different from animals?
3. What are the main reasons people communicate?
4. In what ways do animals communicate with people?
5. In what ways do people communicate with animals?

G. Related Ideas for Further Inquiry:

1. Study people's gestures. Do they mean different things to different people?
2. Study how transportation is related to communication with people.
3. Study gestures and/or hand signals used by people when training pets.
4. Study Activity IV-A-1, "What is the difference between living and nonliving things?"
5. Study Activity IV-A-2, "How many different species of animals are there?"
6. Study Activity IV-A-6, "How do animals protect themselves?"
7. Study Activity IV-J-3, "Should animals be protected?"

H. Vocabulary Builders—Spelling Words:

1) **touching**   2) **sounds**   3) **attractants**
4) **pheromones**   5) **alarm**   6) **protection**

I. Thought for Today:

"The first thing children learn when they get a drum is that they will never get another one."

Ants "communicate" showing the location of a dead milkweed butterfly caterpillar.

A. Problem: *How Do Animals Protect Themselves?*

B. Materials Needed:

1. Pictures and multisensory materials about animals:
   a. running from a predator
   b. hiding in a tree
   c. burrowing into the ground, etc.
2. Books on animals' living habits

C. Procedure:

1. Discuss animal characteristics.
2. Discuss the need for animals to protect themselves.
3. Discuss the roles of "preys" and "predators."
4. Discuss how animals protect themselves, including:
   a. camouflage
   b. venom
   c. speed (run away)
   d. size (of some animals)
   e. stings
   f. teeth, antlers, tusks
   g. hide (ground, tree stumps, etc.)
   h. sounds
5. Discuss things that people use to protect themselves:
   a. clothing
   b. furnaces
   c. air conditioners
   d. health habits
   e. social activities
   f. fire protection
   g. police protection
   h. safety precautions
   i. shelters, etc.

D. Results:

1. Students will learn about preys, predators, and protection techniques.
2. Students will realize that protection is necessary for survival for all animals including human beings.

E. Basic Facts and Supplemental Information:

1. Animals have to protect themselves from other animals, the weather, and sometimes, people.
2. Protection is a constant concern of all animals.

F. Thought Questions for Class Discussions:

1. How do people protect themselves that is similar to the ways animals do?
2. How do people protect themselves differently from the ways animals do?

Beaver building a home

3. How do some groups of people protect themselves from other groups of people?
4. There is a theory in science that says: "survival of the fittest." What do you think this means?

G. Related Ideas for Further Inquiry:

1. Discuss how pets are protected in private homes.
2. Discuss the ways the government protects animals.
3. Study different organizations which lobby for animal protection.
4. Study Activity IV-A-2, "How many different species of animals are there?"
5. Study Activity IV-A-5, "How do animals communicate?"
6. Study Activity IV-J-3, "Should animals be protected?"
7. Study Activity VI-A-1, "What is the balance of nature?"
8. Study Activity VI-A-3, "What is 'biological diversity'?"

H. Vocabulary Builders—Spelling Words:

1) **protect**   2) **camouflage**   3) **venom**   4) **stings**
5) **antlers**   6) **survival**   7) **fittest**   8) **speed**

I. Thought for Today:

"The world could be greatly improved with more vision and less television."

SECTION B: PETS

Activity

IV **B** 1

A. Problem: *What Kinds of Pets Does Our Class Have in Their Homes?*

B. Materials Needed:
1. Chalkboard
2. Chalk
3. Class notebook, album

C. Procedure:
1. Survey the students and list on the chalkboard the different kinds of pets the students have in their homes.
2. Discuss the care and feeding of these pets. See Activity IV-I-4, "How can we make a cage for medium-sized animals?"
3. Have students bring in their small pets or draw pictures of any size pet(s) they have.
4. Place the pictures or drawings in the class notebook-album.
5. Have each student describe his/her pet and some unusual experiences he/she has had with it.

D. Results:
1. Students will list the usual pets—dogs, cats, birds, and fish.
2. Some students will have unusual pets such as turtles, hamsters, rats, gerbils, mice, frogs, snakes, etc.

E. Basic Facts and Supplemental Information:
1. Classroom pets will enrich any classroom environment.
2. Excellent science activities can be developed around a female pet and her young.
3. Responsibility is vital in caring for pets so they do not suffer from lack of food, exercise, or comfort.
4. Before a final decision is made for the selection of a classroom pet, provisions should be made for care of the pet over weekends, holidays, and during vacation time.

F. Thought Questions for Class Discussions:
1. Should people be allowed to keep exotic pets, pets that would live outside of their natural environments?

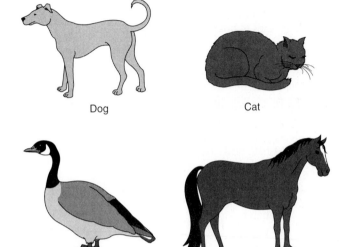

Dog   Cat

Goose   Horse

2. Should animals be used for research?
3. What are some of the problems of lost or stray pets?

G. Related Ideas for Further Inquiry:
1. Visit pet stores for more information on pets and their care.
2. Discuss visits to the zoo.
3. Talk to local veterinarians regarding problems faced by many pets and pet owners.

H. Vocabulary Builders—Spelling Words:
1) **responsibility**   2) **caring**   3) **feeding**
4) **veterinarian**   5) **guinea pigs**   6) **gerbils**

I. Thought for Today:
"Pets are such agreeable friends, they ask no questions, they make no criticisms."

Activity

A. Problem: *What Kind of Pet Should I Have?*

B. Materials Needed:

1. Small pets belonging to students or pictures or drawings of them
2. Cages to house pets temporarily

C. Procedure:

1. Have a discussion about pets in general and those owned by the students.
2. Have students make a list of pets that they know about.
3. Group pets according to major characteristics such as fish, birds, dogs, cats, horses, cows, sheep, ducks, hamsters, etc.
4. Have committees research each of the major types of pet categories as to:
   a. habits
   b. problems
   c. care
   d. food requirements
   e. training, etc.
   and report their findings to the class.

D. Results:

1. Students will learn about pets.
2. They will learn how to care for their pets.
3. They will learn that some animals are hatched from eggs while others are live-bearers.

E. Basic Facts and Supplemental Information:

1. Students can obtain information about pets in many ways, such as:
   a. visiting pet stores
   b. talking to veterinarians
   c. observing their pets
   d. talking to friends and neighbors about their pets.
2. Responsibility for the care of pets must always be assigned whether at home or at school so that pets do not suffer from lack of food, water, exercise, or physical comfort.
3. It is important that the whole family share in the discussion of what kinds of pets should be kept in and/or around the home.

F. Thought Questions for Class Discussions:

1. Why do people want pets?
2. Should people keep exotic pets (animals out of their natural environment)?
3. What should be done with stray pets? lost pets?

4. Should cats be licensed the same as dogs?
5. What kind of medical attention do household pets normally need?

G. Related Topics for Further Inquiry:

1. Find out whether each species of pet is considered a prey, a predator, or both.
2. For art work, draw a pet and use the drawing for a workbook cover.
3. Look for interesting articles about pets, and report to class.
4. Students can bring in pictures of their pets.
5. Do research on training of pets.
6. Have students study the geographic sources of exotic pets.
7. Study Activity IV-B-3, "How do we care for dogs and cats?"
8. Study Activity IV-B-4, "How do we care for hamsters, guinea pigs, gerbils, and/or mice?"

H. Vocabulary Builders—Spelling Words:

1) **pets**   2) **dogs**   3) **cats**   4) **farm**   5) **field**
6) **care**   7) **training**   8) **feeding**   9) **problems**

I. Thought for Today:

"If dogs could talk, they wouldn't be such good friends."

Activity

A. Problem: *How Do We Care for Dogs and Cats?*

B. Materials Needed:
1. Pictures of cats
2. Pictures of dogs
3. Selected dogs and cats of students
4. Printed materials from pet stores or veterinary clinics

C. Procedure:
1. Discuss the different breeds of dogs and cats the students have as pets.
2. Describe other breeds of dogs and cats.
3. Have each student tell how his/her pet is cared for: (a) feeding, (b) exercising, (c) excretion needs, (d) cleaning, (e) sleeping, (f) protecting (g) inoculations for disease prevention.
4. Have each student also tell about his/her pet's problems, idiosyncrasies, tricks, manners, association with other animals, etc.
5. Discuss common problems and diseases of dogs and cats: (a) fleas, (b) ticks, (c) lice, (d) parvovirus, (e) distemper, (f) rabies.
6. Have a student or resource person talk about showing dogs at dog shows or cats at cat shows.
7. Study printed materials obtained from feed stores or veterinary clinics regarding the care of pets.

D. Results:
1. Students will learn about the care and feeding of dogs and cats.
2. They will become more appreciative of all living things.

E. Basic Facts and Supplemental Information:
1. Animal shelters are full of dogs and cats that are lost, strayed, or abandoned because people have not taken proper care of their pets. Every class should have some classroom pet(s): fish, birds, small animals, etc.
2. Cats should have scratching pads (carpet-covered wooden posts).
3. Squirt catnip near the base of the scratching pad.
4. Newly acquired cats should be kept indoors for 10 days to become acquainted with their new home.
5. Litter boxes should be cleaned twice each week.

6. All pets should have proper vaccinations.
7. Most people know how to take care of dogs.
8. Cats are a different species with different needs than dogs.
9. We have about 125 million dogs and cats in the United States.
10. Dogs and cats alone require seven billion pounds of pet food yearly.

F. Thought Questions for Class Discussions:
1. In what ways are dogs and cats like people?
2. In what ways are dogs and cats different from people?
3. Do most pet owners take proper care of their dogs and cats?

G. Related Topics for Further Inquiry:
1. Check with a veterinarian about the care and feeding of dogs and cats.
2. Visit an animal shelter (pound).
3. Study Activity IV-B-2, "What kind of pet should I have?"
4. Study Activity IV-B-4, "How do we care for hamsters, guinea pigs, gerbils, and/or mice?"

H. Vocabulary Builders—Spelling Words:
1) **feeding** 2) **exercising** 3) **excreting**
4) **cleaning** 5) **sleeping** 6) **caring** 7) **pets**
8) **tricks** 9) **hamsters** 10) **guinea pigs**

I. Thought for Today:
"Nothing in the world is friendlier than a wet dog."

Activity

A. Problem: *How Do We Care for Hamsters, Guinea Pigs, Gerbils, and/or Mice?*

B. Materials Needed:
1. Male animal
2. Female animal of same species
3. Two wire mesh pens, about 3′ × 2′ in area, with sides at least 16″ high
4. Four pans for food and water

C. Procedure:
1. Select students for specific duties, such as feeding the animals, cleaning the pens, or recording observations.
2. If desired, place two animals of the opposite sex in the same pen and in time they will mate. Do not cage two males of the same species together because they are apt to fight.
3. Feed the animals a good commercial food product (well-balanced).
4. Keep fresh water in the pen at all times.

D. Results:
1. Students will learn about the care and feeding of animals.
2. Pupils will discover some of the responsibilities of breeding and caring for young animals.

E. Basic Facts and Supplemental Information:
1. All life comes from life, and each species reproduces its own kind of living organism.
2. Life is dependent upon certain materials and conditions.
3. Most animals need food, water, exercise, fresh air, and sunshine.
4. Use caution in handling the females for a short time preceding and following the birth of a litter.
5. Mice and hamsters are usually the most available rodents.
6. Mice and white rats make good pets, and they are a lot of fun to watch.
   a. They are nearsighted and timid.
   b. They are nocturnal and love to explore.
   c. They can produce up to 17 litters a year with 6 to 12 young in each litter.

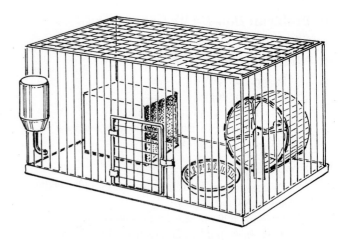

   d. They eat about two ounces of food a day which should include seeds, nuts, dry dog food, bread, cheese, and green vegetables.
   e. Mice should have a litter box which needs to be cleaned every two days.
7. Responsibilities must always be assigned to students so that the pets do not suffer from lack of food, water, exercise, or physical comfort.

F. Thought Questions for Class Discussions:
1. What are some common characteristics of pets?
2. What are the natural habitats of these animals?
3. How do these animals differ from dogs and cats?
4. Should animals be raised for fur coats and/or scientific research?

G. Related Topics for Further Inquiry:
1. Stories can be collected about pets.
2. Students can write creative stories about pets.
3. Students can relate their art work to these activities.
4. Study other Activities in this Section.

H. Vocabulary Builders—Spelling Words:
1) **hamster** 2) **guinea pigs** 3) **gerbils** 4) **mice**
5) **rodents** 6) **exercise** 7) **sunshine** 8) **cleaning**

I. Thought for Today:
"Strolling through the back alley the seventy-four pound mouse cried, 'Here Kitty, Kitty, Kitty.' "

SECTION C: INSECTS AND SPIDERS

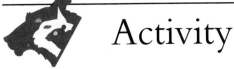

Activity

IV C 1

A. Problem: *How Do Spiders Differ from Insects?*

B. Materials Needed:

Specimens or pictures of spiders

C. Procedure:

1. Collect specimens and pictures of as many spiders as possible.
2. Study the body parts of each of them.
3. Note that the main difference between spiders and insects is the number of legs. Insects have six legs; spiders have eight legs.
4. Most insects have three main body parts while the spiders usually have only two.

D. Results:

1. Students will learn about the main characteristics of spiders.
2. They will learn about spiders' homes.

E. Basic Facts and Supplemental Information:

1. Arachnids include spiders, scorpions, ticks, mites, horseshoe crabs, and king crabs.
2. One of the master engineering jobs is accomplished by the spider in spinning its web with silk-like fibers.
3. Webs are sticky so spiders can catch their prey.
4. The spiders feel a "catch" when the web vibrates.
5. Each spider then paralyzes its prey.
6. Later the spider feeds upon the prey.
7. Spiders do not sting; some bite.
8. Some spiders are nomadic, that is they have no webs or homes.
9. Insects have wings; spiders have none.
10. The head and thorax, usually separate in insects, are combined in the spider to form a cephalothorax which is separate from the abdomen.

F. Thought Questions for Class Discussions:

1. What kinds of spiders have you seen?
2. Where have you seen them?
3. Do spiders fight among themselves?

G. Related Topics for Further Inquiry:

1. Make collections or copies of spiders' webs.
2. Make a spider vivarium.
3. Study: other Activities in this Section.

SPIDERS

Spiders differ in residences

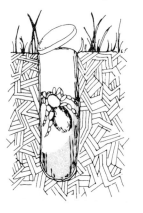

Trap-door spider and nest (Below ground level)

Turret spider and nest (Partially below ground level)

Spiders differ in web design

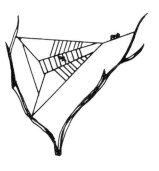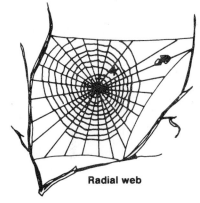

Triangular web

Radial web

H. Vocabulary Builders—Spelling Words:

1) **spider** 2) **cobweb** 3) **radial** 4) **triangular**
5) **trapdoor** 6) **abdomen** 7) **cephalothorax**

I. Thought for Today:

"If it weren't for the last minute, a lot of things wouldn't get done."

A. Problem: *How Do Ants Live?*

B. Materials Needed:

1. Ants, ten to fifteen, any kind
2. Ant house or large jar with screen (See drawing.)
3. Loose soil
4. Water
5. Black construction paper
6. Small moist sponge
7. Honey or sugar
8. Magnifying glass
9. String or masking tape

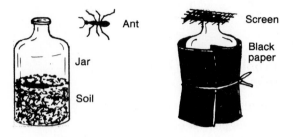

C. Procedure:

1. Fill the jar with loose soil.
2. Dampen soil slightly.
3. Leave sponge in jar (at the top).
4. Place the ants and a small amount of sugar or honey in jar.
5. Cover jar with fine wire screen.
6. Tie or tape black paper around the jar. (Leave about an inch at the top of the jar without paper.)
7. Slip the black paper off for a short period each day to observe the ants at work.
8. It is necessary that ants have water daily.
9. Feed ants bread crumbs, very small meat scraps, honey, and sugar. Caution—too much food will cause mold and odor in the colony.
10. Have students observe ants under a magnifying glass and draw a simple sketch of an ant's main body parts.

D. Results:

1. Students will see that ants build living areas that consist of tunnels and storehouses.
2. Students will learn the major anatomical parts of ants.

E. Basic Facts and Supplemental Information:

1. Ants are social insects.
2. Ants work together to build homes and carry on life processes. They live in a specialized animal society, that is, some ants are workers, some royalty, and some cows.
3. Queens and males both have wings.
4. A simple ant house can be constructed out of glass. The large sides should be 1′ square each, and the small sides 1′ high and 2″ wide each. The

base can be any hard material cut to size. This ant house provides good viewing of ant tunnels. Black paper must still be used to keep the ant house dark.

5. Ant houses are highly motivating devices and stimulate a great amount of interest and curiosity on the part of the students.

F. Thought questions for Class Discussions:

1. How do ants behave differently in their natural environment than they do in a classroom ant house?
2. What kinds of food have you seen ants carry to their natural homes?
3. Are ants strong animals? How large an item in comparison with their body size have you seen them carry or drag?
4. Can ants see? Have you seen two ants meet head-on? What happens?

G. Related Topics for Further Inquiry:

1. Carefully observe ants in their natural habitat.
2. Locate and describe the different kinds of ants.
3. Learn the difference between insects and spiders.
4. Study Activity IV-C-3, "How do bees live?"
5. Study Activity IV-C-5, "How can we collect moths, butterflies, other insects, and spiders?"

H. Vocabulary Builders—Spelling Words:

1) **ants** 2) **aunts** 3) **screen** 4) **paper** 5) **society**
6) **ant house** 7) **dark** 8) **masking tape**

I. Thought for Today:

"We need society and we need solitude just as we need summer and winter, day and night, exercise and rest."—Philip Gilbert Hamerton

Activity

IV **C** 3

A. Problem: *How Do Bees Live?*

B. Materials Needed:

1. Glass bee house, if available
2. Dead bee
3. Pictures of bees
4. Books containing information about bees
5. Magnifying glass
6. Honeycomb (or jar of honey if honeycomb is unavailable)

C. Procedure:

1. Bring a bee house, empty honeycomb, honey, and/or dead bee to class; this will stimulate the interest of the students.
2. The class should list questions about bees and group them around broad areas such as food, habits, structure, etc.
3. The class should then attempt to find answers to their questions by observation and reading.
4. Observe a dead bee under a magnifying glass.
5. Pupils should draw a simple sketch of the main anatomical parts of a bee.

D. Results:

1. Students will learn about the community life of bees.
2. Students will learn about the main body parts of bees.

E. Basic Facts and Supplemental Information:

1. Bees are insects.
2. Life in a beehive is complex, orderly, and interesting. Each bee has its own work to do for the welfare of the entire colony.
3. People often confuse bees, wasps, hornets, and yellow-jackets.
4. Precautions should be cited if live bees are investigated.
5. There are 20,000 species of bees.
6. A new species of bee is invading the United States. It is called the "Killer Bee" because its sting is more deadly than those of typical honeybees.

    These bees are "Africanized honeybees"—the term entomologists prefer. They produce more honey but they attack intruders in greater numbers. To the naked eye, they look no different than the European honeybee commonly found in the United States.
7. Bees communicate where nectar is by "dancing maneuvers" (turning and waggling).

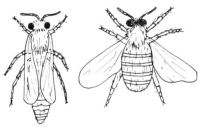

Queen (Female)   Drone (Male)

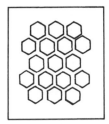

Worker   Honeycomb

F. Thought Questions for Class Discussions:

1. How does the society of a bee compare with that of an ant?
2. What determines the different flavors of honey?
3. What are the specific jobs of the worker bees, drones, and queen bee?

G. Related Topics for Further Inquiry:

1. Study how beeswax is used (candles, cosmetics, pharmaceuticals, dental impressions, etc.).
2. Discuss keeping bees with a local beekeeper.
3. Study Activity III-B-4, "How do bees help plant reproduction?"
4. Study Activity IV-C-1, "How do spiders differ from insects?"
5. Study Activity IV-C-5, "How can we collect moths, butterflies, other insects, and spiders?"

H. Vocabulary Builders—Spelling Words:

1) **queen**   2) **drone**   3) **worker**
4) **honeycomb**   5) **sting**   6) **Africanized**
7) **honeybee**   8) **maneuvers**   9) **nectar**
10) **communicate**

I. Thought for Today:

"Friendships multiply joys and divide griefs."
—*H. G. Bohn*

Activity

A. Problem: *How Do Moths Differ from Butterflies?*

B. Materials Needed:
1. Pictures and/or specimens of moths
2. Pictures and/or specimens of butterflies
3. Reference materials on insects
4. Collected specimens (optional)
   a. *butterflies:*
      1) butterfly net
      2) collecting jars
      3) Riker mounts
   b. *moths: (collect at night)*
      1) lamp
      2) saucer
      3) sugar solution (one teaspoon of sugar to one tablespoon of water)
      4) collecting net
      5) collecting jar
      6) Riker mounts

C. Procedure:
1. Decide whether you want to identify the differences between moths and butterflies by pictures and reference materials or collect specimens and then identify the differences.
2. If you want to collect butterflies, this can easily be done during the day, especially around flowering plants.
3. If you want to collect moths, you can easily do this at night, using a light and a sugar solution to attract them, then using a small net to catch them. Another method to trap moths is to get a large box and cover the top (about two-thirds) with muslin or cheesecloth. Put a small flashlight inside the box. The light will attract the moths and some of them will get caught inside where they can be collected.
4. A collecting jar can be used to kill the insects; the specimens can then be displayed in Riker mounts.

D. Results:
1. Students will be able to distinguish between these two species of insects.
2. If specimens are collected, the students will become junior entomologists.

Butterfly   Moth

E. Basic Facts and Supplemental Information:
1. Both moths and butterflies are insects.
2. Both go through the four stages of development—"metamorphosis." These are: (1) egg, (2) caterpillar, (3) pupa, and finally, (4) adult.
3. Both have three body parts, six legs, and antennae.
4. Butterflies fly during the day; moths fly at night.
5. Moths' bodies are relatively wider than butterflies.
6. Butterflies' antennae always have "knobs" on the ends.
7. When resting, butterflies' wings are erect and over their heads, while moths fold their wings onto their bodies when resting.
8. Butterflies are more colorful because color is their primary mating attractant, while the moths' colors tend to blend in with their environment to serve as a camouflage during the day.
9. Moths use pheromones (smells) to attract mates.

F. Thought Questions for Class Discussions:
1. Would "flutterby" be a better name than "butterfly?" This was one of its early names.
2. Why aren't moths seen during the daytime?
3. What is "phototropism"?

G. Related Topics for Further Inquiry:
1. Do butterflies aid in plant reproduction?
2. Why is it important for moths to blend in with their environment during the day?
3. Do butterflies migrate?

H. Vocabulary Builders—Spelling Words:
1) **butterfly** 2) **moth** 3) **thorax** 4) **abdomen**
5) **antennae** 6) **pheromone** 7) **phototropism**

I. Thought for Today:
"The caterpillar said to the butterfly, 'You'll never get me up in one of those things.'"

Activity

A. Problem: *How Can We Collect Moths, Butterflies, Other Insects, and Spiders?*

B. Materials Needed:
1. Butterfly net
2. Killing jar and cover
3. Carbon tetrachloride, ethyl acetate, or acetone
4. Cotton
5. Envelopes, small
6. Magnifying glass or lens (10 power)
7. Cardboard box, side
8. Dowels (12″–18″)
9. Kitchen sieve (for water insects)
10. Reference materials for identifying insects and spiders

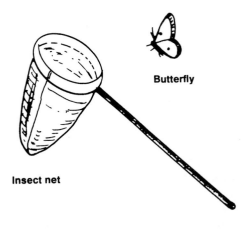

Butterfly

Insect net

C. Procedure:
1. Have class or group take a walk around the campus to look for insects and spiders.
2. Bring all equipment listed under "Materials."
3. Watch for flying insects.
4. Use net to entrap.
5. Use net to scoop along grasses and wooded areas.
6. Work specimens to small end of net.
7. Place killing jar with liquid next to specimen.
8. Have some students select a bush.
9. Specimens will be found in the bush.
10. Have one or two students hold a side of a cardboard box slightly bent in the middle next to bush or under part of it while others use dowels to tap lightly on the bush. Insects will fall onto the cardboard.
11. Also look under rocks and dead wood carefully.
12. If water is nearby use kitchen sieve to collect specimens.
13. After the insects have been killed, place in envelopes for classifying and mounting.

Insect

Cardboard with punched holes

Cotton soaked with carbon tetrachloride

Insect killing jar

D. Results:
1. A walk around campus will be planned.
2. Insects and spiders will be collected.
3. Most specimens will be identified.

E. Basic Facts and Supplemental Information:
1. Students will enjoy this activity.
2. Usually, besides insects and spiders, other animals will be seen and can be identified.

F. Thought Questions for Class Discussions:
1. Where else might insects be found?
2. How do farmers protect their fruits and vegetables from unwanted insects?
3. How is food in the home protected from insects?

G. Related Topics for Further Inquiry:
1. Take field trips to study other plants and animals.
2. Turn on porch light at night and collect flying insects.
3. Students can look for insects and spiders around their homes.
4. Study other Activities in this Section.

H. Vocabulary Builders—Spelling Words:
1) **killing jar** 2) **poison** 3) **sieve** 4) **envelope**
5) **insects** 6) **spiders** 7) **cotton** 8) **specimen**

I. Thought for Today:
"Be thankful if you have a job a little harder than you like. A razor cannot be sharpened on a piece of velvet."

Section D: Reptiles

Activity

A. Problem: *What Are Reptiles?*

B. Materials Needed:

1. Models, specimens or pictures of:
   a. snakes
   b. lizards
   c. turtles
   d. crocodiles
   e. alligators
   f. other reptiles
2. Reference materials on reptiles

C. Procedure:

1. Discuss with class members their experiences with snakes, lizards, turtles, and other reptiles.
2. Discuss the characteristics of common reptiles:
   a. lay eggs on land
   b. have leathery skin or shell
   c. ectothermic—body temperature varies with external temperature (cold-blooded)
   d. have two pairs of legs (except snakes)
   e. have claws on their toes
   f. have scaly skin for body covering
   g. three main groups:
      1) squamates (snakes and lizards)
      2) crocodilians (crocodiles, alligators, caimans, and gavials)
      3) chelonians (tortoises, turtles, and terrapins)
3. Study local reptiles.
4. Relate any unusual characteristics found in reference materials such as:
   a. About 6,500 species of reptiles exist today.
   b. Dinosaurs were reptiles that dominated the Earth for millions of years.
   c. Snakes can spring only half the length of their bodies.
   d. Very few snakes are poisonous.
   e. Lizards and snakes shed their skins from time to time so they can grow.
   f. A few species of crocodiles can reach almost 30 feet in length.
   g. Fertilization takes place inside the body.

D. Results:

1. Students will acquire some basic information about reptiles.
2. Pupils will learn that most snakes are not poisonous and they help keep the rodent population in balance.

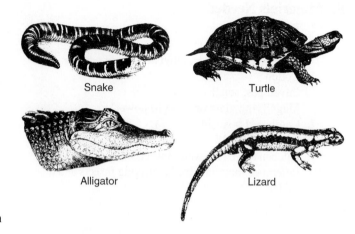

Snake   Turtle

Alligator   Lizard

E. Basic Facts and Supplemental Information:

1. Reptiles are a "class" of animals.
2. They are found primarily in warm climates, especially in the tropics.
3. The Anaconda snake can reach 30 ′ in length.
4. The Marine Leatherback turtle weighs up to 1,500 pounds.
5. Except for snakes, reptiles have four limbs which project from the sides.
6. Reptile hides are valued in the making of shoes, purses, etc. In some parts of the world reptiles are hunted for food.

F. Thought Questions for Class Discussions:

1. Would Canada, Alaska, or Siberia have many reptiles?
2. How do reptiles differ from mammals?
3. How do crocodiles differ from alligators?

G. Related Topics for Further Inquiry:

1. Study reptiles in local zoos.
2. Study the rise and fall of dinosaurs.
3. Study Activity IV-D-2, "What are some characteristics of snakes?"
4. Study Activity IV-D-3, "How do we make a terrarium for reptiles?"

H. Vocabulary Builders—Spelling Words:

1) **snakes**   2) **lizards**   3) **turtles**   4) **tortoises**
5) **crocodiles**   6) **alligators**   7) **reptiles**

I. Thought for Today:

"He swam up the Nile as far as the first crocodile."

Activity

A. Problem: *What Are Some Characteristics of Snakes?*

B. Materials Needed:
1. Pictures of snakes (king, gopher, garter, bull, coral, and rattle)
2. Plaster specimens may be borrowed from local museums, colleges, or universities
3. Reference materials about snakes

C. Procedure:
1. Gather materials and data on snakes from the United States Department of Agriculture.
2. Post pictures on the bulletin board to arouse interest and discussion. Invariably the discussion will lead to poisonous snakes and common misconceptions concerning snakes.
3. Guide the discussion; ask for volunteers to do some research and present their findings to the class.

D. Result:
Better understanding of snakes helps to correct misconceptions; results in less fear of snakes, and helps to protect useful snakes.

E. Basic Facts and Supplemental Information:
There are many more harmless than harmful snakes. Many snakes are helpful to people and should be protected. Most snakes, including poisonous ones, are timid and flee from people if they can. They are not as cunning as many people believe.
1. Characteristics of common snakes:
   a. Of the 136 species of recognized snakes in North America only about 4 species are poisonous. They are: rattlesnakes, coral snakes, copperheads, and water moccasins.
   b. Many of the harmless snakes are helpful to society and should be protected.
      1) Gopher and bull snakes help farmers by eating mice, rats, and gophers.
      2) Black snakes eat moles, frogs, and grasshoppers.
      3) King snakes eat rodents and kill rattlesnakes.
   c. Rattlesnakes (pit viper family) can be recognized by the rattles on their tails and their triangular-shaped heads.
   d. The coral snake is about 15 inches long and has black rings that are bordered on each side by yellow ones; it has a black-tipped head.

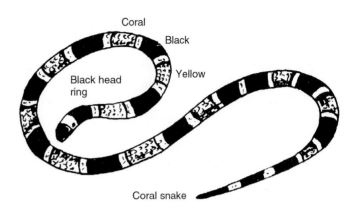

Coral
Black
Yellow
Black head ring
Coral snake

   e. A snake's tongue is used primarily for smelling. It contains no poison.
   f. At most, a snake strikes about half its body length.
2. First aid measures to take in case of snakebite:
   a. Call a doctor.
   b. Tie a tourniquet around the limb above the bite.
   c. Cut an X across the bite to help the bleeding and let the venom out.
3. Do not try to collect poisonous snakes; leave them to the professionals.

F. Thought Questions for Class Discussions:
1. What are some common characteristics of all snakes?
2. What are some common misconceptions about snakes?
3. What snake is most numerous in your locality?

G. Related Topics for Further Inquiry:
1. Compare snakes with other reptiles.
2. Study Activity IV-D-1, "What are reptiles?"
3. Study Activity IV-D-3, "How do we make a terrarium for reptiles?"

H. Vocabulary Builders—Spelling Words:
1) **rattlesnakes**   2) **coral**   3) **poisonous**
4) **harmless**   5) **harmful**   6) **reptiles**
7) **cold-blooded**   8) **helpless**   9) **rodents**

I. Thought for Today:
"Silence is one of the hardest arguments to refute."

A. Problem: *How Do We Make a Terrarium for Reptiles?*

B. Materials Needed:
1. Large glass box for terrarium
2. Plate glass cover
3. Masking tape
4. Sand
5. Small, dry twigs and rocks
6. Material for a hiding place for reptiles
7. Shallow dish or saucer
8. Reptiles
9. Electric light (small, 25-watt bulb for heating) in a flexible lamp

C. Procedure:
1. Fill the bottom of glass box with two inches of sand.
2. Place saucer inside.
3. Add twigs, rocks.
4. Design a place for reptile(s) to hide.
5. Add water to saucer.
6. To assure a fresh supply of air, place a little roll or small ball of masking tape on each corner between the terrarium and the glass cover.
7. If the glass cover is about the same size as the top of the terrarium, it is wise to tape the cover to one side of the terrarium so that the cover can be raised and lowered without fear of slipping and/or breaking.
8. Put reptile(s) in terrarium.
9. Put cover in place.
10. Feed the reptiles worms, live insects, and earthworms.
11. Place light over cover to maintain warm temperature.
12. Assign a small group of students to act as a committee to take care of the reptile(s) for feeding, cleaning the terrarium as needed, and reporting on the progress the reptile(s) is (are) making.

D. Results:
1. Class will learn about the care and feeding of reptiles.
2. Students will learn about the responsibilities of taking care of animals.

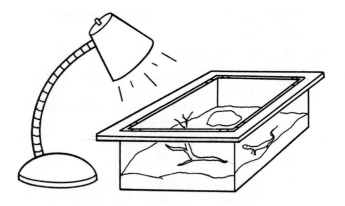

E. Basic Facts and Supplemental Information:
1. Do not use poisonous varieties of snakes in the classroom.
2. The best temperature for a terrarium is about 80° F.
3. Ants, flies, and crickets are good food for snakes and lizards.
4. Feed them live food once a week.
5. Reptiles love to eat soft-bodied insects.
6. Lizards and snakes shed their outermost layer of skin. This is called "molting."
7. Reptiles are cold-blooded animals.
8. Snakes and lizards lay eggs.

F. Thought Questions for Class Discussions:
1. Are reptiles helpful to people?
2. What are some distinct characteristics of reptiles?
3. How do snakes shed their skin?

G. Related Topics for Further Inquiry:
1. Discuss with students their experiences with snakes.
2. Discuss with students their experiences with other reptiles.
3. Visit a zoo and observe reptiles.
4. Study Activity IV-D-1, "What are reptiles?"
5. Study Activity IV-D-2, "What are some characteristics of snakes?"

H. Vocabulary Builders—Spelling Words:
1) **terrarium**   2) **masking**   3) **twig**   4) **reptile**
5) **saucer**   6) **snake**   7) **lizard**   8) **insects**

I. Thought for Today:
"If you wouldn't write it and sign it, don't say it."

Activity

A. Problem: *What Do We Know about Dinosaurs?*

B. Materials Needed:
1. Pictures of dinosaurs
2. Models of dinosaurs
3. Other multisensory materials about dinosaurs
4. Reference materials on dinosaurs

C. Procedure:
1. Ask the class if they have ever heard of dinosaurs.
2. Have them relate what they have found.
3. Show pictures and models of these creatures.
4. Tell the class the dinosaurs existed a long time ago—about 200 million years ago.
5. Discuss appropriate items cited in Section E of this Activity.

D. Results:
1. Students will learn that dinosaurs really existed.
2. Pupils will learn that changes in the environment can cause great changes in animal life.

E. Basic Facts and Supplemental Information:
1. Dinosaurs were:
   a. reptiles.
   b. cold-blooded (body temperature changed with outside air temperature).
   c. land animals.
   d. mostly plant eaters.
2. Dinosaurs had:
   a. four legs; most had two large hind legs and two small front legs.
   b. small heads and small brains.
   c. short, flat, pointed teeth.
3. Dinosaurs:
   a. walked on their hind legs.
   b. varied in looks; some looked like lizards, others like turkeys, turtles, or elephants.
   c. lived in marshy, swampy lands.
   d. varied in size. The largest was Brontosaurus, that ranged up to 80 feet long and weighed up to 40 tons (80,000 pounds).
   e. were oviparous (hatched from eggs).
4. Many dinosaurs were able to live in the water.
5. The Earth's climate became colder and drier about 60 million years ago, and the swamps and marshes dried up. A lot of their vegetation was lost and the dinosaurs became extinct.
6. We know dinosaurs existed because we have found a lot of their fossil remains.
7. The word "dinosaur" means "terrible lizard."

Tyrannosaurus Rex
"King of the Dinosaurs"

8. A flying dinosaur was the pterodactyl (actually glided or soared, did not fly).
9. Tyrannosaurus Rex was the most ferocious and was called "King of the Lizards."
10. The dinosaurs lived in the Mesozoic era which lasted from 65 to 230 million years ago.

F. Thought Questions for Class Discussions:
1. What animals today do you think are the most closely related to dinosaurs?
2. Do all animals "like" the same kind of temperature?
3. What could cause changes in the Earth's temperature?

G. Related Topics for Further Inquiry:
1. Study Activity VI-C-12, "What is the ozone problem?"
2. Study Activity VI-C-5, "What is global warming (the 'Greenhouse Effect')?"
3. Study Part VI, "Ecology."
4. Compare dinosaurs with other animals.
5. Students can make models of dinosaurs with clay or papier-maché.
6. Pupils can make dioramas of habitats of dinosaurs. (Dioramas are three-dimensional scenes, usually in a box.)

H. Vocabulary Builders—Spelling Words:
1) **dinosaurs** 2) **swamps** 3) **marshes**
4) **oviparous** 5) **reptiles** 6) **extinct**

I. Thought for Today:
"The turtle lays thousands of eggs without anyone knowing, but when the hen lays one egg, the whole country is informed."

Section E: Water Animals (Fish and Amphibians)

Activity

A. Problem: *How Can We Identify the Different Species of Fish?*

B. Materials Needed:
1. Pictures of fish
2. Books about fish
3. Multisensory aids about fish

C. Procedure:
1. Compare fish with other animals.
2. Have students relate their experiences regarding fish and fishing.
3. Have them do research on different species of fish.
4. Have them relate the similarities and the differences among the different species.
5. Have them learn the main parts of fish to help them in their descriptions and identifications.

D. Results:
1. Students will learn that there are many species of fish.
2. They will learn the main terminology of fish parts.

E. Basic Facts and Supplemental Information:
1. Seventy-one percent of the Earth's surface is covered with water.
2. Fish live in water.
3. They are classified as vertebrates. They have backbones.
4. The basic body structures of the fish are shown in the sketch.
5. Fish vary in size from about one-half inch to about fifty feet.
6. Some fish live in salt water; others live in fresh water, and some, like the salmon, live in both.
7. Some fish lay eggs, some are live-bearers.
8. Fish are cold-blooded.
9. They breathe by means of gills.
10. Most have fins and scales.
11. Sharks and rays are fish.
12. Humans depend on fish for food.
13. In the future we are going to have more fish farms as our need for proteins grows.

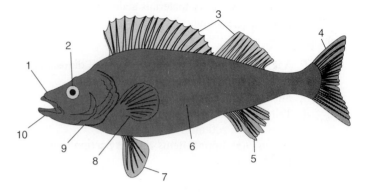

1. Nostrils
2. Gill cover
3. Dorsal fins
4. Caudal fin
5. Anal fin
6. Scales
7. Ventral or pelvic fin
8. Pectoral fin
9. Gills
10. Mandible

F. Thought Questions for Class Discussions:
1. In what ways do fish benefit people other than for food?
2. What are some harmful effects of fish on humans?
3. Do some fish make good pets?

G. Related Topics for Further Inquiry:
1. Compare fish with amphibians.
2. Compare the breathing apparatus of fish (gills) with that of humans.
3. Study the living conditions that fish must have in order to survive.

H. Vocabulary Builders—Spelling Words:
(Use terminology cited in drawing)

I. Thought for Today:
"Nothing grows faster than a fish from the time he bites until he gets away."

A. Problem: *How Should We Collect Seashells?*

B. Materials Needed:
1. Terrestrial globe
2. Pictures of a sea coast
3. Shell specimens
4. Reference books on seashells

C. Procedure:
1. Show the students the globe pointing out the extensive amount of water (71%) on our planet Earth.
2. Point out the many, many coastlines.
3. Briefly describe plant life and animal life found near or in the coastal waters.
4. Discuss how to collect seashells safely when visiting coastal areas:
   a. Check with local experts for:
      1) potential dangers
      2) best hunting spots
      3) types of specimens desired
      4) methods of collecting
   b. Never search alone. Always have an adult partner.
5. Decide on methods of displaying after collecting.
6. It is always more fun to take pictures during the hunting and collecting of seashells.
7. Discuss mollusks:
   a. univalves
   b. bivalves
8. Identify the pictures or specimens collected.

D. Results:
1. Students will gain insight into the innumerable species and specimens found in our oceans.
2. Students will learn a fascinating hobby—collecting seashells.

E. Basic Facts and Supplemental Information:
1. Shells are produced by a wide variety of soft-bodied animals called mollusks.
2. Univalves have only one valve or shell. They are also called gastropods.
3. Abalones are one major type of gastropod.
4. Snails, limpets, and conchs are also members of the univalve family.
5. The bivalves, those with two shells, i.e., oysters, clams, and *pectens* (scallops), make up the bulk of this latter group.

6. For displays, shells should be washed and scrubbed in soapy water and the encrusted materials should be scraped off.

F. Thought Questions for Class Discussions:
1. What other types of sea life live near the homes of mollusks?
2. What do you think happened to the animals that lived in the shells?
3. How have people used seashells?

G. Related Topics for Further Inquiry:
1. Study ocean life.
2. Study tide pool life.
3. Study especially Activity VI-D-4, "How can we protect our oceans and beaches?"
4. Study other Activities in this Section.

H. Vocabulary Builders—Spelling Words:
1) **univalve** 2) **bivalve** 3) **abalone**
4) **coast** 5) **gastropod** 6) **mollusk**
7) **seashells** 8) **environment**

I. Thought for Today:
"A computer analysis reveals that children in grades three to nine see the word 'money' more often than 'love', 'war' more often than 'peace', and 'car' more often than 'family.'"

Activity

A. Problem: *What Are the Differences Between Frogs and Toads?*

B. Materials Needed:
1. Pictures, books, printed materials on frogs and toads
2. Frog eggs and toad eggs if possible
3. Tadpoles of frogs and toads if possible

C. Procedure:
1. Discuss animals in general.
2. Discuss the main characteristics of amphibians.
3. Describe the main characteristics of frogs and toads:
   a. amphibians
   b. undergo metamorphosis:
      1) eggs
      2) tadpoles
      3) adults
   c. over 2,000 species
   d. found all over the world but rarely in polar regions
   e. mating calls stem from large vocal sacs
4. Describe the unique features of frogs:
   a. habitat—basically water or near water
   b. skin—smooth, soft, moist, thin
   c. teeth—small
   d. movement—fast
   e. food—carnivorous: insects and small water animals
   f. bodies—slim
   g. eggs—laid in clumps
5. Describe the unique features of toads:
   a. habitat—basically land
   b. skin—hard, bumpy
   c. teeth—none
   d. movement—erratic, slow
   e. food—insects, small land animals
   f. bodies—fat
   g. eggs—laid in strings (often double strands)
6. If possible, collect eggs and/or tadpoles from nearby lakes, ponds, or streams.

D. Results:
1. Students will learn the differences between frogs and toads.
2. Some classes will have a lot of fun raising frogs and toads from eggs and/or tadpoles.

Tree frog demonstrates air sac

Toad with bumpy skin

E. Basic Facts and Supplemental Information:
1. Toads do not cause warts.
2. Toads and frogs are common prey for many animals, alligators, birds, large fish, etc.
3. A few species of toads have secretions which are poisonous to humans if they contact a person's mucous membranes in the eyes, mouth, etc.

F. Thought Questions for Class Discussions:
1. What animals do you know that are closely related to frogs and toads?
2. Have you ever eaten frog legs?
3. Have you ever heard strange sounds near ponds or lakes especially at night? These could be frogs or toads.

G. Related Topics for Further Inquiry:
1. Compare amphibians to reptiles.
2. Compare amphibians to fish.
3. Study all activities in this Part IV, "Animals."

H. Vocabulary Builders—Spelling Words:
1) **frogs** 2) **toads** 3) **amphibians**
4) **metamorphosis** 5) **oviparous** 6) **tadpoles**

I. Thought for Today:
"Genius begins great works; labor alone finishes them."

Activity

A. Problem: *How Do We Care for a Fresh-Water Aquarium?*

B. Materials Needed:

1. Glass tank and cover
2. Sand
3. Plants (water)
4. Thermometer (aquarium)
5. Fish (start with inexpensive tropical fish)
6. Water
7. Sprinkling can
8. Snails
9. Air pump

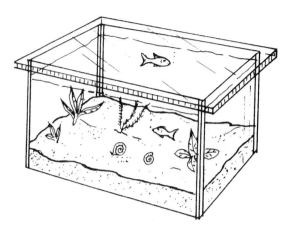

C. Procedure:

1. Place the tank in its permanent position. (Moving the aquarium after it is filled with water may cause a leak.) The tank should be placed in a position that ensures a liberal supply of diffused light. This will result in the active process of photosynthesis.
2. Disinfect plants by putting them in a salt solution (four ounces of salt per gallon of water) for one minute, then washing them in fresh water. All plants, native or purchased, should be disinfected. Use plants sparingly. Too many plants will shut out the light. Too much light encourages the growth of algae and weeds which crowd out cultivated plants. A balance is needed. Floating plants may be added later if desired.
3. Wash glass tank thoroughly. A tank with a rectangular metal frame and a slate or glass bottom is most satisfactory. A tank $10'' \times 10'' \times 16''$ or more is advisable, as it is difficult to keep a smaller tank properly balanced.
4. Wash sand till water is clear. Coarse sand is best for the aquarium.
5. Place a two-inch layer of sand at the bottom of the aquarium. Large pebbles and rocks, as well as ornamental castles, seashells, and the like should never be placed in the aquarium as they encourage algae growth.
6. Put plants in sand. Roots should be spread and well covered with sand. Plants of like species are best grouped together. A plan should be made on paper before the actual planting.
7. Temperature is important. Cold-water fish, including goldfish, thrive at temperatures from 59° to 65° F. Tropical fish require temperatures of 70° to 80° F.

8. Pour water from a sprinkling can into the tank, taking care to disturb the sand as little as possible. The slow pouring of water from a sprinkling can allows it to become aerated.
9. When tap water is used, the tank should be allowed to stand at least 24 hours before putting the fish into it. This allows the water to clear and become thoroughly oxygenated, the plants to take root, and any unwanted gases to dissipate. An air pump should be attached and utilized to continue proper oxygenation of aquarium.
10. Place fish and snails in the aquarium. The water in the aquarium should be approximately the same temperature as that from which the fish are taken. The fish should not be touched with the hands or dropped into the water, as this may injure their scales and lead to development of a fungus disease. They should be allowed to swim out of the container into the tank.
11. After fish have been placed in the aquarium, cover the aquarium with glass in order to prevent evaporation and the collecting of dust.
12. Fresh-water snails are, for all purposes the best scavengers. Certain small fish such as the "weather fish" and catfish also are good scavengers.
13. Feed fish sparingly. It is well to remember that prepared fish food is highly concentrated. Fish should be given only what they can eat within 15 minutes. If food remains at the bottom, too much has been given. Uneaten food should be removed.

14. Feedings should be regular. Twice a week is usually sufficient in cold weather—three times a week in warm seasons. Prepared food can be obtained at aquarium supply stores, pet stores, and grocery markets. This may be supplemented by occasional fresh foods such as tiny scraps of raw beef and chopped lettuce. Live food such as Artemia is also satisfactory.

15. Remove immediately any fish showing signs of illness. Overfeeding, insufficient oxygen, and sudden changes in temperature are the chief causes of sickness in fish. Spotty reddish fins, white fungus on the body, or wobbly body movement are signs of illness. Treatment with salt water has been found best for general use. For a weak bath, one teaspoonful salt to a gallon of water is recommended. For a strong bath, use one tablespoon salt to a gallon of water. A sick fish should be left in the weak bath for 24 hours. This treatment is continued with a new solution until the fish becomes healthy. Salt water treatment is not effective in all types of illness. Consult a book on aquarium care or a knowledgeable person at an aquarium or a tropical fish store.

16. Gasping of fish at the top of the water may be due to an excess of carbon dioxide in the water or a lack of oxygen. If the water is oversaturated or undersaturated with oxygen, the excess or lack is quickly adjusted by exposure with the air above the water. However, since carbon dioxide passes from water to air and air to water very slowly, it takes much longer for an excess of carbon dioxide to dissipate. It has been found that fish cannot take in oxygen at the gills if too much carbon dioxide is in the water. For this reason, fish can suffocate even when plenty of oxygen is present.

D. Results:

1. The aquarium will continue to provide material for discussion and research into the coexistence of various kinds of aquatic life, and also what is required to support that life in various circumstances.

2. The students become aware of the interrelationship between plants and animals. The oxygen needed by the animals is provided by plants and the carbon dioxide needed by the plants is provided by animals. When the oxygen-carbon dioxide relationship is well balanced, it is unnecessary to change the water in the aquarium. If a glass aquarium isn't available, a clear plastic box can be utilized.

3. This is an excellent example of an ecosystem even though it is a relatively small one.

E. Basic Facts and Supplemental Information:

1. The experience of making an aquarium and caring for live animals in the classroom is both interesting and educational. The types of aquaria, sand, fish, scavengers, and plants selected all are factors to be considered.

2. In the newly planted aquarium, algae may develop and fresh water may become cloudy because of uneaten fish food.

3. Snail eggs are the little dots that form on the sides of the aquarium that look as if they were covered with thin cellophane.

F. Thought Questions for Class Discussions:

1. There are both freshwater and salt water aquaria. What are the advantages and disadvantages of each?

2. Which type of green plants survive best?

3. What are the advantages of bushy-type plants?

G. Related Topics for Further Inquiry:

1. Raise guppies. They are easy to raise and quite prolific.

2. Construct and stock a salt water aquarium. (Find specific directions. Salt water fish are more varied and more beautiful.)

3. Study Activity IV-A-1, "What is the difference between living things and nonliving things?"

4. Study Activity IV-E-1, "How can we identify the different species of fish?"

5. Study Activity VI-A-1, "What is the balance of nature?"

6. Study Activity VI-A-3, "What is biological diversity?"

H. Vocabulary Builders—Spelling Words:

1) **aquarium**   2) **sprinkling**   3) **snails**
4) **coarse**   5) **decay**   6) **algae**   7) **oxygen**
8) **carbon dioxide**   9) **ecosystem**

I. Thought for Today:

"This would be a fine world if people always showed as much patience as they do when waiting for fish to bite."

SECTION F: BIRDS

Activity

A. Problem: *How Do Birds Differ from Other Animals?*

B. Materials Needed:
1. Pictures of various birds
2. Chart paper to list the characteristics of birds
3. Bird books
4. Stuffed birds (specimens) if available

C. Procedure:
1. A good motivating technique for studying birds is to have the class walk around the campus to see how many different species of birds they can find.
2. Have students draw simple sketches of the birds they see, noting size, color, and general shape.
3. When students return to class, have them place the sketches on the bulletin board.
4. Place pictures of birds around the room. Have the bird books on the science table. If stuffed birds are obtainable, display them also.
5. See how many different kinds of birds the class can identify.
6. Have students study pictures, books, and specimens about birds.
7. After the study period, list the characteristics of birds on chalkboard.
8. Have students notice that birds have feathers, wings, beaks, but have no teeth. Birds lay eggs; they are not live-bearers.
9. The students should make a chart with the data they have discussed.
10. Have students identify birds by their common names.

D. Results:
1. The students will learn some of the general characteristics of birds.
2. Students will identify some of the local birds.

E. Basic Facts and Supplemental Information:
1. Birds are warm-blooded animals. They have special characteristics which adapt them for food searching, protection, and flight.
2. There are many simple bird feeders and birdbaths which the students might want to build.
3. Few birds are attracted to birdhouses; most are attracted to bird feeders.
4. When referring to a bird's mouthpart, some ornithologists prefer using "bills" for flat appendages and "beaks" for pointed ones.

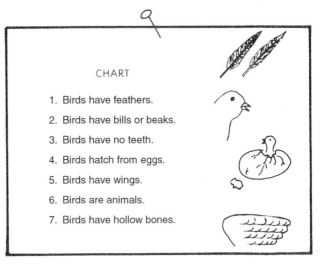

CHART

1. Birds have feathers.
2. Birds have bills or beaks.
3. Birds have no teeth.
4. Birds hatch from eggs.
5. Birds have wings.
6. Birds are animals.
7. Birds have hollow bones.

5. Birds burn 20 times as much energy as land animals (hummingbirds 50 times as much).
6. As birds fly, air moves over their wings which are similar in shape to those of an airplane. This movement of air provides "lift."

F. Thought Questions for Class Discussions:
1. How do the bones of birds differ from the bones of other land animals?
2. Do birds need much energy for flight? How do they adjust to their energy requirements?
3. How are the wings of birds similar to the wings of airplanes? How are they different?
4. Are some birds threatened with extinction?
5. What is the largest bird? the smallest?
6. Do farmers raise birds?

G. Related Topics for Further Inquiry:
1. Study game birds (birds that are hunted).
2. Visit a zoo or aviary to learn about exotic birds.
3. Build a bird feeder for your school.
4. Study other Activities in this Section.

H. Vocabulary Builders—Spelling Words:
1) **feathers**   2) **wings**   3) **beaks**   4) **eggs**
5) **teeth**   6) **songs**   7) **bills**   8) **flight**

I. Thought for Today:
"You can't be a night owl and an early bird."

Activity

A. Problem: *How Do We Classify Common Birds?*

B. Materials Needed:
1. Notebook
2. Pencil
3. Bird identification book(s)

C. Procedure:
1. Quickly peruse bird identification book(s).
2. Have students take a field trip near or around school taking notes on each different bird species they see.
3. In their notebooks, have the students fill in the following data on each different species of bird seen. Compare the number after each bird part with the drawing.
   General (common) name
   Location
   Date
   Color(s)
   Beak (1)
   Throat (2)
   Nape (3)
   Crown (4)
   Eye color (5)
   Back (6)
   Rump (7)
   Belly (8)
   Breast (9)
   Tail (10)
   Wings (11)
   Legs (12)
   Feet (13)

D. Results:
1. Students will learn about and be able to identify the common birds in their locality.
2. Students will learn how to record field observations.

E. Basic Facts and Supplemental Information:
1. Many birds can be recognized by their flight patterns.
2. Adult birds protect their eggs and their young after they are hatched.
3. Song patterns identify species and are significant in communication among or between birds.

4. Other characteristics which could be included are:
   a. Movements on the ground
   b. Flight patterns (soar, glide, undulating, etc.)
   c. Position of wings in flight
   d. Nesting habits
   e. Migration patterns
5. There are more birds than people.
6. Birds have lightweight feathers and hollow bones to make flight easier.
7. Birds have big hearts for their size and strong wing muscles.

F. Thought Questions for Class Discussions:
1. What are some behaviors of birds that are harmful to people?
2. How do birds help us?
3. What do birds eat?

G. Related Topics for Further Inquiry:
1. Make a bird feeder. If you keep it stocked, you will see many different kinds of birds.
2. Take a field trip to a nearby wooded area and look for birds.
3. Study other Activities in this Section.

H. Vocabulary Builders—Spelling Words:
1) **feathers** 2) **bills** 3) **wings** 4) **beaks**
5) **nest** 6) **breast** 7) **nape** 8) **rump**

I. Thought for Today:
"Even the woodpecker owes its success to the fact that it uses its head and keeps pecking away until it finishes the job it starts."

Activity

A. Problem: *What Can We Learn From Birds' Beaks and Feet?*

B. Materials Needed:

Pictures, specimens, books, audiovisual materials that show birds' beaks and feet

C. Procedure:

1. Discuss general characteristics of birds.
2. Discuss differences among birds, particularly their beaks and feet.
3. Birds' existences depend on how they move, feed, and hunt.

D. Result:

Students will learn that beaks and feet of birds differ widely.

E. Basic Facts and Supplemental Information:

1. A bird's beak is an indication of the type of food it eats.
2. Short, stubby beaks show that the bird feeds on nuts and seeds.
3. Curved beaks are used for tearing flesh.
4. Long, narrow beaks are used for probing in shallow waters.
5. Broad, flat beaks are used for dabbing in the mud and water nearby.
6. A bird's foot type is an indication of the life-style of the bird.
7. A webbed foot is used for paddling and swimming.
8. Curved, hooked talons are used for seizing prey.
9. Three toes forward and one back identifies perching birds.
10 Two toes forward and two back indicate that the bird is a climbing creature.

F. Thought Questions for Class Discussions:

1. What different foods do birds eat?
2. Where do birds spend most of the day?
3. Are birds generally helpful or harmful to people?

G. Related Topics for Further Inquiry:

1. Invite a speaker from a local Audubon Club to talk to the class about birds and their habits.
2. Get a good reference book on birds and see how many different kinds of birds you can identify in your community.
3. Study other Activities in this Section.

Birds' beaks

Birds' feet

H. Vocabulary Builders—Spelling Words:

1) **beaks**   2) **bills**   3) **talons**   4) **seeds**
5) **insects**   6) **wadding**   7) **perching**

I. Thought for Today:

"The next best thing to knowing something is knowing where to find it."

Activity

A. Problem: *Why Do Birds Migrate?*

B. Materials Needed:

1. Pictures of birds migrating or appearing to migrate. (See drawing.)
2. Models of birds, if available
3. Reference books about birds

C. Procedure:

1. Discuss bird characteristics.
2. Discuss with students if they notice any difference in the species of birds from season to season.
3. Look up the migration routes of birds.
4. Draw migration routes of birds on maps.

D. Result:

Students will learn that most birds do migrate and they migrate for:

1. food
2. warmth
3. mating, laying eggs, and building nests

E. Basic Facts and Supplemental Information:

1. Some birds migrate great distances.
2. Usually birds in the north fly south during the winter season.
3. Bird migration patterns differ widely. For example:
   a. Bobolinks fly to Argentina.
   b. Wood thrushes fly to Mexico.
   c. House wrens fly to Florida.
   d. Golden plovers fly to Brazil and Argentina.
   e. Artic terns fly to Antarctica.
   f. Ruddy tuonstones (Alaska) fly to Hawaii.
   g. Cliff swallows fly to South America.
   h. Other species fly to Cuba, Jamaica, and Central America.
4. Birds are warm-blooded and therefore are more sensitive to heat and cold.
5. Birds are able to fly long distances because they are light in weight; they have hollow bones and light feathers and are able to expend more than 20 times as much energy as land animals.
6. Ornithologists, scientists who study bird life, have found that birds migrate and navigate by the:
   a. sun
   b. landmarks
   c. semimagnetic compasses in their heads
7. Since birds can fly, they can live anywhere in the world.

Geese migrating in typical V formation. Some birds migrate thousands of miles.

F. Thought Questions for Class Discussions:

1. Do some people migrate?
2. Do other land animals migrate?
3. Do some sea animals migrate?
4. How can land birds migrate over hundreds of miles of ocean?

G. Related Topics for Further Inquiry:

1. Discuss why people move long distances.
2. Study Activity IV-F-1, "How do birds differ from other animals?"
3. Study Activity IV-F-2, "How do we classify common birds?"
4. Study Activity IV-F-3, "What can we learn from birds' beaks and feet?"

H. Vocabulary Builders—Spelling Words:

1) **migration** 2) **visitor** 3) **Mexico**
4) **South America** 5) **Argentina**

I. Thought for Today:

"Fools live to regret their words, wise people to regret their silence."—Will Henry

A. Problem: *How Do Mammals Differ from Other Animals?*

B. Materials Needed:

1. Pictures of mammals
2. Books about mammals
3. Filmstrips or motion pictures about mammals

C. Procedure:

1. Review Activity IV-A-3, "How do we classify living things?"
2. Discuss mammals. Mammals are members of the Phylum Chordata (animals with backbones).
3. Discuss the common characteristics of mammals such as:
   a. comparatively large in size
   b. hairy
   c. warm-blooded
   d. backbones
   e. large brains
   f. born alive (a few rare exceptions are born from eggs)
   g. suckle milk from milk glands
4. Have class describe what pets they have that are classified as mammals.
5. Have class make a list of other animals that are in this classification.
6. Describe or show pictures of other animals that are mammals. These might include:
   a. platypus   i. rabbit
   b. anteater   j. whale
   c. wallaby   k. walrus
   d. shrew   l. aardvark
   e. lemur   m. elephant
   f. bat   n. warthog
   g. sloth   o. tiger
   h. gorilla   p. man
7. View accessible filmstrips, slides, or movies about mammals.
8. Discuss the fact that some mammals are meat eaters while others are primarily vegetarians. Meat eaters must be strong, swift, and smart. Vegetarian animals spend a lot of time searching for leaves, twigs, and tender plant shoots.
9. Discuss the wide range of habitats of mammals: equator to poles, land to water, low to high elevations, etc.
10. If possible, plan a field trip to a zoo.

D. Result:

Students will learn about mammals and that people are included in this animal classification.

E. Basic Facts and Supplemental Information:

1. Other major characteristics of mammals:
   a. move quickly
   b. think fast
   c. body parts consist of head, trunk and appendages
   d. Milk has all the fat, proteins, water, sugar, vitamins, and minerals their young need.
2. There are many sources where information about mammals can be obtained, such as:
   a. pet stores
   b. veterinarians
   c. medical researchers
   d. zoo keepers
   e. farmers
   f. feed stores

F. Thought Questions for Class Discussions:

1. How do mammals differ from other animals?
2. How are mammals similar to other animals?
3. What mammals are very important to people? Why?
4. Is the bat a mammal? (Yes!!)

G. Related Ideas for Further Inquiry:

1. Compare mammals with other members of the Phylum Chordata.
2. Have each student research or report on one particular species in this phylum.
3. Study other Activities in this Section.

H. Vocabulary Builders—Spelling Words:

Use the mammals listed in Procedure C-6.

I. Thought for Today:

"Frustration is not having anyone else to blame but yourself."

A. Problem: *What Are Some Common Jungle, Farm, and Sea Mammals?*

B. Materials Needed:

1. Pictures of animals in these classifications
2. Filmstrips or motion pictures of these animals
3. Reference materials about these animals

C. Procedure:

1. Review Activity IV-G-1, "How do mammals differ from other animals?"
2. Organize three groups of students.
3. Have each group make a thorough study of one of the three groups cited in the problem.
4. Other areas could be included or substituted such as mountain, prairie, or desert.
5. The "jungle group" could study lions, tigers, elephants, zebras, rhinoceroses, hippopotamuses, leopards, etc.
6. The "farm group" could study horses, cows, pigs, goats, sheep, rabbits, dogs, etc.
7. The "sea group" could study whales, porpoises, dolphins, narwhals, and grampuses.
8. Show filmstrips and motion pictures concerning these animals.

D. Results:

1. Students will learn that mammals within a certain environment have common characteristics necessary for their survival.
2. Students can begin to realize the bases of animal classification.

E. Basic Facts and Supplemental Information:

1. The age, maturity, and interests of the students will determine the depth of study of this Activity.
2. Studies of mammals lead up to a study of human beings.
3. Mammals get energy from the food they eat after they have been suckled by their mothers.

F. Thought Questions for Class Discussions:

1. What are some of the environmental factors that determine where certain groups of mammals live?
2. Which area studied has the greatest number of mammals?
3. Which mammal out of each group would you rather be? Why?

G. Related Ideas for Further Inquiry:

1. Study the ecological factors of each species.
2. Make predictions on the future of each species.

3. Study Activity III-A-1, "How do we classify living things?"
4. Study other Activities in this Section.

H. Vocabulary Builders—Spelling Words:

1) **mountain**   2) **prairie**   3) **desert**   4) **jungle**
5) **farm**   6) **animals listed in Procedure**

I. Thought for Today:

"The wishbone will never replace the backbone."

Activity

A. Problem: *Are Human Beings Mammals?*

B. Materials Needed:
1. Pictures of many mammals
2. Pictures of people in many activities
3. Books, pamphlets about mammals

C. Procedure:
1. Review Activities III-A-1, "How do we classify living things?" and IV-G-1, "How do mammals differ from other animals?"
2. Review the main characteristics of mammals:
   a. backbones
   b. large brains
   c. warm-blooded
   d. born alive (few hatch from eggs)
   e. suckle milk from milk glands
   f. body hair
   g. breathe with lungs
   h. seven neck bones
3. Compare the characteristics of humans with other mammals.

D. Result:
Students will learn that humans are part of the animal kingdom and are mammals.

E. Basic Facts and Supplemental Information:
1. One of the shocking experiences of most students is the realization that they are part of the animal kingdom.
2. The teacher can explain that humans are the highest order of animals in that they have three major biological characteristics that set them apart from other animals and they are:
   a. Complex brain (complex reasoning power, creative, problem-solver). For example, humans have created many "new foods" and "new tools."
   b. Prehensile hand (enables humans to be tool-using) (opposable thumb). This has enabled humans to communicate through writing and sign language.
   c. Well-developed voice box (gives humans the power to utter many sounds and, consequently, complex vocal communication).
3. Mammals are a Class in animal classification. They have mammary glands.
4. Humans are omnivores because we eat meats and plants. We eat seeds (parts of plants) such as corn, wheat, rice, oats, barley, and rye.
5. Humans live everywhere on our planet. There are no races of humans; the differences are only physical, ethnic, and cultural.
6. The fact that people can and sometimes do interbreed proves that we are all members of one race—the human race.
7. Humans have the longest period of infant care of any mammal.
8. Humans need food and shelter.
9. Humans are affected by the pranks of nature the same as any other animal: droughts, floods, severe weather, earthquakes, etc.
10. Fertilization takes place within the body as with other mammals. The fertilized egg develops into an embryo.

F. Thought Questions for Class Discussions:
1. What mammals are most like people?
2. Do other mammals ever kill their own kind?
3. Which has the greatest effect on humans, biological inheritance or cultural environment?

G. Related Ideas for Further Inquiry:
1. Discuss how humans cope with varied environments: swimming, flying, space travel, etc.
2. See especially Section V-C, "Nutrition."
3. Study other Activities in this Section.

H. Vocabulary Builders—Spelling Words:
1) **mammal** 2) **backbone** 3) **creative**
4) **prehensile** 5) **complex** 6) **mammary**
7) **hair** 8) **lungs**

I. Thought for Today:
"Humans are the only animal that can be skinned more than once."

Activity

A. Problem: *How Do Mammals Protect Themselves?*

B. Materials Needed:

1. Reference materials on how animals protect themselves
2. Specimens of animals and their means of protection
3. Models of animals and their protective devices

C. Procedure:

1. Review Activity IV-A-6, "How do animals protect themselves?"
2. Discuss with class the animals that they have seen protecting themselves.
3. Discuss prey-predator relationships.
4. Have the class list ways that animals can protect themselves. Such a list will probably include:

   a. strength   k. teeth
   b. running   l. stinging
   c. fangs   m. poisons
   d. claws   n. hiding
   e. shells   o. noise (bark, howl, etc.)
   f. odors   p. hibernation
   g. antlers   q. migration
   h. horns   r. quills
   i. flight (flying)   s. behavior (fighting, etc.)
   j. camouflage   t. grouping (herding)

5. Have class list ways that people protect themselves:

   a. shelter
   b. clothing
   c. warmth
   d. air conditioners
   e. health practices
   f. food
   g. rocks
   h. sticks
   i. weapons
   j. alarm systems

D. Results:

1. Students will realize that in the animal world, animals must be continually on the alert to protect themselves.
2. Students will learn that animals not only protect themselves, but their young as well.
3. Students will learn that protective behavior is highly instinctive.

How does this animal protect itself?

And this one?

E. Basic Facts and Supplemental Information:

1. Life and death are common in the animal world.
2. Life is a continuous struggle for all animals.
3. Scientists have not been able to adequately explain what animal instinct is. Some instinctive behaviors are:

   a. birds migrating
   b. bears hibernating
   c. dogs burying bones
   d. cats purring

F. Thought Questions for Class Discussions:

1. What would happen to birds if they didn't migrate?
2. Why are some animals nocturnal?
3. What part does camouflage play in animal protection?

G. Related Ideas for Further Inquiry:

1. Study animals that are basically classified as "predators."
2. Study animals that are considered "preys."
3. Study other Activities in this Section.
4. Study Activity VI-A-1, "What is the balance of nature?"
5. Study Activity VI-A-9, "Are any animals threatened with extinction?"

H. Vocabulary Builders—Spelling Words:

1) **size**   2) **speed**   3) **hibernation**   4) **migration**
5) **camouflage**   6) **poison**   7) **hiding**   8) **shells**

I. Thought for Today:

"Some people have a wonderful instinct about things, except for the obvious."

A. Problem: *How Can We Make an Earthworm Home?*

B. Materials Needed:

1. Two glass panes about 12″ × 16″ each (Handle carefully.)
2. Two sideboards, 2″ × 2″ × 12″ each
3. Baseboard, 2″ × 4″ × 12″
4. Two support boards, 2″ × 4″ × 20″ each
5. Masking tape
6. Construction paper, dark
7. Nails, 3″ long
8. Hammer
9. Soil, rich garden
10. Leaves, small
11. Earthworms

C. Procedure:

1. Line up support boards about 12″ apart.
2. Nail sideboards to each end of baseboard in an upright position.
3. Center baseboard over support boards as shown in sketch.
4. Nail baseboard to support board.
5. Attach one glass pane to one side of frame by using masking tape.
6. Attach second glass pane to the opposite side of frame by using masking tape.
7. Add rich garden soil and leaves to earthworms' home.
8. Dampen soil slightly to keep moist, but not wet.
9. Collect earthworms. Add earthworms to their home.
10. Cover front and back with construction paper.
11. Cover top with construction paper.
12. Feed earthworms biweekly.
13. Observe worms by removing dark paper for short periods of time.

D. Result:

An earthworm residence has been created.

E. Basic Facts and Supplemental Information:

1. Earthworms can be found by digging in soft, rich soil.
2. The best time to collect them is early in the morning, late at night, or after a rain.
3. Earthworms should be fed finely ground leaves, grasses, meat, and soft insects.

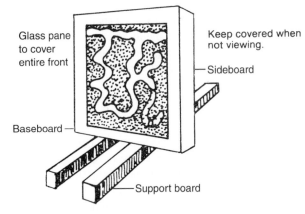

Glass pane to cover entire front

Keep covered when not viewing.

Sideboard

Baseboard

Support board

Earthworm residence

4. Earthworms are part of the classification Annelids, which are segmented worms.
5. The two other major types of worms: are flat worms (Platyhelminths) and round worms (Nematodes).
6. There is one giant earthworm found in Australia which can reach a length of over ten feet (*Megascolides australis*).
7. Fertilization of all earthworms occurs outside of the body and occurs in three stages: (1) egg, (2) larva, and (3) adult.

F. Thought Questions for Class Discussions:

1. How do segmented worms differ from crustaceans?
2. Are there different species of earthworms?
3. How do earthworms help the farmers?

G. Related Ideas for Further Inquiry:

1. Study Section IV-B, "Pets."
2. Study Section IV-I, "Storage and Care."
3. Study Activity IV-H-2, "What are the main characteristics of snails?"

H. Vocabulary Builders—Spelling Words:

1) **earthworms**   2) **segmented**   3) **specimens**
4) **dampen**   5) **support**

I. Thought for Today:

"Look out, not in,
Look up, not down.
Look forward, not backward."

Activity

A. Problem: *What Are the Main Characteristics of Snails?*

B. Materials Needed:
1. Several specimens of garden snails
2. Reference book on mollusks
3. Pane of glass or long, clear, plastic sheet
4. Container for snails (temporary)
5. Newspapers
6. Desk or tabletop

C. Procedure:
1. Place the snails in the temporary container.
2. Place the newspapers on the desk or tabletop.
3. Place the glass pane or flat plastic sheet on the newspapers.
4. Gently place the snails in the middle of the glass pane or plastic sheet.
5. Study their movements. It will take a little time.

D. Results:
1. The snails will begin to move about.
2. The students will learn that after the snails have moved, they will leave a trail of sticky material behind them.

E. Basic Facts and Supplemental Information:
1. Snails are gastropods, which are part of the family of mollusks.
2. Gastropod means "stomach-foot."
3. There are three main groups in the Phylum Mollusks:
   a. Gastropods: limpets, snails, and whelks
   b. Bivalves: clams and mussels (two-hinged joints: oysters, scallops)
   c. Cephalopods: octopuses and squids (small shell hidden inside their bodies)
4. Snails are found on land and in water.
5. Snails have sharp tongues which can quickly tear their food into tiny pieces.
6. Snails have exoskeletons which means their skeletons or supporting system is external and not inside their bodies.
7. Almost all snail shells coil in a clockwise formation when viewed from the front.

F. Thought Questions for Class Discussions:
1. What problems do gardeners have with snails?
2. What are "escargots?"
3. What are the "black dots" formed on the inside of an aquarium's glass sides?

G. Related Ideas for Further Inquiry:
1. Study the snails in the classroom aquarium. They keep the algae in check.
2. Aquarium snails lay eggs. These can be separated and, if they are studied under a microscope, cellular structures are clearly seen.
3. Another exciting Activity is collecting snails from lakes, ponds, and small, slow, shallow flowing streams. They are most abundant around vegetation.

H. Vocabulary Builders—Spelling Words:
1) **snails** 2) **aquarium** 3) **garden**
4) **gastropods** 5) **mollusks** 6) **algae**

I. Thought for Today:
"If animals had reason, they would act just as ridiculous as we do."

SECTION I: STORAGE AND CARE

Activity

A. Problem: *How Do We Make a Simple Vivarium?*

B. Materials Needed:
1. Aquarium
2. Glass cover
3. Charcoal
4. Small rocks
5. Soil
6. Plants
7. Watering can and water
8. Pads, 4 (to keep lid raised slightly)
9. Animal(s) desired (frogs, turtles, toads, lizards, etc.)

C. Procedure:
1. Clean the aquarium thoroughly.
2. Place a handful of charcoal at the bottom—this will help keep the soil sweet.
3. Put in a handful of small, irregularly shaped rocks.
4. Place soil to depth of 1 1/2″ to 2″ in the bottom of the aquarium over charcoal and rocks.
5. Use plants that thrive in a shady place and humid air.
6. Use a small or dwarf variety of slow-growing plant.
7. Use a small sprinkling can for watering.
8. Place in a north window out of direct sunlight, but where it receives a reasonable amount of light.
9. Insert pads on corners under lid so animals can have a fresh supply of air.
10. Frogs, toads, turtles, and lizards are suitable animals for this vivarium.
11. Reproduce animal's natural habitat as closely as possible.

D. Result:
Students will learn about plant environment and the habits of the animal(s).

E. Basic Facts and Supplemental Information:
1. A vivarium is a helpful and interesting way to study animals and plants in their own environment. A homemade vivarium can be made from window panes, wooden supports, and heavy masking tape.
2. Many other types of vivaria can be used such as turtle habitats and hamster cages.

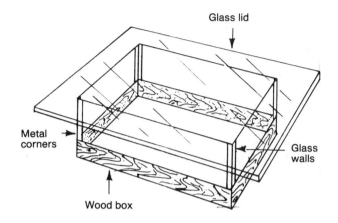

Glass lid · Metal corners · Glass walls · Wood box

3. The following terms are frequently misused and interchanged. Technically:
   a. A "terrarium" contains soils.
   b. A "vivarium" contains soils and water.
   c. An "aquarium" contains only water.

F. Thought Questions for Class Discussions:
1. How does a vivarium differ from a terrarium?
2. What experiments could be done with several similar vivaria?
3. What plants or animals would probably not survive in a vivarium?

G. Related Ideas for Further Inquiry:
1. Study possible animals that would be appropriate for this vivarium.
2. Study Activity III-A-1, "How do we classify living things?"
3. Study Section IV-D, "Reptiles."
4. Study Activity VI-A-1, "What is the balance of nature?"
5. Study Activity VI-A-3, "What is 'biological diversity'?"
6. Study other Activities in this Section.

H. Vocabulary Builders—Spelling Words:
1) **vivarium** 2) **aquarium** 3) **terrarium**
4) **charcoal** 5) **habitat** 6) **soils** 7) **rocks**
8) **sunlight** 9) **plants** 10) **animals**

I. Thought for Today:
"If you carry too many large bundles in both arms at the same time, it will cause your nose to itch."
—*John A. Norment*

A. Problem: *How Do We Build a Small, Simple Cage?*

B. Materials Needed:

1. Widemouth jar
2. Lid with top section removed
3. Screen (3″ × 3″)
4. Cutting pliers or wire cutters
5. A little soil
6. Few leaves
7. Small twigs
8. Animal(s) to be enclosed (insects, spiders, etc.)

C. Procedure:

1. Cut screen to fit inside jar lid.
2. Place screen in lid.
3. Place soil, leaves, and twigs in jar.
4. Place animal(s) in jar.
5. Replace lid and tighten it securely.
6. Place "cage" in a convenient place where temperature, air, and light are most healthful.

D. Results:

1. Students will develop skills in building a small, simple cage.
2. Students will learn about the care and feeding of small animals.

E. Basic Facts and Supplemental Information:

1. Students enjoy making "cages" and caring for insects and spiders. They can also watch various developmental changes of the insects and spiders which can be used for classroom discussion.
2. Students will learn that one main difference between insects and spiders is the number of legs they have—insects, six; spiders, eight.
3. This type of "cage" is easily kept clean and can be adapted to different insects and spiders.
4. The all-around view gives students a clear observation of the animals. This "cage" is very easy to make, and the size of the jar used can be varied according to the need.
5. These make excellent displays of students' work for parents to see.
6. With all live animals, there must be specific plans for their care and feeding over extended weekends, holidays, and long vacation periods.

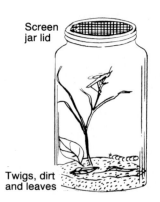

Screen jar lid

Twigs, dirt and leaves

F. Thought Questions for Class Discussions:

1. What other small animals might be kept in such a cage?
2. What are some precautions that must be taken in order to keep the animals alive?
3. Could we test which foods these animals prefer to eat?
4. How do spiders catch their food?
5. Are all spider webs the same?

G. Related Ideas for Further Inquiry:

1. Study Activity III-A-1, "How do we classify living things?"
2. Study Section IV-C, "Insects and Spiders."
3. Study Activity IV-C-1, "How do spiders differ from insects?"
4. Study Activity IV-I-3, "How do we make a wire cage for small animals?"
5. Study Activity IV-I-5, "What should we feed captured animals?"
6. Study Activity VI-A-1, "What is the balance of nature?"
7. Study Activity VI-A-3, "What is 'biological diversity'?"

H. Vocabulary Builders—Spelling Words:

1) **cage** 2) **container** 3) **widemouth**
4) **caterpillar** 5) **insect** 6) **screen** 7) **cutting**
8) **twigs** 9) **soil** 10) **lid** 11) **dirt**

I. Thought for Today:

"Have you noticed that even the busiest people are never too busy to take time to tell you how busy they are."

Activity

A. Problem: *How Do We Make a Wire Cage for Small Animals?*

B. Materials Needed:

1. Pie plates, oatmeal box with cover, or cut out coffee can with lid
2. Fine mesh wire screen to fit inside of finished cage, about 6 inches high (See drawing.)
3. Plaster of Paris (or thick styrofoam)
4. Branch and leaves from shrubbery where animal was found
5. Wire cutters or cutting pliers
6. Masking or cellophane tape
7. Heavy cardboard or leather hinge for top

C. Procedure:

1. Measure the circumference of the can or plate before cutting the screen so that it will not overlap more than 1″.
2. Pull one or two strands of wire off one side of the screen so that it will have loose ends.
3. Shape screen into cylinder so that it will fit into the lids of the can or the plate.
4. Wind loose ends of wire on overlapped portion of screen around screen to form an enclosed cylinder.
5. Mix plaster of Paris and put in bottom of can.
6. Place branch in the desired position and let plaster dry.
7. Cover the plaster with leaves and the cage is completed.
8. The lid placed on top of the screen keeps the animal(s) inside the cage.

D. Results:

1. Students will develop skills in building a small, simple cage.
2. Students will learn about the care and feeding of small animals.

E. Basic Facts and Supplemental Information:

1. This is an easy method by which the students can build an inexpensive cage. It will be useful in their observations of small animals because it is easy to view them. It is exceptionally fine for caterpillars.
2. Every cage should be provided with a shelter area into which the animal(s) can retire to sleep or to hide when excited or fearful. Warm and safe

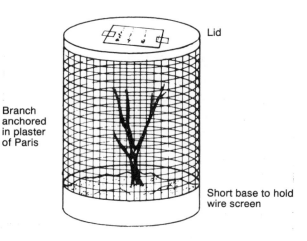

Lid

Branch anchored in plaster of Paris

Short base to hold wire screen

shelters should be provided for female animals that are expecting young.
3. This size cage is particularly suited for many species of insects and spiders.

F. Thought Questions for Class Discussions:

1. What kinds of animals can best be kept in such a cage?
2. What precautions should be taken to keep them alive?
3. What are some "natural" enemies of the animal(s) that you have collected?

G. Related Ideas for Further Inquiry:

1. Study Activity IV-I-5, "What should we feed captured animals?"
2. Study Activity III-A-1, "How do we classify living things?"
3. Study Section IV-C, "Insects and Spiders."
4. Study Section IV-B, "Pets."
5. Study Activity IV-I-2, "How do we build a small, simple cage?"
6. Study Activity IV-I-4, "How do we make a cage for medium-sized animals?"

H. Vocabulary Builders—Spelling Words:

1) **wire**   2) **cage**   3) **screen**   4) **plaster**   5) **branch**
6) **strand**   7) **cutting**   8) **animals**   9) **mesh**

I. Thought for Today:

"Never stop learning—don't get trappped in a mental cage."

Activity

A. Problem: *How Do We Make a Cage for Medium-Sized Animals?*

B. Materials Needed:

1. Galvanized screen (about 1″ or 2″ mesh)
   a. 2 pieces 30″ × 26″—(sides)
   b. 2 pieces 20″ × 26″—(ends)
   c. 1 piece 21″ × 31″—(top)
2. Wire-cutter pliers
3. Wire flooring (optional) (21″ × 31″)
4. 3/8″ plywood for floor of cage (21″ × 31″ if desired)
5. Handsaw

C. Procedure:

1. Cut pieces of wire to specifications. (Other size screens can be substituted if desired.)
2. The sides can be fastened together by either one of the following methods:
   a. Use galvanized wire to tie corners together, spacing the ties about 6″ apart. Wind wire around three times.
   b. When cutting sides of cage, leave 1″ projections of wire on front and back. These can be bent back around the wire of sides of cage.
3. The top is fastened in the same manner along one side only to form a lid.
4. The cage can be placed on a cookie sheet or other flat metal surface. If a bottom for the cage is desired, the four corner wires could be secured to a baseboard by nailing them down.
5. Sand can be placed on the bottom of the cage for ease in cleaning.

D. Result:

A sturdy, practical classroom cage is made.

E. Basic Facts and Supplemental Information:

1. This cage is collapsible for convenience in storing and carrying.
2. The tying of the edges together allows for folding of the cage when not in use.
3. This type of cage can be used for any of the larger pets such as rabbits, setting hens, squirrels, or small raccoons in the classroom.
4. For larger pets, commercial cages work best.
5. Each animal should have:
   a. enough space to move around and be comfortable
   b. an environment as close as possible to its own habitat

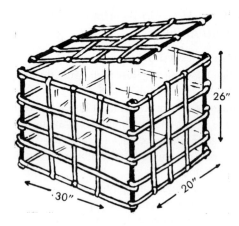

c. a shelter to hide or rest
d. proper food
e. fresh water
f. good ventilation
g. clean cage
h. sufficient food and water during weekends and short vacation periods
i. provision for care and feeding during long vacation periods

F. Thought Questions for Class Discussions:

1. What species of animals could be kept in this cage?
2. What modifications of this cage could be made that would make watering, feeding, and cleaning easier?
3. Could other types of animal cages be utilized?

G. Related Ideas for Further Inquiry:

1. Students can chart growth of small animal(s).
2. Study about the care and feeding of animals in the local zoo.
3. Study Activity IV-I-2, "How do we build a small, simple cage?"
4. Study Activity IV-I-3, "How do we make a wire cage for small animals?"
5. Study Activity IV-I-5, "What should we feed captured animals?"

H. Vocabulary Builders—Spelling Words:

1) **medium** 2) **size** 3) **pliers** 4) **plywood**
5) **galvanizing** 6) **screen** 7) **flooring**
8) **optional**

I. Thought for Today:

"Some minds are like concrete—thoroughly mixed and permanently set."

Activity

A. Problem: *What Should We Feed Captured Animals?*

B. Materials Needed:
1. Appropriate food for animal(s) as cited below
2. Natural food

C. Procedure:
1. Identify the animal(s).
2. Look up appropriate feed for it (them).

D. Result:

Animals will be fed appropriate diets.

E. Basic Facts and Supplemental Information:
1. Animals should be kept in an environment as similar to their natural environment as possible.
2. The temperature range must be considered for each species.
3. Animals should have adequate ventilation.
4. Amount of sunlight should be as close to their natural environment as possible.
5. ANIMAL(S):   SUGGESTED MENUS:

ANIMAL(S):	SUGGESTED MENUS:
a. Ants	Grated dry dog food, dead insects and spiders, food scraps, especially products "sweetened" with sugar or honey
b. Birds	Wild bird seed, breadstuffs, dry breakfast cereals, pieces of raw vegetables and fruits, hard-boiled eggs, vegetable greens
c. Butterflies	Honey, thick sugar solution, nectar
d. Caterpillars	Leaves of plants where animals were found
e. Chickens	Scrap meat, grit, bird seed, cut up hard-boiled eggs, corn
f. Earthworms	Finely ground leaves, grasses, and meat
g. Frogs and Toads	Soft-bodied insects, worms, caterpillars
h. Gerbils	Dry dog food, seeds, lettuce, carrots, grasses
i. Goldfish	Commercial goldfish food, ground dry dog food, oatmeal
j. Grasshoppers	Leaves where animals were found, celery, lettuce
k. Guinea pigs	Dry dog or rabbit food, lettuce, celery, carrots

Animals too young to feed themselves can be fed with a small nursing bottle or an eyedropper.

Carrots

Commercially prepared foods

Lettuce

Celery

l. Guppies	Commercially prepared tropical food; babies require tiny portions
m. Hamsters	Grains, dog biscuits, common vegetables, nuts, commercial hamster food
n. Lizards	Soft-bodied insects, flies, meal worms
o. Mice	Grated dry dog food, bread, meat leftovers, cheese
p. Rabbits	Commercial foods, most common vegetables
q. Snails	Most soft, green vegetables and leaves
r. Snakes	Soft-bodied insects, crickets, earthworms, small pieces of meat (irregular eaters may go days without food)

s. Tadpoles   Fine guppy food, water plants, finely ground meat in small quantities

t. Turtles   Soft-bodied insects, commercial foods, earthworms, lettuce, hardboiled eggs

6. Larger animals can be fed canned dog and/or cat food. Wholesome commercial food can be purchased at a local pet food store.

F. Thought Questions for Class Discussions:

1. Why is natural food best for all animals?
2. Is water just as important as food in caring for animals?
3. How can you tell if an animal is sick?
4. Who is going to be responsible to take care of classroom animals over extended weekends or vacation periods?
5. Have you seen any movies recently that had small animals in them that could be used for classroom pets? Were the animals real or animated?

G. Related Ideas for Further Inquiry:

1. There are many highly potentially scientific activities that can be observed on the school campus:
   a. identifying animals
   b. watching their behaviors
   c. determining how they acquire their food
   d. analyzing preypredator relationships
2. Field trips can be taken to surrounding areas, local parks, and zoos to study the care, feeding, and problems of small animals.
3. There are many resources and resource people in most communities where information about the care, feeding, and problems of small animals can be made available:
   a. pet shops
   b. veterinarians
   c. pet groomers
   d. local farmers
   e. other teachers in different schools and at different grade levels

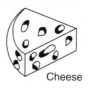
Cheese

Nuts

Eggs

Insects

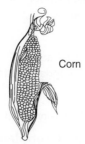
Corn

4. Study Part III, "Plants."
5. Study Activity III-A-1, "How do we classify living things?"
6. Study Activity IV-B-2, "What kind of pet should I have?"
7. Study Activity IV-B-3, "How do we care for dogs and cats?"
8. Study Activity IV-B-4, "How do we care for hamsters, guinea pigs, gerbils, and/or mice?"
9. Study Activity IV-C-2, "How do ants live?"
10. Study Activity IV-D-2, "What are some characteristics of snakes?"
11. Study Activity IV-D-3, "How do we make a terrarium for reptiles?"
12. Study Activity IV-E-4, "How do we care for a fresh-water aquarium?"

H. Vocabulary Builders—Spelling Words:

1) **ants** 2) **birds** 3) **butterflies** 4) **caterpillars**
5) **chickens** 6) **earthworms** 7) **frogs** 8) **turtles**

I. Thought for Today:

"To teach is to learn twice."

Activity

A. Problem: *How Do Animals Help People?*

B. Materials Needed:

Pictures of:

1. Elephants
2. Fish
3. Dogs
4. Rabbits
5. Sheep
6. Camels
7. Horses
8. Cows
9. Other animals

Transportation and recreation

C. Procedure:

1. Discuss animals in general.
2. Show pictures of animals listed in "Materials Needed."
3. Discuss how each specific animal species helps us:
   a. labor-saving
   b. transportation
   c. food
   d. pleasure
   e. research
   f. companionship
   g. clothing
   h. medicine

Food

D. Result:

Students will learn that many animals help us directly and indirectly by providing us with comfort and well-being.

E. Basic Facts and Supplemental Information:

1. The list of animals could be greatly expanded with other animals such as: shellfish, frogs, silkworms, etc.
2. As human population has increased, the animal population has decreased.
3. Many animals have been used in medical research testing which eventually leads to healthier lives for all. The use of animals in medical, cosmetic, etc. research has become a highly controversial issue.
4. Many people use dogs for protection and security.
5. There are many products made from animals:
   a. buttons for clothing
   b. leather for shoes, wallets, purses
   c. costume jewelry
6. Medical science has used animal organs for human replacement parts. The heart valves of pigs have been highly successful replacements for damaged human heart valves.

Clothing

Companionship

F. Thought Questions for Class Discussions:

1. How do plants help people?
2. Do plants help other animals?
3. Do some animals harm people?

G. Related Ideas for Further Inquiry:

1. Select an item listed in "Procedure" and list as many animals as possible that would come under this category.
2. Study Activity IV-J-2, "Why do we hunt and fish for certain animals?"
3. Study Part IV, "Animals."
4. Study Activity III-A-1, "How do we classify living things?"
5. Study other Activities in this Section.

H. Vocabulary Builders—Spelling Words:

Use the animals listed in "Materials Needed."

I. Thought for Today:

"Remember when kids brought teachers apples instead of driving them bananas?"

A. Problem: *Why Do We Hunt and Fish for Certain Animals?*

B. Materials Needed:
1. Pictures of animals
2. Books about animals
3. Newspaper accounts of animals
4. Other multisensory aids about animals
5. Chalkboard
6. Chalk
7. Class or group notebook(s)

C. Procedure:
1. Ask the class how many have ever gone fishing. Have them relate their experiences.
2. Ask the class how many have ever gone hunting. Have them relate their experiences.
3. Have class make a list of all the animals they know that have been hunted or fished for specific reasons.
4. Divide the class into groups or have them work individually and do research on each specific animal listed.

D. Results:
A sample list might start like this:

1. Deer—food
2. Elephants—ivory, work
3. Trout—food
4. Tropical fish—recreation
5. Alligators—skins
6. Birds—food, companionship
7. Abalone—buttons and other items, food
8. Monkeys—research
9. Dolphins—recreation
10. Fish—food, recreation, etc.

E. Basic Facts and Supplemental Information:
1. Many animal species have become endangered and some extinct because of people's activities.
2. We must learn to balance our needs with animals' needs.
3. Many animals have been killed by oil spills, pesticides, and water contamination.
4. Many animals have been fished or hunted for recreational purposes. Some animals have become

endangered and others extinct because of excessive fishing and hunting.
5. Animals are needed to provide the basic proteins for the diets of many people.

F. Thought Questions for Class Discussions:
1. What problems will we have as a result of expanding people population and decreasing animal population?
2. How can we protect our animals?
3. What part do you think greed plays in the loss of some of our animals?

G. Related Ideas for Further Inquiry:
1. Study other activities in Part IV, "Animals."
2. Study other activities in Part VI, "Ecology."
3. This is an excellent activity to combine art and science. Students can draw pictures of their recreational experiences.

H. Vocabulary Builders—Spelling Words:
1) **recreation** 2) **clothing** 3) **endangered**
4) **extinct** 5) **population** 6) **threatened**

I. Thought for Today:
"A racehorse is an animal that can take several thousand people for a ride at the same time."

Activity

A. Problem: *Should Animals Be Protected?*

B. Materials Needed:
1. Newspaper and journal accounts of animals that are threatened with extinction
2. Pictures of threatened animals
3. Multimedia aids if available

C. Procedure:
1. Discuss animals that are in danger of extinction.
2. Discuss animals that are being domesticated by people.
3. Discuss the balance of nature.
4. Discuss whether animals are worth the expense of protection.

D. Results:
1. Students will place a higher value on animal protection.
2. Students will learn that animals are vital in our food web.

E. Basic Facts and Supplemental Information:
1. By selective breeding of nearly extinct animals, scientists hope to increase their populations and return them to their natural environments.
2. There are increasing attempts to overcome the great reduction of numbers of species:
   a. Native condors were captured for breeding. Several pairs have already been released.
   b. Black-footed ferrets are nearing extinction.
   c. Whooping cranes are being bred in captivity.
   d. Red wolves are being bred in zoos.
   e. Coho salmon are being protected by new federal and state laws.
   f. Two international conservation groups recently announced that nearly 5,205 animals are near extinction. This includes:
      1) 25% of the world's mammals
      2) 11% of the world's birds
      3) 20% of the world's reptiles
      4) 25% of the world's amphibians
      5) 34% of the world's fish
   g. All animals have some effect on our lives, either directly or indirectly.

F. Thought Questions for Class Discussions:
1. Should we have concerns about protecting animals throughout the world?
2. Do plants need protection from extinction?
3. Do people need protection from extinction?

Elk

Bison

G. Related Ideas for Further Inquiry:
1. Study Activity III-A-1, "How do we classify living things?"
2. Study Activity VI-A-1, "What is the balance of nature?"
3. Study Activity VI-A-3, "What is 'biological diversity'?"
4. Study Activity VI-D-3, "How can we save our diminishing species?"

H. Vocabulary Builders—Spelling Words:
1) **protection** 2) **survival** 3) **extinct**
4) **condor** 5) **balance** 6) **nature** 7) **world**

I. Thought for Today:
"Success is a journey; not a destination."

PART V

HEALTH

SECTION A   BODY STRUCTURE AND FUNCTION   231
SECTION B   SENSES   239
SECTION C   NUTRITION   249
SECTION D   PERSONAL HEALTH   258
SECTION E   PUBLIC HEALTH   269
SECTION F   FIRST AID   273
SECTION G   SAFETY   281

SECTION A: BODY STRUCTURE AND FUNCTION

Activity

A. Problem: *What Are the Different Systems in Our Body?*

B. Materials Needed:

1. Pictures of different systems of the human body
2. Books, magazines about body systems
3. Puppets (optional)
4. Clay (optional)
5. Art supplies
6. Models of human anatomical parts

C. Procedure:

1. Discuss with class the different systems in body and their main purpose:
   a. respiratory—breathing
   b. digestive—eating
   c. muscular—moving
   d. excretory—eliminating
   e. circulatory—supplying
   f. skeletal—supporting
   g. lymphatic—protecting
   h. reproductive—reproducing
   i. nervous—sensing
   j. external protective—protecting (skin, hair, nails)
2. Discuss the models and let the students handle them.
3. Have students collect pictures showing different systems in action. (Respiratory could be a runner breathing hard, digestive could be a person eating, muscular could be a weight lifter, etc.)
4. Have the students discuss what changes they would make in a person's anatomical construction to make him/her "perfect."
5. Have them draw such changes. (See drawing for example.)
6. By reconstructing this perfect person, what health problems might be encountered?

D. Results:

1. Students will learn about the many different systems in the body and their functions.
2. They will realize that all systems are interrelated.
3. They will learn that all systems are vital to living.

4. They will realize that our bodies are "perfect" now.
5. They will learn that any apparent "perfect change" will cause more complications than benefits.

E. Basic Facts and Supplemental Information:

1. Each system has many component parts; for example, the circulatory system includes the heart, arteries, veins, and many smaller vessels.
2. Stress should be placed on the interdependence of all systems and the care of each.

F. Thought Questions for Class Discussions:

1. Which system do you think is the most important?
2. Which system is the most complex?
3. Which system is the most important for growth?

G. Related Ideas for Further Inquiry:

1. Compare the systems in our body to the "systems" found in an automobile, house, and/or mechanical person (robot).
2. Discuss how all our body's systems are composed of organs, tissues, and cells.
3. Discuss how a problem in one system usually affects most other systems.

H. Vocabulary Builders—Spelling Words:
Use the names of the body systems listed in "Procedure 1."

I. Thought for Today:
"If you are not afraid to face the music, someday you may lead the band."

Activity

A. Problem: *What Different Kinds of Bones and Joints Do We Have?*

B. Materials Needed:
1. Pictures or drawings of human skeleton
2. Pictures or drawings of bones

C. Procedure:
1. Tell class that the main functions of bones in the body are to support it and help it in its movements.
2. Discuss the different types of movements the body can perform.
3. Ask if any of the students have ever broken one of their bones. If so, how did the doctor help with the mending or repair?
4. Ask the class if they have ever found a bone in a field, in the woods, or anywhere.
5. Study the main bones of the body.
6. If chicken bones can be obtained, try to reconstruct a chicken skeleton.
7. Discuss the function of bone marrow (supplies red blood cells).

D. Results:
1. Students will learn that the body has specialized bones and each part adds to body mobility.
2. Students will locate the different kinds of joints:

Kind of Joint:	Location:
Ball-and-socket	Shoulder, hip
Hinge	Elbow, knee, fingers, toes
Pivot	Head on spine
Gliding	Vertebra
Angular	Wrist, ankle
Partially movable	Ribs to spine
	Hip to sacrum
Almost immovable	Cranium, adult

3. Students learn that the body has about 206 different bones, in four main groups:
   a. chest
   b. head
   c. arms and legs
   d. extremities (fingers and toes)

E. Basic Facts and Supplemental Information:
1. Bones are composed primarily of calcium and phosphorus. Growing children should have adequate amounts of these elements in their daily diet.
2. Besides muscles and bones involved in body movement, there are also tendons, cartilage, blood supply, nerves, etc.

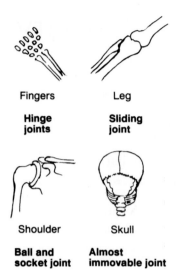

Fingers — Hinge joints

Leg — Sliding joint

Shoulder — Ball and socket joint

Skull — Almost immovable joint

3. Good posture is determined by proper alignment of bones.
4. More than half of your body's 206 bones are in your hands and your feet.
5. The skeleton is the framework of the body.
6. Ligaments hold the bones together.
7. Joints are hinges which enable the bones to move.

F. Thought Questions for Class Discussions:
1. Why do many people suffer from back problems?
2. Why can most boys run faster than girls of the same size?
3. What does "crossbones" mean?
4. Do all animals have bones?
5. How can we take better care of our bones?

G. Related Ideas for Further Inquiry:
1. Students can bring in chicken or turkey bones.
2. Soak a bone in vinegar for several days and then examine it.
3. Older students may want to study the bones in one part of the body such as the arms, legs, or head.
4. String together empty thread spools to simulate the vertebrae.
5. Study other Activities in this Section.

H. Vocabulary Builders—Spelling Words:
Use the words listed under *Kind of Joint* in "Results."

I. Thought for Today:
"Nature does make mistakes; sometimes she puts all the bones in the head and none in the back."

Activity

A. Problem: *How Does Our Heart Work?*

B. Materials Needed:

1. Model of heart
2. Pictures, posters, and/or charts showing the chambers of the heart and the circulatory system

C. Procedure:

1. Discuss the four chambers of the heart:
   a. Left ventricle—starts the blood moving to all parts of the body.
   b. Right atrium—receives blood from all parts of the body.
   c. Right ventricle—starts blood moving to the lungs to be oxygenated.
   d. Left atrium—receives oxygenated blood from the lungs.
2. Have the students make a simple drawing of where the blood circulates and the main blood vessels the body has to transport the blood.
3. Describe the pumping action of the heart.
4. Define the terms:
   a. Systolic—how hard the heart works (contracting).
   b. Diastolic—blood pressure when the heart relaxes (dilating).
5. Blood pressure is usually reported by citing the systolic pressure (upper reading) followed by the diastolic pressure (lower reading). Thus a reading of 120/80 (one twenty over eighty) is the pressure in millimeters of mercury of the systolic and diastolic systems, respectively.

D. Result:

Pupils can better understand how a four-chambered human heart circulates blood throughout the body.

E. Basic Facts and Supplemental Information:

1. Blood circulates to the lungs to give off carbon dioxide and to get oxygen. It then returns to the heart to be pumped to all parts of the body.
2. Our heart pumps about 100,000 times a day and pumps about 3,000 gallons of blood through 60,000 miles of arteries, veins, and capillaries. In an average lifetime it pumps about 73,000,000 gallons of blood.
3. The blood is composed of serum (the liquid part) and white cells, red cells, and platelets (the solid parts). The white cells fight infection, the red cells distribute oxygen and pick up carbon dioxide, and the platelets help in blood clotting.

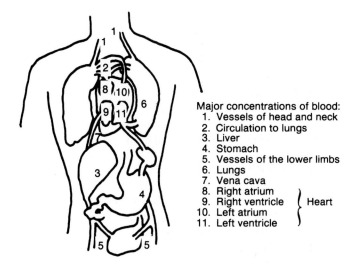

Major concentrations of blood:
1. Vessels of head and neck
2. Circulation to lungs
3. Liver
4. Stomach
5. Vessels of the lower limbs
6. Lungs
7. Vena cava
8. Right atrium ⎫
9. Right ventricle ⎬ Heart
10. Left atrium ⎪
11. Left ventricle ⎭

4. There are four types of blood: Types A, B, AB, and O. These must be matched in blood transfusions.
5. There is also an "Rh" factor that concerns blood clotting (agglutinogen). If a person has it, it is called "Rh positive;" if not, it is called "Rh negative."
6. The heart is about the size of a closed fist and weighs about 12 ounces in men and 9 ounces in women. There are valves which control the flow of blood during pumping motions.
7. The blood starts from the heart in large arteries and ends up in capillaries smaller than the diameter of a human hair.
8. The blood delivers food to every cell in the human body.

F. Thought Questions for Class Discussions:

1. What is heart disease?
2. How serious is heart disease?
3. Is there such a thing as "athlete's heart"?
4. How can we take better care of our hearts?

G. Related Ideas for Further Inquiry:

1. Discuss what happens during accidents which cause bleeding.
2. Study Section V-F, "First Aid."
3. Study other Activities in this Section.

H. Vocabulary Builders—Spelling Words:

1) **artery** 2) **vein** 3) **capillary** 4) **atrium**
5) **ventricle** 6) **platelets** 7) **circulation** 8) **heart**

I. Thought for Today:

"The heart is happiest when it beats for others."

Activity

A. Problem: *How Can We Find Our Pulse?*

B. Materials Needed:

1. Pictures, charts, or sketches of:
   a. human body
   b. forearm
   c. blood vessels in the arm
   d. point where pulse should be taken
2. Clock or watch with second hand

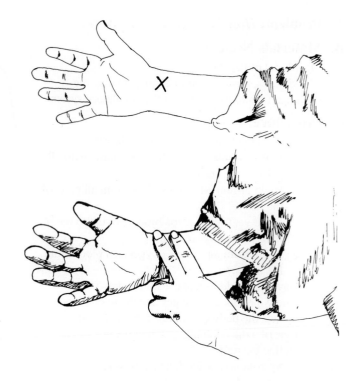

C. Procedure:

1. Briefly explain about the circulatory system.
2. Discuss how the heart pumps food and oxygen to the cells and gets rid of wastes from all our cells.
3. Describe how most blood vessels are deep within the body for protection.
4. Show the chart of the forearm where pulse is to be located (radial artery).
5. Divide class into pairs.
6. Show class, on a student, where pulse can be taken.
   a. forearm
   b. nearest thumb side (radial side)
   c. in cavity between bones (radial and ulna)
   d. about two inches below joint of hand
7. Cite how pulse is taken:
   a. use two of the three middle fingers (never thumb)
   b. press down until throbbing is felt
8. Have students count the number of times the pulse beats (pulsates) for one-half minute.
9. Multiply this number by two.
10. Have students do some exercises and retake pulse.
11. Have students take their pulse, three minutes after exercises and compare findings with previous ones.
12. Have students rest for five minutes and retake pulse.

D. Results:

1. Students will learn something about the circulatory system.
2. Pupils will learn how to take their pulse.
3. Students will learn that the heart beats faster during exercise.

E. Basic Facts and Supplemental Information:

1. While the heartbeat will average around 72 beats per minute, pulse rate ranges are considered normal from 65 to 85.
2. Doctors look not only for the number of beats but also if they are equal in strength and time duration.

3. If students have problems locating pulse on their arm, then have them feel for pulse on the side of the neck, slightly forward of the midline using the three middle fingers.

F. Thought Questions for Class Discussions:

1. Does the heart beat faster in higher altitudes?
2. What is an "athlete's heart"?
3. Why does the heart beat faster when we exercise?
4. How much blood does the heart pump every minute? Compute from data of previous Activity.
5. Does the heart get any rest? (yes, between "beats")

G. Related Ideas for Further Inquiry:

1. Study Activity V-A-1, "What are the different systems in our body?"
2. Study Activity V-A-3, "How does our heart work?"
3. Study other Activities in this Section.

H. Vocabulary Builders—Spelling Words:

1) **pulse** 2) **forearm** 3) **vessels** 4) **midline**
5) **radial artery** 6) **circulation** 7) **heartbeat**

I. Thought for Today:

"Absence makes the heart grow fonder."

Activity

A. Problem: *How Much Air Do Our Lungs Hold?*

B. Materials Needed:

1. Large, clear bowl
2. Large plastic bottle
3. Temporary lid for jar (could be an index card)
4. Plastic tubing (24″ long)
5. Measuring cup
6. Water
7. Sink or tabletop

C. Procedure:

1. Place large bowl in sink or on tabletop.
2. Fill large bowl about one-third full of water.
3. Fill jar with water; measure and record volume of water in jar.
4. Put temporary lid on jar.
5. Invert jar, place it in the large bowl in vertical position. (See drawing.)
6. Remove temporary cap. Have one student hold the jar in upright position.
7. Position plastic tubing in neck of jar so that tubing extends about three inches into the jar.
8. Have another student test his/her lung capacity by taking a deep breath, holding his/her nose and then blowing steadily into the tube until his/her lungs are empty. (*Do not inhale through tube.*)
9. Measure the amount of water left in the jar. Subtract this amount from the original volume of water in jar. This indicates the volume of air replaced in jar from the student's lungs.

D. Results:

1. The water in the plastic bottle will be replaced by the air from the student's lungs.
2. The air will bubble into the bottle.
3. A rough estimate of lung capacity can be determined. (The lungs can never be completely emptied as some air always remains in them.)

E. Basic Facts and Supplemental Information:

1. Air is approximately 78% nitrogen and 21% oxygen.
2. Only the oxygen is utilized by the body.
3. Oxygen is absorbed by the blood and carried to all parts of the body.
4. The heart is the pump that forces the blood to all parts of the body.
5. Oxygen plus food equals energy which we need in order to function.
6. The lungs have as much surface area as a tennis court.
7. The lungs work like the bellows of an accordion.

F. Thought Questions for Class Discussions:

1. Does our body require a greater volume of air in high elevations?
2. How does exercise affect our breathing?
3. What part does carbon dioxide play in our breathing process?

G. Related Ideas for Further Inquiry:

1. Study Activity 1-B-18, "How much oxygen is in the air?"
2. Study Activity V-A-1, "What are the different systems in our body?"
3. Study Activity V-C-2, "What is the food pyramid?"
4. Study Activity II-B-12, "Is carbon dioxide heavier than air? Will carbon dioxide gas support combustion?"
5. Study Activity V-A-8, "What are cells, tissues, and organs?"

H. Vocabulary Builders—Spelling Words:

1) **lungs**   2) **breathing**   3) **bowl**   4) **plastic**
5) **capacity**   6) **measure**   7) **compute**   8) **estimate**

I. Thought for Today:

"If the air doesn't become purer, I'm going to stop breathing it." (Author unknown)

Activity

A. Problem: *How Does Our Skin Help Us?*

B. Materials Needed:

Pictures of people's faces of different ethnic groups

C. Procedure:

1. Have students list the ways they take care of their skin.
2. Have students list the ways that the skin helps us.
3. Discuss items they may have omitted such as:
   a. protects us from bacteria
   b. holds our inner organs inside
   c. protects inner organs from injuries
   d. pigment in skin protects us from ultraviolet radiation from the sun
   e. sensory perceptors give us our senses of feeling: (alarm system) (sense of touch)
      1) heat
      2) pain
      3) pressure
   f. eliminates perspiration (wastes)
   g. keeps us cool (We have more than 1,000,000 sweat glands.)
   h. keeps our body temperature constant (cools us)
   i. supports body hair (Hair on our head grows 25 feet in a lifetime.)
   j. means of identification (fingerprints, footprints)
   k. adds color—all have the same coloring pigment melanin (black). There are no red or yellow skin pigments. Many Orientals have a thicker skin layer which consists of keratin which yields a yellow cast. Native Americans tan easier; skin appears as reddish.
   l. protects us from sun, rain, and other weather conditions
   m. keeps us in touch with the world

D. Result:

Students will learn a lot about their skin and consequently will know how to take better care of it.

E. Basic Facts and Supplemental Information:

1. The skin is the largest body organ.
2. A square inch of skin contains about 250 sweat glands, 72 feet of nerves, 60 hair follicles, and 18 feet of blood vessels.
3. Scientists have produced artificial skin composed of collagen from animal tissue and a silicon film.
4. Your skin weighs twice as much as your brain.

F. Thought Questions for Class Discussions:

1. In what ways do we harm our skin?
2. What did primitive tribes do to harm their skin?
3. Are cosmetics helpful or harmful to the skin?

G. Related Ideas for Further Inquiry:

1. Study the problem of acne.
2. Discuss acupuncture.
3. Have students wet one hand and leave the other hand dry. Moisture or water on the hands will have a cooling effect because of evaporation.
4. Study ways we can protect our skin.
5. Study the effects of ultraviolet rays on our skin.
6. Study other Activities in this Section.

H. Vocabulary Builders—Spelling Words:

1) **skin**   2) **melanin**   3) **keratin**
4) **acupuncture**   5) **cosmetics**   6) **acne**

I. Thought for Today:

"Happiness is having the bell ring just as you are called on to recite."

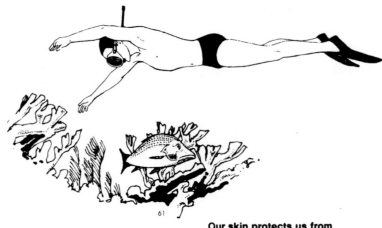

61

Our skin protects us from outside temperatures, water, and disease.

A. Problem: *Are All Fingerprints Different?*

B. Materials Needed:

1. Pictures of people
2. Pictures of different kinds of fingerprints
3. Picture of hands
4. Magnifying glass
5. Inked stamp pad
6. Clean, white paper
7. Paper towels to clean fingers

C. Procedure:

1. With a magnifying glass, look at the top front surfaces of your fingers to see what types of fingerprints they would make.
2. Place one finger on an inked stamp pad and then on a piece of clean, white paper.
3. Draw this fingerprint.
4. Repeat with all other fingers.
5. Compare your fingerprints with those in the pictures to identify the main kind.
6. See if you find any major type of fingerprint: (a) loop, (b) double loop, (c) central pocket loop, (d) whorl, (e) plain arch, or (f) tented arch.

D. Results:

1. Students will learn the basics of fingerprints.
2. They will discover that no two fingerprints are identical.
3. They will see that even their own fingers have different prints.

E. Basic Facts and Supplemental Information:

1. There are many types of fingerprints.
2. Fingerprints are a good form of identification in case of accidents.
3. Fingerprints provide good clues in police work and are as good as leaving one's name and address.
4. These papillary ridges are also found on the soles of the feet and on the palms of the hands.
5. Even identical twins have different sets of fingerprints.
6. The fingerprints on your right hand differ from those on your left hand.
7. With the aid of a computer, a fingerprint can be traced to 1 of 250,000,000 individuals in 4 seconds. This is about the population of the United States.

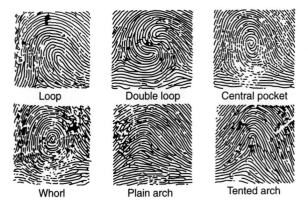

Loop   Double loop   Central pocket

Whorl   Plain arch   Tented arch

8. Focal points in ridgeline patterns are deltas and cores:
   a. delta is the point concerned with divergence.
   b. core is the approximate center point.
9. The shapes of fingerprints do not change with age; the ridges just spread out.
10. Fetuses as young as four months have fingerprint ridges.
11. Current fingerprinting techniques require no ink.

F. Thought Questions for Class Discussions:

1. Do you think everybody should be required to have their fingerprints on record?
2. Do fingerprints change if one skins his/her finger and the skin grows back?
3. Can fingerprints be changed?
4. Could fingerprints be used to locate and identify a lost person?

G. Related Ideas for Further Inquiry:

1. Ask a police officer to talk to the class about the use of fingerprints in investigations.
2. Study Activity V-A-8, "What are cells, tissues, and organs?"
3. Study other Activities in this Section.

H. Vocabulary Builders—Spelling Words:

1) **fingerprint**   2) **loop**   3) **whorl**   4) **arch**
5) **identify**   6) **delta**   7) **core**   8) **pocket**

I. Thought for Today:

"When it comes to picking up dirt, the vacuum cleaner can't compare with the telephone."

A. Problem: *What Are Cells, Tissues, and Organs?*

B. Materials Needed:

1. Onion
2. Thin strip of bacon, raw
3. Picture of heart, liver, and/or spleen
4. Microscope or magnifying glass
5. Pictures of mouth, windpipe, lungs (cross-sectional if possible)
6. Tongue depressor

C. Procedure:

1. Discuss how a body is like an automobile or a house. Each is a complete unit, made up of smaller, intricate parts or sections.
   a. Automobile has chassis, tires, motor, etc. Each of these has component parts.
   b. House has rooms; each room has component parts: windows, floors, walls, ceilings, etc.
2. Discuss the body as a whole entity.
3. Describe how the body is composed of systems.
4. Describe how the systems contain organs.
5. Describe how the organs are composed of tissues.
6. Describe how the tissues are composed of many cells.
7. In other words, the body is composed of:
   a. cells—which form
   b. tissues—which form
   c. organs—which are part of
   d. systems—which form the
   e. whole body.
8. Cut an onion and slice one layer of it very thin.
9. Look at this one layer under a microscope or magnifying glass.
10. Carefully scrape inside the cheek for cheek cells with the tongue depressor.
11. Examine these under a microscope.
12. Examine the strip of bacon under the microscope.

D. Results:

1. Students will see cells under the microscope.
2. Pupils will learn that the body is composed of many parts all working in unison.

E. Basic Facts and Supplemental Information:

1. The body is composed of trillions of cells.
2. While no one has counted them, the human body at birth is estimated to contain 3 trillion (3,000,000,000,000) cells.

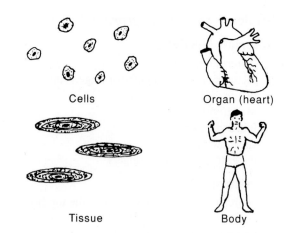

Cells

Organ (heart)

Tissue

Body

3. The most remarkable fact is that each human being started out as one cell.
4. Vitamins and minerals must be supplied by the expectant mother to convert proteins, carbohydrates, and fats into living cells.
5. The main kinds of tissue are muscle, skin, and organ.
6. The main organs of the body are heart, spleen, liver, kidneys, reproductive organs, pancreas, stomach, and lungs.
7. The main systems of the body are the muscular, reproductive, circulatory, lymphatic, digestive, respiratory, and nervous.

F. Thought Questions for Class Discussions:

1. Which systems are involuntary and which are voluntary? (Voluntary are those which individuals can control consciously.)
2. Do all animals have the same kinds of systems?
3. Do plants have the same kinds of systems?

G. Related Ideas for Further Inquiry:

1. Study the main purpose of each body group.
2. Study how the structures of humans differ from the structures of other animals.
3. Study the parts of an individual body cell.
4. Study other Activities in this Section.

H. Vocabulary Builders—Spelling Words:

1) **cells**   2) **tissues**   3) **organs**   4) **systems**
5) **heart**   6) **spleen**   7) **liver**   8) **lungs**

I. Thought for Today:

"One learns much from one's teachers, more from one's colleagues, and most from one's pupils."

SECTION B: SENSES

Activity

A. Problem: *How Many Senses Do We Have? How Do We Receive Information About Our Environment?*

B. Materials Needed:

1. Chart or notebook paper
2. Pen, pencil, marking pen
3. Pictures of sense organs (optional)

C. Procedure:

1. Talk to class about how we know what is in our environment (surroundings).
2. Have students list various sensations or feelings realized from:

   a. warm clothing
   b. aroma of flowers
   c. loud stereo
   d. falling rain
   e. candy bar
   f. orange juice
   g. fuzzy toy
   h. seeing a star
   i. drums
   j. snow

D. Results:

1. Students will be aware of our five main senses.
2. Students will develop a list that might include:

   a. touch
   b. pressure
   c. heat
   d. cold
   e. pain
   f. smell
   g. taste (sweet, sour, bitter, salty)
   h. sight
   i. hearing
   j. balance

E. Basic Facts and Supplemental Information:

1. People refer to the five main senses, but actually we have many more.
2. The sense of touch is made up of special nerve endings in the skin, and these specialized cells detect pressure, pain, heat, and cold. Cold is really the absence of heat.
3. There is also a "sense" of balance. This enables a person to maintain an upright position.
4. There is also a "kinesthetic" sense. A person knows the position(s) of his/her arms, legs, and head, etc.
5. Sense organs send signals to the brain via nerves. The brain interprets these and the body acts accordingly.
6. We have five main organs of sensation:

   a. skin
   b. nose
   c. ears
   d. eyes
   e. tongue

7. Our sense of smell is due to the absorption of chemicals by the mucous membranes in our nostrils.
8. Our sense of sight is due in part to the bathing of lacrimal fluid that keeps our eyes moist and permits light to enter, which strikes the retinal nerve.

F. Thought Questions for Class Discussions:

1. Could we detect our surroundings if we lost all of our senses?
2. If a person loses one sense, are there any ways that it can be replaced?
3. Do you, or any of your friends or family wear glasses, contact lenses, or a hearing aid? How did these help change your/their life?

G. Related Ideas for Further Inquiry:

1. Have students identify 10 objects in a paper sack just using their sense of touch.
2. Discuss what harm could affect our senses.
3. Study other Activities in this Section.

H. Vocabulary Builders—Spelling Words:

Use the words listed in "Results."

I. Thought for Today:

"A child is a thing that stands halfway between an adult and a television screen."

Activity

VB2

A. Problem: *Why Do the Pupils of Our Eyes Change Size?*

B. Materials Needed:
1. Flashlight
2. Drawings of eyes with pupils dilated and contracted

C. Procedure:
1. Define and point out the iris and the pupil of the eye.
2. Have some students stand in a brightly lighted part of the room for one or two minutes and let some others observe the size of the pupils of their eyes.
3. Move the students to a darker area of the room and have the observers report any changes in the size of their pupils.
4. Have students cover their eyes with their hands for a few seconds and then quickly remove them.
5. Discuss what observers saw when this was done.
6. Cover one eye with one hand and repeat. Does one eye react or both?
7. In groups of three, have one student be a test student, a second to alternately shine and remove the flashlight from shining in the eyes of the first student, and the third student should be the observer to note changes. The light should be shone in the student's eyes for only a fraction of a second. The light should be held several feet away. The pupils will respond immediately.
8. Repeat step 7, shining the flashlight on only one eye for a fraction of a second. Did one eye react or both?

D. Result:

The pupils dilate when there is little light and contracts when light approaches the eye. Both eyes react to light stimulation of one eye.

E. Basic Facts and Supplemental Information:
1. Contraction of the pupil of the eye protects it from excessive light. Dilation allows more light to enter when it is dark.
2. Ideas to save your eyes:
   a. Have proper light when you read.
   b. When viewing television, have other lights on in room. Don't view at close range.
   c. The best source of light for reading should be over one shoulder.

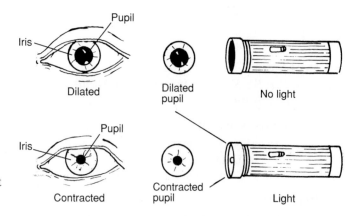

d. Don't read fine print for a long period of time.
e. Never look directly at the sun.
f. Don't read in bright sunlight.
g. Wear protective glasses in any situation where your eyes could be injured.
h. If you have frequent headaches, see a doctor.

F. Thought Questions for Class Discussions:
1. Are our pupils large or small when we watch television?
2. Does the color of our eyes have anything to do with our ability to see?
3. Why do some people wear dark glasses?

G. Related Ideas for Further Inquiry:
1. Should all automobile drivers take eye tests?
2. Should bicyclists take eye tests?
3. Stand in front of a mirror and open and close your eyes. Observe pupils.
4. Study Activity V-B-4, "How do our eyes blend separate colors?"
5. Study Activity V-B-5, "Are there blind spots in our eyes?"
6. Study Activity V-B-7, "How do we see motion?"
7. Study other Activities in this Section.

H. Vocabulary Builders—Spelling Words:
1) **iris** 2) **pupil** 3) **dilate** 4) **contract**
5) **flashlight** 6) **react** 7) **eye** 8) **change**

I. Thought for Today:
"You can lead children to education but you can't make them learn."

Activity

A. Problem: *How Do We See Color?*

B. Materials Needed:

1. Shoe box
2. Construction paper squares of 5″ of various colors
3. Scissors or knife
4. Cellophane tape
5. Cellophane rectangles 3″ × 5″ of various colors

C. Procedure:

1. Cut a rectangular opening about 2″ × 4″ in the top of the shoe box, about 2″ from one end. (See drawing.)
2. Outline the opening with a cellophane tape border.
3. Cut a two 2″ diameter circular opening at the other end of the box top (peephole).
4. Place a square of colored construction paper in the center of the shoe box at the bottom.
5. Tape a piece of the same color cellophane to the rectangular opening in the top of shoe box.
6. Place the shoe box top on the shoe box.
7. Place the shoe box in a well-lighted area.
8. Look through the peephole at the construction paper square.
9. Repeat the experiment using a different color for the construction paper square and the cellophane.
10. Repeat experiment using different color combinations of construction paper and cellophane.

D. Results:

1. If the same color construction paper and cellophane are used, the student will see that particular color.
2. If complementary colors are used for the construction paper and the cellophane, the student will see only dark color (near black). If colors were perfectly complementary, student would see black, the absence of all colors.
3. If adjacent colors are used with a primary color as the cellophane, only the primary color will be seen. (Adjacent colors are colors next to each other in the light spectrum. Red and orange are adjacent colors.)
4. Other unusual and unexpected outcomes will be observed.

E. Basic Facts and Supplemental Information:

1. The primary colors of light are slightly different from paints. They are red, blue, and green.

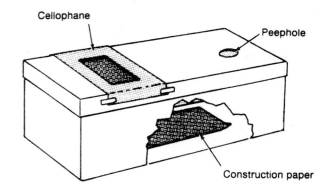

Cellophane

Peephole

Construction paper

2. If the colors appear too dark, point the box toward a window.
3. White light, from the sun or light bulbs, is composed of all colors and can be separated into its component colors by passing it through a prism.
4. For unknown reasons, color blindness affects more men than women.
5. If white light strikes an object of one color, the object absorbs that color but our eyes perceive its complementary color. If we perceive a green object, the object is actually orange, its complementary color.

F. Thought Questions for Class Discussions:

1. Why are clouds usually seen as white?
2. What is the real color of a red dress?
3. If we say an object is blue, is it actually blue?
4. If we call a tree a rock, is it a tree or a rock?
5. What color light is not used by plants?

G. Related Ideas for Further Inquiry:

1. Draw a picture using only one color. Look at it through a similar-colored piece of cellophane.
2. Look at a color blindness chart. Can you see any numbers?
3. Study other Activities in this Section.

H. Vocabulary Builders—Spelling Words:

1) **constructive** 2) **cellophane** 3) **color blindness**
4) **diameter** 5) **scissors** 6) **complementary**

I. Thought for Today:

"Education is not a headful of facts, but knowing how and where to find facts."

Activity

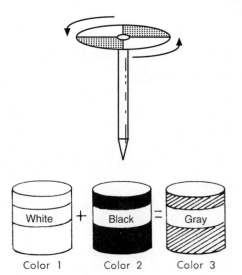

White + Black = Gray

Color 1   Color 2   Color 3

A. Problem: *How Do Our Eyes Blend Separate Colors?*

B. Materials Needed:

1. Tagboard
2. Compass, drawing
3. Paints, water-base: red, orange, yellow, green, cobalt blue, indigo, and violet
4. Scissors
5. Pencil or dowel
6. Thumbtack
7. Protractor
8. Paint brushes

C. Procedure:

1. With compass, draw four disks about six inches in diameter on tagboard.
2. Cut these out with scissors.
3. Divide two of these into four equal sections as shown in drawing.
4. Paint one disk in alternate colors of red and yellow.
5. Paint a second disk in alternate colors of yellow and blue.
6. Paint a third disk in alternate colors of any two colors cited in "Materials Needed."
7. Divide the fourth disk into seven equal sections using the protractor (about 51.5° each—it doesn't have to be exact).
8. Punch a small hole in the center of each disk.
9. Attach disk one to the top of pencil or dowel with thumbtack.
10. Spin the disks; observe and record results.
11. Repeat with the other three disks.

D. Results:

1. When the red and yellow disk is spun, the disk will appear to be orange.
2. When the yellow and blue disk is spun, the disk will appear to be green.
3. The third disk's apparent color when spun will vary with the colors selected.
4. The fourth disk will appear white when spun if the colors are perfect. Since they probably are not perfect, the disk will appear a pale gray.
5. The primary colors of light are slightly different from the primary colors of paints.

E. Basic Facts and Supplemental Information:

1. This phenomenon is called "visual persistency."
2. Each image our eyes receives lasts for a short length of time beyond the actual scene. This produces the effect of mixing colors.
3. When these disks are spun rapidly, our eyes blend the colors into a mixed color.

4. The color "white" is a mixture of all colors.
5. The color "black" is the absence of all colors.
6. The colors cited in "Materials Needed" are primary and secondary colors of light.
7. The primary colors of paint differ from the primary colors of light, consequently the mixing of paints may produce "off-colors."

F. Thought Questions for Class Discussions:

1. Can you figure out what color will be produced before you spin the disk?
2. Will it make any difference how fast the disk is spun?
3. What would happen if we used three colors on the disk?

G. Related Ideas for Further Inquiry:

1. Two different colors of paints can be mixed and tested to see what third color they would produce.
2. Challenge the students to produce specific secondary colors: those formed by mixing two primary colors.
3. Have the students learn the sequence of colors of light by the name of a hypothetical man, ROY G. BIV (*r*ed, *o*range, *y*ellow, *g*reen, *b*lue, *i*ndigo, and *v*iolet).
4. Study Section II-C, "Light and Color."
5. Study other Activities in this Section, especially V-B-3 and V-B-7.

H. Vocabulary Builders—Spelling Words:

1) **mixing**   2) **blending**   3) **visual persistency**
Also use the primary colors cited in "Materials Needed."

I. Thought for Today:

"The politicians were talking themselves red, white, and blue in the face."

Activity

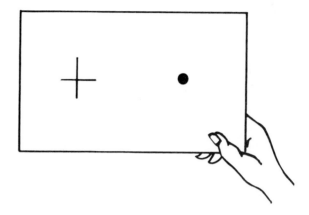

A. Problem: *Are There Blind Spots in Our Eyes?*

B. Materials Needed:
1. 3″ × 5″ cards, plain (one for each student)
2. Pencils
3. Rulers

C. Procedure:
1. Have each student reproduce the card in the sketch using a pencil with black lead.
2. Have each student hold the card at arm's length with the right hand.
3. Have each student close his/her left eye or cover it with his/her hand.
4. Have each student stare at the cross and slowly move his/her hand holding the card toward his/her right eye.

D. Result:
When the card is about halfway toward the right eye, if the student has followed the procedures carefully, the dot will disappear.

E. Basic Facts and Supplemental Information:
1. This blind spot is where the image of the object seen would focus on the retina at the point where the optic nerve joins it. Since there are no light-sensitive cells there, the eye blanks out.
2. In normal viewing, the right eye sees the "blind spot" of the left eye and vice versa.
3. In the middle drawings are two sketches which have double perceptions. What do you see?
4. In the bottom drawing is an illustration of how our brain "sees" for us. We can "see" an equilateral triangle, but in reality, our eyes perceive only three angles—no triangle!
5. You can use the drawing in this book in lieu of a card if you wish. The results will be the same.

F. Thought Questions for Class Discussions:
1. How large a dot can each student make disappear? This can be tested by gradually increasing the size of the dot with a pencil.
2. Why don't we have a blind spot when we are using both eyes?
3. How many times do we blink our eyes in one minute?
4. Study other Activities in this Section.

G. Related Ideas for Further Inquiry:
1. Collect other optical illusions.
2. Study a model of the eye.

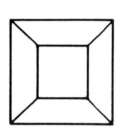

The inner square appears to be first in the back, then in front.

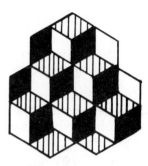

How many blocks do you see? Six or seven?

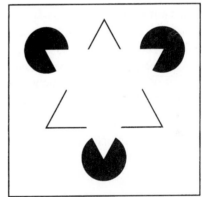

One triangle? Or two?

3. Study Activity V-B-6, "Do our eyes ever deceive us?"

H. Vocabulary Builders—Spelling Words:
1) **blind spot**   2) **length**   3) **cover**   4) **cross**
5) **outwardly**   6) **stare**   7) **illusion**
8) **perspective**

I. Thought for Today:
"If at first you don't succeed, you're running about average."

Activity

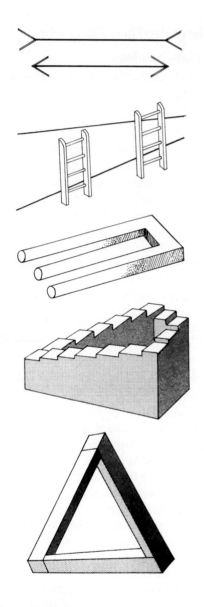

A. Problem: *Do Our Eyes Ever Deceive Us?*

B. Materials Needed:

Drawings of the illustrations depicted

C. Procedure:

1. Briefly describe how our eyes see. (Our eyes receive light, and the light impulses travel to the brain via our optic nerves. The brain interprets these impulses and sometimes is confused.)

2. Have the students look at the sketches and report what they see. In the drawings: Which line is longer? Which ladder is taller? Where is the middle tube attached? Do steps always go up? Is the triangle twisted?

3. Discuss the problems of interpreting three-dimensional objects on a two-dimensional plane.

D. Result:

Students will enjoy these optical illusions, but more important, they will realize why the drawings can be interpreted in several ways.

E. Basic Facts and Supplemental Information:

Start a collection of optical illusions. They are always good for a rainy day.

F. Thought Questions for Class Discussions:

1. Discuss how two people can see the same thing but interpret it differently.

2. Are witnesses to accidents always able to describe the scene or report facts accurately?

3. How important is our brain in seeing?

G. Related Ideas for Further Inquiry:

1. Study the cause of optical illusions.

2. Run other tests on the eyes and seeing.

3. Study Activity V-B-2, "Why do the pupils of our eyes change size?"

4. Study Activity V-B-5, "Are there blind spots in our eyes?"

5. Study Activity V-B-7, "How do we see motion?"

6. Study other Activities in this Section.

H. Vocabulary Builders—Spelling Words:

1) **optical** 2) **illusion** 3) **interpreting**
4) **brain** 5) **problems** 6) **viewing** 7) **seeing**
8) **deceive** 9) **optic** 10) **nerve**

I. Thought for Today:

"Heredity determines the color of a child's eyes, but it is the environment that lights them up."

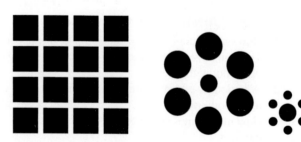

Are there any tiny gray squares at the intersections?

Which center dot is larger?

Activity

A. Problem: *How Do We See Motion?*

B. Materials Needed:

1. Heavy white or light-colored cardboard, 2 1/2″ × 3″
2. Fine string, 36 inches long
3. India ink or black paint
4. One-hole punch
5. Marking pen
6. Scissors

C. Procedure:

1. Punch four holes in the card as shown in the drawing.
2. Cut string in half.
3. Thread each string through two holes on both sides of card, securing ends well. (See drawing.)
4. Use black ink or marking pen to make a heavy vertical line on one side of the card.
5. Do the same to make heavy horizontal line on the opposite side of the card.
6. Wind up the string and card by rotating card 20 to 30 times.
7. Spin the card rapidly by pulling the two loops outwardly.

D. Result:

The two marks will appear to blend, forming a cross.

E. Basic Facts and Supplemental Information:

1. We may conclude that vision persists for a short time in the eye after the object is gone from view. This phenomenon is called "visual persistency."
2. This attribute is used in motion pictures and television.
3. We receive light sensations with our eyes and interpret these with our brain.

F. Thought Questions for Class Discussions:

1. Could you design a test to determine how long a vision persists?
2. What percent of our population has visual handicaps?
3. What percent of our population should be wearing glasses or contact lenses?
4. Do motion pictures move?

G. Related Ideas for Further Inquiry:

1. Study the actual film of a motion picture.
2. Try other designs and combinations besides those illustrated in the drawings.

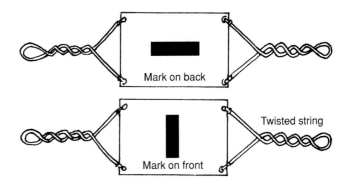

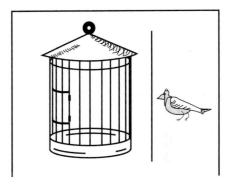

Can you put the bird in the cage
without changing the picture?

3. Study Activity II-C-1, "Does light travel only in a straight line?"
4. Study Activity II-C-3, "What colors of light are in sunlight?"
5. Study Activity V-B-1, "How many senses do we have? How do we receive information about our environment?"
6. Study Activity V-B-2, "Why do the pupils of our eyes change size?"
7. Study Activity V-B-5, "Are there blind spots in our eyes?"
8. Study Activity V-B-6, "Do our eyes ever deceive us?"

H. Vocabulary Builders—Spelling Words:

1) **visual** 2) **persistency** 3) **vertical**
4) **horizontal** 5) **cardboard** 6) **spin**
7) **strong** 8) **wind** 9) **eyes** 10) **brain**

I. Thought for Today:

"Few people ever get dizzy from doing too many good turns."

A. Problem: *How Well Do We Hear?*

B. Materials Needed:

1. Measuring tape (25′ to 50′)
2. List of words to be used
3. Clock

C. Procedure One:

1. Have a student measure a distance of 20′ by drawing a chalk line on the floor.
2. Have the pupil come to the front of the room to be tested. Explain carefully what you are going to do.
3. The student is to turn his/her back and repeat after you the words whispered at a distance of 20′. Care should be taken to whisper in a natural voice, not a forced whisper.

Procedure Two:

1. Have the student hold his/her hand over the right ear.
2. Have another student hold a clock to the left ear and then move slightly away from him/her.
3. When the student being tested can no longer hear the ticking of the clock, he/she is to call, "Stop."
4. Have another student measure the distance between the tested student's ear and the clock.
5. Double check by walking toward the student to see when he/she begins to hear the ticking.
6. Repeat for right ear.

D. Result:

In most cases, the degree of hearing varies between the left and right ear. The distance at which the student hears words and the ticking of the clock determines relative hearing ability.

E. Basic Facts and Supplemental Information:

1. If the average student hears the clock or whisper at 20′, then hearing and correctly repeating the words scores 20–20. The first number represents the hearing distance, the second, the actual distance.
2. If the student cannot hear at 20′, tester moves forward until he/she can hear, and the hearing is rated accordingly, i.e., 10–20, etc.
3. Let pupils place their hands on their throats to discover vibrations of whispered words.
4. Our sense of balance is accomplished by nerves within the inner ear.
5. There are essentially two major types of hearing loss:
   a. "Nerve deafness," when there is a problem with nerve stimulation.
   b. "Bone deafness," when there is some problem with the middle ear bones.

6. We can detect the source of sounds because of the "triangulation" sensed by both of our ears.

F. Thought Questions for Class Discussions:

1. How well do hearing aids re-establish "natural" hearing?
2. What percent of our population has hearing losses? (Youth—about 10%)
3. What percent requires hearing aids? (Youth—about 3%)
4. What is the most beautiful sound you have ever heard?

G. Related Ideas for Further Inquiry:

1. Discuss ways that our hearing can be impaired (sudden loud blasts, loud rock music, etc.).
2. What can we do to protect our ears from loud noises?
3. Have class close their eyes for several minutes being very quiet, and then report on noises heard.
4. What makes our ears "pop" when we go up or down a high hill?
5. Study Activity V-B-1, "How many senses do we have? How do we receive information about our environment?"
6. Study other Activities in this Section.

H. Vocabulary Builders—Spelling Words:

1) **measure** 2) **distance** 3) **whisper** 4) **ticking**
5) **clock** 6) **hearing aids** 7) **nerves**

I. Thought for Today:

"Mother nature is wonderful. Years ago she didn't know we were going to wear glasses, yet look at the way she placed our ears."

Activity

V B 9

A. Problem: *What Can We Learn About Our Sense of Touch?*

B. Materials Needed:

1. Many individual objects which can be handled by students to provide them with different sensations of touch. Such objects might include toothbrush, feather, orange, piece of cloth, fur, spoon, etc.
2. Paper bag containing ten objects such as marbles, small ball, closed safety pin, spoon, eraser, button, shoelace, pine cones, etc.

C. Procedure:

1. Have students write on the chalkboard some different sensations of touch they have experienced such as:
   a. soft—sponge
   b. hard—rock
   c. cold—ice
   d. warm—warm water
   e. mushy—mud
   f. sticky—paste
   g. sharp—edge of knife blade
   h. rough—sandpaper
   i. smooth—marble
   j. small—pencil point
   k. big—mountain
2. Have students go to the touch table and report on how each of the objects feels. (See Materials Needed 1.)
3. Without looking in the paper bag (Materials Needed 2) have some students feel inside and see if they can tell what the objects are. For added fun, pass the bag around and see if each student can remember and list what was in the bag.

D. Results:

1. Students will learn that the sense of touch includes many sensations and is very helpful in learning about our environment.
2. Students will be able to identify some of the objects in the paper bag by their sense of touch.

E. Basic Facts and Supplemental Information:

Our sense of touch is not only located in our fingers, but we have touch sensations all over our bodies. These are nerve endings in the skin which send messages to the brain. These cutaneous senses include the specific senses of pressure, pain, heat, and cold. All feeling sensations are combinations of these.

F. Thought Questions for Class Discussions:

1. When are we totally dependent on our sense of touch for information?
2. When can our sense of touch warn us of dangers?
3. Do babies like to be touched? Why?
4. How important is the sense of touch to blind people?
5. How do blind people read?

G. Related Ideas for Further Inquiry:

1. Discuss what we have learned through our sense of touch.
2. Younger students can discuss sensations in playing with blocks, working with clay, etc.
3. Discuss why we don't feel pain when we get a haircut.
4. Study Activity V-A-1, "What are the different systems in our body?"
5. Study Activity V-B-1, "How many senses do we have? How do we receive information about our environment?"
6. Study other Activities in this Section.

H. Vocabulary Builders—Spelling Words:

Use the words listed in "Procedure."

I. Thought for Today:

"Friendship is the only cement that will ever hold the world together."—Woodrow Wilson

Activity

A. Problem: *How Do We Use Our Sense of Smell?*

B. Materials Needed:

1. Air freshener or deodorizer in spray can
2. Soap
3. Cinnamon
4. Coffee
5. Onion
6. Cloves
7. Vanilla
8. Mint
9. Garlic
10. Lemon extract
11. Sage
12. Fresh flowers
13. Chart paper

C. Procedure:

1. Have students close their eyes.
2. Spray a small amount of air freshener or deodorizer around the room.
3. Tell them to raise their hands quietly if they can smell anything different.
4. Check the distance that fragrance can be detected.
5. Ask class if fragrance can be detected in areas where spray was not seen.
6. Have several volunteers close their eyes and see if they can identify different substances by their smell.
   a. soap
   b. cinnamon
   c. coffee
   d. onion
7. Record their findings.

D. Results:

1. Very, very small parts of air freshener or deodorizer which we call molecules moved about the room.
2. These small parts (molecules) will be detected by the students' sense of smell.
3. The tiny molecules of soap, cinnamon, coffee, and onion will be detected as they circulate within the room because of air currents.

E. Basic Facts and Supplemental Information:

1. A molecule is the smallest part of a substance that retains the properties of that substance.
2. We detect odors when molecules of certain substances reach nerve receptors inside our nose.
3. Our sense of taste comes essentially from our sense of smell.
4. We can recognize about 10,000 different kinds of scents.
5. If you burn a piece of toast you can smell it all over the room.

6. An odor is added to the gas used in our homes to warn and protect us in case of gas leaks.
7. This Activity can also be used to detect air movement.

F. Thought Questions for Class Discussions:

1. Can you tell what is cooking on the stove at home without looking?
2. Can you smell two things at the same time?
3. Can you smell anything if it is in a closed, sealed container?

G. Related Ideas for Further Inquiry:

1. Discuss smoke detectors (molecules in movement during fires).
2. There are many other odors that can be detected when our eyes are closed: garlic, herbs, ammonia, etc.
3. Discuss how air smells different after a rain.
4. Study Activity V-A-8 "What are cells, tissues, and organs?"
5. Study Activity V-A-1, "What are the different systems in our body?"
6. Study Activity V-B-1, "How many senses do we have? How do we receive information about our environment?"
7. Study other Activities in this Section.

H. Vocabulary Builders—Spelling Words:

Use the words listed in "Materials Needed."

I. Thought for Today:

"Experience is a hard teacher because she gives the test first; the lessons come afterwards."

SECTION C: NUTRITION

Activity

v C 1

A. Problem: *What Kinds of Foods Do Our Bodies Need?*

B. Materials Needed:
1. Items, containers, cans, etc., of each of major food groups:
   a. Milk
   b. Meat
   c. Bread-Cereal
   d. Vegetable-Fruit
2. Magazines with food pictures
3. Books about food

C. Procedure:
1. Divide class into four committees, one committee representing each of the four major food groups.
2. Have each committee:
   a. identify common characteristics of their food group
   b. reasons for eating that group of foods
   c. calories of average serving
   d. vitamins
   e. minerals
   f. costs, etc.
3. Each group may produce a notebook showing various foods found in their food group.
4. Have the class as a whole plan a balanced diet for a week. (If the students are old enough, this could be an individual project.)

D. Results:
1. The students will learn that the body needs carbohydrates, fats, proteins, minerals, vitamins, and water.
2. Students will learn that we must eat properly to maintain good health and physical fitness.
3. Cereal, bread, and potatoes are fuel foods, which furnish energy for work and play and keep our bodies warm.
4. Lean meat, eggs, and beans furnish materials for body repair and growth.
5. Tomatoes, milk, and carrots contain vitamins and minerals which keep our bodies in good working order.
6. Sugars and fats have been left out of this Activity because they should be eaten in very limited amounts.

Bread   Meat   Tomato

Potato   Eggs   Lettuce

E. Basic Facts and Supplemental Information:
1. Everyone must eat enough of the right kinds of food every day in order to have a healthy body.
2. The right kinds of foods include those which provide for energy, for body repair and growth, and for the proper functioning of body organs.
3. The average American consumes about 40 tons (36.3 metric tons) of food in a lifetime. Study the "Food Pyramid" in the following Activity.
4. Fibers are a very important part of a good diet; they keep the digestive tract healthy.

F. Thought Questions for Class Discussions:
1. Is candy good for us?
2. What precautions should people take before they diet? while dieting?
3. What are some diseases of malnutrition?

G. Related Ideas for Further Inquiry:
1. Discuss why breakfast should be the largest meal of the day.
2. Discuss the problems of cholesterol.
3. Discuss the importance of frequent medical checkups.
4. Study other Activities in this Section.

H. Vocabulary Builders—Spelling Words:
1) **milk** 2) **bread** 3) **cereal** 4) **tomatoes**
5) **vitamins** 6) **minerals** 7) **proteins**

I. Thought for Today:
"If life hands you a lemon, make lemonade."

Activity

A. Problem: *What Is The "Food Pyramid?"*

B. Materials Needed:

1. Samples, empty cartons or cans, or pictures of items of the six food groups (See drawing.)
2. Reference materials on the above items

C. Procedure:

1. Discuss the need for healthy foods:
   a. growth
   b. energy
   c. disease prevention
2. Discuss what foods contain in general:
   a. carbohydrates (starches and sugars)
   b. proteins
   c. fats
   d. water
   e. vitamins
   f. minerals
3. Discuss calories.
4. Discuss what any pyramid is.
5. Describe the purpose of the Food Pyramid.
   a. Cite the kinds of foods we should eat.
   b. Show the proportions of each food group that we should eat.
6. With the items cited in "Materials Needed" (above), have the class decide which food level each item belongs to.
   a. *Lower Level:*
      1) grains (bread, cereals, rice, pasta, etc.)
      2) recommended servings: 6–11
   b. *Second Level:*
      1) vegetables (carrots, broccoli, lettuce, etc.) servings: 3–5
      2) fruits (oranges, apples, bananas, etc.) servings: 2–4
   c. *Third Level:*
      1) dairy (milk, cheese, yogurt, etc.) recommended servings: 2–4
      2) meats and proteins (beef, chicken, fish, eggs, beans, etc.) servings: 2–3
   d. *Top Level:*
      1) fats and oils (salad oil, salad dressing:) servings: (eat sparingly)
      2) sugars (candy, jams, jellies, etc.) recommended servings: (eat sparingly)

D. Results:

1. Students will learn about a balanced diet.
2. Students will realize that there must be a lot of planning for a balanced diet.

The Food Pyramid
Four Levels — Six Groups

E. Basic Facts and Supplemental Information:

1. The "Food Pyramid" was designed by the U.S. Department of Agriculture.
2. The "Food Pyramid" is designed to:
   a. reduce saturated fats.
   b. increase the amount of fiber.
   c. vary the proportions of the main basic food types.
   d. coincide with the latest medical findings on health and nutrition.

F. Thought Questions for Class Discussions:

1. What food organizations might find fault with this new idea?
2. Are there any bad foods? bad diets?
3. What could you do to change your diet to make it more healthy according to the "Food Pyramid"?

G. Related Ideas for Further Inquiry:

1. Study Activity V-C-1, "What kinds of foods do our bodies need?"
2. Study Activity V-C-3, "What foods contain carbohydrates (starches and sugars)?"
3. Study also Activities V-C-4 and V-C-7.

H. Vocabulary Builders—Spelling Words:

1) **grains** 2) **vegetables** 3) **fruit** 4) **meats**
5) **milk** 6) **cheese** 7) **oils** 8) **fats** 9) **sugars**

I. Thought for Today:

"A young boy with a weekly allowance told his mother after reading a food label: 'Look, even the USDA recommends daily allowances.'"

Activity

A. Problem: *What Foods Contain Carbohydrates (Starches and Sugars)?*

B. Materials Needed:
1. Several 2″ × 4″ pieces of wax paper
2. One 4″ × 6″ piece of white paper for each kind of food to be tested
3. Iodine, tincture (diluted)
4. Foods to be tested: piece of ham, bread, potato, flour, crackers, corn, celery, sugar, candy, etc.
5. Twelve test tubes or small plastic cups
6. Benedict's solution

C. Procedure One:
1. Place each food to be tested on a piece of wax paper or double thickness of regular paper (to prevent possible leakage).
2. Label each food to be tested.
3. Place two drops of iodine on each foodstuff.
4. Observe results.

Procedure Two:
1. Place each item to be tested in a test tube or cup.
2. Label each test tube or cup with the name of the item to be tested.
3. Add several drops of Benedict's solution to each.
4. Record any visible changes.

D. Results:
1. When iodine is placed on the corn, flour, potatoes, crackers, and bread, the touched areas turn purplish-blue. This color indicates starch is present. The ham and celery areas remain a reddish-brown color: no starch.
2. Benedict's solution turns a dark blue-green color in the presence of foods with sugar.

E. Basic Facts and Supplemental Information:
1. If Benedict's solution is unavailable, Clinitest tablets are available at your local pharmacy. They are used by diabetic people to indicate if starch is converted to sugar in the body.
2. Starches and sugars are excellent sources of heat, energy, and calories.
3. Carbohydrates are found in the lower level of the "Food Pyramid" (See Activity V-C-2).
4. Carbohydrates are starches and sugars. They are found mainly in breads and cereals. They are also found in fruits and vegetables.
5. Starches are complex carbohydrates.
6. Sugars are simple carbohydrates which are easily digested. They are found mainly in cane and beet

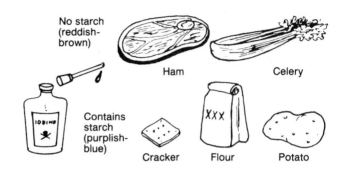

No starch (reddish-brown)

Ham

Celery

Contains starch (purplish-blue)

Cracker

Flour

Potato

sugar (sucrose) and corn syrup which contains fructose.
7. Sugars when listed in ingredients usually end in "ose"—glucose, sucrose, fructose, etc.
8. The healthiest forms of starches are found in natural, unprocessed foods.

F. Thought Questions for Class Discussions:
1. What other foods contain starch?
2. Where do most starches come from?
3. How much starch should a person consume daily?

G. Related Ideas for Further Inquiry:
1. Make a list of common food items that contain starch.
2. Make a list of common food items that contain sugar.
3. Study the different kinds of popular diets. Are they "balanced"?
4. Study the labels on selected foods. Evaluate the ingredients.
5. Study Part III, "Plants."
6. Study Activity V-C-1, "What kinds of foods do our bodies need?"
7. Study Activity V-C-2, "What is the 'Food Pyramid'?"
8. Study Activity V-C-6, "How is food preserved?"
9. Study Activity V-C-7, "Are 'fast foods' good for us?"
10. Study other Activities in this Section.

H. Vocabulary Builders—Spelling Words:
1) **sugar**   2) **starch**   3) **carbohydrates**   4) **iodine**
5) **Benedict's solution**   6) **test**   7) **iodine**
8) **drops**   9) **glucose**   10) **fructose**

I. Thought for Today:
"Minds are like parachutes; they only function when they are open."

Activity

A. Problem: *How Do We Test Foods for Fats?*

B. Materials Needed:
1. Small piece of bacon
2. Peanuts
3. Olive oil or mayonnaise
4. Butter or butter substitute
5. Leafy vegetable
6. Bread
7. Six sheets of paper toweling

C. Procedure:
1. Rub each food to be tested on a sheet of paper toweling.
2. Hold toweling up to the light and notice where the food was rubbed.
3. Notice any change in appearance.

D. Result:
If a translucent grease spot appears, fat is present.

E. Basic Facts and Supplemental Information:
1. Some foods contain much fat and others contain very little. Too many fatty foods in the diet can contribute to intestinal, heart, and circulatory problems.
2. There are tests for proteins, but these are usually too complicated and, therefore, not recommended for classroom study.
3. Medical science has demonstrated that a high-fat diet leads to high cholesterol which is one of the causes of heart and circulatory problems.
4. The "Food Pyramid" places "fats" on top of the pyramid which means that "fats" should be eaten sparingly.
5. Fats are found in various foods and in a variety of forms.
6. Fats are found in foods of animal origin such as meat, poultry, and fish.
7. Some fats are in liquid form such as cooking and salad oils.
8. Most fats are solids and are found in such foods as butter, margarine, shortening, meat trimmings, etc.
9. Nutritionists classify fats as "fatty acids." These are either "saturated" or "unsaturated." Saturated fats tend to raise your cholesterol level.

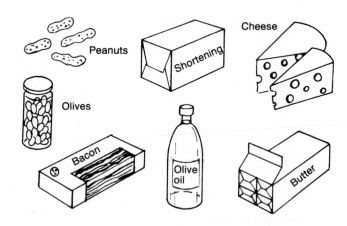

10. Since both butter and margarine contain fats, nutritionists recommend that you minimize either spread.

F. Thought Questions for Class Discussions:
1. What is the difference between fat and protein?
2. How much fat should we eat in a balanced diet?
3. What is cholesterol? What are the latest findings about this substance?

G. Related Ideas for Further Inquiry:
1. Study Activity V-C-1, "What kinds of foods do our bodies need?"
2. Study Activity V-C-2, "What is the 'Food Pyramid'?"
3. Study Activity V-C-3, "What foods contain carbohydrates (starches and sugars)?"
4. Study Activity V-C-5, "How do we make butter?"
5. Study Activity V-C-6, "How is food preserved?"
6. Study Activity V-C-7, "Are 'fast foods' good for us?"
7. Study Section V-D, "Personal Health."

H. Vocabulary Builders—Spelling Words:
1) **mayonnaise** 2) **absorbent** 3) **grease** 4) **fat**
5) **protein** 6) **translucent** 7) **cholesterol**

I. Thought for Today:
"To many of today's parents, youth is stranger than fiction."

Activity

A. Problem: *How Do We Make Butter?*

B. Materials Needed:
1. One-half pint of whipping cream (heavy cream)
2. One or more small jars with lids
3. Colander
4. Salt
5. Crackers (lightly salted)

Whipping cream

C. Procedure:
1. Discuss the different kinds of dairy products (milk, cream, cheese, butter).
2. Put whipping cream into a small jar.
3. Tighten lid and shake cream vigorously until butter forms. (Have students take turns shaking the jar.)
4. Pour buttermilk into separate jar (liquid part).
5. Wash the chunks of butter by placing them in a colander and running water over them.
6. The following steps are optional:
   a. Taste the unsalted butter.
   b. Add salt to the butter and taste.
   c. Put butter on crackers and have a class party.

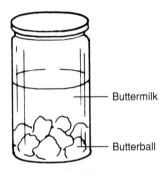
Buttermilk

Butterball

Shake jar vigorously.

D. Results:
1. Butter is formed when the cream is shaken. This is a physical change, not a chemical change.
2. Buttermilk is the by-product of the process of making butter.

Colander

E. Basic Facts and Supplemental Information:
1. Butter is food. It contains fat and cholesterol.
2. Cream is lighter than milk. It rises to the top.
3. Butter contains fats, proteins, and carbohydrates.
4. Butter contains Vitamin A, B vitamins, and C vitamins.
5. Butter also has some minerals—basically sodium, calcium, and iron. Most vitamins and minerals in butter are in very small quantities.

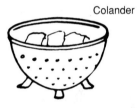
Wash thoroughly.

F. Thought Questions for Class Discussions:
1. What is the difference in caloric value between margarine and butter?
2. What is the difference in the fat and protein content of each?
3. What is "butterfat"?

G. Related Ideas for Further Inquiry:
1. Study the label on a butter carton for specific ingredients.
2. Study how cheese is made.
3. Study how cottage cheese is made.

4. Study Activity V-C-1, "What kinds of foods do our bodies need?"
5. Study Activity V-C-4, "How do we test foods for fats?"
6. Study Activity V-C-6, "How is food preserved?"
7. Study Activity V-C-7, "Are 'fast foods' good for us?"
8. Study Activity V-C-8, "If I'm overweight or underweight, what should I eat?"

H. Vocabulary Builders—Spelling Words:
1) **butter** 2) **whipping** 3) **cream** 4) **colander**
5) **chunks** 6) **buttermilk** 7) **shake**
8) **vigorously**

I. Thought for Today:
Baby octopus to mother: "All I want to know is which are my hands and which are my feet?"

Activity

A. Problem: *How Is Food Preserved?*

B. Materials Needed:
1. Canned food
2. Dried food
3. Pictures of frozen food
4. Salted food
5. Smoked food
6. Irradiated food
7. Pasteurized milk
8. Canned milk

C. Procedure:
1. Discuss the availability of foodstuffs to all people throughout the world.
2. Discuss the problems of food production, distribution, and consumption.
3. Discuss how food must be preserved to ship from the producer to the consumer.
4. Discuss the problems of food spoilage.

D. Results:
1. Students learn that many people throughout the world are underfed and starving to death.
2. Pupils learn the problems of sending food to other countries.
3. Students learn the problems of harvesting the food in one season and eating it in another.
4. Pupils will learn that salting, drying, and smoking removes the liquid and retards bacterial growth in foods.

E. Basic Facts and Supplemental Information:
1. There are almost 6 billion people in the world today.
2. Each year there are about 90 million more individuals to feed.
3. About 18 million people starve annually because of a lack of food.
4. The main problem today is a lack of distribution rather than the production of foods.
5. The world's population is expected to double in the next 50 to 60 years, and this will require twice as much food; there is not that much additional agricultural land available.
6. We are going to have to produce more food per acre of land.
7. We need to find better, faster means of food distribution.
8. We are going to have to find more efficient ways of preserving our foods.

9. Irradiation is being used on some fruits and vegetables to prolong shelf life. There is still a lot of controversy over its use.

F. Thought Questions for Class Discussions:
1. How can we improve our distribution of food supplies?
2. How can we produce more and more food with less and less land?
3. If our lands become polluted, will they contaminate our food?

G. Related Ideas for Further Inquiry:
1. Study population projections and increased food needs.
2. Study why so many people throughout the world are starving.
3. Study Activity V-C-1, "What kinds of foods do our bodies need?"
4. Study Activity V-C-2, "What is the 'Food Pyramid'?"
5. Study Activity VI-A-10, "Is there a world population explosion?"
6. Study Activity VI-C-9, "How does pollution affect food chains and food webs?"
7. Study Activity VI-B-8, "How can we conserve our natural resources?"
8. Study Activity VI-C-8, "What is happening to our topsoil?"

H. Vocabulary Builders—Spelling Words:
1) **canned**   2) **dried**   3) **frozen**   4) **salted**
5) **smoked**   6) **pasteurized**   7) **irradiated**
8) **preserved**   9) **foods**   10) **distribution**

I. Thought for Today:
"The farmer doesn't go to work. He wakes up every morning surrounded by it."

Activity

A. Problem: *Are "Fast Foods" Good for Us?*

B. Materials Needed:

1. Pictures of popular hamburgers, tacos, fish sandwiches, french fries, shakes, soft drinks, etc.
2. Reference books and pamphlets

C. Procedure:

1. Discuss health, nutrition, calories, vitamins, minerals, etc.
2. Have students relate their experiences with eating fast foods.
3. Read authoritative articles about fast foods.
4. Discuss their findings.

D. Result:

Students will learn that fast foods have some nutritional value but have reduced quantities of some basic ingredients. Fast foods also contain some ingredients that are not conducive to optimum health.

E. Basic Facts and Supplemental Information:

1. Fast foods do have some food values.
2. Students will learn that fast foods, light meals, or snacks are usually:
   a. high in calories
   b. very high in fats
   c. very high in salt (about 75% of daily requirement)
   d. low in fiber (fiber is needed to help digestion)
   e. deficient in vitamins A and C and several B vitamins
   f. deficient in iron
   g. high in sugar (a milkshake contains 8 to 14 teaspoons of sugar)

F. Thought Questions for Class Discussions:

1. What would happen to your health if you lived only on fast foods?
2. Would eating fast foods once in a while be harmful?
3. Is it best to try to avoid fast foods?

G. Related Ideas for Further Inquiry:

1. Talk to cooks in fast food establishments and ask about the ingredients used.
2. Study your own fast food the next time you snack out.

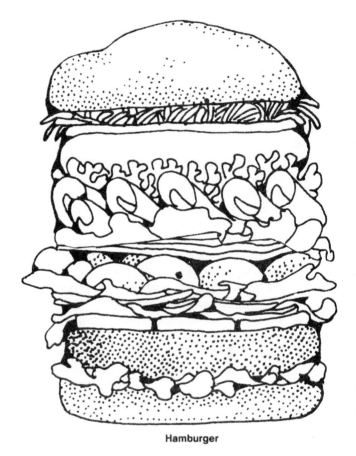

Hamburger

3. Study Activity V-C-1, "What kinds of foods do our bodies need?"
4. Study Activity V-C-2, "What is the 'Food Pyramid'?"
5. Study Activity V-C-3, "What foods contain carbohydrates (starches and sugars)?"
6. Study Activity V-C-4, "How do we test foods for fats?"
7. Study Activity V-C-6, "How is food preserved?"

H. Vocabulary Builders—Spelling Words:

1) **hamburger**   2) **shakes**   3) **french fries**
4) **pizza**   5) **tacos**   6) **calories**   7) **nutritious**

I. Thought for Today:

"A vegetable is a substance used to balance a child's plate while it's being carried to and from the table."

Activity

A. Problem: *If I'm Overweight or Underweight, What Should I Eat?*

B. Materials Needed:

(Tables at end of this Activity)

C. Procedure:

1. Discuss good health practices.
2. Discuss weight in relation to health.
3. Doctors and nutritionists classify body builds in three categories:
   a. endomorph (large)
   b. mesomorph (medium)
   c. ectomorph (thin)
   All are normal.
4. If a person wants to lose weight, he/she should plan a balanced diet with low-calorie foods.
5. If a person wants to gain weight, he/she should plan a balanced diet with high-calorie foods.
6. Stress that proteins are very important for body growth and development.
7. Stress the fact that carbohydrates, fats, and oils are particularly rich in heat, energy, and calories.

D. Result:

Students will become aware that diet can play a major role in weight change.

E. Basic Facts and Supplemental Information:

1. If a person eats more than needed, the body stores the excess in body fat.
2. If a person eats less than needed, the body uses up the excess in body fat.
3. If a body needs energy and there is no fat, the body begins to take proteins from the muscle, thus weakening the person.
4. Exercise also plays a vital role in controlling body weight.

F. Thought Questions for Class Discussions:

1. Are all heavy people overweight?
2. Are all thin people underweight?
3. Is there an ideal weight for each age level?
4. Could a person be overfed and undernourished?

G. Related Ideas for Further Inquiry:

1. Test foods for carbohydrates.
2. Test foods for fats.
3. There is no simple test for protein.
4. Study Activity V-C-1, "What kinds of foods do our bodies need?"

LOW CALORIE FOODS		
FOOD	**MEASURE**	**CALORIES**
Beef	Medium slice	100
Carrots	½ cup	25
Celery	2 stalks	5
Chicken	½ med. broiled	100
Cottage Cheese	Tablespoon	15
Cucumbers	Medium	10
Egg, boiled		70
Jello	½ cup	50
Lettuce	Medium head	25
Milk, reg.	Cup	150
Milk, low fat	Cup	85
Milk, nonfat	Cup	80
Oils, salad	Tablespoon	None
Parsley	Bunch	5
Peppers	Medium	15
Tomatoes	Medium	25

HIGH CALORIE FOODS		
FOOD	**MEASURE**	**CALORIES**
Apple Pie	3 inch serving	350
Beef Hamburger on bun		300
Biscuit		50
Butter	Tablespoon	100
Cheese	One inch cube	125
Chocolate fudge	One inch cube	115
Chocolate malted milk		460
Cream	Tablespoon	70
Cupcake, frosted		250
Hot dog on roll		250
Jellies or Jams	Tablespoon	80
Mayonnaise	Tablespoon	100
Peanut butter	Tablespoon	100
Popcorn, buttered	Cup	170
Potato Chips	10 pieces	100
Sugar, white	Tablespoon	50
Waffle	5" square	250

5. Study Activity V-C-2, "What is the 'Food Pyramid'?"
6. Study Activity V-C-3, "What foods contain carbohydrates (starches and sugars)?"
7. Study Activity V-C-7, "Are 'fast foods' good for us?"

H. Vocabulary Builders—Spelling Words:

1) **overweight**   2) **underweight**   3) **measure**
4) **tablespoon**   5) **ectomorph**   6) **mesomorph**
7) **endomorph**   8) **nutrition**   9) **calories**

I. Thought for Today:

"How can a society that exists on instant mashed potatoes, packaged cake mixes, frozen dinners, and microwave cooking teach patience to its young?"

Activity

A. Problem: *What Should We Look for on Food Labels?*

B. Materials Needed:
1. Cans of food with labels
2. Boxes of food with labels
3. Food labels only
4. Reference materials on labeling

C. Procedure:
1. Discuss food and good health.
2. Explain the difference between natural and processed foods.
3. Relate how additives have been added to food for:

   a. preserving
   b. coloring
   c. sweetening
   d. flavoring
   e. vitamins
   f. stabilizing
   g. consistency
   h. antibiotics
   i. blending
   j. antioxidants
   k. antifoaming
   l. firming
   m. binding
   n. conditioning
   o. drying
   p. peeling
   q. neutralizing
   r. anticaking
   s. bleaching, etc.

4. Study some labels and note in particular the first five items.

D. Results:
1. Students will become aware of the amount and kinds of additives that are put into our foods.
2. They will begin to realize the reasons why some additives are included in our foods.

E. Basic Facts and Supplemental Information:
1. Ingredients listed on labels are in order of quantity in the product. The first item listed is more prevalent than any other; the second item is next most prevalent.
2. Some additives are absorbed better by themselves; some better in combinations with others; and some block the effects of other additives.
3. One big problem is that each additive by itself is probably harmless, but when combined with others, the effects are questionable.
4. Small doses of some additives may be healthful, but in larger doses could be toxic.
5. The safest foods are natural, fresh foods.
6. Other items to look for on food labels:

   a. Calories
   b. Total fat
   c. Cholesterol
   d. Sodium
   e. Carbohydrates
   f. Fiber
   g. Protein
   h. Vitamins
   i. Minerals

F. Thought Questions for Class Discussions:
1. Why are natural foods better than foods with additives?
2. Do you think the more additives, the more dangerous the food might be?
3. What does the term "enriched" mean to you when it appears on a food label?

G. Related Ideas for Further Inquiry:
1. Study the food labels for weights and measures.
2. Study the food labels for expiration dates. Some products have short shelf lives.
3. Study the sugar content of foods. Most sugars end in "ose" such as glucose, fructose, lactose, etc.
4. Study Activity V-C-1, "What kinds of foods do our bodies need?"
5. Study Activity V-C-2, "What is the, 'Food Pyramid'?"
6. Study Activity V-C-6, "How is food preserved?"
7. Study Activity V-C-7, "Are 'fast foods' good for us?"
8. Study Activity V-C-8, "If I'm overweight or underweight, what should I eat?"

H. Vocabulary Builders—Spelling Words:
1) **labels** 2) **additives** 3) **preservatives**
4) **coloring** 5) **flavoring** 6) **sweetening**

I. Thought for Today:
"Never eat any product on which the listed ingredients cover more than one-third of the container."

SECTION D: PERSONAL HEALTH
Activity
v D 1

A. Problem: *How Can We Stay Healthy?*

B. Materials Needed:

Pictures of:

1. Nutritious foods
2. Healthful exercises
3. Wholesome relaxations
4. Clean people

C. Procedure:

1. Show examples of nutritious food. Review Activity V-C-1.
2. Demonstrate and discuss the signs of good health:
   a. Hair—clean and lustrous
   b. Eyes—bright, clear
   c. Ears—clean, free from infection
   d. Skin—healthy color, unblemished
   e. Teeth—clean, properly aligned
   f. Muscles—firm, well-conditioned, ease of movement
   g. General appearance—alert, good posture, proper weight
   h. Good appetite—balanced, regular
   i. Energetic—ambitious
3. Discuss proper rest:
   a. 8 to 10 hours of sleep every night (depending on age)
   b. Adequate ventilation
   c. Rest periods during the day

D. Results:

1. Students will learn that it takes a lot of careful thinking, planning, and exercising to be healthy.
2. Students will learn that they must not take good health for granted.

E. Basic Facts and Supplemental Information:

1. Mental and emotional health are just as important as physical health.
2. More people occupy hospital beds for the mentally ill than the physically ill.

F. Thought Questions for Class Discussions:

1. What do some people do that impairs their health?
2. Do you think it is wise to have regular medical checkups?
3. How do athletes train to get in top physical condition?

G. Related Ideas for Further Inquiry:

1. There are many medical personnel, counselors, and nutritionists who could be called upon to give talks to your class, e.g., district doctor, school nurse, school cafeteria manager, etc.
2. Many community personnel are also excellent health resources.
3. Study Activity V-D-6, "Is smoking bad for our health?"
4. Study Activity V-D-9, "Why should we wash our hands frequently?"
5. Study Activity V-D-10, "Is liquor bad for our health?"

H. Vocabulary Builders—Spelling Words:

1) **healthy** 2) **nutrition** 3) **exercise** 4) **foods**
5) **cleanliness** 6) **emotional** 7) **physical** 8) **rest**

I. Thought for Today:

"Jumping to conclusions is about the only exercise some people get."

Activity

A. Problem: *How Can We Protect Our Eyes?*

B. Materials Needed:

1. Sunglasses: different colors
2. Goggles: various types
3. Reading materials about eyes
4. Multisensory aids about eyes

C. Procedure:

1. Have students list things that are dangerous to their eyes.
2. Show protective devices for eyes.
3. Show different colored sunglasses:
   a. Discuss what causes color.
   b. Have students tell why people wear sunglasses.
   c. Ask students what color sunglasses they like best and why.
   d. Have students read black printing on white paper through different colored sunglasses.
   e. Have students record which color(s) they can see most clearly.
   f. Have them check other colored objects with different colored sunglasses and record results.
   g. Discuss other protective measures for eyes such as:
      1) Don't read in moving objects: cars, trains, etc.
      2) When viewing television, there should be little contrast in room lighting.
      3) Sit at least eight feet away (preferable) from television. (possible radiation damage if closer).
      4) Goggles should be worn if doing dangerous work: filing, grinding, sanding, welding, etc.
      5) Avoid glaring light.
      6) Don't read or do close work for too long a period of time. (Rest frequently; change focus frequently, too.)
      7) Keep sharp objects away from eyes.

D. Result:

Students will learn protective measures for their eyes.

E. Basic Facts and Supplemental Information:

1. Your eyes are wonderful organs that can receive millions of unrelated pieces of information about the outside world almost instantaneously.
2. Eyes are protected with eyelids, eyelashes, tears, and adjustable lenses.
3. Within the retina are "rod cells" which perceive light and "cone cells" which perceive both color and light.

4. The most common eye problems are myopia (nearsightedness), hyperopia (farsightedness), astigmatism (asymmetrical cornea), and presbyopia (inability to focus at close range). Most are easily treated with corrective lenses.
5. About 25% of students have some visual difficulties and about 10% need glasses or contact lenses if they are to do satisfactory classwork.
6. Wearing nonprescription sunglasses for long periods of time can be harmful.

F. Thought Questions for Class Discussions:

1. What is astigmatism?
2. What is color blindness?
3. How can eyes be injured?
4. How can eye injuries be prevented?
5. Should sunglasses be wrap-arounds?
6. Should sunglasses be purchased at just any store or obtained through an optometrist or ophthalmologist?

G. Related Ideas for Further Inquiry:

1. Have school nurse or doctor discuss eye care.
2. Have an optometrist discuss eye examinations and glasses with class.
3. Study other Activities in this Section.

H. Vocabulary Builders—Spelling Words:

1) **glasses** 2) **protective** 3) **television**
4) **glaring** 5) **goggles** 6) **retina**

I. Thought for Today:

"Today's young people need better models, not better critics."

Activity

A. Problem: *How Can We Protect Our Hearing?*

B. Materials Needed:

1. Noise makers such as horns, whistles, etc.
2. Radio
3. Toy automobiles, planes
4. Hearing aids or pictures of hearing aids
5. Advertisements about hearing aids
6. Cotton
7. Pictures of stereos, cassettes, CDs, etc.
8. Reference books about hearing

C. Procedure:

1. Discuss with class the general structure of the ear.
2. Discuss different sound levels from whispers to loud explosions.
3. Discuss the causes of severe hearing losses and deafness:
   a. explosions
   b. mumps, measles, scarlet fever, rubella
   c. improper blowing of nose (should blow one nostril at a time gently)
   d. jumping in water without holding nose
   e. listening to loud music frequently and for long periods of time
   f. aging
4. Discuss with class the ways of protecting one's hearing from loud noises:
   a. cotton in the ears
   b. earmuffs
   c. reducing the volume of radios, CDs, etc.

D. Results:

1. Students will learn that hearing can be impaired or lost if not protected.
2. Barring accident and/or illness, hearing can last a lifetime—if protected.

E. Basic Facts and Supplemental Information:

1. Your hearing is very important because it enables you to detect sounds and provides you with a sense of balance.
2. There are three main parts of the ear.
   a. Outer ear—which we can see
   b. Middle ear—which receives sound, processes it, and sends signals to the brain for interpretation
   c. Inner ear—consists of canals and the cochlea which provide us with our sense of balance.
3. Deafness or impaired hearing is sometimes hereditary or may be caused by external conditions.

4. Continual playing of loud music is the chief preventable cause of loss of hearing.
5. Hearing aids cannot replace normal hearing. They can magnify sounds, but tone and quality cannot be replaced.
6. At the present writing, there are no good binaural hearing aids on the market.

F. Thought Questions for Class Discussions:

1. What can a person do to prevent hearing losses?
2. Do you believe all the advertisements regarding hearing aids?
3. What is the purpose of Sign Language?
4. What is the purpose of lip reading?

G. Related Ideas for Further Inquiry:

1. Check the price of hearing aids. (Some cost more than television sets.)
2. Invite an audiologist to come to the class to explain hearing loss (bone and nerve bases).
3. Interview people who wear hearing aids.
4. Discuss merits of lip reading.
5. Study other Activities in this Section.

H. Vocabulary Builders—Spelling Words:

1) **deafness** 2) **hearing** 3) **impairment**
4) **decibel** 5) **explosion** 6) **protection**

I. Thought for Today:

"Tennis is a game that can't be played without raising a racket."

Activity

A. Problem: *What Kind of Clothing Should We Wear?*

B. Materials Needed:
1. Samples of natural fibers:
   a. sheep—wool   e. cotton
   b. goat—psahm,   f. silk
      pashmina, mohair   g. flax
   c. alpaca/llama—wool   h. rubber
   d. goose—down
2. Samples of synthetic fibers:
   a. polyester   d. acrylic
   b. nylon   e. rayon
   c. orlon
3. Specimens or pictures of unusual clothing
4. Reference materials on clothing
5. Clothing advertisements from newspapers

C. Procedure:
1. Discuss the purpose of clothing as a means of:
   a. keeping warm
   b. keeping cool
   c. protection
   d. attracting attention
      1) type
      2) style
      3) color(s)
   e. self-satisfaction
2. Study the characteristics of fibers and their usefulness in clothing.

D. Results:
1. Students will learn that there are many kinds of fibers and wearing apparel.
2. Students will realize that there are many ways to keep warm or cool as well as to protect themselves with the clothing they wear.
3. Pupils will realize that people select clothing for many reasons and seasons.

E. Basic Facts and Supplemental Information:
1. Some of the characteristics of fibers that might be discussed are:
   a. elasticity
   b. waterproof or water-resistant
   c. weight
   d. shine or gloss
   e. durability
   f. length of fibers
   g. wind resistance
2. Some unusual facts concerning fibers:
   a. Wool retains its warmth when damp.

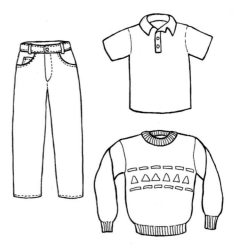

   b. Alpaca/llama fibers are very fine, glossy, and elastic.
   c. Goose down is normally plucked during shedding season with no harm to the geese.
   d. Cotton is one of the most important textiles because of its durability, ease of dyeing, and laundering.
   e. Silk is produced by silkworms that feed on mulberry leaves.
   f. Most synthetic fibers are made from petrochemicals.
   g. The first clothes were animal skins.
   h. Fibers are spun into yarn, and yarn is woven into fabrics.

F. Thought Questions for Class Discussions:
1. What are the different kinds of clothing worn in sports? military uniforms?
2. How does climate affect the choice of clothing?
3. What part does culture play in the choice of clothing?

G. Related Ideas for Further Inquiry:
1. Study the labels on clothing regarding cleaning or laundering.
2. Study how disease is related to improper clothing.
3. Study Activity VII-E-10, "Why are summers warmer than winters?"
4. Study Activity VII-E-4, "Where does rain come from?"

H. Vocabulary Builders—Spelling Words:
Use the list of fibers in the "Materials Needed" section.

I. Thought for Today:
"One good thing about having one suit of clothes—you don't have to make any decisions on what to wear."

Activity

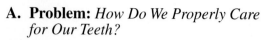

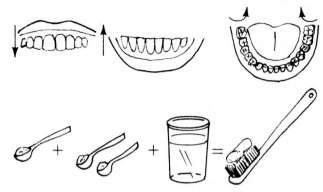

Salt, baking soda, and water make toothpaste

A. Problem: *How Do We Properly Care for Our Teeth?*

B. Materials Needed:
1. Soft, multi-tufted toothbrush
2. Dental floss
3. Colored wall chart of teeth
4. Water irrigating device for teeth

C. Procedure:
1. Discuss some facts about teeth:
   a. There are no substitutes for brushing, water irrigating devices, and flossing.
   b. There is no substitute for professional dental care.
   c. There is no such thing as all-day dental protection.
   d. There are no invisible shields.
   e. Brushing alone does not prevent bad breath (halitosis); there are many causes.
   f. Mouthwashes are effective only for a short period of time.
   g. Salt, water, and baking soda (one part salt to two parts baking soda) are as effective as many toothpastes and have no caustic, toxic, or abrasive effects.
2. Demonstrate how:
   a. upper teeth are brushed downward.
   b. lower teeth are brushed upward.
   c. surfaces of the teeth are brushed in a scooping scrubbing motion.
   d. dental floss is properly used.

D. Result:
Students will learn how:
1. the surfaces of the teeth are cleaned.
2. food is dislodged from between the teeth.
3. plaque (bacteria and polysaccharides that build up around the gums and on the teeth) is reduced or removed.

E. Basic Facts and Supplemental Information:
1. Teeth are vital assets for they enable us to chew our food properly to make digestion easier. When properly cared for, they can be cosmetically attractive.
2. Decay originates when bacteria react on food particles between the teeth and form an acid that destroys the tooth enamel and causes cavities.
3. Plaque is composed of mucous food particles and bacteria. It is the primary cause of tooth decay.

4. Ninety-five percent of people over 5 years of age have tooth decay.
5. By the age of 60, many Americans have only 10 of their 32 permanent teeth left.
6. Always use a soft multi-tufted toothbrush; a firm brush may damage your gums.
7. Use dental floss. The most effective method of disrupting plaque between the teeth and at the gum line is the proper use of dental floss. It can remove up to 80% of plaque and is the most vital part of plaque control. It's a good idea to show students how to use dental floss making sure they use "C's" around the teeth as well as probing between the teeth.

F. Thought Questions for Class Discussions:
1. How could you set up a test to show that acids cause tooth decay?
2. How could you test the relative effectiveness of different kinds of toothpastes and powders?
3. What kind of brushing does your dentist or school nurse recommend? Does he/she recommend any special brand of toothpaste?

G. Related Ideas for Further Inquiry:
1. Invite a dentist or oral hygienist to talk to class about tooth care and dental hygiene.
2. Have students relate visits to dentists.
3. Invite a dental professional to show how teeth can be straightened.
4. Study Activity V-D-1, "How can we stay healthy?"

H. Vocabulary Builders—Spelling Words:
1) **brushing** 2) **flossing** 3) **upward** 4) **downward**
5) **hygienist** 6) **irrigating** 7) **plaque** 8) **bacteria**

I. Thought for Today:
"The main difference between a human and a dog is that if you pick up a starving dog and make him prosperous, he will not bite you."

A. Problem: *Is Smoking Bad for Our Health?*

B. Materials Needed:

1. Wide-mouthed plastic bottle (quart or half-gallon size)
2. Cotton
3. Three or four cigarettes
4. Matches
5. Insect or small rodent
6. Small electric fan

C. Procedure:

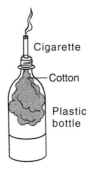

Cigarette

Cotton

Plastic bottle

NOTE: This Activity should be done in a well-ventilated classroom. Open a window so smoke will not be breathed in by teacher or students. If possible, the fan should be set to blow the smoke toward the open window.

1. Explain to class that this bottle filled with air is similar to lungs.
2. Wrap a cigarette with cotton so that it fits snugly into the top of the container. The cigarette should be extended into the air as long as possible.
3. Place the apparatus where all the students can view clearly.
4. Light the cigarette.
5. Squeeze the container and release in a pumping motion.
6. Repeat this procedure a number of times.
7. When this cigarette is lighted and pumped, the apparatus will "smoke" the cigarette.
8. Remove the cotton and cigarette butt quickly, insert the insect or small rodent in the jar and let it stay there for a while.
9. Observe the changes in the air.
10. Observe what happens to the insect or small rodent.

D. Result:

If the insect or rodent is not removed in a short time, it will die. If you do not want it to die, you should remove it from the jar as soon as it becomes groggy, and quickly expose it to fresh air; it will revive.

E. Basic Facts and Supplemental Information:

1. What happens to the insect or rodent is quite extreme because the concentration of the cigarette smoke in the bottle is greater than would be found in a smoke-filled room.
2. The fact that cigarette smoke is detrimental to health, both in the lungs and the circulatory system has been demonstrated so conclusively that there is no doubt whatsoever about the harmful effects of cigarette smoke.
3. Second-hand smoke (passive smoking) is far more damaging to nonsmokers than previously thought. One out of ten cases of lung cancer is caused by "second-hand" smoke (nonsmokers who have been exposed to tobacco smoking over a period of time).
4. Cigarette smoke contains over 4,600 chemicals, whether first-hand or second-hand. Those that doctors are most concerned about are:
   a. nicotine
   b. carbon monoxide
   c. arsenic
   d. alcohol
   e. ammonia
   f. hydrocyanic acid
   g. other acids (11 different kinds)
   h. pyridine
   i. phenols
   j. aldehydes
   k. aromatic hydrocarbons
   l. benzopyrene
5. It is estimated that the health costs of smoking are over $100 billion for health care and the loss of productive work.
6. Each year smoking kills more than 400,000 Americans. This is more than were killed in World War II and Vietnam.
7. Twenty-five percent of Americans over the age of 20 are still smoking, and 70% of these know that smoking is addictive. Nicotine is an addictive drug. It can be as addictive as liquor or cocaine.
8. Fifty million Americans consume 80 million packs of cigarettes every day.
9. Smoking is the largest preventable cause of death and disability in this country.
10. One in five deaths in this country is attributable to smoking.

11. Tobacco companies spend almost $5 billion a year in advertising and promotion to entice youngsters, and a few oldsters, to take up this life-threatening habit.
12. Specifically, cigarette smoking:
    a. impairs the sense of taste
    b. impairs the sense of smell
    c. causes bad breath (smoker's breath)
    d. slows down circulation by constricting blood vessels so the heart has to pump harder, and this causes a rise in blood pressure
    e. robs the body of 10% of its oxygen-carrying capacity
    f. contains tars (like paving material used on streets and highways), and they are carcinogens
    g. contains over 15 known carcinogens
    h. has three deadly agents: (1) nicotine, (2) tars, and (3) carbon monoxide
    i. carbon monoxide replaces the oxygen in the blood (hemoglobin)
    j. causes stomach to secrete acids, producing ulcers
    k. causes 400,000 premature deaths every year
    l. causes 52,000 new cases of lung cancer each year
    m. has crippled the lungs of 50,000,000 people in the United States
    n. entices 1,000,000 new teenagers to start smoking every year
    o. harms tissue in the mouth, throat, larynx, trachea, and lungs
    p. leads to the use of other drugs
    q. is responsible for the sale of 585,000,000,000 cigarettes a year in the United States
    r. has enough nicotine in one pack of cigarettes to kill a person if all the nicotine was in a single dose
    s. produces a hacker's cough
    t. leads to emphysema
    u. leads to heart disease
    v. leads to chronic bronchitis
    w. corrodes the membranes of the lips and palate
    x. stains teeth
    y. leaves nicotine odor in clothing, hair, drapes, upholstered furniture, etc.
    z. shortens lifespan
13. The U.S. Centers for Disease Control and Prevention reports that:
    a. 1,000 lives are lost each week because of "second-hand" smoke.
    b. Second-hand smoke is the third leading cause of preventable death; it follows active smoking and alcohol use.
14. One of six cases of children's lung cancer has definitively been traced to parental smoking in the home.

15. Of all the people who are alive today, fully 500 million will die from tobacco-related diseases, according to estimates from the World Health Organization.
16. Peer pressure is the number one reason young teenagers take up smoking. Parental example is the number two reason.

F. Thought Questions for Class Discussions:

1. Do you think the federal government should declare nicotine "addictive?" The Food and Drug Administration is seriously considering this at the present time.
2. Is nicotine the only harmful ingredient in cigarette smoke?
3. Have you ever been in close quarters with people who are smoking? How did you feel about it? What do you think about it?

G. Related Ideas for Further Inquiry:

1. List the many disadvantages of smoking: health impairment, monetary cost, odor, etc.
2. List the advantages (if any) of smoking.
3. Compare lists.
4. Have a smoker take a big drag on a cigarette and exhale it on a clean white handkerchief. (A big, brown stain will appear.) Ask students if they would like to have a lot of this in their lungs.
5. Open a cigarette filter to examine its contents.
6. Have students discuss any experiences they have had in a smoked-filled room.
7. Estimate the cost of cigarette purchases over a period of several years.
8. Discuss with doctors and nurses the experiences they have had with smokers.
9. Interview ex-smokers on why they decided to quit.
10. Interview smokers on why they are continuing to smoke when all the negative evidence is well-known.
11. Study Activity V-D-1, "How can we stay healthy?"
12. Study Activity V-D-2, "How can we protect our eyes?"
13. Study Activity V-D-7, "How can we protect our skin?"
14. Study other Activities in this Section.

H. Vocabulary Builders—Spelling Words:

1) **nicotine**   2) **smoking**   3) **cigarette**   4) **tar**
5) **carcinogen**   6) **emphysema**   7) **habit**   8) **cough**
9) **peer pressure**   10) **expensive**   11) **deadly**

I. Thought for Today:

"The most incredible creation in the universe is your body. Don't destroy it with cigarette smoking."

Activity

A. Problem: *How Can We Protect Our Skin?*

B. Materials Needed:

Pictures of people with smooth, unblemished skin

C. Procedure:

1. Discuss health in general.
2. Discuss the importance of the skin. (Study Activity V-A-6, "How does our skin help us?"
3. Discuss ways to have a healthier looking skin:
   a. balanced diet
   b. cleanliness
      1) daily, warm bath or shower
      2) adequate rest and exercise
   c. drink 6 to 8 glasses of water daily
4. Ways to help yourself if you have acne or pimples:
   a. keep skin clean
   b. wash affected areas twice daily with unscented soap
   c. use creams and lotions only as prescribed by your dermatologist
   d. squeezing or picking aggravates the condition
   e. avoid chocolate, fatty and fried foods, nuts, sugar-rich food and drinks
   f. see a dermatologist in severe cases
5. Discuss sunburn:
   a. Ultraviolet rays cause sunburn.
   b. Eighty percent of the sun's ultraviolet radiation is scattered by clouds and still hits Earth and people.
   c. A healthy tan is likely to produce an unhealthy skin—even melanoma (skin cancer).
   d. Light-complexioned people are much more prone to skin damage. (Should use tanning lotion, sun blocks)
   e. Eyes need protection, too: gray, brown, and green tinted glasses are best (if red-green color blind, then avoid green).
6. Discuss diseases of the skin (poison oak, poison ivy, etc.).
7. Discuss childhood diseases that affect the skin (usually temporary); chickenpox, measles, mumps, and smallpox.

D. Result:

Students will learn about their skin and ways to protect it.

E. Basic Facts and Supplemental Information:

1. The skin is the largest organ of our body.
2. It protects us from the sun and weather.
3. We should protect our skin for optimum health.

4. Our lips and nose need protection, too.
5. When tanning, do it in small, gradual steps.

F. Thought Questions for Class Discussions:

1. What times of day are easiest to get sunburned?
2. Can you get sunburned in winter? in the Arctic region?
3. Does clothing protect us from the sun?

G. Related Ideas for Further Inquiry:

1. Consult a dermatologist regarding skin care and protection.
2. Discuss how some foods and liquids benefit the skin.
3. Study Activity V-D-9, "Why should we wash our hands frequently?"

H. Vocabulary Builders—Spelling Words:

1) **sunburn**   2) **exercise**   3) **nutrition**
4) **prevention**   5) **acne**

I. Thought for Today:

"The factory that produces the most important product is the home."

Activity

A. Problem: *How Can I Improve My Posture?*

B. Materials Needed:

1. Pictures of students with good posture
2. Pictures of athletes with good posture
3. Multisensory aids dealing with posture

C. Procedure:

1. Discuss the value of good posture:
   a. more agile
   b. more comfortable
   c. less pain (now and later) (especially back pain)
   d. enhance appearance
2. Relate how good posture when standing requires:
   a. head upright and straight
   b. trunk upright and straight with normal curves in spine
   c. legs balanced
3. To check trunk posture, have students stand against the wall with heels and head touching wall. They should be able to slip their hands between their low back and the wall, yet touching both.
4. Good posture when sitting is with a straight back, hips against the back of chair or desk, and bending forward from the pelvis—not the neck. *Avoid slumping.*
5. Have students march around the room and have different students judge their posture.

D. Result:

Students will learn to think about good posture and how it benefits them.

E. Basic Facts and Supplemental Information:

1. There are three types of back curvature to look for in judging good posture:
   a. Lordosis—excess curvature of lower back
   b. Kyphosis—hump back
   c. Scoliosis—sideways curvature of spine. Can be spotted by a difference in the height of shoulders.
2. Posture can be improved by these simple rules:
   a. Stand tall.
   b. Sit tall.
   c. Feet straight ahead.
   d. Sleep on firm mattress.
   e. When lifting objects, bend knees and keep back upright.

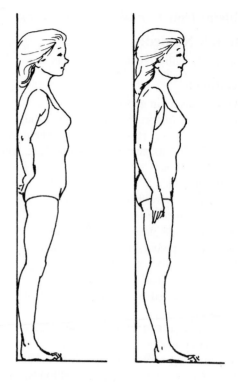

   f. Good fitting shoes:
      1) long arch
      2) transverse arch
   g. Proper clothing
   h. Proper daily exercise
   i. Proper diet
   j. Sufficient rest, sleep

F. Thought Questions for Class Discussions:

1. Why is posture important?
2. Can exercise correct some postural deviations?
3. Do you think people with poor posture look nice?

G. Related Ideas for Further Inquiry:

1. Have school nurse or doctor check students' posture.
2. Discuss activities that could hurt posture.
3. Study Activities in Part V, "Health."

H. Vocabulary Builders—Spelling Words:

1) **posture** 2) **lordosis** 3) **kyphosis**
4) **scoliosis** 5) **upright** 6) **enhance**

I. Thought for Today:

"When Aristotle was asked how he compared educated men to uneducated he replied, 'As much as the living are to the dead.'"

Activity

A. Problem: *Why Should We Wash Our Hands Frequently?*

B. Materials Needed:

1. Eight potatoes
2. Paring knives
3. Eight glass jars that can be sterilized and sealed
4. Heating device to sterilize jars

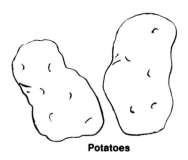

Potatoes

C. Procedure:

1. Sterilize the jars by heating them to 140° F. for 5–10 minutes.
2. Have eight students volunteer to help with the experiment.
3. Send four students to the restroom to wash their hands thoroughly.
4. Leave the other four students with their hands unwashed.
5. Have each of the eight students peel a potato and place it in a sterile jar.
6. Label the jars with either "Hands washed" or "Hands unwashed" as the case may be.
7. Place the jars on the science table and observe from day-to-day to note if any changes occur.

D. Results:

1. In about three to five days the jars labeled "Hands unwashed" will show mold growth on the potatoes.
2. The other jars labeled "Hands washed" will show little or no growth.

E. Basic Facts and Supplemental Information:

1. Our hands come in contact with our environment constantly.
2. Germs are plentiful in our environment.
3. Germs thrive in and on unclean objects.
4. To reduce the germs that contact our bodies, we should wash our hands frequently.
5. We should also try to keep our environment clean (our rooms at home, toys, clothing, bedding, etc.).

F. Thought Questions for Class Discussions:

1. What are some sources of germs?
2. How do people help keep their food clean?
3. How do people preserve their food?
4. Should hands be washed before, after, or before and after going to the restroom?

G. Related Ideas for Further Inquiry:

1. Discover why doctors scrub before surgery.
2. Discuss cleanliness at school and at home.

3. If microscopes are available, many experiments on "dirtiness and cleanliness" can be devised.
4. Examine your fingernails after a full day of work and/or play.
5. Study Activity III-A-1, "How do we classify living things?"
6. Study Activity V-A-8, "What are cells, tissues, and organs?"
7. Study Section V-C, "Nutrition."
8. Study Activity V-D-1, "How can we stay healthy?"
9. Study Activity V-D-4, "What kind of clothing should we wear?"
10. Study Activity V-D-5, "How do we properly care for our teeth?"
11. Study Activity V-D-7, "How can we protect our skin?"
12. Study Activity V-E-3, "How can we fight disease?"

H. Vocabulary Builders—Spelling Words:

1) **washed**   2) **unwashed**   3) **sterile**   4) **germs**
5) **volunteer**   6) **disease**   7) **potato**   8) **clean**

I. Thought for Today:

"Instruction ends in the classroom, but education ends with life."

Activity

A. Problem: *Is Liquor Bad for Our Health?*

B. Materials Needed:

1. Empty beer can
2. Empty wine bottle
3. Empty whiskey bottle
4. Rubbing alcohol
5. Earthworm
6. Saucer

C. Procedure:

1. Have students relate experiences they have observed with alcoholic beverages without citing names or relationships.
2. Discuss why some young people drink:
   a. they think they are grown-up
   b. to show off
   c. to escape from reality
   d. peer pressure
3. Describe beverages that contain alcohol.
4. Tell the students that it is not what you drink but how much alcohol you consume that affects you and can make you drunk or cause your death.
5. Place some alcohol in the saucer.
6. Place earthworm in the saucer.
7. Observe results.

D. Results:

1. The earthworm will die.
2. Students will learn about the harmful effects of drinking alcoholic beverages.
3. Students will learn the reasons people start to drink alcoholic beverages.

E. Basic Facts and Supplemental Information:

1. Alcoholism is a serious major health problem in the United States.
2. Beer contains 2–5% alcohol; wines, 8–17% alcohol.
3. Whiskey, gin, vodka, rum contain 40–50% alcohol.
4. Alcohol is a depressant, not a stimulant.
5. Alcohol dulls the nerve centers in the brain.
6. Muscular coordination is affected.
7. Visual acuity is reduced.
8. Forty percent of all automobile fatalities are caused by drinking drivers.
9. Drinking by drivers and pedestrians is said to cause 30,000 highway deaths a year in the U.S.
10. Alcohol leads to brain damage—usually to delirium tremens (horrifying hallucinations).
11. Seventy percent of adults drink.
12. There are 13,000,000 compulsive alcoholics in the United States.
13. All alcoholic drinks contain ethyl alcohol (C_2H_5OH).
14. Ninety percent of alcohol consumed gets into the bloodstream in one hour.
15. If a 150 pound person drinks two beers, the alcohol level in his/her blood = 0.05%
    .10% affects motor activity
    .20% affects the midbrain (sleep)
    .50% could produce death from respiratory failure.
16. Alcohol causes cirrhosis of the liver.
17. Alcohol is involved in 31% of the homicides and 36% of the suicides in the United States.
18. Half of all crimes are committed by people under the influence of alcohol.
19. "Don't let peer pressure lead to beer pressure."

F. Thought Questions for Class Discussions:

1. Are there any good arguments for drinking alcoholic beverages?
2. Do you think some people drink for social reasons?
3. Do you think some people drink because they are persuaded or influenced by friends? advertisements? peers?

G. Related Ideas for Further Inquiry:

1. Visit a grocery store and observe the size of the liquor section.
2. Have the school nurse discuss the problems of alcohol.
3. Have a lecture from a recovering alcoholic.
4. Have a debate on whether alcoholic beverages should be outlawed.
5. Study Activity V-D-1, "How can we stay healthy?"
6. Study Activity V-D-6, "Is smoking bad for our health?"

H. Vocabulary Builders—Spelling Words:

1) **alcohol**   2) **drinking**   3) **beer**   4) **wine**
5) **whiskey**   6) **earthworm**   7) **depressant**

I. Thought for Today:

"If you drink like a fish, swim, don't drive."

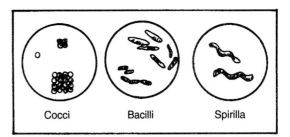

Cocci   Bacilli   Spirilla

A. Problem: *What Makes People Ill?*

B. Materials Needed:

Books, pamphlets, pictures, charts, newspaper clippings, and/or multisensory aids on sickness and disease

C. Procedure:

1. Discuss good health and feeling well.
2. Ask the students if they have ever been sick.
3. Ask them how they felt when they were sick.
4. Ask if they know what causes illness.
5. Tell them we don't know all the answers, but some common causes are microorganisms (microbes) such as:
   a. bacteria—microscopic plants that are pathogenic (cause disease). The two most common are:
      1) staphylococcus
      2) streptococcus
   b. viruses—thousands of times smaller than bacteria, live only in a living cell; a collection of chemicals coated with a protein that attacks living cells. They cause:
      1) chickenpox   5) mumps
      2) colds   6) polio (myelitis)
      3) influenza   7) rabies
      4) measles   8) smallpox
   c. protozoa (one-celled animals) cause:
      1) dysentery (one form)
      2) malaria
      3) sleeping sickness
   d. fungus causes:
      1) athlete's foot
      2) ringworm
      3) infections in ear and lungs
   e. worms that cause disease are:
      1) tapeworms
      2) hookworms
6. Diseases can be carried in the air, live in water, or carried by other animals such as houseflies, fleas, rats, cockroaches, and ticks.
7. The best protection against illnesses are:
   a. proper nutrition,
   b. proper exercise,
   c. cleanliness,
   d. controlling stress,
   e. avoiding tobacco, alcohol, and other drugs, and
   f. avoiding people who are ill.

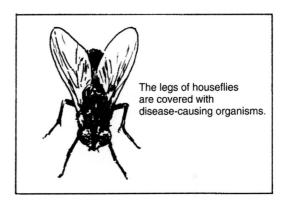

The legs of houseflies are covered with disease-causing organisms.

D. Result:

Students will learn that cleanliness and good health habits can ward off many diseases.

E. Basic Facts and Supplemental Information:

1. Many people can become ill from animals that carry disease.
2. Bites and stings of animals can also cause people to become ill.

F. Thought Questions for Class Discussions:

1. How can you get rid of houseflies?
2. Are water wells hazardous?
3. Why is milk pasteurized?

G. Related Ideas for Further Inquiry:

1. Discuss how people spread disease.
2. Discuss how the food industry protects people from disease.
3. Students could work on individual projects each focusing on one specific disease.
4. Study other Activities in this Section.

H. Vocabulary Builders—Spelling Words:

1) **disease**   2) **health**   3) **cause**   4) **bacteria**
5) **viruses**   6) **nutrition**   7) **cleanliness**

I. Thought for Today:

"We live in a mixed up world; now a car is a necessity and walking is a luxury."—Monta Crane

Activity

A. Problem: *How Can We Prevent Disease?*

B. Materials Needed:

Books, pamphlets, pictures, charts, and/or multisensory aids on microorganisms

C. Procedure:

1. Discuss health.
2. Discuss illnesses.
3. Discuss ways people prevent disease:
   a. Pasteurize milk
   b. Cook foods
   c. Put chlorine in drinking water and swimming pools
   d. Aerate and add chemicals to drinking water; filter it
   e. Spray swamps and ponds
   f. Sneeze and cough in disposable tissues
   g. Can foods
   h. Freeze foods
   i. Build sewage disposal plants
   j. Add preservatives to foods
   k. Take care of your health
   l. Study pure food and drug laws
   m. Be careful to avoid bites, stings, and poisonous plants
   n. Frequent medical checkups
   o. Stay in healthy environment
   p. Wash hands frequently
4. Discuss ways that each student can personally prevent disease:
   a. Proper nutrition
   b. Proper exercise
   c. Personal cleanliness
   d. Minimizing stress
   e. Avoiding tobacco, alcohol, and other drugs
   f. Avoiding people who are ill

D. Results:

1. Students will learn that there are many ways to prevent disease.
2. Pupils will recognize that the best way to prevent disease is by positive thinking and good personal health habits.

E. Basic Facts and Supplemental Information:

1. The most important points in preventing disease are to get proper rest and exercise, eat nutritious foods, and drink 6 to 8 glasses of water daily.
2. If there is any doubt about a serious disease developing, consult a doctor immediately.

3. Use the "Food Pyramid" as a guide to nutritious eating. Study Activity V-C-2.
4. Mental health is as important as physical health. We should avoid stress and try to solve our problems intelligently.

F. Thought Questions for Class Discussions:

1. When should a doctor be consulted?
2. Should you ever take any medication without advice from a doctor?
3. Why is rest so important in curing disease?

G. Related Ideas for Further Inquiry:

1. Plan a trip to a sewage plant, food processing plant, and/or local water plant.
2. Talk to the school custodian about maintaining a healthy environment in the school.
3. Study "health heroes."
4. Conduct Petri dish experiments with prepared gelatin. Sterilized contents will show signs of bacterial growth when bacteria come in contact with test material (prepared gelatin). This usually takes 3 to 5 days to develop.
5. Study other Activities in this Section

H. Vocabulary Builders—Spelling Words:

1) **contaminants**   2) **sewage**   3) **sanitation**
4) **pasteurization**   5) **prevention**   6) **disease**

I. Thought for Today:

"The end of school brings home to parents what teachers have known for nine months."

Activity

A. Problem: *How Can We Fight Disease?*

B. Materials Needed:

Books, pamphlets, pictures, charts, newspaper clippings, and/or multisensory aids about healthy people and sick people

C. Procedure:

1. Discuss symptoms of ill health, disease, and/or injury
   a. Fever
   b. Chills
   c. Headache
   d. Upset stomach
   e. Pain(s)
   f. Skin eruption or rash
   g. Broken bone
   h. Abrasion (bruise)
   i. Laceration (cut)
   j. Sneezing
   k. Coughing
   l. Running nose
   m. Difficulty in breathing
   n. Toothache
   o. Earache
   p. Excessive tearing of eyes, etc.
2. Inform the students that:
   a. In any disease, with the possible exception of minor colds, a doctor should be seen to avoid its developing into something more serious.
   b. One of the worst things a person can do is to treat themselves when ill or injured; they can do more harm than good.
3. Tell the pupils that the best treatments include:
   a. consulting their doctor
   b. prescribed medication
   c. rest
   d. reduced diet
   e. more fluids
   f. cleanliness

D. Results:

1. Students will learn that there are many symptoms foretelling disease.
2. Students will learn that fighting disease often requires professional treatment.

E. Basic Facts and Supplemental Information:

1. Aspirin and other pain relievers should be taken according to a doctor's prescription only because of possible serious side effects.

2. Temperature should be taken. Above average temperatures are caused by the body's effort to destroy foreign organisms.
3. Doctors have many diagnostic tools to determine the type of illness they can treat:
   a. blood tests
   b. biopsies
   c. endoscopic tests
   d. body scans
      1) CT scanning
      2) magnetic resonance imaging (MRI)
   e. microbiological tests, etc.

F. Thought Questions for Class Discussions:

1. Are home remedies always safe?
2. Is over-the-counter medication wise to use?
3. Is prevention the best medicine?
4. What are contagious diseases?

G. Related Ideas for Further Inquiry:

1. Have students check home medicine cabinets with a parent; medication on hand is:
   a. for whom?
   b. for what purpose?
   c. outdated?
      (Medication should always be kept out of reach of children.)
2. Consult with doctor or school nurse to find the best methods for fighting disease.
3. Study other Activities in this Section.

H. Vocabulary Builders—Spelling Words:

1) **prevention** 2) **fighting** 3) **medicine**
4) **drugs** 5) **illness** 6) **diagnosing**

I. Thought for Today:

"There are only two things children will share willingly—communicable diseases and their mother's age."

Activity

A. Problem: *How Does the Government Protect our Health and Safety?*

B. Materials:

1. Toy cars
2. Empty medicine bottle
3. Glass of water
4. Empty, clean can with label
5. Pictures of meat, food
6. Pictures of unsanitary conditions
7. Toy fire engine
8. Toy ambulance
9. Model of street traffic control lights
10. Model of hospital

C. Procedure:

1. Describe to the class how important it is to be healthy and to practice safety.
2. There are many examples of governmental regulations that can be effectively used in a lesson on health and safety. A few examples might be:
   a. speed limits
   b. traffic controls: lights, lanes, rules
   c. unsafe drinking water (Only about 50% of our drinking water is relatively safe.)
   d. honest weights and measurements (meat, canned food, gasoline, etc.)
   e. licenses (for competent services)
   f. police and fire protection
   g. accident help (ambulance, hospital, paramedics)
   h. inspections for health and safety
   i. record keeping
   j. clinics
   k. waste disposal
3. Have a school administrator or school nurse discuss health services and safety inspections of the school.
4. Discuss why the government conducts inspections and establishes health laws.
5. Discuss with students "Who is the government?" (The government is really all of us and our representatives.)

D. Results:

1. Students will learn that our government helps to protect our health and safety.
2. Pupils should learn that the best health and safety precautions are their own behaviors.

Government Inspected

Water	Milk
Drugs	Meat

E. Basic Facts and Supplemental Information:

1. The FDA (Food and Drug Administration) attempts to keep our foods and drugs safe. Unfortunately they are understaffed and cannot be as effective as they should be.
2. In threats of specific diseases, the government frequently offers free immunizations.
3. The government is always trying to reduce our traffic casualties. There are about 50,000 deaths and several million injuries per year due to automobile accidents in the United States.

F. Thought Questions: For Class Discussions

1. What do you think would happen to us if the government stopped protecting us from impure foods and drugs and unsafe environmental conditions?
2. Would you eat in any public eating place if you thought the food might be unclean?
3. Should people on bicycles know and obey the traffic signals?
4. Do school custodians protect your health and safety?

G. Related Ideas for Further Inquiry

1. Discuss public health dangers.
2. Find out what governmental agencies in your community are concerned with health.
3. Study Part VI, "Ecology."
4. Study other Activities in this Section.

H. Vocabulary Builders—Spelling Words:

1) **government** 2) **health** 3) **safety**
4) **inspections** 5) **clinics** 6) **protect**
7) **regulations** 8) **licenses** 9) **unsanitary**

I. Thought for Today:

"Today is the tomorrow you worried about yesterday, and all is well."

SECTION F: FIRST AID

Activity

A. Problem: *What Can You Do for a Cold?*

B: Materials Needed:
1. Pictures of people sneezing
2. Pictures of pallid (pale or wan) people

C. Procedure:
1. Discuss known information about colds:
   a. Viral infections—over 100 cold-causing viruses have been identified.
   b. Spread in droplets of moisture expelled while coughing or sneezing.
   c. Infection is in upper respiratory tract. Symptoms are:
      1) stuffed nose
      2) sneezing
      3) sore throat
      4) headache
      5) muscular aches and pains
      6) moderate fever
      7) coughing
      8) feel weak
2. Tell the students that there is no known medicine that will help cure a cold. Antibiotics will not affect viruses.
3. It usually takes about a week to overcome the infection.
4. All you can do is to make yourself more comfortable by:
   a. drinking more liquids
   b. eating light diet
   c. keeping warm
   d. resting
   e. If temperature is above normal (98.6° F.) consult a doctor.
   f. One or two aspirins or analgesics every 4 hours (depending on age of patient) will alleviate fever and aches. This should be done under parental guidance.
   g. A sore throat can be helped by gargling with salt water (teaspoonful in a glass of warm water).
   h. Cough can be alleviated by inhaling steam for 5 minutes. (Boil a pot of water; hold your head over pot, not too close or steam will burn); put a towel over your head and the pot (like a tent) and inhale through your nose and exhale through your mouth.

D. Result:
Students will learn that colds run their courses and only the symptoms can be eased.

E. Basic Facts and Supplemental Information:
1. The average number of colds that a person gets each year is 2 or 3.
2. Colds can be caused by any number of viruses and bacteria; most are viral infections.
3. Colds are caught especially when the body's resistance is low. The infected membrane secretes large quantities of mucus.

F. Thought Questions for Class Discussions:
1. What are safeguards for reducing the number of colds one gets?
2. Why does the body increase its temperature during times of infection?
3. What do white cells do to fight colds?

G. Related Ideas for Further Inquiry:
1. Study Section V-D, "Personal Health."
2. Study Section V-E, "Public Health."
3. Study other Activities in this Section.

H. Vocabulary Builders—Spelling Words:
1) **virus**   2) **infection**   3) **liquids**   4) **fever**
5) **sneezing**   6) **coughing**

I. Thought for Today:
"Adolescence is not so much a period as an exclamation point."

Activity

A. Problem: *What Should We Do for Cuts and Wounds?*

B. Materials Needed:
1. Pictures of cuts and wounds
2. First aid pamphlet (Red Cross has several great ones)
3. Multisensory materials on cuts and wounds
4. First aid kit

C. Procedure:
1. Ask if any of the students have ever been cut or wounded.
2. Have them describe the cause of the accident.
3. Have them describe what first aid measures were taken.
4. Teach them simple first aid measures about cuts and wounds. Include the following and determine the seriousness of the wound:
   a. *Non-serious wound:*
      1) Clean the wound with soap and warm water.
      2) Wipe foreign matter away from the wound.
      3) May put on antibacterial ointment— precautionary measure
      4) Cover wound with dry, sterile dressing such as gauze pad or bandage.
      5) Change dressing when wet or dirty.
   b. *Serious wound: (deep cuts) (lacerations)*
      1) Stop bleeding with compress (handkerchief) or hold with fingers over the wound.
      2) Avoid tourniquets except in extreme cases because if they are left on too long, they kill healthy cells. If used, they should be released every 20 minutes.
      3) Use ice packs to inhibit blood flow.
      4) Clean the wound with water.
      5) Wash the wound with antiseptic soap and water.
      6) If available, wash the wound with hydrogen peroxide.
      7) Get medical help.
      8) A tetanus shot is a must within 24 hours of a possible infection. Normally a child has received three to five shots of tetanus before entering school, usually combined with diphtheria and pertussis vaccines.
5. After the discussion on first aid techniques, consider some hypothetical injuries. Have the students describe what they would do and then have them perform the necessary treatment(s).

D. Result:
Students will learn some simple first aid procedures for common cuts and wounds.

E. Basic Facts and Supplemental Information:
1. Bruises are called contusions and should improve within 24 hours. They do not break the skin, therefore ice packs are the preferred treatment. (They are usually the result of a hard blow.)
2. Tears in the skin are called lacerations.
3. Cuts in the skin are called incisions (knife-like cuts).
4. Scrapes in the skin that cause bleeding are called abrasions (like a skinned knee).
5. Remember, in serious cases a doctor must be consulted.

F. Thought Questions for Class Discussions:
1. What are the dangers of not treating a wound or cut promptly?
2. What symptoms indicate an infection in cuts and wounds?
3. Is there such a thing as a clean cut or wound?

G. Related Ideas for Further Inquiry:
1. Have the school nurse talk to class about cuts and wounds.
2. Show students various medications and bandages that can be used with cuts and wounds.
3. Study other Activities in this Section.

H. Vocabulary Builders—Spelling Words:
1) **incision** 2) **wound** 3) **abrasion**
4) **laceration** 5) **contusion** 6) **bleeding**

I. Thought for Today:
"Strangers are friends that you have yet to meet."

Activity

A. Problem: *What Should You Do if You Get Something in Your Eye?*

B. Materials Needed:
1. Pictures of the eye(s)
2. Model of the eye(s)
3. Clean handkerchief

C. Procedure:
1. Discuss structure of the eye.
2. Ask the class if anyone ever had something get in their eye.
3. Ask what they did about it.
4. Demonstrate the best procedures for removing foreign objects from the eye:
    a. Examine eye by:
       1) Pull down the lower eyelid.
       2) Roll back the upper eyelid.
    b. If a speck is on either lid, moisten the corner of a clean cloth or handkerchief and try to remove it.
    c. If speck is in the eye, pull the upper lid down over the lower lid. This increases the flushing action of the eye.
    d. Hold for several minutes.
    e. If speck is still in the eye, close eye and *gently* push on upper lid, moving from the outer portion to the inner portion (toward the nose). This is the direction of tear flow.
    f. Examine the eye again.
    g. If speck is still in eye, moisten cloth tip and swab from ear-side to nose-side *gently*. (Best to have an adult do this.)
    h. If still no success, place a gauze pad over the eye and get to an ophthalmologist.

D. Result:
Students will learn the techniques of removing foreign substances from the eye.

E. Basic Facts and Supplemental Information:
1. The eye must be treated very carefully and gently.
2. If there is any activity where the eye might be harmed, goggles should be worn. Give some examples: using tools, paint, or chemicals.

F. Thought Questions for Class Discussions:
1. Why do people wear eyeglasses or contacts?
2. What occupations require goggles?
3. Do glasses completely protect the eyes?

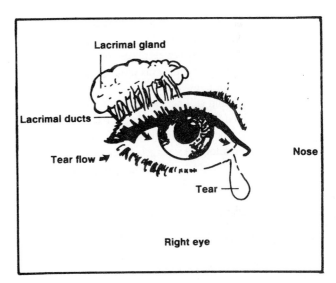

G. Related Ideas for Further Inquiry:
1. Have the school nurse demonstrate techniques for removing foreign substances from the eye(s).
2. Discuss protective devices for the eyes: glasses, goggles, eye shields, etc.
3. Study Activities V-B-2 to V-B-7.

H. Vocabulary Builders—Spelling Words:
1) **something** 2) **speck** 3) **eyelid**
4) **flush** 5) **examine** 6) **lacrimal ducts**

I. Thought for Today:
"Mother's Day is from 7 A.M. to midnight."

Activity

A. Problem: *What Should You Do in Case of a Nosebleed?*

B. Materials Needed:

Books, pamphlets, and/or multisensory aids about nose bleeds (possible causes and what to do about them)

C. Procedure:

1. Discuss blood circulation about the nose.
2. Ask class if anyone has ever had a nosebleed.
3. Ask student(s) what they did about it.
4. Discuss the best procedure which should include:
   a. Stand up.
   b. Blow nose gently. (in case of partial clot or to remove mucus which might be infected).
   c. Remain calm
   d. Hold head back.
   e. Hold this position for about 10 minutes.
   f. If still bleeding, squeeze your nostrils together and hold for a full 5 minutes. (Bleeding should stop.)
   g. If bleeding hasn't stopped, then pack nostril(s) with a plug of sterile gauze, elevate head, and place cold, wet towels across face. Breathe through the mouth. This plug can be left in safely for a few hours.
   h. If bleeding still persists call your doctor.
   i. If bleeding is ever severe, go to a hospital emergency room immediately. Also, phone your doctor.

D. Result:

Students will learn what to do for nosebleeds.

E. Basic Facts and Supplemental Information:

1. Because nosebleeds are usually scarey for youngsters, reassurance is a necessity.
2. The sight of blood frightens young students.
3. If a child is known to be a hemophiliac, a doctor should be consulted immediately no matter how slight the bleeding might be.
4. Bleeding is also called hemorrhaging.
5. Ice or icepacks, if available, can be applied as this constricts the blood vessels and slows or stops the bleeding.

Hold head back.

6. Your nose is the main gateway to your respiratory system.
7. Your nose filters, humidifies, and warms the air as it moves to your lungs.
8. Normal breathing occurs 12 to 20 times a minute.

F. Thought Questions for Class Discussions:

1. What activities might cause nosebleeds?
2. Why are cold applications good for all types of bleeding?
3. Do you think placing the tongue under the upper lip would help stop a nosebleed?

G. Related Ideas for Further Inquiry:

1. Study Section V-D, "Personal Health."
2. Study Section V-E, "Public Health."
3. Have the school nurse talk to the class about nosebleeds.
4. Study other Activities in this Section.

H. Vocabulary Builders—Spelling Words:

1) **nosebleed**   2) **hemorrhage**   3) **circulation**
4) **nostril**   5) **elevate**   6) **bleeding**

I. Thought for Today:

"A lot of people lose their health trying to become wealthy, and then lose their wealth trying to get back their health."

Activity

A. Problem: *How Can We Help a Person with Injuries to the Arms or Legs?*

B. Materials Needed:
1. Triangular bandage
2. Roller bandages
3. Sterile compresses
4. First aid pamphlets

C. Procedure:
1. Discuss why first aid should be learned.
2. Demonstrate some of the uses of triangular bandages.
3. Show how to apply roller bandages.
4. Illustrate the uses of sterile compresses.
5. Let the students practice by using triangular and roller bandages.
6. Let the students check each other's bandages for correct application (with the teacher overseeing, of course).

D. Result:
The students will learn some of the correct techniques for administering first aid.

E. Basic Facts and Supplemental Information:
1. It is never too early to learn how to take care of ourselves and to aid others when accidents occur. Students should learn when to and when not to use bandages. The American Red Cross has excellent printed materials on first aid.
2. If you suspect dislocation(s), don't try to "put it back." Get help. If bone(s) return or snap back, a doctor still needs to be seen because frequently there is damage to the ligaments and blood vessels.
3. Roller bandages should be twisted (turned over) every other wrapping for best binding.
4. Remember "first aid" means first aid only, and it should be followed up immediately by "second aid" which is medical help.

F. Thought Questions for Class Discussions:
1. What is the first thing a person should do in case of a serious accident?
2. Why is it dangerous to move a person with a broken limb?
3. If a person has multiple first aid needs, how do you determine which problem should be taken care of first?

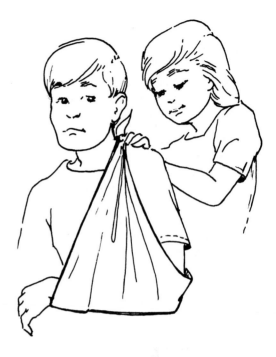

4. Cardiopulmonary resuscitation recommends the sequence should be: (1) A, (2) B, (3) C.
   A = Airway—Clear any obstructions
   B = Breathing—Breathe for the person if necessary
   C = Circulation—Restore the blood flow.

G. Related Ideas for Further Inquiry:
1. Simulate aftermath of earthquakes, tornadoes, or auto accidents.
2. Study Activity V-A-2, "What different kinds of bones and joints do we have?"
3. Study Activity V-A-3, "How does our heart work?"
4. Study Activity V-A-4, "How can we find our pulse?"
5. Study other Activities in this Section.

H. Vocabulary Builders—Spelling Words:
1) **triangular**   2) **roller**   3) **sterile**   4) **doctor**
5) **pamphlets**   6) **apply**   7) **practice**   8) **first aid**
9) **compresses**   10) **bandages**

I. Thought for Today:
"We are all faced with a series of great opportunities disguised as insoluble problems."

A. Problem: *What Should We Do in Case of Burns? Scalds?*

B. Materials Needed:

Books, pamphlets, pictures, charts, and/or multisensory aids about sunburn, other burns, scalds, as well as the seriousness of these burns and possible treatment.

C. Procedure:

1. Discuss how people get accidentally burned.
2. Ask the class if any of them have ever been burned.
3. Ask those, what treatment was administered.
4. Discuss proper treatment:
   a. If skin isn't broken:
      1) Immediately put the 'burned' part (finger, hand, etc.) in clean, cold water.
      2) Apply ice.
      3) Keep it cold for about 20 minutes to ease pain.
      4) Then, mix a couple tablespoons of baking soda in a quart of lukewarm water. Soak dressing and apply to burn.
   b. If skin is broken, see a doctor as soon as possible.
   c. If clothing is on fire, smother fire by having victim roll on ground or smother with blanket. If clothing adheres to burn, cut out clothing but do not try to pull it off skin.
   d. Scrub hands to prevent contamination.
   e. Don't apply ointments, oils, or antiseptics.
   f. Many burns on young children are from the sun. Caution the students.
   g. If skin is blistered, don't break skin to drain blisters.
   h. Burns over 40% of the body are considered life-threatening.

D. Result:

Students will learn that minor burns can be treated at home, and that severe burns require medical attention.

E. Basic Facts and Supplemental Information:

1. If burn is from chemicals, flush the burned area thoroughly with water to dilute and remove chemicals.
2. Burns can be serious. Stress the need for prevention.
3. Many serious burns are complicated by shock.

4. Burns are categorized by degrees.
   a. First degree—reddens the skin
   b. Second degree—blisters the skin
   c. Third degree—breaks the skin
5. Many weather reports now include ultraviolet radiation indexes which indicate how long a person can stay in the sun without harmful effects.

F. Thought Questions for Class Discussions:

1. Where in the home might burns or scalds occur?
2. Where in school might burns or scalds occur?
3. Where outside the home might burns or scalds occur?

G. Related Ideas for Further Inquiry:

1. Study Part II-B, "Fire and Heat."
2. Invite a paramedic to speak to class about fire and burns.
3. Study other Activities in this Section.

H. Vocabulary Builders—Spelling Words:

1) **burns** 2) **scalds** 3) **broken** 4) **degrees**
5) **prevention** 6) **blisters** 7) **treatment**

I. Thought for Today:

"If Washington is the seat of government then the taxpayer is the pants pocket."

Activity

A. Problem: W*hat Should We Do for a Bite or a Sting?*

B. Materials Needed:
1. Pictures of a bee, wasp, yellow-jacket and hornet
2. Pictures of poisonous spiders
3. Pictures of poisonous snakes
4. Picture of a scorpion
5. Pictures of mean-looking dogs and cats

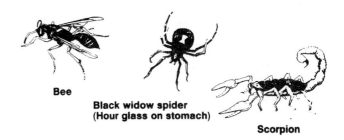

Bee

Black widow spider
(Hour glass on stomach)

Scorpion

C. Procedure:
1. Show pictures of poisonous animals that can bite or sting.
2. Ask students to describe any bite or sting they might have had.
3. Describe and have students simulate correct procedures for insect stings.
   a. Remove stinger gently. (Use sterile needle, tweezers, or knife blade. Do not squeeze or additional poisons might be squeezed into wound.)
   b. Run water over and around the sting (eases pain and dilutes venom).
   c. Apply calamine lotion (relieves itching) or baking soda solution (one teaspoon per pint of water).
   d. If there are multiple stings or bites or if a person is allergic, give antihistamines (if formerly doctor-prescribed) and get medical help immediately.
4. Describe and have students simulate procedures for bites or stings of poisonous spiders or scorpion.
   a. Keep victim quiet.
   b. Cover victim with blanket or extra clothing.
   c. Pack ice around the wound (slows the spread of poison).
   d. These can be fatal, so get victim to doctor or emergency hospital immediately.
5. Procedure in case of dog, cat, or wild animal bite:
   a. Wash bite wound with antiseptic soap or detergent solution.
   b. Rinse well with running water or salt solution.
   c. Cover wound and get medical help as quickly as possible.
   d. Report wound to police or health official; your doctor may do this.
   e. The most serious concern is whether or not the animal is rabid (has rabies).

   f. Any animal (after inflicting bite) should be confined or quarantined for 15 days.
   g. If rabies is suspected, the animal should be anesthetized and examined by a veterinarian or health clinic.

D. Result:
Students will learn that bites and stings can be dangerous or even fatal, so first aid is vital.

E. Basic Facts and Supplemental Information:
1. For non-poisonous snake bites, just clean and dress the wound.
2. For poisonous bites, get medical help quickly. (This is more important than opening the wound and sucking out poison. This can be done on way to medical help.)
3. Children's (human) bites can be more infectious than other animal bites—get medical help quickly.

F. Thought Questions for Class Discussions:
1. How can you prevent bites and stings?
2. Why are most bites and stings treated with alkalines?
3. When would it be wise to have a first aid kit nearby?

G. Related Ideas for Further Inquiry:
1. Study about the treatment for bites of rabid animals.
2. Collect pictures of poisonous animals.
3. Discuss protective clothing.
4. Study other Activities in this Section.

H. Vocabulary Builders—Spelling Words:
1) **wasp** 2) **hornet** 3) **scorpion** 4) **rabid**
5) **treatment** 6) **stinger** 7) **infection**

I. Thought for Today:
"Cats are so unpredictable. You just never know how they will ignore you next."

Activity

A. Problem: *How Can Breathing Be Restored in Drowning or Shock?*

B. Materials Needed:
1. Student volunteers
2. Handkerchiefs
3. Plastic squares
4. *The National American Red Cross First Aid Book*

C. Procedure:

The teacher, doctor, school nurse, and/or members of the fire department rescue squad could conduct the following activity:

1. Discuss ways that breathing might be stopped or impaired: drowning, poisonous gases, shock, choking, etc.
2. Discuss different ways that artificial respiration has been done in the past (rolling over logs, holding legs up, etc.). Death comes quickly if air doesn't get into the lungs.
3. Demonstrate mouth-to-mouth resuscitation as the preferred method.
   a. Start as quickly as possible.
   b. Bend neck back, keep one hand underneath the neck.
   c. Pinch nose, keep closed.
   d. Cover mouth with handkerchief or plastic square with hole in it. (In real cases, must use mouth directly if no cover is available.)
   e. Take a deep breath and blow into victim's mouth. (If you cannot, blow into victim's nose.)
   f. If a small child or infant, blow into both nose and mouth.
   g. After blowing in, remove your mouth and listen for air exhalation.
   h. Repeat about 12 times a minute for adults, 20 times a minute for children.
   i. Keep respiration going until breathing is restored or there is no possibility of recovery.

D. Results:
1. Students will learn how to do mouth-to-mouth resuscitation.
2. Students will gain confidence in the effectiveness of this procedure.

E. Basic Facts and Supplemental Information:
1. A doctor, fire department members, or paramedics should be summoned as quickly as possible in an emergency.

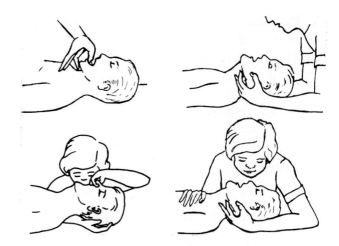

2. Cardiopulmonary resuscitation (CPR) should also be taught to older students. Everyone should learn this technique.
3. Many needless deaths occur because no one has administered artificial respiration or CPR effectively and soon enough.

F. Thought Questions for Class Discussions:
1. Should people ever swim alone?
2. What would cause people to be in a state of shock?
3. If a person is not breathing and bleeding, which of these should be taken care of first?

G. Related Ideas for Further Inquiry:
1. Doctors, nurses, or paramedics can present this Activity effectively.
2. Check with Red Cross for appropriate pamphlets.
3. Study Activity V-A-5, "How much air do our lungs hold?"
4. Study Activity V-F-5, "How can we help a person with injuries to the arms or legs?"
5. Study other Activities in this Section.

H. Vocabulary Builders—Spelling Words:
1) **breathing**   2) **drowning**   3) **resuscitation**
4) **artificial**   5) **victim**   6) **mouth-to-mouth**

I. Thought for Today:
"A young person is a theory; an old person is a fact."—Ed Howe

SECTION G: SAFETY

Activity

v G 1

A. Problem: *What School Safety Drills Should We Know?*

B. Materials Needed:

For safety drills:

1. Cards
2. Posters
3. Pictures
4. Other multisensory aids

C. Procedure:

1. Tell class that this is going to be a lesson on "Safety."
2. Have students discuss the importance of "Safety."
3. Discuss with class what emergencies might happen while at school and what should be done in case of fire, earthquake, tornado, air raid, flood, and accidents:
   a. Listen for alarm or warning.
   b. Follow directions.
   c. Don't panic.
   d. Move according to instructions.
4. Demonstrate the proper procedures for a "Drop Drill":
   1) Get under a desk or table.
   2) Back should be toward window.
5. After drill or emergency:
   a. Wait for all-clear instructions.
   b. Return to normal activities.

D. Results:

1. Students will realize the importance of safety.
2. Students will know what to do in an emergency.

E. Basic Facts and Supplemental Information:

1. All states have laws regarding emergency drills, especially regarding frequency—usually once or twice a month.
2. Many fire deaths are caused by carelessness and panic.
3. Stress classroom safety rules:
   a. Listen and follow directions carefully.
   b. Be considerate of others.
   c. Wear goggles as needed in science activities.
   d. Orderly behavior at all times
   e. Cooperate with teacher and other students.
   f. When in doubt, check with teacher.
   g. Treat chemicals with respect, etc.

F. Thought Questions for Class Discussions:

1. Do you live in an earthquake zone?
2. Do you live in a tornado zone?

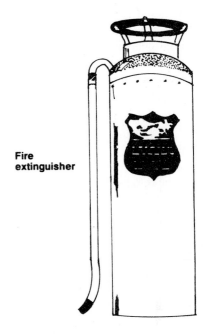

Fire extinguisher

3. What would you do if you were the first to spot a fire on campus?
4. What other emergencies might happen on campus?

G. Related Ideas for Further Inquiry:

1. Locate fire extinguishers and fire boxes on campus.
2. Invite a firefighter to talk to class.
3. Have custodians discuss emergency procedures.
4. List emergency numbers that can be used at home.
5. Have students memorize these numbers.
6. Study Activity V-G-2, "How can we prevent accidents?"
7. Study Activity V-G-3, "What traffic signals should we know?"
8. Study Activity V-G-4, "What safety precautions should we take when riding bicycles, skateboards, or in-line skates?"

H. Vocabulary Builders—Spelling Words:

1) **safety**   2) **drill**   3) **alarm**   4) **earthquake**   5) **tornado**   6) **cooperate**   7) **directions**

I. Thought for Today:

"A skeptic is a person who, seeing the handwriting on the wall, claims it is a forgery."

Activity

A. Problem: *How Can We Prevent Accidents?*

B. Materials Needed:
1. Pictures of traffic accidents
2. Empty medicine bottles
3. Empty gasoline can
4. Pictures of containers with poisonous chemicals
5. Pictures of write-ups of other accidents
6. Matches
7. Knife
8. Bulletin board

C. Procedure:
1. The most effective way to teach accident prevention is to keep a running record of each accident found in the media or occurring to a class member. Some clippings or notices should be kept on the bulletin board. Some typical accidents might be:
   a. traffic accidents
   b. falls
   c. fires
   d. poisonous chemicals (medicine cabinet and garage)
   e. contaminated or spoiled food, etc.
   f. burns
   g. cuts and wounds
   h. swimming accidents
2. Students should make suggestions on how each type of accident might have been prevented.
3. A safety check of the homes can be conducted.
4. Divide class into four sections and have each section work on one of the four main areas of accidents:
   a. highways and freeways
   b. work
   c. play
   d. home

D. Result:
Students will become more conscious of accident potentials and hopefully reduce the number of accidents happening to young people.

E. Basic Facts and Supplemental Information:
1. Accidents are the leading cause of death and injury to young people.
2. Types of home fatalities for young children:
   a. Fires, burns   50%
   b. Firearms   23%
   c. Falls   6%
   d. Poisons   3%
   e. Miscellaneous   18%

3. The primary cause of fatalities to children outside the home is automobile accidents.
4. This activity could be part of a health unit on first aid.

F. Thought Questions for Class Discussions:
1. What kinds of accidents could occur at school? in the homes? on the playground? in swimming pools?
2. What kinds of accidents could kill people?
3. Who are the people who are employed to take care of people who have accidents?

G. Related Ideas for Further Inquiry:
1. Interview nurses about accidents.
2. Visit a fire station or have a firefighter talk to class.
3. Ask a police officer to speak to class about traffic accidents.
4. Study Activity V-G-1, "What school safety drills should we know?"
5. Study Activity V-G-3, "What traffic signals should we know?"
6. Study Activity V-G-4, "What safety precautions should we take when riding bicycles, skateboards, or in-line skates?"

H. Vocabulary Builders—Spelling Words:
1) **accident** 2) **prevent** 3) **traffic** 4) **burns**
5) **falls** 6) **swimming** 7) **poisons** 8) **fires**

I. Thought for Today:
"Accident statistics prove the road to heaven is paved."

Activity

A. Problem: *What Traffic Signals Should We Know?*

B. Materials Needed:

1. Area of the playground with chalk-marked traffic lanes
2. Traffic light mock-ups
3. Railroad signal gate-guard mock-up
4. Cards with "WALK," "DON'T WALK," and "WAIT" on them
5. Chalk
6. Traffic dioramas and models
7. Pictures of traffic and traffic signs

C. Procedure:

1. The teacher can mark an intersection with chalk on the playground or use a diorama in class to include traffic lanes and pedestrian crosswalks.
2. Demonstrate correct pedestrian procedures used with "Stop Sign."
3. Teacher should discuss the following traffic color signals:
   a. Red—stop
   b. Yellow—caution (or slow)
   c. Green—go
4. Teacher should discuss lanes for automobiles and pedestrian crosswalks.
5. The teacher uses the traffic light mock-up (or the circle cut-outs) to have each student react to various traffic signals in the street layout by walking, stopping, or waiting.
6. The teacher should repeat the activity using only the "WALK," "DON'T WALK," and "WAIT" cards.
7. The teacher can explain the function of railroad signal drop-gates.
8. When class is back inside, pictures of traffic can be studied for safe and unsafe practices.
9. If the school has school crossing guards, the teacher should play this role and have students walk through typical situations.

D. Result:

Students will learn the rules of the road and traffic safety procedures for pedestrians.

E. Basic Facts and Supplemental Information:

1. In the U.S., the number one cause of death and injury among people from birth through 24 years of age is traffic accidents.
2. Most traffic signals are on a 60-second cycle, and the students should be taught patience and safety in waiting.

 Green  Red

International adopted signs

3. Most pedestrian accidents occur after school hours between 3 P.M. and 6 P.M.
4. A traffic safety bulletin board and a felt board demonstration are two great teaching devices to use for this Activity.

F. Thought Questions for Class Discussions:

1. Could a pedestrian be right and still be injured or killed in a traffic accident?
2. What precautions should a pedestrian take if there are no traffic signals or pedestrian crossing lanes?
3. How can traffic accidents be reduced?

G. Related Ideas for Further Inquiry:

1. Have students draw a simple traffic light and color appropriate signals.
2. Post pictures of traffic accidents on bulletin board. Be discreet—not too graphic.
3. Discuss controlled and uncontrolled intersections.
4. Play-act out traffic hazards. (Toy vehicles are excellent models of automobiles or bicycles.)
5. Have a crossing guard speak to class.
6. Study Activity V-G-1, "What school safety drills should we know?"
7. Study Activity V-G-2, "How can we prevent accidents?"
8. Study Activity V-G-4, "What safety precautions should we take when riding bicycles, skateboards, or in-line skates?"

H. Vocabulary Builders—Spelling Words:

1) **traffic**   2) **signal**   3) **walk**   4) **accidents**
5) **stop sign**   6) **caution**   7) **wait**   8) **fatalities**

I. Thought for Today:

"Drive as if you owned the other car."

A. Problem: *What Safety Precautions Should We Take When Riding Bicycles, Skateboards, or In-line Skates?*

B. Materials Needed:
1. Bicycle
2. Area on the playground marking off traffic lanes with chalk
3. Model of traffic light

C. Procedure:
1. Discuss the mechanical problems that might develop with a bicycle such as:
   a. brake failure
   b. broken chain
   c. gears slipping
   d. flat tire, etc.
2. Teach and/or review directional arm signals for drivers of bicycles and cars.
3. Teach and/or review traffic signals.
4. Describe bicycle accessories that help with bicycle safety such as:
   a. helmets
   b. reflectors
   c. lights
   d. horns
   e. viewing rods with flags
   f. rear view mirror
5. Simulate normal traffic signals and have a student demonstrate by walking a bicycle through the correct procedures at intersections for each sequence of lights.
6. Have one student walk a bicycle and a second student walk by his/her side to demonstrate proper arm signals for each type of turn and stop.
7. Discuss the do's and don'ts of bicycle riding.
   a. Do watch for other vehicles.
   b. Do practice safe riding.
   c. Do follow the rules of the road.
   d. Do stay in lanes marked for bicycles.
   e. Don't be a show-off on a bicycle.
   f. Don't ride on the sidewalk.
   g. Don't ride at night without lights, etc.
8. Discuss the differences between riding a bicycle, a skateboard, and in-line skates regarding:
   a. safety precautions
   b. crossing streets (the "rules of the road" must be obeyed)
   c. courtesy to all pedestrians
   d. laws for riding on sidewalks, streets, in parks, etc.

Look both ways before crossing the street.

D. Results:
1. Students will learn about bicycle safety in a safe area.
2. Pupils will learn the legal and ethical differences in safety and courtesy when riding a bicycle and using a skateboard or in-line skates.

E. Basic Facts and Supplemental Information:
Bicycle accidents and traffic deaths among youngsters are far too high, and most are due to carelessness and lack of bicycle safety education.

F. Thought Questions for Class Discussions:
1. Should bicycle riders be licensed the same as automobile drivers?
2. Are bicycle riders who break the law given traffic violation tickets?
3. Can bicycles be legally ridden on sidewalks in your community?

G. Related Ideas for Further Inquiry:
1. Discuss bicycle problems at uncontrolled intersections.
2. Discuss the concept of right of way.
3. Study Activity V-G-2, "How can we prevent accidents?"
4. Study Activity V-G-3, "What traffic signals should we know?"
5. Study other Activities in this Section.

H. Vocabulary Builders—Spelling Words:
1) **safety** 2) **precaution** 3) **bicycle** 4) **look**
5) **intersection** 6) **uncontrolled** 7) **lights**
8) **signals** 9) **skates** 10) **in-line skates**

I. Thought for Today:
"In large cities, the rush hour is when the traffic is almost at a standstill."

Activity

"No, I don't go with strangers!!!"

A. Problem: *Should We Be Friendly with Strangers?*

B. Materials Needed:
1. Pictures of many adults
2. Pictures of children
3. Pictures of missing children
4. Newspaper accounts of missing children

C. Procedure:
1. The details of the lesson will depend on the age level of the class.
2. Collect stories of children who:
   a. are missing
   b. have been kidnapped
   c. have been murdered
3. Explain to students what to do and what not to do if a stranger approaches them for any reason. (They usually entice children with gum, candy, toys, or a story about taking them home because their parents want them.)
4. Role play different situations. (Acting out is important because many can describe what they should or shouldn't do but they can't act it out.) Acting out is more realistic.
5. Create situations and ask students to act out such examples as:
   a. becoming separated from parent in a shopping mall
   b. being home alone and seeing a stranger at your front door
   c. walking home and seeing some stranger following you
   d. having a person stop his (her) car close to you and asking for information
6. Ask students if they can identify a child molester by a picture.
7. Ask students if they can identify, by a picture, a child who might be molested.

D. Results:
1. Students will become aware that there are dangers involved in talking to strangers.
2 Students will gain some experience in how to deal with a stranger.

E. Basic Facts and Supplemental Information:
1. About a million children are reported missing every year.
2. Police officers are always good friends.

F. Thought Questions for Class Discussions:
1. Can you tell a good stranger from a bad one?
2. What would you do if you saw your best friend talking to a stranger?
3. If a stranger picked up a friend in an automobile what should you do? (Get the license plate number, call police.)

G. Related Ideas for Further Inquiry:
1. Discuss hazards of playing alone.
2. Invite a police officer to talk to the class about missing children.
3. Study Activity V-G-1, "What school safety drills should we know?"
4. Study Activity V-G-2, "How can we prevent accidents?"
5. Study Activity V-G-3, "What traffic signals should we know?"
6. Study other Activities in this Section.

H. Vocabulary Builders—Spelling Words:
1) **strangers** 2) **friendly** 3) **missing**
4) **children** 5) **approaches** 6) **suspicious**

I. Thought for Today:
"The way most people who fish catch fish is by the tale."

Activity

A. Problem: *What Should We Do if We Get Lost in the Woods?*

B. Materials Needed:

1. Wristwatch
2. Matches
3. Rocks or pebbles
4. Miniature tent
5. Stick
6. Compass
7. Flashlight

C. Procedure:

1. Describe how people get lost in the city and in rural areas.
2. Tell the students that even the people who know the woods (hikers, foresters, scientists) get lost once in a while.
3. Have the students learn some basic rules:
   a. Since panic is the number one problem, sit down and give yourself time to calm down and think.
   b. If someone knows roughly where you are, don't go anywhere—help will come to you. Always tell someone where you are going.
   c. If you have matches or a lighter, make a fire and keep it going day and night. A smoky fire in the daytime can be seen from long distances, and this can be made by using green or wet wood and brushes.
   d. Find an open clearing and make a large "HELP" sign out of rocks, limbs, or trenches in snow.
   e. Conserve your energy and strength.
   f. If nobody knows your whereabouts, then try to walk out in a straight line.
      1) Estimate direction of nearest help.
      2) If you have a compass, use it; if not, walk in a straight line by lining up high landmarks.
   g. Many people have gone hungry in the woods with many kinds of edible plants surrounding them.
4. Demonstrate procedures with materials listed above.
5. If you have a portable radio it can be used to determine direction of signal by turning it until a station comes in loud and clear. If you know the location of the station, this will help you get your bearings.
6. If you are with friends and have walkie-talkies, make plans ahead of time to check with others at designated time intervals. This saves batteries and keeps all individuals regularly informed as to each other's whereabouts.

D. Result:

Students will learn a few basic safety rules if they get lost in the woods.

E. Basic Facts and Supplemental Information:

1. If a stream is found, it should be noted that water will follow the deepest path down and consequently the shortest.
2. Noisemakers should be attempted by blowing across reeds, cans, or spent cartridges.
3. A wristwatch can be used as a compass. You can also use the shadows cast by trees for general directions.
4. Hikers should never hike alone.
5. Bearings of mountain peaks or unusual physical features can help determine placement.
6. People can go weeks without food, days without water, but only hours in extreme cold. Keeping warm should be the primary concern.

F. Thought Questions for Class Discussions:

1. What should a person take along when going into some large wooded area where one might get lost?
2. What is the buddy system?
3. Is it safe to go hiking alone?

G. Related Ideas for Further Inquiry:

1. Talk to forest rangers about safety.
2. Discuss with sporting goods salesmen about safety equipment needed in the woods.
3. Study Activity I-D-5, "How can we make a compass?"

H. Vocabulary Builders—Spelling Words:

1) **lost** 2) **woods** 3) **help** 4) **hikers** 5) **panic** 6) **compass** 7) **direction** 8) **warm** 9) **water**

I. Thought for Today:

"When I don't have anything to worry about, I begin to worry about that."

PART VI

ECOLOGY

SECTION A   Ecosystems   288
SECTION B   Conservation   298
SECTION C   Pollution   308
SECTION D   Pollution Solutions   321

A. Problem: *What Is the Balance of Nature?*

B. Materials Needed (On Ecology):

1. Books
2. Magazines
3. Newspaper accounts
4. Pictures
5. Animal cut-outs
6. Drawing supplies

C. Procedure:

1. Discuss ecosystems (biotic communities and their environments).
2. Describe several biotic communities (the interrelationships of all living things).
3. Discuss some of the ecosystems that include humans.
4. Describe some of the limitations of environments:
   a. temperature
   b. food supplies
   c. oxygen
   d. water
   e. land types, soil
5. Discuss the problems of doubling all existing animals (including humans).
6. Discuss the terms "food chain" and "food web."
   a. Food chain—consists of a direct line of energy transfer from the:
      1) sun to plant (producer) to
      2) herbivore to
      3) primary consumer to
      4) secondary consumer to
      5) tertiary or final consumer.
   b. Food web—consists of all the possibilities of food sources and their interrelationships.
7. Students should draw charts of food chains and food webs that they have studied either at school or at home.

D. Results:

1. Students will learn about biotic communities and ecosystems.
2. Students will discover that as animal populations expand, plant foods decrease.

E. Basic Facts and Supplemental Information:

1. Ecosystems are "balanced" when the numbers of plants and animals remain about the same and the physical environment is relatively stable.
2. Most plants and animals can adapt to minor changes in the physical environment.

Plants, animals, and the physical environment

3. Many species of animals have become extinct because their ecosystems were dramatically changed in one way or another.
4. Many more species are in danger of becoming extinct.
5. The two terms, biotic community and ecosystem, are going to become increasingly important in the language of all people, especially with the pressure of growing populations and the corresponding reductions of food supplies per person.

F. Thought Questions for Class Discussions:

1. Do we change ecosystems when we spray with strong insecticides?
2. Are there any animals that are 100% bad?
3. What changes will there be in the food web if our human population doubles?

G. Related Ideas for Further Inquiry:

1. Study the local school community as an "ecosystem."
2. Study Activity VI-A-2, "What is the 'Triangle of Life'?"
3. Study Activity VI-A-3, "What is 'biological diversity'?"
4. Study Activity VI-A-7, "How do people destroy habitats?"
5. Study Activity VI-A-9, "Are any animals threatened with extinction?"
6. Study Activity VI-A-10, "Is there a world population explosion?"

H. Vocabulary Builders—Spelling Words:

1) **biological** 2) **balance** 3) **nature** 4) **ecosystem**
5) **herbivores** 6) **consumers** 7) **food** 8) **web**
9) **extinct** 10) **increasing** 11) **decreasing**

I. Thought for Today:

"When we were in school the hard stuff meant algebra"

Activity

A. Problem: *What Is the "Triangle of Life"?*

B. Materials Needed:
1. Pictures of specimens in the various levels:
   a. Person
   b. Large fish or land animal
   c. Small fish or small land animal
   d. Small plant-eating organism
   e. Small plant (energy producer)
   See sketch for sample ideas.
2. Chalkboard or bulletin board

C. Procedure:
1. At a convenient time, when a problem or question of food arises, question class on their previous knowledge of the "Triangle of Life."
2. Discuss what a triangle is.
3. Draw a triangle on the board and make five sections by drawing four lines parallel to the base line as shown in drawing.
4. Have students make a copy of this.
5. Label the sections.
6. Have students fill in the name of a specific organism that lives in each section.
7. Place appropriate picture of the same or similar organism on the board.
8. Cite that each section represents the number of organisms that live in that section. Since the lowest section is the largest, there could be billions of organisms living there. The next section could represent millions, the next thousands, the next hundreds, and the top, tens. This is true in nature so that every level will feed on a lower level, and the lower level being much more plentiful will continue to flourish.
9. Discuss how all living things must have other things to feed on in order to exist.
10. Cite the problems that would exist if there were an equal number of all species. This would mean that a person could eat one carrot, one apple, one kind of fish, or one of anything in a lifetime.
11. Fortunately, nature provides more organisms on the lower section to reproduce and feed those on the higher sections. Because of this all species continue to exist.

D. Result:
Students will gain a new understanding of the relationships of numbers in the food chains and food webs.

E. Basic Facts and Supplemental Information:
1. The food triangle applies to plants in the food chain as well as animals.

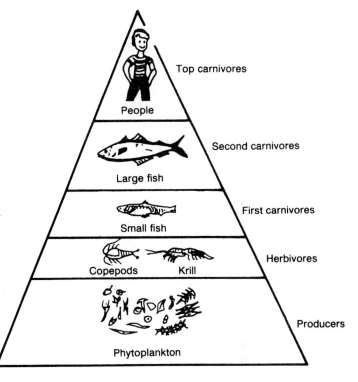

Top carnivores — People
Second carnivores — Large fish
First carnivores — Small fish
Herbivores — Copepods   Krill
Producers — Phytoplankton

2. Humans have greatly interfered with many food "triangles of life" (building dams, clearing land for businesses, homes, highways, etc.).

F. Thought Questions for Class Discussions:
1. Why has the cost of shrimps and crabs climbed faster than most other foods?
2. Have humans developed new food triangles?
3. Do pesticides interfere with food triangles?

G. Related Ideas for Further Inquiry:
1. Study Activity VI-A-1, "What is the balance of nature?"
2. Study Activity VI-A-3, "What is 'biological diversity'?"
3. Study Activity VI-A-7, "How do people destroy habitats?"
4. Study Activity VI-A-9, "Are any animals threatened with extinction?"

H. Vocabulary Builders—Spelling Words:
1) **triangle**   2) **living**   3) **species**   4) **individual**
5) **numbers**   6) **carnivores**   7) **herbivores**

I. Thought for Today:
"One of the first things children learn at school is that other children get allowances."

A. Problem: *What Is "Biological Diversity"?*

B. Materials Needed:

1. Small planted area around the school campus
2. Reference materials on small animals
3. Notebooks
4. Drawing materials (pencils, paper, rulers, etc.)

C. Procedure:

1. Select a "plot" of land at or near school.
2. Have students make a rough drawing of the area.
3. Have students study the area for all forms of living organisms. This might contain:
    a. insects
    b. spiders
    c. worms
    d. bees
    e. flies
    f. beetles
    g. lizard(s)
    h. grasses
    i. weeds
    j. flowers
    k. trees
    l. bushes
    m. mosses
    n. butterflies
4. In their drawing, have students indicate where each organism was seen.
5. Have students look up the scientific name and/ or common name of each.
6. Have pupils draw lines from one organism to another in which there was any kind of relationship. These might include:
    a. spider—fly (food)
    b. insect—grass (hiding) protection
    c. bees—flowers (pollinating)
7. Discuss other items of "biological diversity" and the interrelationships of organisms.

D. Results:

1. Students will learn that there are many organisms that live within a very small area.
2. Students will become familiar with reference materials on classification.
3. Students will learn that all organisms have many interrelationships.

E. Basic Facts and Supplemental Information:

1. Taxonomists' estimates of the number of plant and animal species that exist on Earth vary from 3 million to 30 million.

A variety of plants and animals

2. Biological diversity (biodiversity) is the total variety of life on Earth.
3. Species of plant and animal life are rapidly dwindling in the United States and the rest of the world.
4. Life is very complicated, interrelated, and mutually dependent.

F. Thought Questions for Class Discussions:

1. On what species are people very dependent?
2. What role does the physical environment play in maintaining organisms?
3. How have people disturbed other organisms?

G. Related Ideas for Further Inquiry:

1. Study Part III, "Plants."
2. Study Part IV, "Animals."
3. Study Activity VI-A-1, "What is the balance of nature?"
4. Study Activity VI-A-2, "What is the 'Triangle of Life'?"
5. Study Activity VI-A-5, "How do we make a simple ecosystem?"
6. Study Activity VI-A-8, "What controls animal populations?"
7. Study Activity VI-A-9, "Are any animals threatened with extinction?"
8. Study Activity VI-A-7, "How do people destroy habitats?"

H. Vocabulary Builders—Spelling Words:

1) **biological** 2) **diversity** 3) **species**
4) **interdependent** 5) **organisms** 6) **taxonomy**

I. Thought for Today:

"A mule makes no headway while he is kicking; neither does a person."

Activity

A. Problem: *What Are the Largest Ecosystems in the World?*

B. Materials Needed:

1. World globe
2. Maps showing large areas of land
3. Reference books on geography and climate

C. Procedure:

1. Write the following terms on the chalkboard:
   a. icecaps
   b. tundra
   c. temperate deciduous forests
   d. tropical rain forests
   e. savannahs
   f. deserts
   g. temperate coniferous forests
   h. mediterranean
   i. grasslands
   j. jungles
   k. coastal waters
   l. oceans
2. Show on the globe a few of the most prominent geographic areas and large ecosystems.
3. Have students volunteer to form study groups for the main large ecosystems citing main differences such as:
   a. location
   b. climate:
      1) weather
      2) humidity
      3) temperature ranges
   c. land, soils
   d. water supply
   e. animals, animal products
   f. plants, plant products
   g. minerals
   h. economic value
   i. unusual characteristics, etc.

D. Results:

1. Students will realize that the Earth has many large, varied ecosystems.
2. Pupils will have gained some research information regarding ecosystems.

E. Basic Facts and Supplemental Information:

1. Ecosystems can vary from macroscopic to microscopic.

2. Large ecosystems vary greatly in all the elements of which they are composed.
3. Temperate climates are cold and wet.
4. Tropical climates are warm and wet.
5. Half of all plant and animal species live in the rain forests.
6. We have been burning down the world's forests to make room for farms, residences, and roadways.

F. Thought Questions for Class Discussions:

1. What label would you put on the classification of the large ecosystem in which you reside?
2. Are there sharp boundaries between the large ecosystems?
3. Should we be concerned about the distant, large ecosystems?

G. Related Ideas for Further Inquiry:

1. Draw maps showing the location of the large ecosystems.
2. Make a detailed study of one large ecosystem.
3. Study plate tectonics.

H. Vocabulary Builders—Spelling Words:

Use the terms cited in C-1.

I. Thought for Today:

"Don't believe the world owes you a living. The world owes you nothing— it was here first."

A. Problem: *How Do We Make a Simple Ecosystem?*

B. Materials Needed:
1. Five-gallon water container (glass)
2. Large cork
3. Sealing wax or paraffin
4. Gravel (small pebbles), sand
5. Fresh-water plants (aquarium types)
6. Water
7. One small aquarium-type fish (goldfish is best)
8. Water snails
9. Stick or dowel about 20″ long to affix water plants

C. Procedure to Construct:
1. Fill container with water to about 3″ from the top.
2. Add sand and gravel.
3. With stick, place plants in gravel and sand bottom. (Plants might have to be weighted.)
4. Have some floating plants as well.
5. Let stand for 24 hours.
6. Place snails and fish in container.
7. Place cork on top and seal with wax or paraffin.
8. Place container near window.

Procedure to Teach:
1. Explain to class the fundamentals of an ecosystem (plants, animals, environment in balance).
2. Explain the oxygen and carbon dioxide cycle. (Plants in daytime give off oxygen and take in carbon dioxide; animals give off carbon dioxide and take in oxygen.)
3. Explain to class that you are going to make an ecosystem with the fish and snails as the animals, the plants as the plants, and the air and the water in the container as the environment. Sealing the environment makes it a closed community.
4. Ask the class how long they think the fish will live.

D. Results:
1. The students will learn more about ecosystems.
2. The fish should live for the entire semester without being fed.

E. Basic Facts and Supplemental Information:
1. If the fish becomes too large or too sluggish, open the container and place the fish in a regular aquarium.
2. The students may keep a record of their observations, noting any changes in any of the plants, snails, or fish.

A biotic community

3. A complete ecosystem consists of:
   a. producers (produce food for other organisms)
   b. consumers (consume plants and/or animals)
   c. decomposers (recyclers)
   d. materials
4. Some organisms may be producers and/or consumers and/or decomposers.

F. Thought Questions for Class Discussions:
1. What would happen if there were no plants placed in the container?
2. What would happen if several large fish were placed in the container?
3. Does this prove that plants give off oxygen?

G. Related Ideas for Further Inquiry:
1. Study Part III, "Plants."
2. Study Part IV, "Animals."
3. Study Activity VI-A-1, "What is the balance of nature?"
4. Study Activity VI-A-2, "What is the 'Triangle of Life'?"
5. Study Activity VI-A-3, "What is 'biological diversity'?"

H. Vocabulary Builders—Spelling Words:
1) **biotic**   2) **community**   3) **wax**   4) **paraffin**
5) **gravel**   6) **gallon**   7) **fish**   8) **balanced**

I. Thought for Today:
"Many a child who watches television for hours will go down in history—not to mention arithmetic, English, and science."

A. Problem: *Do We Belong to an Ecosystem?*

B. Materials Needed:
1. Notebook paper
2. Pens
3. Pencils
4. Compasses (for drawing)

C. Procedure:
1. Describe what an ecosystem is: living and nonliving interrelationships.
2. Give several examples of ecosystems:
   a. lake or pond community
   b. farm community
   c. forest community
   d. desert community
3. Ask the class if they think they are part of an ecosystem now.
4. Have them draw four large concentric circles.
5. Label them from inside out:
   a. Classroom
   b. School Building
   c. School Grounds
   d. School Community
6. Ask them to fill in all elements that they can in each of these areas as shown in the illustration.

D. Results:
1. Students will realize that they are a part of many ecosystems.
2. They will realize that ecosystems consist of animals, plants, and things.

E. Basic Facts and Supplemental Information:
1. Individuals are one element in a complex web of living things in natural surroundings.
2. Every element that affects an individual, whether living or nonliving, is part of that individual's ecosystem:
3. No living organism lives in complete isolation from all others.
4. Plants and animals that live in the same habitat share the same air, water, ground, and climate as all others.
5. Without plants and animals, no human being can survive.
6. An "ecosystem" includes all plants, animals, and the physical environment.
7. A "biotic community" focuses only on the interrelationships of plants and animals.
8. This is an excellent activity for each student to begin to realize his/her place in nature and the interrelationships of all living and nonliving things.

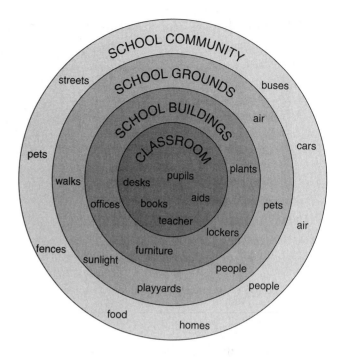

F. Thought Questions for Class Discussions:
1. Can our homes be considered an ecosystem?
2. Can our planet be considered an ecosystem?
3. What is the difference between an ecosystem and a biological community?
4. Are the oxygen, nitrogen, water, and carbon cycles part of our ecosystem?
5. Are the sun, moon, and stars part of our ecosystem?

G. Related Ideas for Further Inquiry:
1. Have each student study the ecosystem of his/her home and local community.
2. Study Part III, "Plants," Part IV, "Animals," and other Sections of this Part.
3. Study Activity VI-A-1, "What is the balance of nature?"
4. Study Activity VI-A-3, "What is 'biological diversity'?"

H. Vocabulary Builders—Spelling Words:
1) **ecosystem** 2) **biotic** 3) **community**
4) **nonliving** 5) **concentric** 6) **environment**

I. Thought for Today:
"Most of us would be better off financially if it weren't for the extravagances of our neighbors."

Ecology **293**

Activity

A. Problem: *How Do People Destroy Habitats?*

B. Materials Needed:

1. Large box
2. Scrap cardboard
3. Pieces of wood or blocks
4. Miniature toys
   a. cars
   b. houses
   c. bridges
   d. shops
5. Maps of local areas

C. Procedure:

1. Study maps of local areas.
2. Construct a diorama of the local community. (A diorama is a three-dimensional scene in a box.)
3. Study the main activities that people in your community are involved in such as:
   a. working
   b. recreating
   c. shopping
   d. schooling
4. Construct another diorama of your community as it existed 30, 40, or 50 years ago or whatever time frame you choose. (You may want to construct both dioramas simultaneously.)
5. Have the class interview parents and long-time residents to determine how the community looked historically.
6. Study the flora and fauna that existed prior to the "late growth" of your locality.
7. Compare these with the ones that are currently in the community.

D. Results:

1. Students will visualize the differences in their neighborhood that have occurred through the years.
2. They will realize that a lot of flora and fauna have disappeared as a result of the increased number and activities of human beings.

E. Basic Facts and Supplemental Information:

1. When people move into a pristine area, plants are destroyed and animals move out.
2. Wetlands have given way to developers.
3. Desertification has increased as human population expands.
4. Forests have been replaced by human artifacts.

Habitat destruction

5. When Homo sapiens expand in numbers, they destroy natural habitats and replace them with towns and cities.
6. Habitats are also reduced by people by hunting, fishing, and polluting the environment.

F. Thought Questions for Class Discussions:

1. Are all species important to people?
2. Should we be concerned about species that are threatened with extinction?
3. Should we try to preserve some natural habitats—even if it means losing some jobs?

G. Related Ideas for Further Inquiry:

1. Study Part III, "Plants."
2. Study Part IV, "Animals."
3. Study Activity VI-A-1, "What is the balance of nature?"
4. Study Activity VI-A-2, "What is the 'Triangle of Life'?"
5. Study Activity VI-A-3, "What is 'biological diversity'?"
6. Study Activity VI-A-5, "How do we make a simple ecosystem?"
7. Study Activity VI-A-8, "What controls animal populations?"
8. Study Activity VI-A-9, "Are any animals threatened with extinction?"
9. Study Activity VI-A-10, "Is there a world population explosion?"

H. Vocabulary Builders—Spelling Words:

1) **Homo sapiens**   2) **habitats**   3) **species**
4) **extinction**   5) **threatened**   6) **pollution**

I. Thought for Today:

"We are not out of the woods-yet."

Activity

A. Problem: *What Controls Animal Populations?*

B. Materials Needed:

1. Pictures of fishing gear
2. Pictures of hunting equipment
3. Pictures of various animals whose populations have been affected by people
4. Pictures or news items concerning traps, cages, etc.

C. Procedure:

1. Discuss food chains.
2. Review Activity VI-A-5, "How do we make a simple ecosystem?"
3. Show the students pictures of items listed in the "Materials Needed."
4. Discuss how people kill animals for food and sport.
5. Discuss other ways that animals lose their lives.
6. Students may want to read stories or do research about unusual food chains or food webs. This might include:
   a. salmon
   b. wolves
   c. lemmings
   d. tuna
7. Discuss how animals kill other animals.
8. Discuss "preys" and "predators."

D. Results:

1. Students will learn about food chains and food webs.
2. Pupils will learn that animal populations are controlled by:
   a. predators
   b. environment
   c. disease
   d. humans
      1) hunting
      2) poisoning
      3) encroaching on animal habitats
   e. animals themselves

E. Basic Facts and Supplemental Information:

1. Humans have wiped out some animal species and have endangered many more.
2. Animals tend to balance themselves naturally if left alone.

F. Thought Questions for Class Discussions:

1. Do endangered species ever make a comeback?
2. Do humans overhunt and overfish?
3. Who should control sport hunting and fishing?
4. Who should control hunting and fishing of endangered species?
5. Should we be concerned about all plants? all animals?

G. Related Ideas for Further Inquiry:

1. Study Part III, "Plants."
2. Study Part IV, "Animals."
3. Study Activity VI-A-1, "What is the balance of nature?"
4. Study Activity VI-A-2, "What is the 'Triangle of Life'?"
5. Study Activity VI-A-3, "What is 'biological diversity'?"
6. Study Activity VI-A-9, "Are any animals threatened with extinction?"
7. See other Activities in this Section.

H. Vocabulary Builders—Spelling Words:

1) **control** 2) **animal** 3) **population** 4) **hunting**
5) **fishing** 6) **wolves** 7) **predators** 8) **disease**

I. Thought for Today:

"An ecologist wants to clean up the world; an environmentalist wants you to clean up your yard."

Activity

A. Problem: *Are Any Animals Threatened with Extinction?*

B. Materials Needed:

Pictures and accounts of as many of the following as possible:

1. Eastern elk
2. Passenger pigeon
3. American alligator
4. Southern bald eagle
5. Columbian white-tailed deer
6. Utah prairie dog
7. Ivory-billed woodpecker
8. Whooping crane
9. Wolves
10. Sea otter
11. Giant panda
12. Hawk
13. Pine martin
14. Polar bears
15. Leopards (five species)
16. Black-footed ferret
17. Sea turtles
18. Whales
19. Condors
20. Peregrine falcon
21. Masked bobwhite
22. Kirtland's warbler
23. Eskimo curlew
24. American crocodile

C. Procedure:

1. Have students study the general characteristics of each of the major species in which these animals are found (elk, pigeons, eagles, etc.).
2. Emphasize the interrelationships of these animals to other animals in their species.
3. Describe how these endangered animals are interrelated with resident plants.
4. Study the reasons why animals become endangered, extinct?

D. Results:

1. The students will learn that the first two animals listed are now extinct.
2. The rest of the animals and many others are being threatened with extinction.

E. Basic Facts and Supplemental Information:

1. The *Worldwatch* magazine reported that 70% of the biologists believe that the world is in the midst of the fastest mass extinction of living things in the 4.5 billion year history of our planet.
2. The scientists rated biodiversity loss as a more serious problem than the depletion of the ozone layer, global warming, or pollution and contamination.
3. Defenders of wildlife claim that there are 1,900 animal species nearing extinction.
4. Hawaii, thought to be isolated, is an example of what has happened:
   a. Outside predators have been introduced.
   b. Humans have entered the scene.

Alligator

Passenger pigeon

   c. Both have reduced fresh-water fish, land mullusks, and birds by over 36%.
5. Conservationists have helped slow the extinction rate by setting up sanctuaries, refuges, and zoos. These have helped the grizzly bear, bison, African cheetah, condors, turtles, whooping cranes, etc. These represent only a small number of the total threatened animal species.

F. Thought Questions for Class Discussions:

1. Should people wear the furs of animals of endangered species?
2. What happens when the balance of nature is disturbed?
3. If an animal becomes extinct, can it ever be restored?
4. What can you do to keep nature's beautiful plants and animals from being destroyed?
5. What would happen to us if all the animals were to disappear?
6. What would happen to us if all the plants were to disappear?

G. Related Ideas for Further Inquiry:

1. Visit a zoo.
2. Visit a fish hatchery.
3. Visit a game refuge.
4. Study how the government protects some animals.
5. Study Activity VI-A-1, "What is the balance of nature?"
6. Study Activity VI-A-2, "What is the 'Triangle of Life'?"
7. Study Activity VI-A-3, "What is 'biological diversity'?"
8. Study Activity VI-A-7, "How do people destroy habitats?"

H. Vocabulary Builders—Spelling Words:

1) **pigeon** 2) **alligator** 3) **eagle** 4) **woodpecker**
5) **wolves** 6) **bears** 7) **birds** 8) **wildlife**

I. Thought for Today:

"The dictionary is the only place where success comes before work."

Activity

A. Problems: *Is There a World Population Explosion?*

B. Materials Needed:

About population statistics:

1. Magazines
2. Newspapers
3. Chart paper
4. Pencils

C. Procedure:

1. Have students look at all the evidence, statistics, etc. they can collect in regard to the population explosion.
2. Chart these findings for the world.
3. Chart these findings for the United States.
4. Discuss what these findings mean in the way of buildings, medical care, food, water, power, schools, smog, pollution, wastes, etc.

D. Results:

1. Students will see that there is a fast and steady rise in population in the United States and throughout the world.
2. Pupils will realize that this added growth will create many new problems, particularly in the areas of food, fresh water, health care, education, and housing. Feeding more people with less farmland will be the number one concern.

E. Basic Facts and Supplemental Information:

1. The world's population in 1975 was 4 billion.
2. The world's population is expected to reach 8 billion in the year 2020. It is now about 6 billion.
3. The United States is adding 2.4 million people to its population every year.
4. The world is adding 90 million more people to its population every year.
5. The population in "hungry" countries is doubling twice as fast as it is in "well-fed" countries.
6. Vital statistics: (world wide)

Year	Population	Time to Double
6,000 B.C.	5,000,000	Doubled @
1650 A.D.	500,000,000	1200 yrs.
1850	1 billion	200 yrs.
1930	2 billion	80 yrs.
1975	4 billion	45 yrs.
2010	8 billion	35 yrs.
2900	100 people/sq. yd.	(estimated)

7. Even though the U.S. birthrate has dropped, there are still more women of childbearing age than old people; consequently we are recording more births than deaths.

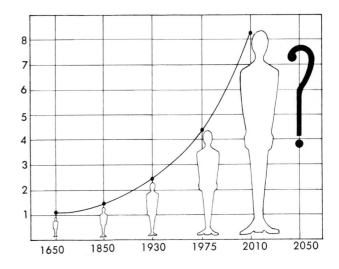

8. More people mean more:
   a. dirty air
   b. fresh water contamination
   c. urban sprawl
   d. loss of wildlife
   e. loss of farmland
   f. traffic congestion
   g. waste disposal problems, etc.

F. Thought Questions for Class Discussions:

1. Will there be enough food, water, and clean air in 2020?
2. Will there be beautiful rivers, forests, and wildlife in 2020?
3. Do you think there is enough space for all people, world-wide?
4. Do we act the same in crowded areas as we do where there is plenty of space?
5. What can we start doing now that will assure our growing population of an adequate food supply in the coming years?

G. Related Ideas for Further Inquiry:

1. Study Activity VI-A-1, "What is the balance of nature?"
2. Study Activity VI-A-2 "What is the 'Triangle of Life'?"
3. Study Activity VI-A-3, "What is 'biological diversity'?"
4. Study other Activities in this Section.

H. Vocabulary Builders—Spelling Words:

1) **population** 2) **explosion** 3) **evidence**
4) **statistics** 5) **graph** 6) **starvation** 7) **double**

I. Thought for Today:

"The glory of young people is their strength; of old people, their experience."

SECTION B: CONSERVATION

Activity

VI B 1

A. Problem: *How Does Running Water Affect Our Soil?*

B. Materials Needed:
1. Large cookie sheet with edges
2. Soil, finely ground
3. Water
4. Pitcher
5. Catch basin

C. Procedure:
1. Discuss with students the importance of rain:
   a. agricultural growth
   b. fills lakes, enlarges rivers, etc.
   c. provides drinking water
2. Cite how rain is formed and discuss the water cycle.
3. Discuss how light rain is valuable.
4. Cite how heavy rains can cause severe damage such as flooding and its consequences.
5. Stress the fact that all rains cause some soil erosion.
6. Have students prepare a sample of how running water causes some soil erosion by having one student build a mound of soil at one end of a slightly raised cookie sheet.
7. Place catch basin in best place to collect water.
8. Have another student fill up the pitcher with water and slowly pour a little water over the top of the mound of soil.

D. Results:
1. The "flowing" water will carry some soil with it where it will collect at the lower end of the cookie sheet.
2. Students will be able to visualize a simple form of soil erosion.

E. Basic Facts and Supplemental Information:
1. Soil erosion is a major problem.
2. Soil erosion occurs as a result of rain, wind, and poor agricultural practices.
3. Monsoons in the Far East bring some of the heaviest rains, cause the greatest flooding, and account for much loss of precious topsoil—topsoil needed for the growth of crops.

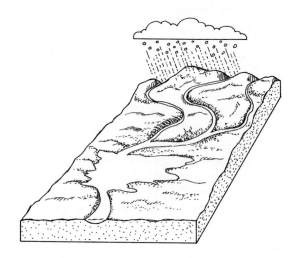

4. Since 1972 the world has lost nearly 500 billion tons of topsoil through erosion, and during this same period of time we added 1.8 billion more mouths to feed.
5. Running water causes gullying.
6. Loosened soil causes landslides; homes have been lost from loosened soil.

F. Thought Questions for Class Discussions:
1. How can we prevent soil erosion?
2. Can topsoil be replenished?
3. What is topsoil?

G. Related Ideas for Further Inquiry:
1. Study conservation procedures in your community.
2. Study the types of soil found in your locality.
3. Study Section VII-C, "Earth's Crust."
4. Study Activity VI-B-2, "How does moving air affect our soil?"
5. Study Activity VI-B-9, "How can we conserve our fresh water?"

H. Vocabulary Builders—Spelling Words:
1) **running**   2) **water**   3) **soil**   4) **erosion**
5) **topsoil**   6) **dirt**   7) **conservation**   8) **gullying**

I. Thought for Today:
"A lot of good soil is lost when children wash their hands."

Activity

A. Problem: *How Does Moving Air Affect Our Soil?*

B. Materials Needed:
1. Electric fan
2. Small flats, approximately 8″ × 8″ of:
   a. grass-covered soil
   b. scattered plants
   c. rocks
   d. gravel
   e. sand
   f. clay soil
   g. humus soil, etc.
   h. fine, loose soil

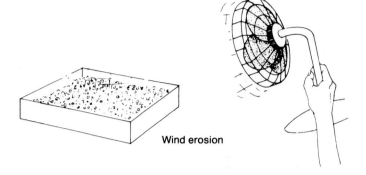

Wind erosion

C. Procedure:
1. Have the class describe what they have seen the wind do to different types of soil.
2. Test each soil by placing the electric fan close by, turning it on, and studying the effects of strong moving air on the soil.

D. Results:
1. The wind will blow away loose soil.
2. The wind will blow away fine soil or sand.
3. The wind will have little effect on planted areas, rocks, or gravel.

E. Basic Facts and Supplemental Information:
1. Severe winds cause a lot of damage to property.
2. Strong winds blow away valuable topsoil.
3. Powerful winds may form gullies.
4. We need soil to grow food.
5. Without soil we would have no grass, plants, or trees.
6. Soil is a complex mixture of:
   a. rocky material
   b. minerals
   c. remains of living things
7. Wind is air in motion; it rarely stops moving.
8. Along the equator, there is an area of low pressure where the trade winds meet. This area is called the "doldrums." There is very little wind, consequently sailing ships are frequently "becalmed" in this area.
9. The strongest winds are about six miles above the Earth. These "jet streams" are only a few hundred miles wide, but their length frequently stretches halfway around the world. They usually travel at about 125 m.p.h. but have been recorded at double this figure.

10. It takes about a thousand years to develop one inch of topsoil.
11. We have lost several inches of topsoil in some of our best farming areas because of poor conservation practices.

F. Thought Questions for Class Discussions:
1. What can a farmer do to keep topsoil from being blown away?
2. Could we survive without our topsoil?
3. What are some other causes of soil erosion?
4. How can we stop soil erosion?

G. Related Ideas for Further Inquiry:
1. Study the soils in your community.
2. Study the conservation practices in your locality to prevent soil erosion.
3. Study Section I-B, "Air."
4. Study Section III-C, "Soils and Germination."
5. Study Section VII-C, "Earth's Crust."
6. Study Activity VI-B-1, "How does running water affect our soil?"
7. Study Activity VI-B-6, "How can we conserve our forests, especially the rain forests?"
8. Study Activity VI-B-9, "How can we conserve our fresh water?"

H. Vocabulary Builders—Spelling Words:
1) **moving** 2) **affect** 3) **electric** 4) **plants**
5) **clay** 6) **rocks** 7) **gravel** 8) **humus**
9) **planted**

I. Thought for Today:
"If you are looking for a helping hand, look at the end of your shirt sleeve."

Activity

A. Problem: *How Can We Conserve Our Wildlife?*

B. Materials Needed:
1. Classroom pets
2. Bird feeders
3. Classroom plants
4. Pictures of:
   a. zoos
   b. wetlands
   c. refuges
   d. local, state, and national parks
5. Media accounts of the problems of wildlife

C. Procedure:
1. Show students the classroom pet(s).
2. Show students a classroom plant.
3. Remove these from the view of students.
4. Ask the students if they would like to have these removed permanently.
5. Tell them this is what is happening to many, many species all over the world. Species are being "removed" permanently for various reasons.
6. Cite these important facts:
   a. Many millions of plant and animal species have become extinct since life began on Earth.
   b. Most of these died out because of natural causes.
   c. In the last three centuries, humans have greatly speeded up the "extinction process" almost 1,000 times by:
      1) excessive hunting and fishing
      2) destroying habitats
      3) draining wetlands
      4) mining
      5) polluting the environment
      6) collecting animals
      7) killing for animal parts for unscientific health reasons and body decorations
7. Discuss the interrelationships of various animals.
8. Discuss the interrelationships of plants and animals.
9. Study various ecosystems.
10. Stress the need to protect all wildlife, plants, and animals.
11. Show pictures of the methods used by people to protect wildlife (zoos, refuges, sanctuaries, etc.)

D. Results:
1. Students will learn that a lot of our wildlife is in danger.
2. Pupils will begin to develop ideas of how they can individually help protect our wildlife.

Panda

E. Basic Facts and Supplemental Information:
1. "Extinct" means that a species has disappeared. None is known to exist.
2. "Endangered" refers to a species that is threatened with extinction.
3. "Threatened" signifies that a species has numbers severely decreased and could be placed on the endangered list.
4. We do not know the exact number of species (plants, animals, etc.) that exist, but estimates vary between 3 and 30 million. Only about 300,000 have been classified.
5. There is no doubt that the numbers are decreasing at faster and faster rates.
6. The primary cause is the human factor— increasing encroachment into the habitats of species.

F. Thought Questions for Class Discussions:
1. How do you think we can slow down the loss of wildlife?
2. Are you in favor of creating more refuges for wildlife?
3. What would happen to us if all other animal life were to become extinct?

G. Related Ideas for Further Inquiry:
1. Study our efforts to stop wildlife extinction of certain species by setting up refuges, breeding, and returning new animals to their old habitats or new ones.
2. Study Part III, "Plants."
3. Study Part IV, "Animals."

H. Vocabulary Builders—Spelling Words:
1) **conserve** 2) **wildlife** 3) **extinction**
4) **endangered** 5) **threatened** 6) **species**

I. Thought for Today:
"Do you know how to tune a piano? tuna salad?"

Activity

A. Problem: *How Can We Conserve Energy (and Money) in Our Homes?*

B. Materials Needed:

Pictures or actual articles that use electricity in our homes:

1. can opener
2. toothbrush
3. frypan
4. toaster
5. fan
6. lamp
7. television set
8. computer
9. dishwasher
10. washing machine
11. air conditioner
12. dryer, etc.

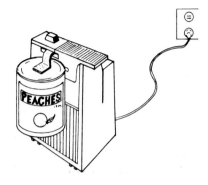

C. Procedure:

1. Discuss how great-grandmother and great-grandfather lived around 1900.
2. Describe how (with no electricity in the home) there were no electric lights, electric appliances, TVs, VCRs, microwave ovens, electronic games, etc.
3. Have students list all the electrical appliances they have in their homes.
4. Have them go over the list and classify them as:
   a. absolutely essential
   b. desirable, but not essential
   c. could do without
5. Have students go over the list one more time and check to see if each item is used for:
   a. convenience—comfort
   b. health—cleanliness
   c. entertainment—recreation
6. Have students go over the list and cite ways that the use of these electric appliances could be reduced.
7. Discuss our sources of power and how every time we use an electrical device we are adding to air pollution through our coal or fuel oil burning power plants or to water and land pollution if we use atomic power plants.

D. Results:

1. Students will learn that our great-grandparents lived without electricity and had cleaner air.
2. Pupils will realize that we have many, many electrical appliances and a lot of pollution.
3. The class will learn that some possible means of reducing our power needs are by:
   a. eliminating or reducing night advertising
   b. reducing our home lights
   c. having all sporting events in the daytime
   d. encouraging thrift
   e. increasing electric rates on a sliding scale
   f. free advertising of the problem

g. reducing our population growth through education and abstinence
h. avoiding or keeping the use of electrical appliances to a minimum

E. Basic Facts and Supplemental Information:

Electricity in the homes can be reduced by cutting down on the use of essential items and eliminating the nonessential items. People hold different views on what is essential and what is not essential in their homes.

F. Thought Questions for Class Discussions:

1. Which is more valuable or important: electric gadgets or clean air?
2. Should power be rationed? or taxed for heavy use?
3. Do you think today's young people would like to "go back" to the days of their great-grandparents in order to have clean air?
4. Would it be possible to return to those times?

G. Related Ideas for Further Inquiry:

1. Have students make specific recommendations on how electricity could be saved in the home such as:
   a. keep thermostat higher in summer, lower in winter
   b. close chimney vents when appropriate
   c. wash clothes in warm water
   d. proper ventilation
   e. close drapes in summer
   f. install or improve insulation
   g. turn out lights when not in use
2. Study Section II-B, "Fire and Heat."
3. Study other Activities in this Section.

H. Vocabulary Builders—Spelling Words:

1) **electricity** 2) **essential** 3) **desirable**
4) **thermostat** 5) **appliances** 6) **conservation**

I. Thought for Today:

"Teaching children to count is not as important as teaching children what counts."

Activity

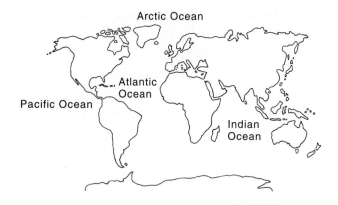

Arctic Ocean

Atlantic
Ocean

Pacific Ocean

Indian
Ocean

A. Problem: *How Can We Conserve Our Oceans?*

B. Materials Needed: (found on beaches)

1. Empty cans
2. Empty bottles
3. Paper goods
4. Empty plastic containers
5. Styrofoam cups
6. Wooden objects
7. Metal objects
8. Miscellaneous debris
9. Also include media reports of ocean contamination

C. Procedure:

1. Have students describe their visits to the beaches, citing the debris they saw.
2. Discuss how our beaches are becoming contaminated.
3. Show the materials collected above.
4. Discuss sewage disposal.
5. Discuss agricultural runoffs.
6. Cite the problems of industrial wastes.
7. Have students discuss ways of protecting our oceans from contamination.

D. Results:

1. Students will realize that our oceans are becoming polluted and that some evidence of this is found on our beaches.
2. Pupils will realize that private citizens, farmers, industrialists, etc. all contribute to ocean pollution.
3. Pupils will learn that the more we pollute the oceans, the greater will be the loss of ocean life, which is a vital part of the food supply for many nations.

E. Basic Facts and Supplemental Information:

1. The oceans comprise 71% of the surface of the Earth.
2. Most of the ocean floor is flat and lies one to three miles below the surface.
3. Attributes of the oceans that affect people are its waves, tides, currents, and temperatures.
4. Coastal zones are vital to life on Earth because most of the fresh oxygen supplies come from phytoplankton, which live along the coasts.
5. If phytoplankton are decimated by pollution and contamination, we are losing a vital need of all living creatures.

6. The four main oceans are Pacific, Atlantic, Indian, and Arctic.
7. There are billions of tons of salt in the oceans.
8. When sea water evaporates, it leaves the salt behind.
9. Ours is the only known planet in our solar system that has oceans. The others are too hot or too cold.
10. Since the Earth is spinning, it makes water in the northern hemisphere flow clockwise and in the southern hemisphere counterclockwise.
11. The oceans have currents because of the Earth's rotation, the winds, and the differences in salt concentration. The heavier salt water moves downward.
12. The ocean currents carry the pollutants we dump in our coastal waters to other areas.

F. Thought Questions for Class Discussions:

1. Should we use the oceans as garbage dumps?
2. Who should control the oceans?
3. Should any nation be allowed to pollute the oceans? or overfish them?

G. Related Ideas for Further Inquiry:

1. Collect public information from the media on ocean pollution.
2. Study ocean life.
3. Study phytoplankton particularly.
4. Study the chemicals found in the ocean.
5. Study Section I-C, "Water."
6. Study Section IV-E, "Water Animals (Fish and Amphibians)."

H. Vocabulary Builders—Spelling Words:

1) **oceans** 2) **cans** 3) **bottles** 4) **plastics**
5) **beaches** 6) **debris** 7) **phytoplankton**

I. Thought for Today:

"The best thing I know of between the United States and Europe is the Atlantic Ocean."

Activity

A. Problem: *How Can We Conserve Our Forests, Especially the Rain Forests?*

B. Materials Needed:
1. Display of wood products such as:
   a. blocks
   b. pencils
   c. wooden toys
   d. toy furniture
2. Pictures of wooden furniture
3. Picture of house under construction

C. Procedure:
1. Ask class what products are made of wood.
2. Ask class how long these wood products usually last.
3. Inquire as to where we get new supplies of wood.
4. Discuss with class:
   a. America burned forests to clear lands, and we have lost three-quarters of our original forests.
   b. Many countries are now burning some of the rain forests to clear the land.
   c. Watersheds hold water.
   d. Trees prevent soil erosion on slopes.
5. Discuss with class the value of trees as a source of our oxygen (supplies about 25%) and saving our trees.
6. Discuss methods of reducing forest fires.
7. Discuss activities that could help preserve our forests:
   a. Smokers need to be extremely careful to put out their cigarettes.
   b. Eliminate fungi and insects that attack the trees.
   c. Reduce the items cited in E-8.
   d. Reduce off-road vehicular travel.

D. Result:
Students will learn that forests are precious and should be conserved.

E. Basic Facts and Supplemental Information:
1. Trash consists of 59% paper (wood product) and 10% of wood itself.
2. It takes 17 trees to make a ton of paper.
3. Much of our packaging is unnecessary.
4. We have to think more of tree rotation (like crop rotation) rather than just destroying without any thought of reforestation.
5. More than half of all animal and plant species live in the tropical rain forests which support life because they are warm and wet.
6. Tropical rain forests are not only in South America but also in Africa, Asia, and Australia.

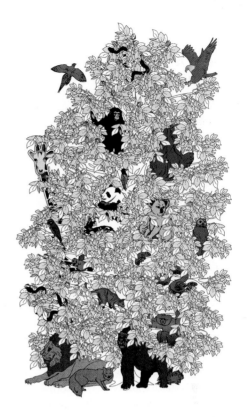

7. Since 1945, more than half of the world's rain forests have been destroyed.
8. The threats to forests stem from:
   a. the need for lumber
   b. the need for more farmlands
   c. the need for more residences
   d. mining operations
   e. oil explorations

F. Thought Questions for Class Discussions:
1. What would we do without lumber?
2. What is meant by "rain forests"?
3. How do forests regulate the amount of water below the surface of the Earth?

G. Related Ideas for Further Inquiry:
1. Study Section II-B, "Fire and Heat."
2. Study Part III, "Plants."
3. Study Activity VI-A-1, "What is the balance of nature?"

H. Vocabulary Builders—Spelling Words:
1) **forest** 2) **rain** 3) **furniture** 4) **burned**
5) **watershed** 6) **conservation**

I. Thought for Today:
"Democracy is a small hard core of common agreement surrounded by a rich variety of individual differences."

Activity

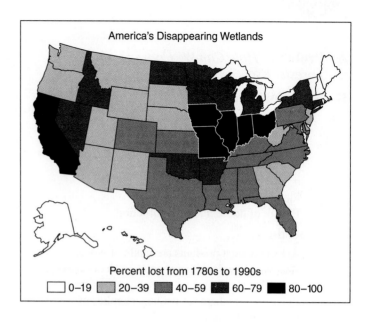

America's Disappearing Wetlands

Percent lost from 1780s to 1990s

☐ 0–19 ▨ 20–39 ▨ 40–59 ▨ 60–79 ■ 80–100

A. Problem: *How Can We Protect Our Wetlands?*

B. Materials Needed:

1. Reference materials on:
   a. swamps
   b. bogs
   c. marshes
   d. estuaries, etc.
2. Two sponges
3. Water
4. Pictures of wetlands
5. Maps of wetlands (if available)
6. Bulletin board
7. Large tray
8. Book (to support tray)
9. Desk or tabletop.

C. Procedure:

1. Define "wetlands."
   Wetlands are lands that are saturated with surface or ground water for all, or a good portion, of the time.
2. Display pictures of wetlands on the bulletin board.
3. With student help set up the tray on desk or tabletop.
4. Place a dry sponge to one side of the tray.
5. Wet second sponge and wring carefully so that it is not dripping, but still wet.
6. Place this sponge next to first sponge.
7. Raise one end of the tray with book.
8. Add equal amounts of water to both sponges.
9. Observe results.
10. Add vital information about wetlands. (See Part E.)
11. To protect our wetlands we must prevent encroachment by human beings.

D. Results:

1. Students will be able to define "wetlands."
2. Pupils will learn the value of wetlands.
3. The wet sponge will absorb water more quickly than the dry sponge.

E. Basic Facts and Supplemental Information:

1. Wetlands form vital ecosystems for plants and animals.
2. One-third of our endangered plants and one-third of our endangered animals are dependent on wetlands.
3. The United States originally had about 220 million acres of wetlands. Today there are only about 100 million acres left.
4. California, Iowa, Indiana, and Missouri have lost over 87% of their wetlands. Connecticut has lost over 50% of its coastal wetlands, and Florida has lost over 50% of its everglades.
5. The values of wetlands are:
   a. provide food for wildlife
   b. provide water for wildlife
   c. help control floods
   d. filter water naturally
   e. homes for wildlife
   f. naturally beautiful
6. Wetlands have been altered or destroyed to build cities, roads, industries, and farms.

F. Thought Questions for Class Discussions:

1. Should wetlands be protected?
2. How important is it to save our wetlands?
3. Should we reclaim some of our wetlands?
4. What policies should we establish in regard to our wetlands?

G. Related Ideas for Further Inquiry:

1. Study any wetlands in or near your community.
2. Study the different kinds of wetlands.
3. Study Activity VI-A-1, "What is the balance of nature?"
4. Study Activity VI-A-3, What is 'biological diversity'?"
5. Study Activity VI-A-9, "Are any animals threatened with extinction?"

H. Vocabulary Builders—Spelling Words:

1) **wetlands** 2) **marshes** 3) **swamps** 4) **bogs**
5) **estuaries** 6) **lagoons** 7) **wildlife**

I. Thought for Today:

"A shallow thinker seldom makes a deep impression."

Activity

A. Problem: *How Can We Conserve Our Natural Resources?*

B. Materials Needed:

1. Models or pictures of tractors, excavators
2. Dioramas of land before and after strip mining
3. Specimens or pictures of our most common natural resources (minerals, chemicals, etc.)

C. Procedure:

1. Describe the problems of food, energy, and recreational needs.
2. Cite the dilemmas we are having and will have over land use. As our population increases, shall our priorities for land use be with residences, nonresident urban uses, farming, or mining? Some of the arguments for farming and mining are cited below:

   a. *Farming:*
      1) Soil, sun, and rain produce food, fiber, and wood to feed, clothe, and shelter us.
      2) The topsoil must produce more grains, vegetables, and fruits to feed an ever-growing population here and abroad.
      3) Our lands produce the hay and greens for our pasture animals.
      4) Our farmlands must produce millions of bales of cotton to help clothe us.
      5) Our water must be kept clean and flowing to protect the animal life forms that help feed us and to quench our thirst.
      6) Our lands must provide an adequate supply of trees for housing and industry.

   b. *Mining:*
      1) More and more people are demanding more and more energy and more and more material goods.
      2) Most minerals lie close to the Earth's surface.
      3) Coal, our largest nonrenewable source of energy, also lies close to the Earth's surface.
      4) We have built bigger and bigger machines to strip the Earth of its precious resources and in so doing have destroyed the trees, flowers, and grasses.

   c. Problem: The lands we use for gathering needed minerals are the same lands that feed, clothe, and shelter us. There is no land to spare.

   d. One of our strip mining diggers stands nearly 200' high, has a boom 310' long and scoops up 325 tons of earth with each scoop.

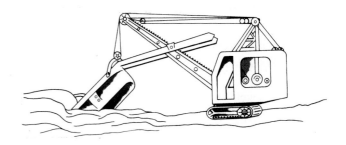

   e. We are losing almost 5,000 acres of topsoil to strip miners every week.

3. Using models and dioramas, show what strip mining does to the earth.

D. Result:

This lesson certainly should stimulate thinking as to what we should do about our natural resources.

E. Basic Facts and Supplemental Information:

1. As of 1999, we have lost over 2.6 million acres of potential agricultural lands to strip miners.
2. Twenty percent of our best agricultural lands have already been lost to cities and highways.

F. Thought Questions for Class Discussions:

1. Is strip mining worth the price we are paying? we will have to pay?
2. How long does it take to produce an inch of topsoil naturally? (1,000 years)
3. Should we insist on costlier, more dangerous types of mining, namely underground?

G. Related Ideas for Further Inquiry:

1. Study Section III-C, "Soils and Germination."
2. Study Section VII-C, "Earth's Crust."
3. Study Activity VI-B-7, "How can we protect our wetlands?"
4. Study other Activities in this Section.

H. Vocabulary Builders—Spelling Words:

1) **strip mining** 2) **survive** 3) **tractors**
4) **excavating** 5) **diorama** 6) **farming**
7) **mining** 8) **natural** 9) **resources**

I. Thought for Today:

"Some get lost in thought because it is such unfamiliar territory."

A. Problem: *How Can We Conserve Our Fresh Water?*

B. Materials Needed:
1. Chalkboard
2. Chalk
3. Class-constructed survey form

C. Procedure:
1. Have class list on the chalkboard all the ways water is used around their homes. Parenthetical figures indicate an estimate of the average amount of gallons and/or gallons per unit of time of water used. The list will probably include:
   a. watering garden (60/hr)
   b. bathtub (25)
   c. showers(s) (5/min)
   d. washing machine (40)
   e. dishwasher (25)
   f. toilet (6)
   g. drinking, cooking (5)
   h. refilling aquaria (if any); watering houseplants (2/week)
2. Have the students make a home survey of the amount of water used during a one-week period.
3. Discuss and describe the sources of water for your community.
4. Study the home survey sheets for ways that water can be conserved.
5. If a water bill can be obtained, determine approximately how much money could be saved by conserving water.

D. Results:
1. Pupils will learn that conservation pays.
2. Parents, too, will become more conservation-minded.

E. Basic Facts and Supplemental Information:
1. As our population grows, more water will be needed.
2. As business and industry grow, more water will be needed.
3. There is no source of fresh water other than rain. Rivers and wells get their water from rain.
4. We can get fresh water from the ocean (desalinization) but at the present time it is very costly.
5. Our wells and aquifers are being drained slowly. Contamination in them is increasing, some near the danger zone.

F. Thought Questions for Class Discussions:
1. Will increasing the price of water solve our water shortage problem?
2. Will cloud seeding increase our water supply?
3. Do you think we will ever have to ration water for everybody?
4. Where does your community get its fresh water?

G. Related Ideas for Further Inquiry:
1. If your community had its water supply cut in half, how would you budget your supply?
2. Study Section I-C, "Water."
3. Study Section VII-C, "Earth's Crust."
4. Study Section VII-E, "Weather."
5. Study other Activities in this Section.

H. Vocabulary Builders—Spelling Words:
1) **conserve** 2) **water** 3) **garden** 4) **bathtub**
5) **dishwasher** 6) **showers** 7) **sprinkling**
8) **drinking** 9) **aquifer** 10) **cooking**

I. Thought for Today:
"Teachers affect eternity; they can never tell where their influence stops."

A. Problem: *What Is Recycling? Salvaging?*

B. Materials Needed:

1. Florence flask
2. Single-hole stopper
3. Stand and clamps
4. Heating device
5. Pyrex jar
6. Pyrex tubing
7. Piece of toweling
8. Dirt
9. Leaves
10. Salt
11. Food dye
12. Gloves
13. Wet rag
14. Water

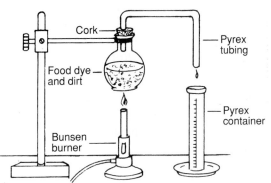

This symbol tells you that the product can be recycled. It does not mean that the product is made of recycled materials.

This symbol tells you that the product has been made with a minimum of 50% recycled materials.

C. Procedure:

1. Discuss with class the necessity of recycling and salvaging. (If we used things only once, we would soon run out of things to use.)
2. Discuss biodegradable (naturally decomposable) items.
3. Discuss how we now recycle and salvage some materials that we use.
4. Place some dirt, leaves, salt, and colored water in a Florence flask.
5. Place glass tubing connections in rubber stopper and fit on flask. (Tubing can be bent by gently warming over heating device and carefully rotating and bending as tubing gets hotter. Use gloves as a safety precaution against burns.)
6. Heat contents with Bunsen burner, hot plate, or Sterno.
7. Place wet rag around tubing to cool liquid.
8. Clear water will come out the condensed side.
9. Have class name other items that have been recycled or salvaged; paper, cars, metals, and glass.

D. Results:

1. The water has been recycled.
2. Pure water has been salvaged.
3. Students will learn about using materials over and over again.

E. Basic Facts and Supplemental Information:

1. Many discarded items made of paper, glass, metals, tires, plastic, cloth, etc. can be returned to industry for new products or energy. Recycling of this sort requires a major focus involving careful planning.
2. Even nonusable garbage can be used for landfills.
3. Some items can be burned, and if complete burning takes place the only products will be water and carbon dioxide. Incomplete burning will produce carbon monoxide, smoke, sulphur dioxide, nitrous oxides, etc.
4. Our landfills are rapidly filling up; most large cities have a shortage of landfill areas.

5. Goodwill Industries of America has been recycling discarded furniture, clothing, and household items for over 70 years.

F. Thought Questions for Class Discussions:

1. Should we worry about salvaging and recycling, or should we let the next generation worry about itself?
2. Are some solid items biodegradable? (It takes glass about 100 years, aluminum about 1,000 years, and plastics many thousands of years to disintegrate.)
3. Should we separate our garbage into salvageable and nonsalvageable items?

G. Related Ideas for Further Inquiry:

1. Make a collection of items that could be recycled. *Look for symbols on packaging.* (See drawings.)
2. Make two lists of disposable items: one that is recyclable and one that is biodegradable.
3. List items that would make good compost (plant enrichment).
4. Students might want to develop a compost site for a school garden. A school gardener can make some good suggestions.
5. Study other Activities in this Section.

H. Vocabulary Builders—Spelling Words:

1) **recycle** 2) **salvage** 3) **compost** 4) **reusable**
5) **biodegradable** 6) **landfills** 7) **pyrex**

I. Thought for Today:

"Nothing is more confusing than people who give good advice but set bad examples."

SECTION C: POLLUTION

Activity

VI C 1

A. Problem: *What Are the Main Pollution Problems?*

B. Materials Needed:

1. Newspaper accounts of pollution
2. Pictures of air, water, and land pollution
3. Glass of water
4. Clean, empty jar
5. Clear jar filled with dirt
6. Clear jars filled with various debris, wastes, garbage, etc.
7. Model car
8. Empty cans of sprays (paints, pesticides, etc.)
9. Models or pictures of farm animals
10. Bulletin board
11. Science table or desk, etc.

C. Procedure:

1. Display materials on desk or science table.
2. Mount pictures on the bulletin board.
3. Ask students if they know what these articles have in common.
4. Review other Activities in this section with class.
5. Let the students handle the articles during the discussions.
6. Discuss some of the main pollution disasters:
   a. mercury poisoning in a bay off Japan (brain and nerve damage)
   b. herbicide leaks in Italy (poisoned people, killed domestic animals)
   c. chemical leak in India (killed 2,500 people)
   d. nuclear reactor accident in Russia (radiation poisoning)
   e. oil spills (many) (pollutes beaches, kills wildlife)
   f. sewage contamination
   g. acid rain
   h. ozone layer destruction, etc.
7. Discuss ways that pollution can be prevented or minimized.

D. Results:

1. Students will learn that there are many pollution problems and ALL of them are caused by people.
2. Pupils will begin to think about methods that could prevent or reduce pollution.

Fire, Friend or Foe?

E. Basic Facts and Supplemental Information:

1. The Earth is billions of years old.
2. People have been on our planet for only thousands of years.
3. In this comparatively short time, people have ransacked the Earth for food, energy, shelter, and material "benefits" with little regard for present or future resources.
4. The world's population is increasing faster than we can supply food and other resources for them.
5. We must develop a philosophy of "sustainability."
6. We must think in terms of renewable resources.
7. We must accept recycling, salvaging, reusing as a way of life.

F. Thought Questions for Class Discussions:

1. Is the Earth a "spaceship"?
2. Is there anywhere in space where we can pick up new resources?
3. What is "sustainability"?
4. Have we been good custodians of our planet Earth?

G. Related Ideas for Further Inquiry:

1. Study the nonrewable resources of our planet.
2. Study the renewable resources of our planet.
3. Interview community personnel who are involved with resources of our planet.

H. Vocabulary Builders—Spelling Words:

1) **pollution**   2) **problems**   3) **nonrenewable**
4) **sustainability**   5) **hazards**   6) **custodians**

I. Thought for Today:

"Soil erosion almost always occurs when children wash their hands."

Activity

A. Problem: *What Are Nonrenewable Resources? Renewable Resources?*

B. Materials Needed:
1. For "nonrenewable":
   a. Newspaper accounts of pollution
   b. Pictures of air, water, and land pollution
   c. Oil can, empty
   d. Piece of coal
   e. Mineral samples (ores)
2. For "renewable":
   a. Glass of water
   b. Clear, empty jar
   c. Clear jar filled with dirt
   d. Picture of the sun
   e. Picture or model of dam
3. Bulletin board
4. Science table or desk

C. Procedure:
1. Display materials on science table or desk.
2. Mount pictures on the bulletin board.
3. Ask students if they know what these have in common.
4. Have pupils define "nonrenewable" and "renewable."
5. Have a discussion about which of our resources are renewable and which are nonrenewable.
6. Let the students handle the materials during the discussion.
7. Discuss some of the problems that will occur as our nonrenewable resources are used up.
8. Discuss the consequences of these.
9. Review Activities VI-A-4 and VI-A-5.

D. Results:
1. Students will learn that some of our resources are being "used up."
2. Students will realize that everyone needs to do their part as individuals to conserve nonrenewable resources. They will realize that continued misuse and waste will lead to dire consequences for everyone.

E. Basic Facts and Supplemental Information:
1. The world's population is now about 6 billion.
2. It is expected to double in about 45 years.
3. We will then have to provide twice as many resources as we now have.
4. Food and energy are going to be the two main concerns.

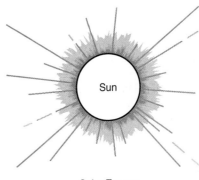

Solar Energy

5. We may be able to solve our energy problem with solar energy.
6. Our food problem will not be an easy one to solve; it is something to work and plan for before shortages become a universal reality.

F. Thought Questions for Class Discussions:
1. How can we double our food supply?
2. Should we continue to use up our fossil fuels—our largest nonrenewable energy resource?
3. Should we continue to cut down our trees for energy?
4. What plans should we be making now for future generations?

G. Related Ideas for Further Inquiry:
1. Have the class create a plan (some plans) for "sustainability"—living within the availability of present resources without diminishing current supplies.
2. Interview community personnel who are involved with any of our present day resources.
3. Study Activity VI-C-1, "What are the main pollution problems?"
4. Study Activity VI-C-8, "What is happening to our topsoil?"
5. Study Activity VI-C-9, "How does pollution affect food chains and food webs ?"

H. Vocabulary Builders—Spelling Words:
1) **renewable** 2) **nonrenewable** 3) **sustainability**
4) **energy** 5) **planning** 6) **planet**

I. Thought for Today:
"You can't climb the ladder of success with both hands in your pockets."

Activity

A. Problem: *How Do Automobiles Pollute the Air?*

B. Materials:

1. Model cars
2. Pictures of suburbia
3. Pictures of gravestones
4. Chart paper or chalkboard

C. Procedure:

1. Discuss the ways automobiles contribute to the destruction and pollution of our environment: exhaust fumes, abandoned cars, cutting down trees to build new highways, etc.
2. Make a list of these on chart paper or a chalkboard.
3. Discuss what life would be like without automobiles.
4. Compare lifestyles of automobile and horse-and-buggy eras.
5. Have students list the advantages and disadvantages of automobiles.

D. Results:

1. Students will learn that automobiles pollute the environment in many ways.
2. Students will learn that automobiles provide advantages and disadvantages.

E. Basic Facts and Supplemental Information:

1. About 75% of outside noise is made by automobiles.
2. About 80% of the air pollution comes from automobiles burning gasoline and oil.
3. Highways and streets destroy natural land.
4. Cars uproot residents by contributing to urban sprawl.
5. Heavy automobile traffic clogs streets, highways, and freeways.
6. Automobiles in the U.S. kill thousands of people (about 50,000 per year), and they injure millions every year (about 2 to 3 million).
7. Millions of automobiles are also abandoned and clutter up the countryside.
8. Automobile exhausts include:
   a. carbon monoxide
   b. nitrogen oxides
   c. hydrocarbons
   d. detergents
   e. antioxidants
   f. lubricants
   g. metal deactivators

h. deposit modifiers
   i. anti-rust agents
   j. anti-icing agents
9. The horsepower of automobiles ranges from about 100 to 300. Horsepower is a unit of energy that is needed to lift 550 pounds a distance of one foot in one second.
10. There are over 200 million cars, trucks, and buses in the United States adding to our pollution problems.

F. Thought Questions for Class Discussions:

1. Is the automobile worth the problems it has caused?
2. Have you ever seen an abandoned car? What should be done about this problem?
3. How effective have smog control devices been on automobiles?
4. Would you be willing to give up the automobile if it would guarantee clean air?

G. Related Ideas for Further Inquiry:

1. Study booklets and handouts from the state automobile agency or local motor clubs.
2. Have the students answer some of the questions on the state drivers' license test (speed, smog checks, etc.).
3. Interview automobile mechanics regarding automobile pollution.
4. Study Section II-E, "Simple Machines."
5. Study Activity VI-C-4, "How are our homes adding to the pollution problems?"
6. Study Activity VI-C-5, "What is global warming (the "Greenhouse Effect")?"
7. Study Activity VI-C-9, "How does pollution affect food chains and food webs?"
8. Study Section V-D, "Personal Health."

H. Vocabulary Builders—Spelling Words:

1) **automobiles** 2) **pollute** 3) **ecology**
4) **highways** 5) **exhausts** 6) **smog** 7) **urban**
8) **abandoned** 9) **gasoline** 10) **lubricants**

I. Thought for Today:

"Automobiles continue to be driven at two speeds— lawful and awful."

A. Problem: *How Are Our Homes Adding to the Pollution Problems?*

B. Materials Needed:

Pictures of:

1. Gas, electric, or oil furnace
2. Uncovered garbage can
3. Stereo
4. TVs and VCRs
5. Gas or electric stove
6. Electric appliances
7. Fireplace
8. Leaf blower

C. Procedure:

1. Discuss the different kinds of pollution found in and around the home:
   - a. noise
   - b. garbage
   - c. sprays
   - d. insecticides
   - e. motor oil
   - f. gasoline
2. Discuss some means of reducing wastes and pollution:
   - a. recycling
   - b. reusing
   - c. conserve fuels where possible
   - d. keep home, yard, and garage clean
3. Have students develop a specific list of home practices they might do in order to reduce home pollution. See "Basic Facts and Supplemental Information" for possible items.

D. Results:

1. Students will learn about wastes and pollution and some methods to reduce them.
2. Students will realize that pollution made in one home spreads to other areas directly and indirectly. (Electrical conveniences in homes cause air pollution everywhere. Sewage affects others in cost of treatment or pollution of waters and land.)

E. Basic Facts and Supplemental Information:

Suggestions to promote good ecology at home:

1. Use only white paper towels, tissue, and napkins. (Dyes pollute.)
2. Reuse shopping bags.
3. Use a lunch box instead of a paper bag.
4. Reduce use of electricity during peak hours.
5. Do not waste water.
6. Take newspapers, aluminum cans, glass, and recyclable plastics to recycling center, or separate for pick-up if this is done in your neighborhood.

7. Compost or bury garbage.
8. Encourage drivers in your home to drive less or car pool.
9. Walk or bicycle when convenient and safe.
10. Don't buy products or packaging that will eventually pollute the air (combustibles, sprays, etc.).
11. Protect wildlife.
12. Take shorter showers instead of baths.
13. Use a low-phosphate or phosphate-free detergent.
14. Reduce air conditioner use in summer and furnace use in winter.
15. Use recyclable plastics. (Some plastics are not biodegradable and worse, they are made from oil.)
16. Avoid styrofoam products.
17. Plant a tree.

F. Thought Questions for Class Discussions:

1. Can you think of any other things to do at home that will help our environment and help avoid pollution?
2. Do you think any of the damage done by pollution can be corrected? What and how?
3. Do you think it is time that we started a major program to reduce pollution everywhere?

G. Related Ideas for Further Inquiry:

1. Study Section VI-D, "Pollution Solutions."
2. Study Section II-G, "Current Electricity."
3. Study Section VI-B, "Conservation."
4. Make a home survey of "Pollution" activities.
5. Study other Activities in this Section

H. Vocabulary Builders—Spelling Words:

1) **home** 2) **furnace** 3) **garbage** 4) **electric**
5) **noise** 6) **wastes** 7) **sewage** 8) **plastics**

I. Thought for Today:

"If you really want to know what an enormous job it is to clean up the environment, start cleaning out your garage."

Activity

VI **C** 5

A. Problem: *What Is Global Warming (the "Greenhouse Effect")?*

B. Materials Needed:
1. Flannel board
2. Large orange, flannel, semicircle
3. Smaller, dark-color, flannel circle
4. Tiny circles of flannel (any color)
5. Many thin white or orange flannel strips

C. Procedure:
1. Place large semicircle at top of flannel board. This is the sun.
2. Place the smaller circle at the bottom of flannel board. This is the Earth.
3. Place tiny circles at random between the "Sun" and "Earth." These are "air pollutants." Air pollutants consist of particulate matter, carbon dioxide gas, and other gases.
4. Place thin strips of flannel as shown in sketch. These are rays of the sun.
5. Discuss what a greenhouse is.
6. Discuss how the air is full of particles such as:
   a. smoke
   b. soot
   c. industrial gases
   d. automobile exhausts
   e. aerosprays
   f. salt particles
   g. ashes, etc.
7. Using the flannel board, show how the sun's rays strike the Earth, bounce back to hit the particles, and bounce back to the Earth again.
8. Explain that this "double warming" raises the temperature of the Earth's surface. This is called the "Greenhouse Effect."
9. Also tell the class that some of the rays that are reflected back from the Earth to the air miss the particles and return to space.

D. Result:
Students will learn by visualization a very difficult concept, the "Greenhouse Effect."

E. Basic Facts and Supplemental Information:
1. If the Greenhouse Effect was the only additional factor affecting the Earth's atmospheric temperature, our Earth would gradually warm up and cause some or all of the polar caps to melt.
2. If the polar caps melt, this would increase the water level all over the Earth up to 30 feet,

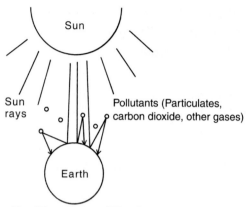

The "Greenhouse Effect"

flooding many of our coastal cities and low elevation lands. The latest predictions are that the ocean water levels will rise about ten feet (three meters) in the next 100 years if the current trend continues.
3. Global warming is caused by people producing too much carbon dioxide and other pollutant gases in many ways.
4. These gases act as a blanket and retain the heat that would normally escape into the atmosphere from doing so.
5. This blanket permits the sun's short wave radiation to pass through, but reflects the Earth's long-range heat radiation that tries to escape.
6. When we burn oil, coal, or wood we release a lot of carbon dioxide into the atmosphere.

F. Thought Questions for Class Discussions:
1. Would this effect decrease the Earth's land area?
2. What would this do to our present harbors?
3. How would this affect people who live or work along the coast?

G. Related Ideas for Further Inquiry:
1. Study Section VII-C, "Earth's Crust."
2. Study Section VII-E, "Weather."
3. Study other Activities in this Section.

H. Vocabulary Builders—Spelling Words:
1) **Greenhouse Effect**   2) **particles**   3) **rays**
4) **pollutants**   5) **global**   6) **warming**

I. Thought for Today:
"He's the kind of a person who adds more heat than light to a discussion."

Activity

A. Problem: *Are Our Lakes and Rivers Becoming Polluted?*

B. Materials Needed:

Articles on fresh-water pollution found in:

1. Magazines
2. Newspapers
3. Library books
4. Pictures of lakes
5. Pictures of rivers

C. Procedure:

1. Discuss the beauty of our lakes and rivers.
2. Ask students if they know of any lakes or rivers in the area.
3. If so, inquire as to what condition they are in. clean? polluted?
4. If there are some nearby water areas, have some students visit them and report to the class what they have seen.

D. Results:

Students will learn that our lakes and rivers are being polluted by:

1. sewage
2. garbage
3. paper
4. plastics
5. cans
6. oil and gasoline
7. chemicals
8. junk

E. Basic Facts and Supplemental Information:

1. The larger the lake, the more the pollution.
2. Four out of five of our Great Lakes are greatly polluted. Some headway is being made by the strict enforcement of laws by the United States and Canada reducing the amounts of pollutants dumped into the Great Lakes by private industries and local city governments.
3. Our inland waters are still being polluted by sewage, phosphates, pesticides, soils, and other toxic materials.
4. The Environmental Protection Agency ranks the following waterways that have shorelines that exceed government standards of pollution in terms of mileage by the following percentages:

Tampa Bay	66%
Cuyahoga River (Ohio)	58%
Monongahela River (Pa., W.Va.)	55%
Savannah River	49%
Ohio River	46%
Lake Ontario	46%
Lake Erie, western shore	45%
Mobile Bay	43%
Niagara River	40%
Lower Hudson River	36%
Green River (Wyo.)	33%
Lower Colorado River	31%
Mohawk River (N.Y.)	30%
Cumberland River (Tenn., Ky.)	27%
Lower Missouri River	27%
Narragansett Bay	26%
Tennessee River	23%
Upper Mississippi River (Rock Island to Cairo, Ill.)	23%
Illinois River	21%

Source: U.S. News and World Report

F. Thought Questions for Class Discussions:

1. What would happen if we could not use our fresh waters?
2. If you had the authority, what would you do to clean up the fresh waters?
3. Whose responsibility is it to clean up our fresh waters?
4. Estuaries are also in deep trouble because these areas are where rivers and streams meet the oceans.
5. The longer the river, the more pollution it picks up.

G. Related Ideas for Further Inquiry:

1. Study Section I-C, "Water."
2. Study Activities VI-C-1 and VI-C-9.
3. Study other Activities in this Section.
4. Study Section VII-C, "Earth's Crust."

H. Vocabulary Builders—Spelling Words:

1) **lakes** 2) **rivers** 3) **estuary** 4) **sewage**
5) **chemicals** 6) **plastics** 7) **trash** 8) **discards**

I. Thought for Today:

"The politician's promises of yesterday are the taxes of today."

Activity

A. Problem: *How Safe Is Our Drinking Water?*

B. Materials Needed:
1. Glass of clear water
2. Glass of dirty (impure) water

C. Procedure:
1. Allow class to examine the two glasses of water.
2. Ask the students how they would feel about drinking from one or both glasses. Do not let anyone drink from the impure water.
3. Discuss with class what we are doing to our drinking water:
   a. pouring harmful chemicals into the water
   b. dumping sewage into some of our waters
4. Study newspaper and magazine reports on our drinking water. (Some are very shocking.)

D. Result:
Students will learn that about 50% of our drinking water already is or is very close to being considered unsafe for drinking.

E. Basic Facts and Supplemental Information:
1. Dirty (impure) water can carry many water-borne diseases such as typhoid, dysentery, and cholera.
2. In the last 10 years, there have been 125 outbreaks of disease from polluted drinking water.
3. Each year there are more than 500 new chemical pollutants developed, and many of these end up in our drinking water.
4. Drinking water directly from some rivers and streams is dangerous because they usually have dangerous numbers of microorganisms in them.
5. Sources of fresh water supplies include:
   a. aquifers—deep underground water supplies
   b. wells
   c. reservoirs
   d. rivers and streams
   e. lakes and ponds
6. The average American home uses about 107,000 gallons (480,000 liters) of water every year. This is miniscule compared to the demands of industry and farming.
7. Water is the most common chemical compound on Earth.
8. More substances will dissolve in water than in any other liquid.
9. Only 2.8% of the Earth's water is fresh, and of that small proportion only 6% is liquid, available for drinking; 90% is contained in the polar icecaps, and the remainder in water vapor in the atmosphere.

10. Ninety-eight percent of the Earth's liquid fresh water is underground.
11. The amount of water on the Earth has remained the same for about the last 5 billion years.

F. Thought Questions for Class Discussions:
1. Do you think we should have some federal standards for drinking water?
2. Do you know how safe water is in your community?
3. Is well water being polluted by underground pollutants?

G. Related Ideas for Further Inquiry:
1. Study "aquifers."
2. Study "eutrophication."
3. Interview personnel from your local community water supplier.
4. Study: Part I-C, "Water."
5. Study: Part V-E, "Public Health."
6. Study other Activities in this Section.

H. Vocabulary Builders—Spelling Words:
1) **water**   2) **drinking**   3) **harmful**   4) **chemicals**
5) **typhoid**   6) **dysentery**   7) **cholera**

I. Thought for Today:
"We may never succeed in curing poverty, but with prices and taxes the way they are, we're sure going to cure wealth."

Activity

A. Problem: *What Is Happening to Our Topsoil?*

B. Materials Needed:
1. Tray (with raised edges) full of soft dirt
2. Water
3. Electric fan
4. Model tractor
5. Model truck
6. Reference books on lands and soils
7. Small cans of fruits
8. Small cans of vegetables
9. Desk or table
10. Old book (to raise tray)

C. Procedure:
1. Discuss the importance of topsoil for growing our food or raising farm animals for food.
2. Set the tray on the desk or table.
3. Raise the tray slightly at one end with the book.
4. Aim the fan over the tray so that a little dirt dust will appear and blow away. Tell the class that this is what happens on windy days or when the farmland is cultivated with heavy farm equipment.
5. Pour a little water on the raised end of the tray. Tell class this is what happens in heavy rains when the farmland is not contoured to prevent runoff.
6. Cite some of the statistics mentioned in "Basic Facts and Supplemental Information."
7. Ask the students what might be done to slow down or prevent future soil erosion.

D. Results:
1. Students will realize that we are losing some of our precious topsoil.
2. Wind and water (rains and floods) are the two main physical causes of topsoil losses.

E. Basic Facts and Supplemental Information:
1. It takes about 1,000 years for nature to make one good inch of topsoil.
2. Originally topsoil is rich in organic materials, but frequently minerals are taken out by groundwater.
3. The subsoil, the layer immediately below the topsoil, is less rich in organic materials but far richer in minerals.
4. Soil is a complex mixture of small rocky materials, dissolved and redeposited minerals, and the remains of plant and animal life.
5. The main types of soil are:
   a. humus　　　　d. clay
   b. loam　　　　 e. sand
   c. peat　　　　 f. silt

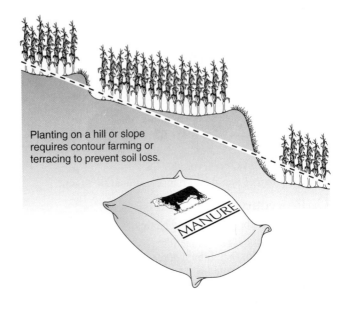

Planting on a hill or slope requires contour farming or terracing to prevent soil loss.

MANURE

6. Soil is eroded by:
   a. slanted terrains
   b. weathering
   c. flooding
   d. poor agricultural practices

F. Thought Questions for Class Discussions:
1. Why do farmers enrich topsoil?
2. Recent statistics show that we are slowly losing our topsoil. What could we do to reverse this trend?
3. Does the loss of some of our forest areas affect topsoil?

G. Related Ideas for Further Inquiry:
1. Interview some local farmers to find out their concerns about topsoil.
2. Collect news reports on topsoil, foods, hungry and starving people.
3. Make a survey of the soil types found in your community.
4. Contact the Soil Conservation Service for current data and problems.
5. Study Activity VI-C-9, "How does pollution affect food chains and food webs ?"

H. Vocabulary Builders—Spelling Words:
1) **topsoil**　2) **humus**　3) **loam**　4) **clay**
5) **peat**　6) **cultivate**　7) **enrich**

I. Thought for Today:
"What this country needs is dirtier hands and cleaner minds."

A. Problem: *How Does Pollution Affect Food Chains and Food Webs?*

B. Materials Needed:

Pictures or models of:

1. Plants
2. Herbivores (plant-eating animals)
3. First-level carnivore (meat-eating animals)
4. Second-level carnivore (larger carnivores that eat first-level carnivores)
5. Flannel board and flannel cutouts (optional)

C. Procedure:

1. Describe several food chains:
   a. carrot, rabbit, people
   b. kelp, fish, tuna, people
   c. grass, cow, people
   d. kelp, small fish, large fish, people
2. Discuss ways pollution affects each of these:
   a. grass—harmed by air pollutants
   b. animals—harmed by insecticides
   c. people—harmed by increased irritants from all sources
3. If desired, these processes can be effectively shown on a flannel board adding one step in the food chain at a time.
4. Food webs can also be explained in a similar way except that instead of a straight-line, chain pattern, a circular pattern can be shown with several alternative food sources for each higher-level organism.

D. Results:

1. Students will learn about food chains and food webs.
2. Students will learn that some poisons become more concentrated as they move up the food chain, and the more concentrated they are, the more damaging they are to the organisms involved. Poisoning organisms destroys the natural food chains and food webs.
3. Students will learn that pollution anywhere affects our food supply.

E. Basic Facts and Supplemental Information:

1. Poisons build up in organisms.
2. Poisons tend to stay in the organism that eats them.
3. For example, if a phytoplankton picks up one unit of mercury (a poison) it will have one unit of mercury in its body.
4. If a small fish eats 1,000 phytoplankton, it will acquire 1,000 units of mercury.

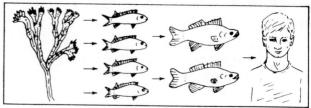
A food chain

5. If a large fish eats 50 small fish, it will acquire 50 times 1,000 or 50,000 units of mercury.
6. If a large mammal or a person eats two large fish, then 2 times 50,000 or 100,000 units of mercury will be ingested.
7. Large mammals and people can become very seriously ill because of this buildup of mercury.
8. Japanese individuals who ate a lot of fish that were contaminated developed very deformed bodies—a symptom of mercury poisoning.
9. Other toxic materials act in a similar fashion.
10. Phytoplankton are important because they supply us with about 75% of our oxygen supply.

F. Thought Questions for Class Discussions:

1. How can people avoid poisoning themselves (regarding pollution)?
2. Do you think people should go back to living like they did 100 years ago? What would be the advantages? the disadvantages?
3. What is the difference between a food chain and a food web?

G. Related Ideas for Further Inquiry:

1. Study Section IV-E "Water Animals (Fish and Amphibians)."
2. Study Section IV-G, "Mammals."
3. Study Section V-C, "Nutrition."
4. Study Activity VI-A-3, "What is 'biological diversity'?"
5. Study Activity VI-C-1, "What are the main pollution problems?"
6. Study Activity VI-C-2, "What are nonrenewable resources? renewable resources?"

H. Vocabulary Builders—Spelling Words:

1) **plants**   2) **herbivores**   3) **carnivores**
4) **insecticides**   5) **mercury**   6) **phytoplankton**

I. Thought for Today:

"A little learning is a dangerous thing—just ask any kid who comes home with a bad report card."

A. Problem: *What Should We Do with Our Wastes?*

B. Materials Needed:

1. Trash collected around school stored in quart jars
2. Quart jars filled with other typical wastes that would be discarded in homes, businesses, industries, and farms

C. Procedure:

1. Have students collect sample wastes around school and place each sample in quart jar for easy viewing.
2. Bring in other sample discards from business, industry, farms, and homes.
3. Discuss the source of each "waste" and why it was discarded.
4. Cite the present means of disposing of our wastes (garbage, sewage, and farm and business wastes).
5. Discuss landfills and the problems we face as they fill up.

D. Results:

1. Students will expand their concept of "wastes."
2. Students will realize that waste disposal is now and will become a greater problem as current landfills are filled.

E. Basic Facts and Supplemental Information:

1. All living organisms produce waste products.
2. All living organisms' natural wastes are recycled by the ecosphere.
3. Living organisms called decomposers eat dead and decaying material so that it can be used again and again. This is natural recycling.
4. Humans produce unnatural wastes that are not naturally recyclable.
5. Many waste products are not biodegradable: tin, glass, plastic, etc.
6. We have been dumping most of our solid wastes in landfills.
7. The average person discards about 2,000 pounds of garbage and other waste products every year.
8. Each year about 110 tons of sulphur dioxide is released into the atmosphere. This gas is one of the main gases causing acid rain.
9. Automobiles spew millions of tons of exhaust into our atmosphere. These include deadly carbon monoxide and nitrogen oxide which contribute to acid rain.
10. We are "hiding" our wastes in the air, in the waters, and on and under surface land.
11. Landfills are controlled land depressions where waste materials and garbage are dumped, compacted, and covered.
12. The problem is that we are running out of land space to create new, needed landfills.

F. Thought Questions for Class Discussions:

1. Would you like a landfill in your community?
2. What action should we take now for future wastes? reduction? elimination? new sites?
3. What are "toxic wastes"?

G. Related Ideas for Further Inquiry:

1. Study how your community disposes of its wastes.
2. Do some research into other methods of disposing of our regular and toxic wastes.
3. Study Activity VI-C-1, "What are the main pollution problems?"
4. Study Activity VI-C-2, "What are nonrenewable resources? renewable resources?"

H. Vocabulary Builders—Spelling Words:

1) **wastes**   2) **hazardous**   3) **toxic**
4) **landfills**   5) **disposal**   6) **refuse**

I. Thought for Today:

"Fifty years ago the only water pollution people knew about was the Saturday night bath."

Activity

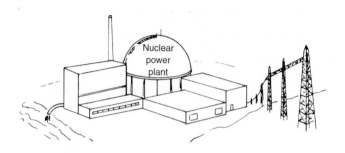

A. Problem: *Are There Hazards in Using Nuclear Energy?*

B. Materials Needed:
1. Pictures of regular steam-generating plants and atomic power plants
2. Sketches of generating systems of both (if available)

C. Procedure:
1. Discuss the need for power and electricity:
   a. more people
   b. more labor-saving devices
2. Briefly describe the steps in developing electricity from a steam plant.
   a. Coal is burned.
   b. Heat changes water into steam.
   c. Steam turns generators.
   d. Generators create electricity.
   e. Electricity is sent to homes, schools, factories, etc.
3. Briefly describe the steps in developing electricity from an atomic power plant:
   a. Atoms are split, creating heat.
   b. Heat changes water into steam.
   c. The rest of the steps are identical to those above.
4. Discuss the waste products of each:
   a. Fossil fuels, especially coal, pollute the air.
   b. Atomic power residues make water warmer and slightly radioactive.
   c. Atomic furnaces produce wastes which stay radioactive for tens of thousands of years.
   d. The problem is where to put these wastes.
   e. Many nuclear power plants have had major disasters including radiation leaks.
5. Discuss the pros and cons of coal-burning power plants and nuclear power plants.

D. Result:
Students will be better able to make comparisons between nuclear and non-nuclear power plants.

E. Basic Facts and Supplemental Information:
1. Most people come to the conclusion that atomic power plants are far more ecologically sound than coal-burning plants.
2. One argument for nuclear power plants is that it stops strip mining of our lands.
3. Many people are concerned about the possibility of nuclear accidents. The Three Mile Island Nuclear Plant in Pennsylvania has been our worst accident to date. The accident spewed radioactive gas and steam into the atmosphere, and there was great concern that a nuclear meltdown would occur.
4. The Soviet Union had a nuclear power plant mishap in Chernobyl in 1986 which sent radiation across Europe, but they reported only 31 deaths in the Soviet Union. There have been many other effects from this such as large increases in cancer rates of people in the affected areas.
5. It should also be noted that the chance for a nuclear explosion to take place is very, very remote as the amount of materials needed for a nuclear explosion approximates about 95% of fissionable materials, and the nuclear power plants are working at about a 5% level.
6. There are now about 250 nuclear power plants scattered throughout the world.

F. Thought Questions for Class Discussions:
1. If you had to develop more electricity for your country, which method would you employ?
2. Are there ways to create electricity other than fossil fuels or nuclear energy?
3. Should we stop producing nuclear power until we can safely dispose of its wastes?

G. Related Ideas for Further Inquiry:
1. Study Activity I-A-2. "What are atoms? molecules?"
2. Study Section II-G, "Current Electricity."
3. Study other Activities in this Section.

H. Vocabulary Builders—Spelling Words:
1) **nuclear** 2) **power** 3) **generating** 4) **atomic**
5) **labor-saving** 6) **wastes** 7) **accidents**

I. Thought for Today:
"If you started counting in the year one and counted until this moment, you could not have counted enough atoms to cover a pinhead."

Activity

A. Problem: *What Is the Ozone Problem?*

B. Materials Needed:

On ozone:

1. Books
2. Pamphlets
3. Pictures
4. Charts
5. Multisensory aids
6. Newspaper articles

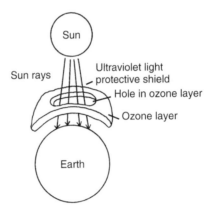

C. Procedure:

1. Describe what ozone is. (A form of oxygen which has three atoms to a molecule while regular oxygen has two.)
2. Tell the class about the ozone layer. It is a layer, a shield, that protects us from harmful ultraviolet radiation. It is about 15 to 30 miles above the Earth.
3. Two holes have developed in this layer. The first and largest ozone hole is above Antarctica in the Southern Hemisphere. This hole has reached the size of the continental United States.
4. A second and smaller hole has developed in the Northern Hemisphere.
5. The holes vary in size depending on the latitude and seasons.
6. Other findings show that:
   a. Chlorofluorocarbon (frequently abbreviated CFC) propellants damage the ozone layer.
   b. From 1957 to 1975 there was no apparent change in the ozone layer. Since 1975 the "ozone hole" has slowly increased in size.
   c. Ozone thinning leads to skin cancer.
   d. Increased ozone would lead to a decrease in Vitamin D and would harm bone development.
   e. Actually there are no "holes," only a great thinning.

D. Results:

Students will learn that:

1. Ozone is a form of oxygen.
2. The ozone layer protects us from the dangerous ultraviolet radiation from the sun.
3. The thickness of the ozone layer appears to be diminishing every year.

E. Basic Facts and Supplemental Information:

1. The CFCs are catalysts that break down ozone into oxygen. Since catalysts remain unchanged, the CFCs continue to act and break down more ozone, causing an increase in the size of the "ozone hole."
2. Refrigerators and aerosol sprays which contained CFCs are slowly being replaced with carbon dioxide and hydrocarbons which do not destroy the ozone layer.
3. While the United States and a few other countries have stopped using chlorofluorocarbon propellants, other countries have not, and so the holes in the ozone layers have continued to grow.
4. Chlorofluorocarbons release chlorine which destroys ozone.
5. Other factors in ozone depletion might be from soils from tree cutting or atmospheric winds.
6. If CFCs continue to be used, then in 50 years the ozone layer will be reduced by 5% to 10%. This would cause an additional 40,000,000 skin cancer cases and 800,000 deaths.
7. The most recent findings have indicated that the ozone layer is also thinning over parts of Canada and the United States.

F. Thought Questions for Class Discussions:

1. Do you think we are still polluting our environment?
2. Are you concerned about the ozone problem?
3. Do you think exhausts from jet planes might be part of the problem? (Most scientists think so.)

G. Related Ideas for Further Inquiry:

1. Study Section I-B, "Air."
2. Study Section I-C, "Water."
3. Study other Activities in this Section.

H. Vocabulary Builders—Spelling Words:

1) **ozone**   2) **layer**   3) **chlorofluorocarbons**
4) **antarctic**   5) **arctic**   6) **protective**

I. Thought for Today:

"A hole is nothing at all but you can break your neck in it."

A. Problem: *Is Noise Pollution a Problem?*

B. Materials Needed:

1. Noisemakers:
   a. pictures of musical instruments
   b. toy planes
   c. toy trains
   d. toy cars
   e. radio
2. Cotton
3. Pictures of noisemakers:
   a. jackhammers
   b. television
   c. bells
   d. stereos
   e. boom boxes
4. Picture of, or actual hearing aid

C. Procedure:

1. Have class remain absolutely quiet for about five minutes while they make a list of all the sounds they hear (mostly outside sounds).
2. Have them discuss the loudest sound they ever heard.
3. Have them discuss the softest sound they ever heard.
4. Describe how continually listening to loud noises causes hearing loss such as:
   a. jackhammer working
   b. industrial production machinery
   c. loud rock music
   d. jet engines
5. Have students put cotton in their ears and then talk to them.
6. Tell them this is all they will hear if they continue to listen to loud noises or loud music.
7. Use each of the noisemakers and have students describe the loudness.
8. Show them a picture of or an actual hearing aid and briefly describe its functions and limitations.
9. Tell the class that statistically speaking, about 10% of all students have a hearing problem, and that 3% of the students should be using a hearing aid in order to hear properly in class. Stress that a student should be no more self-conscious about wearing a hearing aid than eyeglasses or contact lenses.

D. Results:

1. Students will become aware of noise pollution and how it can permanently impair their hearing.

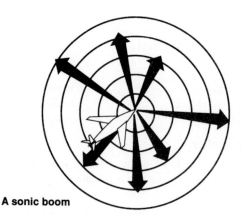

A sonic boom

2. Students will have experienced what it would be like to have a hearing loss.

E. Basic Facts and Supplemental Information:

1. Noise pollution is a real problem in some areas and in some vocations.
2. It is a serious problem in that there are no immediate symptoms, just a gradual loss of hearing.

F. Thought Questions for Class Discussions:

1. Why do jet plane guides wear "earmuffs" when directing planes on the runways?
2. How do earmuffs protect the ears?
3. What kinds of occupations could cause hearing problems?

G. Related Ideas for Further Inquiry:

1. Ask an audiologist to talk to the class and run a "mock hearing test."
2. Study Activity V-B-1, "How many senses do we have? How do we receive information about our environment?"
3. Study Activity V-B-8, "How well do we hear?"
4. Study Activity VI-C-1, "What are the main pollution problems?"
5. Study Activity VI-C-3, "How do automobiles pollute the air?"
6. Study other Activities in this Section.

H. Vocabulary Builders—Spelling Words:

1) **noise**   2) **instruments**   3) **hearing**
4) **cotton**   5) **decibel**   6) **jackhammer**

I. Thought for Today:

"One of our troubles today stems from the fact that too many adults, and not enough children, believe in Santa Claus."

SECTION D: POLLUTION SOLUTIONS

Activity

VI D 1

A. Problem: *How Can We Help Solve the Pollution Problems?*

B. Materials Needed:
1. Colored paper towels or tissue
2. Wire clothes hanger
3. Glass bottle
4. Newspaper
5. Lunch box
6. Pictures of litter, strip-mined lands, hovels, automobile junkyards, etc.

C. Procedure:
1. Discuss the problems of pollution.
2. Students can do research on or class can discuss ways in which each one can personally help with pollution solutions.
3. Discuss how America is made up of states: states have counties, counties have cities, cities have schools, and schools have classrooms.
4. To make America beautiful, the class should start with its own room.
5. After the classroom is neat, initiate a clean campus campaign.
6. After the campus is cleaned up, the class or school might make a list of ways in which we all can help solve our pollution problems such as:
   a. Have students make a list of actions that they can do individually or collectively that will help our environment.
   b. Discuss with students what each is doing to save our planet.
   c. Post on the bulletin board items describing environmental problems and activities that alleviate them.

D. Results:
1. Students will learn about many pollution problems.
2. Students will know what they can do to help alleviate the pollution problems.

E. Basic Facts and Supplemental Information:
Solving the problems of pollution is everyone's responsibility. With everyone helping a little, a lot can be accomplished. Students will learn that they can:

1. Use only white paper towels, paper napkins, or tissue. (Dyes pollute water.)

**Don't be a
LITTER-BUG!**

2. Use cloth towels instead of paper towels *when possible.*
3. Use a lunch box rather than paper bags.
4. Reduce the amount of electricity consumed in the home, particularly electric appliances. (Electricity requires generating plants which produce pollution.)
5. Save newspapers and magazines. (One ton of recycled paper saves 17 trees.)
6. Use both sides of writing paper at home and at school.
7. Walk and bicycle rather than ask parent(s) or adult(s) to drive automobiles.
8. Compost or bury garbage (especially vegetable trimmings).
9. Return wire coat hanger to the cleaners.
10. Use containers that disintegrate easily (paper or cardboard).
11. Plant trees and vegetable gardens.
12. Stop littering.
13. Avoid wasting water.
14. Avoid buying products or clothes made from endangered species.
15. Use reusable shopping bags (cloth and net types).
16. Avoid suntan lotions when swimming in a lake, river, or ocean.
17. Use biodegradable soap and cleaning products.
18. Refuse to buy overpackaged items.
19. Initiate rummage sales.
20. Recycle paper, plastic, glass, and metal products.
21. Ride in car pools.
22. Promote wildlife.
23. Practice soil conservation.
24. Don't ride in or drive off-road vehicles that scar the environment.

25. Choose biodegradable products marked "cruelty free" or "not tested on animals."
26. Take more showers, fewer baths.
27. Use rechargeable batteries.
28. Properly dispose of toxic substances.
29. Remember the 5 Rs in helping our environment:
    Recycle
    Reuse
    Reduce
    Repair
    Refuse (excess packaging, wasting)
30. Talk about and practice ecology.

F. Thought Questions for Class Discussions:
1. Why should we keep America clean?
2. Who should be responsible for keeping America clean?
3. How can vandalism be stopped?
4. Who "owns" the forests, parks, highways, city roads, beaches, etc.?
5. What will happen if we don't think ecologically?
6. Is pollution everybody's responsibility or just the government's?

G. Related Ideas for Further Inquiry:
1. Have students check in their homes on ways that can improve the environment.
2. Have students add other activities to the list cited in "Basic Facts and Supplemental Information" to help our planet.
3. Study Section VI-A, "Ecosystems."
4. Study Section VI-C, "Pollution."
5. Study Activity VI-D-2, "What is the best way to get rid of our nontoxic wastes?"
6. Study Activity VI-D-3, "How can we save diminishing species?"
7. Study Activity VI-D-4, "How can we protect our oceans and beaches?"
8. Study Activity VI-D-5, "Are detergents harmful to our environment?"
9. Study Activity VI-D-6, "What better ecological means of transportation do we have other than automobiles?"
10. Study Activity VI-D-7, "What is 'sustainability'?"

H. Vocabulary Builders—Spelling Words:
1) **pollution** 2) **solution** 3) **recycle** 4) **reuse**
5) **reduce** 6) **repair** 7) **refuse** 8) **research**

I. Thought for Today:
"Thanks to the miles of superhighways under construction, America will soon be a wonderful place to drive—if you don't have to stop."

Activity

A. Problem: *What Is the Best Way to Get Rid of Our Nontoxic Wastes?*

B. Materials Needed:
1. Empty cans
2. Newspapers
3. Glass containers (nonreturnable)
4. Plastic bags
5. Pictures of garbage
6. Pesticide

C. Procedure:
1. Discuss some of the ways that we presently get rid of wastes:
   a. burn
   b. bury
   c. dump in the ocean
   d. recycle
   e. litter
2. Discuss whether these are good or bad practices.
3. Have class determine which materials should be recycled.
4. Have students make a survey of items in a grocery store that are packed in throw-away containers.
5. Discuss the attitude of people who would rather throw something away than try to save it, recycle it, or return it.

D. Results:
1. Students will learn that the problem of wastes is a serious problem and that it is getting worse all the time as more and more people use more and more materials which must be disposed of.
2. Pupils will realize that some scarce materials can be reclaimed or recycled.

E. Basic Facts and Supplemental Information:
1. Getting rid of wastes is everybody's job.
2. Glass can be broken into many small pieces and used as a base for roadbeds.
3. Meltable products can be reclaimed.
4. Some materials can be burned with a minimum of air pollution while others produce highly toxic pollutants.
5. Newspapers can be recycled.
6. In 1994 alone, people threw out more than 100 million tires, 30 billion bottles, 60 billion cans, 9 million automobiles, 4 million tons of plastics, 1 million television sets, and uncounted millions of other appliances.

7. One of our biggest problems is finding new disposal sites because many sites have been filled and many others are almost full.

F. Thought Questions for Class Discussions:
1. Can you think of any constructive ways to get rid of our waste products?
2. Do you think we should levy a tax on disposable items?
3. Should we pass laws to prevent throw-away packaging for one-way containers?

G. Related Ideas for Further Inquiry:
1. Study Section VII-C, "Earth's Crust."
2. Study Section VI-C, "Pollution."
3. Study Activity VI-D-1, "How can we help solve the pollution problems?"
4. Study Activity VI-D-4, "How can we protect our oceans and beaches?"
5. Study Activity VI-D-7, "What is 'sustainability'?"

H. Vocabulary Builders—Spelling Words:
1) **solids** 2) **wastes** 3) **litter** 4) **recycle**
5) **throw-aways** 6) **reuse** 7) **nontoxic**

I. Thought for Today:
"The mind is a wonderful thing. It starts working the minute you're born and never stops until you get up to speak in public."

Activity

A. Problem: *How Can We Save Diminishing Species?*

B. Materials Needed:
1. Pictures of threatened species
2. Models of endangered species
3. Media reports of diminishing species

C. Procedure:
1. Show the pictures and models of the species to the class.
2. Ask if they know what they have in common.
3. Discuss whether these species should be preserved.

D. Results:
1. Students will realize that many plant and animal species are threatened with extinction.
2. Pupils will learn some of the reasons why these species should be preserved.

E. Basic Facts and Supplemental Information:
1. Millions of species have become extinct since life began on Earth.
2. Before 1700, most of these species died from natural causes.
3. Human beings have aided in speeding up extinction by:
   a. destroying habitats
   b. polluting the environment
   c. collecting rare species
   d. using species for undesirable purposes
   e. over-fishing and over-hunting
4. Present estimates place the number of species now living on Earth between 3 and 30 million.
5. Current statistics cite that we are losing about 50,000 species per year.
6. The greatest percentage of losses are with mammals—large animals closest to us on the classification lineage.
7. The main reasons why all species (plants and animals) should be preserved:
   a. balancing of habitats
   b. source of medical supplies
   c. source of our oxygen supplies (phytoplankton and trees)
   d. food
   e. shelter
   f. clothing
   g. recreation
   h. beauty (pleasant surroundings)

Giant panda   Bald eagle   Humpback whale

Indian tiger   Northern spotted owl   Mountain gorilla

Utah prairie dog   Sea turtle   Leopard

8. Animals can be preserved in and by
   a. wildlife preserves
   b. zoos
   c. restricting hunting
   d. restricting fishing
   e. stopping poaching
   f. breeding farms

F. Thought Questions for Class Discussions:
1. Should we be concerned about the diminishing species?
2. Do animals have any rights?
3. Are people more important than animals?
4. Should trees be burned for energy?

G. Related Ideas for Further Inquiry:
1. Collect media accounts of threatened species.
2. Talk to zookeepers, pet store owners, and veterinarians about endangered species.
3. Study Part III, "Plants."
4. Study Activity IV-A-1, "What is the difference between living and nonliving things?"
5. Study Section IV-B, "Pets."
6. Study Section IV-J, (Animal) "Resources."
7. Study Activity VI-D-1, "How can we solve the pollution problems?"
8. Study Activity VI-D-7, "What is 'sustainability'?"

H. Vocabulary Builders—Spelling Words:
1) **diminishing** 2) **threatened** 3) **endangered**
4) **extinct** 5) **poaching** 6) **habitats**

I. Thought for Today:
"Animals are such agreeable creatures, they ask no questions, they make no criticisms."

Activity

A. Problem: *How Can We Protect Our Oceans and Beaches?*

B. Materials Needed:

1. Reference materials on oceans, beaches, seashore life, etc.
2. Multisensory aids on oceans and beaches
3. Newspaper accounts of damages to our oceans and beaches

C. Procedure:

1. Discuss with class the importance of our oceans and beaches:
   a. supply us with food
   b. transportation system:
      1) people
      2) food supplies
      3) equipment
   c. recreation areas
   d. water evaporation supplies us with needed rain
   e. minerals (We can and are mining the oceans.)
   f. phytoplankton (microscopic organisms that live along the seashores and supply us with about 75% of our oxygen)
2. Discuss with students their experiences with visits or trips to beaches and oceans.
3. Study ocean life.
4. Show available and appropriate multisensory aids about our beaches and oceans.

D. Results:

1. Students will learn that our beaches and oceans are vital to us.
2. Students will learn that about 70% of the Earth's surface is covered by oceans.
3. Students will learn that we are polluting our oceans by:
   a. industrial wastes
   b. agricultural runoffs (pesticides, fertilizers, etc.)
   c. domestic sewage
   d. chemical contaminants from many sources
4. Our beaches are becoming more contaminated with litter and dumping of wastes.

E. Basic Facts and Supplemental Information:

1. The oceans are full of plant and animal life from microscopic bacteria to huge whales.
2. Many of the substances that are now dumped in the oceans could be recycled and reclaimed.
3. One of the great threats to our ocean life is the dumping of plastics. Untold numbers of sea birds, sea turtles, whales, seals, sea lions, and other

marine mammals die annually after becoming entangled in or ingesting discarded plastics.
4. Oil spills, too, have become more frequent as more oil is transported over the ocean waters.
5. Most of the ocean life is along the coasts, and it is along the ocean fronts that we are greatly contaminating the oceans.
6. In 1991, over 2,000 beaches were closed because of sewage dumping. California, New York, Florida, Connecticut, New Jersey, and Hawaii were the hardest hit.

F. Thought Questions for Class Discussions:

1. How should we dispose of our sewage? our chemical wastes?
2. Who should be responsible for keeping our beaches clean?
3. Who should be responsible for keeping our oceans free from contamination?
4. Do you think it is safe to eat lobsters, crabs, oysters, mussels, etc.?

G. Related Ideas for Further Inquiry:

1. Interview commercial fishermen to determine their main problems.
2. Write to state agencies that are involved with maintaining our beaches and seashore life to find the kinds of problems that exist and the means to reduce them.
3. Study Activities VI-D-1, VI-D-2, and VI-D-7.
4. Study other Activities in this Section.

H. Vocabulary Builders—Spelling Words:

1) **oceans** 2) **beaches** 3) **seashores**
4) **phytoplankton** 5) **plastics** 6) **sewage**
7) **dumping** 8) **wastes** 9) **oil spills**

I. Thought for Today:

"I love the ocean—especially from the beach."

Activity

A. Problem: *Are Detergents Harmful to Our Environment?*

B. Materials Needed:

1. Detergent boxes that have ingredients showing phosphates as one of the ingredients
2. Other detergent boxes that do not show phosphates as one of the ingredients

C. Procedure:

1. Discuss the difference between soaps and detergents. (Soaps are made from fats; detergents from manufactured chemicals.)
2. Discuss the difference between detergents that contain phosphates and those that don't. (Both provide cleaning, but phosphates cause serious problems to the environment.)
3. Fifty percent of all phosphates in American inland waters comes from detergents.
4. Inform the class that phosphates over-fertilize algae and other plant life which is excellent for farmers, but it depletes the oxygen in lakes and ponds.
5. Several states and many counties and cities have now banned detergents that contain phosphates.
6. Many manufacturers have reduced their phosphates in detergents.
7. Only 15% of U.S. communities are near inland waters where problems could develop from detergents.
8. Discuss with class the fact that when oxygen is removed from the water, water animals will die.

D. Results:

1. Students will see that manufactured chemicals can do a lot of damage (especially by hastening the "eutrophication" of lakes and ponds).
2. Pupils will realize that soaps and detergents without phosphates are beneficial in removing harmful bacteria from clothes and body.

E. Basic Facts and Supplemental Information:

1. We, and our immediate environment, would be awfully unsanitary without soaps and detergents.
2. Water can dissolve many things; it cannot dissolve grease.
3. Laundry soaps leave scum in the water.
4. Laundry detergents remove both dirt and grease, leaving no scum.

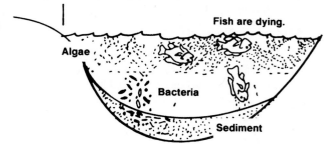

Phosphates enter body of water.

Fish are dying.

Algae

Bacteria

Sediment

5. Doctors recommend frequent washing of hands with soaps or detergents to remove harmful bacteria.
6. Many phosphate substitutes are dangerous.
7. Phosphates were really never tested for their long-term effects on the environment.
8. Eutrophication of lakes is the destruction of animal life in the lakes because of a great reduction in the oxygen supply in the water.

F. Thought Questions for Class Discussions:

1. Is your favorite lake being destroyed by phosphates?
2. Would you like to fish in a lake in the last stages of eutrophication?
3. Should we make it illegal to use phosphates in cleaning items?

G. Related Ideas for Further Inquiry:

1. Study Section I-C, "Water."
2. Study Section VI-C, "Pollution."
3. Study Section V-E, "Public Health."
4. Study Activity VI-D-I, "How can we help solve the pollution problems?"
5. Study Activity VI-D-2, "What is the best way to get rid of our nontoxic wastes?"
6. Study Activity VI-D-4, "How can we protect our oceans and beaches?"
7. Study Activity VI-D-7, "What is 'sustainability'?"

H. Vocabulary Builders—Spelling Words:

1) **lakes** 2) **ponds** 3) **eutrophication**
4) **oxygen** 5) **phosphates** 6) **detergents**

I. Thought for Today:

"For every minute you're angry, you lose sixty seconds of happiness."

A. Problem: *What Better Ecological Means of Land Transportation Do We Have Other than Automobiles?*

B. Materials Needed:

1. Toys and/or pictures of:
   a. cars (large and small)
   b. bicycles
   c. buses
   d. taxi cabs
   e. trains
   f. people
   g. motorcycles
   h. monorail system
2. Resource person in charge of automobile emission test

C. Procedure:

1. Discuss the problem of automobile pollution.
2. Have students watch the number of cars that go past the school with only one or two people in them.
3. Have the students list the other kinds of transportation available that could be used instead of automobiles.
4. If toys are not available, then students could draw pictures, make mobiles of different kinds of land transportation, or make a transportation collage.
5. Have resource person discuss emission and state control laws.

D. Results:

1. Students will learn about automobiles and pollution.
2. Students will learn that there are many ways to help cut down automobile exhausts, e.g.,
   a. walk
   b. bicycle
   c. motorcycle
   d. public transportation
   e. car pools
   f. use smaller horsepower cars
   g. keep motors clean and in good repair
   h. use smog devices on cars
   i. alternative fuels

E. Basic Facts and Supplemental Information:

1. The time is fast arriving when more catastrophes are going to demand the reduction of fossil fuel burning in cars and power plants.

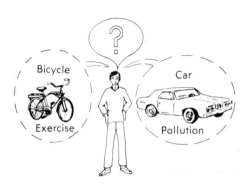

2. Walking and bicycling are healthier than riding in cars. They are great exercise.
3. We need electric automobiles.

F. Thought Questions for Class Discussions:

1. What public means of transportation carries more people than any other each day in the United States? (Be careful—answer at end of next question.)
2. Do you think car pools should be made mandatory? Why or why not? (Ans.—elevators)
3. As far as transportation is concerned, do you think there were more problems in the "horse and buggy days" than there are now?
4. What harm is done to our bodies from automobile exhausts?

G. Related Ideas for Further Inquiry:

1. Make a transportation collage.
2. Make a survey of the homes of the class to determine if they use any other means of transportation besides automobiles.
3. Study Section I-B, "Air."
4. Study Section VI-C, "Pollution."
5. Study Activity VI-D-1, "How can we help solve the pollution problems?"
6. Study Activity VI-D-2, "What is the best way to get rid of our nontoxic wastes?"
7. Study Activity VI-D-7, "What is 'sustainability'?"

H. Vocabulary Builders—Spelling Words:

1) **ecology**   2) **transportation**   3) **bicycles**
4) **motorcycles**   5) **catastrophe**   6) **public**
7) **mass transit**   8) **buses**   9) **healthier**

I. Thought for Today:

"The greatest lesson in life is to realize that even fools are right sometimes."—Winston Churchill

Activity

A. Problem: *What Is "Sustainability?"*

B. Materials Needed:
1. Several cans of food
2. Several cans of oil
3. Bottle of water
4. Empty milk carton
5. Pictures of:
   a. trees, shrubs, and other plants
   b. wildlife
   c. atmosphere

C. Procedure:
1. Explain to class that we are all passengers on a great spaceship—Planet Earth.
2. Tell the class that each spaceship must carry its own supplies. There is no other place where we can stop and replenish them.
3. Our spaceship cannot use up or destroy more resources than it can subsequently develop. This is called "sustainability." It is the key to our survival.
4. Ask the class what they would do if there were no more of the items listed in "Materials Needed" 5.
5. Challenge them to propose alternatives for our food, water, oil, etc., if these items were to become scarce, nonexistent, or unfit for human consumption.

D. Results:
1. Students will begin to realize that our planet has limited resources.
2. Students will learn that if life on our planet is to survive, we must use our resources more intelligently and not waste or destroy them.
3. They will learn that "sustainability" should be the main criterion for the use of many of our earthly supplies.

E. Basic Facts and Supplemental Information:
1. Our air is becoming more polluted.
2. Our population is expected to double in the next century.
3. Doubling the planet's population will double the need for water, living space, food, energy, and all the other basic resources we need.
4. Our agricultural lands are being diminished as new residences, streets, buildings, etc. are developed.
5. Our wildlife is being depleted.

F. Thought Questions for Class Discussions:
1. Can the world support twice as many people? ten times as many?
2. How can we prevent millions of people from starving to death every year?
3. Should we continue to bury our garbage and dump our wastes in the oceans?
4. Do you think "sustainability" is a good idea?
5. If we double the number of people in the world, will we double the amount of air pollution? water pollution?
6. Will there be enough food, water, and natural resources for our grandchildren?

G. Related Ideas for Further Inquiry:
1. Study the difference between renewable and nonrenewable sources of energy.
2. Study the problems of soil erosion.
3. Study the causes of droughts.
4. Study Activity VI-D-1, "How can we help solve the pollution problems?"
5. Study Activity VI-D-2, "What is the best way to get rid of our nontoxic wastes?"
6. Study Activity VI-D-3, "How can we save diminishing species?"
7. Study Activity VI-D-4, "How can we protect our oceans and beaches?"
8. Study Activity VI-D-6, "What better ecological means of land transportation do we have other than automobiles?"
9. Study Section VII-C, "Earth's Crust."

H. Vocabulary Builders—Spelling Words:
1) **sustainability**   2) **conserve**   3) **recycle**
4) **reuse**   5) **sewage**   6) **wastes**   7) **wildlife**

I. Thought for Today:
"One of our biggest problems is heir pollution."

PART VII

EARTH AND SPACE

SECTION A   Universe   330

SECTION B   Solar System   337

SECTION C   Earth's Crust   351

SECTION D   Gravity   360

SECTION E   Weather   369

SECTION A: UNIVERSE
Activity

A. Problem: *How Big Is the Universe?*

B. Materials Needed:

1. Sketches and drawings about the universe
2. Books about astronomy
3. Multisensory aids on the universe
4. Diagrams as shown in drawings

C. Procedure:

1. Assign students the task of looking up at the sky at night and reporting what they have seen.
2. Ask them how far they can see in the night sky.
3. Ask them what is up in the sky.
4. Tell them that we use the term "universe" to include everything that exists in space:
   a. stars
   b. sun (another star)
   c. moon
   d. planets (like our Earth)
   e. "shooting stars"
   f. and many other "things"
5. Explain the drawings:
   (The "dot" represents one object; the "circle" a much larger object containing the first.)
   a. *Top Drawing:*
      1) You are a student in our classroom.
      2) The classroom is in the school.
      3) The school is in the community.
      4) The community is in the state.
      5) There are many, many states in all the countries, 50 in the United States.
   b. *Bottom Drawing:*
      1) The Earth is in the solar system.
      2) The solar system is in our galaxy, the Milky Way.
      3) The Milky Way is in our supercluster, a large group of galaxies.
      4) Our supercluster is part of the universe.
      5) There are millions of superclusters in the universe.
6. Explain that measuring the universe is an impossible concept even for scientists. No one can grasp the vastness of space.

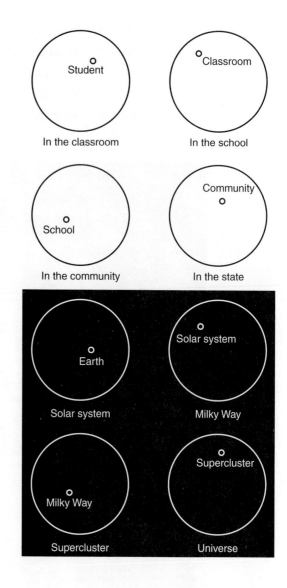

7. Select additional information from the items below depending on the age, ability, and interest of your group.
   a. Begin with known distances: miles from home to school, miles to grandma's and grandpa's house, or the farthest students have traveled from their homes.

b. Ask them how long it took to get there.

c. Compare this to the distance to the moon—240,000 miles away.

d. Compute time to get to the moon if driving a spaceship at the speed of a car traveling 60 miles per hour—(240,000 divided by 60) (answer in hours). (This would take 167 days.)

e. Compare this to the sun which is 93,000,000 miles away. A person traveling at 60 m.p.h. would require 178 years to get there.

f. Relate the following statistics even though they are mind-boggling:

1) The diameter of the Earth is 7,926 miles.

2) The diameter of the sun is 865,400 miles.

3) The diameter of our solar system is 7,340,000,000 miles.

4) The diameter of the solar system can also be measured in light-years. A light-year is the distance light travels in a year. Light travels at 186,200 miles per second. A light-year equals 5.88 trillion miles (5,880,000,000,000).

5) The solar system measures a little over .001 light-years across.

6) The diameter of the Milky Way is 100,000 light-years. It contains about 200 billion stars.

7) The diameter of our supercluster is 40 million light-years. It contains about 2,500 galaxies.

8) The diameter of the known universe has been estimated to be from 12–13.4 billion light-years in diameter. It contains millions of superclusters.

D. Results:

1. Students will be aware of the vastness of space.

2. Students will realize the difficulty of comprehending large numbers.

3. Pupils will begin to realize how small each person is in the large universe.

E. Basic Facts and Supplemental Information:

1. All celestial bodies are in motion.

2. It takes our solar system 200 million years to make one revolution around our galaxy, the Milky Way.

3. The most recent studies of time and distances in the universe tend to support the "Big Bang" theory because all celestial bodies are moving away from each other just as lettering does on an expanding balloon.

4. The Earth is near the center of the solar system.

5. The solar system is near the edge of the Milky Way.

6. The Milky Way is between the center and the edge of our supercluster.

7. We're really not sure of the relative position of the supercluster in the universe.

F. Thought Questions for Class Discussions:

1. Does our planet seem very large to you now?

2. Is our sun far away?

3. Is a week very long?

G. Related Ideas for Further Inquiry:

1. Construct a bulletin board full of news items that pertain to objects in the universe.

2. Take a field trip to an observatory.

3. Discuss the universe with astronomers and/or cosmologists.

4. Study Activity VII-A-2, "What kinds of heavenly bodies are there?"

5. Study Activity VII-A-3, "Why do the stars move?"

6. Study Activity VII-A-5, "What are constellations?"

7. Study Activity VII-A-6, "What are galaxies?"

H. Vocabulary Builders—Spelling Words:

1) **light-year** 2) **Solar System** 3) **Milky Way**
4) **Supercluster** 5) **universe** 6) **vast**

I. Thought for Today:

"To love the world is no problem. It's the person next door that is the problem."

Activity

A. Problem: *What Kinds of Heavenly Bodies Are There?*

B. Materials Needed:

1. Astronomy charts
2. Model spaceships
3. Books and pictures on space

C. Procedure:

1. Discuss travel by planes.
2. Discuss the difference between plane travel and space travel (leaving Earth's atmosphere).
3. Ask the class to list all the different kinds of heavenly bodies that they know about outside the Earth's atmosphere.
4. Have them read books and pamphlets about space and space travel.

D. Results:

1. Students will learn that there are many kinds of heavenly bodies.
2. They will realize that space is vast.

E. Basic Facts and Supplemental Information:

1. All heavenly bodies are contained in the universe.
2. No one knows whether our universe is finite or infinite, how it got started, or exactly how old it is.
3. Many astronomers believe that the universe was created 12 to 13.4 billion years ago from a great explosion called the "Big Bang."
4. Only about 30% of the cosmic material is known.
5. Known heavenly bodies consist of galaxies, superclusters, star clusters, constellations, supernovas, novas, stars, and quasars that emit light.
6. Planets, asteroids, meteors, satellites, and comets do not emit light.
7. The balance of known objects in space consists of gas, radiation, and dust and includes nebulae and rays (gamma, X-rays, ultraviolet, and infrared).
8. Black holes, recently confirmed objects in space, are highly dense objects whose gravity is so strong that they pull in everything around them, even light. Since they don't emit any light, they are black and consequently they are called "black holes."
9. The Van Allen radiation belts lie within our atmosphere and protect us from strong ultraviolet radiations.

10. In 1993, our spacecraft Galileo photographed a tiny satellite, a moon ("Dactyl") one mile wide, encircling the 34-mile-long asteroid, "Ida."

F. Thought Questions for Class Discussions:

1. Would you like to take a space trip to another galaxy? (Even if it took 25–50 years?)
2. What would be some of the problems you might realize on such a trip?
3. Do you think there could be other planets like the Earth where conditions would be similar and life could exist? (Scientists estimate that there could be about 10,000,000 planets like the Earth in our universe.)

G. Related Ideas for Further Inquiry:

1. Visit an observatory.
2. Study Section I-A, "Matter."
3. Study Part II, "Energy."
4. Study all Activities in this Section.
5. Study Activity VII-A-1, "How big is the universe?"
6. Study Activity VII-A-5, "What are constellations?"
7. Study Activity VII-A-6, "What are galaxies?"

H. Vocabulary Builders—Spelling Words:

Use the heavenly bodies cited in E-5

I. Thought for Today:

"An eminent scientist has announced that, in his opinion, intelligent life is possible on several planets— including the Earth!"

A. Problem: *Why Do Stars Move?*

B. Materials Needed:
1. Reference books on stars
2. Star charts
3. Chalkboard
4. Chalk
5. World globe
6. Multisensory aids if available
7. Paper figure
8. Cellophane tape

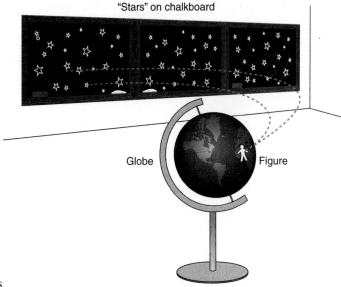

"Stars" on chalkboard

Globe   Figure

C. Procedure:
1. Ask the class what the night sky looks like.
2. Ask them if the stars move.
3. Ask them if they know why.
4. Draw some "stars" on the chalkboard over a wide area.
5. Tape the paper figure on the center of the globe as shown in sketch.
6. Discuss how the Earth rotates. It spins from west to east.
7. Move the globe slowly in this direction.
8. Ask the students what "stars" the figure on the globe would see when he/she first saw the "stars."
9. Ask if the figure could see all the stars at the first viewing.
10. Slowly move the globe so that the figure gets a different view of the sky.
11. Ask how the stars would appear to move to the observer.

D. Results:
1. As the globe moves, the viewer will get a different perspective of the sky.
2. Since the viewer is moving west to east, the stars will appear to move east to west.

E. Basic Facts and Supplemental Information:
1. If the viewer were standing at the North Pole, the stars would appear to move in concentric circles.
2. If the viewer were standing at the equator, the stars would appear to move in a straight line from east to west.
3. The Earth rotates once every 24 hours. Consequently the stars will look the same every night at the same time.
4. Actually the earth rotates every 23 hours and 56 minutes.
5. If the sun didn't shine during the day, we could see the stars all the time. The stars are "out" all the time.

6. Since the stars are so far away, they appear to be stationary, but all heavenly bodies are in constant motion.
7. Stars vary in distances from the Earth, yet they all appear to be the same distance away.
8. Stars appear to move in the same direction as the sun—from east to west.

F. Thought Questions for Class Discussions:
1. What is the difference between a star and a planet?
2. Is our sun a star?
3. Does the sun move?

G. Related Ideas for Further Inquiry:
1. Make star charts of constellations by punching holes in heavy tagboard and placing it against a window for viewing.
2. Locate the North Star.
3. Make a constellation viewer by punching holes in the bottom of a tin can and then looking through the bottom of the can at a light source for viewing.

H. Vocabulary Builders—Spelling Words:
1) **stars** 2) **sun** 3) **movement**
4) **nighttime** 5) **rotation** 6) **turning**

I. Thought for Today:
"Of the billions of stars in the universe we can only see about 3,000 with our naked eye."

Activity

A. Problem: *How Can We Find the North Star?*

B. Materials Needed:

1. Star charts
2. Pictures of constellations
3. Astronomy books, pamphlets
4. Compass
5. Star chart as shown in drawing.

C. Procedure:

1. Ask the class if they could find their direction if they got lost at night.
2. Tell them the best positive way is to find the North Star (Polaris).
3. Show the class the star chart.
4. The best way to find the North Star is to first locate the constellation called the Big Dipper (Ursa Major) ("Big Bear").
5. The best way to locate this constellation is to locate north on a compass at night and look for a constellation that resembles a cooking pot with a long handle. (See drawing.)
6. If they can find this, then they should locate the "pointers." These are the two stars on the outside edge of the "pot."
7. The pointers point in the same direction as the open side of the pot, directly to the North Star. (See drawing.)
8. If the Big Dipper is down too close to the horizon, look for the constellation Cassiopeia. (It looks like a "W" or an "M".) It has seven well-lighted stars, and the two stars in the center point in the general direction of the North Star.
9. Once you know where north is, you won't need a compass anymore.

D. Results:

1. Students will be able to find the North Star (Polaris).
2. Pupils will become more aware of heavenly bodies.

E. Basic Facts and Supplemental Information:

1. The North Star is in the constellation Ursa Minor ("Little Bear") (Little Dipper).
2. This constellation also looks like a long-handled cooking pot with the North Star on the "handle."
3. If you face the North Star with arms outstretched, the left hand will be pointing West, your right

hand will be pointing East, and South will be in back of you.

4. If you lived at the North Pole, the North Star would be directly over your head. If you lived at the equator, the North Star would be on the horizon. The angle from the horizon to the point above us then equals 90°. Consequently, the number of degrees we live above the equator (our latitude) is equal to the height of the North Star above the horizon. If we lived at 38° north latitude, the height of the North Star would be 38°.

F. Thought Questions for Class Discussions:

1. Who would need to know what direction north is?
2. If you lived at 45° north latitude, how many degrees above the horizon would the North Star be?
3. What constellation (not shown in drawing) is between the Big Dipper and the Little Dipper?

G. Related Ideas for Further Inquiry:

1. Study Section VII-E, "Weather."
2. Study Section VIII-C, "Space Travel."
3. Study Activity VII-A-2, "What kinds of heavenly bodies are there?"
4. Study Activity VII-A-5, "What are constellations?"
5. Study Activity VII-A-6, "What are galaxies?"

H. Vocabulary Builders—Spelling Words:

1) **North Star** 2) **Polaris** 3) **Ursa Major**
4) **Ursa Minor** 5) **Cassiopeia** 6) **pointers**

I. Thought for Today:

"The simple realization that there are other points of view is the beginning of wisdom."

A. Problem: *What Are Constellations?*

B. Materials Needed:
1. Astronomy books
2. Astronomy pamphlets
3. Star charts
4. Constellation cardboards (punched holes in cardboard or heavy tagboard showing constellations). These are best viewed by placing in windows and letting the light show through holes.

C. Procedure:
1. Ask the students if they have ever studied the stars at night.
2. Ask them if they have ever tried to draw pictures or make designs from groups of stars as seen in the night sky.
3. Tell them that constellations are groups of stars that astronomers and ancient observers have created pictures of for reference.
4. Have the students see if they can locate the following constellations in printed materials or night skies:
   a. Big Dipper (Ursa Major) ("Big Bear")
   b. Little Dipper (Ursa Minor) ("Little Bear")
   c. Cassiopeia
   d. Orion
   e. Southern Cross
   f. Hydra
   g. Boötes
   h. Corona Borealis
   i. Hercules
   j. Cepheus
   k. Lyra
   l. Pegasus
   m. Pisces
   n. Pleiades (*scientifically a "star cluster"*)
   o. Taurus
   p. Gemini
   q. Cancer
   r. Leo
   s. Virgo
   t. Libra
   u. Andromeda
   v. Perseus
   w. Draco
   x. Ophiuchus
   y. Auriga
   z. Aquarius

D. Results:
1. Students will learn the location of some constellations.
2. Pupils will have fun while learning the constellations.

E. Basic Facts and Supplemental Information:
1. Ancients grouped stars together and named them after mythological persons, animals, or inanimate objects. These were used as references for directions.

2. Although the stars in a constellation look close together, they are actually billions of miles apart.
3. Another star chart can be made by punching holes in the bottom of a tin can, with each hole representing a star. Use a flashlight or hold the can up to a window for viewing.
4. Most astronomers list 88 different constellations.

F. Thought Questions for Class Discussions:
1. Can you create other pictures with the stars?
2. Are the brightest stars closest to us?
3. How can you tell the difference between a planet and a star when viewing the sky at night?

G. Related Ideas for Further Inquiry:
1. Study Activity VII-B-5, "What makes day and night?"
2. Study Activity VII-B-7, "How does the length of day and night change from season to season?"
3. Study Activity VII-A-1, "How big is the universe?"
4. Study Activity VII-A-2, "What kinds of heavenly bodies are there?"
5. Study Activity VII-A-4, "How can we find the North Star?"
6. Study Activity VII-A-6, "What are galaxies?"

H. Vocabulary Builders—Spelling Words:
Use the names of the constellations in "Procedure."

I. Thought for Today:
"Superior to kind thought is a kind word. Superior to a kind word is a kind deed."

A. Problem: *What Are Galaxies?*

B. Materials Needed:

1. Books or pamphlets about astronomy
2. Pictures, charts, and/or multisensory aids about galaxies

C. Procedure:

1. Have students describe what they see in the sky on a clear night.
2. Tell them the stars tend to group themselves into pictures which we call constellations.
3. Many stars make up constellations.
4. Billions of stars make up galaxies.
5. Our galaxy is called the Milky Way.
6. Break the class into groups and have them study all the information they can find about our galaxy such as:
   a. It is spiral in shape.
   b. It is 100,000 light-years across.
   c. It is traveling through space at 481,000 m.p.h.
   d. It is rotating and the outer part is rotating faster than the inner part.

D. Results:

1. Students will learn about our galaxy, the Milky Way.
2. Pupils will realize that galaxies are very large.

E. Basic Facts and Supplemental Information:

1. A light-year is the distance light travels in a year. Light travels 186,200 miles per second (300,000 km./sec.), or about 6 million million miles (about 9.5 million million kilometers).
2. People will never be able to travel to distant galaxies or even to the nearest star in our own galaxy for lack of time and supplies.
3. The top drawing shows a top view of our Milky Way.
4. The bottom drawing shows a side view.
5. Galaxies are like a collection of bubbles in space surrounded by empty space.
6. On a clear night you can see a big, broad band of light in the sky. This is part of our galaxy.

F. Thought Questions for Class Discussions:

1. Would you like to visit another galaxy? (There might not be any planets there.)
2. Would you like to spend half your life aboard a spaceship?
3. Do motion pictures and television accurately portray space realities?

Our Milky Way galaxy from the top looking down.

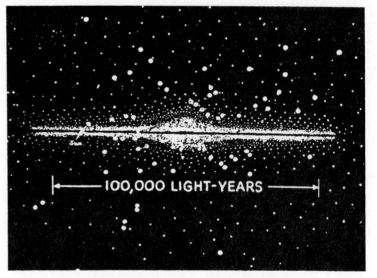

Side view of our galaxy—the Milky Way.

G. Related Ideas for Further Inquiry:

1. Study Part VII, "Earth and Space."
2. Study Section VIII-B, "Satellites."
3. Study other Activities in this Section.
4. Use star charts to locate constellations.

H. Vocabulary Builders—Spelling Words:

1) **galaxy** 2) **astronomy** 3) **constellation**
4) **space** 5) **traveling** 6) **Milky Way**

I. Thought for Today:

"While science has made giant strides in communication in recent years, there is still a lot to be said for paying attention."

SECTION B: SOLAR SYSTEM
Activity

VII B 1

A. Problem: *What Are Planets?*

B. Materials:
1. Large bulletin board
2. Construction paper, different colors
3. Straight pins or thumbtacks
4. Colored yarn

C. Procedure:
1. Plan a solar system bulletin board display.
2. See the "Planet Table" in the following Activity, VII-B-2.
3. From the chart construct a scale that would represent various diameters and distances from the sun for each planet. The following may be used.
   a. Using scale 1″ = 16,000 miles, you can depict the sun by making a curved arc 62 1/2″ in diameter at one side of bulletin board.
   b. Using a different scale of 1″ = 36 million miles, place Mercury cutout of construction paper one inch from arc of sun.
4. Have students figure out how far the other planets should be placed from the sun. Place them where they belong.
5. Cut out planets from different colors of construction paper and size indicated in chart on page 339.
6. With colored yarn make orbits for each planet going around sun. (Only partial orbits can be depicted.)

D. Results:
1. Students will learn about the planets' relative sizes, distances from sun, and orbits.
2. An understanding of the Earth's position will be learned in relation to our solar system.

E. Basic Facts and Supplemental Information:
1. Planets are celestial bodies like the Earth, and including the Earth, revolve around the sun.
2. Five planets—Mercury, Venus, Mars, Jupiter, and Saturn—can be seen at night with the unaided eye if conditions are right (clear sky, observable position).
3. Mercury, Venus, Earth, and Mars are terrestrial planets.
4. The largest planets, Jupiter, Saturn, Uranus, and Neptune, are gaseous and have rings. All are multi-ringed.

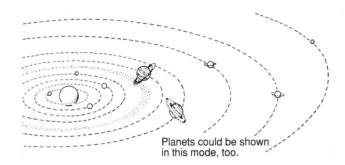
Planets could be shown
in this mode, too.

5. Pluto is the smallest planet. It is composed of frozen gases and has a moon, Charon, which is about 875 miles in diameter, about one-half the size of Pluto. Pluto's eliptical orbit made it closer to the sun than Neptune during the period 1979 to 1999. It is now back to its normal outermost position.
6. The first confirmed planet outside of our solar system has been found orbiting around a neutron star in the constellation Virgo. Since then up to 17 more planets have been found to exist in our universe. Astronomers are finding new ones almost monthly.

F. Thought Questions for Class Discussions:
1. How did we find out that all planets beyond Mars have rings around them?
2. Why doesn't the Earth shoot off into space or fall into the sun?
3. Do you think life could exist on other planets?

G. Related Ideas for Further Inquiry:
1. A larger and more accurate scale can be developed on the schoolyard.
2. Visit an observatory.
3. Look for planets at night in the sky. (They shine with a steady light while stars twinkle.)
4. Study Activity VII-B-2, "How is the Earth different from other planets?"
5. Study Activity VII-B-3, "Is the Earth round?"
6. Study other Activities in this Section.

H. Vocabulary Builders—Spelling Words:
Use the names of the planets in our solar system.

I. Thought for Today:
"For every person with a spark of genius, there are a dozen more with ignition troubles."

Activity

A. Problem: *How Is the Earth Different from Other Planets?*

B. Materials Needed:
1. World globe
2. Planisphere (model of the Earth, moon, and sun) if available
3. Reference materials about our planet
4. Bulletin board
5. Multisensory materials

C. Procedure:
1. Read reference materials about the Earth.
2. Show whatever multisensory materials are available.
3. Discuss the pertinent information about the Earth cited in Section E of this activity.
4. Construct a bulletin board display comparing the planets.
5. Use the world globe and/or planisphere to show some of the Earth' s characteristics.

D. Results:
1. The students will learn that the Earth is a very unique planet in our solar system.
2. Students will learn how to construct a comparable bulletin board display.
3. Students will learn that we are living on a spaceship which needs attention and care.

E. Basic Facts and Supplemental Information:
1. The Earth is one of nine planets in our solar system.
2. The Earth rotates on its axis and is tilted about 23 1/2 degrees from its orbital path.
3. This tilt causes the Northern Hemisphere to have summer when the tilt is toward the sun and winter when the tilt is away from the sun.
4. The Earth orbits around the sun in one year (365 ¼ days).
5. The Earth rotates on its axis once every day (23 hours, 56 minutes).
6. The Earth has one moon. This affects our tides.
7. The Earth is the third planet away from the sun (about 93,000,000 miles away).
8. If we were much closer to the sun, we would sizzle; if we were much farther away, we would freeze.
9. The Earth has an atmosphere composed primarily of nitrogen (78%), oxygen (21%), and a variety of gases making up the balance.

Our planet Earth

10. The troposphere, the lower layer of our atmosphere, is where our weather occurs and makes life possible.
11. The sun sends to the Earth about 99.9% of the energy we need to heat the land, oceans, and air—three important factors in creating our weather and climates.
12. A layer of ozone concentrated about 15–30 miles above the Earth protects us from most of the sun's harmful ultraviolet radiation.
13. Air pollution can cause changes in our weather and climate. The burning of fossil fuels and biomass releases carbon dioxide into the atmosphere which forms a "blanket." Therefore, heat that is normally reflected back into space is reflected back to the Earth instead, giving us the "Greenhouse Effect."
14. Water covers 70% of the Earth's surface.
15. The Earth's gravity keeps us and our atmosphere from being lost in space.
16. The Earth is part of the solar system and our solar system is part of the Milky Way Galaxy, which is composed of billions of stars.
17. The core of the Earth is a very hot molten mass that ranges from 4,000–8,000° F. Thanks to our mantle and crust, we are insulated from this extreme heat. Actually our crust is composed of large pieces of land mass which float on the molten core. The shifting of adjacent land masses (tectonic plates) causes earthquakes.
18. Our planet has seven major land masses called continents. They are:
    a. North America
    b. South America
    c. Europe
    d. Asia
    e. Africa
    f. Australia
    g. Antarctica

19. The planet Earth is our spaceship traveling through space at breakneck speeds.
20. As passengers aboard our spacecraft, we must take good care of it and be careful of its provisions.
   a. There are millions of species of plant and animal life that exist on our planet, but these are being reduced at faster and faster rates as people encroach on their habitats.
   b. Our population is expected to double in the next 35–50 years, causing problems in supplying sufficient food and fresh water to all our passengers.
   c. Our rain forests are being depleted. Our wetlands are being dramatically reduced.
   d. Our natural resources are being used up.
   e. Our landfills are being topped.

F. Thought Questions for Class Discussions:

1. How have people changed the surfaces of the Earth?
2. How would life be different if we lived on the moon?
3. What are some dangers to people's existence on our planet?

4. What are we doing to our air?
5. What are we doing to our water?
6. Are we taking good care of our natural resources?

G. Related Ideas for Further Inquiry:

1. Have students try to locate planets in the night skies.
2. Study Activity VII-B-1, "What are planets?"
3. Study Activity VII-B-3, "Is the Earth round?"
4. Study Activity VII-B-6, "How does the sun help us?"
5. Study Part VI, "Ecology."
6. Study Section VII-C, "Earth's Crust."
7. Study Section VII-D, "Weather."

H. Vocabulary Builders—Spelling Words:

1) **planet**   2) **moon**   3) **axis**   4) **rotation**
5) **revolution**   6) **seasons**   7) **atmosphere**

I. Thought for Today:

"Isn't it amazing that we don't get dizzy on our spinning Earth?"

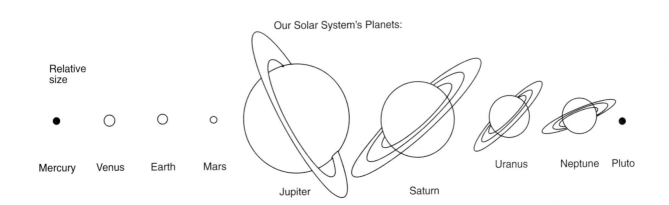

Our Solar System's Planets:

Relative size

Mercury   Venus   Earth   Mars   Jupiter   Saturn   Uranus   Neptune   Pluto

BASIC INFORMATION ABOUT THE PLANETS IN OUR SOLAR SYSTEM

Name:	Diameter:	Miles from Sun:	Rotation Time:	Revolution Time:	Moons:
Mercury	3,000 miles	36 million	59 days	88 days	0
Venus	7,550 miles	69 million	243 days	225 days	0
Earth	7,926 miles	93 million	24 hours	365¼ days	1
Mars	4,200 miles	142 million	25 hours	687 days	2
Jupiter	88,700 miles	484 million	10 hours	12 years	16
Saturn	74,000 miles	891 million	11 hours	29 years	22
Uranus	29,000 miles	1.8 billion	18 hours	84 years	15
Neptune	28,000 miles	2.8 billion	18 hours	165 years	8
Pluto	1,460 miles	3.7 billion (ave.)	6 days	248 years	1
Sun	865,400 miles	0	25–35 days	0	9 (planets)

Activity

A. Problem: *Is the Earth Round?*

B. Materials Needed:

1. World globe
2. Toy ship

C. Procedure:

1. Ask class if any of them have been at the beach and seen ships or sailboats disappear over the horizon.
2. Have these students recount their experiences.
3. Place globe where students can see it. Emphasize its roundness.
4. Hold the globe steady with one hand.
5. Take the toy ship with the other hand and move it on the globe away from the students until it moves out of their line of sight.

D. Result:

The toy ship disappears from the students' view. (The top of the ship disappears last.)

E. Basic Facts and Supplemental Information:

1. Explain that when ships disappear over the horizon (as did the toy ship) it is an indication that the Earth is round.
2. Astronauts have taken pictures of the Earth from space which have proved the roundness of the Earth.
3. Points on Earth can be located by "longitude" and "latitude." Longitude is measured in degrees east or west of the "prime meridian," which is located in Greenwich, England. Latitude is measured in degrees north or south of the equator.
4. Aristarchus of Samos (310–230 BC) was a Greek astronomer and was the first to maintain that the Earth rotates and revolves around the sun. The values he obtained, by using geometry, were inaccurate because of faulty observation.

F. Thought Questions for Class Discussions:

1. What evidence do we have that the Earth is round?
2. What are some problems that we have in launching a spacecraft from the United States to the moon because our Earth is round?

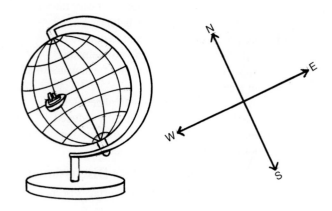

3. What are some possible reasons for the Earth being round (spherical) rather than square, cubical, or elliptical in shape?
4. Did people always know that the world is round?
5. Is the Earth perfectly round?

G. Related Ideas for Further Inquiry:

1. Research solar eclipses to help prove the world is round.
2. Study Activity VII-B-1, "What are planets?"
3. Study Activity VII-B-2, "How is the Earth different from other planets?"
4. Study Activity VII-B-4, "Does the sun revolve around the Earth?"
5. Study Activity VII-B-5, "What makes day and night?"
6. Study Activity VII-B-6, "How does the sun help us?"
7. Study Activity VII-B-7, "What causes seasons?"
8. Study Section VII-A, "Universe."

H. Vocabulary Builders—Spelling Words:

1) **earth** 2) **round** 3) **globe** 4) **ship**
5) **disappear** 6) **shape** 7) **horizon** 8) **curved**

I. Thought for Today:

"Those who go round in circles will never become 'big wheels.' "

A. Problem: *Does the Sun Revolve Around the Earth?*

B. Materials Needed:

1. Orrery, if available (model of the solar system with balls of various sizes and movable arms to show movement of sun, moon, and planets)
2. Pictures of the sun and the Earth
3. Large card marked "SUN"
4. Large card marked "EARTH"

C. Procedure:

1. Ask class how the sun moves in the sky.
2. Tell them that the sun is a body in space and so is the planet Earth.
3. Have one student stand in front of class and turn around slowly. Explain that this movement is called "rotation."
4. Have a second student stand on one side of the first student.
5. Have the first one hold the card "SUN" and the second one hold the card "EARTH."
6. Have the "EARTH" rotate slowly without turning his/her head.
7. Ask the "EARTH" how the "SUN" appears to move.
8. May have to repeat demonstration several times and with several students.
9. If an orrery is available, use it to explain the rotation of the Earth. To a person on Earth, it appears that the sun revolves around the Earth. This apparent motion is due to the rotation of the Earth.

D. Results:

1. Students will learn that the Earth rotates, and consequently it appears that the sun moves around the Earth.
2. The pupils will learn the difference between "actual movement" and "apparent movement."

E. Basic Facts and Supplemental Information:

1. The Earth rotates on its own axis once each day.
2. The Earth revolves around the sun once each year. Its path is called its "orbit."
3. The length of time each day the sun can be seen changes because of the tilt of the Earth's axis and its rotation.
4. The sun is a star and is like a furnace burning up fuel. Its life expectancy is about 5 billion more years.

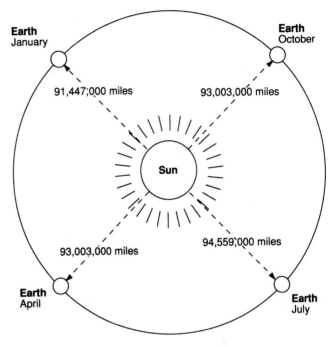

Orbit of the earth around the sun

F. Thought Questions for Class Discussions:

1. Does the Earth revolve around the moon, or does the moon revolve around the Earth?
2. Why doesn't the Earth stop spinning (rotating)?
3. Why does the sun look bigger in the morning and in the evening than it does at midday?

G. Related Ideas for Further Inquiry:

1. Study Section VII-A, "Universe."
2. Study Section VIII-B, "Satellites."
3. Study other Activities in this Section.

H. Vocabulary Builders—Spelling Words:

1) **rotation** 2) **revolution** 3) **apparent**
4) **orbit** 5) **sun** 6) **Earth** 7) **motion**

I. Thought for Today:

"If you're feeling low, don't despair; the sun has a sinking spell every night, but it comes back up every morning."

A. Problem: *What Makes Day and Night?*

B. Materials Needed:

1. World globe
2. Flashlight or slide projector
3. Cellophane tape
4. Plain paper

C. Procedure:

1. Darken the room.
2. Have one student shine the flashlight or slide projector on the globe. This represents the sun's rays; the globe represents the Earth.
3. Ask the students what causes night; what causes day.
4. Cut a piece of paper and tape it on the globe to represent your city so the students can see where they live.
5. Rotate the globe and show what happens to their city as the Earth rotates.
6. Ask the students how long it takes for the Earth to rotate once. If you make it clear to them where the sun is shining to start with, they may be able to figure out for themselves that the Earth rotates once a day. Have them work with the globe and light source to gain additional understanding.

D. Result:

The students will learn that the Earth rotates once each day. This causes darkness (night) in half of the world while it is light (day) in the opposite half.

E. Basic Facts and Supplemental Information:

1. The rotation of the Earth, not the movement of the sun, causes day and night.
2. The Earth is divided into time zones, otherwise it would be the same time for everybody all around the world.
3. We have four time zones in the continental United States:
   a. Pacific
   b. Mountain
   c. Central
   d. Eastern
4. Alaska is on Alaskan Standard Time and is one hour earlier than Pacific Standard Time.
5. Hawaii is on Hawaiian-Aleutian Standard Time and is two hours earlier than Pacific Standard Time.
6. Daylight Saving Time doesn't change the length of time or day. We just change our clocks by moving them forward one hour. This is done in the spring. In the fall we set our clocks back one hour.

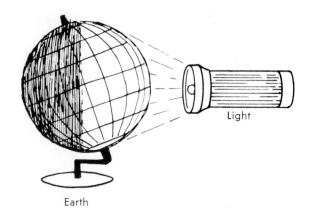

Light

Earth

We can remember this by the expression, "SPRING ahead and FALL back."

F. Thought Questions for Class Discussions:

1. Can you figure out if the Earth rotates from east to west or west to east?
2. Why, during some times of year, are days longer than nights and at other times nights longer than days?
3. How do we know the axis of the Earth tilts in relation to the sun?
4. If it is 1:00 P.M. in New York, what time is it in California?
5. Can you see farther in the daytime or nighttime? (Be careful—hint: stars?)

G. Related Ideas for Further Inquiry:

1. Discuss time zones in relation to friends or relatives who live in other parts of the country.
2. Discuss rotation and revolution.
3. Study Activity VII-B-1, "What are planets?"
4. Study Activity VII-B-2, "How is the Earth different from other planets?"
5. Study Activity VII-B-4, "Does the sun revolve around the Earth?"
6. Study Activity VII-B-6, "How does the sun help us?"
7. Study Activity VII-B-7, "How does the length of day and night change from season to season?"
8. Study other Activities in this Section.

H. Vocabulary Builders—Spelling Words:

1) **day** 2) **night** 3) **rotation** 4) **Earth**
5) **globe** 6) **flashlight** 7) **dawn** 8) **dusk**

I. Thought for Today:

"Daylight saving time just makes some people tired one hour earlier."

A. Problem: *How Does the Sun Help Us?*

B. Materials Needed:

On the sun:

1. Books
2. Pamphlets
3. Pictures
4. Charts
5. Multisensory aids

C. Procedure:

1. Have students draw a picture which includes the sun.
2. Ask the class how the sun helps us.
3. Make a list of these items and write them on the chalkboard.
4. Add your own items which might include:
   a. getting energy (All the Earth's energy for plants and people comes from the sun.)
   b. keeping us warm
   c. keeping all plants growing
   d. keeping all animals growing
   e. lets us see in the daytime (provides light)
   f. find our direction
   g. tell time
   h. causes seasons
   i. one source of Vitamin D
   j. gives us a tan
   k. gives us time to play

D. Results:

1. Students will learn that the sun is our main source of energy and without it no life can exist on Earth.
2. Pupils will know that our sun is a star and that the energy is derived by nuclear fusion.

E. Basic Facts and Supplemental Information:

1. The Earth receives only a very small part of the sun's total energy output.
2. The Earth receives only one-half of one billionth of the total amount of the sun's output.
3. The sun shines in all directions.
4. Of the total amount of the sun's radiation that the Earth receives, 43% is absorbed, 42% is reflected, and 15% is held in our atmosphere.
5. The sun is an atomic furnace releasing energy.
6. Most astronomers believe that our planet was made from stardust left over from the sun.
7. The sun is about 93 million miles away.
8. The sun is really just another star.

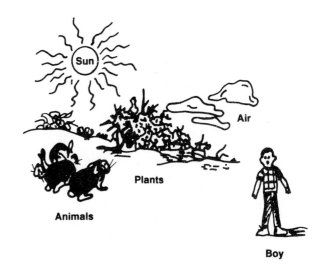

9. It is a ball of hot, luminous gases, primarily hydrogen and helium.
10. The energy that it creates is accomplished by atomic fusion.
11. Its temperature is about 25 million degrees Fahrenheit (14 million degrees Centigrade).
12. The sun some day will use up all its energy and "die," but we won't have to worry because it is expected to last 5 billion more years.

F. Thought Questions for Class Discussions:

1. What steps are necessary to convert the sun's energy to our energy?
2. Which planet is the hottest? Which is the coldest? Why?
3. Which planet, other than ours, would be most apt to have living organisms on it?

G. Related Ideas for Further Inquiry:

1. Study the three main stages in the life of stars (and our sun): red giant, white dwarf, and black dwarf.
2. Study Activity VII-B-1, "What are planets?"
3. Study Activity VII-B-2, "How is the Earth different from other planets?"

H. Vocabulary Builders—Spelling Words:

1) **energy** 2) **warm** 3) **alive** 4) **plants**
5) **animals** 6) **output** 7) **growing**

I. Thought for Today:

"It has been observed that a person who laughs, lasts."

A. Problem: *How Does the Length of Day and Night Change from Season to Season?*

B. Materials Needed:

1. Desk, table, or stand
2. World globe
3. Filmstrip projector (Flashlight may be substituted.)
4. Compass
5. Chalkboard pointer or yardstick

C. Procedure:

1. Place globe on desk or table.
2. Place filmstrip projector about 15′ from the globe.
3. Darken the room.
4. Turn the projector on.
5. Shine the light from the projector to the globe. (The light side represents daytime; the dark side, nighttime.)
6. Using compass, tilt the globe northward until the elevation of the axis above the horizontal is the same as the latitude of the school. (If your community is located at 38° North Latitude, then the globe should be tilted 38° from the horizontal position. You can estimate tilt, it doesn't have to be exact.)
7. Slowly rotate the globe on its axis noting the amount of light on the North Pole and South Pole.
8. Select another point on the globe, and as the globe rotates, determine if it receives no light, all light, more than half, or less than half of the light during one rotation.
9. Move the projector to the floor and repeat rotation.
10. Move the projector to a high level and repeat rotation.

D. Results:

1. Students will visualize that the North Pole is opposite the South Pole as to lightness and darkness.
2. Pupils will learn that lightness and darkness change as the seasons change (moving the projector up and down).

E. Basic Facts and Supplemental Information:

1. In the spring and fall the axis of the Earth is neither tilted toward nor away from the sun, thus providing equal amounts of night and day.
2. In the Northern Hemisphere during the summer, the axis of the Earth is tilted toward the sun. The

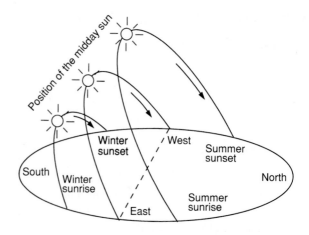

daylight arc is longer than the nighttime arc, therefore, the days are longer than the nights.

3. In the Northern Hemisphere during winter, the axis of the Earth is tilted away from the sun. The daylight arc is shorter than the nighttime arc, therefore, the days are shorter and the nights are longer.

F. Thought Questions for Class Discussions:

1. If you could live where the daylight was the longest, where would you live in the summer? winter? autumn? spring?
2. Check with the weather bureau to find the average temperature of your locality for a winter month and a summer month. Is there much difference?
3. What is the international date line? Why is it necessary?

G. Related Ideas for Further Inquiry:

1. Design a test to prove that our Earth tilts at 23 1/2 degrees from its orbital plane.
2. Discuss how plants, animals, and people adjust to each season.
3. Study Section VII-E, "Weather."
4. Study all Activities in this Section.

H. Vocabulary Builders—Spelling Words:

1) **length** 2) **day** 3) **night** 4) **season**
5) **orbit** 6) **tilt** 7) **summer** 8) **winter**

I. Thought for Today:

"Winter is the season in which people try to keep the house as warm as it was in the summer when they complained about the heat."

Activity

A. Problem: *Why Is the Sky Blue?*

B. Materials Needed:

1. Prism
2. Light source
3. Quart jar
4. Milk
5. Slide projector or flashlight
6. Two chalkboard erasers

C. Procedure One:

1. Ask the class what colors the sky has been that they have observed.
2. Ask if they know why the sky is normally blue on a clear day.
3. Demonstrate how a prism breaks white light into its component parts.
4. Tell the class how our atmosphere acts like a prism.
5. Inform the students that if the Earth had no atmosphere the sky would have no color.
6. The gases and dust in our atmosphere break up the sunlight.
7. The blue part is more scattered than the other colors, consequently we see more blue.

Procedure Two:

In a darkened room:

1. Add milk to a jar of water a drop at a time.
2. Continually stir the mixture.
3. In a darkened room with projector or flashlight, shine the beam through the jar.
4. To see the beam of light, strike two chalkboard erasers together over the light beam to get chalk particles into the air.
5. Observe the jar through its side.
6. Observe the jar through the front (opposite side of beam entrance).

D. Results:

1. Procedure One:
   The prism breaks the light into a rainbow of colors.
2. Procedure Two:
   a. When the contents of the jar are viewed from the side, they appear blue.
   b. When the contents of the jar are viewed from the front, they appear reddish-yellow.
3. From both activities, students will learn why the sky is blue during the day and why it has a reddish cast at sunrise or sunset.
4. Technically, red light has almost twice the wavelength of blue light. The shorter the wavelength, the more the light is scattered.
5. Students will also begin to realize that the shorter the wavelength of a particular color of light, the more that color is scattered.

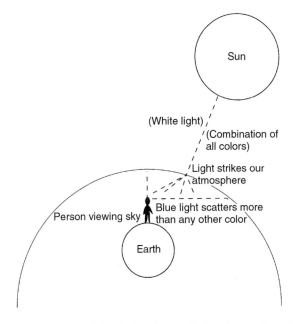

6. Most particles in the air are slightly larger than the wavelengths of light and, therefore, when the light hits the particles it is scattered.

E. Basic Facts and Supplemental Information:

1. Blue light is scattered more. This is why in the prism experiment, the blue color is bent the most of any color.
2. In the second procedure, the blue and violet waves scatter quite easily and can be seen from the side view.
3. In the second procedure, the long red waves move through the mixture (like the mixture in our atmosphere) with little scattering.

F. Thought Questions for Class Discussions:

1. What makes color?
2. What makes a rainbow?
3. Why do some clouds look white and others gray or black?

G. Related Ideas for Further Inquiry:

1. Study Section VI-C, "Pollution."
2. Study Activity VII-B-6, "How does the sun help us?"
3. Study Activity VII-E-7, "What causes a rainbow?"
4. Study other Activities in this Section.

H. Vocabulary Builders—Spelling Words:

1) **sky**   2) **blue**   3) **atmosphere**   4) **scatter**
5) **gases**   6) **dust**   7) **colors**   8) **prism**

I. Thought for Today:

"If most of us are ashamed of shabby clothes and shoddy furniture, let us be more ashamed of shabby ideas and shoddy philosophies."

A. Problem: *How Does the Moon Travel?*

B. Materials Needed:

1. World globe
2. Flashlight or slide projector
3. Chalkboard
4. Three cards labeled: "Earth," "Moon," and "Sun"
5. Flannel board and cutouts (optional)

C. Procedure:

1. Discuss with the class the concepts of rotation (spinning on its axis) and revolution (moving around another body).
2. Discuss the causes of day and night, and length of a day, a month, and a year.
3. Use the flashlight or slide projector to explain day and night. (See Activity VII-B-5.)
4. Have three students come to the front of the room and explain the relative movements of the Earth, moon, and sun. Let one student be the sun; another student, the moon; and the third student, the Earth. Have each of these students individually go through the motions of his/her celestial body, holding up his/her labeled card, while the other two remain stationary.
    a. The "Sun" "rotates" slowly over a fixed point.
    b. The "Earth" "revolves" around the sun slowly and "rotates" on its axis much faster.
    c. The "Moon" "revolves" around the Earth once and "rotates" once. It keeps one side facing the Earth all the time.
5. If space permits, have all three "celestial bodies" move at the same time in their regular patterns. If room is not available in the classroom, conduct this activity outside.

D. Result:

Students will become more aware of the effect the sun and moon have on the Earth, and the relative movements of each.

E. Basic Facts and Supplemental Information:

1. This activity could be conducted on the school campus, with the orbit of the Earth around the sun chalked on the surface of the school yard to more accurately show the relative distance between all three celestial bodies.
2. The moon travels from west to east around the Earth. The moon rises about 50 minutes later each night. It travels completely around the Earth from

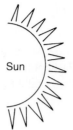

one full moon to another. This takes approximately 27.3 days.

3. The moon is approximately 240,000 miles from the Earth.
    a. Its diameter is 2,160 miles.
    b. While the moon is rotating on its axis and revolving around the Earth, its apparent motion of rising later each day is due to the rotation of the Earth.

F. Thought Questions for Class Discussions:

1. What are some problems astronauts have in trying to land on the moon with a spaceship?
2. Why is it that we can't see the moon on some nights?
3. What causes the moon to change apparent shapes?
4. Why does the moon look larger when it first rises (near the horizon) than it does when it is higher (overhead)? (There is more distortion because the line of sight contains more particles in the air.)

G. Related Ideas for Further Inquiry:

1. Study the position of the moon and see how it moves over several hours of time.
2. Study Activity VII-B-5, "What makes day and night?"
3. Study Activity VII-B-10, "Why does the moon appear to change shape?"
4. Study Activity VII-B-11, "What causes an eclipse?"
5. Study Section VIII-B, "Satellites."

H. Vocabulary Builders—Spelling Words:

1) **moon** 2) **travel** 3) **Earth** 4) **rotation**
5) **revolution** 6) **celestial** 7) **orbit** 8) **axis**

I. Thought for Today:

"Time is what we want the most, and what we use the worst."

Activity

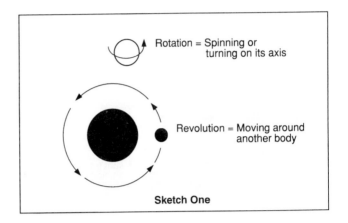

Rotation = Spinning or turning on its axis

Revolution = Moving around another body

Sketch One

A. Problem: *Why Does the Moon Appear to Change Shape?*

NOTE: This is a very difficult concept and should be undertaken over a period of time. A good start is to review Activity VII-B-5, "What makes day and night?" Then have the students observe the changes in the moon's appearance for a complete month.

B. Materials Needed:

1. World globe or large ball
2. Electric lamp
3. Slide projector
4. Bulletin board (preferably covered with light blue construction paper)
5. Flannel board, approximately 24″ × 36″ (preferably light blue color)
6. Colored construction paper: yellow, orange, dark green, light green, black, and white
7. Glue, paste, or cellophane tape
8. Colored yarn

C. Procedure One (See Sketch One.):

1. Move chairs and desks to the sides of the room.
2. Set the lamp on a desk in the middle of the room.
3. Turn lamp on.
4. Darken the room, except for the lamp.
5. Demonstrate the term "rotation" by having one student turn around slowly while staying in one spot. This rotation could be the sun, moon, Earth, or any other celestial body.
6. Demonstrate the term "revolution" by having another student walk around the lamp. This revolution could be any celestial body that moves around another, such as the Earth orbiting the sun, the moon orbiting the Earth, or any celestial body orbiting around another celestial body.
7. Have two students move as the Earth and moon do. The student representing the Earth should walk very, very slowly around the sun (lamp) in a large circle while the second student walks around the first student with his/her face always toward the student who represents the Earth.

Procedure Two (See Sketch Two.):

1. From the construction papers, cut out the following representations:
   a. the sun (approximately 12″ in diameter) and its rays (yellow or orange) (The rays could be represented by colored yarn.)

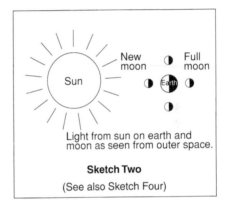

Light from sun on earth and moon as seen from outer space.

Sketch Two

(See also Sketch Four)

   b. the Earth (approximately 4″ in diameter, dark green on the half that will be away from the sun and light green on the half that will be closest to the sun)
   c. four moons (each half white and half black, 2″ in diameter)
2. Place the construction paper "sun" on one side of the flannel board, explaining that the sun gives off light in all directions. (See Sketch Two.)
3. Place the construction paper "Earth" about halfway to the side of the flannel board, with the light half facing the "sun."
4. Place the four moons around the "Earth" as shown in Sketch Two labeling the positions of the "New Moon" and the "Full Moon." (These show four positions of the moon at different times of the month.)
5. While the light side of the moon always faces the sun, the shape of the moon depends on where we view it from Earth.

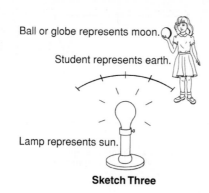

Ball or globe represents moon.

Student represents earth.

Lamp represents sun.

Sketch Three

Phases of the moon

New Moon	Waxing Crescent	First Quarter	Waxing (Gibbous)
Full Moon	Waning (Gibbous)	Last Quarter	Waning Crescent

as seen from the earth
Sketch Four

The crescent shape appearances of the moon are due to the light from the sun shining on a *ball-shaped* moon as seen from earth.

Procedure Three (See Sketch Three.)

1. Place a light in a high position (tabletop or desk).
2. Draw an arc on the floor with a piece of chalk to represent 1/13 of the Earth's path around the sun. The arc should be part of a circle about 12 feet in diameter. This represents the time the moon orbits the Earth and the Earth's partial orbit around the sun in one month's time.
3. Divide the arc into 4 equal parts and mark them as shown in Sketch Three.
4. Darken the room.
5. Have a student hold the globe or ball just over his/her head.
6. Have him/her make one slow rotation in his/her walk along the arc, noting the change of the shape of the light on the globe or ball. (Have class report viewing changes.)

Procedure Four (See Sketch Four.)

1. From the construction paper, cut out four white moons and four black moons, each about 10 to 12 inches in diameter.
2. Cut out portions of circles of the opposite color to affix to the moon cutouts as shown in the drawings.
3. Glue, paste, or tape these cutouts to the moons.
4. Mount the "moons" on the bulletin board.
5. Label each phase as shown.
6. Compare this display with the actual observations of the moon during the month.

D. Results:

Major concepts pupils learn through these procedures:

1. At any one time, half of the Earth and half of the moon are in darkness and half in lightness (night and day).
2. "Rotation" means a body turns on its axis.
3. "Revolution" means a body orbits another body.
4. The moon rotates once for every revolution it makes around the Earth consequently we see only one side of the moon.
5. Our perspective of the shape of the moon's lighted side is caused by the sun shining on it.
6. The moon rotates once and revolves around the Earth once every 27.3 days.
7. The moon revolves around the sun about 13 times a year, not exactly once a month.

E. Basic Facts and Supplemental Information:

1. If an orrery is available, be sure to use it to supplement the activities cited.
2. Important facts about the moon:
   a. The moon is a satellite revolving around the Earth.
   b. It is about 1/3 the size of the Earth; its diameter is about 2,160 miles.
   c. The moon is approximately 240,000 miles from the Earth.
   d. Although continually changing, each phase lasts about three and a half days.
   e. When there is an increase of light on the moon as seen from the Earth each day, it is "waxing." If decreasing, it is "waning."

F. Thought Questions for Class Discussions:

1. How would the Earth appear to change in shape if we were on the moon?
2. If it were possible to view the Earth and moon from the sun, how would they appear to change in shape?
3. What causes an eclipse of the moon? of the sun?

G. Related Ideas for Further Inquiry:

1. Visit an observatory.
2. Study Activity II-C-1, "Does light travel only in a straight line?"
3. Study Activities VII-B-1, VII-B-5, VII-B-9, and VII-B-11.

H. Vocabulary Builders—Spelling Words:

1) **phase** 2) **quarter** 3) **waxing** 4) **waning**
5) **gibbous** 6) **rotation** 7) **revolution**

I. Thought for Today:

"What we learn with pleasure, we never forget."

A. Problem: *What Causes an Eclipse?*

B. Materials Needed:
1. World globe (or large ball)
2. Table or desk
3. Tennis ball (to represent the moon)
4. Ice pick
5. Slide projector
6. Wire

C. Procedure:
1. With ice pick, *carefully* punch two holes on opposite sides of tennis ball.
2. Put wire through holes with loop on top to manipulate it. (Demonstration is more realistic when shadow of your hand is not on the globe as you rotate tennis ball.)
3. Set globe on desk or table.
4. Set up slide projector 10 to 15 feet from globe.
5. Darken room; turn on projector.
6. Revolve tennis ball around the globe so light from projector will cast shadows.
7. Revolve moon (tennis ball) until it falls within the shadow cast by the Earth (lunar eclipse).
8. Revolve the tennis ball close to Earth until it comes between the Earth and the sun, throwing its own shadow over the Earth. This will produce a partial or total eclipse, depending on the observer's position on globe (solar eclipse).

D. Result:
Students learn that the shadows of the Earth and moon are what causes eclipses of the moon and sun. When the moon has light from the sun cut off by the Earth, it is a lunar eclipse (eclipse of the moon). When the Earth has light cut off by the moon, it is a solar eclipse (eclipse of the sun).

E. Basic Facts and Supplemental Information:
Solar eclipses are visible on limited sections of the Earth because of the relatively small shadow cast by the moon. Lunar eclipses are visible over large areas of the Earth's surface because they are caused by the Earth casting a shadow on the moon. (The Earth is much larger than the moon.)

F. Thought Questions for Class Discussions:
1. Do we have lunar eclipses every month?
2. Do other planets have moons?
3. Can we see both sides of the moon during one day, one week, or one month? Why or why not? (Hint: It rotates once for every revolution it makes around the Earth.)

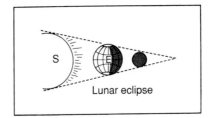
Lunar eclipse

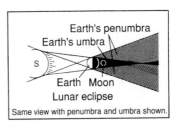
Earth's penumbra
Earth's umbra
S
Earth Moon
Lunar eclipse
Same view with penumbra and umbra shown.

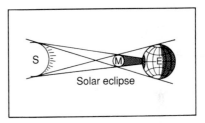
Solar eclipse

G. Related Ideas for Further Inquiry:
1. Discuss what causes the Earth's umbra and penumbra.
2. Discuss what we can learn during an eclipse.
3. Study Section VII-A, "Universe."
4. Study other Activities in this Section.

H. Vocabulary Builders—Spelling Words:
1) **eclipse** 2) **sun** 3) **moon** 4) **shadow**
5) **globe** 6) **umbra** 7) **penumbra** 8) **orbits**

I. Thought for Today:
"Science can predict an eclipse of the sun many years in advance, but cannot accurately predict the weather over the weekend."

Activity

A. Problem: *What Causes Tides?*

B. Materials Needed:
1. Large ball depicting sun
2. Small ball depicting Earth
3. Smaller ball depicting moon (styrofoam balls work well)
4. Wide rubber band
5. Four cup hooks
6. Three supports: one for the sun, one for the Earth, and one for the moon. (The sun's support may be stationary. The Earth's and moon's supports should be movable.)
7. Attach cup hooks and balls to rubber band as shown in drawing.

C. Procedure:
1. Explain that heavenly bodies attract each other. The sun attracts the Earth and the Earth attracts the sun. The Earth attracts the moon and the moon attracts the Earth.
2. Discuss how the moon attracts the Earth and moves the oceans toward the moon.
3. Discuss how the sun attracts the Earth and moves the oceans toward the sun.
4. Explain how the moon exerts a greater pull because it is so much closer to the Earth.
5. By the use of the apparatus made, the direction of pull can be demonstrated by the direction of the rubber band. (See drawing.)
6. Move the moon to various positions around the Earth.
7. Explain when the sun, moon, and Earth are in a straight line, the pull is greatest. These tides are called spring tides and occur twice a month. When the moon, Earth, and sun form a right triangle (one week later) the tides are smallest and are called neap tides.
8. Discuss the causes of high and low tides each day. (The Earth's rotation and its relation to the position of the moon.)
9. Discuss the causes of incoming tides. (The oceans are getting closer to the moon.)

D. Results:
1. Students will learn that the sun and moon cause the tides.
2. Pupils will learn that the moon has a much greater effect on tides than the sun.

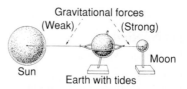

Gravitational forces
(Weak)   (Strong)
Sun   Earth with tides   Moon

3. Students will be able to differentiate the terms "spring tides," "neap tides," "incoming tides," and "ebb tides."

E. Basic Facts and Supplemental Information:
1. The daily newspapers usually report the time of high tides and low tides each day.
2. Normally there are two bulges of the Earth at the same time—one facing the moon and one on the opposite side.
3. Usually there are two high tides and two low tides every day due to the Earth's rotation.
4. The shape of the seacoast has a great effect on the height and range of tides.
5. Remember that "spring tides" are the tides with the highest waters.
6. "Neap tides" occur when the pull of the sun and the moon are weakest; the tides are at their lowest level.
7. "Ebb tides" are those periods when the waters are receding.

F. Thought Questions for Class Discussions:
1. In some parts of the world the daily tides are less than 2 feet high, while in other parts of the world they are as great as 70′ high. Why?
2. How can tides be used to help us?
3. Do you think tides could be used to generate electricity?

G. Related Ideas for Further Inquiry:
1. Students can check the location of the moon at high tide and at low tide.
2. Study Activity VII-B-11, "What causes an eclipse?"
3. Study Activity VII-B-10, "Why does the moon appear to change shape?"
4. Study other Activities in this Section.

H. Vocabulary Builders—Spelling Words:
1) **tide** 2) **gravity** 3) **attract** 4) **spring**
5) **neap** 6) **rotation** 7) **heavenly** 8) **pull**

I. Thought for Today:
"Patience is bitter but its fruit is sweet."

Earth's crust

A. Problem: *What Are the Natural Surfaces Found on the Earth's Crust?*

B. Materials:

1. Reference materials on the Earth's crust
2. Multisensory aids on the different surfaces of the Earth:
   a. world globe
   b. maps
   c. pictures
   d. films, filmstrips, slides, etc.
   e. dioramas, models, etc.
   f. bulletin board

C. Procedure:

1. Briefly discuss the position of the Earth in our solar system.
2. Discuss the uniqueness of our planet and those characteristics that make life possible:
   a. atmosphere (nitrogen, oxygen, etc.)
   b. temperature range
   c. natural resources
   d. wildlife
   e. balance of nature, etc.
3. Show the students the world globe and start a list on the bulletin board of the different kinds of natural surfaces found on our planet. These should include:

   a. oceans   n. estuaries
   b. mountains   o. deserts
   c. volcanoes   p. icecaps
   d. glaciers   q. islands
   e. valleys   r. plateaus
   f. rivers   s. lagoons
   g. geysers   t. mesas
   h. forests   u. plains
   i. waterfalls   v. peninsulas
   j. caves   w. deltas
   k. lakes   x. canyons
   l. ponds   y. straits
   m. bays   z. hills, etc.

4. Have students read reference materials for additional surfaces.
5. Use whatever multisensory aids are available to further study the surfaces of our planet.
6. Some students might want to build dioramas, models, or mobiles showing some special features of our planet.

7. Continually integrate the importance of our various natural surfaces to provide:
   a. food   c. transportation
   b. shelter   d. recreation, etc.

D. Results:

1. Students will learn there are many different types of surfaces found on our planet.
2. Students will realize that we must take care of the Earth's surface in order for us to survive.

E. Basic Facts and Supplemental Information:

1. Other surfaces that might be studied are glaciers, geysers, forests, waterfalls, caves, ponds, bays, estuaries, crops, other plants, etc.
2. The surfaces of the Earth are continually changed by nature and people.
   a. People change the surfaces of the Earth by building cities, streets, bridges, highways, residences, planting crops, etc.
   b. Nature changes the surfaces by rain, wind, erosion, volcanic eruptions, earthquakes, etc.

F. Thought Questions for Class Discussions:

1. The population of the world will probably double in the next 50 years. What will this do to the natural surfaces of the Earth?
2. Should we preserve some of our natural surfaces? which ones?
3. How are animals affected by people's interferences with changing Earth's natural surfaces?

G. Related Ideas for Further Inquiry:

1. Study Part III, "Plants."
2. Study Part IV, "Animals."
3. Study Activity VII-C-2, "What kinds of rocks are there?"
4. Study Activity VII-C-5, "What causes earthquakes?"
5. Study Activity VII-C-6, "What causes a volcano to erupt?"
6. Study Section VII-E, "Weather."

H. Vocabulary Builders—Spelling Words:

1) **oceans** 2) **mountains** 3) **valleys** 4) **rivers**
5) **lakes** 6) **deserts** 7) **icecaps** 8) **continents**

I. Thought for Today:

"When you come right down to it, the problem isn't the environment, but the people who spoil it."

Activity

A. Problem: *What Kinds of Rocks Are There?*

B. Materials Needed:

1. Reference books about rocks
2. Tables about rock characteristics (See Tables, next page)
3. Pictures of rocks
4. Rock collections (could be brought in by students)
5. Hammer
6. Vinegar or dilute hydrochloric acid
7. Eyedropper
8. Multisensory aids

C. Procedure:

1. Discuss rocks using multisensory aids to motivate and stimulate students' questions.
2. Ask students to collect as many different kinds of rocks as they can.
3. Make a display of the rocks.
4. With reference books, have pupils identify as many as possible.
   a. Being careful of fingers, tap the rock sample with the hammer to determine its relative hardness.
   b. The students can use 6 to 8 drops of vinegar to test samples, or the teacher can test with dilute hydrochloric acid. (The students should never be allowed to use acids for these tests.)
5. Have students label rocks and give characteristics of each type. (See next page.)
6. Plan a field trip to increase the classroom collection.

D. Results:

1. Some rocks when hit will break into small pieces; some will chip and some will remain in one piece.
2. Some rocks will bubble when vinegar or dilute acid is placed on them showing the presence of carbonates. Rocks are carbonates or silicates.
3. Students will learn to identify the main types of rock formations.

E. Basic Facts and Supplemental Information:

1. This activity is always motivating for students.
2. Students are natural collectors, and this activity makes use of this natural curiosity.
3. With a little persuasion from the teacher, many students will start their own rock collections.
4. Rocks are classified by their color, hardness, cleavage, size, etc.
5. Rocks usually contain a mixture of minerals.

6. It's fun to collect minerals.
7. Minerals are building blocks of rocks.
8. There are over 2,000 known minerals.
9. Twenty of them make up 95% of the Earth's crust.
10. Minerals contain no living or once living material. Silver, gold, and diamonds are minerals (and also elements). Diamonds are pure crystalline carbon.
11. Semiprecious stones such as sapphires, rubies, and emeralds are also minerals.
12. Minerals have definite physical characteristics; rocks do not.
13. Characteristics of minerals to look for:
    a. luster (glossy or dull)
    b. crystalline
    c. appearance when split
    d. color
    e. hardness (See Moh's Scale—next page.)
    f. magnetic or not
    g. acid test (white vinegar is best for elementary students to use. Many minerals contain calcium carbonate ($CaCO_3$) and will bubble when acid is placed on them.)
    h. Older students may want to test specimens with a smelting or heat test to determine if sulphur or metals are present.
    i. Older students may want to use a flame test. A small sample is heated in a flame. Different substances have different colors when heated. Extreme caution should be taken when heating rocks. Long tongs and gloves should be worn by the students. Better yet—the instructor should perform this part of the rock test.

14. Rocks are of three major types:
   a. Sedimentary—formed by mineral deposits from oceans or rivers.
   b. Igneous—formed by cooling of hot lava.
   c. Metamorphic—formed by a combination of igneous and sedimentary rocks.

F. Thought Questions for Class Discussions:

1. Why do we need to know anything about rocks?
2. How many ways can you name in which rocks are helpful or harmful to us?
3. How do rocks differ?

G. Related Ideas for Further Inquiry:

1. Make a campus survey to study the different kinds of rocks.
2. Have students make a survey of the different kinds of minerals that are found in homes.
3. Interview a jeweler about his/her work with minerals (and rocks).
4. Study Activity I-A-1, "What are the three states of matter?"
5. Study Activity I-A-2, "What are atoms? molecules?"
6. Study Activity I-A-3, "What are elements? compounds? mixtures?"
7. Study Activity I-A-8, "How do materials combine?"
8. Study Activity VII-C-1, "What are the natural surfaces found on the Earth's crust?"
9. Study Activity VII-C-5, "What causes earthquakes?"
10. Study other Activities in this Section.

H. Vocabulary Builders—Spelling Words:

1) **sapphire** 2) **diamond** 3) **silver** 4) **gold**
5) **crystalline** 6) **carbon** 7) **luster** 8) **scratches**

I. Thought for Today:

"A rolling stone gathers no moss, but it gains a certain polish."

COLOR TABLE

EXTERNAL COLOR	STREAK TEST	EXAMPLE
Blue or white Green, purple, white	White	Calcite
Gray or green	White	Fluorite
Blue–green	White	Talc
Gray	White	Apatite
Pale yellow	Gray	Galena
Orange–yellow	Dark green	Pyrite
Gray; Red–brown	Green–black	Chalcopyrite
Bright green	Red–brown	Hematite
Brown	Pale green	Malachite
Black	Ochre yellow	Limonite
	Black	Magnetite

HARDNESS TABLE (MOH'S SCALE)

HARDNESS NUMBER	HARDNESS TEST	EXAMPLE
1	Scratches easily with a fingernail	Talc
2	Scratches with a fingernail	Gypsum
3	Scratches with a pin or penny	Calcite
4	Scratches easily with a knife	Fluorite
5	Scratches with a knife	Apatite
6	Knife will not scratch rock; rock will not scratch glass	Feldspar
7	Scratches glass easily	Quartz
8	Scratches quartz easily	Topaz
9	Scratches topaz easily	Corundum
10	Scratches all other rocks	Diamond

SIZE TABLE

NAME	SIZE IN INCHES	(METRICS)
Boulder	More than 10 inches across	(25 cm)
Cobble	2½ to 10 inches across	(6–25 cm)
Pebble	⅛ to 2½ inches across	(30 mm–6 cm)
Granules	¹⁄₁₆ to ⅛ inches across	(15–30 mm)
Sand	¹⁄₆₄ to ¹⁄₁₆ inches across	(5–15 mm)
Silt	As fine as scouring powder	(—)
Clay	Particles can only be seen with microscope	(—)

Activity

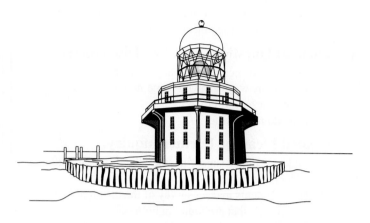

A. Problem: *What Are Some Characteristics of Oceans?*

B. Materials Needed:

1. Maps of the oceans
2. Pictures of ships on the oceans
3. Pictures of plants and animals that live in the oceans
4. Glass of water
5. Salt shaker
6. Thermometer
7. Pictures of beaches
8. Reference books on:
   a. tides
   b. waves
9. Specimens of ocean life:
   a. seashells
   b. coral
10. Multisensory aids on oceans

C. Procedure:

1. Ask the class if they have taken trips on or to the ocean(s).
2. Have them recount their experiences.
3. Discuss the values of oceans:
   a. food
   b. transportation
   c. recreation
      1) swimming
      2) boating
      3) surfing
      4) fishing
4. Discuss several ecosystems of the oceans.
5. Discuss some unusual characteristics of the oceans as time and interest permit:
   a. tides   e. underwater volcanos
   b. currents   f. tsunamis
   c. waves   g. El Niño
   d. water evaporation
6. Show any multisensory aids available.
7. Show selected tests with salt water.

D. Results:

1. Students will learn that oceans cover a large portion of the Earth's surface.
2. They will know that in spite of the names that we have given them, there is really only one gigantic ocean that surrounds all of the Earth's land masses.

E. Basic Facts and Supplemental Information:

1. The oceans cover 70% of the surface of the Earth.

2. There are four main oceans:
   a. Atlantic   c. Indian
   b. Pacific   d. Arctic
3. Sea water averages between 3.3–3.7% salt.
4. On the ocean floor are hidden mountain ranges, valleys, and vast open plains.
5. There are many underwater volcanos.
6. Underwater earthquakes cause vibrations which trigger tsunamis, giant waves that rush through the ocean surface at hundreds of miles per hour with waves which have been recorded as high as 250′. These sweep into coastal areas and destroy everything in their paths.
7. Tides result from the gravitational force of the sun and predominantly the moon.
8. Currents are the result of prevailing winds.
9. El Niño conditions are basically the result of warming temperatures in the oceans causing excess water evaporation and rains.

F. Thought Questions for Class Discussions:

1. Who owns the oceans? Who should?
2. Who should control fishing rights in the oceans?
3. Should we dump our sewage into the oceans?

G. Related Ideas for Further Inquiry:

1. Study the different kinds of materials that are polluting our oceans.
2. Study what causes waves.
3. Collect specimens of seashells and corals.
4. Study Activity VII-C-1, "What are the natural surfaces found on the Earth's crust?"

H. Vocabulary Builders—Spelling Words:

1) **names of the oceans**   2) **terms in Procedure 5**

I. Thought for Today:

"Love the sea? I dote upon it—from the beach."

Activity

A. Problem: *Where Do We Get Our Natural Gas?*

B. Materials Needed:

1. Chart
2. Map
3. Overhead projector and transparencies (optional)
4. Reference materials on natural gas

C. Procedure:

1. Ask class if they use natural gas in their homes.
2. Ask them where natural gas is used: stove? fireplace? water heater?
3. Ask them if they know where natural gas comes from.
4. Use a chart, draw a sketch, or have a transparency ready to show a typical gas well.
5. Explain to class that at first, early drilling only went down several hundred feet.
6. Describe how much more gas is needed because we have more people and increased demand.
7. Show students, using a picture or sketch, that gas companies today are digging deeper and deeper to explore for more gas, and already some companies are digging to the 7 mile depth.

D. Result:

Students will learn that natural gas is "mined" with oil and is now being sought at deeper and deeper levels as our shallow supplies have been used up.

E. Basic Facts and Supplemental Information:

1. Natural gas is formed by the decomposition of organic matter.
2. Natural gases are those bubbles that arise when probing stagnant waters.
3. Another term for natural gas is rock gas which may be in the form of petroleum.
4. Natural gas is stored in natural underground tanks (rock formations where gas can be piped out as supplies are needed).

F. Thought Questions for Class Discussions

1. How do you think the expression, "cooking with gas" originated?
2. Do you think we will ever run out of our supply of natural gas?
3. Is it cheaper to cook with gas or electricity?

G. Related Ideas for Further Inquiry:

1. Interview local gas personnel.
2. Have students read and interpret gas meter readings.

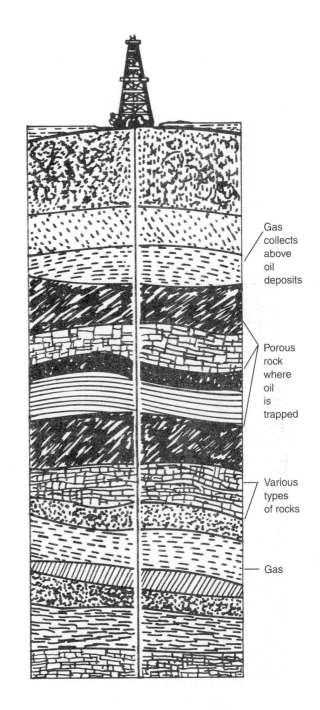

Gas collects above oil deposits

Porous rock where oil is trapped

Various types of rocks

Gas

3. Study Part II, "Energy."
4. Study other Activities in this Section.

H. Vocabulary Builders—Spelling Words:

1) **gas**   2) **electricity**   3) **wells**   4) **drilling**
5) **petroleum**   6) **natural**   7) **decomposition**

I. Thought for Today:

"One solution to the energy problem is to hole up all the government red tape and use it for fuel."

A. Problem: *What Causes Earthquakes?*

B. Materials Needed:

1. Three samples of carpeting or
   Three pieces of clay or
   Three blocks of wood, 2″ × 4″ × 12″
2. Tabletop or desk
3. Desk cover (if clay is used)

C. Procedure:

1. Briefly describe the composition of the Earth:
   a. hot, solid inner core
   b. hot, liquid outer core
   c. warm, variable thick mantle
   d. crust, made up of many layers 5 to 25 miles thick.
2. Tell the class that the carpeting, clay, or wood represent the layers of the Earth's crust. The layers can be represented by different pieces of carpeting, different colors of clay, or markings on the wood blocks.
3. Describe the pressures that act on the Earth's Surface: hot gases, winds, rains, glaciers, etc.
4. Floating on the Earth's molten core are land masses called "continental drifts" or more commonly, "plate tectonics." These plates rub, bump, move over or under other plates, causing vibrations and cracks (faults). Any of these movements cause earthquakes.
5. If blocks of wood are used, place the three blocks together.
6. Move one block forward and show how the Earth has moved along a fault line.
7. Replace the blocks so that the three are again lined up in their original position.
8. Lift two adjoining blocks up or holding all three, let one move downward.
9. Explain that this is what causes earthquakes—the resettling of the portions of the earth's crust caused by internal pressures.
10. Explain that the strength of earthquakes is measured by a Richter scale from "1" up.

Each subsequent number is ten times greater than the preceding number. A reading of "3" is 100 times greater than a reading of "1." Most earthquakes are reported in tenths such as 4.6, 3.5, or 2.8.

D. Results:

1. The movement of the blocks demonstrates Earth movements which produce earthquakes.

Carpeting, clay or wood

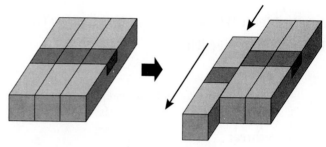

horizontal movement

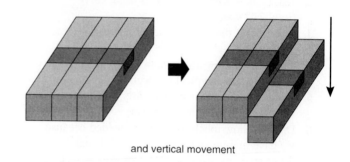

and vertical movement

2. Students will realize that the Earth has natural cracks or "faults" which are in a constant state of stress and sometimes produce earthquakes.

E. Basic Facts and Supplemental Information:

1. The shifting of the Earth as represented by the movement of the blocks usually occurs under the surface of the Earth and usually does not break the surface.
2. When an earthquake occurs, its vibrations travel rapidly through the body of the Earth.
3. These vibrations are detected by seismographs.

F. Thought Questions for Class Discussions:

1. What causes the different layers of the Earth?
2. What are fault lines?
3. If an earthquake happened in one area, what are the chances that it can happen in that area again?

G. Related Ideas for Further Inquiry:

1. Have students interview people who have been in a major earthquake.
2. Study all Activities in this Section.

H. Vocabulary Builders—Spelling Words:

1) **earthquake** 2) **crust** 3) **seismograph**
4) **Richter Scale** 5) **erosion** 6) **pressure**

I. Thought for Today:

"To err is human, but when the eraser wears out before the pencil, you're overdoing it."

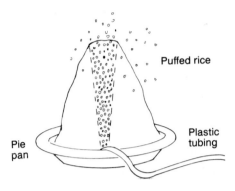

Puffed rice

Pie pan

Plastic tubing

A. Problem: *What Causes a Volcano to Erupt?*

B. Materials Needed:

1. Pie pan
2. Length of plastic tubing, about 15″ long
3. Salt and flour paste
4. Puffed rice
5. Dry, ground cereal
6. Tempera paint (brown)
7. Carbonated soft drink in a bottle or can
8. Water

C. Procedure:

1. Have a class committee do the research on the shape, general appearance, and structure of a volcano.
2. Students can make a paste of flour, salt, and water.
3. From this paste students can make a model of a volcano. A vertical cone-shaped hole should be left in the center. A plastic tube should be connected to the bottom of this hole. (See drawing.)
4. When paste has hardened, paint volcano brown with tempera paint.
5. Place some puffed rice cereal in the cavity.
6. Have a student blow, with great force, into the end of the plastic tube.
7. Open the soft drink bottle or can and notice the bubbles and some liquid droplets escaping.

Soft drink

D. Results:

1. The increased air pressure caused by the student blowing into the plastic tube will cause the "puffed rice" volcano to erupt.
2. Gas pressure forces the bubbles to spray out of the bottle or the can.

E. Basic Facts and Supplemental Information:

1. Volcanic eruptions are due to gas pressures that build up from the molten material from the Earth's core and reach the mantle and crust of the Earth.
2. This demonstration could lead to a discussion on the formation of mountains by pressure from the Earth's core.
3. Eruptions from volcanos cause major influences on the atmospheric environment by spewing carbon dioxide, nitrogen dioxide, and particulates into the air.

F. Thought Questions for Class Discussions:

1. In what way is the "erupting" model volcano similar to a real volcano erupting on Earth?

2. What causes the internal pressures within the Earth?
3. What pollutants from volcanos affect the atmosphere the most?

G. Related Ideas for Further Inquiry:

1. Combine this activity with art work.
2. Study Activity II-A-2, "What are renewable sources of energy?"
3. Study Activity VII-C-1, "What are the natural surfaces found on the Earth's crust?"
4. Study Activity VII-C-4, "Where do we get our natural gas?"
5. Study Activity VII-C-5, "What causes earthquakes?"
6. Study Activity VII-C-7, "What are geysers?"
7. Study other Activities in this Section.

H. Vocabulary Builders—Spelling Words:

1) **volcano**   2) **erupt**   3) **cone**   4) **pressure**
5) **simulate**   6) **puffed rice**   7) **plastic**

I. Thought for Today:

"If you think you have somebody eating out of your hand, it's a good idea to count your fingers."

A. Problem: *What Are Geysers?*

B. Materials Needed:

1. Small open can
2. Water
3. Cookie sheet with raised edges
4. Dirt
5. Heating element (hot plate works best)
6. Tissue paper
7. Rubber band
8. Work table

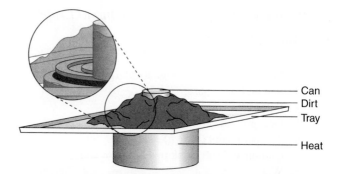

Can
Dirt
Tray
Heat

C. Procedure:

1. Place tray on work table.
2. Place small can on tray.
3. Fill can with water.
4. Cover top of can with tissue paper.
5. Secure with rubber band.
6. Make a pile of dirt that will just cover the can.
7. Place the heating element under the cookie sheet.
8. Keep students away from apparatus.
9. Discuss geysers.
10. Turn on the heating element.

D. Results:

1. The water will boil.
2. The steam will force its way through the tissue paper and move the dirt off the top.
3. Students will learn that geysers are formed by the Earth heating the soil and causing water to change to steam.

E. Basic Facts and Supplemental Information:

1. If you prefer, you could use a can of a carbonated soft drink that is at room temperature to liken to a geyser when the can is opened quickly.
2. Molten rocks below the Earth's crust reach temperatures of 1,800° F (1,000° C.)
3. This energy source is called geothermal energy.
4. "Old Faithful" in Yellowstone National Park is a geyser that erupts approximately every 45 minutes.
5. About twenty countries now use geothermal energy.
6. In order to use geothermal energy, the molten (or very hot) rocks have to be near the surface of the Earth and the surface of the Earth has to be relatively thin.
7. The molten area or hot rocks are from about 5–30 miles below the Earth's surface.
8. Most geothermal projects work cold water down to the "hot areas."

F. Thought Questions for Class Discussions:

1. What are "hot springs?"
2. Where does the molten rock get its heat?
3. Is geothermal energy a "renewable" source of energy?

4. Can steam ever be over 212° F. (100° C.)?
5. Do you think we can ever tap the core of the Earth for energy?

G. Related Ideas for Further Inquiry:

1. Study geothermal energy.
2. Research the geothermal projects that various countries are using for energy.
3. Study hot springs, natural mud baths.
4. Study Activity VII-C-1, "What are the natural surfaces found on the Earth's crust?"
5. Study Activity VII-C-2, "What kinds of rocks are there?"
6. Study Activity VII-C-4, "Where do we get our natural gas?"
7. Study Activity VII-C-6, "What causes a volcano to erupt?"

H. Vocabulary Builders—Spelling Words:

1) **geyser**   2) **steam**   3) **energy**   4) **erupt**
5) **crust**   6) **molten**   7) **geothermal**

I. Thought for Today:

"He is more apt to contribute heat than light to a discussion."

Activity

A. Problem: *What Is the "Water Table"?*

B. Materials Needed:
1. Glass container or jar
2. Water glass
3. Water
4. Gravel
5. Sand
6. Chalkboard and colored chalk or overhead projector and transparencies

C. Procedure:
1. Draw a sketch of the water table as shown in Drawing 1, using blue for the water, and brown for land areas.
2. Label different kinds of water:
   a. rivers
   b. swamps
   c. lakes
   d. estuaries
   e. wetlands, etc.
3. Explain that where the land surface dips below the top of the water table, ground water flows to the surface forming rivers, swamps, or lakes.
4. Mix the sand and gravel together in the glass container (Drawing 1) until it is about half full.
5. Add water until it reaches a level about halfway up the mixture.

D. Results:
1. The water will be seen about halfway up the mixture. This water represents ground water. The upper level of ground water is called the water table.
2. Students will visualize the level of the "water table."
3. Pupils will begin to recognize the value of the "water table."

E. Basic Facts and Supplemental Information:
1. The water table varies from location to location. In some desert areas, the water from water tables is being tapped so that productive crops can be grown.
2. Some underground lakes never reach the surface of the Earth.
3. Some dumping of toxic wastes on land reaches the underground water and pollutes water wells miles away.
4. The water table is dependent on the amount of water present. If we use up the water, the water level drops.
5. The bottom of the ground water lies on nonporous, impervious rocks.

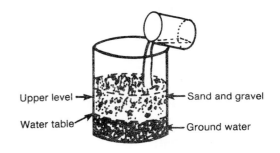

Drawing 1

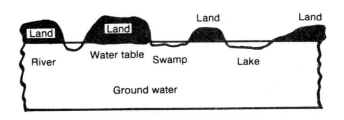

Drawing 2

6. Water wells have to be deep enough to account for dropping levels of water.

F. Thought Questions for Class Discussions:
1. What is the difference between water table and watershed?
2. Is it ever possible to reach the water table with a small shovel just by digging a small hole?
3. Does the water table move up and down? How could you prove it does or does not?

G. Related Ideas for Further Inquiry:
1. Talk to people you know who use well water.
2. Research your community for any water tables that can be studied first-hand.
3. Study Section I-C, "Water."
4. Study Section VII-E, "Weather."
5. Study Activity VII-C-1, "What are the natural surfaces found on the Earth's crust?"
6. Look up "aquifers." Find out what they are and where they are located.

H. Vocabulary Builders—Spelling Words:
1) **ground water**   2) **water table**   3) **river**
4) **swamp**   5) **lake**   6) **estuary**   7) **wetland**

I. Thought for Today:
"There is a mad scramble to improve just about everything in the world except people."

SECTION D: GRAVITY

Activity

A. Problem: *Do Heavy Objects Fall Faster Than Light Ones?*

B. Materials Needed:
1. Any solid articles of contrasting size and weight such as:
   a. Two old books
   b. Toy block
   c. Yarn, tightly wound
   d. Old flashlight battery
   e. Chalkboard eraser
   f. Rock
2. Two or three other objects of varying sizes

C. Procedure:
1. Plan to drop two articles from the above list at the same time from the same height, but have them vary in size and weight.
2. Have class predict beforehand which will reach the ground first.
3. Drop the test items.
4. Repeat with different objects, still varying in size and weight.

D. Results:
1. All solid objects will fall to earth with the same speed when wind resistance is neglected.
2. Most students are amazed at the result of these tests.

E. Basic Facts and Supplemental Information:
1. A light and a heavy solid object fall to Earth at equal times.
2. The size or weight of the object makes no difference in its falling speed.
3. Tightly wound yarn may fall a little slower than solid objects because of wind resistance.
4. The first, accurate tests of gravity were done by Galileo who dropped three unequal weights from the Leaning Tower of Pisa in the 16th century. All three hit the ground at about the same time. (Wind resistance had little effect.)
5. Freely falling objects, skydivers and parachutists, before their chutes open, fall at about 9.8 meters per second.
6. Each second of fall increases their speed by 9.8 meters per second, so that their speed at the end of two seconds is 19.6 meters per second and 29.4 meters per second after three seconds of free fall.

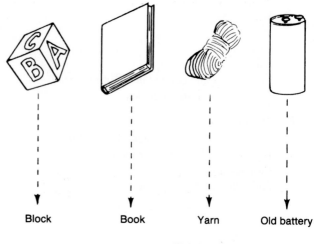

Block   Book   Yarn   Old battery

(Tightly packed)

F. Thought Questions for Class Discussions:
1. Why does a rock fall faster than a feather?
2. Will a rock and a feather fall at the same speed if placed in a vacuum?
3. Do all objects fall at an even rate of speed or do they fall faster and faster?

G. Related Ideas for Further Inquiry:
1. Place a feather on a book and drop them on a soft landing place that can't harm the book.
2. Drop a flat piece of paper to the floor and ask class where it will land. (Can't predict with any accuracy because of the zillions of air molecules that will affect it on its downward path.)
3. Study Section I-A, "Matter."
4. Study Activity VII-D-2, "Does gravity always work in the same direction?"
5. Study Activity VII-D-4, "How does gravity affect swinging objects?"
6. Study Activity VII-D-5, "How fast is gravity?"
7. Study Activity VII-D-8, "Can a rolling cylinder defy gravity?"
8. Study other Activities in this Section.

H. Vocabulary Builders—Spelling Words:
1) **gravity** 2) **heavier** 3) **size** 4) **weight**
5) **drop** 6) **predict** 7) **speed** 8) **resistance**

I. Thought for Today:

"No one needs a smile so much as one who has none to give."

Activity

A. Problem: *Does Gravity Always Work in the Same Direction?*

B. Materials Needed:
1. World globe
2. Four paper dolls
3. Cellophane tape
4. Unbreakable objects which can be dropped:
   a. chalkboard eraser
   b. old book
   c. magazine
   d. rock, etc.

C. Procedure:
1. Ask the class to point in the direction of "up."
2. Tell them to point in the direction of "down."
3. Drop one of the objects listed above.
4. Ask which direction it fell.
5. Ask what caused it to fall.
6. Drop another object on the floor.
7. Ask what direction it fell.
8. Scotch tape the four paper dolls to the globe. (See drawing.)
9. Ask students to point to the direction an object would fall if a student was at the North Pole, South Pole, Equator, or any other point on the globe.

D. Results:
1. All objects will fall "down."
2. All objects will fall toward the center of the Earth.
3. Gravity attracts objects on the Earth to the center of the Earth.
4. Students will learn that the "down" direction means toward the center of the Earth, and the "up" direction means away from the center of the Earth.

E. Basic Facts and Supplemental Information:
1. The Earth has a force which attracts objects toward its center. This is called "gravity."
2. We cannot see gravity, but we can see its effects.
3. The gravitational pull of the Earth on an object gives it its weight.
4. All bodies—people, animals, things, planets, etc., have gravitational pulls on all other people, animals, things, and planets, etc. We can say that every object in the universe attracts every other body.
5. The force of gravity, the gravitational pull, depends upon the mass of the objects and the distances they are apart.

Earth

F. Thought Questions for Class Discussions:
1. Could people live on the Earth if there were no gravity?
2. Do our space shuttles have problems with the gravitational pull of the Earth?
3. Does it take much work to overcome the force of gravity?

G. Related Ideas for Further Inquiry:
1. See other Activities in this Section.
2. Test falling objects to see if they fall at the same speed.
3. Study how the Earth and moon affect each other with their "gravitational pulls."
4. Study Activity VII-D-1, "Do heavy objects fall faster than light ones?"
5. Study Activity VII-D-4, "How does gravity affect swinging objects?"
6. Study Activity VII-D-9, "Do people have a center of gravity?"

H. Vocabulary Builders—Spelling Words:
1) **gravity** 2) **force** 3) **weight** 4) **Earth**
5) **direction** 6) **down** 7) **center**

I. Thought for Today:
"The old saying, 'What goes up must come down' is no longer true."

A. Problem: *How Does Gravity Affect the Time of Falling Sticks of Different Lengths?*

B. Materials Needed:

1. One-foot dowel
2. Two-foot dowel
3. Three-foot dowel
4. Table

C. Procedure:

1. Discuss falling objects and gravity with class. Have them relate their experiences with these.
2. Clear the tabletop.
3. Place the three dowels together in a vertical position as shown in the sketch.
4. While still holding them, lean all three to a slight angle off the vertical so that when released all three will fall independently to the tabletop.
5. Ask the class to hypothesize (guess) which dowel will strike the tabletop first and why.
6. Release the dowels.

D. Results:

1. The shorter dowel will strike the tabletop first.
2. The middle dowel will strike the tabletop second.
3. The longest dowel will strike the table last.

E. Basic Facts and Supplemental Information:

1. Gravity affects all objects with an equal force. Excluding wind resistance, a feather and a brick would fall at the same speed and if dropped from equal heights would hit the ground at the same time.
2. The time it takes an object to fall depends on its height above the ground (tabletop in this activity) and its center of gravity.
3. The center of gravity can be considered as the point where all the weight is concentrated.
4. Since the center of gravity in each dowel will be in the center of the stick, the longest dowel will have a higher center of gravity and thus take a longer time to fall to the tabletop.
5. Gravity is the force that pulls objects together regardless of whether they are large or small.

F. Thought Questions for Class Discussions:

1. Who has the higher center of gravity, a tall boy or a short girl?
2. Does a bowling pin have a high or low center of gravity?
3. Are moving automobiles affected by gravity?

G. Related Ideas for Further Inquiry:

1. See Section II-E on "Simple Machines." Determine how gravity affects each of these.
2. Study why sailboats sometimes turn over (capsize).
3. Study the stability of cars, bicycles, motorhomes, etc.
4. Study Activity VII-D-2, "Does gravity always work in the same direction?"
5. Study Activity VII-D-4, "How does gravity affect swinging objects?"
6. Study Activity VII-D-5, "How fast is gravity?"

H. Vocabulary Builders—Spelling Words:

1) **gravity**   2) **center**   3) **stability**
4) **falling**   5) **dowels**   6) **height**

I. Thought for Today:

"Teenagers are people who have a burning desire to be different by dressing alike."

Activity

A. Problem: *How Does Gravity Affect Swinging Objects?*

B. Materials Needed:
1. High support (top of chalkboard)
2. Various lengths of string
3. Enlarged protractor drawn on board
4. Proportionate weights, (e.g., 5, 10, 15 grams)
5. Chart like that shown in sketch
6. Watch with a second hand

C. Procedure:
1. Attach longest string to the top of support with the enlarged protractor behind it.
2. Attach the largest weight to the other end.
3. Raise the weight in about a 90° arc.
4. Release the weight.
5. Time the number of swings it makes in one minute.
6. Record the swings in chart.
7. Repeat using the next heaviest weight.
8. Repeat with lighter and lighter weights.
9. Use a second string about three-fourths the length of the first and repeat with all the weights, timing all the swings; record data.
10. Repeat with shorter and shorter lengths of strings.
11. Repeat with smaller and smaller arcs such as: 75°, 60°, 45°, and 30°.
12. Discuss the forces that are involved in these experiments:
    a. gravity   c. potential energy
    b. kinetic energy   d. wind resistance

D. Results:
1. Weights do not affect swing time.
2. Arcs do not affect swing time.
3. Lengths of string do affect swing time.

E. Basic Facts and Supplemental Information:
1. Class can be arranged in groups with each group working on one constant.
2. Pendulums will always swing in a straight line unless left for a long period of time when they would begin to rotate due to the rotation of the Earth.
3. Grandfather's clocks use pendulums with double arms to correct for expansion and contraction due to changes in room temperature.
4. The longer the pendulum, the greater the swing time.

F. Thought Questions for Class Discussions:
1. How does gravity affect the motion of a pendulum?
2. If you wanted a pendulum to swing slower, what would you do?

Pendulum Swing Time:

Length of String:		Weight:		
90° Arc	10	5	10	15
	20			
	40			
	80			
75° Arc	10	5	10	15
	20			
	40			
	80			
60° Arc	10	5	10	15
	20			
	40			
	80			
30° Arc	10	5	10	15
	20			
	40			
	80			

3. At what point does the pendulum weight have maximum kinetic energy? maximum potential energy?

G. Related Ideas for Further Inquiry:
Simplified experiments can be conducted using the following setups:

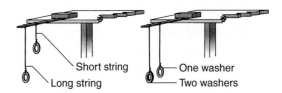

Short string
Long string

One washer
Two washers

H. Vocabulary Builders—Spelling Words:
1) **pendulum** 2) **swing time** 3) **length** 4) **arc**
5) **angle** 6) **kinetic** 7) **potential** 8) **energy**

I. Thought for Today:
"If you can keep your head while everybody else is losing theirs, you'll be a head taller."

A. Problem: *How Fast Is Gravity?*

B. Materials Needed:
1. Student
2. Crisp one dollar bill

C. Procedure:
1. Discuss falling objects such as rocks thrown up in the air, trees that are cut down, fly balls in baseball, etc.
2. Ask the students if gravity is "slow" or "fast."
3. Ask a student if he/she is "slow" or "fast." (reaction time)
4. Tell student that you will give him/her a dollar if he/she is faster than gravity.
5. Have him/her come to the front of the room.
6. Have him/her spread his/her thumb and forefinger about an inch and a half apart.
7. Tell this student that you are going to drop a one dollar bill vertically between his/her thumb and forefinger and that if it can be grabbed before it passes through his/her fingers he/she can keep it. Student must not move the hand—only the fingers. Hold the dollar bill a few inches above the student's spread fingers. Wait a few seconds—then drop it.

Ready?

Grab!

D. Results:
1. The student will not be able to grab the dollar bill.
2. Your dollar will be safe.
3. Gravity is faster than reaction time.

E. Basic Facts and Supplemental Information:
1. It takes time for the eye to see the dollar bill although light travels very fast.
2. It takes time for the eye to send a message to the brain.
3. It takes time for the brain to interpret the message.
4. It takes time for the brain to send a message to the fingers.
5. It takes time for the fingers to close.
6. The total time is called "reaction time."

F. Thought Questions for Class Discussions:
1. If the dollar bill were folded and held higher, and dropped in a similar fashion, would your dollar be safe?
2. Does the size of a dropped object make any difference?
3. Does the weight of a dropped object make any difference?

G. Related Ideas for Further Inquiry:
1. Study Section I-A, "Matter."
2. Study Section I-B, "Air."
3. Study Activity VII-D-1, "Do heavy objects fall faster than light ones?"
4. Study Activity VII-D-6, "Can you balance a pencil on the tip of your finger?"
5. Study Activity VII-D-9, "Do people have a center of gravity?"

H. Vocabulary Builders—Spelling Words:
1) **dollar** 2) **thumb** 3) **forefinger** 4) **keep**
5) **fast** 6) **speed** 7) **gravity** 8) **reaction**

I. Thought for Today:
"The world is moving so fast these days that the person who says it can't be done is generally interrupted by someone doing it."

Activity

A. Problem: *Can You Balance a Pencil on the Tip of Your Finger?*

B. Materials Needed:

1. Two ice picks
2. Several pencils

C. Procedure:

1. Challenge several students to see if they can balance a pencil on their forefinger.
2. Have the apparatus shown in the picture prepared ahead of time. This should be done very *carefully* by inserting the ice picks in the pencil with handles down and out, and on opposite sides of the pencil.
3. Tell the class that you can balance a pencil very easily.
4. Bring out the apparatus and perform the balancing act.
5. Discuss gravity, the center of gravity, and why the pencil is balanced.

D. Results:

1. The students will not be able to balance a pencil on their forefingers.
2. The teacher (or a student) carefully handling the apparatus will succeed in balancing the pencil on his/her forefinger.

E. Basic Facts and Supplemental Information:

1. This seemingly magic balancing is due to the fact that the center of gravity of the pencil is below the point where the pencil rests on the forefinger.
2. In this setup the pencil will balance perfectly regardless of its position on the finger.
3. The pencil can be made to balance at some very odd angles by very carefully changing the points of attachment of the ice picks.
4. The amazing thing about gravity is that we don't know what it is or what causes it.
5. We do know that two bodies mutually attract each other whether it is the sun and the Earth, the Earth and the moon, or the Earth and a person. This attraction is called "gravity."
6. In all of the unusual balancing modes, note that the center of gravity of the apparatus is well below the balancing point.

F. Thought Questions for Class Discussions:

1. What is the center of gravity?

2. Why do the ice pick handles need to fall below the point of attachment?
3. If three ice picks were attached, would it still be possible to balance the pencil on your forefinger?

G. Related Ideas for Further Inquiry:

Try this surprising balance.
(Be sure hammer head is well under tabletop.)

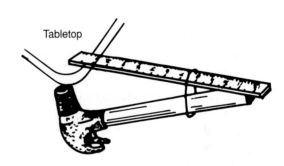

Tabletop

1. Study Section I-A, "Matter."
2. Study Activity VII-D-1, "Do heavy objects fall faster than light ones?"
3. Study Activity VII-D-5, "How fast is gravity?"

H. Vocabulary Builders—Spelling Words:

1) **balance** 2) **center** 3) **gravity** 4) **pencil**
5) **ice pick** 6) **attract** 7) **apparatus** 8) **magic**

I. Thought for Today:

"You could get rich manufacturing crutches for lame excuses."

Activity

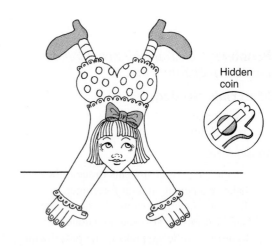

Hidden coin

A. Problem: *Is It Easy to Become a Gymnast?*

B. Materials Needed:
1. Tagboard, light cardboard, or heavy paper
2. Cellophane tape
3. Two coins (same weight)
4. Scissors
5. Crayons or tempera paints
6. Pencil
7. Glue
8. Piece of string
9. Attachment devices for string

C. Procedure:
1. Carefully draw an outline of a gymnast of your choice on the tagboard, cardboard, or paper, making sure that his/her nose or chin will be the balancing point. (See drawing.)
2. Draw another gymnast exactly the same size and shape. (This is the reverse side.)
3. With crayons or paints, color your gymnast with bright colors.
4. With cellophane tape attach one coin to each hand (on the reverse side of the gymnast).
5. Glue front and reverse sides of gymnast together. Coins will be hidden and the front and reverse sides of the gymnast will match.
6. Secure the string to the attachment devices.
7. Carefully place your gymnast on the string as shown in drawing. One hand will be in front of the string; one hand will be behind the string.
8. Ask the class why the gymnast doesn't fall off.

D. Results:
1. The gymnast will balance on the string.
2. The students will be amazed.

E. Basic Facts and Supplemental Information:
1. The "trick" of the apparatus is that the "center of gravity" is below the nose or chin of the gymnast thus preventing it from falling over or down.
2. Gravity is one of the least understood of the major forces that exist in the universe.

F. Thought Questions for Class Discussions:
1. What keeps people in an upright position?
2. How do airplanes overcome gravity?
3. Are astronauts concerned with gravity?

G. Related Ideas for Further Inquiry:
1. Study Section I-A, "Matter."
2. Study Section I-B, "Air."
3. Study Section II-F, "Movement and Resistance."
4. Study Activity VII-D-1, "Do heavy objects fall faster than light ones?"
5. Study Activity VII-D-5, "How fast is gravity?"
6. Study Activity VII-D-6, "Can you balance a pencil on the tip of your finger?"
7. Study other Activities in this Section.

Here is another amazing balancing act.

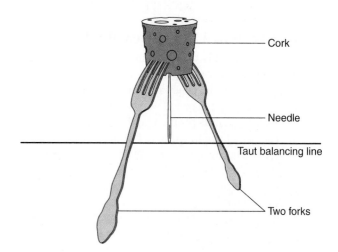

Cork

Needle

Taut balancing line

Two forks

H. Vocabulary Builders—Spelling Words:
1) **gymnast**   2) **gravity**   3) **balance**   4) **string**
5) **coins**   6) **center**   7) **force**   8) **glue**

I. Thought for Today:
"Character is made by what you stand for; reputation, by what you fall for."

SECTION E: WEATHER
Activity

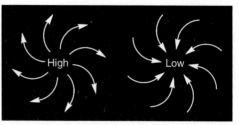

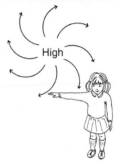

A. Problem: *What Makes the Wind Blow?*

B. Materials Needed:
1. Weather maps (if possible, from local newspaper)
2. Map of the United States or chalkboard drawing of the United States
3. Chalk

C. Procedure:
1. Locate highs (high pressure areas) and lows (low pressure areas) on weather map or sketch them as shown in the illustration.
2. Explain causes of air pressure changes: heating, cooling, movements, etc.
3. Explain how gases move from high concentration areas to low concentration areas. (Air is a mixture of gases.)
4. Review Activities in Section I-B, "Air."

D. Result:
Pupils will learn that winds are masses of air in motion.

E. Basic Facts and Supplemental Information:
1. Highs and rising pressures usually indicate fair weather.
2. Lows and falling pressures usually indicate poor weather.
3. High pressure areas normally rotate clockwise in the Northern Hemisphere and counterclockwise in the Southern Hemisphere.
4. Low pressure areas normally rotate counterclockwise in the Northern Hemisphere and clockwise in the Southern Hemisphere.
5. To locate the center of a high pressure area, stand with your back to the wind then turn about 45° to your right. Extend your arms. Your right arm will point to the high pressure area, the left to the center of the low pressure area. Since winds usually move in an easterly direction you can tell whether fair weather or poor weather is approaching. Local conditions and weak masses and fronts may vary the conditions.
6. In coastal areas, during the day, the land heats up faster than the oceans so a land breeze develops. During the night, the oceans are warmer than the land so a sea breeze develops.
7. Pressure and temperature are the two main factors in producing wind.

8. The rotation of the Earth is a major cause of winds. Since the Earth rotates from east to west, the prevailing winds blow from west to east.
9. Winds are named from their source.
   a. A "north wind" blows from the north to the south.
   b. A "land breeze" blows from the land to the sea.
   c. A "sea breeze" blows from the sea to the land.

F. Thought Questions for Class Discussions:
1. Are winds affected by the Earth's rotation?
2. Are winds affected by friction on the Earth?
3. Do winds at high altitudes behave similarly to winds close to the Earth's surface?

G. Related Ideas for Further Inquiry:
1. Study Section I-B, "Air."
2. Build a wind vane.
3. Study "wind socks" at a local airport.
4. Study Activity VII-E-2, "How can we make a wind vane?"
5. Study Activity VII-E-3, "Is there water in the air? What causes dew?"
6. Study Activity VII-E-12, "How do we read a weather map?"
7. Study Activity VII-E-13, "What are 'warm fronts?' 'cold fronts'?"

H. Vocabulary Builders—Spelling Words:
1) **wind** 2) **weather** 3) **pressure** 4) **temperature**
5) **hemisphere** 6) **northern** 7) **southern**
8) **extend** 9) **clockwise** 10) **counterclockwise**

I. Thought for Today:
"Philosophy is common sense in a dress suit."

A. Problem: *How Can We Make a Wind Vane?*

B. Materials Needed:

1. Drinking straw
2. Straight pin
3. Pencil with eraser
4. Feather or strip of paper (See drawing.)
5. Cellophane tape or rubber cement
6. Scissors
7. Fan (optional)

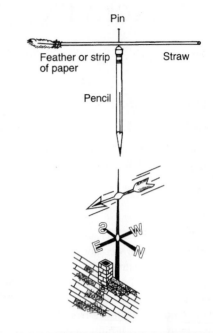

C. Procedure:

1. With scissors, make a longitudinal cut about 2″ from one end of the straw, making a split.
2. Insert the feather or paper strip into the split end.
3. Secure with cellophane tape or rubber cement.
4. Put a pin halfway between ends of apparatus.
5. Push pin into eraser of pencil.
6. Turn straw around a few times to make sure it turns easily.
7. Check vane with wind sources:
   a. outside
   b. in front of fan if available

D. Results:

1. The wind vane will point in the direction from which the wind is blowing.
2. Students will learn that winds move weather vanes.
3. As they study winds more, they will learn that North winds blow *from* the *North*. (Ocean movements are named in the direction they flow—just the opposite of winds.)

E. Basic Facts and Supplemental Information:

1. Wind vanes and wind socks can be studied.
2. If any student has ever been sailing, he/she might describe how wind conditions affected the boat.
3. You might want to have the class try to fly kites to show the effects of the wind.
4. Winds are named from their source. North winds blow from the north, sea breezes from the sea, and land breezes blow from the lands to the seas.
5. Do pilots consider wind conditions when flying? on the ground?
6. How do wind socks help pilots?

F. Thought Questions for Class Discussions:

1. Does wind help to dry laundry hung outside?
2. What makes the wind change directions?
3. What are some bad effects of wind? good effects?

G. Related Ideas for Further Inquiry:

1. Study how sailing boats use the wind.
2. Study weather maps.
3. Study the classification of winds.

BEAUFORT WIND SCALE

Number	Map Symbol	Descriptive Word(s)	Velocity (Miles/Hour)
1		Calm	1–3
2		Light breeze	4–7
3		Gentle breeze	8–12
4		Moderate breeze	13–18
5		Fresh breeze	19–24
6		Strong breeze	25–31
7		Moderate gale	32–38
8		Fresh gale	39–46
9		Strong gale	47–54
10		Full gale	55–63
11		Whole gale	64–75
12		Hurricane or violent storm	above 75

4. Make a permanent weather vane out of plywood shaped like an arrow using a dowel for support and a nail as pivot.
5. Study Activity VII-E-1, "What makes the wind blow?"
6. Study Activity VII-E-6, "How are clouds formed? What kinds of clouds are there?"
7. Study Activity VII-E-12, "How do we read a weather map?"
8. Study Activity VII-E-13, "What are 'warm fronts'? 'cold fronts'?"
9. Study other Activities in this Section.

H. Vocabulary Builders—Spelling Words:

1) **vane** 2) **weather** 3) **north** 4) **south**
5) **feather** 6) **dowel** 7) **cellophane** 8) **cement**

I. Thought for Today:

"Being grown up means that we can have our own way—at our own expense."—Hal Rogers

Activity

A. Problems: *Is There Water in the Air?*
What Causes Dew?

B. Materials Needed:
1. Two water glasses
2. Water
3. Ice cubes

C. Procedure:
1. Fill one glass about two-thirds full of water.
2. Fill the second glass about half full of water and add ice until the levels of water in the two glasses are the same.
3. Set aside until droplets form on the outside of second glass.
4. Ask the class where the droplets came from. (Some answers will surprise you, such as "the glass leaks," "spilled over," etc.)

D. Results:
1. Water droplets will form on the outside of the glass which has ice in it.
2. No droplets will form around the glass that has no ice in it.

E. Basic Facts and Supplemental Information:
1. There is always water in the air.
2. Water vapor which condenses upon cooling is called dew. Clouds and fog are tiny condensed droplets of water on small particles of matter: sand, dust, etc.
3. Fog and clouds are the same thing. Fog is in contact with the ground, clouds are above the ground.
4. When dew freezes it is called frost.
5. The amount of water in the air is called "humidity."
6. The percentage of water that the air can hold at a specific temperature is called "relative humidity."
7. When the humidity is 100% the water vapor condenses back into water and forms fog, clouds, or rain.
8. We are uncomfortable when the humidity is high because it is difficult for us to get rid of our natural perspiration.

F. Thought Questions for Class Discussions:
1. What causes fog?
2. How is dew beneficial? harmful?

No ice   With ice

3. What is humidity?
4. What is relative humidity?
5. What is hail? snow? sleet?

G. Related Ideas for Further Inquiry:
1. Study the weather reports on "humidity."
2. Study the general feelings of class members when the weather is very dry.
3. Study the general feelings of class members when the weather is very humid.
4. Study Activity VII-E-1, "What makes the wind blow?"
5. Study Activity VII-E-2, "How can we make a wind vane?"
6. Study Activity VII-E-4, "Where does rain come from?"
7. Study Activity VII-E-5, "How can we measure rainfall?"
8. Study Activity VII-E-7, "What causes a rainbow?"
9. Study Activity VII-E-11, "How is fog formed?"
10. Study Activity VII-E-12, "How do we read a weather map?"
11. Study Activity VII-E-13, "What are 'warm fronts'? 'cold fronts'?"

H. Vocabulary Builders—Spelling Words:
1) **fog** 2) **clouds** 3) **condense** 4) **dew**
5) **frost** 6) **ice** 7) **droplets** 8) **glass**
9) **outside** 10) **hail**

I. Thought for Today:
"Science can predict an eclipse of the sun many years in advance but cannot accurately predict the weather over the weekend."

Activity

A. Problem: *Where Does Rain Come From?*

B. Materials Needed:

1. Teakettle
2. Small pot or saucepan
3. Electric plate, or heating apparatus
4. Water
5. Ice cubes

C. Procedure:

1. Add water to pot.
2. Add ice to water in pot.
3. Add water to teakettle.
4. Bring water in teakettle to boiling point so steam is rising from spout.
5. VERY CAREFULLY, when steam is rising from kettle, hold pot of ice over spout so steam from spout will strike bottom and sides of pan.

D. Result:

The steam from the kettle, upon striking the cold pan, is cooled and condenses to form droplets of water on the outside of the pan. These droplets collect and fall from the pan like rain falling from a cloud.

E. Basic Facts and Supplemental Information:

1. Water, when heated, rises in the form of vapor (gas) into the air. Upon striking cool air, the vapor condenses into tiny droplets of water or moisture. These droplets collect upon particles of dirt, dust, ash, or salt in the air to form clouds. When condensed further, this moisture falls from the clouds in the form of rain. This demonstration can be used effectively by the pupils in the classroom to further their understanding of how rain is formed. Used in conjunction with demonstrations of how fog and clouds are formed, the combined demonstrations can be very effective. The visible part of what we call steam is actually small droplets of water (liquid). Water vapor (gas) is invisible.
2. All life on Earth is dependent upon rain.
3. Rains water the seeds of plants which enables them to grow.
4. Rains fill our lakes and rivers and provide us with our drinking water.
5. Excess rains cause flooding which damages our homes, our crops, and some businesses.
6. The temperature of the air in the cloud and the surrounding atmosphere determines whether precipitation will be rain, snow, hail, or sleet.

Pot of ice water

F. Thought Questions for Class Discussions:

1. How does rain help us?
2. Is rain ever harmful to us?
3. What would happen if it never rained?
4. Can you see steam (gaseous water)?

G. Related Ideas for Further Inquiry:

1. Study weather maps.
2. Study how weather personnel forecast weather.
3. Make a rain gauge using a coffee can and a ruler standing upright inside.
4. Study Section I-C, "Water."
5. Study Activity VII-E-3, "Is there water in the air? What causes dew?"
6. Study Activity VII-E-5, "How can we measure rainfall?"
7. Study Activity VII E-6, "How are clouds formed? What kinds of clouds are there?"
8. Study Activity VII-E-7, "What causes a rainbow?"
9. Study Activity VII-E-8, "What is lightning?"
10. Study Activity VII-E-9, "What is thunder?"
11. Study Activity VII-E-11, "How is fog formed?"
12. Study Activity VII-E-12, "How do we read a weather map?"
13. Study Activity VII-E-13, "What are 'warm fronts'? 'cold fronts'?"

H. Vocabulary Builders—Spelling Words:

1) **rain** 2) **steam** 3) **vapor** 4) **condensing**
5) **teakettle** 6) **spout** 7) **boiling** 8) **ice water**

I. Thought for Today:

"American youngsters tend to live as if adolescence were a last fling at life, rather than a preparation for it."

Activity

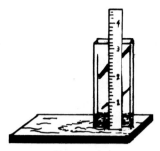

Rain gauge

A. Problem: *How Can We Measure Rainfall?*

B. Materials Needed:

1. Baseboard (approximately 6″ × 8″)
2. Piece of wood (1″ × 1″ × 6″)
3. Nails
4. Hammer
5. Ruler (or piece of yardstick)
6. Wide, straight-edged glass or plastic container or quart milk carton
7. Wire

C. Procedure:

1. Nail piece of wood to baseboard as shown in drawing.
2. Nail ruler or piece of yardstick with zero edge at baseboard to upright piece of wood.
3. Wire the container to the measuring device.
4. When it rains, place apparatus out in an open area.
5. Record reading(s) when desired. Reading should be to the nearest tenth of an inch.

D. Results:

1. Students will construct a rain gauge.
2. Students will learn how to read a rain gauge.

E. Basic Facts and Supplemental Information:

1. The students may want to use a magnifying glass for more accurate reading.
2. Charts and graphs of rainfall can be made.
3. Simpler rain gauges can be made with only a ruler and a glass container. Nail polish can be used for marking. (See bottom drawing.)

F. Thought Questions for Class Discussions:

1. Would the readings be inaccurate if the rain seemed to be falling diagonally?
2. What is the average annual rainfall in your community?
3. About how much rain does an average rainfall bring to your community?
4. Would a wide container collect a higher level of water than a narrow one?

G. Related Ideas for Further Inquiry:

1. Check weather maps in local newspapers during rainy seasons.
2. Study Section I-C, "Water."
3. Study Activity VII-E-3, "Is there water in the air? What causes dew?"
4. Study Activity VII-E-4, "Where does rain come from?"

Simple rain gauge

5. Study Activity VII-E-6, "How are clouds formed? What kinds of clouds are there?"
6. Study Activity VII-E-7, "What causes a rainbow?"
7. Study Activity VII-E-8, "What is lightning?"
8. Study Activity VII-E-9, "What is thunder?"
9. Study Activity VII-E-12, "How do we read a weather map?"
10. Study Activity VII-E-13, "What are 'warm fronts'? 'cold fronts'?"

H. Vocabulary Builders—Spelling Words:

1) **measure** 2) **rainfall** 3) **calibrate** 4) **ruler**
5) **container** 6) **indicator** 7) **gauge** 8) **graph**

I. Thought for Today:

"Don't pray for rain if you're going to complain about the mud."

Activity

A. Problem: *How Are Clouds Formed?*
What Kinds of Clouds Are There?

B. Materials Needed:

1. Reference book on clouds
2. Cotton and cotton balls
3. Tagboard, black
4. Pictures of clouds
5. Bulletin board
6. Glue or rubber cement

C. Procedure:

1. Study the different cloud types found in the reference books.
2. Reproduce the various cloud types by using cotton and cotton balls and gluing the cotton on the tagboard.
3. Mount the cotton clouds and pictures on the bulletin board.
4. Describe the type of weather that is usually associated with each type of cloud.
5. Explain that clouds are formed when water evaporates from the oceans, lakes, rivers, etc., rises into the air, condenses into droplets of water, and then joins together to form clouds.

D. Results:

1. Students will become familiar with the various types of cloud formations, and will associate the chart mountings and pictures with the actual cloud types.
2. Pupils will begin to learn that different cloud formations are weather prognosticators.

E. Basic Facts and Supplemental Information:

Weather is predictable, and observing clouds is one of the means of predicting future weather conditions. There are ten major cloud formations. Four of the most easily identified and the type of weather they portend are:

1. Nimbostratus—Generally indicates turbulent weather conditions. The fast-rising updrafts normally cause rain and hail.
2. Stratus—Associated most often with outside edges of cyclone (low pressure area) and hence good weather usually follows (little vertical movement of air to cause rain). (A high pressure area is called an anticyclone.)
3. Cirrus—Usually precede low pressure areas (cyclones). These are often the first warnings of an approaching hurricane (tropical cyclone). They may be associated with fair weather. If they move fast and change into sheets, they forecast bad weather. If they dissipate, fair weather will follow.

Nimbostratus   Stratus

Cirrus   Cumulus

4. Cumulus—Generally are signs of good weather, unless they continue into the night. If so, rain is probable.
5. Other cloud types are:
   a. Cirrostratus—usually bring rain within 12 hours
   b. Altostratus—could develop into rain clouds
   c. Stratocumulus—dry weather
   d. Altocumulus—temporary, good weather coming
   e. Cumulonimbus—showers and thunderstorms

F. Thought Questions for Class Discussions:

1. Do the clouds you see in the sky help to predict what the weather will be for the next day?
2. By looking at clouds, can you tell whether or not they are rain clouds?
3. What makes clouds change in size, shape, and color?

G. Related Ideas for Further Inquiry:

1. Have students go outside and try to classify the clouds they see.
2. Study Activity VII-E-12, "How do we read a weather map?"
3. Study Activity VII-E-13, "What are 'warm fronts'? 'cold fronts'?"

H. Vocabulary Builders—Spelling Words:

1) **predict**   2) **weather**   3) **forecasting**
4) **formation**   5) **specific cloud types mentioned in Basic Facts and Supplemental Information.**

I. Thought for Today:

"The value of a book is not the book but in the subsequent behavior of its readers."

Activity

A. Problem: *What Causes a Rainbow?*

B. Materials Needed:

Books, pamphlets, pictures, charts, and/or multisensory aids about weather conditions which cause rainbows

C. Procedure:

1. Ask students if they have ever seen a rainbow.
2. Have them describe what it looked like and the weather conditions.
3. Review Activity II-C-3, "What colors of light are in sunlight?"
4. Inform students that:
   a. The air about the Earth is composed of many tiny particles, including dust, ash, salt, and water vapor. As the sunlight passes through the water droplets, white light is separated into its component colors. Since blue light is refracted more than the other colors, our sky is blue.
   b. A rainbow is a spectrum that is produced when the sun shines during or immediately after a rain shower. The raindrops act as tiny prisms and break the sunlight into all the colors of the rainbow, and they form a beautiful arch.

D. Results:

1. Students will learn that rainbows are formed during light rains by water droplets in the air acting like minute prisms.
2. Pupils will learn that some rainbows do not form a complete arch because there are no raindrops present to complete the arch.

E. Basic Facts and Supplemental Information:

1. Sunlight hits the raindrops that have a different density than the air thus producing a rainbow effect.
2. Each droplet acts like every other droplet thus causing a pattern.

F. Thought Questions for Class Discussions:

1. Why can't rainbows appear directly overhead?
2. How long can rainbows last?
3. Can rainbows best be seen against dark or light backgrounds?

G. Related Ideas for Further Inquiry:

1. You can make a real rainbow by spraying a garden hose in the air in the late afternoon when the sun is low on the horizon.
2. A second method is to put a glass of water on a window sill when the sun is low on the horizon. A

Girl-made rainbow

Natural rainbow

white piece of tagboard will show the rainbow if placed on the floor near the elevated glass so that the glass acts like a prism.

3. Study Section II-C, "Light and Color."
4. Study Activity VII-E-4, "Where does rain come from?"
5. Study Activity VII-E-5, "How can we measure rainfall?"

H. Vocabulary Builders—Spelling Words:

1) **rainbow** 2) **prism** 3) **droplet** 4) **particles**
5) **spectrum** 6) **reflected** 7) **refracted**

I. Thought for Today:

"It's better to look where you are going rather than to see where you have been."

Activity

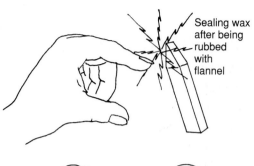

Sealing wax after being rubbed with flannel

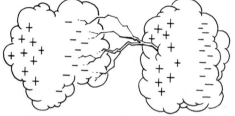

Lightning is very hot; 27,000° F. or hotter.

A. Problem: *What Is Lightning?*

B. Materials Needed:

1. Piece of wool
2. Piece of flannel
3. Piece of silk
4. Glass rod
5. Stick of sealing wax

C. Procedure:

1. Rub the glass rod briskly with the three pieces of material, one at a time.
2. Note any differences.
3. Rub the three pieces of material on the sealing wax, one at a time.
4. Place the sealing wax near your finger.
5. Note any differences.
6. Ask class if anyone has ever had an "electric shock" when walking on a carpet and touching a metal object such as a doorknob.

D. Result:

When the glass rod is rubbed with the flannel a crackling sensation should be experienced, but not with the silk or the wool. A spark should occur when the wax is rubbed with the flannel, but not with the silk or the wool.

E. Basic Facts and Supplemental Information:

1. Lightning is a huge electrical spark produced during severe weather.
2. Fast-rising air rubs against the water droplets in the cloud and charges them electrically.
3. One side of the cloud becomes positively charged while the other side becomes negatively charged.
4. Sometimes the force of the fast-rising air is strong enough to rip the cloud in two so that each half has a different electrical charge.
5. When the force of attraction between the positive and negative charged parts of a cloud, or between two clouds, becomes great enough, a huge spark of electricity, called lightning, flows from the negatively charged part to the positively charged part.
6. Lightning can jump between two sides of the same cloud, between two clouds of different charges, from a cloud to the Earth, and sometimes even from the Earth to a cloud.
7. During thunderstorms people should avoid open areas, especially those that contain good conductors of electricity.
8. It is the movement of electrons from one atom to another that makes atoms become electrically charged.

F. Thought Questions for Class Discussions:

1. What is a lightning rod?
2. What should you do if you are caught (outdoors) in a lightning storm?
3. Is lightning related to static electricity?
4. Is it a good idea to go swimming during an electrical storm?

G. Related Ideas for Further Inquiry:

1. See Activity I-A-2, "What are atoms? molecules?"
2. See Activity I-E-1, "What is static electricity?"
3. Study Activity VII-E-1, "What makes the wind blow?"
4. Study Activity VII-E-4, "Where does rain come from?"
5. Study Activity VII-E-6, "How are clouds formed? What kinds of clouds are there?"
6. Study Activity VII-E-9, "What is thunder?"
7. Study Activity VII-E-12, "How do we read a weather map?"
8. Study Activity VII-E-13, "What are 'warm fronts'? and 'cold fronts'?"
9. Study other Activities in this Section.

H. Vocabulary Builders—Spelling Words:

1) **lightning**   2) **thunderstorm**   3) **charged**
4) **negative**   5) **positive**   6) **flannel**   7) **silk**
8) **cracking**   9) **dangerous**   10) **careful**

I. Thought for Today:

"What the weatherman saves for a rainy day is probably an alibi."

Activity

A. Problem: *What Is Thunder?*

B. Materials Needed:

Small paper bags

C. Procedure:

1. Discuss with class their experiences and ideas about thunder.
2. Bring out the following points:
   a. Lightning flashes are big sparks of electricity.
   b. Lightning is very hot.
   c. Air is suddenly made hot and expands.
   d. Sudden movement of expanded air makes thunder.
3. Give several students paper bags and have them inflate them by blowing into them.
4. Let each student pop his/her paper bag. (A few at a time works well, and never close to another student's ear.)

D. Results:

1. Loud noises will result.
2. Students will learn something about sound and the cause of thunder.

E. Basic Facts and Supplemental Information:

1. The loud noise results from the sudden movement of air out of the bag. Lightning heats the air causing it to expand suddenly, and this makes the loud noise that we call thunder. This is the sound produced by the rapid heating and expansion of the air through which lightning passes. The rumbling that thunder makes is really a series of sounds that are bounced off the clouds. This is similar to air compression and its rapid expansion in the firing of a cannon. It is also similar to the rapid movement of air which is caused when an airplane goes faster than sound. This is what we call a sonic boom.
2. If you count the number of seconds between the time you see the lightning and the time you hear the thunder and multiply this number by 5, you will get a good approximation of the distance in miles to the storm cloud. Sound travels about 5 miles per second. Light travels at 186,000 miles per second. Because light travels so fast, we just assume it to be instantaneous when doing this fast approximation.

Bang!

F. Thought Questions for Class Discussions:

1. Why does a loud noise result when you stick a pin in an inflated balloon?
2. What are some other ways in which you might cause air to move rapidly enough to make noise?
3. Does the bang of a flat tire represent the same principle?

G. Related Ideas for Further Inquiry:

1. Study Section II-D, "Sound."
2. Study Activity V-B-8, "How well do we hear?"
3. Study Activity VII-E-4, "Where does rain come from?"
4. Study Activity VII-E-5, "How can we measure rainfall?"
5. Study Activity VII-E-6, "How are clouds formed? What kinds of clouds are there?"
6. Study Activity VII-E-7, "What causes a rainbow?"
7. Study Activity VII-E-8, "What is lightning?"
8. Study Activity VII-E-11, "How is fog formed?"
9. Study Activity VII-E-12, "How do we read a weather map?"
10. Study Activity VII-E-13, "What are 'warm fronts'? 'cold fronts'?"

H. Vocabulary Builders—Spelling Words:

1) **thunder** 2) **expansion** 3) **lightning**
4) **electrical** 5) **heating** 6) **sonic boom**
7) **flashes** 8) **sparks** 9) **clouds**

I. Thought for Today:

"Glass blowers will never produce anything as fragile as the human ego."

Activity

A. Problem: *Why Are Summers Warmer than Winters?*

B. Materials Needed:

1. Flashlight
2. Chalk
3. Yardstick

C. Procedure:

1. Make a chalk mark on the floor.
2. Darken the room.
3. Have a student hold a flashlight about one yard above the mark and vertically shine the flashlight on the mark.
4. Have a second student draw a circle with chalk around the spot of light.
5. Moving the flashlight horizontally about one yard from the original spot, shine the light at the same mark on the floor. (The beam will be slightly slanted.)
6. Draw a line on the floor around the spot of the beam of light.
7. Compare the areas of light projection.

D. Result:

The second drawing will be larger than the first.

E. Basic Facts and Supplemental Information:

1. The sun is hotter when directly above us than when it is setting. The same amount of sunlight is given off by the sun in winter as in summer, but the light (heat) is distributed over a wider area and therefore, each small area receives less light (heat). In other words the slanting rays cover a wider area, thus the same amount of energy is not received in winter as it is in the summer at any one point.
2. The second most important factor in determining the Earth's temperature is the length of time the sun shines each day. Because of the tilt of the Earth, the length of each day is much longer in the summertime than during the wintertime (about two hours longer in the midline of the United States).
3. A slide projector could be used instead of a flashlight and the beam could be focused on a wall.
4. We have four seasons on Earth:
   a. Spring—March 21 to June 21
   b. Summer—June 21 to September 23
   c. Fall—September 23 to December 21
   d. Winter—December 21 to March 21

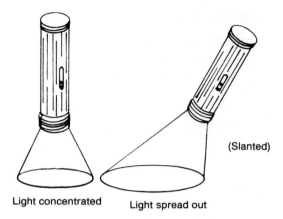

(Slanted)

Light concentrated   Light spread out

5. "Spring equinox" occurs on March 21 when the days and nights are equal in length. From this day on the days get longer and the nights get shorter.
6. "Fall equinox" occurs on September 23 when the days and nights are equal in length. From this day on the days get shorter and the nights get longer.

F. Thought Questions for Class Discussions:

1. What causes the sun's rays to hit any spot on Earth at 90°? to slant less than 90°?
2. Is there any difference in seasons between the Northern and Southern Hemispheres? Why or why not?
3. How do scientists measure light intensity?
4. Is the sun ever directly overhead in your community?

G. Related Ideas for Further Inquiry:

1. Study Part II, "Energy."
2. Study: Section II-C, "Light and Color."
3. Study: Section VII-B, "Solar System."
4. Study Activity VII-E-6, "How are clouds formed? What kinds of clouds are there?"
5. Study Activity VII-E-12, "How do we read a weather map?"
6. Study Activity VII-E-13, "What are 'warm fronts'? 'cold fronts'?"
7. Study other Activities in this Section.

H. Vocabulary Builders—Spelling Words:

1) **summer** 2) **winter** 3) **direct** 4) **slanting**
5) **area** 6) **chalk** 7) **energy** 8) **light**

I. Thought for Today:

"There's one thing to be said for inviting trouble, it usually accepts."

A. Problem: *How Is Fog Formed?*

B. Materials Needed:

1. Clean, dry, empty, quart glass bottle or jar
2. Two ice cubes, frozen together
3. Water
4. Gooseneck desk lamp with 100-watt bulb film projector, or strong flashlight
5. Electric hot plate
6. Teakettle or pan

C. Procedure:

1. Discuss with students the problems of driving an automobile in a fog.
2. Discuss with class the problems of an airplane flying in a fog.
3. Boil water in teakettle or pan.
4. CAREFULLY and very slowly (to prevent cracking) pour a small amount of boiling water into the glass bottle or jar and swish it around.
5. Pour this water out.
6. Set lamp to one side of bottle or jar.
7. Turn the lamp on.
8. Carefully add a small amount of boiling water to the glass bottle or jar.
9. Quickly place ice cubes over mouth of bottle covering mouth as completely as possible.
10. Hold bottle in front of lighted lamp.
11. Keep the ice cubes over mouth of the bottle to prevent escape of steam.

D. Results:

1. The warm moist air will rise from the hot water and meet the cool air under the ice cubes.
2. The moisture in the warm, moist air will be cooled forming tiny droplets of water forming fog.
3. When held in front of light, the fog will be seen swirling around in the bottle.

E. Basic Facts and Supplemental Information:

The air of our atmosphere (represented by the cool air from the ice cubes) cools faster than the water in bodies of water on the Earth (represented by hot water in bottle). The moist warm air rising from these bodies of water comes in contact with the cooled air and condenses, thereby forming fog. This demonstration can be used effectively for class presentation by pupils.

F. Thought Questions for Class Discussions:

1. How is fog dangerous to people?

Ice

Fog

Boiling water

2. What is the difference between fog and clouds? (They are identical except that fog touches the ground and clouds are all in the air.)
3. Is fog basically water that is in a gaseous, liquid, or solid state?

G. Related Ideas for Further Inquiry:

1. Discuss with class the problems of safety of all people in foggy conditions.
2. See Section I-C, "Water."
3. Study Activity VII-E-1, "What makes the wind blow?"
4. Study Activity VII-E-2, "How can we make a wind vane?"
5. Study Activity VII-E-3, "Is there water in the air? What causes dew?"
6. Study Activity VII-E-4, "Where does rain come from?"
7. Study Activity VII-E-5, "How can we measure rainfall?"
8. Study Activity VII-E-6, "How are clouds formed? What kinds of clouds are there?"
9. Study Activity VII-E-10, "Why are summers warmer than winters?"
10. Study Activity VII-E-12, "How do we read a weather map?"
11. Study Activity VII-E-13, "What are 'warm fronts'? 'cold fronts'?"

H. Vocabulary Builders—Spelling Words:

1) **fog** 2) **condense** 3) **droplets** 4) **preheat**
5) **frozen** 6) **boiling** 7) **lamp** 8) **dangers**

I. Thought for Today:

"Science is nothing but trained and organized common sense."

A. Problem: *How Do We Read a Weather Map?*

B. Materials Needed:

1. Weather maps from local newspaper(s)
2. Reference materials on weather
3. Multisensory aids on weather

C. Procedure:

1. Discuss weather conditions in your locality.
2. Ask students to discuss unusual weather that they have experienced.
3. Show whatever multisensory materials are available about weather.
4. Study weather maps and particularly weather symbols pointing out:
   a. isotherms—equal temperature lines
   b. weather conditions include: (1) fair, (2) rain, (3) snow, (4) thunderstorms, (5) ice
   c. weather fronts are: (l) warm, (2) cold, (3) occluded
   d. pressure areas indicate: (1) highs, (2) lows, (3) troughs
   e. jet stream
5. Discuss media reports of weather predictions.

D. Results:

1. Students will learn how to read weather maps.
2. Students will become weather prognosticators.

E. Basic Facts and Supplemental Information:

1. One of the first things we do each morning is to check the weather.
2. What clothes we wear and activities we engage in depend on the weather.
3. Severe weather conditions can have very disruptive effects on our lives.
4. Weather has six main components:
   a. temperature
   b. pressure
   c. wind
   d. humidity
   e. precipitation
   f. cloudiness
5. Weather predictions also include:
   a. dangers of ultraviolet radiation
   b. data on "particulate matter."
6. Scientists who specialize in studying weather are called "meteorologists."
7. Meteorologists study weather fronts to predict major weather conditions.

8. Warm fronts are indicated by semicircles on the isobars (lines of equal pressure).
9. Cold fronts are indicated by small triangles on the isobars.
10. An occluded front (mixed) would have both semicircles and small triangles on the isobars.
11. The heavy lines with the arrows indicate the flow of the "jet stream."

F. Thought Questions for Class Discussions:

1. How can you predict that a storm is approaching in your area?
2. What would determine if a period of good weather is approaching your locality?
3. What causes changes in weather?

G. Related Ideas for Further Inquiry:

1. Study the "jet stream" and how it effects weather conditions.
2. Study other Activities in this section, especially Activities VII-E-6 and VII-E-13.

H. Vocabulary Builders—Spelling Words:

1) **weather** 2) **fronts** 3) **temperature**
4) **pressure** 5) **wind** 6) **humidity**
7) **precipitation** 8) **cloudiness** 9) **warm**
10) **cold**

I. Thought for Today:

"Whether it's cold or whether it's hot, we shall have weather, whether or not."

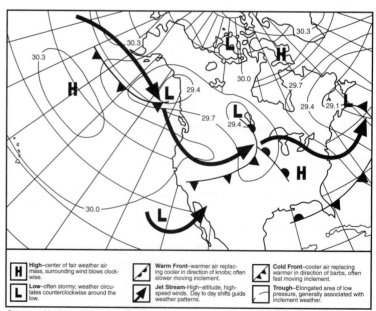

Source: National Weather Service

Activity

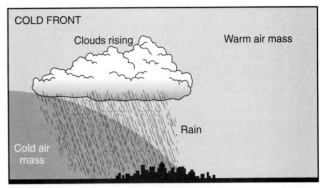

COLD FRONT

Clouds rising

Warm air mass

Rain

Cold air mass

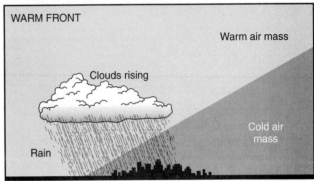

WARM FRONT

Warm air mass

Clouds rising

Cold air mass

Rain

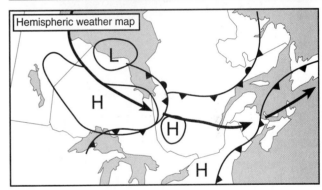

Hemispheric weather map

A. Problem: *What Are "Warm Fronts" and "Cold Fronts?"*

B. Materials Needed:
1. Newspaper weather maps
2. Books on meteorology
3. Newspaper clippings on weather conditions

C. Procedure:
1. Have students bring in newspaper articles that concern weather. May be an accident caused by slippery roads or ???
2. Read accounts of weather from newspaper clippings.
3. Discuss different kinds of weather.
4. Review appropriate weather Activities in this Section.
5. Define "fronts" as the boundaries between large air masses.
6. Discuss the characteristics of "fronts."
   a. Cold fronts usually form over polar regions.
   b. Warm fronts usually form over tropical waters.
   c. Activity on the fronts depend upon:
      1) temperature   4) wind speed
      2) pressure   5) clouds
      3) humidity   6) jet stream

D. Results:
1. Students will learn how to read weather maps.
2. Students will be able to predict upcoming weather conditions.
3. Pupils will realize that weather affects our lives in many ways.

E. Basic Facts and Supplemental Information:
1. Fronts may be "occluded" (mixed conditions).
2. If a cold front overtakes a warm front, it causes the warm front to rise because it is less dense.
3. When the warm air is forced upward, clouds are pushed up, and as they cool they are less capable of holding moisture, so precipitation results.
4. If a warm front overtakes a cold front, it rides up over it because it is less dense. The clouds in the warm front are pushed up, and as they become colder they can no longer hold their moisture; consequently, rain develops.

F. Thought Questions for Class Discussions:
1. What is a cyclone? anticyclone?
2. What weather conditions would probably follow dropping barometer readings? rising barometer readings?
3. What cloud types are associated with good weather? poor weather?

G. Related Ideas for Further Inquiry:
1. Study other Activities in this Section.
2. Develop a weather calendar for your classroom. (Indicate each day's main type of weather.)
3. Develop a class weather station. Predict the weather for your community.

H. Vocabulary Builders—Spelling Words:
1) **warm front**   2) **cold front**   3) **occluded**
4) **precipitation**   5) **barometer**   6) **weather**

I. Thought for Today:
"The sophisticated equipment of today's weatherperson is what enables him/her to explain in greater detail, why he/she was wrong."

PART VIII

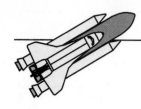

AVIATION, SATELLITES, AND SPACE TRAVEL

SECTION A   Aviation   383
SECTION B   Satellites   389
SECTION C   Space Travel   396

A. Problem: *What Are the Different Kinds of Aircraft?*

B. Materials Needed:
1. Pictures or models of:
   a. Monoplanes   f. Gliders
   b. Biplanes   g. Hang gliders
   c. Seaplanes   h. Dirigibles
   d. Amphibians   i. Balloons
   e. Helicopters   j. Space shuttle
2. Other multisensory aids about aircraft

C. Procedure:
1. Ask the class if they have ever flown in an airplane or some other type of aircraft.
2. Have them discuss their experiences.
3. List all the different types of aircraft and explain their functions.
4. With multisensory aids, show appropriate films, slides, transparencies, etc.

D. Result:
Students will realize that there are many different types of aircraft, each with its own special function(s).

E. Basic Facts and Supplemental Information:
1. Aircraft can be divided into two main categories:
   a. Lighter-than-air
   b. Heavier-than-air
2. Most planes built today are monoplanes (one set of wings).
3. Satellites which carry people cannot be classified as aircraft because they fly above the air.
4. Helicopters have no wings: they have rotating blades.
5. Gliders have no engines or propellers.
6. Hang gliders are used exclusively for recreation.
7. A new aircraft is now being designed. It is a scramjet. It will be able to take off from land and go into orbit and/or used for space travel.

F. Thought Questions for Class Discussions:
1. How do each of these aircraft stay aloft?
2. How do pilots know which direction they are flying?
3. How do aircraft bring the people of the world together?

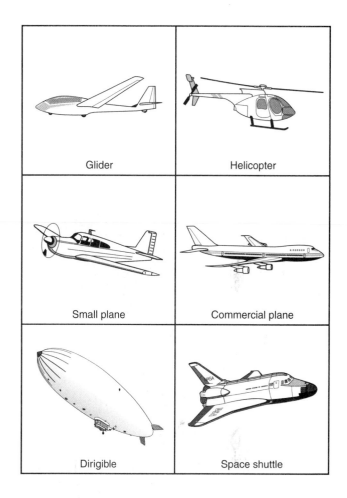

Glider   Helicopter

Small plane   Commercial plane

Dirigible   Space shuttle

G. Related Ideas for Further Inquiry:
1. Take a field trip to an airport.
2. Create a teaching unit about the airport or about air transportation.
3. Study Section I-B, "Air."
4. Study Section VII-E, "Weather."
5. Study other Activities in this Section.

H. Vocabulary Builders—Spelling Words:
Use the terms listed in "Materials Needed."

I. Thought for Today:
"Despite all the talk about supersonic transports, no engineer has ever been able to concoct anything that can go faster than a vacation."—**Roger Allen**

A. Problem: *What Are the Main Parts of an Airplane?*

B. Materials Needed:

1. Models or pictures of propeller-driven planes
2. Models or pictures of jet planes
3. Models or pictures of other kinds of planes
4. Newspaper accounts of airplane:
   a. accidents
   b. unusual facts
   c. new developments, etc.
5. List of names of airplane parts cited in Procedure, item 4 (below). Write these names on chalkboard or bulletin board.

C. Procedure:

1. Discuss various modes of transportation.
2. Discuss the strengths and problems of each.
3. Describe the special characteristics of airplanes.
4. Ask students to paste labels on models or pictures depicting the parts listed below:
   a. fuselage
   b. cabin
   c. propeller(s) or jet engines
   d. main wing
   e. horizontal stabilizer
   f. elevators
   g. tail assembly
   h. rudder
   i. ailerons
   j. vertical stabilizer
   k. engine nacelle
   l. landing gear
   m. flaps, etc.
5. Have pupils describe the function of each of the parts listed above.
6. Discuss with students the problems of airplanes in flight.
7. Compare the engine of an airplane with that of an automobile.
8. Compare the control systems of an airplane to those of a bicycle or automobile.

D. Results:

1. Students will learn the names of the various airplane parts.
2. Students will enjoy matching names to picture parts.
3. Pupils will learn that propulsion systems and control mechanisms vary greatly depending on their purpose and environment.

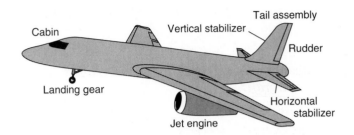

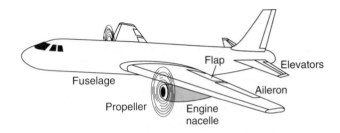

E. Basic Facts and Supplemental Information:

1. There are many other parts not listed here that some students may know about, such as landing lights, missile mounts, extra tanks, etc.
2. Different planes have differently shaped parts.
3. Planes vary in size, purpose, speed, costs, etc.

F. Thought Questions for Class Discussions:

The best thought questions for this activity are to have the students name the main function for each part.

G. Related Ideas for Further Inquiry:

1. Study Section I-B, "Air."
2. Study Section VII-E, "Weather."
3. Study Activity VIII-A-1, "What are the different kinds of aircraft?"
4. Study Activity VIII-A-3, "How does an airplane get 'lift' from its wings?"
5. Study Activity VIII-A-5, "How does an airplane propeller work?"

H. Vocabulary Builders—Spelling Words:

Use the names of the various airplane parts cited in "Procedure."

I. Thought for Today:

"Our new faster-than-sound jet planes are wonderful. You can eat dinner in London and get indigestion in New York City."

Activity

A. Problem: *How Does an Airplane Get "Lift" From Its Wings?*

B. Materials Needed, Procedure One:
   1. Piece of paper 10″ × 4″
   2. Pencil
   3. Paste or cellophane tape

   Materials Needed, Procedure Two:
   1. Strip of writing paper 3″ × 6″
   2. Book

C. Procedure One:
   1. Paste or tape ends of paper together.
   2. Curve surfaces until it takes the shape of a cross section of an airplane wing.
   3. Slip pencil through loop, hold up the wide end for a moment, and blow across the *upper* surface of the paper wing until the wing moves.

   Procedure Two:
   1. Place one end of the paper in the book (which is standing up) so that the weight of the paper causes it to bend over, away from you. (See drawing.)
   2. Blow gently across the surface of the curved paper.

D. Results:
   1. In the first procedure, the paper wing will rise.
   2. In the second procedure, the paper sheet will rise.
   3. The students will begin to develop a concept of "lift" on airplane wings.

E. Basic Facts and Supplemental Information:
   1. Air flowing over the wing is thinner on top and the airplane develops "lift" because there are more molecules below the wing than above. The same is true for the "paper wing." More molecules provides greater "lift."
   2. In an actual plane in flight, more than 3/4 of the entire weight of the plane is held up by the reduced air flow on top of the wings, and only 1/4 by the force of the air on the bottom of the wings.
   3. There are four major forces acting on a plane:
      a. Lift—from air flowing over wing(s)
      b. Gravity—attraction to the Earth
      c. Thrust—power from engine(s)
      d. Drag—resistance from the air

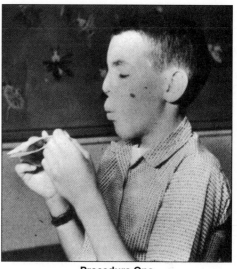

Procedure One

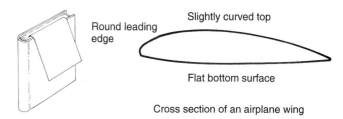

Round leading edge

Slightly curved top

Flat bottom surface

Cross section of an airplane wing

Procedure Two

F. Thought Questions for Class Discussions:
   1. What is Bernoulli's Principle?
   2. Is lift a problem in space travel?
   3. Is the turning of an airplane accomplished by lift?
   4. How does gravity affect lift?

G. Related Ideas for Further Inquiry:
   1. If any student has a model airplane, ask him/her to bring it to class and explain how it works.
   2. Study Section I-B, "Air."
   3. Study Section VII-E, "Weather."
   4. Study all Activities in this Section.

H. Vocabulary Builders—Spelling Words:
   1) **lift** 2) **curved** 3) **surface** 4) **pressure**
   5) **underneath** 6) **gravity** 7) **thrust** 8) **drag**

I. Thought for Today:
   "Air travel is wonderful. It allows you to pass motorists at a safe distance."

Activity

A. Problem: *How Does a Pilot Control an Airplane?*

B. Materials Needed:

1. Plyboard for frame
2. Apple crate (if available; if not, use comparable lumber)
3. Scrap lumber
4. Screw eyes
5. Flexible wire
6. Leather for hinges
7. Ball-and-socket device
8. Tools: pliers, handsaw, hammer, screwdriver
9. Books, articles, etc. about the nomenclature of airplanes

C. Procedure:

1. Have students study the main parts of a plane's control system.
2. Define control terms: pedals, stick, ailerons, rudder, and stabilizers.
3. Outline airplane on plyboard frame.
4. Using apple crates and/or scrap lumber, build wings so that controls can be attached.
5. Construct pedals and stick and attach to ailerons, rudder, and stabilizers as shown in drawing.
6. Pedals should be hinged to base with wires going to rudder.
7. Stick should be a ball-and-socket joint or near facsimile at the base so that when the stick is moved from side to side, the aileron on the side toward which the stick is moved rises and the opposite aileron depresses.
8. The stick should also have wires running to the horizontal stabilizers so that when the stick is moved forward the stabilizers depress and when the stick is pulled back the stabilizers elevate.
9. One apple crate can be used as a pilot's seat.

D. Results:

1. An understanding of an airplane's control system will be learned as the students see and move the pedals and stick.
2. They will begin to realize the effects of air pressure against the various movable parts of the airplane.

E. Basic Facts and Supplemental Information:

1. Students can make the model, thereby gaining experience and knowledge about planes.
2. Two good alternatives to the construction of a whole plane is to build mock-ups of the various

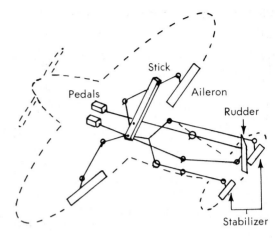

movable parts or create a large drawing and explain in detail how the major parts operate.
3. Aileron, rudder, and stabilizers are movable parts controlling the plane and are operated by the pedals and stick.
4. These controls operate like ships' rudders by extending part of air stream which pushes that part of plane, thus changing direction(s).
5. Stabilizers aid the plane in moving up and down. When the stick moves back, the stabilizers move up helping the plane to rise.
6. Rudders are used for turning. When the stick moves to the left, the rudder moves toward the left, and the plane moves in that direction.
7. Ailerons are used for banking plane and balance. If one goes up, the other goes down. The aileron that is turned up forces that side of the plane to go down.

F. Thought Questions for Class Discussions:

1. What are trim tabs?
2. How else does a pilot control a plane in flight?
3. What is the function of the propeller?
4. What is drag?

G. Related Ideas for Further Inquiry:

1. If any students have model planes, have them bring them to class for study.
2. Study Section I-B, "Air."
3. Study Section VII-E, "Weather."
4. Study other Activities in this Section.

H. Vocabulary Builders—Spelling Words:

1) **pedal**   2) **stick**   3) **rudder**   4) **aileron**
5) **stabilizer**   6) **flight**   7) **maneuver**   8) **thrust**

I. Thought for Today:

"The wife of a pilot is the only woman who is glad to see her husband down and out."

A. Problem: *How Does an Airplane Propeller Work?*

B. Materials Needed:

1. Top of large tin can or metal disc
2. Wooden rod or dowel
3. Large spike or nail
4. Metal file
5. Two small nails
6. Empty spool (from thread)
7. Cord or heavy string
8. Ruler
9. Tin snips
10. Cutting pliers
11. Hammer
12. Awl

C. Procedure:

1. For construction of propeller, use top of large tin can or lightweight metal disc about 6″ in diameter. (Lightweight metal is important because it gives a better flight.)
2. Find center of disc. Draw diameter lines to determine this point. (The center point will be at the intersection.)
3. Mark disc as shown in Fig. 1.
4. **CAREFULLY** cut out propeller with tin snips and smooth edges with file. (Twist ends slightly in opposite directions. Make them of equal pitch.)
5. To make a rotary:
   a. Drive a nail part way into the rod or dowel (the handle).
   b. Place the spool on the nail so that it can spin freely.
6. Remove the heads from the two small nails with cutting pliers and drive them into the top of the spool. Make sure they are directly opposite each other.
7. Punch two small holes in the center of the propeller with awl so that it will fit loosely over the two nails and rest on top of the spool.
8. Place propeller on spool nails.
9. Wind a few feet of strong cord around the spool. Be sure the cord is wound evenly around the spool to avoid tangles and to make a smoother, more successful flight.
10. Hold wooden rod vertically and pull out briskly on cord.

D. Result:

Propeller will spin rapidly and rise into the air.

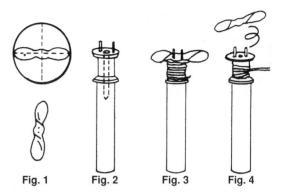

Fig. 1   Fig. 2   Fig. 3   Fig. 4

E. Basic Facts and Supplemental Information:

1. The pitch or bend in the tin causes a change in air pressure above and below the propeller as it spins. It cuts through the air like a propeller on a boat or a ship cuts through the water to drive the boat or ship forward.
2. There are many games and contests that can be played by students to add fun and interest to use of this propeller.

F. Thought Questions for Class Discussions:

1. How does a propeller on a plane compare to that of a boat?
2. How many ways can people lift objects into the air?
3. Would a four-bladed propeller of equal diameter have more lifting power than a two-bladed propeller?

G. Related Ideas for Further Inquiry:

1. Students can make paper windmills and test their operations.
2. Pupils can study propellers on model boats and planes.
3. Study Section I-B, "Air."
4. Study Section VII-E, "Weather."
5. Study other Activities in this Section.

H. Vocabulary Builders—Spelling Words:

1) **propeller** 2) **airplane** 3) **rotary** 4) **vertical**
5) **briskly** 6) **pitch** 7) **thrust** 8) **drag**

I. Thought for Today:

"Airplane fares have been increasing considerably so that even the cost of going up is going up."

A. Problem: *How Does a Parachute Work?*

B. Materials Needed:
1. Large handkerchief
2. Four pieces of string of equal length
3. Metal ring, rock, or other weight

C. Procedure:
1. Tie a string to each corner of the handkerchief.
2. Tie the other ends of the strings together.
3. Tie the weight to the place where the strings are joined.
4. Fold the handkerchief so the weight is in the middle and covered.
5. Throw the "parachute" as high as possible.

D. Result:
Parachute will open and descend slowly.

E. Basic Facts and Supplemental Information:
1. As the parachute falls, it cups the air, and this added air pushes up against the cloth, causing an upward pressure. This causes the "parachute" to descend slowly because any force going in one direction impedes the progress of a force going in the other direction.
2. A parachute is a very important device for saving the lives of pilots whose planes have to be abandoned in flight for whatever reasons.
3. A parachutist in free fall would accelerate at the rate of 32.2 feet (9.8 meters) per second.
4. This increase would last about 14 seconds until it equaled the force of gravity. At that time the free fall would remain steady without further acceleration.
5. One more factor must be taken into account, and that is air resistance which slows the rate of acceleration.
6. The final speed of a free falling object is called its "terminal velocity."

F. Thought Questions for Class Discussion:
1. What will happen to the parachute if only two corners are tied instead of four?
2. By changing the weight position on the string, can we influence the direction in which the parachute will fall?

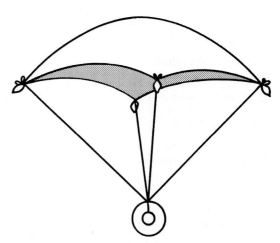

Handkerchief parachute

3. How does this toy parachute differ from a real one?
4. What would happen if two adjacent strings were a little shorter than the other two?

G. Related Ideas for Further Inquiry:
1. Study Section I-B, "Air."
2. Study Section VII-E, "Weather."
3. Study Activity VIII-A-1, "What are the different kinds of aircraft?"
4. Study Activity VIII-A-3, "How does an airplane get 'lift' from its wings?"
5. Study other Activities in this Section.

H. Vocabulary Builders—Spelling Words:
1) **parachute**   2) **handkerchief**   3) **weight**
4) **upward**   5) **pressure**   6) **device**   7) **safety**
8) **rescue**   9) **descend**   10) **acceleration**

I. Thought for Today:
"The person who said: 'What goes up must come down' must have lived before they invented taxes, postal rates, and space probes."

A. Problem: *Why Does Water Stay in a Fast-Swinging Bucket?*

B. Materials Needed:

1. Bucket with a handle on the top
2. Supply of water
3. Planted area on school campus

C. Procedure:

1. Fill a bucket about one-half full of water.
2. Have a student hold it to one side over a sink or planted area and invert it quickly.
3. Fill the bucket about one-half full again.
4. Have the student hold the bucket to his/her side and gently swing the bucket back and forth, the way a pendulum swings.
5. Keep increasing the height of the swing until it is about six inches below the horizontal plane.
6. When the swing reaches this height, quickly accelerate the swing very rapidly so that it goes all the way around.
7. Swing it around in a circle several times, then gradually decelerate the swing until the bucket can be set down.

D. Results:

1. When the bucket is held to one side and inverted, the water falls out.
2. When the water in the bucket is swung quickly around, the water stays in the bucket.

E. Basic Facts and Supplemental Information:

1. In order to fully understand this phenomenon one must study Newton's Laws of Motion. His laws applicable to this activity are:
   First Law: An object in motion continues in motion along a straight line unless acted upon by some external force.
   Second Law: The mass of a body accelerates in direct proportion to the force applied to it.
   Third Law: For every action there is an equal and opposite reaction.
2. When the bucket is held to one side and inverted, the force of gravity makes the water fall out.
3. In this activity with the bucket swinging in a full circle, Newton's Laws apply as follows: The bucket has a tendency to move in a straight line but this is changed by:

   a. *gravity*—a force pulling the bucket of water down toward the center of the Earth.
   b. *centripetal force* which is applied by the student and directed toward the center of the swing.

F. Thought Questions for Class Discussions:

1. What do you think would happen if the speed of the swing became slower and slower?
2. Can this principle be used to train astronauts for their weightlessness in space?
3. Why do you think our space vehicles bend their flight paths soon after their initial vertical takeoffs?
4. Can you name some rides at amusement parks that use centripetal force to hold riders in position?

G. Related Ideas for Further Inquiry:

1. Study Section I-B, "Air."
2. Study Section I-C, "Water."
3. Study Activity II-F-3, "What is inertia? momentum?"
4. Study other Activities in this Section.

H. Vocabulary Builders—Spelling Words:

1) **bucket**   2) **water**   3) **centripetal**   4) **gravity**
5) **momentum**   6) **speed**   7) **direction**   8) **inertia**

I. Thought for Today:

"Don't kill your ideas, execute them!!!"

Activity VIII **B** 2

A. Problem: *What Direction Will a Circular Moving Ball Go if All External Forces Are Removed?*

B. Materials Needed:

1. Pie tin
2. Marble
3. Tin snips
4. Metal file

C. Procedure:

1. Cut one quarter of the pie tin out as shown in drawing. File edges to make smooth.
2. Place marble near the edge of the remaining 3/4 portion.
3. Ask students to guess which direction the marble will go if it is pushed quickly along the flat edge and then released.
4. Discuss reasons for guesses.
5. Push marble as mentioned.

D. Result:

The marble will exit in a straight line along a perpendicular tangent to the radius.

E. Basic Facts and Supplemental Information:

1. Part of Newton's first law of motion states that a body in motion will continue to move in a straight line unless acted on by some external force.
2. When the edge in the pie tin no longer acted on the marble, the marble continued to move in the direction it was going when the edge was removed. This was a straight line.
3. As it exited, there were no forces pushing it to either side.
4. Inertia is the term we use to show the condition of the body. We say that a body at rest tends to stay at rest unless acted on by some external force, and/or a body in motion tends to stay in motion unless acted on by some external force (Newton's first law of motion). Inertia is the condition of the body at rest or in motion. It requires a force to overcome inertia either in moving it if it is at rest or slowing or stopping it if it is in motion.
5. If a pie tin is not available, an aluminum foil pie pan could be substituted.
6. Momentum is a property of matter in motion. It is a force dependent on the mass and its velocity that keeps a body in motion at the same speed and moving in the same direction unless acted upon by some external force.

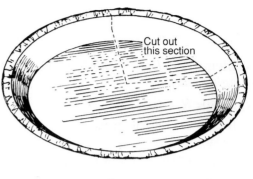

Cut out this section

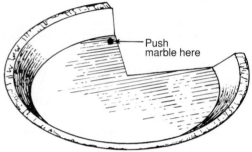

Push marble here

F. Thought Questions for Class Discussions:

1. What forces are acting on satellites? our moon? on the Earth itself?
2. Does inertia play a role in stopping an automobile or a bicycle?
3. Which helps us more, inertia or gravity?

G. Related Ideas for Further Inquiry:

1. Study Section II-E, "Simple Machines."
2. Study Activity II-F-3, "What is inertia? momentum?"
3. Study Activity II-F-5, "What is sliding friction? rolling friction?"
4. Study other Activities in this Section.

H. Vocabulary Builders—Spelling Words:

1) **force** 2) **direction** 3) **marble** 4) **Newton**
5) **motion** 6) **tangent** 7) **speed** 8) **external**

I. Thought for Today:

"It's unfortunate that ignorance isn't painful."

Activity

A. Problem: *How Does a Rocket Work?*

B. Materials Needed:

1. Elongated balloon
2. Monofilament fishline
3. Paper clips
4. Rubber bands
5. Screw eyes to fasten line to wall

C. Procedure:

1. Fasten screw eyes to opposite walls.
2. Put fishline through screw eyes; tighten line and knot tautly.
3. Bend several paper clips so that they form an eye at one end that goes around the fishline.
4. Curve the middle part of the paper clip so that it roughly takes the shape of the balloon.
5. Attach a rubber band to each paper clip making a loop at the other end of the paper clip.
6. Slide the apparatus to one end of the line.
7. Insert balloon between curved part of paper clips and rubber bands. (They make a harness.)
8. Explain Newton's Third Law of Motion. This simply stated is ". . . for every action there is an equal and opposite reaction."
9. Blow up balloon; tightly close open end.
10. Release the balloon.

D. Result:

The balloon will shoot across the room with great speed.

E. Basic Facts and Supplemental Information:

1. The air in the balloon, upon being released, will push against the air that was outside the balloon and will cause the balloon to move forward.
2. In other words, the "action" of the balloon moving forward is "equal and opposite" to the released air moving backwards.
3. The following are all examples of Newton's Third Law of Motion, "For every action there is an equal and opposite reaction":
   a. high jumper in a track meet
   b. motorboat speeding
   c. sailboat sailing into the wind
   d. frog jumping off a lily pad
   e. sitting on a chair

F. Thought Questions for Class Discussions:

1. How many examples of Newton's Third Law of Motion can you think of?
2. Does this principle apply to a ball being kicked or hit?

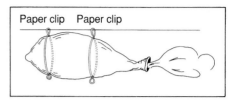

Paper clip   Paper clip

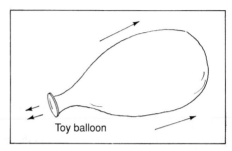

Toy balloon

3. What were Newton's First and Second Laws of Motion? See Activity VIII-B-1, Section E-1.
4. How is the movement of the balloon similar to the motion of a jet plane?
5. What makes the balloon stop moving?
6. Would the balloon move if released in outer space?
7. If a student is on roller skates and facing a wall, what will happen if the student pushes against the wall? Why?

G. Related Ideas for Further Inquiry:

1. An easy alternative activity to demonstrate this principle is to blow up the balloon and release it immediately.
2. Study Section I-B, "Air."
3. Study Section VII-B, "Solar System."
4. Study Section VIII-A, "Aviation"
5. Study Section VIII-C, "Space Travel."

H. Vocabulary Builders—Spelling Words:

1) **rocket** 2) **elongated** 3) **fishline** 4) **Newton**
5) **action** 6) **reaction** 7) **balloon** 8) **released**

I. Thought for Today:

"Don't forget that people will judge you by your actions, not intentions. You may have a heart of gold— but so does a hard-boiled egg."

Activity

A. Problem: *How Is a Spaceship Launched?*

B. Materials Needed:

1. Flannel board (blue background preferred)
2. Flannel board cutouts of:
   a. first stage rocket
   b. second stage rocket
   c. third stage rocket
   d. nose cone (with satellite)

C. Procedure:

1. Assemble all stages to form one complete spacecraft.
2. Discuss some of the major problems of putting a satellite in orbit.
3. Cite the fact that in order to put a satellite 300 miles in orbit above the Earth requires a speed of 18,000 miles per hour and to leave the Earth's gravitational pull requires a speed of 25,000 miles per hour.
4. Tell the class that weight is an important hindrance in overcoming gravity.
5. Inform the class that as the fuel to drive the rocket upward is consumed, it is unnecessary to carry the empty fuel containers, therefore our rockets have been designed in stages so that the containers could be dropped off when emptied.
6. Illustrating with the flannel cutouts, show how the three stages are eliminated one at a time.
7. Explain in detail how a typical shuttle is placed in orbit:
   a. The first stage is ignited and the rocket takes off.
   b. The rocket attains a speed of 4,000 miles per hour and jettisons the first stage. (Remove first stage from flannel board.)
   c. Second stage is ignited. (Since air resistance is now less, we don't need as much fuel so second container is smaller.)
   d. The rocket attains a speed of 10,000 miles per hour and jettisons the second stage. (Remove second stage from flannel board.)
   e. Third stage is ignited and attains a speed of 25,000 miles per hour which is the "escape velocity."

D. Result:

Students will be able to visualize how the three stages of rockets (with or without satellites) are ignited, shot into space, and dropped off.

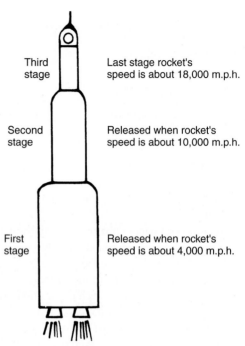

Space rocket with satellite

Third stage — Last stage rocket's speed is about 18,000 m.p.h.

Second stage — Released when rocket's speed is about 10,000 m.p.h.

First stage — Released when rocket's speed is about 4,000 m.p.h.

E. Basic Facts and Supplemental Information:

In addition to attaining the correct height and speed, the last stage must also put the rocket on its correct glide path. In order to accomplish this, after the initial stage has been fired straight up, the rocket is programmed to roll toward its final (orbital) path, so in this demonstration, the roll-over pattern should also be included.

F. Thought Questions for Class Discussions:

1. What are some of the major problems that might be (and have been) encountered in the space program?
2. What additional design problems did we have in landing on and returning from the moon?
3. What happens to the jettisoned fuel containers?

G. Related Ideas for Further Inquiry:

1. Study Section I-B, "Air."
2. Study Section VII-A, "Universe."
3. Study Section II-F, "Movement and Resistance."
4. Study Section VII-D, "Gravity."
5. Study other Activities in this Section.

H. Vocabulary Builders—Spelling Words:

1) **escape**   2) **velocity**   3) **roll-over**
4) **stage**   5) **rocket**   6) **fuel**   7) **thrust**

I. Thought for Today:

"Sometimes the best helping hand you can get is a good, firm push."

Activity

A. Problem: *What Is a Space Station?*

B. Materials Needed:

1. Pictures or drawing of space stations
2. Reference materials about space stations
3. Newspaper accounts of the progress we are making with the international space station now being constructed in space
4. Materials needed to construct a miniature mock-up space station (optional)

C. Procedure:

1. Tell the class, "We are going to plan a space station and we need volunteers to serve in three committees:
   a. Group 1 will have the responsibility of designing controls, instruments, and equipment.
   b. Group 2 will plan all the services needed.
   c. Group 3 will make a list of supplies needed.
2. Give them ample time to plan their space venture in a space station.
3. Have them cite the potential problems that a space station crew might have living aboard a space station for a year.
4. (Optional) Have them construct a mock-up space station in miniature.

D. Results:

1. Students will learn about the supplies needed for an extended stay in space.
2. Students will realize the services required during space travel.
3. They will realize that space ventures are full of problems and dangers.
4. If they build a mock-up space station, they will learn about the coordination needed for all goods and services required of space living.

E. Basic Facts and Supplemental Information:

1. The Soviet Union already has a space station in orbit called "Mir" which means "peace."
2. The United States launched a space station "Skylab" in 1973. It reentered Earth's atmosphere in 1980 and disintegrated.
3. A Russian astronaut stayed aboard Mir, the Russian space station, for 326 days, but left in a weakened condition. He did regain full strength.
4. The United States and Russia are now in a joint program developing a new space station. Elements

of the space station are being produced in the United States, Russia, Canada, Japan, Italy, Britain, Germany, and France.

5. The station will spread over an area 118 yds. × 81 yds. (108 m. × 74 m.) and will circle the Earth at an altitude of 220 miles.
6. It will require 73 space launches by three nations over a 55-month period.
7. It is scheduled to be completed in 2002.

F. Thought Questions for Class Discussions:

1. What would be some of the benefits of having a permanent space station?
2. Would you like to spend a year in space on a space station?
3. What would be some of the major problems of living in space?

G. Related Ideas for Further Inquiry:

1. Study Section I-B, "Air."
2. Study Section VII-B, "Solar System."
3. Study Section V-D, "Personal Health."
4. Study Section VI-A, "Ecosystems."
5. Study other Activities in this Section.

H. Vocabulary Builders—Spelling Words:

1) **station**   2) **space**   3) **instruments**
4) **supplies**   5) **service**   6) **astronauts**

I. Thought for Today:

"One secret of success is to be able to put your best foot forward without stepping on anybody's toes."

A. Problem: *What Keeps a Satellite in Orbit?*

B. Materials Needed:

1. Ping-pong ball
2. Filament tape
3. Four or five rubber bands (may use a rubber ball and long rubber line from a paddle ball)

C. Procedure:

1. Drop the ping-pong ball on the table.
2. Interlock the rubber bands or use the rubber line.
3. Tape the rubber bands to another ping-pong ball.
4. Slowly swing rubber bands, with ball attached, in a circular motion. Note the distance from your hand.
5. Increase the speed of circular swing. Note the distance in this case.
6. Discuss why the ping-pong ball falls to the tabletop, and why the distance from the hand increases as the ball revolves at a greater speed.

D. Results:

1. The ping-pong ball will fall to the tabletop.
2. In step 4 above, as the ball moves slowly, it revolves at a certain distance from the hand.
3. In step 5 above, as the speed is increased, the ball moves farther from the hand.

E. Basic Facts and Supplemental Information:

In the first experiment there was one major force acting on the ball and that was gravity, causing the ball to fall. In the second experiment there were two forces acting on the ball. One was gravity and the second was centripetal force generated by the muscles of the hand and wrist. Gravity tends to pull the ball to the center of the Earth. The momentum of the ball tends to move it in a straight line perpendicular to the rubber bands, but the centripetal force tends to move the ball toward the hand and wrist. The balancing of gravity and the centripetal force causes the ball to revolve around the hand and wrist. This adds momentum to the ball. As more centripetal force is applied, the ball will move farther away. As centripetal force is decreased, the ball will move closer to the hand. Earth satellites have only two forces acting on them, gravity and centripetal force. Earth satellites are sent high into space and given an initial thrust to start them revolving. Since a body in motion continues to stay in motion, the satellites continue to revolve. Because there is a very light density of air even at high altitudes, these satellites will slow down, come closer to Earth, meet denser air and slow down still more. This continues until the satellites finally fall to Earth or burn up as they meet denser and denser air.

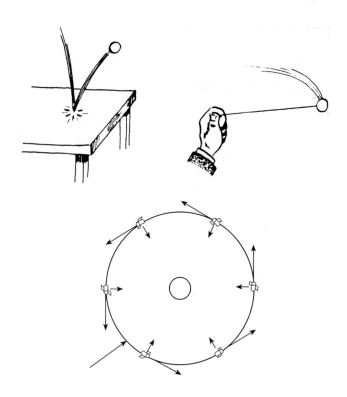

F. Thought Questions for Class Discussions:

1. What happens to the position of our satellites that maintain an orbit of about 22,300 miles from Earth?
2. Could Earth satellites circle the globe in any direction?
3. What are some potential dangers to our satellites in orbit around the Earth?
4. Are there dangers to us from falling space junk?
5. Have you seen pieces of tires from trucks lying on highways? What causes the pieces to fly off from the tire?

G. Related Ideas for Further Inquiry:

1. Study Activity II-F-3, "What is inertia? momentum?"
2. Study Section VIII-A, "Aviation."
3. Study other Activities in this Section.

H. Vocabulary Builders—Spelling Words:

1) **satellite** 2) **orbit** 3) **circular** 4) **momentum**
5) **distance** 6) **centripetal** 7) **gravity** 8) **inertia**

I. Thought for Today:

"You can't get through this world without making mistakes. The person who makes no mistakes does nothing, and that is a mistake."

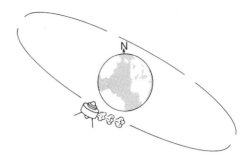

A. Problem: *What Good Are Artificial Satellites?*

B. Materials Needed:
1. Models or pictures of satellites
2. Pictures of occupations described in Results (D-3 below)
3. Weather maps
4. Rocks, mineral specimens

C. Procedure:
1. Discuss the development of artificial satellites.
2. Have students find out about the different kinds of satellites.
3. Discuss the purposes of satellites.

D. Results:
Students will learn that:
1. Up to now there have been over a thousand artificial satellites.
2. Most of them have been used for bouncing television pictures and sending messages over long distances, even between continents.
3. Satellites are helping:
   a. farmers—improve farm practices
   b. fishermen—locate water depths, temperatures
   c. foresters—locate best woods (soft, hard, etc.)
   d. industrialists—best location for factories
   e. geologists—locate "faults," shifting glaciers, etc.
   f. hydrologists—water movement, pollution, better use
   g. mineralogists—locate deep sources of minerals
   h. map makers—better, up-to-date, more detailed
   i. ecologists—detect water, air pollution
   j. conservationists—locate forest fires early
   k. sailors—report best course for sailing
   l. city planners—up-to-date maps, locate pollution
   m. military—monitoring military installations of other nations
   n. teachers—to relay school lessons

E. Basic Facts and Supplemental Information:
1. A space station is an artificial satellite.
2. Russia has a space station, MIR-1, in orbit now.
3. The United States and Russia are planning on a joint construction of a space station scheduled for completion in the year 2002.

4. Many modern instruments on satellites can see or "feel." These instruments are cameras and remote sensors.
5. Different objects can be detected by the energy patterns that are emitted and/or reflected.
6. We now use cameras with folded optics which increase their seeing power by a series of mirrors within the camera.
7. We also have multiband cameras which can take pictures simultaneously of the visible and infrared portions of the spectrum.
8. Microwave devices, and radar, can detect cloud formations and changes of foliage.
9. Magnetometers can locate buried minerals by their magnetic anomalies.

F. Thought Questions for Class Discussions:
1. Can you think up any other uses of Earth satellites?
2. Would you like to be aboard a space station where you could work and perform scientific experiments?
3. What would be some problems of people living on a space station?

G. Related Ideas for Further Inquiry:
1. Study Section I-B, "Air."
2. Study Section VII-A, "Universe."
3. Study Activity II-F-3, "What is inertia? momentum?"
4. Study other Activities in this Section.

H. Vocabulary Builders—Spelling Words:
Use the occupations cited in "Results."

I. Thought for Today:
"One who thinks only of oneself is hopelessly uneducated."

Earth travelling through space

A. Problem: *How Is Our Planet (Earth) Like a Spaceship? How Is It Different?*

B. Materials Needed:
1. Pictures and models of Earth
2. Pictures and models of spaceships

C. Procedure:
1. Have class list all similarities between our planet traveling in space and a spaceship traveling in space.
2. Have class list any differences between our planet traveling in space and a spaceship traveling in space.

D. Results:
1. Students will gain a new and broader concept of our planet.
2. They will learn that there are no space stations for the Earth to take on new supplies.

E. Basic Facts and Supplemental Information:
1. Earth and spaceship's similarities include:
   a. passengers
   b. oxygen supply
   c. food supply
   d. water resources
   e. mineral resources
   f. livable temperature range
   g. space to move about
   h. communication systems
2. Differences include:
   a. living plants
   b. living animals
   c. waterfalls
   d. caves
   e. buildings
   f. highways
   g. bridges, etc.

F. Thought Questions for Class Discussions:
1. Are we destroying our Earth's oxygen supply?
2. Are we destroying our Earth's water supply?
3. Are people interfering with the Earth's temperature through increased pollution?
4. Are we wasting our Earth's mineral resources?
5. Are we overpopulating the Earth?

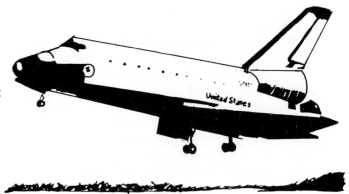

Spaceship (Our "shuttle")

G. Related Ideas for Further Inquiry:
1. Study Section VII-B, "Solar System."
2. Study Section V-D, "Personal Health."
3. Study Section VIII-B, "Satellites."
4. Study Activity VIII-C-2, "What are some of the problems of space travel?"
5. Study Activity VIII-C-3, "What is a space shuttle?"

H. Vocabulary Builders—Spelling Words:
1) **passengers** 2) **oxygen** 3) **water**
4) **resources** 5) **temperature** 6) **space**

I. Thought for Today:
"How would you like to be an astronaut just about to be shot into space and realize that the many parts of your spacecraft were all procured from the lowest bidder?"

Activity

A. Problem: *What Are Some of the Problems of Space Travel?*

B. Materials Needed:

1. Jumpsuits or substitute clothing
2. Large paper bag with cellophane front
3. Mock-up spaceship of cardboard boxes with controls

C. Procedure

1. Build a mock-up spaceship.
2. Plan on the crew members.
3. Determine destination.
4. Plan needs of voyagers (supplies and equipment):
   a. oxygen
   b. food and water
   c. sleeping quarters
   d. exercise area
   e. heating apparatus or equipment (sun will be on one side only.)
   f. propellants for escape velocity
   g. means of controlling spacecraft from: roll, pitch, swaying (yawing), etc.
   h. living in weightlessness
   i. means of controlling speed
   j. games or recreation
   k. communication system with Earth
   l. design your instrument panel
   m. re-entry equipment and/or landing equipment
   n. intercom
   o. bathroom facilities
   p. equipment for experiments to be performed aboard the spaceship
   q. cameras
5. Take your simulated trip.

D. Result:

Students will realize that space travel is not just fun, but a lot of hard work with many discomforts.

E. Basic Facts and Supplemental Information:

1. An impossible concept to teach is the element of time aboard a spacecraft because time on a spacecraft is far different from time on Earth.
2. Albert Einstein's theories of relativity involve the differences between "time on Earth" and "time in space travel."
3. Space begins where the Earth's atmosphere has so little density that it no longer affects objects passing through it. The atmosphere becomes thinner and thinner above the earth: 99% of the

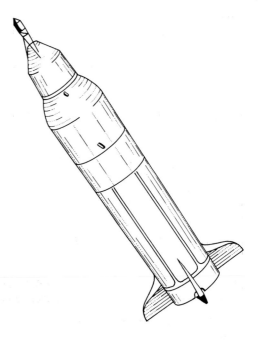

atmosphere lies below 20 miles. There is enough air at 75 miles to make meteors glow from friction against it. At 100 miles up there is still enough air that satellites are slowed up and dropped to lower levels. For all practical purposes we can say that space begins at 100 miles up.

F. Thought Questions for Class Discussions:

1. What other problems might arise in a long space journey?
2. What problems might be encountered from outside sources?
3. What safety precautions should be taken into account?

G. Related Ideas for Further Inquiry:

1. Study Activity VIII-B-5, "What is a space station?"
2. Study Section I-B, "Air."
3. Study Section VII-B, "Solar System."
4. Study Section V-C, "Nutrition."
5. Study Section V-D, "Personal Health."
6. Study Section V-G, "Safety."
7. Study other Activities in this Section

H. Vocabulary Builders—Spelling Words:

1) **space**   2) **travel**   3) **oxygen**   4) **water**
5) **weightlessness**   6) **food**   7) **recreation**
8) **propellants**   9) **supplies**   10) **equipment**

I. Thought for Today:

"Money can build a house, but it takes love to make it a home."

Activity

A. Problem: *What Is a Space Shuttle?*

B. Materials Needed:

1. Models of space shuttles
2. Drawings of space shuttles
3. Newspaper and magazine accounts of recent space shuttle flights

C. Procedure:

1. Students can design and build space shuttles or obtain models, pictures, or drawings of them.
2. Discuss the unique problems of space shuttles. See Activity VIII-C-2.
3. Discuss the differences between manned Earth satellites and space shuttles.
4. Plan a space shuttle mission to the moon and back.
5. Make a list of supplies needed. Supplies are those items that must be replenished.
6. Make a list of equipment needed. These need not normally be replaced. Some such items would be:
   a. navigational equipment
   b. maneuvering devices
   c. communicating systems, etc.

D. Results:

1. Students will learn that space shuttles are controlled, maneuverable from takeoff to landing.
2. Pupils will realize that space shuttles require carefully planned supplies and thoroughly tested equipment.
3. Class members will become cognizant of the concerns and inherent dangers of space travel.

E. Basic Facts and Supplemental Information:

1. Space shuttles save the government a lot of money because they are reusable.
2. Women have joined some of the crews aboard the space shuttles.
3. We lost one space shuttle crew on January 28, 1986.
4. There is always a risk in space flights.
5. A space shuttle coasting in space is in free flight. There are no forces acting on it such as thrust, friction, pressure—only the gravitational pull of the Earth, moon, sun, planets, etc., and its own inertia. The gravitational pull and its own inertia keep it in orbit.
6. Besides trained astronauts, civilian experts have been conducting scientific experiments aboard the space shuttles.
7. At the present time, the international space station is being constructed primarily by the United States

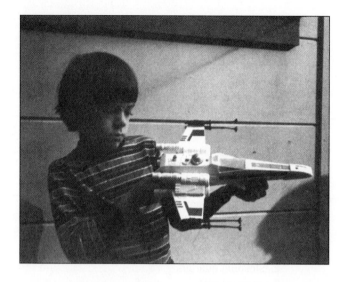

and Russia. Space shuttles are being used to ferry supplies, equipment, and parts of the space station itself to this orbiting project.

8. One of the biggest problems facing space travelers in any long duration flights is weightlessness. Because the body is not working against gravity, muscles, tendons, bones, cartilage, etc. tend to weaken. So far, returning astronauts have regained their former physical condition without any noted problems.

F. Thought Questions for Class Discussions:

1. What are the dangers in a space shuttle flight?
2. What does the Earth look like from outer space?
3. How can space shuttles benefit us?
4. Would you like to orbit the Earth aboard a space shuttle?

G. Related Ideas for Further Inquiry:

1. Study Section I-B, "Air."
2. Study Section VII-B, "Solar System."
3. Study Section V-D, "Personal Health."
4. Study Section VIII-A, "Aviation."
5. Study Section VIII-B, "Satellites."
6. Study other Activities in this Section.

H. Vocabulary Builders—Spelling Words:

1) **shuttle** 2) **space** 3) **manned**
4) **free flight** 5) **friction** 6) **gravitational**
7) **dangers** 8) **inertia** 9) **momentum**

I. Thought for Today:

"Science is only a tool. The harm or good it does depends on how people use it."

Activity

A. Problem: *How Do Astronauts Maneuver Spacecraft?*

B. Materials Needed:

1. Model of a spacecraft
2. Sketch of a spacecraft on chalkboard (or an overhead transparency)

C. Procedure:

1. Show the class the model or illustration.
2. Discuss space flights in general, including forward thrust.
3. Discuss the terms "rotation" and "axis" to be sure the class understands these terms.
4. Talk to the class about the dangers of the spaceship twisting or turning in launching or maneuvering.
5. Cite the three kinds of maneuvering problems that might occur or are desired, demonstrating each with the model or illustration.
   a. roll—rotation along the longitudinal axis (length of spaceship)
   b. yaw—rotation along the vertical axis (right and left motion)
   c. pitch—rotation along the short horizontal axis (up and down motion)
6. When students have become proficient in identifying each movement separately, use various combinations of any two maneuvering problems.
7. For top level, mature students you can combine all three maneuvers.
8. Describe to class that there are central mechanisms which work to stop each kind of rotation, like an exhaust thrust. For each mechanism that turns the spaceship one way, there is another that turns it the opposite way (to correct it).
9. If a spacecraft rotates in one direction, by knowing what rotation is involved, the astronaut could start a mechanism that would have the opposite effect, thus neutralizing any undesired rotation.

D. Result:

Students will learn that spaceships may twist, turn, and tumble, but there are mechanisms aboard to steady them.

E. Basic Facts and Supplemental Information:

1. By the use of these mechanisms it is possible to steer a spaceship in any direction in three-dimensional space.
2. Gyroscopes are used to keep the spaceship in a stabilized position.

3. Using these controls it is possible for one spacecraft to join another spacecraft or a space station.
4. Each spaceship has a redundancy system aboard in case of a failure of one vital part.
5. On a long journey, a spacecraft is deliberately rolled to keep the craft from overheating on the side facing the sun.

F. Thought Questions for Class Discussions:

1. What other dangers exist aboard a spaceship?
2. What would happen if one system failed?
3. What is weightlessness?
4. In space is there any "up" or "down"?

G. Related Topics and Activities:

1. Study Section I-B, "Air."
2. Study Section VIII-B, "Satellites."
3. Study Section V-D, "Personal Health."
4. Study Section II-F, "Movement and Resistance."

H. Vocabulary Builders—Spelling Words:

1) **roll** 2) **yaw** 3) **pitch** 4) **rotate**
5) **maneuver** 6) **controls** 7) **redundant**
8) **redundancy** 9) **axis** 10) **rotation**

I. Thought for Today:

"When everything is coming your way, you're probably in the wrong lane."

GLOSSARY

Science words and expressions, as well as other words needing explanation, are included in this Glossary. Words are broken down into their basic syllables.

ab a lo ne: large, univalve shellfish.

a bra sion: scraping or wearing away, usually skin damage.

ab so lute zer o: the lowest possible temperature (0° K., –459.67° F, or –273.15° C.).

ab sorb: to take in, or suck up, liquids.

ac cel er a tion: the capacity to gain speed.

ac id: a substance, sour to taste, which dissolves in water. In chemical tests acids turn blue or litmus red.

ac id rain: rain from the burning of fossil fuels, particularly sulphur dioxide and nitrogen dioxide.

a corn: the nut, or fruit, of an oak tree.

ac tion: the act or process of doing.

ad ap ta tion: a change in structure, form or habits to fit different conditions.

ad di tive: any substance added to food or drink to enhance its flavor, color, or life span.

AIDS: disease affecting the immune system, usually fatal.

ai ler on: hinged surface on the trailing edge of an airplane's wing to aid in banking and turning.

air craft: machine for flying in the air; either lighter or heavier than air.

al co hol: usually means *ethyl,* or *grain,* alcohol, a colorless liquid with a strong odor formed by the action of organisms on sugar. Alcohol has many uses in science and industry.

al gae: group of plants that have chlorophyll but do not have true roots, stems, or leaves.

al ka line: water soluble substance with hydroxide ions (OH⁻).

al li ga tor: a large reptile with a long body, four short legs, a thick skin, and a long tail. Alligators live in rivers and marshes in warm parts of America.

al ni co mag net: a very strong permanent magnet made of aluminum, nickel, cobalt, and iron.

al tim e ter: instrument for measuring heights; most frequently used in planes for determining altitude.

a lu mi num: a silvery, metallic metal, used for its lightness.

am mo nia: a solution in water of a gas obtained by distilling organic bodies containing nitrogen.

am phet a mine: drug to overcome fatigue, mental depression; also used in diets.

am phib i an: usually refers to members of the class Amphibia, which includes frogs, toads, and salamanders. The young of these animals are hatched and develop in water, but the adults of many species emerge from the water to live on land.

am pli tude: the size of vibration or the height of a wave.

a nat o my: the science of body structure in plants and animals.

a nem i a: reduction in red blood cells or hemoglobin in the blood.

an e mom e ter: instrument that measures wind speed.

an i mal: any living organism that has senses and can move.

an nu als: plants that live for about one year.

an ode: positive pole on a battery.

an ten nae: feelers on the head of an insect.

an thrax: a contagious disease, attended by fever, of human beings and animals.

an ther: top of the stamen in plants.

an thra cite: hard coal which gives much heat and little smoke.

an ti dote: something that hinders or removes the effects of poison or disease.

an ti sep tic: a solution which will check or prevent the growth of bacteria; a disinfectant.

an ti tox in: a substance produced in living tissues of plant or animal to check or hinder or make neutral a bacterial poison that produced it.

ap o gee: point that is the greatest distance from the Earth of orbiting objects.

ap pa ra tus: the equipment, tools, device, or appliance by which a process of work or play is carried on.

a quar i um: tank or bowl in which water plants and water animals are kept.

a rach nid: any of a large group of small arthropods including spiders, scorpions, mites, etc. An arachnid is air-breathing, has four pairs of walking legs, and no antennae; the body is usually divided into two regions.

Ar chi me des: early Greek who invented the screw to raise water.

Ar chi me des' Prin ci ple: a floating object displaces the weight of water equal to its own weight.

ar ter y: any of the blood vessels that carry blood away from the heart.

ar thro pod: one of a large group of invertebrate animals having segmented (jointed) bodies and legs. Insects, arachnids, and crustaceans are arthropods.

ar ti fi cial: made or contrived by human labor; not natural.

as cend: move upward, climb.

a scor bic ac id: vitamin C.

as ter oid: any one of the very small bodies revolving around the sun between the orbit of Mars and the orbit of Jupiter.

a stig ma tism: defect of the eye, or lens of the eye, that makes objects look indistinct or gives imperfect images.

as tro naut: person trained to fly in space.

as tron o mer: a scientist who studies the earth's relation to the sun, moon, stars, and other heavenly bodies.

a stron o my: study of stars, planets, and other space objects.

at mos phere: the air that surrounds the Earth.

atom: the smallest particle of an element that can exist. Atoms are the very small particles that make up molecules.

a tom ic: pertaining to an atom or atoms.

a tom ic en er gy: energy from the nucleus of the atom.

at tract: to draw to oneself as a magnet draws iron filings toward itself.

au to mat ic: able to move or act without help from another source.

ax is: an imaginary line around which a body rotates.

back bone: the bony column tht extends along the middle of the back in man, mammals, birds, reptiles, and fishes; the spine. The backbone consists of many separate bones, called vertebrae, held together by muscles and tendons and separated by pads of cartilage. The backbone protects the spinal cord, which it encloses.

bac te ria: a group of plant organisms, too small to be seen without a microscope.

bak ing so da: sodium carbonate; used in baking as leavening agent.

bal ance: an apparatus for weighing.

Bal ance of Nature: ample food supply for all organisms.

ball-and-sock et joint: a flexible skeletal joint formed by a ball or knob of one bone fitted into the cupped end of another bone. The shoulder and hip are ball-and-socket joints. As such they permit some motion in every direction.

bar bi tu rate: drug used as a sedative or pain deadener.

bas es: chemicals that react opposite to acids; contain hydroxyl ions.

ba sic: in chemistry, an alkaline, having the properties of a base.

beak: bill or nib of a bird.

bea ver: amphibious animal, found in lakes and ponds; builds underwater homes.

Ben e dicts So lu tion: a chemical solution used to test for sugar(s).

Ber nouil li's Prin ci ple: a fast moving fluid has less pressure sideways than it does forward.

bi cus pid: a double-pointed tooth; human adults have eight such teeth.

bi o de grad a ble: easily decomposable, especially biologically.

bi o tic com mun i ty: area where living things are mutually dependent.

bite: seizing by teeth or mouth.

blind spot: a round spot on the retina of the eye not sensitive to light.

blood ves sel: any of many tubes in the body through which blood flows. The three types of blood vessels are arteries, veins, and capillaries.

blow hole: hole for breathing located in the top of the head of whales and some other air-breathing animals. The blowhole usually has a flap of skin that keeps water out of the animal's lungs.

boil er: a container for heating liquids.

boil ing point: point where a liquid changes to a gas.

brain: the part of the nervous system enclosed in the skull.

breed ing: process of developing or propagating plants or animals.

burns: injury due to excessive heat.

buoy an cy: quality of floating on the surface of a liquid such as water.

butter milk the slightly acid liquid left after churning butter.

caf feine: the stimulant found in coffee and tea.

cal ci um: silver-white chemical element found in limestone.

cal o rie: unit of heat. Heat required to raise one gram of water one degree centigrade.

Cal o rie: (Big "C" calorie): Unit of heat, a thousand times that of "small c calorie." This unit is used in evaluating foods.

cam ou flage: disguise, change appearance.

cap il lar y: a small blood vessel with very thin walls. A network of capillaries joins the arteries and veins.

car bo hy drates: sugars and starches.

car bon: chemical element found in diamonds, graphite, and organic compounds.

car bon cy cle: sequence of states that the element passes through.

car bon di ox ide: a heavy, colorless, odorless gas present in the air. Green plants use carbon dioxide to make food.

car bon mon ox ide: a deadly gas, usually the product of incomplete combustion.

car di o pul mon a ry re sus ci ta tion: a method of restoring breathing and/or heartbeat to a victim.

car ni vore: flesh-eating animal.

car te sion di ver: A floating device that can be made to rise or sink.

car ti lage: the firm, tough, flexible substance that forms parts of the skeleton of vertebrates; gristle.

Cas si o pe ia: a northern constellation between Andromeda and Cepheus.

cath ode: negative pole on a battery.

ce les ti al: having to do with space, sky.

cell: the unit of living matter, usually microscopic, of which all plants and animals are made. Cells vary in form according to their use.

Cel si us: scale for measuring heat with water freezing at zero degrees and water boiling at one hundred degrees.

cen ti grade: same as Celsius.

cen trif u gal: apparent force moving away from center.

cen trip e tal: moving toward the center.

chain re ac tion: chemical reactions where each step is initiated by former step.

char ac ter is tic: a special quality or feature.

chem i cal: a substance obtained when two or more substances act upon one another to cause permanent change.

chem is try: the study of elements and compounds and the reactions they undergo.

chlam y di a: most common, severe venereal disease.

chlo rine: a heavy poisonous gas used in liquid form as a disinfectant.

chlo ro fluor o car bons: chemicals used in sprays destroying ozone.

chlo ro phyll: the green-colored material in the cells of green plants.

chol er a: an acute disease of the stomach and intestines.

cho les ter ol: a substance contained in all animal fats.

chrys a lis: a form of an insect when it is encased in a pupa, cocoon.

cir cuit: a complete path made of conductors through which an electric current can flow from the source of electrical energy and back again.

cir cu late: move around, move through a closed system as the blood moves through the blood vessels, or as air moves through a hot-air heating system.

cir cum fer ence: boundary line of a circle, every point in circumference of a circle is at the same distance from the center.

cit rus: relating to fruits such as the orange, lemon, lime, and grapefruit.

clas si fy: to arrange in groups, usually according to certain structures or functions.

clay: fine-grained earth, usually silicates.

clock wise: moving in the direction of the hands on a clock.

cloud: a visible mass of condensed watery vapor in the atmosphere.

coal: combustible solid mineral used for burning and heating.

co caine: drug, narcotic, local anesthetic, addictive.

cold-blood ed: having blood that is about the same temperature as the air or water around the animal; having blood that changes its temperature as the temperature of the surroundings changes.

com bus tion: the act of burning.

com et: a bright heavenly body with a starlike center and often with a cloudy tail of light.

com mu ni ca ble: that which can be spread or communicated from person to person or place to place, as a disease.

com mu ni ca tion: imparting knowledge, opinions, or facts.

com pare: to find out or point out how things are alike and how they differ.

com pass: an instrument for showing directions; it consists of a free-turning magnetic needle; an instrument for drawing a circle.

com pli men tar y: two or more things that enrich other(s).

com pound: to put together.

com press: a pad of folded cloth.

com pres sion: the act of pushing together or bunching up.

con cave: lens shallower in the center.

con clu sion: final decision.

con den sa tion: change of a gas or vapor into a liquid.

con dense: to change from a gas to a liquid.

con duc tion: the passing of heat from one particle to another. The particles vibrate but do not move from one place to another.

cones: the seed-bearing part of pine, cedar, fir, and other evergreen trees, light receptive cells in the eyes.

con ser va tion: preservation; avoidance of waste.

con stel la tion: a group of stars that seems to form a picture in the sky.

con ta gious: that which is communicable, catching, as a disease; can be spread from person to person.

con tam i nate: to spoil or make impure by contact with waste matter or impurities.

con test ing: competing with others for something, fighting; struggling.

con ti nen tal code: scheme of dots and dashes used in telegraphy.

con tin ent: one of the seven large land masses of Earth.

con tour far ming: following natural ridges and furrows to avoid soil erosion.

con tract: to draw together or to make shorter; to shrink or become smaller.

con vection: the movement of particles of a liquid or a gas from a cold place to a warmer one. The movement is somewhat circular, the colder material pushing the warmer material sideways and upward.

con vex: lens thicker in the center.

core: inner part as the Earth's core.

cor ne a: the transparent part of the outer coat of the eyeball. It covers the iris and the pupil.

coun ter clock wise: moving in the opposite direction of the hands on a clock.

CPR: See cardiopulmonary resuscitation.

cray fish: a freshwater animal of the class Crustacea that looks like a small lobster; a similar but larger saltwater shellfish.

croc o dile: large, amphibious lizard, rounded nose.

crus ta cean: any of a group of water animals having tough shells, jointed bodies and legs, and gills for breathing. Crabs, lobsters, and shrimps are crustaceans.

crys tal: a solid substance with a regular shape.

cu ta ne ous: pertaining to the skin.

dam: a framework to obstruct water.

DDT: potent, persistent, pesticide; contaminates food, causes many birds to lay eggs with too thin shells.

de cay: to rot; also, material that has rotted, as tooth decay.

dec i bel: a unit for measuring the volume of sound.

de cid u ous: a tree or bush that sheds its leaves annually.

de com po si tion: to separate into simpler elements.

de flate: to let the air or gas out of an inflated object.

de ger mi nat ed: that grain from which the germ has been removed.

de gree: a step in the scale; a stage in a process; a unit for measuring temperature.

de hy dra tion: the process of removing water from food and other substances; drying.

del ta: the deposit of earth and sand that collects at the mouth of some rivers. A delta is usually three-sided.

den si ty: the mass per unit volume of a substance.

den tin: the hard material of which the main part of the tooth is composed.

de press ant: a substance that pulls down, or lowers.

der ma tol o gist: medical doctor who specializes in the study of the skin.

de sa li ni za tion: removal of salt from sea water.

de scend: move downward.

des ert: dry, barren land.

de ter gent: a cleansing substance.

dew: condensed water from the air.

di ag no sis: the identification of a disease by its symptoms.

di a phragm: the partitions or walls of tissues, sinew, or muscle, for the purpose of separating and protecting adjoining parts in the body or in instruments.

di a stol ic: the pressure of the heart when it is in a state of relaxation.

di et: the kind and amount of food and drink that a person or animal usually eats.

di gest: to change (food) within the stomach and intestines so that it can be absorbed by the body.

di ges tive juice: a juice produced by the body for use in the digestion of food.

di late: to make wider or larger.

di no saur: an extinct reptile of the Mesozoic era.

dir ig i ble: a balloon type airship.

dis ease: an illness or weakened condition of health.

dis in fec tant: something that destroys bacteria and/or viruses.

dis solve: to make liquid; to become liquid, especially by putting or being put into a liquid. When a solid has dissolved completely, it cannot be separated from the liquid by filtering.

dis til la tion: a process where liquids are separated into their component parts by heating and condensing.

do mains: small, jumbled parts of a piece of iron or steel and when aligned become a magnet.

down ers: slang term for drugs that are depressing.

drag: in air travel, the resistance of the gaseous medium on the airship.

drone: nonworking male of most bee species.

drought: a long period with no rain.

drug: prescribed medicine, narcotic, habit-forming; also illegal medicines.

dry ice: solid carbon dioxide, refrigerant.

dys en ter y: a painful disease of the intestines.

earth quake: undulating movement of the earth's crust.

e clipse: a darkening of the sun or the moon.

e col o gist: a scientist who studies the relation of living things to their community and to each other.

ec o sys tem: area where living things are mutually dependent.

egg: oval bodies laid by birds, fish, and reptiles; reproductive cell.

e lec tric it y: form of energy resulting from the flow of electrons.

e lec trode: material used to make an electric cell.

e lec tro mag net: a piece of iron that becomes a temporary magnet when an electric current passes through wire coiled around it.

e lec tron: particle that moves rapidly around the nucleus of an atom. Every electron has a negative charge.

e lec tro scope: a device for detecting small changes in electricity.

el e ment: a part; that cannot be detected or separated without chemical analysis.

e lim i na tion: the act of getting rid of, removing.

El Niño: major changes in the weather pattern due to abnormally high ocean temperatures.

e lo de a: an aquatic plant often used in aquariums. It floats beneath the surface, but its roots can take hold in the soil under low-water conditions.

em bry o: an unborn or unhatched offspring.

em phy se ma: an abnormal swelling of body tissue, often found in the air sacs in the lungs.

en dan gered species: an organism threatened with extinction.

en er gy: ability to do work or to act; capacity for work.

en vir on ment: surroundings of an organism.

en zyme: a catalyst that helps bring about chemical changes in the body.

e ro sion: process of eating away or of being worn away gradually. In nature, wind and water cause most erosion of rock and soil.

es cape ve loc i ty: the speed of spaceship to overcome earth's gravity.

es tu ar y: wide tidal mouth of a river, an arm of the sea.

Eu sta chi an tube: slender canal between the pharynx and the middle ear.

eu troph i ca tion: process(es) of aiding nutrition.

e vap o rate: to change from a liquid into a gas. Molecules of the liquid escape from its surface into the air in the form of vapor.

e vap o ra tion: the process of evaporating.

ev er green: having green leaves throughout the year.

ex cre tion: the act of expelling waste matter.

ex er cise: movement, put into action, train.

ex ert: to use; put into use; use fully.

ex hale: breathe out.

ex pand: to grow large or cause to grow larger.

ex pec to rate: to spit.

ex per i ment: to test; a test that is made to find out something.

ex tinc tion: no longer existing.

ex tin guish: put out a fire.

Fahr en heit: a thermometer on which the boiling point of water is 212° and the freezing point is 32°.

fam ine: scarcity of food, destroy with hunger.

fast food: food that can be prepared and served quickly particularly at a snack bar or restaurant.

fa tigue: tiredness or weariness.

fats: greasy or oily substances of the body. Also oils and parts of meat or other foods that yield oils and grease.

fault: a break in a mass of rock in which one part slides past another part.

fer men ta tion: the chemical change which causes milk to sour, apple juice to turn to vinegar, and starches to turn to sugars.

ferns: any of a group of plants having roots, stems, and leaves, but no flowers, and reproducing by spores instead of seeds.

fer tile: capable of growing, producing fruit or vegetation.

fer til i za tion: the joining of male and female gametes.

fer ti li zer: any material to improve the quality of the soil.

fil a ment: thread-like; part of the stamen bearing the anther.

fil ter: a device for passing liquids or gases through some substance in order to remove certain particles; the material (often paper) through which a liquid or gas passes so that certain things can be removed; to put a material through a filter.

fire: active burning, combustion.

fire box: the place in which fuel is burned in a furnace or boiler.

fire ex tin guish er: device for putting out fires.

fire tri an gle: the three elements needed for fires; heat, material, and oxygen.

fish: vertebrate animals living in water and breathing with gills.

fis sion: a method of reproduction in which one-celled living thing divides, forming two new individuals; the splitting of large atoms such as uranium atoms into smaller atoms, releasing atomic energy.

flesh: the soft part of the body that covers the bones and is covered by skin. Flesh consists mostly of muscles and fat; the soft part of fruits and vegetables.

flood: an overflowing of water on land.

floss ing: act of using dental threads to scrape teeth.

flow er: part of the plant that contains the reproductive organs.

fog: a thick, cloud layer of water suspended in the atmosphere or near the Earth's surface.

food chain: a series of organisms, each of which is eaten by the next organism.

food web: the relationships of many organisms which can be eaten by many other organisms.

force: any cause that produces changes in, starts, or stops motion of, an object.

fore cas ting: predicting, estimating.

form: a shape; to shape or make; a condition or state.

fos sil: preserved remains of a living thing.

fos sil fu els: materials from the past that are used for energy.

frac tion al dis til la tion: removing each material separately by continuing to increase temperature.

frame work: a support or skeleton; the stiff parts that give shape to something.

freez ing point: the temperature at which a liquid freezes or changes to a solid. The freezing point of water at sea level is 32 degrees Fahrenheit or 0 degrees Centigrade.

fre quen cy: the number of times any action occurs.

fric tion: the rubbing of one body against another.

frost: white, frozen dew.

fuel: a substance, or mixture of substances, that can be burned to produce heat or some other form of energy.

ful crum: balance point on a lever.

fun gi: any of a group of plants without flowers, leaves, or green coloring matter.

fu sion: the combining of small atoms, such as hydrogen, forming larger atoms and releasing atomic energy.

gal ax y: a huge group of stars.

gam etes: reproductive cells in plants and animals.

gar ter snake: a common, harmless snake that is brown or green with long yellow stripes.

gas: a material, like air, that is neither a solid nor a liquid, they move about freely, spreading apart until they fill all the available space.

gas, nat u ral: gas that is extracted from the Earth.

gas oline: a fuel from petroleum used in internal combustion engines.

gen er a tor: a device for transforming mechanical energy into electric energy.

ge o graph ic North Pole: one end of the axis about which the Earth rotates. The axis is an imaginary line through the center of the Earth. The geographic North Pole marks the most northerly point on the Earth.

geo graph ic South Pole: one end of the Earth's axis. The geographic South Pole is the most southerly point on the Earth.

ge ol o gist: scientist who studies the Earth.

ge o therm al: relating to the internal heat of the Earth.

ger mi na tion: starting to grow or develop, sprouting.

germs: microscopic animals or plants that cause disease.

gey ser: a spring of hot water that gushes into the air.

gill: in certain water animals, a body structure used for breathing. The gill takes in oxygen from the water habitat and sends out carbon dioxide.

gla cier: a large mass of ice, formed from snow, that moves slowly down a mountainside or sloping valley, or outward from a center as in a continental glacier. The movement of glaciers causes erosion and piling up of soil and rocks.

glands: small organs in the body which produce different substances to be used by or discharged from the body.

gold: heavy, yellow, metallic element that is a precious metal.

gon or rhe a: a serious venereal disease that affects mucous membranes.

gourd: a climbing plant like a squash; hollowed shell of same.

grass es: plants with blade-like leaves, single seed and includes barley, oats, rye, and wheat.

grav i ty: natural force that tends to move objects toward the center of the Earth or other celestial body.

Green house Ef fect: rising of the atmosphere's temperature due to pollutants that reflect Earth's radiant heating toward Earth.

guin ea pig: a small, fat mammal in the rat family with short ears and short tail.

gul ly: a small valley or a ditch cut by running water.

gup py: a very small, usually brightly colored fish that lives in tropical freshwater.

hab i tat: the place where an animal or plant lives and grows.

half-life: time of a radioactive material to lose half of its original substance.

hal lu ci na tion: apparent perception by senses that are not actually present.

ham ster: small, short-tailed rodent with large cheek pouches.

har mon ics: mixed tones and overtones.

hear ing graph: a graph that shows a person's hearing range or ability.

heart: a small muscle that pumps the blood to all parts of the body and back again.

heat: quality of being hot from molecular action.

Heim lich Ma neu ver: a first aid procedure to help a choking person.

hel i cop ter: type of aircraft that gets its left by horizontal, overhead revolving blades.

he li um: second lightest element, a gas, used in airships and balloons.

hem i sphere: half of a sphere; the Earth is divided into a Northern Hemisphere and a Southern Hemisphere by the equator.

he mo phil i a: a condition in which the blood fails to clot quickly.

hem or rhage: escape of blood from a broken vessel.

herb i cides: chemicals used to destroy unwanted plants.

her bi vore: any animal that feeds on plants.

her pes: a viral infection of the skin or mucous membrane(s).

hi ber nate: to spend the winter in a sleep or in an inactive condition. In true hibernation, body processes are slowed.

highs: high pressure air masses identified with good weather.

ho mog e nized: blended or mixed by force into one part, as homogenized milk.

Ho mo sa pi ens: only living species of the genus Homo is the human being.

hor i zon: the line where the Earth and sky meet.

hu mid i ty: dampness and moisture of the air.

hu mus: soil made from decaying leaves and other vegetable matter.

hur ri cane: a violent storm with winds from 70 to 100 m.p.h. usually with rain and thunder.

hy dro car bons: chemical compounds that contain only hydrogen and carbon. Four groups of hydrocarbons are found in automobile exhausts.

hy dro chlor ic acid: a solution of hydrogen chloride gas in water.

hy dro e lec tric: having to do with the production of electricity by water power.

hy dro gen: a gas, the lightest of all elements.

hy drol o gist: an expert in the study of water.

hy drom e ter: a device to determine the specific gravity of liquids (thickness and weight).

hy drox ide: a metallic compound containing the "OH" ion.

hy poth e sis: an educated guess, a proposition made for reasoning.

ice: solid form of water.

Ice house Ef fect: lowering of the atmosphere's temperature due to pollutants that prevent the sun's radiation from striking the Earth by reflecting back the sun's rays before they strike the Earth.

ig ne ous: of or having to do with fire; produced by fire, great heat, or the action of a volcano.

il lu sion: misapprehension of the state of affairs.

im age: the view seen by the reflection of light rays.

im mu ni za tion: the state of being immune or protected from a disease.

in can des cent: to glow with heat.

in ci sion: a cut or gash.

in ci sor: tooth having a sharp edge for cutting.

in clined plane: sloping, flat surface.

in cu ba tor: an apparatus for hatching eggs artificially.

in er ti a: tendency to remain in the state one is in whether stationary or in motion.

in fec tion: a condition or disease caused by contact with certain harmful organisms.

in flate: distend, puff up.

in fra red: wavelength greater than red end of visible light.

in hale: to breathe in, to draw into the lungs.

in ner ear: the innermost part of the ear. The inner ear is made up of several canals that are filled with fluid. This part of the ear is connected to the brain by a nerve. When the fluid vibrates, it sets up impulses in this nerve which are received in the brain as sound.

in sect any member of a group of small invertebrate animals having a body that has three parts, three pairs of legs, two feelers, and usually two pairs of wings.

in sec ti cides: chemicals used to kill insects.

in stru ment: a tool, mechanical device.

in su la tion: a material or materials that covers another to prevent loss of heat or electricity.

in ten si ty: amount of heat, light, or sound per unit.

in tes tine: the part of the digestive system that extends from the lower end of the stomach. It receives food from the stomach, digests it further, and absorbs it. The intestine consists of two parts: the small intestine, a coiled tube that is about 22 ft. long in the adult; and the large intestine, a thicker tube about 5 ft. long.

in ver sion: act of being inverted or reverse.

in ver te brate: without a backbone; an animal without a backbone. All animals except fishes, amphibians, reptiles, birds, and mammals are invertebrates.

i o dized: having had iodine added.

i ris: the colored area that surrounds the pupil of the eye.

i ron: a metal that rusts easily and is strongly attracted by magnets; a mineral important to the body.

ir ra di a tion: emitting atomic or subatomic rays or particles.

jet stream: strong winds that circle the Earth about 6 miles (10 kilometers) above the Earth.

joint: in an animal, a place where two bones are joined together by ligaments. The movable joints are kept moist by a liquid. Some joints are not movable.

Kel vin: a temperature scale measured in Celsius degrees with absolute zero equal to −273° C.

ki net ic en er gy: the energy of a body that is in motion which includes its mass and its velocity.

king dom: one of the main sub-divisions of all living things.

Kra ka to a: the volcano that produced the greatest noise known.

lac er a tion: a jagged tear or cut.

la goon: enclosed body of water near an ocean or lake.

land fill: waste material used to reclaim land and/or burying rubbish.

lar va: the form in which most insects hatch from the egg, wingless and sometimes wormlike.

lar ynx: a hollow muscular organ forming an air passage to the lungs and holding the vocal cords.

Lat in: language of the ancient Romans. It is still used in science and religion.

lat i tude: distance north or south of the equator, measured in degrees.

la va: molten rock flowing from a volcano; rock formed by the cooling of this molten rock.

lay er: one thickness or fold

leaf: flat usually green plant part growing from stem

leg umes: vegetables that have pods, such as peas and beans.

lens: the part of the eye, glasses, or camera, that focuses light to form clear images.

lev er: a bar resting on a pivot used to lift heavy objects.

leu ke mi a: a disease in which there is an extra large number of white blood cells.

lift: upward force on an airplane wing caused by upper curved surface of the wing which thins the air over the wing causing greater pressure below the wing.

lig a ment: a band of strong tissue that connects bones or holds parts of the body in place.

light ning: discharge or flash of electricity in the sky.

lime: calcium oxide, used in neutralizing soil acids.

lime stone: a sedimentary rock formed under water, usually from the remains of sea animals.

lines of force: invisible lines from one pole of a magnet to the other pole that indicate the direction in which the force of the magnet is acting.

liq uid: a material that is not a solid or a gas and that can flow freely like water and take the shape of its container.

li quor: alcoholic beverages.

lit mus pap er: a paper whose dye turns red in acid conditions and blue in alkaline.

lit ter: that which is scattered about needlessly.

liv er wort: a plant that is somewhat amorphous like a moss.

liz ard: large groups of reptiles with thin bodies and four legs, live in hot, dry areas.

loam: vegetable matter with clay and sand.

lo co mo tion: moving from one place to another.

lode stone: a kind of iron ore, called magnetite, that attracts iron and some kinds of steel just as a magnet does.

lows: low pressure air masses identified with poor weather.

lu bri cate: to oil to reduce friction.

lu mi nous: giving off light.

lungs: the breathing organs found in the chest of many animals with backbones.

lymph: colorless fluid containing white blood cells.

ma chine: a mechanical vehicle.

mag gots: wormlike larvae of an insect.

mag ma: liquid, molten rock from the Earth's mantle or crust. It cools to form igneous rock.

mag net: a piece of iron, steel or alloy that attracts or repels iron or other like substances.

mag net ic: having the properties of a magnet.

mag net ic pole: each end of a magnet.

mag ne tize: to give something the properties or qualities of a magnet.

mag ni fy ing glass: a lens which enlarges the viewing area.

mam mal: any number of a group of warm-blooded vertebrates that have fur or hair and that produce milk to feed their young.

mam ma ry: of the human female breast, milk secreting gland.

man u fac tured: having been made by people, and not the result of a natural cause.

mar ble: the metamorphic crystallized form of limestone, white or colored; it is capable of taking a high polish.

mar i jua na: poisonous drug made from hemp leaves and flowers.

mass: volume.

meat: the flesh of an animal, the muscles of an animal.

me di a: the main means of mass communication; the middle layer of the wall of the artery or other vessel.

melt ing point: the temperate at which a solid substance begins to melt or become liquid.

mem brane: a thin, soft layer of tissue in the body of an animal or plant.

met a mor phic: characterized by change of form; having to do with change of form. A metamorphic rock is one that has been changed to a different form by heat, pressure, or both.

met a mor pho sis: change of form, example—tadpoles to frogs.

me te or ite: a large meteor that falls to the earth before it is completely burned up.

mi cro scope: a magnifying instrument that has lens or combination of lenses for making objects appear larger aid of light.

mid dle ear: in humans, the cavity of the ear that is separated from the other ear by the eardrum, and which contains three small bones called the hammer, the stirrup, and the anvil. The cavity of the middle ear is filled with air and is connected to the throat by a tube.

mi gra tion: a move from one place to settle in another.

milk: fluid secreted by female mammals to feed their young.

Milky Way: our galaxy.

mil lion: one thousand thousand; 1,000,000.

min er als: inorganic substances; substances that are neither vegetable nor animal in nature.

mix ture: two or more substances mixed together but not chemically combined. Each of the substances has it own properties and doesn't change when in contact with the other substance or substances present.

moist: slightly wet or damp.

mol e cule: the smallest particle into which a substance can be divided without changing the chemical nature of that substance.

mol lusk: invertebrates that live in water which includes oysters, clams, mussels, snails, squids, and octopi.

mo men tum: force with which a body moves. It is equal to its mass times its velocity.

mo ne ra: one-celled animals without any definite structure; recently named a kingdom.

moss: any of various very small, soft, green or brown plants that grow close together like a carpet on the ground, on rocks, on trees, etc.

moth ball: naphthalene or camphor which repels moths.

moun tain: large mass of earth and rock above ground level.

mul ti-sen sor y: pertaining to two or more senses.

mus cle: a bundle of fibers, made up of cells, that contracts or extends to move a part of the body.

musk rats: a North American water rodent, somewhat like a rat but larger.

nar cot ic: a substance that eases pain and may cause sleep.

na sal pas sage: air pathway inside the head extending from the nostrils to the throat.

nat u ral: found in nature, not artificial.

nec tar: a sugary liquid found in the flowers of some plants.

nerv ous sys tem: a network of nerves and nerve centers in a person or animal. In man, the central nervous system is made up of the brain and spinal cord.

neu trons: neutral charge masses that lie within the nucleus of atoms.

New ton: formulator of the Laws of Motion.

ni a cine: nicotine acid, a vitamin, the lack of produces pellagra, (red, dry, skin, and a sore mouth).

niche: area in which an organism usually lives.

nic o tine: the drug contained in tobacco.

ni trates: soluble salts needed by plants and animals for growth; used to fertilize the soil.

ni tro gen: a colorless, odorless gas that constitutes about four-fifths of the Earth's atmosphere.

non mag net ic: lacking the properties of a magnet; not attracted by a magnet.

non re new a ble: any substance that cannot be restored or replaced.

nu cle ar: having to do with the nucleus (center) of the atom.

nu cle us, plural nu cle i: the part of a cel that controls much of what happens in the cell . . . the central part of an atom.

nu tri ent: a food substance that gives nourishment to the body.

nu tri tion: nourishment; food; the act or process of absorbing food or nourishment.

oat: edible seed, small grain, thought to reduce cholesterol.

ob ser va tion: the act of seeing and noting; something seen and noted.

oc clud ed front: where the cold front overtakes the warm front.

oc cu py: to take up; to fill.

o cean: a great body of salt water, there are five main oceans.

o cean og ra pher: scientist who studies the oceans.

Old Faith ful: a natural, large geyser in Yellowstone National Park.

om nivore: animal that eats both plants and other animals.

or bit: the curved path that a planet follows around the sun or one object around another.

or gan: a main part of an animal or plant, made up of several kinds of tissues.

or gan ic: having characteristics of living organisms; natural.

or gan isms: any living beings.

or nith ol o gist: scientist that studies birds.

os mos sis: movement of a liquid through a semi-permeable membrane.

out er ear: in humans, the visible part of the ear and the passageway leading to the middle ear. The eardrum separates the outer ear from the middle ear.

o var y: female reproductive organ where ova are produced.

o vule: part of the ovary of seed plants that contain germ cells.

ox i da tion: the combination of an element with oxygen.

ox ide: compound of oxygen with another element or radical.

ox y gen: a colorless, odorless gas that makes up part (about one fifth) of the air. It supports burning and is necessary to animal life. Oxygen is a chemical element.

ox y gen cy cle: sequence of states that the element passes through.

oys ter: a kind of shellfish or mollusk that has a rough, irregular shell. It is an important food.

o zone: An allotrope of oxygen with three atoms to the molecule; pungent, colorless, unstable gas with powerful oxidizing properties.

o zone lay er: a layer in the stratosphere that absorbs most of the sun's ultraviolet radiation.

pan cre as: gland near the stomach that secretes digestive fluid into the duodenum and insulin into the blood.

pan da: a white and black bearlike animal found in Asia.

par a chute: a rectangular or umbrella-shaped canopy allowing a person or object to descend slowly from a height.

par al lel: at or being the same distance apart like railroad tracks.

par a site: a living thing that must live in or on another living thing in order to get food, shelter, or something else that it needs. A parasite gives nothing in return to the animal or plant it lives on.

par ti cle: a very small bit of material.

pas teur i za tion: a process which is used to destroy harmful bacteria in milk and other liquids. The liquid is kept at a temperature of between 140° and 150° Fahrenheit for a certain period of time, then chilled.

pen du lum: weight suspended by a rod or string to regulate movements.

per en ni als: plants lasting a year or longer.

per i gee: the elliptical point which is closest to the Earth or other orbiting body.

per i scope: an apparatus with tube and mirrors permitting the viewer to see objects on a higher plane; used in submarines.

per ma nent: lasting; intended to last; not for a short time only.

per son al i ty: the quality of being a person, habitual patterns of a person.

per spi ra tion: sweat.

pes ti cides: chemicals used to kill unwanted animals.

pet al: leaf of a corolla.

Pe tri dish: small transparent container (dish and lid) used in scientific research particularly in studying bacterial growth.

phar ynx: tube that connects the mouth with the esophagus.

pher o mones: a chemical substance secreted by one animal to attract another of the same species.

phos phates: salts of phosphorus that stimulate growth, many times excessive such as in ponds and lakes.

phos pho rus: one of the minerals found in and necessary to the health of teeth and bones.

pho to syn the sis: process by which plant cells make sugar from carbon dioxide and water in the presence of chlorophyll and light.

pho to tro pism: attracted toward or away from light.

phy lum: a taxological classification below kingdom.

phy to plank ton: microscopic, aquatic plants that produce most of the world's oxygen supply.

pis til: the seed-bearing part of a flower, contains the ovary, stigma, and often the style.

pitch: tone level.

pith: spongy tissue of corn stalk, or rind fruit.

plague: a contagious, epidemic disease.

plan et: 1. an object or body that travels about the sun in an orbit. The sun's planets are Mercury, Venus, Earth, Mars, Jupiter, Saturn, Uranus, Neptune, and Pluto.

plants: a tree, shrub, or herb; non-mobile organism.

plaque: scum-like substance that covers teeth; main cause of tooth decay.

plas ter of paris: fine, white plaster for making molds.

plas tics: chemicals that can be molded.

poach: catch or trap animals illegally.

poi son: a substance, usually a drug that causes severe sickness or death.

Po la ris: the North Star.

pole: place where the force of a magnet is strongest; either end of the earth's axis.

pol len: grain-like discharge from the male part of the flower containing the gamete that fertilizes the female ovule.

pol lute: contaminate, defile the environment.

pol lu tion: state of being unclean or impure.

pop corn: a variety of Indian Corn with small kernels that pop open when heated.

pore: a very small opening in the skin or in a covering of a plant.

po tas si um: one of the minerals necessary to maintain good health.

po ten tial en er gy: the energy of a body that is obtained by its position in space.

pre cip i ta tion: rain, snow, sleet or hail.

pre da tor: any animal that preys on other animals.

pres er va tion: to keep from injury or destruction.

pres sure: force pushing on a particular area.

prey: a living organism that is eaten by predators.

pri mate: the most highly developed order of animals including humans, apes, lemurs, and monkeys.

pri sm: a triangular, transparent block used to separate light rays.

pro pel ler: a revolving shaft with blades especially to move a ship, boat, or airplane.

pro tein: a nourishing food element, important to all living cells, animal or plant.

pro tis ta: one classification of living things; contains amoebas, euglena, and diatoms; has animal and plant characteristics.

pro tons: positive charge masses that lie within the nucleus of atoms.

pro to pla sm: material comprising the living part of a cell.

pro to zo a: a group of one-celled, microscopic animals.

pul ley: a grooved wheel or set of wheels for a rope or chains to lift weights by changing direction and force applied.

pulse: the regular beating of blood against the wall of an artery caused by the pumping of the heart. The pulse is best felt on the wrist near the base of the thumb or at the side of the neck.

pump: a device that moves liquid or gas from one area to another.

pu pa: the cocoon or case stage in the development of an insect; the stage which follows the larva.

pu pil: the opening at the center of the iris of the eye. The pupil regulates the amount of light that enters the eye and expands in dim light and contracts in bright light.

pur pu ra: a disease that colors skin purple from escaping blood from its vessels.

Py rex: hard, heat-resistant type of glass.

qua sar: star-like celestial object that appears very bright and very distant.

rad: a measurement of radiation.

ra di ant en er gy: energy that is given off as rays by a hot object. The sun is a source of radiant energy.

ra di a tion: act or process of giving off light or other kinds of radiant energy; the energy radiated.

ra di a tion de tect or: a device that senses small amounts of radiation.

ra di a tor: a heating device consisting of a set of pipes through which steam or hot water passes; a device for cooling circulating water, i.e., the radiator of an automobile.

rad i o ac tiv i ty: radiation given off by the disintegration of atoms of particular substances.

rain bow: an arc consisting of all colors of the spectrum due to water vapor acting like a prism.

rain for est: tropical woodlands that provide much of the oxygen and mild climates.

re act or: a facility where matter is converted into energy.

re claim: to bring back, to keep from being lost or destroyed.

re cycle: to reclaim and reuse needed materials.

re flec tion: the bouncing back of light, heat, or sound from a surface.

ref use: waste material; garbage; rubbish.

rel a tive: having a relationship or connection to one another.

rem: a measure of radiaiton about one roentgen of an X-ray (*R*adiation *E*quivalent in *M*an.).

re new a ble: capable of being restored to its original state or supply.

re pel: to push away, or to drive back. Magnetic poles that are alike repel each other.

re pro duce: to produce its own kind, as an animal produces young or a plant produces seeds.

rep tile: a cold-blooded vertebrate that creeps or crawls and that is covered with scales or bony plates. Snakes, lizards, turtles, alligators, and crocodiles are reptiles.

re sis tance: opposing, power to resist as force, disease, or electricity.

re sour ces: stock or supply that can be used; available assets.

re spi ra tory: the system of organs used for breathing.

re sus ci ta tion: bring back or come back to consciousness.

ret i na: the membrane lining of the back part of the eyeball; the part of the eye that receives images of vision.

re use: use needed materials over again.

rev o lu tion: a movement of one body around another such as the moon around the Earth or Earth around the sun.

ri bo fla vin: vitamin B-2.

Rich ter Scale: a scale representing the strength of earthquakes (Scale: 0–10).

Ri ker box: container or mount for the collection of insects.

riv er: a large stream of water emptying into a larger body of water.

rock: a piece of mineral material.

roc ket: a self-propelling device operated by means of gas escaping from a nozzle or jet at the rear of a combustion chamber.

ro dent: any of a group of mammals having teeth especially adapted for gnawing wood and similar material. Rats, mice, squirrels, hares, and rabbits are rodents.

roent gen: a unit of X-ray radiaiton.

roll: to move around an object's horizontal axis.

roots: part of plant below surface that provides food, water, and stability to the plant.

ro ta tion: any object that turns around on its own axis.

rud der: a vertical device on a plane or ship for controlling horizontal movements.

rye: a cereal plant, a grass.

sal a man der: an amphibian shaped somewhat like a lizard, closely related to the frogs and toads.

sa li va: a digestive juice produced by glands in the mouth. Saliva keeps the mouth moist and aids in the digestion of food.

sal vage: act of saving reusable materials.

sand dune: a mound or ridge of loose sand heaped up by the wind.

sand stone: a sedimentary rock formed mostly of grains of sand that have been pressed together over a long period of time.

san i ta tion: the elimination of harmful conditions.

sat el lite: any object that revolves around another object.

scald: to burn or injure with a hot liquid or gas.

scale: one of the thin, flat, hard plates forming the outer covering of snakes, lizards, and some fishes; a series of spaces marked by lines and used in measuring distances; an instrument for weighing materials.

scale of dis tance: a scale found on a map or globe for measuring distances between places.

scav en ger: one who, or that which, cleans up dirt and filth.

sci ence prin ci ples: rules or laws of science.

sco li o sis: abnormal lateral curvature of the back.

scor pi on: gray lizard with a curved tail, and poisonous sting.

sea shell: shell of a salt water mollusk, whole or part.

sea son: one of the four periods of the year: spring, summer, autumn, winter.

se cre tions: substances released into the body.

sec tion: a part cut off; part; division; slice.

sed i ment: material that settles to the bottom of a liquid.

sed i men tary: of sediment; having something to do with sediment; formed from sediment as sedimentary rocks.

seed: the part of a flowering plant that will develop into a full plant.

seis mo graph: an instrument that records the force and direction of earthquakes.

son ic boom: the loud, explosive noise from sound waves made by a plane travelling at speeds faster than the speed of sound.

sound ing board: a board with upright nails to test materials for sound.

sen sa tion: the feeling or experience caused by action on the sense organs.

sense or gan: the eye, ear, or other part of the body by which a person or an animal receives information about the surroundings. The messages from such organs are interpreted in the brain as sensations of heat, color, sound, smell, etc.

sen si tive: easily affected or influenced.

se pal: a leafy division of the calyx.

ser ies: objects placed one after the other.

shale: a sedimentary rock formed from hardened clay or mud. Shale splits easily into thin layers.

shoul der: a body joint to which an arm, foreleg, or wing is attached.

silt: fine particles of sand and/or soil.

si phon: a device for transferring liquids from one level to a lower one.

skel e ton: the bony structure of a body. The skeleton is a frame to which muscles and tendons are attached.

skull: the bony framework of the head.

slate: a bluish-gray metamorphic rock, made from shale, that splits easily into thin smooth layers.

smog: air pollution of smoke and fog, also other air pollutants.

smoke: the vaporous and solid materials arising from something burning.

snail: a creepy animal that has curved, protective shell.

snake: legless reptile with an elongated body and tapering tail.

Snel len Chart: eye chart to determine visual acuity.

soil wa ter: water that occurs in the soil. It is absorbed by the roots of plants and provides the minerals they need.

so lar sys tem: the sun and the other heavenly bodies that move around it.

sol id: a kind of material that has shape and size; it is not a liquid or a gas; not hollow; hard; firm; strongly put together.

so lu tion: a combination of substances, especially a liquid formed by dissolving one substance in another; answer to a problem.

space: unlimited room or place extending in all directions; a part or place marked off in some way.

space ship: a rocket-propelled vehicle for travelling in outer space.

space shut tle: a self-contained vehicle that can enter space and return.

space sta tion: a structure designed to orbit above the Earth.

spe cies: a group of animals or plants that have certain permanent characteristics in common.

spec i men: part of a real thing; a representation of a group.

spec trum: series of colored light bands from the division of a prism.

sperm: male gamete; the male reproductive fluid containing the spermatozoa and semen.

spi der: a small animal with eight legs, no wings, and a body with two main divisions. It belongs to the arachnid group.

spi nal col umn: the backbone.

spi nal cord: the thick, whitish bundle of nerves enclosed by the spinal column.

spleen: an abdominal organ that maintains the condition of the blood.

spore: a single cell capable of growing into a new plant or animal. Ferns produce spores.

sprout: to begin to grow; shoot forth; a shoot of a plant.

stag nant: having become dirty and impure from standing still, as of air and water.

sta lac tite: formation of lime, shaped like an icicle hanging from the roof of caves.

sta lag mite: formation of lime, shaped like a cone that is built up from the floor of caves.

sta men: male reproductive organ in flowers, within the petals.

state: the condition of a person or thing; the structure or form of a material; the three states that materials are solid, liquid, and gas.

stat ic e lec tric i ty: electrical discharges that result from moving objects.

stem: stalk of a plant.

ster ile: free from living germs.

steth o scope: an instrument used in examination of a person's chest to convey sounds.

stig ma: the part of the pistil that receives the pollen in fertilization.

stim u lant: anything that increases bodily or mental activity.

stim u lus: whatever makes a living thing act in response to it.

sting: a prick or wound from a plant or animal.

stoma: a small opening such as a pore.

sto ma ta: more than one stoma. The stomata of green leaves regulate the passage of water vapor out of the plant. The carbon dioxide that green leaves use for food making enters through the stomata.

stran ger: a person who is not familiar, a foreigner.

stream: a small river.

strip min ing: surface mining; many times leaving earth scarred.

stron ti um: a pale yellow, metallic element; a by-product of atomic bombs.

struc ture: arrangement of parts; a building or something built.

style: the narrow extension of the ovary in plants.

sub ma rine: a warship that can operate under water and carries torpedoes.

suck ing coil: electrical device that moves a central core.

su crose: a sugar obtained from sugar cane.

suc tion: the creation of a partial vacuum causing a gas or liquid to move from the high pressure area to a lower pressure area.

sug ar: sweet substance from sugar cane or sugar beets, a carbohydrate.

su per clus ter: associated group of galaxies.

sul phur: a pale yellow nonmetallic element.

sul phur di ox ide: an air pollutant that is a nonflammable, nonexplosive, colorless gas: found in acid rain.

sun spot: a dark, cooler area on the surface of the sun.

su per sti tion: a belief or practice based on ignorant fear or mistaken reverence.

sur face ten sion: the cohesion of liquid molecules that act like a "skin" on the surface.

sur viv al: remaining alive.

sur viv al ad ap ta tion: any special means that a species has developed to promote the survival of its kind.

swamp: spongy, low ground filled with water, a marsh or bog.

sweat: moisture given out by glands in the skin of some vertebrates. As sweat evaporates, it lowers the body temperature.

symp toms: signs or indications of a disease or illness.

syn thet ic: not of natural growth or development; made artificially; made of artificial products.

sys tol ic: the contraciton of the heart.

tad pole: an undeveloped frog or toad. At this stage of development, the animal has gills and a tail and must live in water.

tan gent: a straight line that touches an arc, rounded surface.

taste bud: any of certain small groups of cells on the tongue or lining of the mouth that serve as organs of taste.

tel e graph: system of transmitting messages by making and breaking electrical connections.

tel e scope: an instrument for making distant objects appear closer.

tem per a ture: the extent to which anything is hot or cold, given as degrees. The temperature of freezing water is 32° Fahrenheit; the temperature of boiling water is 212° Fahrenheit.

tem po rary: lasting for a short time only.

ten sion: the stress of part of a body or material in equilibrium.

ter ra cing: flattening land from sloped areas to prevent soil erosion.

ter rar i um: an enclosure in which small land plants and/or small animals are kept, contains soil only.

ther mal pol lu tion: pollution of the atmosphere due to abnormal heating.

ther mom e ter: an instrument for measuring temperature.

ther mo stat: device that automatically regulates temperature.

tho ri um: a heavy, gray radioactive element.

thrust: a sudden push or lunge.

thun der: loud, crashing noise due to rapid expansion of heated air usually caused by lightning.

thy roid: pertaining to the large gland which lies near the throat in human beings.

tide: the rise and fall of the ocean; occurs about once every twelve hours.

tis sue: the cells and substance around them which form the bodies of plants and animals.

toad: a small animal somewhat like a frog, which starts life in water but usually leaves it to live on land. The toad returns to the water to deposit its eggs.

top soil: the upper part of the soil; surface soil.

tor na do: violent wind with a funnel-shape cloud that destroys much in its path.

tour ni quet: device for stopping severe bleeding by compressing blood vessel with bandage by twisting with stick.

tox ic: of or relating to poisons.

tox ins: poisons produced by chemical changes in animal and plant tissue.

tra che a: the main tube that carries air to and from the lungs.

trans lu cent: letting light pass through without being transparent.

trans par ent: easily seen through.

tran spi ra tion: passing off vapor from the surface as from leaves of plants or skins of animals.

tree: a tall, woody, perennial plant with many branches.

tri an gle of life: the graphic display of all predator-prey relationships.

tro po sphere: the lowest layer of the Earth's atmosphere between the Earth and the stratosphere about 8 miles (13 kilometers) thick.

tsu na mi: giant waves caused by underground earthquakes.

tu bers: thickened, underground stems of plants, such as in potatoes or dahlias.

tung sten: one of the chemical elements. It is a rare metal used in making steel and for electric-lamp filaments.

tur tle: fresh and salt water reptiles with soft body in a hard shell.

ty phoon: a violent, cyclonic windstorm, usually near the China Sea, a hurricane.

ul tra vi o let light: a type of electromagnetic radiation that is shorter than visible light most blocked out by the ozone layer.

un du lat ing: moving back and forth in waves.

u ni verse: all of the cosmos, totality of space.

up pers: slang term for drugs that are stimulators.

vac ci na tion: the act of injecting killed or weakened organisms into the blood of people to make them immune to a particular disease, such as smallpox or polio.

vac u um: an enclosed empty space from which all of the air has been removed.

vane: pointer showing the direction of the wind; a blade on a windmill or propeller.

vein: one of the three kinds of blood vessels. The veins carry the blood that is returning to the heart from all parts of the body.

ve loc i ty: speed in a particular direction.

ve ne re al dis ease: a disease transmitted by sexual intercourse.

ve nom: poisonous fluid secreted by snakes, scorpions, etc.

ven ti late: to change or purify air in a room by circulating fresh air.

ven tri cle: either of the two lower chambers of the heart that receive blood.

ver te bra: any of the bones of the backbone.

ver te brate: any animal that has a backbone. Fishes, amphibians, reptiles, birds, and mammals are vertebrates.

vet er in ar i an: a doctor who specializes in the treatment of animals.

vi brate: to move rapidly back and forth or up and down.

vi bra tion: quick movement to and fro, up and down, in and out, back and forth as in an earthquake.

vi rus: group of disease producing agents, very small, and dependent upon their host for reproduction and growth.

vis cos i ty: the ease of which a substance flows.

vi su al per sis ten cy: the ability to see an object after it is gone from view.

vi tal: essential or very important to life; having the qualities of living bodies.

vi ta mins: elements found in many foods that are important and necessary to the physical development of man, animals, and plants.

vi var i um: an enclosure in which small plants and/or animals are kept; contains soil(s) and water.

vol ca no: mountain having an opening through which ashes and lava are expelled; an opening in the Earth's surface out of which lava, steam, etc., pour.

volt: electromagnetic force; difference of potential that would carry one ampere of current against one ohm of resistance.

vol ta ic wet cell: a device that produces electricity by chemical change.

vol ume: the amount of space that a material takes up.

warm-blood ed: having warm blood. The body temperature of different warm-blooded animals is from 98° to 112° Fahrenheit. It is relatively constant for each animal.

wasp: winged insect with a slender body and biting mouth parts; has a vicious sting.

wastes: unwanted, formerly used products.

wa ter cy cle: sequence of states that water passes through.

wa ter lev el: the height of the surface of still water.

wa ter shed: area drained by a river or rain.

wa ter ta ble: the level below which the ground is saturated with water.

wa ter va por: water in a gaseous state. The term is used for vapor formed below the boiling point of water. At boiling point and higher it is called steam.

wat tling proc ess: method of conserving land by building fences in gullies to prevent excessive soil erosion.

waves: the up and down movement of water or sound.

wax: dull yellow substance secreted by bees for building cells.

weath er: the state of the atmosphere which includes temperature, pressure, humidity, and winds.

weath er ing: the physical and chemical changes that take place in rocks when they are exposed to conditions at the Earth's surface.

weath er vane: instrument that indicates wind direction.

weight: the amount of force with which gravity pulls down on any object.

wet lands: damp or wet areas of land which include swamps, bogs, lagoons, marshes, etc.

wind: motion of the air.

wind break: a shelter from the wind to prevent soil erosion.

wind pipe: the hollow tube that extends from the throat to the lungs.

wood chuck: a North American marmot; the groundhog.

worm: long, slender, creeping animal with a soft belly living underground.

wreath: a twisted, circular band of flowers or leaves.

X-rays: electro-magnetic radiation; can't be seen; used in medicine and dentistry for examinations.

xy lem: the tissue that carries water through a plant.

yaw: to move back and forth sideways from intended course.

zoo: place where wild animals are kept.

Index

Abalone, 207
Abandoned, 310
Abdomen, 197, 200
Abrasion, 274
Absolve, 83
Absorbent, 252
Absorption, 89
Acceleration, 388
Accidents, 282, 283, 318
Acidic, 13
Acne, 236, 265
Action, 130, 131, 391
Acupuncture, 236
Additive, 257
Afloat, 47
Africanized honeybee, 199
Ailerons, 384, 386
AIR, 19–38, 158, 235
Air pressure, 33, 36, 38
Airplanes, 23, 385, 387
Alarm, 191, 281
Alcohol, 8, 268
Algae, 148, 210, 220
Alkaline, 13
Alligator, 202, 296
Aluminum, 58, 90
Ammonia, 13
Amount, 50
Amphibians, 208, 383. *See also*
WATER ANIMALS
Amplitude, 105
Andromeda, 335
Angles, 94, 101, 363
Angular, 232
ANIMALS, 295, 343
   birds, 211–214
   classification, 187–192
   insects and spiders, 197–201
   mammals, 215–218
   pets, 193–196
   reptiles, 202–205
   resources, 227–229
   storage and care, 221–226
   water animals, 206–210
   worms and snails, 219–220
Annuals, 172
Ant, 226
Ant house, 198
Antarctic, 60, 319
Antennae, 200
Anther, 157
Antlers, 192
Ants, 198, 225
Apparatus, 62, 177, 365
Apparent, 101
Appliances, 133, 301
Apply, 277
Aquarium, 21, 182, 209–210,
   220, 221
Aquarius, 335
Aquifer, 39, 306
Arc, 362
Arch, 237
Archimedes' Principle, 44, 52
Arctic, 60, 319
Area, 50
Argentina, 214
Armature, 144

Artery, 233
Artificial, 280
Ascend, 25, 26, 53
Ashes, 88
Asteroids, 332
Astronauts, 393
Astronomy, 336
Atmosphere, 29, 32, 35, 339, 345
Atomic, 318
Atoms, 3, 18
Atrium, 233
Attach, 33
Attractants, 191
Attraction, 56, 57, 58, 64, 65, 66,
   67, 68
Audiovisual, 107
Auriga, 335
Automobiles, 33, 310
AVIATION, 383–388
Axis, 339, 346, 399
Axle, 114, 119

Backbone, 217
Bacteria, 148, 262, 269
Baking soda, 13, 42, 91
Balance, 22, 115, 229, 239, 292,
   365, 366
Ball-and-socket, 232
Balloons, 22, 26, 30, 86, 383, 391
Bandages, 277
Bar, 63
Barbs, 158
Bark, 176
Barometer, 381
Basic, 13
Bathing, 39
Bathtub, 306
Battery, 135, 136, 138, 140, 144
Beaches, 302, 325
Beak, 211, 212, 213
Beaker, 41
Bears, 296
Beer, 268
Bees, 157, 199
Beetles, 188
Benedict's solution, 251
Bent, 92
Bernoulli's Principle, 22, 36, 38
Bicycles, 33, 284, 327
Big Dipper, 335
Bills, 211, 212, 213
Biodegradable, 307
Biological, 288, 290
Biotic, 292, 293
Biplanes, 383
Bird, 226
BIRDS, 211–214
Birds, 225, 296
Bivalve, 207
Black, 89
Black snake, 203
Bleeding, 274, 276
Blending, 242
Blind spot, 243
Blisters, 278
Block, 125
Blotter, 141
Blue, 345

Board, 30, 125
BODY STRUCTURE AND
   FUNCTION, 230–238
Bogs, 304
Boil, 6, 83
Boiling, 372, 379
Boiling point, 7, 8, 31
Bottle, 21, 34, 40, 111
Bottom, 28
Bowl, 61, 235
Brain, 244, 245
Brakes, 122
Branch, 223
Bread, 249
Breaking, 34
Breast, 211
Breathe, 171
Breathing, 235, 280
Brisk, 65, 66, 69
Broken, 278
Brushing, 262
Bubbles, 42
Buds, 179
Bulb, 97, 135, 139, 140
Bulletin board, 102
Buoyancy, 42, 43, 47
Burns, 278, 282
Burrs, 158
Butter, 253
Butterfly, 185, 200, 225, 226
Buttermilk, 253

Cabin, 383
Cage, 222, 223
Calibrate, 373
Calla lily, 170
Calorie, 255, 256
Camel, 227
Camouflage, 192, 218
Cancer, 335
Candle, 20, 25, 68, 84, 87, 88, 91
Cannon, 129
Capacity, 235
Capillary, 175, 233
Carbohydrate, 251
Carbon, 37, 88, 353
Carbon dioxide, 2, 91, 149,
   171, 210
Carcinogen, 264
Card, 123
Cardboard, 29, 36, 92, 177, 245
Carnations, 170
Carnivores, 289, 316
Carotenoids, 178
Cartesian diver, 53
Cassiopeia, 334, 335
Cat, 194
Catastrophe, 327
Caterpillar, 222, 225, 226
Caution, 87, 283
Celestial, 346
Cellophane, 95, 102, 185, 241
Cells, 143, 238
Celsius, 40, 82–83
Center, 365, 366, 368
Centigrade, 83
Centimeter, 54
Centripetal, 389, 394

Cephalothorax, 197
Cepheus, 335
Ceramic, 90
Cereal, 249
Chair, 27
Chamber, 28
Change, 240
Charcoal, 221
Charges, 68
Charred, 87
Cheese, 250
Chemical change, 5
Chemical reaction, 42
Chemicals, 5, 10, 161, 314
Chicken, 226
Chickens, 225
Chimney, 20
Chlorofluorocarbons, 319
Chlorophyll, 178
Cholera, 314
Cholesterol, 252
Chunks, 253
Cigarette, 264
Cinnamon, 248
Circuit, 132, 135, 136, 137, 144
Circuit breaker, 138
Circular, 65, 394
Circulation, 20, 233, 234, 276
Circulatory, 231
Citric acid, 42
City planners, 395
Clamp, 62
Clapper, 144
Classification, 147
Clay, 161, 166, 315
Clays, 299
Clean, 267
Cleaning, 195, 196
Cleanliness, 258, 269
Climate, 160
Clinics, 272
Clock, 246
Clothespin, 10
Clothing, 228
Cloudiness, 380
Clouds, 371, 377
Coast, 207
Coastal waters, 291
Cobalt blue, 242
Cobweb, 197
Coffee, 17, 248
Coin, 123
Colander, 253
Cold, 239, 247, 380
Cold front, 381
Cold-blooded, 203
Collection, 185
Color, 89, 94, 95, 96, 102, 153,
   168, 170, 184. *See also*
   LIGHT AND COLOR
Color blindness, 241
Coloring, 257
Comb, 66, 69
Combustible, 15
Combustion, 20, 37, 80, 88, 91
Comets, 332
Communication, 104, 107,
   134, 199

Community, 292, 293
Compass, 61, 63, 286
Complementary, 95, 241
Complex, 217
Compost, 307
Compounds, 4, 9
Compress, 277
Compression, 23, 28, 33
Compute, 235
Concave lens, 99–100
Concentric, 293
Condensation, 6, 31, 55, 177
Condense, 371, 379
Condensing, 372
Condor, 229
Conduction, 25, 81, 89, 90, 106, 139
Cone, 87, 106, 357
CONSERVATION, 298–307
Conservationists, 395
Conserve, 300, 306, 328
Constant, 130
Constellation, 332, 336
Construction, 95
Constructive, 241
Consumers, 147, 288
Container, 183, 222
Contaminants, 270
Contamination, 39
Continents, 351
Contract, 2, 40, 46, 85, 240
Contrast, 184
Controls, 295, 399
Contusion, 274
Convection, 25, 81
Converge, 100
Convex lens, 99–100
Cooking, 306
Cooling, 84, 85
Cooperate, 281
Copper, 4, 58, 140, 141
Coral snake, 203
Core, 237
Cork, 28, 32, 129, 138
Corona Borealis, 335
Cosmetics, 236
Cotton, 320
Cough, 264, 273
Cover, 243
Cow, 216, 227
Cream, 253
Creative, 217
Creeping, 190
Crocodile, 202
Cross, 243
Crushed ice, 6, 41
Crust, 356, 358
Crystalline, 353
Crystals, 17
Cultivate, 315
Current, 132, 141
Current detector, 141
CURRENT ELECTRICITY, 132–144
Curved, 340
Custodians, 308
Cutting, 222, 223
Cycles, 105

Dampen, 219
Dangerous, 46
Dangers, 379
Dashes, 142
Dawn, 342
Deadly, 264
Deafness, 104, 260

Debris, 302
Decay, 210
Deceive, 244
Decibel, 108, 260, 320
Deciduous, 153
Decomposition, 10, 355
Decorative, 179, 182
Decrease, 79
Deflate, 33, 86
Defy, 62
Degrees, 278
Dehydration, 10
Delta, 237
Density, 47, 48
Dependent, 104
Depressant, 268
Depth, 111
Descend, 25, 34, 53, 388
Desert, 216
Deserts, 291, 351
Desirable, 301
Desk, 84
Detergents, 326
Deviation, 60
Dew, 6, 371
Diagnosing, 271
Diagonal, 101
Diameter, 95, 241
Diamond, 353
Dicots, 154
Diffusion, 16–17
Digestive, 231
Dilate, 240
Diminishing, 324
Dinosaur, 205
Diorama, 305
Direction, 38, 63, 120, 281, 361, 389, 390
Dirigibles, 383
Dirt, 222, 298
Disappear, 102, 340
Disease, 160, 267, 269, 270, 295
Dishwasher, 306
Disks, 17
Displace, 28, 54
Disposals, 317
Dispose, 87
Dissolve, 12, 17
Distance, 115, 119, 246, 394
Distillation, 8
Distribution, 254
Diversity, 290
Doctor, 110, 277
Dog, 194, 216, 227
Doll, 98
Dolphin, 216
Doorbell, 144
Dots, 142
Double convex, 100
Dowel, 22, 103
Downward, 262
Draco, 335
Drafts, 20
Drag, 119, 122, 385, 387
Dried, 254
Drill, 281
Drilling, 355
Drinking, 29, 268, 306
Driving, 120
Drone, 199
Droplets, 177, 371, 375, 379
Drops, 251
Drought, 39
Drowning, 280
Drugs, 271
Dry cell, 137

Dry ice, 2
Drying, 51
Dusk, 342
Dust, 345
Dysentery, 314

Eagle, 296
Ear, 106
Eardrum, 108
Ears, 110
EARTH AND SPACE
    earth's crust, 351–359
    gravity, 360–368
    solar system, 327–350
    universe, 330–336
    weather, 369–382
Earthquake, 281, 356
EARTH'S CRUST, 351–359
Earthworm, 219, 225, 226, 268
Eclipse, 349
Ecologists, 395
Ecology, 310, 327
ECOLOGY
    conservation, 298–307
    ecosystems, 288–297
    pollution, 308–320
    pollution solutions, 321–328
ECOSYSTEMS, 210, 288–297
Ectomorph, 256
Egg, 211
Eggmobile, 131
Elastic, 30, 367
Electric, 144, 299, 311
Electric circuit, 135
Electrical, 377
Electricity, 65, 132, 134, 135, 301, 355. See also CURRENT ELECTRICITY; STATIC ELECTRICITY
Electrolytes, 140
Electromagnet, 143, 144
Electron, 3, 18, 68, 140
Electrons, 132
Elements, 3, 4, 9
Elephant, 216, 227
Elevate, 276
Elevators, 384
Elongated, 391
Embryo, 165
Emit, 97
Emotional, 258
Emphysema, 264
Endangered, 228, 300, 324
Endomorph, 256
ENERGY, 70–144, 309, 343, 358, 363, 378
Engine nacelle, 384
Enhance, 266
Enrich, 315
Environment, 207, 293
Equal, 128
Erosion, 298, 356
Erupt, 357, 358
Escape, 37
Essential, 301
Estimate, 37, 235
Estuary, 304, 313, 359
Eutrophication, 326
Evaporate, 11
Evaporation, 3, 17, 49–50
Evergreens, 153
Evidence, 297
Examine, 275
Excavating, 305
Excreting, 195
Excretory, 231

Exercise, 195, 196, 258, 265
Exert, 29, 38
Exhale, 171
Exhaust, 310
Expand, 2, 30, 34, 40, 46, 85
Expansion, 377
Expensive, 264
Explosion, 260, 297
External Protective, 231
Extinct, 228, 229, 324
Extinction, 188, 205, 294, 300
Extinguish, 20, 80, 91
Eye, 179, 240, 243, 244, 245
Eyedropper, 43, 53, 103, 170
Eyelid, 275

Fahrenheit, 40, 82–83
Falls, 282
Farm, 194, 216
Farmers, 395
Farming, 305
Fat, 250, 252
Fatalities, 283
Faucet, 69
Feather, 211, 212
Feeding, 193, 194, 195
Fertilization, 156
Fever, 273
Fibrous, 173
Field, 194
Filament, 135, 137
Filings, 9, 11
Filter, 102
Finger, 32
Fingerprint, 237
Fire, 15, 282
FIRE AND HEAT, 79–91
Fire triangle, 80
FIRST AID, 273–280
Fish, 227, 292. See also WATER ANIMALS
Fishermen, 395
Fishing, 295
Fishline, 391
Fittest, 192
Flame, 87, 88
Flaps, 384
Flashlight, 92, 93, 135, 240, 342
Flavoring, 257
Flight, 211, 386
Flip, 123
Flood, 39
Flooring, 224
Florist, 172
Flossing, 262
Flotation, 42, 43, 44
Flow, 132
Flowerpot, 162, 164, 169
Flowers, 150, 154, 155, 164, 172, 174
Flush, 275
Flying, 190
Fog, 371, 379
Food, 254, 258, 397
Force, 34, 114, 115, 116, 118, 121, 122, 123, 124, 128, 129, 131, 361, 366, 390
Forearm, 234
Forecasting, 374
Forest, 303
Foresters, 395
Formation, 374
Fractional, 8
Free flight, 398
Freezing, 40, 41, 46, 83
French fries, 255

Frequency, 105
Fresh water, 39
Friction, 116, 119, 125, 126, 127, 398
Frog, 208, 225, 226
Frost, 371
Frozen, 254, 379
Fructose, 251
Fruit, 150, 250
Fuel, 392
Fulcrum, 115
Fungi, 148, 159
Funnel, 20, 28, 110
Furnace, 26
Fuse, 138
Fuselage, 383

Galaxies, 332
Galaxy, 336
Gallon, 292
Galvanizing, 224
Garden, 182, 220
Gardener, 172
Gardens, 306
Gas, 2, 5, 345, 355
Gasoline, 310
Gastropod, 207, 220
Gauge, 373
Gear, 114, 120
Gemini, 335
Generating, 318
Geologists, 395
Geothermal, 358
Gerbil, 193, 196, 225
Germination, 161, 162, 163, 164, 165
Germs, 267
Geyser, 358
Gibbous, 348
Glaring, 259
Glass, 29, 65, 123, 139, 177
Glasses, 21, 259
Gliders, 383
Gliding, 232
Global, 312
Globe, 340, 349
Glucose, 251
Gluons, 18
Glycerin, 183
Goat, 216
Goggles, 259
Gold, 353
Goldfish, 225
Gourd, 181
Government, 272
Grain, 155, 156, 250
Gram, 54
Grampuses, 216
Graph, 297, 373
Grass, 152, 164
Grasshopper, 225
Grasslands, 291
Gravel, 292, 299
Gravity, 35, 62, 121, 122, 350, 360, 361, 362, 364, 365, 366, 367, 368, 385, 389, 394, 398
Grease, 168, 252
Green, 242
Greenhouse effect, 312
Ground water, 359
Growth, 154, 165, 167
Guinea pig, 193, 195, 196, 225
Gullying, 298
Guppies, 225
Gymnast, 366

Habit, 264
Habitat, 188, 221, 294, 324
Hail, 371
Hair, 217
Hair root, 173
Hamburger, 255
Hamster, 195, 196, 225
Hang gliders, 383
Hard, 247
Hard-boiled, 34, 47
Harvesting, 160
Hazard, 308, 317
HEALTH
    body structure and function, 230–238
    first aid, 273–280
    nutrition, 249–257
    personal health, 258–268
    public health, 269–272
    safety, 281–286
    senses, 239–248
Hearing, 104, 108, 110, 111, 239, 260, 320
Hearing aid, 246
Heart, 233
Heartbeat, 234
Heat, 10, 31, 50, 79, 84, 85, 90, 239. See also FIRE AND HEAT
Heating, 377
Heavenly, 350
Helicopters, 383
Help, 51
Hemisphere, 369
Hemorrhage, 276
Herbaceous, 176
Herbivores, 288, 289, 316
Hercules, 335
Hibernation, 218
Hiding, 218
Highways, 310
Hinge, 232
Hinged, 181
Hippopotamus, 216
Homo sapiens, 294
Honeybee, 199
Horizon, 340
Horizontal, 103, 245
Horizontal stabilizer, 384
Hornet, 279
Horse, 216, 227
Horseshoe magnet, 57, 63
Hose, 92, 106, 132
Hum, 109
Humans, 188
Humidity, 380
Humus, 161, 162, 166, 169, 171, 315
Hunting, 295
Hydra, 335
Hydrologists, 395
Hydrometer, 47
Hygienist, 262

Ice, 5, 45–46, 371
Ice pick, 365
Ice water, 372
Icebergs, 46
Icecaps, 291, 351
Identification, 189
Identify, 237
Identity, 7
Illness, 271
Illusion, 243, 244
Image, 98, 100
Impairment, 260
Incision, 274

Incline, 125
Inclined plane, 114, 116
Increase, 79
Indicator, 373
Indigo, 242
Industrialists, 395
Inertia, 123, 124, 130, 367, 389, 394, 398
Infection, 273, 278, 279
Inflate, 33, 86
Inflation, 23
Infrared, 81, 94
Inhale, 171
Ink, 15
In-line skates, 284
Insecticides, 316
INSECTS AND SPIDERS, 185, 188, 189, 197–201, 204, 213, 222
Inspections, 272
Instruments, 320, 393
Insulate, 135, 138, 139, 143
Intact, 92
Intensity, 105
Interdependent, 290
Interpreting, 244
Intersection, 284
Invisible, 15
Iodine, 251
Iris, 239
Iron, 4, 11
Iron filings, 63, 64
Irradiated, 254
Irregular shape, 52
Irrigating, 262
Irritability, 14, 187

Jackhammer, 320
Jet engines, 384
Jungle, 216

Kelvin, 83
Keratin, 236
Killing jar, 201
Kindling, 80
Kinetic, 81, 363
King snake, 203
Knife, 61, 170, 180, 184
Knife switch, 136, 138, 143
Kyphosis, 266

Label, 257
Labor-saving, 318
Laceration, 274
Lacrimal ducts, 275
Lagoons, 304
Lake, 326, 351, 359
Lamp, 379
Landfills, 307, 317
Landing gear, 384
Layer, 319
LEAVES, STEMS, AND ROOTS, 43, 150, 151, 168, 173–178, 183, 184
Lemon, 141
Lemon juice, 13, 15
Length, 84, 112, 243, 363
Lenses, 103
Leo, 335
Leopard, 216
Leptons, 18
Lever, 114, 115
Libra, 335
Licenses, 272
Lid, 222
Lift, 27, 122
LIGHT AND COLOR, 92–103, 164, 378

Lightened, 96
Lighter, 46
Lighting, 376, 377
Lights, 284
Light-year, 331
Lima bean, 162, 163, 167, 174
Lines for force, 64
Lion, 216
Liquid, 2, 6, 40, 48, 106, 169, 175, 273
Litmus paper, 13
Litter, 323
Little Dipper, 335
Liver, 238
Living things, 187
Lizard, 202, 204, 225
Loam, 161, 166, 315
Locking, 101
Locomotion, 14, 187
Lodestone, 56
Loop, 22, 237
Lordosis, 266
Lubricants, 310
Lubrication, 125, 126
Luminous, 97
Lungs, 217, 235, 238
Luster, 353
Lymphatic, 231
Lyra, 335

Machines, 126. See also SIMPLE MACHINES
Magic, 15, 62
Magnet, 9, 11, 56, 57, 58, 62, 143
Magnetic field, 63
MAGNETISM, 56–64
Magnifying glass, 103, 159
Main wing, 384
MAMMALS, 188, 215–218
Mammary, 217
Maneuver, 386
Map makers, 395
Marbles, 4, 48, 390
Marsh, 205, 304
Mask, 168
Masking tape, 198
Mass, 54
Mass transit, 327
Matches, 25
Materials, 9
MATTER, 2–18
Mayonnaise, 252
Measure, 52, 235, 246, 256, 373
Measuring tape, 61
Meat, 250
Mechanical advantage, 116
Medicine, 43, 271
Mediterranean, 291
Medium, 224
Melanin, 236
Melting, 5, 46
Melting point, 5, 7
Mercury, 316
Mesh, 120, 223
Mesomorph, 256
Messteorph, 256
Metal, 139
Metamorphosis, 208
Meteors, 332
Meterstick, 127
Metric system, 52
Mexico, 214
Mice, 196, 225
Midline, 234
Migration, 214
Military, 395
Milk, 249, 250

Milky Way, 331, 336
Mineral, 249
Mineralogists, 395
Mining, 305
Mirror, 97, 98, 101
Mixing, 242
Mixtures, 4, 8, 41
Model, 142
Moist, 159, 162
Moisture, 51
Molds, 159
Molecules, 3, 5, 10, 12, 17, 40,
    79, 81, 85, 106
Mollusk, 207, 220
Molten, 358
Momentum, 123, 124, 130, 367,
    389, 394, 398
Monera, 148
Monocots, 154
Monoplanes, 383
Moon, 339, 346, 349
Morse Code, 142
Moth, 200
Mothball, 17, 42
Motion, 79, 121, 130, 390
Motorcycles, 327
Mountains, 216, 351
Mouth-to-mouth, 280
MOVEMENT AND
    RESISTANCE, 12,
    121–131, 333
Moving, 38
Muscular, 231
Mushy, 247
Music, 111

Nape, 211
Narwhals, 216
Natural, 305
Nature, 229, 288
Neap, 350
Nectar, 199
Needle, 61, 131
Negative, 65, 68, 69
Nerve, 244, 246
Nervous, 231
Nest, 211
Neutral, 65
Neutrinos, 18
Neutrons, 3, 18
Newspaper, 88, 183, 184
Newton's Laws of Motion, 121,
    130, 390, 391
Nicotine, 264
Night time, 333
Nitrogen, 37
Noise, 320
Nonliving things, 14, 187, 293
Nonrenewable, 308, 309
Nontoxic, 323
North Pole, 60
North Star, 334
North-seeking, 57
Nosebleed, 276
Nostril, 276
Novas, 332
Nuclear, 318
Nucleus, 18, 147
Nursery, 155, 160, 172
NUTRITION, 249–257, 258,
    265, 269
Nutritious, 255

Observation, 174
Occluded, 381
Oceans, 55, 291, 302, 325, 351
Oil, 126, 250

Oil spills, 325
Onion, 248
Ophiuchus, 335
Opposite, 128
Optical, 244
Optional, 224
Orange, 242
Orbit, 3, 344, 346, 349, 394
Ore, 9
Organisms, 147, 290
Organs, 238
Orion, 335
Osmosis, 175
Ounces, 119
Outwardly, 243
Ovary, 156
Overweight, 256
Oviparous, 205, 208
Oxygen, 2, 15, 37, 80, 163, 171,
    210, 326, 396, 397
Ozone, 319

Pain, 108, 239
Paint, 96
Pamphlets, 277
Paper clip, 62, 64
Parachute, 158, 388
Paraffin, 292
Parallel, 65, 132, 136, 137
Parallel circuit, 137
Partial, 27, 31
Partially movable, 232
Particles, 88, 312, 375
Passengers, 396
Pasteurization, 270
Pasteurized, 254
Pattern, 26, 101, 168
Peat, 315
Pedal, 386
Peer pressure, 264
Pegasus, 335
Pendulum, 363
Penumbra, 349
Perching, 213
Perennials, 172
Periscope, 101
Permanent, 56, 62
Perseus, 335
Persistency, 245
PERSONAL HEALTH,
    258–268
Perspective, 243
Petroleum, 355
PETS, 193–196
Phase, 348
Pheromone, 191, 200
Phloem, 176
Phosphates, 326
Photosynthesis, 147, 149, 168, 178
Phototropism, 200
Physical, 258
Physical change, 5, 7, 11
PHYSICAL WORLD, 1–69
Phytoplankton, 302, 316, 325
Pig, 216
Pigeon, 296
Pineapple, 180
Ping-Pong, 38
Pisces, 335
Pistil, 157
Pitch, 105, 108
Pith, 57
Pith balls, 67
Pivot, 232
Pizza, 255
Planet, 309, 332, 339
Planning, 309

Plano-concave, 100
Plano-convex, 100
PLANT GROWTH, 167–172
Planters, 181
Plants, 221, 299, 316, 343
PLANTS
    fun with, 170–185
    growth, 167–172
    parts and classification, 146–153
    roots, stems and leaves, 173–178
    seeds and reproduction, 154–159
    soils and germination, 160–166
Plaque, 262
Plaster, 223
Plastic, 35, 43, 86, 90, 110, 163,
    171, 183, 235, 311, 313,
    325, 357
Platelets, 233
Pleiades, 335
Pliers, 137, 224
Plunger, 27
Plywood, 224
Poaching, 324
Pocket, 237
Pods, 155, 158
Pointers, 334
Poison, 201, 218, 282
Poisonous snake, 203
Polaris, 334
Pollen, 156, 157
Pollination, 154
Pollinization, 157
Pollutants, 312
Pollute, 310
POLLUTION, 294, 308–320
POLLUTION SOLUTIONS,
    321–328
Ponds, 326
Population, 228, 295, 297
Porous, 27
Porpoises, 216
Positive, 65, 68, 69
Posture, 266
Potato, 141, 267
Potential, 363
Potting soil, 180
Power, 120, 318
Practice, 277
Prairie, 216
Precautions, 31, 129, 284
Precipitation, 55, 380, 381
Predator, 188
Predators, 295
Preheat, 379
Prehensile, 217
Preservative, 257
Preserve, 179, 254
Pressure, 21, 22, 23, 27, 29, 30,
    32, 35, 127, 239, 356,
    357, 369, 380, 385, 388
Prevent, 282
Prevention, 265, 270, 271, 278
Prey, 188
Primary colors, 96
Primary root, 173
Prism, 94, 100, 345, 375
Producers, 147
Projector, 93
Propellants, 397
Propeller, 384, 387
Propulsion, 131
Protect, 272
Protection, 191, 192, 229, 260
Protective, 259, 319
Protein, 249, 252
Protista, 148

Protons, 3, 18
Protoplasm, 14, 187
Protractor, 61
Public, 327
Pull, 121
Pulley, 114, 117–118
Pulse, 234
Pump, 30
Punched, 32
Puncture, 22
Pupil, 240
Push, 121
Pyrex, 37, 307

Quarks, 18
Quarter, 348
Quasar, 332
Queen bee, 199

Rabbit, 216, 225, 227
Rabid, 279
Radial, 197
Radial artery, 234
Radiation, 25, 81
Radiator, 39
Radio, 107
Radish, 162, 163
Rain, 303, 372
Rainbow, 94, 375
Rainfall, 373
Raise, 62
Ratio, 120
Rattlesnake, 203
React, 240
Reaction, 48, 128, 130, 131,
    364, 391
Receptacle, 137
Records, 107
Recreation, 228
Rectangle, 95
Recycle, 307, 322, 323, 328
Red, 242
Reduce, 322
Reflected light, 97
Reflection, 89, 98, 102, 375
Refraction, 94, 375
Refrigerator, 40
Refuse, 317, 322
Regulation, 272
Released, 391
Renewable, 309
Repair, 322
Repel, 67, 68
Reproduction, 156, 157, 165, 231
REPTILES, 202–205
Repulsion, 56, 57, 58, 66
Research, 322
Resistance, 115, 116, 121,
    122, 360
Resonating, 111
Resources, 305, 396
Respiration, 14, 187
Respiratory, 231
Respire, 168
Responsibility, 193
Rest, 123, 258
Resuscitation, 280
Retina, 259
Reusable, 307
Reuse, 322, 323, 328
Reverse, 98
Revolution, 339, 341, 346, 348
Rhinoceros, 216
Richter scale, 356
Riker box, 185
Ripe, 180
Rise, 26, 37

River, 351, 359
Rocket, 391, 392
Rocks, 221, 299, 352
Rodent, 189, 196, 203
Roller, 277
Rolling friction, 125
Roll-over, 392
ROOTS, STEMS, AND
    LEAVES, 150, 151,
    173–178
Rope, 118
Rotary, 387
Rotation, 333, 339, 341, 342,
    346, 348, 350, 399
Rough, 247
Round, 340
Rubber, 53, 92, 110, 139
Rudder, 384, 386
Ruler, 84
Rump, 211

SAFETY, 104, 129, 272,
    281–286
Sail, 26
Sailors, 395
Sailor's dilemma, 54
Salt water, 47
Salted, 254
Salvage, 307
Sand, 4, 11, 166
Sanitation, 270
Sapphire, 353
SATELLITES, 332, 389–395
Savannahs, 291
Scalds, 278
Scale, 111, 116, 118, 119
Scatter, 345
Scissors, 26, 115, 241
Scoliosis, 266
Scorpion, 279
Screen, 27, 198, 222, 223, 224
Sea mammal, 216
Sea shells, 207
Seaplanes, 383
Seashores, 325
Seasons, 153, 339, 344
Secondary colors, 96
Secondary root, 173
Secret, 15
SEEDS AND
    REPRODUCTION,
    154–159, 213
Seeing, 244
Segmented, 219
Seismograph, 356
SENSES, 239–248
Series, 132
Series circuit, 135
Serrated, 178
Sewage, 270, 311, 313, 325, 328
Shadow, 93
Shake, 253
Shakes, 255
Shallow, 15, 180
Shape, 340
Sharp, 247
Sheep, 216, 227
Sheet, 93
Shells, 218
Ship, 340
Short circuit, 138
Showers, 306
Shuttle, 398
Sideways, 36
Sieve, 201
Sight, 239
Signal key, 142

Signals, 283, 284
Silt, 166
Silver, 89, 353
Similar, 177
SIMPLE MACHINES, 114–120
Simulate, 357
Sink, 29, 44
Siphon, 23, 35
Size, 218, 224, 360
Skates, 284
Skeletal, 231
Skin, 236
Sky, 345
Sleeping, 195
Sliding friction, 125
Smell, 239, 248
Smog, 310
Smoke, 20, 88, 254, 264
Smooth, 247
Snail, 210, 220, 225
Snake, 202, 225
Sneezing, 273
Soap, 248
Socket, 139, 140
Soft, 247
Soft drink, 32
SOILS AND GERMINATION,
    160–166, 221, 222, 298
SOLAR SYSTEM, 327–350
Solids, 2, 6, 84, 106, 323
Solute, 11, 12
Solution, 12, 322
Solvent, 11, 12
Sonic boom, 377
SOUND, 104–113, 191
Source light, 97
SOURCES, 71–79
South America, 214
South Pole, 60
Southern Cross, 335
South-seeking, 57
Space, 21, 336, 393, 396, 397,
    398. See EARTH
    AND SPACE
Space shuttle, 383
SPACE TRAVEL, 396–399
Spark, 65
Speaking, 109, 113
Species, 290, 294, 300
Specimen, 154, 185, 201, 219
Speck, 275
Spectrum, 94, 375
Speed, 51, 120, 130, 192, 218,
    389, 390
Sperm, 156
Spider, 189, 197, 201. See also
    INSECTS AND
    SPIDERS
Spin, 245
Spiral, 25
Splatter, 7
Spleen, 238
Sponge, 164
Spool, 36
Spout, 372
Spray, 184
Sprinkle, 63, 306
Sprout, 160, 167
Square, 98
Stability, 362
Stabilizers, 386
Stalk, 170
Stamen, 157
Star, 175
Star clusters, 332
Starch, 251

Stare, 243
Stars, 332, 333
Starvation, 297
Statistics, 297
STATIC ELECTRICITY, 65–69
Station, 393
Stationary, 127, 128
Steam, 2, 5, 31, 32, 129, 131,
    358, 372
Steel, 90
STEMS, ROOTS AND
    LEAVES, 150, 151,
    173–178
Sterile, 267, 277
Stethoscope, 110
Stick, 386
Sticky, 247
Stimuli, 14, 187
Sting, 192, 199
Stinger, 278, 279
Stop sign, 283
Straight line, 92
Straighten, 175
Strand, 223
Strangers, 285
Stream, 69
String, 113, 181
Strip mining, 305
Strong, 245
Style, 156
Styrofoam, 57, 67
Sublimation, 2, 5
Submarine, 42, 53
Substance, 10
Suction, 27
Suffocate, 28
Sugar, 4, 10, 11, 12, 149, 250, 251
Sulfur, 9
Sun, 333, 349
Sunburn, 265
Sunlight, 165, 221
Sunshine, 168, 196
Supercluster, 331, 332
Supernovas, 332
Supplies, 39, 393
Support, 64, 67, 219
Surface, 46, 50, 53, 103, 126
Survival, 192, 229
Survive, 305
Suspension, 62
Sustainability, 308, 309, 328
Swamp, 205, 359
Swamps, 304
Sweet potato, 179
Sweetening, 257
Swimming, 47, 190, 282
Swing time, 363
Switch, 144
Symmetrical, 175
Systems, 238

Tadpole, 208, 226
Tail assembly, 384
Talking, 109
Talons, 213
Tangent, 390
Tape, 110
Taproot, 173
Tar, 264
Taste, 239
Taurus, 335
Taut, 113
Taxonomy, 290
Teachers, 395
Teakettle, 372
Teeter-totter, 115
Teeth, 211

Telegraph, 142
Television, 107, 259
Temperature, 5, 7, 40, 41, 50,
    51, 79, 80, 83, 86, 162,
    369, 380, 396
Temporary, 56
Tension, 112, 175
Terminal, 135, 136, 138, 139,
    143, 144
Terrarium, 172, 182, 204, 221
Tertiary, 96
Test, 251
Test tube, 8, 41
Testing, 50
Thermometer, 7, 41, 83, 85
Thermostat, 301
Thickness, 48, 112
Thorax, 200
Thread, 26, 38, 62, 67
Threatened, 228, 294, 324
Threshold, 108
Throat, 109
Throw-aways, 323
Thrust, 87, 122, 385, 386,
    387, 392
Thumb, 35
Thumbtack, 36, 47
Thunder, 377
Thunderstorm, 376
Ticking, 246
Tiger, 216
Tilt, 21
Time, 51
Tire, 30, 33
Tissue, 238
Toad, 208
Tomato, 249
Tone, 111
Toothpick, 15
Topsoil, 166, 298, 315
Tornado, 281
Tortoise, 202
Touch, 62, 239
Touching, 191
Toxic, 317
Tractors, 305
Traffic, 282, 283
Training, 194
Transcriptions, 107
Translucent, 252
Transpiration, 55, 177
Transportation, 327
Trapdoor, 197
Trash, 313
Travel, 92, 397
Treatment, 278, 279
Triangle, 80
Triangular, 197, 277
Trick, 195
Trough, 91
Trowel, 182
Tubing, 28, 30, 35, 67, 110
Tundra, 291
Turning, 333
Turtle, 202, 226
Twig, 43, 204
Twigs, 222
Typhoid, 314

Ultraviolet, 94
Uncontrolled, 284
Underweight, 256
Univalve, 207
UNIVERSE, 330–336
Unsanitary, 272
Unwashed, 267
Upright, 266

Upward, 36, 262
Urban, 310
Ursa Major, 334
Ursa Minor, 334

Vacuum, 27, 31, 35
Valleys, 351
Vane, 370
Vapor, 6, 372
Variation, 60
Vast, 331
Vegetable, 173, 250
Vein, 178, 233
Velocity, 392
Venom, 192
Ventilation, 162
Ventricle, 233
Vertical, 38, 245
Vertical stabilizers, 384
Vessels, 234
Veterinarian, 193
Vibration, 105, 106, 108, 109,
    112, 113
Victim, 280
Viewing, 101, 244
Vigorously, 69, 253
Vinegar, 13, 91, 169
Violet, 242

Virgo, 335
Virus, 269, 273
Viscosity, 48
Visitor, 214
Visual, 245
Visual persistency, 242
Vitamin, 249
Vivarium, 182, 221
Vocal cords, 109, 113
Voice, 109
Volcano, 357
Voltaic, 140
Voltmeter, 140, 141
Volume, 44, 52, 54
Volunteer, 267

Wad, 34
Wadding, 213
Wait, 283
Walk, 190, 283
Waning, 348
Warm, 247, 312, 380
Warm front, 381
Washed, 267
Wasp, 279
Waste, 311, 317, 318, 323,
    325, 328

WATER, 21, 39–55, 131, 158,
    166, 169, 174, 286, 306,
    389, 396, 397
WATER ANIMALS, 206–210
Water cycle, 55
Water table, 359
Watered, 179
Waterlogged, 44
Watershed, 303
Wax, 89, 113, 125, 292, 348
WEATHER, 369–382
Weather vane, 23
Wedge, 114
Weight, 22, 44, 54, 84, 115, 118,
    122, 360, 361
Wells, 355
Wetland, 304, 359
Whale, 216
Wheel, 114, 119
Whipping, 253
Whiskey, 268
Whisper, 108, 246
Whorl, 237
Wick, 87
Widemouth, 222
Width, 112
Wildlife, 296, 300, 304, 328

Wind, 51, 245, 369, 380
Wine, 268
Wing, 211, 212
Wire, 223
Wires, 112
Wolves, 295, 296
Wood, 90
Wooden, 36, 67, 125
Woodpecker, 296
Woods, 286
Woody, 176
Wool, 68
Work, 114
Worker bee, 199
World, 229
WORMS AND SNAILS,
    219–220
Wound, 274

Xylem, 170, 176
Xylophone, 111

Yardstick, 127
Yarn, 181
Yellow, 242

Zebra, 216
Zinc, 140, 141